KT-526-179

EnCase® Computer Forensics

The Official EnCE®: EnCase Certified Examiner

Study Guide

Third Edition

Steve Bunting

PARK LEARNING CENTRE
UNIVERSITY OF GLOUCESTERSHIRE
P.O. Box 220, The Park
Cheltenham GL50 2RH
Tel: 01242 714333

WILEY

John Wiley & Sons, Inc.

Senior Acquisitions Editor: Jeff Kellum
Development Editor: David Clark
Technical Editors: Jessica M. Bair and Lisa Stewart
Production Editor: Eric Charbonneau
Copy Editor: Kim Wimpsett
Editorial Manager: Pete Gaughan
Production Manager: Tim Tate
Vice President and Executive Group Publisher: Richard Swadley
Vice President and Publisher: Neil Edde
Media Project Manager 1: Laura Moss Hollister
Media Associate Producer: Doug Kuhn
Media Quality Assurance: Marilyn Hummel
Book Designer: Judy Fung
Compositor: Craig Johnson, Happenstance Type-O-Rama
Proofreaders: Jen Larsen and James Saturnio, Word One New York
Indexer: Ted Laux
Project Coordinator, Cover: Katherine Crocker
Cover Designer: Ryan Sneed

Copyright © 2012 by John Wiley & Sons, Inc., Indianapolis, Indiana

Published simultaneously in Canada

ISBN: 978-0-470-90106-9

ISBN: 978-1-118-21940-9 (ebk.)

ISBN: 978-1-118-05898-5 (ebk.)

ISBN: 978-1-118-21942-3 (ebk.)

No part of this publication may be reproduced, stored in a retrieval system or transmitted in any form or by any means, electronic, mechanical, photocopying, recording, scanning, or otherwise, except as permitted under Sections 107 or 108 of the 1976 United States Copyright Act, without either the prior written permission of the Publisher, or authorization through payment of the appropriate per-copy fee to the Copyright Clearance Center, 222 Rosewood Drive, Danvers, MA 01923, (978) 750-8400, fax (978) 646-8600. Requests to the Publisher for permission should be addressed to the Permissions Department, John Wiley & Sons, Inc., 111 River Street, Hoboken, NJ 07030, (201) 748-6011, fax (201) 748-6008, or online at www.wiley.com/go/permissions.

Limit of Liability/Disclaimer of Warranty: The publisher and the author make no representations or warranties with respect to the accuracy or completeness of the contents of this work and specifically disclaim all warranties, including without limitation warranties of fitness for a particular purpose. No warranty may be created or extended by sales or promotional materials. The advice and strategies contained herein may not be suitable for every situation. This work is sold with the understanding that the publisher is not engaged in rendering legal, accounting, or other professional services. If professional assistance is required, the services of a competent professional person should be sought. Neither the publisher nor the author shall be liable for damages arising herefrom. The fact that an organization or Web site is referred to in this work as a citation and/or a potential source of further information does not mean that the author or the publisher endorses the information the organization or Web site may provide or recommendations it may make. Further, readers should be aware that Internet Web sites listed in this work may have changed or disappeared between when this work was written and when it is read.

For general information on our other products and services or to obtain technical support, please contact our Customer Care Department within the U.S. at (877) 762-2974, outside the U.S. at (317) 572-3993 or fax (317) 572-4002.

Wiley publishes in a variety of print and electronic formats and by print-on-demand. Some material included with standard print versions of this book may not be included in e-books or in print-on-demand. If this book refers to media such as a CD or DVD that is not included in the version you purchased, you may download this material at http://booksupport.wiley.com. For more information about Wiley products, visit www.wiley.com.

Library of Congress Control Number: 2012941757

TRADEMARKS: Wiley, the Wiley logo, and the Sybex logo are trademarks or registered trademarks of John Wiley & Sons, Inc. and/or its affiliates, in the United States and other countries, and may not be used without written permission. EnCase and EnCE are registered trademarks of Guidance Software, Inc. for all such names used in the manual. All other trademarks are the property of their respective owners. John Wiley & Sons, Inc. is not associated with any product or vendor mentioned in this book.

10 9 8 7 6 5 4 3 2 1

Dear Reader,

Thank you for choosing *EnCase Computer Forensics—The Official EnCE: EnCase Certified Examiner Study Guide, Third Edition*. This book is part of a family of premium-quality Sybex books, all of which are written by outstanding authors who combine practical experience with a gift for teaching.

Sybex was founded in 1976. More than 30 years later, we're still committed to producing consistently exceptional books. With each of our titles, we're working hard to set a new standard for the industry. From the paper we print on to the authors we work with, our goal is to bring you the best books available.

I hope you see all that reflected in these pages. I'd be very interested to hear your comments and get your feedback on how we're doing. Feel free to let me know what you think about this or any other Sybex book by sending me an email at nedde@wiley.com. If you think you've found a technical error in this book, please visit http://sybex.custhelp.com. Customer feedback is critical to our efforts at Sybex.

Best regards,

Neil Edde
Vice President and Publisher
Sybex, an Imprint of Wiley

To Donna, my loving wife and partner for life, for your unwavering love, encouragement, and support.

Acknowledgments

Any work of this magnitude requires the hard work of many dedicated people, all doing what they enjoy and what they do best. In addition, many others have contributed indirectly, and without their efforts and support, this book would not have come to fruition. That said, many are people deserving of my gratitude, and my intent here is to acknowledge them all.

I would like to first thank Maureen Adams, former Sybex acquisitions editor, who brought me on board with this project with the first edition and tutored me on the fine nuances of the publishing process. I would also like to thank Jeff Kellum, another Sybex acquisitions editor, for his work on the second edition and most recently the third edition. Jeff guided me through the third edition, trying to keep me on schedule and helping in many ways. I would also like to thank David Clark, developmental editor. David allowed me to concentrate on content while he handled the rest. In addition to many varied skills that you'd normally find with an editor, David has a strong understanding of topic material and has himself written in the technical field, which helped in so many ways. In addition, with several hundred screen shots in this book to mold and shape, I know there is a graphics department at Sybex deserving of my thanks. To those folks, I say thank you.

A special thanks goes to Jessica M. Bair of Guidance Software, Inc. In addition to being a friend and mentor of many years, Jessica was the technical editor for the first edition and again for the third addition. She worked diligently, making sure the technical aspects of both editions are as accurate and as complete as possible.

I would also thank Lisa Stewart, also of Guidance Software, Inc. Lisa is also a friend and colleague of many years. She reviewed the final material for technical accuracy and, as usual, did a superb job of catching those final details and keeping things as accurate as humanly possible.

The study of computer forensics can't exist within a vacuum. To that extent, any individual examiner is a reflection and product of their instructors, mentors, and colleagues. Through them you learn, share ideas, troubleshoot, conduct research, grow, and develop. Over my career, I've had the fortune of interacting with many computer forensics professionals and have learned much through those relationships. In no particular order, I would like to thank the following people for sharing their knowledge over the years: Keith Lockhart, Ben Lewis, Chris Stippich, Grant Wade, Ed Van Every, Raemarie Schmidt, Mark Johnson, Bob Weitershausen, John Colbert, Bruce Pixley, Lance Mueller, Howie Williamson, Lisa Highsmith, Dan Purcell, Ben Cotton, Patrick Paige, John D'Andrea, Mike Feldman, Mike Nelson, Steve Mahoney, Joel Horne, Mark Stringer, Dustin Hurlbut, Fred Cotton, Ross Mayfield, Bill Spernow, Arnie "A. J." Jackson, Ed Novreske, Steve Anson, Warren Kruse, Bob Moses, Kevin Perna, Dan Willey, Scott Garland, and Steve Whalen. I'd also like to thank my fellow ATA Cyber instructors who have shared their knowledge and friendship over the past few years while we trained law enforcement officers together around the world. They are Scott Pearson, Steve Williams, Lance Mueller, Art Ehuan, Nate Tiegland, Gerard Myers, Tom Bureau, and Scot Bradeen. Those who teach, learn.

Every effort has been made to present all material accurately and completely. To achieve this, I verified as much information as possible with multiple sources. In a few instances, published or generally accepted information was in conflict or error. When this occurred, the information was researched and tested, and the most accurate information available was published in this book. I would like to thank the authors of the following publications because I relied on their vast wealth of knowledge and expertise for research and information verification:

Carrier, Brian. *File System Forensic Analysis*. Boston: Addison-Wesley, 2005.

Carvey, Harlan. *Windows Forensics and Incident Recovery*. Boston: Addison-Wesley, 2005.

Carvery, Harlan. *Windows Registry Forensics: Advanced Digital Forensic Analysis of the Windows Registry*. Burlington: Syngress, 2011.

Carvey, Harlan. *Windows Forensic Analysis Including DVD Toolkit*. Burlington: Syngress Publishing, 2007.

Carvey, Harlan. *Windows Forensic Analysis Toolkit, Third Edition: Advanced Analysis Techniques for Windows 7*. Burlington: Syngress Publishing, 2012.

Hipson, Peter. *Mastering Windows XP Registry*. San Francisco: Sybex, 2002.

Honeycutt, Jerry. *Microsoft Windows XP Registry Guide*. Redmond, WA: Microsoft Press, 2003.

Kruse, Warren G. II, and Jay G. Heiser. *Computer Forensics: Incident Response Essentials*. Boston: Addison-Wesley, 2002.

Mueller, Scott. *Upgrading and Repairing PCs*, 17th Edition. Indianapolis, IN: Que Publications, 2006.

These books are valuable resources and should be in every examiner's library. In addition to these publications, I relied heavily on the wealth of information contained in the many training, product, and lab manuals produced by Guidance Software. To the many staff members of Guidance Software who have contributed over the years to these publications, I extend my most grateful appreciation.

Last, but by no means least, I would like to acknowledge the contributions by my parents and my loving wife. My parents instilled in me, at a very young age, an insatiable quest for knowledge that has persisted throughout my life, and I thank them for it along with a lifetime of love and support. My best friend and loving wife, Donna, encouraged and motivated me long ago to pursue computer forensics. Although the pursuit of computer forensics never ends, without her support, sacrifices, motivation, sense of humor, and love, this book would never have been completed.

Thank you, everyone.

About the Author

Steve Bunting   is a senior forensic examiner for Forward Discovery, Inc. In that capacity, he conducts digital examinations on a wide variety of devices and operating systems. He responds to client sites and carries out incident response on compromised systems. He consults with clients of a wide variety of digital forensics and security, as well as electronic discovery matters. He develops and delivers training programs both domestically and abroad.

Prior to becoming a senior forensic examiner with Forward Discovery, Steve Bunting served as a captain with the University of Delaware Police Department, where he was responsible for computer forensics, video forensics, and investigations involving computers. He has more than 35 years' experience in law enforcement, and his background in computer forensics is extensive.

While with the University Police Department's computer forensics unit, Bunting conducted hundreds of examinations for the University Police Department and for many local, state, and federal law enforcement agencies on an wide variety of cases, including extortion, homicide, embezzlement, child exploitation, intellectual property theft, and unlawful intrusions into computer systems. He has also testified in court on several occasions as a computer forensics expert.

As an instructor, Bunting has taught several courses for Guidance Software, makers of EnCase, serving as a lead instructor at all course levels, including the Expert Series (Internet and Email Examinations). Also, he has instructed computer forensics students for the University of Delaware and is also an adjunct faculty member of Goldey-Beacom College. Bunting has taught various forensics courses internationally as well as developing and teaching courses for the Anti-Terrorism Assistance Program Cyber Division.

Bunting is a speaker and an author. Besides the previous editions of this book, he also coauthored the first and second editions of *Mastering Windows Network Forensics and Investigation*.

Some of Bunting's industry credentials include EnCase Certified Examiner (EnCE), Certified Computer Forensics Technician (CCFT), and Access Data Certified Examiner (ACE). He was also the recipient of the 2002 Guidance Software Certified Examiner Award of Excellence and has a bachelor's degree in Applied Professions/Business Management from Wilmington University and a Computer Applications Certificate in Network Environments from the University of Delaware.

Contents at a Glance

Contents

Table of Exercises

Introduction

This book was designed for several audiences. First and foremost, it was designed for anyone seeking the EnCase Certified Examiner (EnCE) credential. This certification has rapidly grown in popularity and demand in all areas of the computer forensics industry. More and more employers are recognizing the importance of this certification and are seeking this credential in potential job candidates. Equally important, courts are placing increasing emphasis on certifications that are specific to computer forensics. The EnCE certification meets or exceeds the needs of the computer forensics industry. Moreover, it has become the global gold standard in computer forensics certification.

This book was also designed for computer forensics students working either in a structured educational setting or in a self-study program. The chapters include exercises, as well as evidence files on the publisher's website, making it the ideal learning tool for either setting.

Finally, this book was written for those with knowledge of EnCase or forensics who simply want to learn more about either or both. Every topic goes well beyond what's needed for certification with the specific intent of overpreparing the certification candidate. In some cases, the material goes beyond that covered in many of the formal training classes you may have attended. In either case, that added depth of knowledge provides comprehensive learning opportunities for the intermediate or advanced user.

The EnCE certification program is geared toward those who have attended the EnCase Intermediate Computer Forensics training or its equivalent. To that extent, this book assumes the reader has a general knowledge of computer forensics and some basic knowledge of EnCase. For those who may need a refresher in either, you'll find plenty of resources. Many users may have used earlier versions of EnCase and have not yet transitioned to EnCase 7. Those users may benefit by starting with Chapter 6, which discusses the EnCase environment, which has radically changed with the release of EnCase 7.

The chapters are organized into related concepts to facilitate the learning process, with basic concepts in the beginning and advanced material at the end. At the end of each chapter, you will find the "Summary," "Exam Essentials," and "Review Questions" sections. The "Summary" section is a brief outline of the essential points contained in the chapter; the "Exam Essentials" section explains the concepts you'll need to understand for the examination.

I strongly urge you to make full use of the "Review Questions" section. A good way to use the questions is as a pretest before reading each chapter and then again as a posttest when you're done. Although answering correctly is always important, it's more important to understand the concepts covered in the question. Make sure you are comfortable with all the material before moving to the next chapter. Just as knowledge is cumulative, a lack thereof impedes that accumulation. As you prepare for your certification examinations (written and practical), take the time to thoroughly understand those items that you may have never understood. The journey along the road to certification is just as important as the destination.

What Is the EnCE Certification?

Guidance Software, Inc., developed the EnCE in late 2001 to meet the needs of its customer base, who requested a solid certification program covering both the use of the EnCase software and computer forensics concepts in general. Since its inception, the EnCE certification has become one of the most recognized and coveted certifications in the global computer forensics industry. You might ask why, but the answer is simple. The process is demanding and challenging. You must have certain knowledge, skills, and abilities to be able to pass both a written and a practical examination. For certain, it is not a "giveaway" program. You will work hard, and you will earn your certification. When you are certified, you'll be proud of your accomplishment. What's more, you will have joined the ranks of the elite in the industry who have chosen to adhere to high standards and to excel in their field. Remember, in the field of computer forensics, excellence is not an option; it is an operational necessity.

Why Become EnCE Certified?

The following benefits are associated with becoming EnCE certified:

- EnCE certification demonstrates professional achievement.
- EnCE certification increases your marketability and provides opportunity for advancement.
- EnCE certification enhances your professional credibility and standing when testifying before courts, hearing boards, and other fact-finding bodies.
- EnCE certification provides peer recognition.

EnCE certification is a rigorous process that documents and demonstrates your achievements and competency in the field of computer forensics. You must have experience as an investigator and examiner, and you must have received training at the EnCase Intermediate Computer Forensics level or other equivalent classroom instruction before you can apply for the program. Next, you will have to pass both a written and a practical examination before receiving your certification. EnCE certification assures customers, employers, courts, your peers, and others that your computer forensics knowledge, skills, and abilities meet the highest professional standards.

How to Become EnCE Certified

Guidance Software publishes on its website the most current requirements and procedures for EnCE certification, which is at www.guidancesoftware.com/computer-forensics-training-ence-certification.htm. Generally, the process, as it currently exists, is as follows, but it could change. Therefore, always check the website for the most accurate procedure. To become EnCE certified, you must do the following:

- Have attended 64 hours authorized computer forensic training (online or classroom) *or* have 12 months computer forensic experience. Register for the test and study guide, which includes completion of the application and payment of required fees.

- Have all application and supporting documents verified by Guidance Software prior to authorization for exam.

- Pass the written test with a minimum score of 80 percent. The test is administered with ExamBuilder or during the Guidance Software EnCE Prep Course. You are given two hours to complete this test.

Complete the practical examination within 60 days with a minimum score of 85 percent. These requirements are quoted directly from Guidance Software's website and are current as of the publication date of this book. You should check the website before you apply to make sure you are complying with the most current requirements. You can find the requirements, the application form, and other important information relating to the EnCE certification program here:

www.guidancesoftware.com/computer-forensics-training-ence-certification.htm

How to Use This Book and the Publisher's Website

We've included several testing features, both in the book and on the publisher's website, which can be accessed at: www.sybex.com/go/ence3e. Following this introduction is an assessment test that you can use to check your readiness for the actual exam. Take this test before you start reading the book. It will help you identify the areas you may need to brush up on. The answers to the assessment test appear after the last question of the test. Each answer includes an explanation and tells you in which chapter this material appears.

As mentioned, to test your knowledge as you progress through the book, each chapter includes review questions at the end. As you finish each chapter, answer the review questions and then check to see whether your answers are right—the correct answers appear in the Appendix A of this book. You can go back to reread the section that deals with each question you got wrong to ensure that you answer the question correctly the next time you are tested on the material. You'll also find 100 flashcard questions on the publisher's website for on-the-go review. Download them onto your mobile device for quick and convenient reviewing.

In addition to the assessment test and the review questions, you'll find two bonus exams on the publisher's website. Take these practice exams just as if you were actually taking the exam (that is, without any reference material). When you have finished the first exam, move on to the next exam to solidify your test-taking skills. If you get more than 85 percent of the answers correct, you're ready to take the real exam.

Also included on the publisher's website are the following:

- Evidence files for use with the EnCase forensic software

- Guidance Software's *EnCase Legal Journal*

- Information on the Guidance Software Forensic and Enterprise products

Guidance Software's *EnCase Legal Journal*

The most important aspect of any computer forensic examination is the legal admissibility of the evidence found. Guidance Software's full-time legal staff provides case law research and litigation support for its EnCase Forensic and EnCase Enterprise customers. As part of its support, Guidance Software provides the *EnCase Legal Journal*.

The *EnCase Legal Journal* was updated in late 2011 with the most up-to-date case law, and it is provided on the publisher's website in a PDF file. Updates to the *EnCase Legal Journal* are available for download from a link on the EnCE FAQ's web page on the Guidance Software website: www.guidancesoftware.com/computer-forensics-training-ence-faqs.htm.

The EnCE written exam includes six legal questions, whose answers are found in the *EnCase Legal Journal*. Individuals preparing for the EnCE exam are strongly encouraged to review this document.

You can contact Guidance Software's legal staff by email at customerservice@guidancesoftware.com.

Tips for Taking the EnCE Exam

When taking the EnCE written test, here are a few tips that have proven helpful:

- Get a good night's rest before your test.

- Eat a healthy meal before your test, avoiding heavy fats and starches that can make you lethargic or drowsy.

- Arrive at your class or testing site early so that you won't feel rushed. Once there, stretch, relax, and put your mind at ease.

- Read each question carefully. Some questions ask for one correct answer, while other questions ask you to select all answers that are correct. Make sure you understand what each question is asking, and don't rush to a quick answer.

- If you don't answer a question, it will be scored as a wrong answer. Given that, it's better to guess than leave an answer blank.

- When you aren't sure of an answer, eliminate the obviously incorrect answers. Consider the remaining choices in the context of the question. Sometimes a keyword can lead you to the correct answer.

- You'll be provided with scratch paper at your examination station. As soon as you sit down and you can start, write down formulas, memory aids, or other facts you may need before starting the exam. Once you do that, you can relax, knowing you have committed those memory items to paper, freeing your memory to work on the questions. You might think of it as being somewhat analogous to the process by which RAM frees up memory space by writing it to the swap file.

Important: Hardware Requirements and Configuring EnCase 7

In past editions, I have not addressed the ideal hardware configuration for running EnCase. However, with EnCase 7 I feel I must address this matter, as it is critical to using EnCase 7. EnCase 7 changed, and with it our hardware and configurations also must change. To be blunt, if you don't change and provide an adequate hardware environment, you won't have a good experience using EnCase 7. Conversely, if you provide EnCase 7 with the proper computing resources and configure them properly, you will be delighted with the features and performance of EnCase 7.

Guidance Software has published a recommended set of hardware specifications upon which I will expound and speak much more forcefully. Those specifications (summarized in Table 1) are found at: `http://download.guidancesoftware.com/ADlkyEKTv9Dwc77R5rnLOCbRPyHOsC/47tjQ24rmxcbIDESZsIpBlaict49llscMsOOVTjszsVQw862ZZ dCajXnSXeLBk9KXCsBTyxXA7kg%3D` or `http://tiny.cc/sjmzgw`.

TABLE 1:   Guidance Software Hardware Recommendations

Component	Recommended Specifications
Memory	16 GB
Storage Drives	Drive 1: Operating System and page file Drive 2: Evidence Drive 3: Primary Evidence Cache—this drive should be as fast as possible
CPU	Quad-core i7
Operating System	Windows 7 (64-bit) or Windows Server 2008 (64-bit)

TABLE 2:   Author's Hardware Recommendations

Component	Recommended Specifications
Memory	16 GB (more is better, though!)
Storage Drives	Drive 1: Operating System and page file (use SSD) Drive 2: Evidence (RAID 5 delivers high throughput for reads) Drive 3: Primary Evidence Cache—(use SSD in RAID 0 configuration)
CPU	Quad-core i7
Operating System	Windows 7 (64-bit) or Windows Server 2008 (64-bit)

EnCase 7 throughout its range of functions relies upon a high volume of reads and writes to the evidence cache. Some data that used to reside in RAM in previous versions of EnCase (mounted compound files for example) is now stored in evidence cache. It only makes logical sense to have the fastest possible throughput for both reads and writes to the evidence cache, which with today's technology would be SSDs (solid state drives) configured in a RAID 0 configuration. For those concerned about data loss in a RAID 0, rest assured that EnCase 7.04 has resolved that issue with a backup feature that backs up your evidence cache and your case files every 30 minutes.

Along the same lines, the Encase Evidence Processor will make a very large number of reads and writes to cache files and temporary files on the operating system drive. Aside from that, the O/S drive is a very busy drive on any platform and especially on a forensics platform. It only makes sense, then, to use an SSD for your operating system. Considering all the cost that goes into a computer forensics platform, this added cost is insignificant. When you see the performance increase you get by having your O/S on an SSD, you'll never question the decision to have done so!

Finally, you want to have your evidence files available on the local system bus and available for fast reads. A hardware-based RAID 5 offers fast throughput for read activity and provides the added benefit of redundancy in the event of a single drive failure in the RAID 5. If you get near twice the speed when EnCase reads your evidence files, that cuts processing time in half for that portion of the task.

For those of you contemplating storing evidence cache on network-attached storage, don't do it. Performance will be miserable. If you attempt to process evidence files over network resources, you can expect lowered performance. You would do well to reserve network storage for backup purposes, which would be for EnCase's backup feature and redundant copies of evidence files. Even a fiber-connected SAN is a shared resource and that bandwidth is shared. EnCase 7 is at its best when throughput to all data is optimized.

If you are running anti-virus software, you will do well to disable it while running EEP and various other resource-intensive processing routines in EnCase. Further, you should disable Windows indexing and searching as this consumes resources and isn't usually a feature an examiner uses on a forensic platform.

I recently tested two systems. They were nearly identical, except that one machine was using platter-based storage and the other was using SSD-based storage and RAID 5 with a SAS controller for evidence files. The latter processed the evidence using the EnCase Evidence Processor in less than a third of the time taken by the former. When you're looking at days to process evidence, that effectively means one day instead of three days, two days instead of six days, and so forth. The advantages of configuring EnCase 7 with SSDs can't be overstated. You will see EnCase 7 shine if you provide it with the proper resources.

I have summarized my hardware recommendations in Table 2. They are more robust and specific than those recommended by Guidance Software, but you will have a much improved experience with EnCase 7 if you follow them.

SSDs do wear out and, with time, you may experience degraded performance as their memory cells are depleted. Just when that occurs will depend on brand, quality, usage, and so forth. On the other hand, platter-based drives also wear out and are much slower. Thus there is no perfect solution and much depends on your budget and your tolerance to slower performance, along with other factors.

Assessment Test

1. You are a computer forensic examiner tasked with determining what evidence is on a seized computer. On what part of the computer system will you find data of evidentiary value?

   A. Microprocessor or CPU

   B. USB controller

   C. Hard drive

   D. PCI expansion slots

2. You are a computer forensic examiner explaining how computers store and access the data you recovered as evidence during your examination. The evidence is a log file and was recovered as an artifact of user activity on the _____, which was stored on the _____, contained within a _____ on the media.

   A. partition, operating system, file system

   B. operating system, file system, partition

   C. file system, operating system, hard drive

   D. operating system, partition, file system

3. You are a computer forensic examiner investigating a seized computer. You recovered a document containing potential evidence. EnCase reports the file system on the forensic image of the hard drive is File Allocation Table (FAT). What information about the document file can be found in the FAT on the media? (Choose all that apply.)

   A. Name of the file

   B. Date and time stamps of the file

   C. Starting cluster of the file

   D. Fragmentation of the file

   E. Ownership of the file

4. You are a computer forensic examiner investigating media on a seized computer. You recovered a document containing potential evidence. EnCase reports the file system on the forensic image of the hard drive is New Technology File System (NTFS). What information about the document file can be found in the NTFS master file table on the media? (Choose all that apply.)

   A. Name of the file

   B. Date and time stamps of the file

   C. Starting cluster of the file

   D. Fragmentation of the file

   E. Ownership of the file

5. You are preparing to lead a team to serve a search warrant on a business suspected of committing large-scale consumer fraud. Ideally, you would assign which tasks to search team members? (Choose all that apply.)

   A. Photographer

   B. Search and seizure specialists

   C. Recorder

   D. Digital evidence search and seizure specialists

6. You are a computer forensic examiner at a scene and have determined you will seize a Linux server, which, according to your source of information, contains the database records for the company under investigation for fraud. What is the best practice for "taking down" the server for collection?

   A. Photograph the screen and note any running programs or messages, capture volatile data, and so on, and use the normal shutdown procedure.

   B. Photograph the screen and note any running programs or messages, capture volatile data, and so on, and pull the plug from the wall.

   C. Photograph the screen and note any running programs or messages, capture volatile data, and so on, and pull the plug from the rear of the computer.

   D. Photograph the screen and note any running programs or messages, capture volatile data, and so on, and ask the user at the scene to shut down the server.

7. You are a computer forensic examiner at a scene and are authorized to seize only media that can be determined to have evidence related to the investigation. What options do you have to determine whether evidence is present before seizure and a full forensic examination? (Choose all that apply.)

   A. Use a DOS boot floppy or CD to boot the machine, and browse through the directory for evidence.

   B. Use a forensically sound Linux boot CD to boot the machine into Linux, and use LinEn to preview the hard drive through a crossover cable with EnCase for Windows.

   C. Remove the subject hard drive from the machine, and preview the hard drive in EnCase for Windows with a hardware write blocker such as FastBloc/Tableau.

   D. Boot the computer into Windows and use Explorer search utility to find the finds being sought.

8. You are a computer forensic examiner at a scene and have determined you will need to image a hard drive in a workstation while on-site. What are your options for creating a forensically sound image of the hard drive? (Choose all that apply.)

   A. Use a regular DOS boot floppy or CD to boot the machine, and use EnCase for DOS to image the subject hard drive to a second hard drive attached to the machine.

   B. Use a forensically sound Linux boot CD to boot the machine into Linux, and use LinEn to image the subject hard drive to a second hard drive attached to the machine.

   C. Remove the subject hard drive from the machine, and image the hard drive in EnCase for Windows with a hardware write blocker such as FastBloc/Tableau.

   D. Use a forensically sound Linux boot CD to boot the machine into Linux, and use LinEn to image the hard drive through a crossover cable with EnCase for Windows.

9. You are a computer forensic examiner and have imaged a hard drive on site. Before you leave the scene, you want to ensure the image completely verifies as an exact forensic duplicate of the original. To verify the EnCase evidence file containing the image, you should do which of the following?

  A. Use a hex editor to compare a sample of sectors in the EnCase evidence file with that of the original.

  B. Load the EnCase evidence files into EnCase for Windows, and after the verification is more than halfway completed, cancel the verification and spot-check the results for errors.

  C. Load the EnCase evidence files into EnCase for DOS, and verify the hash of those files.

  D. Load the EnCase evidence files into EnCase for Windows, allow the verification process to finish, and then check the results for complete verification.

10. You are a computer forensic examiner and need to verify the integrity of an EnCase evidence file. To completely verify the file's integrity, which of the following must be true?

  A. The MD5 hash value must verify.

  B. The CRC values and the MD5 hash value both must verify.

  C. Either the CRC or MD5 hash values must verify.

  D. The CRC values must verify.

11. You are a computer forensic examiner and need to determine what files are contained within a folder called `Business documents`. What EnCase pane will you use to view the names of the files in the folder?

  A. Tree pane

  B. Table pane

  C. View pane

  D. EnScripts pane

12. You are a computer forensic examiner and need to view the contents of a file contained within a folder called `Business documents`. What EnCase pane will you use to view the contents of the file?

  A. Tree pane

  B. Table pane

  C. View pane

  D. EnScripts pane

13. You are a computer forensic examiner and are viewing a file in an EnCase evidence file. With your cursor, you have selected one character in the file. What binary term is used for the amount of data that represents a single character?

  A. A bit

  B. A nibble

  C. A byte

  D. A word

14. You are a computer forensic examiner and need to search for the name of a suspect in an EnCase evidence file. You enter the name of the suspect into the EnCase keyword interface as John Doe. What search hits will be found with this search term with the default settings? (Choose all that apply.)

   A. John Doe

   B. John D.

   C. john doe

   D. John.Doe

15. You are a computer forensic examiner and need to determine whether any Microsoft Office documents have been renamed with image extensions to obscure their presence. What EnCase process would you use to find such files?

   A. File signature analysis

   B. Recover Folders feature

   C. File content search

   D. File hash analysis

16. You are a computer forensic examiner and want to reduce the number of files required for examination by identifying and filtering out known good or system files. What EnCase process would you use to identify such files?

   A. File signature analysis

   B. Recover Folders feature

   C. File content search

   D. File hash analysis

17. You are a computer forensic examiner and want to determine whether a user has opened or double-clicked a file. What folder would you look in for an operating system artifact for this user activity?

   A. Temp

   B. Recent

   C. Cookies

   D. Desktop

18. You are a computer forensic examiner and want to determine when a user deleted a file contained in a Windows 7 Recycle Bin. In what file is the date and time information about the file deletion contained?

   A. $ROF5B7C.docx

   B. $IOF5B7C.docx

   C. INFO2

   D. deleted.ini

19. You are a computer forensic examiner and want to determine how many times a program was executed. Where would you find information?

A. Temp folder

B. Registry

C. Recycle Bin

D. Program Files

20. You are a computer forensic examiner and want to examine any email sent and received by the user of the computer system under investigation. What email formats are supported by EnCase? (Choose all that apply.)

A. Outlook PSTs

B. Outlook Express

C. America Online

D. MBOX

E. Lotus Notes NSF

F. Microsoft Exchange EDB

Answers to Assessment Test

1. **C.** The hard drive is the main storage media for most computer systems; it holds the boot files, operating system files, programs, and data, and it will be the primary source of evidence during a forensic examination of a computer system. See Chapter 1 for more information.

2. **B.** A file system is nothing more than system or method of storing and retrieving data on a computer system that allows for a hierarchy of directories, subdirectories, and files. It is contained within a partition on the media. File systems are the management tools for storing and retrieving data in a partition. Some operating systems require certain file systems for them to function. Windows needs a FAT or NTFS file system, depending on its "flavor" or version, and won't recognize or mount other systems with its own native operating system. See Chapter 1 for more information.

3. **C, D.** A major component of the FAT file system is the File Allocation Table (FAT), which, among other functions, tracks the sequence of clusters used by a file when more than one cluster is allocated or used. In addition to tracking cluster runs or sequences, the FAT tracks the allocation status of clusters, assuring that the operating system stores data in clusters that are available and that those storing data assigned to files or directories aren't overwritten. FAT does not track file ownership. The other information about the file is stored in directory entries. See Chapter 2 for more information.

4. **A, B, C, D, E.** A file system used by the Windows operating system, starting with Windows NT, is the NTFS file system. NTFS, compared to FAT file systems, is more robust, providing stronger security, greater recoverability, and better performance with regard to read, write, and searching capabilities. Among other features, it supports long filenames, a highly granular system of file permissions, ownership and access control, and compression of individual files and directories. The master file table in NTFS contains, among other items, the name of a file, the date and time stamps of the file, the starting cluster of a file, the fragmentation of a file, and the ownership of a file. See Chapter 2 for more information.

5. **A, B, C, D.** After the area is secure, the search team enters the area and begins their job. Before anything is touched or removed, the scene is recorded through a combination of field notes, sketches, video, or still images. Once the area has been recorded to show how things were initially found, the search team begin its methodical search and seizure process. Search teams often consist of the following functions:

   - *Recorder*: Takes detailed notes of everything seized

   - *Photographer*: Photographs all items in place before seized

   - *Search and seizure specialist*: Searches and seizes and bags and tags traditional evidence (documents, pictures, drugs, weapons, and so on)

   - *Digital evidence search and seizure specialist*: Searches and seizes and bags and tags digital evidence of all types

   See Chapter 3 for more information.

6. A. For Linux and Unix servers, photograph the screen, noting any running programs or messages, and so on, and use the normal shutdown procedure.

In many cases, the user will need to be root to shut down the system. If it's a GUI, right-click the desktop, and from the context menu, select Console or Terminal. At the resulting prompt, look for # at the right end. If it doesn't appear, type **su root**. You will be prompted for a password. If you have it, type it. If you don't have it, you'll probably have no choice but to pull the plug if the system administrator isn't available or can't be trusted. When at root, note the # at the end of the prompt. When at root, type **shutdown -h now**, and the system should halt. See Chapter 3 for more information.

7. B, C. The purpose of the forensic boot disk is to boot the computer and load an operating system, but to do so in a forensically sound manner in which the evidentiary media is not changed. Using a regular DOS boot disk will change the evidence. EnCase provides many options for previewing subject hard drives before seizure. See Chapter 4 for more information.

8. B, C, D. The purpose of the forensic boot disk is to boot the computer and load an operating system but to do so in a forensically sound manner in which the evidentiary media is not changed. Using a regular DOS boot disk will change the evidence. EnCase provides many options for imaging subject hard drives. See Chapter 4 for more information.

9. D. The verification of EnCase evidence files is conducted in EnCase for Windows and starts automatically when an EnCase evidence file is added to EnCase. The verification must be allowed to complete to confirm the validity of the image. See Chapter 5 for more information.

10. B. When an EnCase evidence file containing an MD5 hash value is added to a case, EnCase verifies both the CRC and MD5 hash values. Both must verify to confirm the complete integrity of the EnCase evidence file. See Chapter 5 for more information.

11. B. In the EnCase environment, the Table pane contains a list of all objects (files) within a folder selected in the Tree pane. This pane has columns for the metadata of each file, including the name. Also, there is no EnScripts pane. See Chapter 6 for more information.

12. C. In the EnCase environment, the View pane allows you to view the contents of a file, both in the Text and Hex tabs. Also, there is no EnScripts pane. See Chapter 6 for more information.

13. C. A single character stored on digital media is composed of eight bits, each either 0 or 1. This set of 8 bits is known as a *byte*. See Chapter 7 for more information.

14. A, C. By default, EnCase will find both uppercase and lowercase versions of a search term. The other terms could be found with a properly crafted GREP expression. See Chapter 7 for more information.

15. A. Until a file signature analysis is run, EnCase relies on a file's extension to determine its file type, which in turn determines the viewer used to display the data. A file signature analysis is initiated or run from within the EnCase Evidence Processor. Once a file signature is run, EnCase will view files based on file header information and not based on file extension. This is critical for viewing files whose extensions are missing or have been changed. See Chapter 8 for more information.

16. D. File hashing and analysis, within EnCase, are based on the MD5 hashing algorithm. When a file is hashed using the MD5, the result is a 128-bit value. The odds of any two dissimilar files having the same MD5 hash is one in 2^{128}, or approximately one in 340 billion billion billion billion. Using this method, you can statistically infer that the file content will be the same for files that have identical hash values and that the file content will differ for files that do not have identical hash values. This can be used to identify known good or system files. See Chapter 8 for more information.

17. B. Certain actions by the user create link files without their knowledge. Because the user is creating virtual "tracks in the snow," such files are of particular forensic interest. Specifically, when a user opens a document, a link file is created in the Recent folder, which appears in the root of the user folder named after the user's logon name in legacy versions of Windows, but now appears deep down in the roaming branch of the user's AppData folder. The link files in this folder serve as a record of the documents opened by the user. See Chapter 9 for more information.

18. B. The INFO2 file is a database file containing information about the files in a legacy Windows Recycle Bin. Current Windows Recycle Bins use pairs of $I and $R files, with the former containing the file deletion metadata and he later being the deleted file. When you look at files in the Recycle Bin, you are really looking at the contents of all of the $I files. Thus, when a file is sent to the Recycle Bin, the following information is placed these files: the file's original filename and path (entered twice, once in ASCII and again in Unicode) and the date and time of deletion. See Chapter 9 for more information.

19. B. The Windows registry contains a great deal of information and artifacts about user activity on a computer system, including the number of times a particular program is executed. See Chapter 10 for more information.

20. A, B, C, D, E, F. EnCase 7 supports all of the listed email formats. See Chapter 10 for more information.

Computer Hardware

ENCE EXAM TOPICS COVERED IN THIS CHAPTER:

- ✓ Computer hardware components
- ✓ The boot process
- ✓ Partitions
- ✓ File systems

Computer forensics examiners deal most often with the media on which evidentiary data is stored. This includes, but is not limited to, hard drives, CDs, DVDs, flash memory devices, smart phones, tablets, and even legacy floppies and tapes. Although these devices might be the bane of the examiner's existence, media devices don't exist in a void, and knowledge of a computer's various components and functions is a must for the competent examiner.

As an examiner, you may be called upon to explain how a computer functions to a jury. Doing so requires you know a computer's function from a technical standpoint and that you can translate those technical concepts into real-world, easy-to-understand terms.

As an examiner, you may also be subjected to a *voir dire* examination by opposing counsel to challenge your competence to testify. Acronyms are hardly in short supply in the field of computing—some well-known and meaningful, others more obscure. Imagine being asked during such an examination to explain several of the common acronyms used with computers, such as RAM, CMOS, SCSI, BIOS, and POST. If you were to draw a blank on some obscure or even common acronym, picture its impact on your credibility.

Some acronyms are difficult to remember because their meaning is often obscure or meaningless. A good example is TWAIN, which stands for **Tech**nology **W**ithout **a**n **I**nteresting **N**ame.

You may encounter problems with a computer system under examination or with your own forensic platform. Troubleshooting and configuration require knowledge of the underlying fundamentals if you are to be successful.

Thus, the purpose of this chapter is to provide you with a solid understanding of the various components of a computer and show how a single spark of electricity brings those otherwise dead components to life through a process known as *booting* the computer. In addition, you'll learn about the drive partitions and file systems used by computer systems.

Computer Hardware Components

Every profession has, at its core, a group of terms and knowledge that is shared and understood by its practitioners. Computer forensics is certainly no exception. In this section, I discuss the various terms used to describe a computer's components and systems.

Case   The case, or chassis, is usually metal, and it surrounds, contains, and supports the computer system components. It shields electrical interference (both directions) and provides protection from dust, moisture, and direct-impact damage to the internal components. It is sometimes erroneously called the *central processing unit* (CPU), which it is not.

Read-Only Memory (ROM)   This is a form of memory that can hold data permanently, or nearly so, by virtue of its property of being impossible or difficult to change or write. Another important property of ROM is that it is nonvolatile, meaning the data remains when the system is powered off. Having these properties (read-only and nonvolatile) makes ROM ideal for files containing start-up configuration settings and code needed to boot the computer (ROM BIOS).

Random Access Memory (RAM)   A computer's main memory is its temporary workspace for storing data, code, settings, and so forth. It has come to be called RAM because it exists as a bank of memory chips that can be randomly accessed. Before chips, tape was the primary media, and accessing tape was—and still is—a slow, linear or sequential process. With the advent of chips and media on drives (both floppy and hard drives), data could be accessed randomly and directly and therefore with much greater speed. Hence, *random access memory* was the name initially given to this type of memory to differentiate from its tape predecessor. Today most memory can be accessed randomly, and the term's original functional meaning, differentiating it from tape, has been lost to history. What distinguishes RAM from ROM, among other properties, is the property known as *volatility*. RAM is usually volatile memory, meaning that upon losing power, the data stored in memory is lost. ROM, by contrast, is nonvolatile memory, meaning the data remains when the power is off. It is important to note, however, that there are nonvolatile forms of RAM memory known as nonvolatile random access memory (NVRAM), and thus you should not be quick to assume that all RAM is nonvolatile.

The computer forensic examiner, more often than not, encounters computers that have been shut down, seized, and delivered for examination. Important information in RAM (the computer's volatile memory) is lost when the computer's plug is pulled. All is not lost, however, because this data is often written to the hard drive in a file called the *swap file*. This swap file, in its default configuration, can grow and shrink in most Microsoft Windows systems, which means this data can be in the swap file itself, as well as in unallocated clusters and in file slack as the swap file is resized. Unallocated clusters and file slack are areas containing data that is no longer in an allocated file. I'll cover them in detail in Chapter 2. What's more, if the computer was in the hibernate mode, the entire contents of RAM are written to a file named hiberfil.sys so that the contents of RAM can be restored from disk. In fact, the system can be restored in the time it takes to read the hiberfil.sys file into RAM. It should be no surprise to learn that the hiberfil.sys file is the same size as the system's RAM memory size!

Power Supply   The power supply transforms supply voltage (120VAC or 240VAC) to voltages and current flows required by the various system components. DC voltages of 3.3 volts, 5 volts, and 12 volts are provided on a power supply for an ATX form factor motherboard.

The standard molex power connector used frequently by examiners has four wires providing two different voltages (yellow = 12VDC+, black = ground, black = ground, red = 5VDC+).

Motherboard or Mainboard   This component is the largest printed circuit card within the computer case. It is mounted on "stand-offs" to raise it above the case, providing a space for airflow and preventing contact or grounding of the printed circuits with the case. The motherboard typically contains the following: the CPU socket, BIOS, CMOS, CMOS battery, Real-Time Clock (RTC), RAM memory slots, Integrated Drive Electronics (IDE) controllers, Serial Advanced Technology Attachment (SATA) controllers, Universal Serial Bus (USB) controllers, floppy disk controllers, Accelerated Graphics Port (AGP) or Peripheral Component Interconnect (PCI) Express video slots, PCI or PCI Express expansion slots, and so forth. Many features that once required separate expansion cards are now offered onboard, such as Small Computer System Interface (SCSI) controllers, network interface (Gigabit Ethernet and wireless), video, sound, and FireWire (1394a and b).

Microprocessor or CPU   The brains of the unit, the CPU is a massive array of transistors arranged in microscopic layers. The CPU performs data processing, or interprets and executes instructions. Accordingly, most of the computer's function and instructions are carried out in this unit. Modern processors generate enormous amounts of heat, and quickly and efficiently eliminating heat is essential to both the function and survival of the component.

Heat Sink and Fan   At the very least, a heat sink and fan will be attached to the CPU to keep it cool. The heat sink interfaces directly with the CPU (or other heat-generating chip), usually with a thermal compound sandwiched between. The heat sink consists of a high-thermal conductance material whose job it is to draw the heat from the chip and to dissipate that heat energy into the surrounding air (with the assistance of the fan, with an array of cooling fins). Some high-end platforms will have thermal solutions (heat sinks and fans) mounted to RAM memory, chipsets, hard drives, and video cards. Water-cooling systems are becoming more popular with gamers. Use caution working around these systems because water and electricity are usually at odds; therefore, damage to systems can occur.

Hard Drive   This is the main storage media for most computer systems; it holds the boot files, operating system files, programs, and data. It consists of a series of hard thin platters revolving at speeds ranging from 4,800 to 15,000 revolutions per minute (RPM). These platters (which are magnetized) are accessed by heads moving across their surfaces as they spin. The heads can read or write, detecting or creating microscopic changes in polarity, with positive changes being 1s and negative changes being 0s—which is why we refer to the binary system of "1s and 0s."

Hard drive platters have an addressing scheme so that the various locations where data is stored can be located for reads and writes. Originally this addressing scheme involved the CHS system (C = Cylinder, H = Head, and S = Sector). A *sector* is the smallest amount of space on a drive that can be written to at a time. A sector contains 512 bytes that can be used by the operating system. Each side of the platter is formatted with a series of concentric circles known as *tracks*. Sectors are contained in the tracks, and originally each track contains the same number of sectors. A *cylinder* is a logical construct; it is a point on all the platters where the heads align along a vertical axis passing through the same sector number on all the platters. There are two *heads* for each platter, one for each side (side 0 and side 1). Depending on the number of platters present, the heads will be numbered. To determine the number of bytes present on a hard drive, a formula is used: $C \times H \times S \times 512$ = total storage bytes. The C is the total number of cylinders, the H is the total number of heads, the S is the number of sectors per track, and 512 is a constant that represents the number of bytes in a sector usable by the operating system (OS).

This formula holds true as long as the number of sectors per track remains the same for all tracks, which applies to older, lower-capacity hard drives. This system, however, has limitations for hard drive storage capacity. The limitations reflect how densely populated (sectors per track) the inner tracks are. The outer tracks, by contrast, can always hold more data than the inner tracks and contain wasted storage space. To overcome this limitation, Zoned-Bit Recording (ZBR) was developed; in ZBR, the number of sectors per track varies in zones, with the outer zones containing more sectors per track than the inner zones. This system has vastly improved data storage capacities.

The formula, however, is not valid for modern drives, because the number of sectors per track is no longer constant if ZBR is present. To address the larger-capacity hard drives, a new addressing scheme has been developed, called Logical Block Addressing (LBA). In this system, sectors are addressed simply by sector number, starting with sector zero, and the hard drive's electronics translate the sector number to a CHS value understood by the drive. To determine the storage capacity of hard drives using ZBR, you determine the total LBA sectors and multiply that number by 512 (bytes per sector). The product yields the total storage capacity of the drive in bytes (total LBA sectors × 512 = total storage capacity in bytes).

Depending on their electrical interface or controller, hard drives can be Advanced Technology Attachment (ATA), which is now often called PATA to differentiate parallel from serial with the advent of SATA; SATA (Serial ATA); or SCSI.

Solid State Drive (SSD)   SSDs do away with moving parts altogether, and all data is stored, currently, on NAND memory chips of the same type found in USB thumb drives. This data is persistent and is therefore dubbed nonvolatile. You may also encounter a hybrid drive that is a traditional hard drive (spinning magnetic platter storage) with an SSD. These drives attempt to combine the advantages of both types of drives into one drive. SSD drives are rapidly evolving in terms of speed and storage capacity. As of 2011, you will find them mostly in portable computing devices, but in time, they will become mainstream storage devices in desktop computers as well. SSDs have several different form factors. You may find them in standard hard disk drive (HDD) housings for compatibility with existing technologies. You may find them in a boxed format designed to fit a rack mount system. You may also find them in various bare board form factors to install via a connector to the motherboard. Finally, you may find them in a ball grid array in which the memory chips are soldered directly onto the system motherboard. The latter saves space and energy and will no doubt be used more often in the future. To further complicate matters, the various form factors employ various types of connectors, including SATA, mini-SATA, proprietary connections, and direct solder connections.

Small Computer Systems Interface (SCSI)   SCSI is an electronic interface that originated with Apple computer systems and migrated to other systems. It is a high-speed, high-performance interface used on devices requiring high input/output, such as scanners and hard drives. The SCSI BIOS is an intelligent BIOS that queues read/write requests in a manner that improves performance, making it the choice for high-end systems. SCSI drives do not use the master-slave pin configurations of the IDE counterparts. Rather, they are assigned ID numbers that are most often set by pinning jumpers.

Integrated Drive Electronics (IDE) Controller   IDE is a generic term for any drive with its own integrated drive controller. Originally there were three types, but only one survived; it is known as Advanced Technology Attachment (ATA). Officially, the IDE interface today is called ATA, and the two names will often be used interchangeably. Two IDE connectors are found on the motherboard, one labeled *primary IDE* and the other *secondary IDE*. Each is capable of handling two IDE devices (hard drive, CD, DVD), for a maximum of four IDE devices. Of the two devices on the same IDE ribbon cable, one is the *master*, and the other is the *slave*. One places jumpers on pins to designate the master or slave status. Typically the boot hard drive will be attached to the primary controller, and it is the master if two devices are present on that IDE channel. Alternatively, you could use the Cable Select (CS) method of pinning by which the assignment of master-slave is done automatically, provided you use a cable that properly supports CSEL (another way of abbreviating Cable SELect) signaling. On an 80-conductor IDE/ATA cable using CS, the drive at the end of the cable will be assigned as master, and the drive assigned to the middle connector will be the slave.

Serial Advanced Technology Attachment (SATA) controller   By the beginning of this century, IDE (ATA) hard drives had been around for a long time, but the electronic circuitry by which the data was sent had reached its upper limit (133 megabytes per second, or MBps). In August 2001, a new standard, known as SATA 1.0, was finalized and approved. SATA uses serial circuitry, which allows data to be sent, initially, at 150 MBps. SATA II standards, released on October 2002, have found their way into the market, with SATA II drives now delivering buffer-to-host transfer rates of 300 MBps. Unlike IDE drives, SATA drives require no "pinning." SATA ports can be found on most modern motherboards, and they often have RAID 0 available to them. IDE drives are starting to disappear and are being replaced by SATA drives. Even though IDE drives are being phased out, forensic examiners can expect to see them around for a long time, because they were in use for more than 10 years.

Serial Attached SCSI (SAS)   SCSI drives reached their limit as they, like their ATA drive counterparts, relied upon parallel bus technology for data transmission. As SATA replaced ATA using a serial bus technology, SAS replaced SCSI with a point-to-point serial bus technology. SAS continues to use the SCSI command set. SAS drives and tape drives are usually found in the high-end computers (servers, data centers, and so on). SAS offers backward compatibility with generation-two SATA drives, meaning you can attach a SATA drive (second generation) to an SAS backplane, but you can't attach an SAS drive to any SATA backplane. As you might expect, SAS drives use yet another connector—several actually—all of which are much smaller than their SCSI predecessor connectors. SAS currently supports speeds of 6 Gbps, with 12 Gbps expected in late 2012.

Redundant Array of Inexpensive Disks (RAID) First I'll clear the air on the acronym RAID. It means Redundant Array of Independent Drives (or Disks), and it is also known as Redundant Array of Inexpensive Drives (or Disks). Thus, the letter *I* can mean inexpensive or independent, and the letter *D* can mean drives or disks. But if you find yourself in an argument over this at your next geek cocktail party, don't bet the ranch because either combination of these words is correct. A RAID is an array of two or more disks combined in such a way as to increase performance or increase fault tolerance. In a RAID 0, data is striped over two or more disks, which increases performance by reducing read and write times. However, if any disk fails in a RAID 0, all data is lost. In a RAID 1, data is mirrored over the drives in the array. A RAID 1 does not increase performance, but it does create redundant data, thereby increasing fault tolerance. In a RAID 5 configuration, typically data is stored on three drives, although other configurations can be created. Data is striped over two drives, and a parity stripe is created on the third. Should any one drive fail, it can be "rebuilt" from the data of the other two. RAID 5 achieves fault tolerance and increased performance. RAID 0 + 1 is a relatively new type of RAID. It is typically configured with four drives; one pair is used for striping data, and the other pair is a mirror of the striped pair. With this configuration, you again achieve high performance and fault tolerance. RAID 0 + 1 can also be found as RAID 1 + 0. While similar, with the former (0+1), the stripe is built before the mirror. With the latter (1+0), the mirror is built before the stripe. Rather than digress into a discussion of the performance issues of these two different configurations, over which reasonable technicians can find grounds for dispute, we'll move on.

Floppy Drive Floppy drives used to be primary storage devices. Currently they are used to store and move small amounts of data, since the capacity of the 3.5-inch floppy is only 1.44 MB of data. Forensic examiners often use them as boot drives to boot systems for DOS acquisitions, which is a method of acquiring data using a DOS boot disk. I'll cover this extensively in Chapter 4. Floppy drives are being phased out in lieu of CD/DVD drives and USB thumb drives.

When going out into the field to image a system, always pack a spare internal 3.5-inch floppy drive. You may have to do a DOS acquisition, and the target system may not be equipped with a floppy drive. Or, the one present may be defective, and a CD boot may not be an option. Note that EnCase v7 retired the DOS version of EnCase (en.exe) that can load from a floppy disk. Linux EnCase (linen) is available, which uses 32-bit processing vs. only 16-bit in DOS. However, linen will not fit on a floppy disk, so a CD-ROM drive would be used.

Compact Disc – Read-Only Memory (CD-ROM) or Compact Disc – Read/Write (CD-RW) Drive   CD drives use laser beams to read indentations and flat areas as 1s and 0s, respectively. The data is formatted into a continuous spiral emanating from the center to the outside. (In contrast, hard drive data is formatted into concentric circles.) CD-ROM is read-only technology, whereas CD-RW permits writing to CD media in addition to reading.

Digital Versatile Disc – Read-Only Memory (DVD-ROM) or Digital Versatile Disc – Read/Write (DVD-RW)   DVD drives use a technology similar to that of CD drives. The laser beam used with DVDs is a shorter wavelength, creating smaller pits and lands, which are actually depressions and elevations in the physical surface. The result is a spiral track that is more densely populated with data. Couple this improvement with layered spiral tracks, and the gain in data storage capacity is tremendous. Whereas a CD stores, at most, approximately 700 MB of data, a DVD can hold 8 GB to 17 GB of data, with higher densities on the horizon.

USB Controller   Universal serial bus (USB) is a external peripheral bus standard capable of high-speed serial input/output (USB 1.1 = 1.5 Mbps, USB 2 = 480 Mbps, and USB 3 = 5 Gbps). It was developed to facilitate Plug and Play for external devices, without the need for expansion cards and configuration issues.

USB Port   This is a rectangular-shaped port connected to the USB controller, with pins for four conductors (1: cable power, 2: data negative, 3: data positive, and 4: ground—all surrounded by shielding). These ports are used for USB connections, which can be external storage devices, cameras, license dongles, keyboards, mice, and so forth.

IEEE 1394   Also known as FireWire (the name licensed by Apple) or iLink (Sony), 1394 is yet another high-speed serial I/O standard. Its Plug and Play capabilities are on a parallel with USB. The 1394 standard comes now in two speeds. The 1394a standard is the original version, moving data at 400 Mbps. The 1394b standard is the latest version, moving data at 800 Mbps, with gigabit speeds planned soon. 1394 allows "daisy chaining" of devices, with a maximum of 63 nodes.

IEEE 1394a Ports   FireWire ports are similar to USB ports, except that one end is slightly rounded or pointed. There are six wires/pins in a 1394 connection, with two pairs of clock and data lines, plus two for power (one positive, one negative). FireWire ports are used primarily for external high-speed storage devices, cameras, multimedia systems, and so forth.

IEEE 1394b Ports   FireWire 800 or IEEE 1394b ports are rectangular in shape with a dimpled inset to make them unique. Whereas 1394a used six conductors, 1394b uses nine conductors. Of the three additional conductors, two are used for shielding (A Shield and B Shield). The added shielding provides an improved signal and higher transfer rate, allowing 1394b to have data rates of 786.432 Mbps, usually rounded to 800.

Thunderbolt Ports   Just when everyone thought that USB3 was fast, and it is at 5 Gbps, Apple debuted Thunderbolt in February 2011. Developed by Intel and brought to market by Apple, Thunderbolt is a serial connection interface for peripherals being connected to a computer via an expansion bus. Up to seven devices can be daisy-chained on a Thunderbolt port, up to two of which can be high-resolution monitors using DisplayPort. The speed of Thunderbolt, however, is what caused the real shockwave. Thunderbolt can move data at 10 Gbps, and that is bidirectional. For forensics, this is great news because moving more data faster is always in great demand.

Target Disk Mode (TDM) and Thunderbolt

For those who use TDM to boot Macintosh systems for imaging, you are accustomed to seeing the FireWire symbol when booting successfully into TDM. If the machine supports Thunderbolt, you will see a Thunderbolt icon when booting to TDM. If the machine has both FireWire and Thunderbolt, you will see both icons. That is not to say, however, that you will get full Thunderbolt speed from TDM. Tests of Thunderbolt in TDM are showing speeds slightly faster than FireWire 800. It does, however, provide another means of extracting data from a Macintosh system. More on that later.

Expansion Slots (ISA, MCA, EISA, VL-Bus, PCI, AGP, PCI Express)   Expansion slots are populated by "cards" whose purpose is to connect peripheral devices with the I/O bus on the motherboard so that these peripheral devices can communicate with the CPU. There are several types of peripheral devices, and they expand the capabilities of the PC. Expansion slots come in different flavors, or speeds, that have evolved over time. Rarely do you encounter the older types, such as the Industry Standard Architecture (ISA, 8 bit and 16 bit in 1981 and 1984, respectively), IBM Micro Channel Architecture (MCA, 32 bit in 1986), or Extended Industry Standard Architecture (EISA, Compaq and Generic, 32 bit in 1986). The VESA Local Bus (VL-Bus, named after the VESA Committee that developed it) was in use during 1992 to 1994 and appears as a legacy slot on some older PCI bus systems still in use. The VL-Bus slot uses the 16-bit ISA plus an extension to handle legacy 16-bit and newer 32-bit cards. The Peripheral Component Interconnect (PCI) bus was born in 1992 and is still in use today. It exists primarily as a 32-bit card, but some high-end systems provide a 64-bit PCI interface. After 10 years, in July 2002 the PCI design had reached its upper speed limit and was replaced with the PCI Express 1.0 specification, which is finding its way into the mainstream market. The former was based on parallel data communications, whereas the latter was based on serial data communications, with serial facilitating faster data communications. Sandwiched between the PCI and the PCI Express was the Accelerated Graphics Port (AGP). AGP was based on PCI, with enhancements, but was connected separately from the PCI bus and joined via a direct pathway for exclusive video/graphics use by the system. PCI Express replaces AGP altogether for graphics. PCI Express coexists on most new boards with "legacy" PCI slots, with the latter slated for extinction as the market shifts to PCI Express (which is expected to be the dominant PC bus architecture for the next 10 to 15 years). In laptops, extension cards are called *PC Cards* (also called *PCMCIA cards* after the organization that created them, the Personal Computer Memory Card International Association). *PC Card* is the trademarked name assigned by the PCMCIA.

These cards, which are about the size of a credit card, plug into an externally accessible slot and serve the same purpose for laptops as do the other extension cards for PCs.

Sound Card   A sound card is the circuitry for recording or reproducing multimedia sound. The circuitry can be found in the form of an extension card, a sound codec (compression/ decompression module) chip on the motherboard, or hardware integrated into the motherboard's main chipset. These hardware devices have interfaces for microphones, headphones, amplified speaker output, line-in, CD player input, and so forth. The sound card hardware requires a software counterpart in the form of a driver in order to function.

Video Card (PCI, AGP, PCI Express)   In its most basic form, the video card is the circuitry or interface for transmitting signals that appear as images on the computer display or monitor. High-end cards can perform video capture as well. The circuitry can be found, as with the sound card, in the form of an extension card, as a dedicated chip on the motherboard, or integrated into the motherboard's main chipset. Current display adapters use the 15-pin Video Graphics Array (VGA) analog connectors or the Digital Video Interface (DVI) analog/ digital connector. Like the sound card, the video card requires a software counterpart in the form of a driver in order to function. Both sound and video have undergone extreme improvements over time. Sound used to be used only for troubleshooting and in the form of beeps. Video used to be monochrome for text-only displays. Both are now capable of combining to deliver rich sound and three-dimensional (3D) graphics for movies and games.

Real-Time Clock (RTC)   RTC is the system clock for storing the system date and time, which is maintained by means of a battery when the system powers down. This battery is often called the *CMOS battery*, and the chip hosting the RTC is often called the *CMOS chip* (as the chip material itself is produced using the Complementary Metal-Oxide Semiconductor process). Officially, however, the CMOS chip is called the RTC/NVRAM. I've already explained the RTC component. NVRAM stands for nonvolatile random access memory, meaning that the data remains when the system powers down, and the data can be accessed randomly rather than in linearly. The NVRAM stores the basic configuration data that we have come to call *CMOS data*, which is the amount of installed memory, type of floppy and hard disk drives, and other start-up configuration settings.

CMOS   Complementary Metal-Oxide Semiconductor is the process by which the RTC/ NVRAM chip is produced. CMOS is often used in lieu of RTC/NVRAM (the official term) and may be used in the context of the CMOS settings, which includes the system date/time (RTC) and the basic configuration data.

CMOS Battery   To maintain critical configuration data when the system is turned off, the RTC/NVRAM chip is powered by a battery. These batteries have a long service life. The battery is usually a dime-sized silver disk mounted on the motherboard. On some systems (Dallas Semiconductor or Benchmarq), the battery is built into the chip itself. The expectation is that they will last 10 years, which is longer than the service life of most computer systems. Some systems use no battery at all, instead using a capacitor to store a charge to be used when the system is off. Some systems use a combination of battery and capacitor so that the capacitor can power the chip during battery changes so that the data is never lost.

One of the configuration settings retained by the RTC/NVRAM, aka CMOS chip, is the boot or BIOS access passwords. One of the methods for bypassing these passwords is to remove the CMOS battery and allow the chip to lose its settings when the power is removed, reverting to factory defaults.

BIOS   BIOS stands for Basic Input Output System and is a combination of low-level software and drivers that function as the interface, intermediary, or layer between a computer's hardware and its operating system. They load into RAM from three possible sources:

- From the motherboard ROM (ROM BIOS)
- From the adapter card ROM (examples, video card, SCSI card)
- From disk in the form of device drivers

The acronyms BIOS and CMOS (RTC/NVRAM) are often confused and erroneously used interchangeably. They are separate systems, although closely interrelated and interdependent. The user interface for the settings stored in RTC/NVRAM memory is accessed through a setup program contained within the BIOS. The settings stored in RTC/NVRAM are read by the BIOS during boot and applied for your system configuration.

Two Important Settings in RTC/NVRAM for Examiners

Computer forensic examiners should be concerned with at least two important settings stored in RTC/NVRAM, which is accessed by the BIOS software most often called Setup. Setup is accessed during system boot using a special key or combination of keys, such as F1, F2, F12, Esc, or Delete. Usually the key or combination of keys will be displayed as the system boots. Those two settings are as follows:

- System Date and Time
- Boot Order

The first setting is important to help establish a baseline for system time, and the second may have to be changed by the examiner if the drive must be imaged in place through the use of a boot floppy disk or CD.

Extensible Firmware Interface (EFI)   In 2000, engineers released the first version of EFI, an improved interface designed to replace the old BIOS firmware used historically in all IBM PC–compatible computers. This interface sits between the operating system and the computer's firmware and hardware. In 2005 Intel renamed EFI to Unified EFI (UEFI) to reflect its contributions to the specification. In March 2007 Intel released its latest version of the specification (as of this writing), which is 2.1. UEFI is also still called EFI, and both are often called the BIOS, not out of correctness but out of habit.

Intel uses the Intel Innovation Framework as an implementation that supports EFI and also supports legacy PC BIOS by means of a compatibility support module or CSM. This implementation was originally called Tiano but has since been dubbed simply Framework.

When EFI is used instead of the traditional BIOS, an EFI boot manager is used. The EFI boot manager selects and loads the operating system, and a dedicated boot loader is no longer needed.

Intel's Itanium systems, released in 2000, were among the first to use EFI. Most Intel boards shipped since 2006 use Framework-based firmware, with Intel chipsets starting with Intel 945 supporting EFI. During 2006 Apple launched its first Intel-based Macintosh computers, all of which used EFI and Framework. Despite built-in support for EFI in Intel products, as of this writing, Apple is the only major vendor to take advantage of EFI.

Mouse Port   The mouse port is the interface port in which the mouse is connected to the computer. Older systems use a serial port, and newer systems use a PS/2 (mini-DIN type) connection. Although most computers still provide the PS/2 port option, the mouse you purchase today will probably ship with the USB interface. You can purchase PS/2 adapters from computer hardware stores.

Keyboard Port   This is the interface port into which the keyboard is connected to the computer. Old systems use a five-pin round port, and newer systems use the PS2 connection. As with the mouse, most systems today ship with PS2 ports, but keyboards ship usually with USB connections.

Network Interface Card (NIC)   The NIC is an extension card used to connect the computer to a network. This functionality is available via USB connection and is built into most workstation and laptop motherboards currently manufactured. Ethernet is the most common type of network in use, but Token Ring is still found in some legacy environments. The type of network deployed determines which type of network adapter, Ethernet or Token Ring, will be used. Each NIC has a unique hardware address or serial number coded into its memory. This address is called its Media Access Control (MAC) address. The Data Link Layer (DLL) protocol uses this address to identify and communicate with other NICs on the same network. This address is 48 bits, or six sets of hexadecimal values, and consists of two parts. The first three hexadecimal values identify the manufacturer. The second set of three hexadecimal values is a unique serial number applied by the manufacturer to the specific card. Most network cards today are rated at 10/100 Mbps; however, Gigabit Ethernet (1,000 Mbps) is quite common as well. Another type of network is the wireless network, whereby the network packets are sent via radio waves instead of over wires. Wireless NICs are typically PCI or USB or are offered as on board the motherboard. All three types require an antenna to receive the signal.

Modem   A modem, which stands for modulate/demodulate, is used to connect a computer to other computers using a telephone as the signal carrier. The modem takes your computer's digital signals and *modulates*, or transforms, them to analog signals for transmission over telephone lines. On the receiving end, the modem *demodulates*, or transforms, the analog signals from the telephone line back to digital signals that the receiving computer can understand.

First Responder Hint

Upon discovering that a target computer is connected to a network (telephone, wired, wireless), one of your first concerns should be the potential for the destruction of data via remote connection. Disconnect the network connection, or if it's wireless (such as a laptop), turn off the Wireless button. If the Wireless switch is not present, you may need to power down the machine immediately. Keep in mind, though, that a decision to "pull the plug" must be weighed against the loss of possible evidence by doing so. Running processes, network connections, and data in volatile RAM will be lost once you pull the plug. If your case depends on this volatile data, you may opt to provide a shield to block wireless transmissions while you capture the volatile data.

Parallel Port   The parallel port is a relatively large port used primarily for legacy printer connections, although some other devices are known to use this connection. *Parallel* describes a method of transmitting data in which data is sent down parallel electrical paths at the same time. Parallel data transmission suffers limitations at high speeds with timing issues, cable length limitations, and other problems. It is being replaced by serial data transmission methods and technologies, primarily USB.

Serial Port   The serial port is an I/O port used for connecting devices that use serial data transmission connections. The most common serial port you'll encounter is the RS-232 connection. Older workstations have two serial ports but can support four; however, only two at a time can be used because each pair uses the same hardware resources. Many modern workstations no longer have a serial port.

Watch That Terminology!

The realm of computer forensics is still relatively new, and it's newer still with regard to law enforcement. Our job as computer forensic examiners is not limited to conducting examinations. I find myself having to explain and educate those around me. This includes co-workers, supervisors, attorneys, judges, and, most important, the jury.

I have witnessed countless reports, search warrants, and testimonies in which improper terms were used to describe a computer. I have read police reports where officers have requested examinations on CPUs and computer cases. Better yet, I have observed one search warrant signed by a judge allowing the computer forensic examiner to conduct a search of a computer monitor. Apparently, the officer witnessed something of evidentiary value on the screen and wanted it examined!

If as an examiner you are confronted with inaccurate terminologies describing the device to be examined, you do not have the legal authority to actually examine the device just because the request has been approved. In such scenarios, the police reports have to be corrected and the search warrant amended before you perform any examinations.

The Boot Process

At this point, I have discussed a vast array of computer system components and systems. Next I'll cover the boot process. Computer system components are useless pieces of silicon, copper, gold, and tin until they are awakened by a spark of electricity, which follows a predetermined path, testing the various system components, establishing configuration settings, and loading pieces of code—all of which culminates in the loading of a functional operating system, custom-configured to your particular hardware and software environment. The process by which this occurs is the *boot process*, named for the process of "pulling yourself up by the bootstraps." It is the process by which PC computer systems come to life, and it's the process that computer forensics examiners must understand and may be called upon to describe.

The boot process begins when the user presses the power switch and starts the system. When this occurs, the following steps take place regardless of the operating system:

1. When you press the power switch, the process initiates the Power On Self-Test (POST). Before the power leaves the power supply, the power supply conducts its own POST, making sure voltages and current levels are acceptable. The electrical current from the power supply follows a predetermined path to the CPU. Any residual data in the CPU is erased. This signal also resets a CPU register called the *program counter.* In the case of ATs and later computers, this value is F000. The value describes the address of the next piece of code to be processed. In this case, the address of F000 corresponds to the beginning of a boot program in the ROM BIOS.

2. The boot program (sometimes called *bootstrap*) in the ROM BIOS initiates a series of system checks. The first step in the process is to run a set of instructions or code intended to check the CPU and the POST process, matching it against a set of values stored in the BIOS chipset. The CPU and POST must first be checked before they can be relied on to check the rest of the system. As long as the values match and they "pass," the POST process continues to the next step.

3. Signals are sent from the CPU to the system bus (main electrical pathway) to ensure that the bus is properly functioning. If this test passes, POST continues to the next step.

4. The CPU next tests the RTC, or system clock. This clock keeps all system electrical signals in synchronization. If the RTC passes its POST check, POST continues to the next step.

5. POST next tests the system's video components. The video memory is tested, as are the signals sent by this device. The video's BIOS is added to the overall system BIOS, which is stored in RAM. It is only at this point in the boot process that the user will see anything on the screen.

6. In the next phase of POST, the system's main memory, RAM, is tested. Data is written to RAM. The data is read and compared to the original data sent. If it matches, it passes; if it doesn't match, it doesn't pass. Depending on the system settings, the user

may see the "countdown" as the volume of RAM is tested. If all the RAM memory passes this test, POST continues with the next step.

7. The CPU next tests to see whether a keyboard is properly attached and whether any keys are pressed. If you've ever accidentally left a book or papers on a keyboard during boot, you'll no doubt recall the error beep and screen message from this test! Assuming a successful test, POST continues to the next step.

8. POST next sends signals over specific bus pathways to determine which drives (floppies, CDs, hard drives, and so on) are available to the system.

9. The results of the POST are compared to the expected system configuration settings that are stored in CMOS, which you have learned is properly called RTC/NVRAM. If the settings do not match, the user is given the opportunity to update the configuration through the Setup utility. If it passes, the next step in POST occurs.

10. If any other system component contains its own BIOS, it is loaded into the overall BIOS in RAM at this time. A typical example is a SCSI BIOS. Plug and Play runs next, configuring any Plug and Play devices, configuring systems resources, and writing those settings to RAM. At this point, the system is ready to load a specific operating system.

11. The bootstrap code (boot program) has finished one of its two primary missions, that of conducting the POST. Its final task is that of searching the available drives for an operating system according to the order set forth in the boot sequence. Thus, the ROM BIOS boot code looks to the first sector of the default boot hard drive (first on the list in the boot sequence) for the master boot record (MBR) and, finding it, reads it into memory and tests it for a valid signature. The "signature" is hex 55AA (also sometimes rendered 0x55AA, as discussed in Chapter 2), located at the last two bytes of this sector. If this doesn't match, an error message is returned; otherwise, the boot process continues. Figure 1.1 shows a hard drive with both an MBR and a VBR (volume boot record), and Figure 1.2 shows a floppy disk that has only a VBR.

12. The MBR contains a 64-byte partition table located at byte offsets 446 to 509. Each of up to four partitions is described by 16 bytes in the 64-byte table. The MBR reads its own partition table for the *boot indicator byte* that marks one of the partitions as the active partition. One partition must be active to boot, and there can't be more than one partition marked as active. The absence of an active partition or more than one partition marked as active will result in an error message. The MBR reads the VBR of the partition marked as active, loads it into memory, and conducts the same signature test carried out with the MBR, looking for the last two bytes of the VBR to read as hex 55AA. If the signature test fails, an error message is returned. If it passes, the VBR code executes or runs. The VBR code or program searches for and runs the operating system on that volume. What happens next in the boot process depends on the operating system that is loaded on that active bootable partition.

FIGURE 1.1   Hard disk drive with MBR and VBR

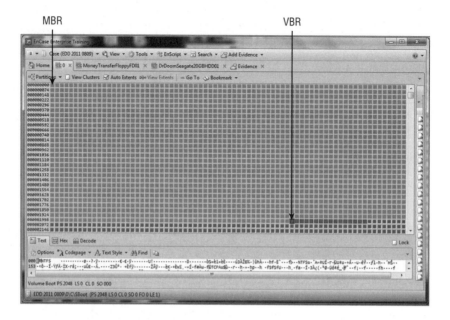

FIGURE 1.2   Floppy disk drive with VBR only

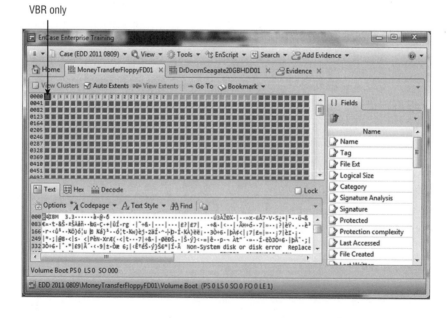

The MBR pertains to hard disk drives only. If the bootable media is removable (for example, a floppy disk or USB flash drive), there is no MBR. Rather, only a VBR is located at the first sector. Thus, when the boot is from a floppy, the VBR only is read and executed because there is no MBR on a floppy.

Up through step 12, the boot process is the same whether you're booting to DOS or to Windows. Steps 13 to 17 will be different for Windows NT/2000/XP, Windows Vista, Windows Server 2003/2008, and Windows 7. I'll first describe how to boot to DOS, in steps 13 through 17. Next, I'll explain how to boot to Windows.

DOS boot:

13. The code in the VBR locates and executes the initial or primary system file, which is IO.SYS (IBMBIO.COM for IBM systems). As part of execution, SYSINIT (a subroutine of IO.SYS) runs. This code copies itself into the highest region of contiguous DOS memory. The code next locates and reads MSDOS.SYS, copying it into low memory and overwriting that portion of IO.SYS in low memory that contains the initialization code (SYSINIT), because it is no longer needed there.

14. SYSINIT runs MSDOS.SYS (or IBMDOS.COM for IBM systems). MSDOS.SYS initializes basic device drivers and checks on the status of system equipment. It also resets the disk system, resets and initializes various devices that are attached to the system, and sets default system parameters. It works with the system BIOS to manage files, execute code, and respond to hardware signals.

15. With the DOS file system running and active, SYSINIT (contained within IO.SYS) resumes control of the boot process. SYSINIT reads the CONFIG.SYS file as many times as there are statements within it to process. The DEVICE statements are processed first, in the order in which they appear, followed by the INSTALL statements in the order of their appearance. Once they are done, if a SHELL statement is present, it is run. If none is present, the default shell with default parameters (COMMAND.COM) is run. SYSINIT is now complete, so COMMAND.COM is written into the section of memory previously occupied by SYSINIT.

16. If the file AUTOEXEC.BAT (.bat is the extension for batch files) is present, COMMAND.COM will run it. Each command in the batch file is executed. If one of the batch commands calls for launching an application or shell, then the user is presented with that interface or prompt. Otherwise, when the batch commands have been executed, the user sees a blinking cursor at a DOS prompt.

17. If no AUTOEXEC.BAT file is present, COMMAND.COM runs the DATE and TIME commands and displays a copyright message, and then the user is shown a blinking cursor at a DOS prompt. The entire process appears in Figure 1.3.

FIGURE 1.3 The boot process (DOS)

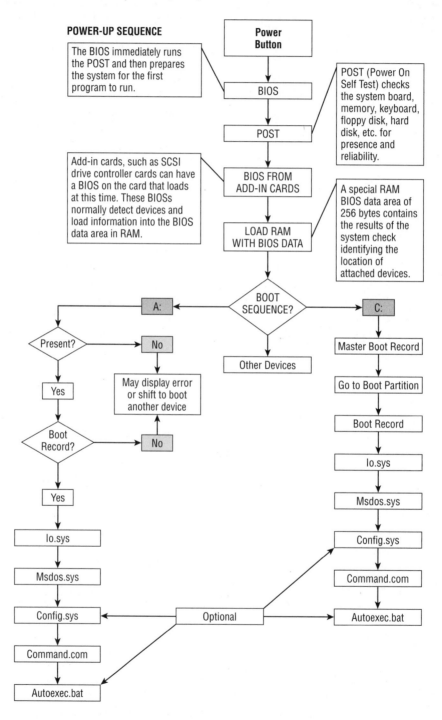

Windows NT/2000/XP boot:

18. The code in the VBR locates and runs the primary system file, which in the case of the various flavors of Windows NT is NTLDR (often called *NT Loader*). NTLDR places the processor in the "protected" mode, starts the file system, and reads the contents of the BOOT.INI file. Start-up options and initial boot menu options are determined by the contents of the BOOT.INI file. If dual booting is configured and the other operating system is a non-NT type such as Linux, BOOTSEC.DOS runs. If SCSI drives are attached to the system, another file (NTBOOTDD.SYS) containing the SCSI drivers executes.

19. NTDETECT.COM executes and searches the system for installed hardware and passes configuration data to NTLDR. If more than one hardware profile exists, NTDETECT determines the correct profile for the current hardware and runs that profile.

20. The configuration data obtained in the previous step by NTDETECT is passed by NTLDR to NTOSKRNL.EXE. NTOSKRNL.EXE is the code that loads the kernel, the Hardware Abstraction Layer (HAL), and the system registry information.

21. The next step in the NT boot process is that of loading drivers and code for networking systems, typically TCP/IP. Simultaneously, services that are configured to run at start-up load and run. One of the services is the logon service; it provides the user with a logon prompt, unless configured otherwise. When the user successfully logs on, the current configuration status is considered "good" and is updated into the system registry as Last Known Good Configuration.

22. As logon occurs, device detection takes place as a simultaneous process. If new devices are detected, Plug and Play assigns system resources, extracts drivers from the DRIVER.CAB file, and completes the configuration and mounting of those devices. If drivers can't be found, the user is prompted to provide them. When done, the user has a graphical user interface (GUI) that allows them to interact with their system and its unique environment of software and hardware.

If the boot is to Windows Vista, Windows Server 2008, or Windows 7, the process, beginning at step 13, differs slightly from that of its Windows predecessors (NT/2000/XP/ Server 2003). The boot code in the Windows Vista (and newer) VBR loads a file named BOOTMGR, which is the Windows Boot Manager, instead of NTLDR. Just as NTLDR reads the BOOT.INI file, BOOTMGR reads the BCD file located in the Boot folder, which is located in the root of the system volume. The BCD file is a database of boot-time configuration data.

BCD (which stands for Boot Configuration Data) is a file located in the Boot directory, which in turn is located in the root of the system volume. This file contains a database of boot-time configuration data, and, interestingly, the file format is the same as that of a registry hive file. This is significant because it means EnCase can mount it when you right-click and then select View File Structure. Just as the BOOT.INI file contained menu entries presented by NTLDR, BCD contains the menu entries presented by the Windows Boot Manager. Those boot options can include, but are not limited to, Windows Vista (and newer) boot options, such as booting a prior version of Windows NT, resuming Windows Vista (and newer) from hibernation, or loading and executing a volume boot record.

In previous Windows versions, NTLDR loaded the kernel (`NTOSKRNL.EXE`), passing boot configuration information in the process. But Windows Vista's (and newer) Windows Boot Manager invokes `WINLOAD.EXE`, which in turn loads the kernel (`NTOSKRNL.EXE`) and boot-class device drivers. Thus, the process is similar but has differences.

Partitions

Partitions and *volumes* are terms that are often used interchangeably. Usually this doesn't cause a problem because typically they are the same thing. There are, however, some subtle differences, and defining the terms and understanding the differences is an important part of being a professional.

A *partition* is a collection of consecutive sectors within a volume, and those sectors are addressable by a single file system specific to and contained within that partition.

A *volume*, by subtle contrast, is a collection of addressable sectors that are used by an operating system or an application to store data. The addressable sectors in a volume do not have to be consecutive—and therein lies the difference. Rather, they need only give the appearance of being consecutive. When a volume consists of a single partition, the two are functionally the same. When a volume spans more than one partition or drive, the difference becomes self-evident.

Volumes are logical storage units that are assigned drive letters by the operating systems. Theoretically, most operating systems can support up to 24 volumes, using the letters C through Z and reserving A and B for floppy drives. If a single physical hard drive were installed in a system, that drive could, in theory, be partitioned into 24 volumes. Recall from the earlier discussion, however, that the partition table contained in the master boot record permits only four 16-byte entries for four partitions. How then could such a system support 24 logical volumes?

The answer lies with the extended partition system. One of the four defined partitions in the MBR partition table can be an extended partition. The disk space assigned to the extended partition is further subdivided into logical volumes by the operating system. Each subpartition of the extended volume contains a partition table located in the first sector of that subpartition. That table defines its own subpartition and, optionally, points to another partition table in yet another subpartition. This "nesting" of subpartitions within the extended partition can extend as far as letter assignments permit, and each "nested" subpartition will have a partition table describing itself and pointing to the next level down until done. Seldom will you ever encounter more than few partitions, but in theory, you could encounter the upper limit of 24!

The partition types you can encounter are many and are usually specific to the operating system(s) on the host computer. The fifth byte within each 16-byte partition entry (byte offset 446–509 of the MBR) will determine the partition type/file system for each defined partition. The same holds true for partition tables within the extended partition and their subpartitions. The first byte of each of the four partition table entries determines which partition is active and therefore is the boot partition. Only one partition can be active.

Hex 80 denotes the active partition. The other three partition entries, if defined, will have hex 00 for the first byte in their respective entries. Table 1.1 defines the partition table fields.

TABLE 1.1   Partition Table Fields Defined*

Offset (Decimal)	Name	Length	Description
446	Boot Byte	1 byte	Boot status; hex 80 is active and bootable. Otherwise, it is hex 00.
447	Starting Head	1 byte	For CHS mode, this is the start head or side of the partition.
448	Starting Cylinder & Sector	2 bytes (16 bits)	For CHS mode, the starting cylinder is 10 bits, and the starting sector is the next 6 bits, for a total of 16 bits.
450	Partition Type	1 byte	This is the partition type/file system.
451	Ending Head	1 byte	For CHS mode, this is the ending head or side of the partition.
452	Ending Cylinder & Sector	2 bytes (16 bits)	For CHS mode, the ending cylinder is 10 bits and the ending sector is the next 6 bits, for a total of 16 bits.
454	Relative Sector	4 bytes (32 bits or Dword)	For LBA mode, this is the number of sectors before the partition, which is the starting sector of the partition.
458	Total Sectors	4 bytes (32 bits or Dword)	For LBA mode, this is the total number of sectors in the partition.

* Fields repeat three more times, if partitions are defined, starting at offsets 462, 478, and 494.

Typically FAT12, FAT16, FAT32, NTFS, and exFAT partitions and file systems are used when running the various flavors of the Windows operating systems. These partitions can be created by utilities that ship with the Windows operating system, such as FDISK, DISKPART, or Disk Manager. Other partition types that are often encountered are Linux Native (EXT2/3/4 and Reiser) and Swap partitions, Solaris (UFS), and Mac OS X (HFS+), all of which are supported in EnCase 6. As with Windows operating systems, partitioning utilities ship with these operating systems. You can also use third-party partitioning utilities to create partitions of varied types, such as Symantec's PartitionMagic and V-Communications' Partition Commander.

Using Disk Manager (Windows 2000 and newer), the formatting is done when you use the Create a New Partition Wizard. If a partition is created with FDISK, the partition must be formatted with the high-level format command before it can be used. When you use the format command to format a FAT12/16/32 partition, the following activity occurs:

1. The disk is scanned for errors, and bad sectors are marked.

2. Drive heads are placed at the first cylinder of the partition, and a DOS VBR is written.

3. FAT1 is written to Head 1 Sector 2. Immediately following FAT1, FAT2 is written. The entries in the File Allocation Table (FAT) are mostly null, except that bad clusters are marked.

4. A blank root directory is written.

5. If the /s parameter is selected, the system files are transferred.

6. If the /v parameter is selected, the user is prompted for a volume label.

The following information is written during the FDISK or disk partitioning process:

- The MBR, which contains the MBR booting code

- The partition table entries

- The MBR signature

It is during the high-level formatting process (format) that the VBR is typically written, along with other file system features.

Somewhat new to the scene is exFAT, which is a proprietary file system developed by Microsoft for flash media. It was actually released in Windows Embedded CE in 2006 but has remained rather obscure until 2010. Gone are the file size limits imposed by FAT, and many examiners will find this file system very useful because it has cross-platform read-write functionality between Windows and OS X, with Linux soon to follow. Windows Vista (SP 1) and newer versions of Windows support exFAT. Legacy versions of Windows (XP and Server 2003) support this format if they have Service Pack 2 or newer and have a special patch update. EnCase recognizes this file system starting with version 6.14.

Examining the Partition Table

In this exercise, you will use EnCase to decode the information contained in the partition table.

1. With EnCase open and a case started, choose Add Evidence ≻ Add Local Device ≻ Next. Select your own boot drive, and select the physical device, not the logical device.

2. From the Evidence ≻ Table tab, double-click your drive to open and parse its file structure.

3. From the resulting Entries View, place your cursor on the root or on Entries in the Entry pane. This will force your devices to appear in the Table pane to the right.

4. Select your device in the Table pane (blue check), go to the Device drop-down list on the toolbar, and choose Disk View. The Disk View will open in its own tab.

5. In the Disk View, go to the first sector, which is sector zero. (This applies to MBR-type partitions only.) Place your cursor on that sector. In the bottom pane, choose the Hex View.

6. Locate and sweep (select by clicking and dragging) bytes 446–509. With these 64 bytes selected, right-click the selected area, and choose Bookmark and then Raw Text.

7. From the Destination Folder tab, choose a new folder and name it Partition Table.

8. On the menu bar, select the drop-down list under View and choose Bookmarks.

9. From the Bookmarks tab, look at the tabs in the bottom section of the Data View pane.

10. First go to the Text tab and see your bookmarked data in this view.

11. Next go to the Hex tab and likewise view your bookmarked data in hex format.

12. Finally, go to the Decode tab; in this view you will see several view types organized in folders.

EXERCISE 1.1 *(continued)*

13. In the Windows folder, choose Partition Entry, and the partition table will be parsed and in the pane to the right, as shown here.

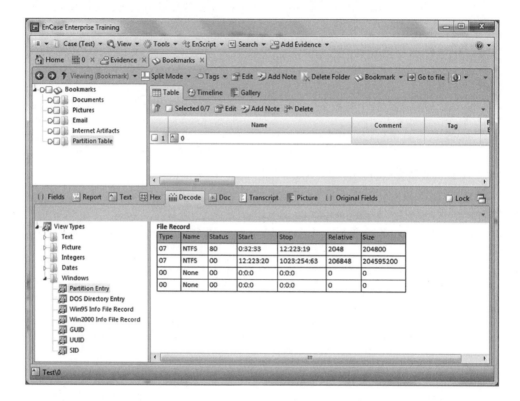

The purposes of this exercise are twofold. The primary and obvious purpose is to use EnCase to examine a partition table. The secondary purpose is to encourage you, the examiner, to use EnCase to examine your own hard drive, which is a good technique for examining known configurations and otherwise conducting research.

Often FDISK is used to remove the partition, rendering the drive unreadable and causing the user to believe the data is gone. All that really occurs is that the partition table entry is removed. Because each defined and formatted partition contains a VBR, which is untouched by FDISK, the examiner can use EnCase to recover a deleted partition. Simply locate and select the VBR, right-click, and choose Add Partition from the context menu. I cover this technique in detail in Chapter 10.

File Systems

I have, thus far, made reference to *file systems* in the discussion of partitions and volumes, but I have not yet defined them or described their function and importance in data storage and retrieval. In this section, I'll discuss file systems in a generic sense. In the chapter that follows, I'll cover specific file systems in detail.

A file system is nothing more than a system or method of storing and retrieving data on a computer system that allows for a hierarchy of directories, subdirectories, and files. File systems must be consistent between systems using the same file system. If a library used the Dewey Decimal System to store books in one library, a user could go to another library using the same file system and locate a book in that library. Even though the book would be stored in different physical locations in both libraries, a common file system would enable the user to find the book using a common filing and locating system. Computer systems are no different in this regard.

A file system needs its own structural or organization files and data, and the other component is the user data. Because a file system is contained within a partition, there must be data or files that describe the layout and size of the file system, as well as how large the data storage units (clusters, blocks, and so on) will be. The data storage units, which are groups of sectors that hold content data, are referred to as *allocation units*, *clusters*, *blocks*, and similar names depending on the file system being used. A file system needs to have a method or convention for naming data and therefore a system of filenames. Filenames are usually contained in directory entries or as an attribute or field in a database of file and directory names. Filenames have to be linked to actual data comprising that filename so that the operating system can locate the data. Thus, there must be an attribute or *metadata* (data within data describing data) to point to where the data starts. This is done, usually, via a directory entry (FAT systems) or an entry (field or attribute) in a file table such as the master file table (MFT) in NTFS systems.

Because the data may be larger than one allocation unit can hold, there must be a system that tracks the containing data storage units (clusters, blocks, and so on). In a FAT system, these clusters are linked together in the file allocation table. In NTFS, the clusters containing the data are described by data runs in the MFT. The operating system must know the size of the data so it knows where the data ends in an allocation unit, and that data is typically stored in a directory entry or as an attribute or field in a database of filenames, such as the MFT.

Finally, any file system must have a system that tracks allocation unit usage and availability. Without this function, data could be overwritten. In a FAT system, this is accomplished with the file allocation table. In NTFS and other systems, this is accomplished by the single-purpose volume bit map (VBM), which is an array of bits, with each representing an allocation unit. A 0 means it is available for use, and a 1 means it is allocated.

At a minimum, a file system needs to have the functions described thus far. Most file systems contain much more information about the files they store and have metadata in the form of file attributes about the data. This information may take the form of dates and times for last written, file creation, and last modified. It may also take the form of file permissions or access control lists (ACLs).

In summary, when a partition is created, its boundaries and type are set forth in a partition table. The *type* is something akin to a zoning ordinance where a given piece of real estate is supposed to be used for a specific purpose. A piece of real estate could be zoned as residential, while a partition type could, similarly, be declared as having a type of Linux Swap. A real estate parcel is described in a deed by its meets and bounds as determined by a survey. A partition's *meets and bounds* are described, similarly, in a partition table by its starting point, ending point, and size, based on a survey conducted by the partitioning utility.

When a partition is formatted, among other things, the data structures needed for its specific file system are created. Although these file system type structures are usually consistent with the file system type declared in the partition table, they do not have to be. One could have a FAT32 file system located in a partition type declared as a Linux Swap. This would be somewhat analogous to someone placing a business on real estate zoned for residential use. If you were using Linux for the operating system, Linux does not rely on the partition type; if instructed to mount the partition as FAT32, it would do so since the structure for FAT32 is present regardless of the declared type. Linux ignores the "zoning laws." Windows, however, strictly obeys zoning laws and would not permit an office in a residential zone. Windows relies on declared partition types for mounting partitions and file systems and would not mount a FAT32 partition declared as a Linux Swap partition or any other type not a FAT32. In this manner, partitions and file systems can be hidden from Windows.

File systems are the management tools for storing and retrieving data in a partition. Some operating systems require certain file systems for them to function. Windows needs a FAT or NTFS file system, depending on its version and won't recognize or mount other systems with its own native operating system. Third-party software can enable mounting and reading (sometimes writing) other file systems from within the Windows environment. EnCase and VMware are two examples. Many different file system schemes have been developed, and more will be forthcoming as computing evolves. In the next chapter, I'll cover FAT in detail.

Summary

This chapter explained the computer's components, as well as its boot process, partitions, and file systems. I covered computer hardware components, including their acronyms, attributes, functions, and purpose. In addition, I covered the two major components of the boot process. The first is the Power On Self-Test, in which the major components are tested and initialized (added to the system). The second consists of the bootstrap code locating a bootable drive and loading the specified operating system.

I also defined and described partitions and volumes. A partition is a collection of consecutive sectors within a volume and is a container for a file system, with specific boundaries and properties. A volume is a collection of addressable sectors that are used by an operating system or an application to store data. A volume is assigned a drive letter by the operating system; it may be limited to a single partition, or it may span partitions or physical hard drives. Finally, I discussed file systems and their purpose, function, and necessary generic components.

Exam Essentials

Know computer hardware components.   Understand the proper terminology, acronyms, purpose, and function of the various computer hardware components.

Be familiar with the boot process.   Understand and be able to describe the POST process. Understand and be able to describe the process by which the system boots and loads an operating system.

Understand partitions and volumes.   Understand and be able to describe partitions and volumes, what the differences are, and how they are created. Understand the MBR and VBR, where they are found, their contents (boot code, partition table, signature), and how and when they are created. Understand a partition table, where it is located, its structure, length, and general properties.

Understand file systems in general.   Understand the purpose of a file system as a means to store and retrieve data. Be familiar with the functional components of any generic file system so as to be able to apply them to specific file systems.

Review Questions

1. What is the definition of a CPU?

    A. The physical computer case that contains all its internal components

    B. The computer's internal hard drive

    C. A part of the computer whose function is to perform data processing

    D. A part of the computer that stores and manages memory

2. What is the BIOS?

    A. BIOS stands for Basic Input Output System and is a combination of low-level software and drivers that function as the interface, intermediary, or layer between a computer's hardware and its operating system.

    B. BIOS stands for Bootstrap Initialization Operating System and is a combination of low-level software and drivers that function as the interface, intermediary, or layer between a computer's hardware and its operating system.

    C. BIOS stands for Boot-level Input Output System and is a combination of low-level software and drivers that function as the interface, intermediary, or layer between a computer's hardware and its operating system.

    D. BIOS stands for Boot Initialization Operating System and is a combination of low-level software and drivers that function as the interface, intermediary, or layer between a computer's hardware and its operating system.

3. What is the definition of POST?

    A. A set of computer sequences the operating system executes upon a proper shutdown

    B. A diagnostic test of the computer's hardware and software for presence and operability during the boot sequence prior to running the operating system

    C. A diagnostic test of the computer's software for presence and operability during the boot sequence prior to running the operating system

    D. A diagnostic test of the computer's hardware for presence and operability during the boot sequence prior to running the operating system

4. Is the information stored on a computer's ROM chip lost during a proper shutdown?

    A. Yes

    B. No

5. Is the information contained on a computer's RAM chip accessible after a proper shutdown?

    A. Yes

    B. No

6. Can information stored in the BIOS ever change?

    A. Yes

    B. No

7. What is the purpose or function of a computer's ROM chip?

    A. Long-term or permanent storage of information and instructions

    B. Temporary storage area to run applications

    C. Permanent storage area for programs and files

    D. A portable storage device

8. Information contained in RAM memory (system's main memory), which is located on the motherboard, is _____.

    A. volatile

    B. nonvolatile

9. What is the maximum number of drive letters assigned to hard drive(s) partitions on a system?

    A. 4

    B. 16

    C. 24

    D. Infinity

10. The smallest area on a drive that data can be written to is a _____, while the smallest area on a drive that a file can be written to is a _____.

    A. bit and byte

    B. sector and cluster

    C. volume and drive

    D. memory and disk

11. The size of a physical hard drive can be determined by which of the following?

    A. The cylinder $\times$ head $\times$ sector

    B. The cylinder $\times$ head $\times$ sector $\times$ 512 bytes

    C. The total LBA sectors $\times$ 512 bytes

    D. Adding the total size of partitions

    E. Both B and C

12. Which is not considered exclusively an output device?

    A. Monitor

    B. Printer

    C. CD-RW drive

    D. Speaker

13. The electrical pathway used to transport data from one computer component to another is called what?

 A. Bus

 B. RAM

 C. CMOS

 D. BIOS

14. What is the main component of a computer to which essential internal devices such as CPU, memory chips, and other chipsets are attached?

 A. BIOS

 B. Motherboard

 C. Expansion card

 D. Processor

15. IDE, SCSI, and SATA are different types of interfaces describing what device?

 A. RAM chips

 B. Flash memory

 C. CPUs

 D. Hard drives

16. What do the terms master, slave, and Cable Select refer to?

 A. External SCSI devices

 B. Cable types for external hardware

 C. Jumper settings for internal hardware such as IDE hard drives and CD drives

 D. Jumper settings for internal expansion cards

17. What can you assume about a hard drive that is pinned as CS?

 A. It's an IDE drive.

 B. It's a SATA drive.

 C. It's a SCSI drive.

 D. All of the above.

18. What is found at Cylinder 0, Head 0, Sector 1 on a hard drive?

 A. Master boot record

 B. Master file table

 C. Volume boot record

 D. Volume boot sector

19. What is the first sector on a volume called?

    A. File allocation table

    B. Volume boot record or sector

    C. Master boot record

    D. Volume boot device

20. Which of the following is incorrect?

    A. The MBR is typically written when the drive is partitioned with FDISK or DISKPART.

    B. A file system is a system or method of storing and retrieving data on a computer system that allows for a hierarchy of directories, subdirectories, and files.

    C. The VBR is typically written when the drive is high-level formatted with a utility such as format.

    D. The partition table is contained within the MBR and consists of a total of 16 bytes, which describes up to four partitions using 4 bytes each to do so.

Chapter

2

File Systems

ENCE EXAM TOPICS COVERED IN THIS CHAPTER:

- ✓ FAT12 file system
- ✓ FAT16 file system
- ✓ FAT32 file system
- ✓ Other file systems (NTFS, CD, and exFAT file systems)

In the previous chapter, we made many references to file systems and discussed generally what a file system is and its functional purpose. We referenced some file system names, such as FAT, NTFS, and Linux's EXT2/3/4. In this chapter, we thoroughly cover the File Allocation Table (FAT) file system's internal structures and function, and we touch on the New Technology File System (NTFS) and CD file systems.

The FAT file system has been around for nearly a quarter of a century and will be with us for the foreseeable future. It is still used with floppy drives, Flash media, and USB thumb drives, and it can still be used, optionally, with Windows XP and Windows Vista. In fact, Flash media in all of its various flavors (thumb drives, memory sticks and cards, and so forth) has given a resurgence to FAT file systems, because they nearly all come formatted in FAT. It is truly the one cross-platform file system that is both readable and writable by all major operating systems. Windows 2000, Windows XP, Windows Server 2003, Windows Vista, Windows Server 2008, and Windows 7 default to NTFS, but if upgrading to a newer operating system, they default to the former file system. If that former file system happened to be FAT, FAT will be the default. Thus, as a computer forensics examiner, you will encounter many cases involving FAT from both legacy and new systems for years to come.

In this chapter, you will learn about the data structures of the FAT file system, which consists of two major components: the File Allocation Table and the directory entries. You will learn how the directory entries store filenames and attributes (metadata), how the FAT is used both to track the allocation status of the data storage area (organized as *clusters*) and to link together the clusters used to store data. You will understand how the FAT system has been tweaked over the years to handle increasingly larger data storage devices. Finally, you will be exposed briefly to various CD file systems, the components of the NTFS file system, and features of the newest file system from Microsoft, exFAT. I'll also explain the similarities and differences among all these systems.

FAT Basics

The first major component of the FAT file system is the directory entry. In all versions of the FAT file system (FAT12, FAT16, and FAT32), every file and directory is referenced and described in a separate directory entry. The directory entry is 32 bytes in length and contains the file's or directory's name, its size in bytes, its starting extent (or beginning cluster), and other file attributes or metadata (created, last-accessed, and last-written time stamps, and so on). None of the data content exists in the directory entry; rather, data content is stored in data allocation units called *clusters*. Clusters consist of one or more sectors, and a cluster is the smallest unit in which a file or directory can be stored. If a file's size exceeds the amount that can be contained in one cluster, it is assigned as many additional clusters as are needed to contain its data. The directory entry tracks only the starting cluster and does not track the other clusters used by a file.

The other major component of the FAT file system is the File Allocation Table, or FAT, which, among other functions, tracks the sequence of clusters used by a file when more than one cluster is allocated or used. In addition to tracking cluster runs or sequences, the FAT also tracks the allocation status of clusters, assuring that the operating system stores data in clusters that are available, and that clusters storing data assigned to files or directories aren't overwritten. The FAT also tracks bad clusters, marking them as such so they won't be used.

The FAT file system comes in three versions that have evolved over time to accommodate the continual development of larger-capacity hard drives. The three versions of FAT are FAT12, FAT16, and FAT32. The number following FAT describes the size of the entries in the FAT.

In a FAT12 system, the table is an array of 12-bit entries, with each 12-bit sequence representing a cluster, starting at cluster 0 and ending with the last cluster in the volume. The theoretical maximum number of clusters for a 12-bit array is 4,096 (2^{12}), but certain values are reserved, making 4,084 clusters the largest number of clusters supported by a FAT12 system.

Similarly, a FAT16 system has 16-bit FAT entries, and a FAT32 has 32-bit entries (although only 28 are used). Taking into account certain reserved values, a FAT16 system supports up to 65,524 clusters, and a FAT32 supports up to a theoretical maximum of 268,435,445 clusters (but the master boot record [MBR] imposes a limit of 67,092,481 clusters, which makes FAT32 capable of supporting a partition size of 2 terabytes). There are some other differences between FAT12/16 and FAT32, but the major difference lies in the number of clusters they can support, as shown in Table 2.1.

TABLE 2.1   Maximum number of sectors supported by FAT types

FAT type	Maximum number of clusters supported
FAT12	4,084
FAT16	65,524
FAT32	67,092,481

The Physical Layout of FAT

The FAT file system, as shown in Figure 2.1, has a distinctive physical layout consisting of three major components:

- Reserved area (volume boot sector)
- FAT (File Allocation Table) area
- Data storage area (directory entries and data content)

FIGURE 2.1   Physical layout of FAT showing the three major components

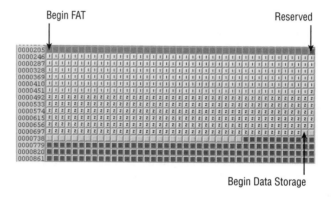

Reserved Area

The reserved area consists of the volume boot sector, often abbreviated as simply *boot sector.* The size of this reserved area is defined within the boot-sector data, but most often FAT12 and FAT16 systems use only one sector for this data. (See Figure 2.2.)

With FAT32 systems, the size of this area is likewise defined in the boot sector, but because it contains significantly more data, it will be several sectors in length (sectors 0, 1, and 2, with backups at sectors 6, 7, and 8), and the reserved area will usually be 32 sectors in length. (See Figure 2.3.) The backup copy of the boot sector (see Figure 2.4) is unique to FAT32 and runs if volume sector 0, the boot sector, is corrupted. Although its location is specified in the boot sector (as a sector number at byte offsets 50–51 in the boot sector), Microsoft standards call for it being located at volume sector 6. It makes sense to have the backup boot sector located in a standard location. If its location were variable and that variable location relied on data in sector 0, a corrupted sector 0 could destroy the system's ability to find its backup boot sector.

FIGURE 2.2   Reserved area (boot sector) of the FAT12 file system using only one sector

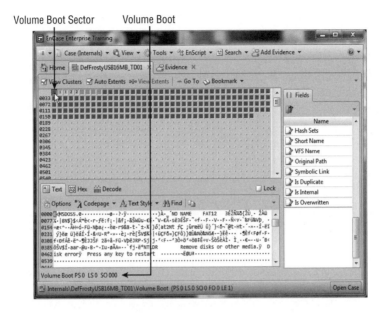

FIGURE 2.3   Reserved area of a FAT32 file system using 32 sectors

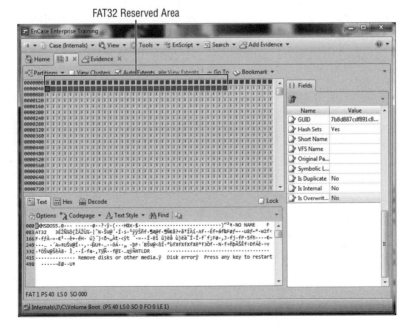

FIGURE 2.4   Backup boot sector unique to the FAT32 file system

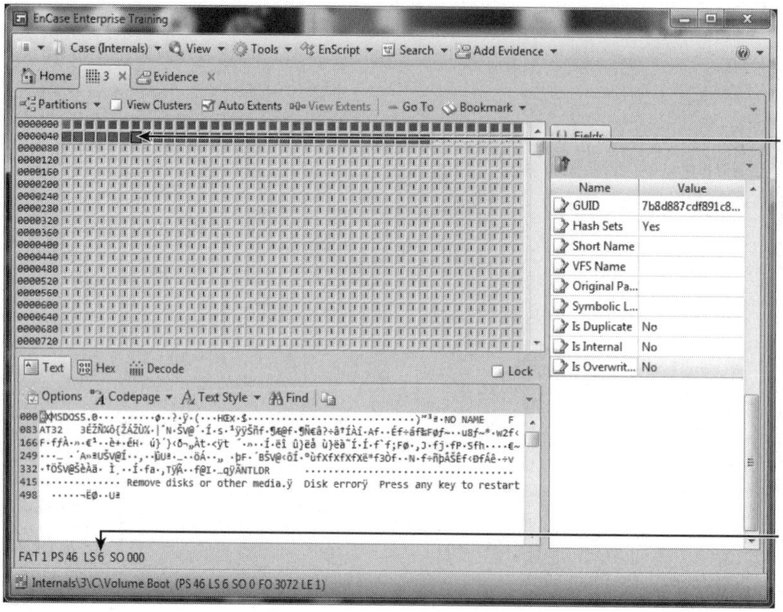

Backup boot sector in FAT32 volume, located at volume sector number 6

Volume sector 6

Also unique to FAT32 is a data structure known as File System Information, or the FSINFO. Its location is specified as a sector number at byte offsets 48–49 in the boot sector, but it is typically found in sector 1, immediately following the boot sector and sandwiched between the boot sector (sector 0) and sector 2, which is a continuation of the FAT32 bootstrap code. Additionally, a backup copy of the FSINFO is maintained in the sector immediately following the backup boot sector, which is sector 7 (the backup boot sector is, by standard, located in sector 6). Its purpose is to provide information to the operating system about the number of free clusters available to the system and the location of the next free cluster. Interestingly, this data is only "suggested" information for the operating system and may or may not be used. Also, this data may or may not be updated or accurate; often the backup copy does not match the primary. Nevertheless, it is a feature unique to FAT32.

The volume boot sector, also called the *volume boot record* (VBR), is located at the first sector of the logical volume. It is the first sector of the reserved area; in FAT12/16, it is often the only sector in the reserved area. The boot sector contains four distinct segments:

- Jump instruction to the boot code (first 3 bytes).

- BIOS parameter block, or BPB (bytes 3–61 for FAT12/16 and bytes 3–89 for FAT32).

- Boot code and error messages (bytes 62–509 for FAT12/16 and bytes 90–509 for FAT32). Note: FAT32 boot code continues at sector 2, bytes 0–509.

- Signature (bytes 510–511; should be 0x55AA).

The jump instruction tells the machine where to find the beginning of the OS bootstrap code located in that sector. Bytes 3–35, as well as bytes 0–2, have the same structure and purpose for all three versions of FAT. Bytes 36–61 have a structure and purpose unique to FAT12/16, while bytes 36–89 have a structure and purpose unique to FAT32. The area beyond byte 61 for FAT12/16 and beyond byte 89 for FAT32, except for bytes 510–511 (the boot sector signature), is used for the bootstrap code, referenced in the first 3 bytes, as well as for error messages.

The BPB is nothing more than a database of sorts, with defined fields that set forth the parameters of the partition and the file system within. The boot sector can be demystified by breaking down the data into its components, as shown in Table 2.2 and Table 2.3.

TABLE 2.2   Volume boot sector format—FAT12/16 file system

Byte offset (decimal)	Name or description and purpose
0–2	Assembly jump instruction to bootstrap code found in this sector, usually 0xEB3C90.
3–10	OEM ID in ASCII; indicates the OS that formatted the volume: Win95 = MSWIN4.0 Win2K/XP/Vista = MSDOS5.0 Linux = mkdosfs (When Linux mkfs msdos command is used to create.)
11–12	Bytes per sector; usually 512, but 1,024, 2,048, or 4,096 may occur.
13	Sectors per cluster; value must be a power of 2 and greater than 0. Typical values are 1, 2, 4, 8, 16, 32, or 64.
14–15	Number of sectors in the reserved area. FAT12/16 is typically one.
16	Number of FATs; typically, this is 2, with FAT1 and FAT2 (FAT2 is a duplicate of FAT1 for redundancy). According to Microsoft, some small devices can have only one FAT!
17–18	Maximum number of 32-byte directory entries in the root directory. This is typically 512 for FAT12/16 and 0 for FAT32.
19–20	16-bit integer describing the number of sectors in the partition. If 0, the number exceeds 65,536 and the byte offset 32–35 is a 32-bit integer describing the number of sectors in the partition.

TABLE 2.2 Volume boot sector format—FAT12/16 file system *(continued)*

Byte offset (decimal)	Name or description and purpose
21	Media descriptor; according to Microsoft, 0xF8 should be used on non-removable media (hard disks), and 0xF0 should be used for removable media. This entry is duplicated in the first entry of the FAT where cluster 0 would be described, but since there is no addressable cluster 0 or 1, this value is used instead.
22–23	16-bit integer that describes number of sectors used by each FAT in FAT12/16. For FAT32, expect a value here of 0.
24–25	Sectors per track value for interrupt 13h, typically 63 for hard disks.
26–27	Number of heads value for interrupt 13h, typically 255 for hard disks.
28–31	Number of hidden sectors before the start of the partition, typically 63 for the first volume on a hard disk.
32–35	32-bit integer describing the number of sectors in the partition. If 0, the number does not exceed 65,536 and is described as a 16-integer in bytes 19–20. Only one of the two (19–20 or 32–35) and not both must be set to 0.
36	Interrupt 13h drive number, which is 0x00 for floppies or 0x80 for hard drives.
37	Not used except by Windows NT; should typically be 0.
38	Extended boot signature to determine the validity of the three fields that follow. If 0x29, the next three fields are present and valid. If otherwise, expect 0x00.
39–42	Volume serial number; used with the field that follows to track volumes on removable media. With some OSs this value is generated using a date/time seed value at time of creation.
43–53	Volume label in ASCII; the volume label is optionally given by the user at the time of creation. Its limit is 11 bytes, and it should match the value in the root directory of FAT12/16. If none is given by the user, "NO NAME" should appear here.
54–61	File system type at time of formatting. Shown in ASCII as FAT, FAT12, or FAT16. It is not used after formatting and could be altered.
62–509	Bootstrap program code and error messages.
510–511	Signature value; 2 bytes and should be 0x55AA.

TABLE 2.3   Volume boot sector format—FAT32 file system

Byte offset (decimal)	Name or description and purpose
0–2	Assembly jump instruction to bootstrap code found in this sector, usually 0xEB3C90.
3–10	OEM ID in ASCII; indicates the OS that formatted the volume: Win95 = MSWIN4.0 Win98 = MSWIN4.1 Win2K/XP/Vista = MSDOS5.0 Linux = mkdosfs
11–12	Bytes per sector; usually 512, but 1,024 or 2,048 or 4,096 may occur.
13	Sectors per cluster; value must be a power of 2 and greater than 0. Typical values are 1, 2, 4, 8, 16, 32, or 64.
14–15	Number of sectors in the reserved area. FAT12/16 is typically one.
16	Number of FATs; typically, this is 2, with FAT1 and FAT2 (FAT2 is a duplicate of FAT1 for redundancy). According to Microsoft, some small devices can have only one FAT!
17–18	Maximum number of 32-byte directory entries in the root directory. This is typically 512 for FAT12/16 and 0 for FAT32.
19–20	16-bit integer describing the number of sectors in the partition. If 0, the number exceeds 65,536, and the byte offset 32–35 is a 32-bit integer describing the number of sectors in the partition.
21	Media descriptor; according to Microsoft, 0xF8 should be used on nonremovable media (hard disks), and 0xF0 should be used for removable media. This entry is duplicated in the first entry of the FAT where cluster 0 would be described, but since there is no addressable cluster 0 or 1, this value is used instead.
22–23	16-bit integer that describes the number of sectors used by each FAT in FAT12/16. For FAT32, expect a value here of 0.
24–25	Sectors per track value for interrupt 13h, typically 63 for hard disks.
26–27	Number of heads value for interrupt 13h, typically 255 for hard disks.
28–31	Number of hidden sectors before the start of the partition, typically 63 for the first volume on a hard disk.

TABLE 2.3   Volume boot sector format—FAT32 file system *(continued)*

Byte offset (decimal)	Name or description and purpose
32–35	32-bit integer describing the number of sectors in the partition. If 0, the number does not exceed 65,536 and is described as a 16-integer in bytes 19–20. Only one of the two (19–20 or 32–35) and not both must be set to 0. When FAT32, this number cannot be 0.
36–39	32-bit integer describing the number of sectors used by one FAT on FAT32 partition; bytes 22–23 must be set to 0 for FAT32.
40–41	A series of bit-field values used in FAT32 to describe how multiple FATs are written to. If bit 7 is off (value 0), then FAT is duplicated. If it is on (value 1), then duplication is disabled and only the FAT referenced in bits 0–3 is active. Bits 0–3 are valid only if bit 7 is "on" and duplication is not occurring. Bits 4–6 and 8–15 are reserved. The default is 0x0000, meaning that FAT1 and FAT2 are replicated.
42–43	The major and minor version numbers of the FAT32 volume, with the high byte being the major and the low byte being the minor. Expect values of 0x00 and 0x00.
44–47	Cluster number where the root directory begins, usually cluster 2. Remember that cluster 2 is the first addressable cluster, and on a FAT32 starts immediately after FAT2 ends. Entries in FAT for clusters 0 and 1 are used for purposes other than addressing clusters.
48–49	Sector number for where FSINFO can be found, usually 1; a backup FSINFO follows sector 6 (location of backup boot sector) and is found at sector 7.
50–51	Sector number for location of backup boot sector, which defaults to sector 6.
52–63	Reserved and not currently used.
64	Interrupt 13h drive number, which is 0x00 for floppies or 0x80 for hard drives.
65	Not used except by Windows NT; should typically be 0.
66	Extended boot signature to determine the validity of the three fields that follow. If 0x29, the next three fields are present and valid. If otherwise, expect 0x00.
67–70	Volume serial number; used with the field that follows to track volumes on removable media. With some OSs this value is generated using a date/time seed value at time of creation.
71–81	Volume label in ASCII; volume label is optionally given by the user at the time of creation. Its limit is 11 bytes, and it should match the value in the root. If none is given by the user, "NO NAME" should appear here.

TABLE 2.3   Volume boot sector format—FAT32 file system *(continued)*

Byte offset (decimal)	Name or description and purpose
82–89	File system type at time of formatting. Shown in ASCII as FAT32. Not used after formatting and could be altered.
90–509	Bootstrap program code and error messages. Note: FAT32 boot program code continues at sector 2, bytes 0–509.
510–511	Signature value; 2 bytes and should be 0x55AA.

FAT Area

The second major physical feature of the FAT file system is the File Allocation Table itself, which begins with the sector that follows the last sector of the reserved area. By default, there are usually two FATs (FAT1 and FAT2) in a FAT file system, as shown in Figure 2.5. The exact number of FATs, the size of a FAT, and the total size for all FATs are specified in the boot sector as described earlier.

FIGURE 2.5   Default FAT configuration showing FAT1 (selected) immediately followed by FAT2

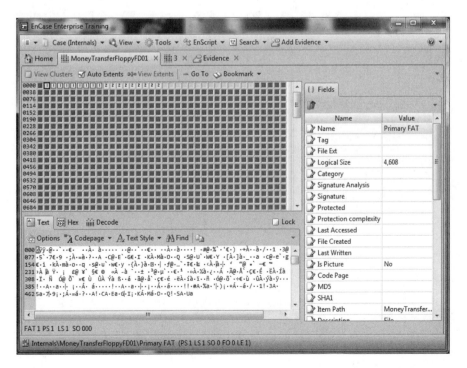

The FAT, as previously mentioned, has two purposes:

- To account for the allocation status of a cluster
- To find the clusters that follow the starting cluster (if any) for any given file or directory

FAT1 starts immediately following the reserved sectors. FAT2, a duplicate of FAT1, is a default configuration and immediately follows FAT1. A second FAT (FAT2) is, however, not required, and a system could be configured to have only one FAT. FAT1 and FAT2 are equal in size and normally a duplicate image of each other.

Each cluster on the file system will be represented sequentially starting with cluster 0 in the table, with each entry or array of bits depending on which version of FAT is used. For FAT12, each entry is 12 bits; for FAT16, each entry is 16 bits; and for FAT32, each entry is 32 bits, with 28 used and 4 in reserve. Remember that cluster 2 is the first addressable cluster in all versions of FAT. With FAT12/16, cluster 2 starts immediately following the fixed-length root directory. With FAT32, cluster 2 starts immediately following the end-of-file allocation tables.

The first 16-bit FAT entry in a FAT16 file system is for nonaddressable cluster 0, which is used to store the value for the media type. As you can see in Figure 2.6, this value is 0xFFF8, or 0xF8 because the leading 0xFF is ignored in this case. This value (0xF8) should match the value at byte 21 in the boot sector (0xF8 should be used on nonremovable media, and 0xF0 should be used for removable media). As you can see in Figure 2.7, this value is 0xF8.

FIGURE 2.6   FAT entry for nonaddressable cluster 0, which contains the value for the volume media type, in this case 0xF8

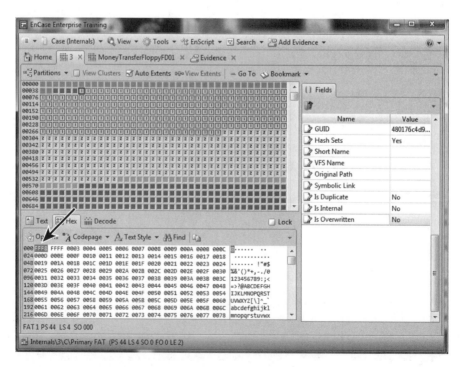

FIGURE 2.7 Byte offset 21 in the boot sector should and does match value in cluster entry 0 (Figure 2.6), which in this case is 0xF8.

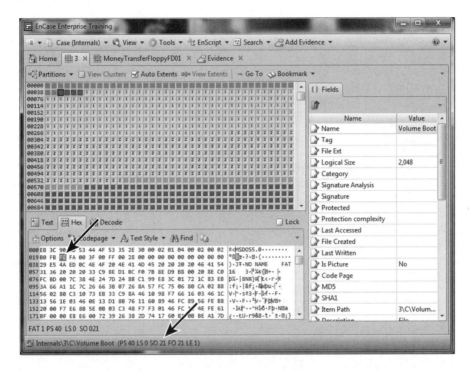

The FAT entry for nonaddressable cluster 1, shown in Figure 2.8, is used to store the value for the "dirty status" of the file system. If a file system was not properly "dismounted," usually from an improper system shutdown, this value is used to track that status, causing the OS to prompt the user to check the file system during a reboot. This value may or may not be accurate in this regard.

The third 16-bit entry in the FAT16 table represents cluster 2, which is the first addressable cluster in the FAT file system. For this entry and all others that follow in FAT1, certain values will be present:

- Unallocated; represented by the value of 0, meaning that the cluster is available for use by the operating system to store a file or directory.

- Allocated; its value will be represented by the next cluster used by the file, unless it is the last cluster used by the file (see item 3).

- Allocated; the last cluster used by the file. This will be populated by the end-of-file marker, which is a value greater than 0xFF8 for FAT12, greater than 0xFFF8 for FAT16, and greater than 0xFFFF FFF8 for FAT32.

- Bad cluster; not available for use by the operating system. This value will be 0xFF7 for FAT12, 0xFFF7 for FAT16, and 0xFFFF FFF7 for FAT32.

FIGURE 2.8 FAT entry for nonaddressable cluster 1, which contains the value for the "dirty status" of the file system

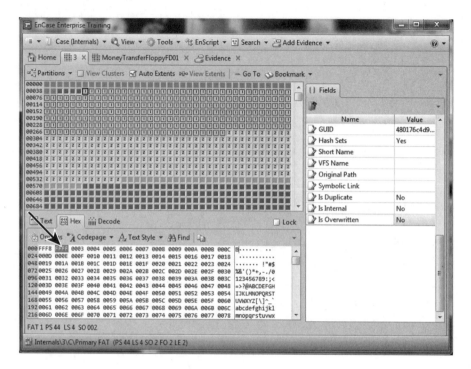

Data Storage Area

The third major physical component of the FAT file system is the data area. The data area contains the clusters used to store directory entries and their data.

Location of Root Directory

With FAT12/16, the root directory is the first part of the data area, which immediately follows at the end of the FAT area. The root directory is a fixed-length feature with FAT12/16 systems; a maximum of 32 sectors are allowed for it. Each directory entry is 32 bytes in length. I cover its structure in depth later in this chapter. Because a root directory in FAT12/16 systems has a maximum of 32 sectors, the number of bytes available to the root directory is 16,384 bytes (32 sectors × 512 bytes per sector). Since each directory entry is a fixed-length entry consisting of 32 bytes, the maximum number of directory entries in a FAT12/16 system is 512 entries (16,384 bytes divided by 32 bytes per entry). Cluster 2 immediately follows the root directory in a FAT12/16 system, followed by all the clusters contained within the defined partition.

As the size of software and hard disk capacity grew in the mid-1990s, the limitations of FAT12/16 file systems necessitated the development of the FAT32 file system. From our previous discussions, you already know that FAT32 allows for a greater number of clusters than its FAT12/16 predecessors. FAT32 also overcame the limitation of 512 entries in the root directory by making the directory "dynamic"—in that its size is not fixed and it can appear anywhere in the data area. When you examine the data area of a FAT32 system, you will see a difference at the very beginning. With FAT12/16, cluster 2 started after the fixed-length root directory, as shown in Figure 2.9. With FAT32, cluster 2 starts immediately following the end of the FAT area, as shown in Figure 2.10. Interestingly, even though the root directory can occur anywhere in the data area of a FAT32 file system, it almost always begins with cluster 2.

FIGURE 2.9   FAT12/16 physical layout, showing the fixed-length root directory immediately following the FAT

Root Directory, marked with green squares, is 32 sectors long, its length is fixed, and it starts immediately following the FAT area.

No clustering numbering is yet present!

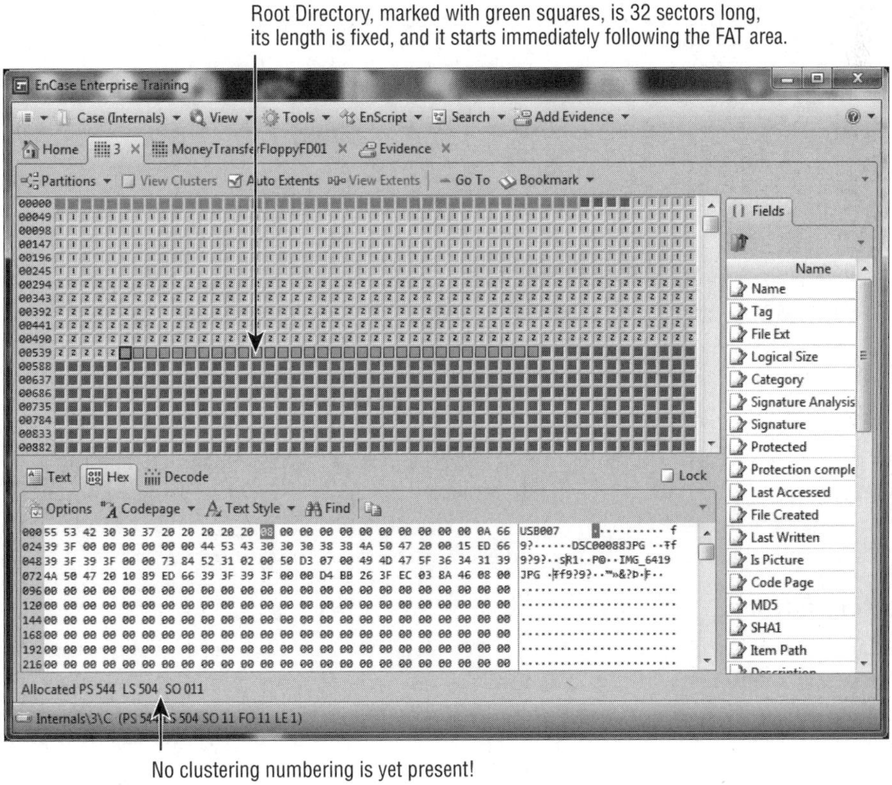

FIGURE 2.10   FAT32 physical layout, showing cluster 2 starting immediately after the FAT

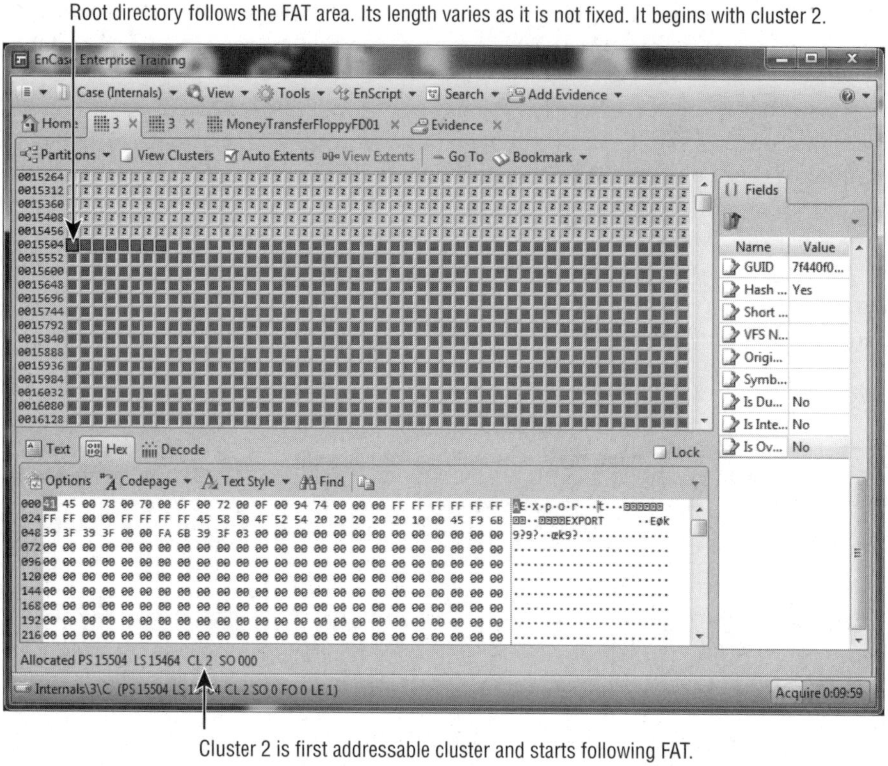

Root directory follows the FAT area. Its length varies as it is not fixed. It begins with cluster 2.

Cluster 2 is first addressable cluster and starts following FAT.

As previously mentioned, the data area contains the clusters that include the directory entries and the contents of the files and directories. FAT12/16 file systems keep the root directory outside, and prior to the cluster structure, which fixes its size and imposes a limitation on the number of directory entries, it can hold up to 512 entries. FAT32 places the root directory inside the cluster area and thereby imposes no limit on its size.

Directory Entries

Thus far, I've mentioned directory entries, but I haven't yet fully described their function, let alone their internal structures. The directory entry is a critical component of the FAT file system. For every file and directory within a partition, a directory entry exists. Regardless of which version of FAT is used, each directory entry is 32 bytes long. Within these 32 bytes, the name of the file or directory, its starting cluster, and its length are described, along with other metadata or attributes. These directory entries are found in the cluster(s) allocated to the file's parent directory.

In this and many systems, the parent directory keeps track of its children, be they files or subdirectories. If parent directory structures are deleted, children can become orphaned, and thus you have lost files or folders, which are files and folders for which no parent directory structure can be found.

A 32-byte directory has sufficient space to name a file or folder (directory) using an "8 dot 3" DOS naming convention, with a maximum of eight characters for the filename and three characters for its extension. No "dot" (a period) actually exists in the directory entry. Should a long filename exist, an attribute set in the metadata is created, and a series of 32-byte entries, sufficient to contain the long filename, will precede its main 32-byte entry. Table 2.4 displays the data structure for the FAT directory structure. Table 2.5 shows the bit-flag values for the various file or directory attributes.

TABLE 2.4   Data structure for FAT directory entry

Byte offset (decimal)	Description
0	First character of the filename or status byte.
1–7	Characters 2–8 of the filename.
8–10	Three characters of the file extension.
11	Attributes (detailed in Table 2.5).
12–13	Reserved.
14–17	Created time and date of file; stored as MS-DOS 32-bit date/time stamp.
18–19	Last accessed date; no time is stored in FAT!
20–21	Two high bytes of FAT32 starting cluster; FAT12/16 will have zeros.
22–25	Last written time and date of file; stored as MS-DOS 32-bit date/time stamp.
26–27	Starting cluster for FAT12/16; two low bytes of the starting cluster for FAT32.
28–31	Size in bytes of file (32-bit integer). Note: will be 0 for directories!

Determining the starting cluster for a FAT12/16 partition is a snap. You merely decode the 2 bytes at byte offsets 26–27 as a 16-bit little endian integer, and you have the value. When the partition is FAT32, things get interesting. The data you need to make this determination is in two different locations and must be combined in the correct order to arrive at the correct value. To illustrate how this is done, consider the following hex values as constituting a FAT32 directory entry: 48 49 42 45 52 46 49 4C 53 59 53 26 18 02 C2 4C 25 30 26 30 **12 00** 6A 4A 26 30 **03 00** 00 80 F8 0F. The bold values constitute the high bytes and low bytes, respectively, of this 32-bit value. To properly combine and calculate this value, you must enter the hex values into a scientific calculator in the following order: 00 12 00 03. This converts the stored values to little endian. The resulting decimal value for this starting cluster would be 1,179,651.

In the previous note, I mentioned the term *little endian*. For those of you not familiar with the term, it is, in essence, reverse-byte ordering. This is a method of storing a number so that its least significant byte appears first in the first hexadecimal number in the case of a 2-byte value. Thus, in the case of a hexadecimal value of FDBA, the little endian method would cause the number to be stored as BAFD, while the big endian method would cause the number to be stored as it is, or FDBA. Intel microprocessors use the little endian method, and Motorola microprocessors use the big endian method. If you'd like to understand more about hexadecimal and integers, jump ahead to Chapter 7, "Understanding, Searching For, and Bookmarking Data."

TABLE 2.5 Bit flag values for attribute Field at byte offset 11

Bit flag values (binary)	Description
0000 0001	Read only
0000 0010	Hidden file
0000 0100	System file
0000 1000	Volume label
0000 1111	Long file name
0001 0000	Directory
0010 0000	Archive

Attributes' bit flag values can be combined, and the resultant hex value will reflect those combinations. If a file were a read-only hidden system file, it would have the following bit flags turned on: 0000 0111. The hex value representing such a combination would be 0x07.

When long filenames are used—ones that exceed the length of the DOS 8 dot 3 limit or contain "illegal" DOS 8 dot 3 characters—special entries are created in the directory entry to accommodate filenames up to 255 characters in length (including the length of the path). When a long filename is created, an "8 dot 3 alias" is created as the filename in the 32-byte entry. It is done according to the following scheme (Windows 9*x*/ME):

- The first three characters of the extension (following the dot) are used as the extension of the 8 dot 3 alias.

- The first six characters of the filename (spaces ignored) are rendered to uppercase and become the first six characters of the 8 dot 3 alias file name. Any "illegal" DOS 8 dot 3 characters are converted to underscores.

- Two characters are added to the six characters. Character 7 is a tilde (~). Character 8 is the numeral 1. If another file exists that has the same alias name, the 1 sequences to 2, and so forth, until a number is assigned for which there is no duplicate alias file name.

If you were to create a file named SQL + Oracle Hacks.hash, the resultant 8 dot 3 alias filename would be SQL_OR~1.HAS. The spaces are ignored, and the plus (+), which is illegal, becomes an underscore (_). All characters become uppercase. After the *r* in *Oracle*, the six-character limit has been reached, and the characters ~1 are appended. The alias extension, HAS, is the first three characters of the long file name (LFN) extension.

> Windows NT/2000/XP/Vista/7 handles alias creation with a slightly different scheme. The first six legal DOS characters in a long file name are used as the alias; they are appended with ~1 if the first six characters are unique. If not, ~2, and so forth, is used. For the extension, the first three legal characters of the LFN extension are used for the alias extension. As if that weren't enough, yet another scheme is applied by Windows NT/2000/XP/Vista/Win7 whereby the first two characters of the LFN are taken for the first two characters of the alias. The LFN is hashed, and the next four characters are the hexadecimal values of that hash. Characters 7 and 8 are ~5. The ~5 remains constant for all subsequent aliases, with only the hash values, and hence the hex values, changing.

The long filename itself is stored in a series of 32-byte entries that immediately precede the directory entry containing the 8 dot 3 alias. The long filename is stored in accordance with the convention described in Table 2.6.

TABLE 2.6   Long file name storage scheme

Byte offset	Description
0	Sequence number used to link together multiple LFN entries. 0xE5 if deleted or unallocated. Typically the first LNF entry above the alias 8 dot 3 entry contains the beginning of the LFN, and they build on top of each other until the end is reached.
1–10	LFN characters 1–5 in Unicode.
11	Attributes.
12	Reserved.
13	Checksum.
14–25	LFN characters 6–11 in Unicode.
26–27	Reserved.
28–31	LFN characters 12–13 in Unicode.

Viewing Directory Entries Using EnCase

Directory entry raw data can be viewed, analyzed, and bookmarked in EnCase. For any file of interest, determine its parent folder, and place that parent folder in the table pane, placing focus on it by highlighting it. Figure 2.11 shows how to determine the parent folder for file of interest. The parent folder for the file of interest is OSXBoot16GBBase. Figure 2.12 shows this folder in the table pane and highlighted. In the view pane, choose the text. FAT directory entries in the view pane, shown also in Figure 2.12, will appear in red when viewed in EnCase.

FIGURE 2.11   File of interest and its parent directory. Note that the arrows show the linkage between the file (right arrow), its parent directory shown in the full path (down arrow), and its parent directory (left arrow).

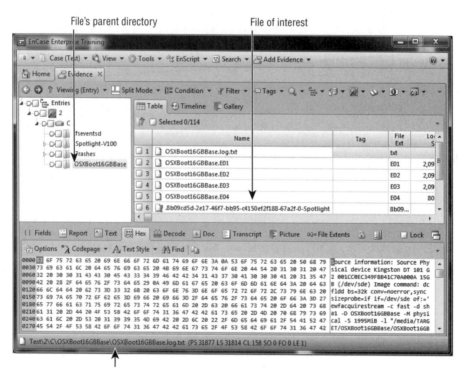

The entries shown in Figure 2.12 are displayed with 32 bytes per line. Since each entry is 32 bytes in length, each directory entry sits on a line by itself, making the data easy to see and analyze. This view didn't magically appear; rather, it was created using EnCase's Text Styles feature. The feature is accessed by following these steps:

1. Select Text Style tab under the Text view.
2. From the drop-down menu, choose Text Styles.

FIGURE 2.12   Directory entries in bottom pane shown in red of parent folder selected in right pane

32-byte directory entry for file of interest (note that parent directory is selected in table pane)

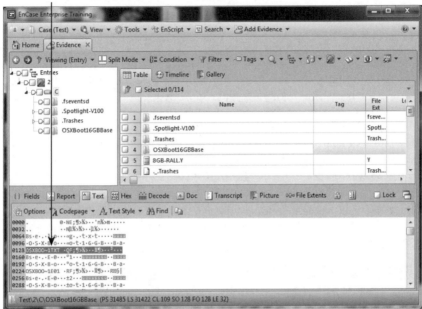

3. Click New and name it **FAT Directory.**
4. Choose Max Size and set the Wrap Length to 32, as shown in Figure 2.13.

FIGURE 2.13   Creating a custom text view for 32-byte directory entries

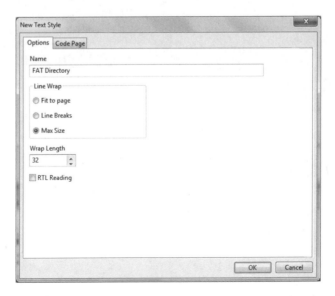

5. On the Code Page tab, select Other, and then select ISO-6937 or its nearest equivalent for the code page.

6. When done, click OK, and select your newly-created code page for viewing directory entries.

When you use this custom view, each of your directory entries will appear on a separate line.

At this point, you could examine directory entries of interest for the selected parent folder. You could bookmark individual byte values within any directory entry using the byte offsets and descriptors in Table 2.3. Although very precise and demonstrative of your forensic prowess, it is painstakingly slow and tedious work. Alternatively, if you were to "sweep" the 32 bytes making up the directory entry, bookmark it as raw text, go to the bookmark view, select the Decode tab, and for a view type choose DOS Directory Entry under the Windows folder, EnCase would decode the information for you and allow you to have the information in a bookmark, as shown in Figure 2.14 and Figure 2.15. In Exercise 2.1, you use EnCase to decode this information for you.

FIGURE 2.14   A 32-byte directory entry, selected, bookmarked, and viewed as a DOS directory entry. EnCase decodes the directory entry information and places it in a bookmark.

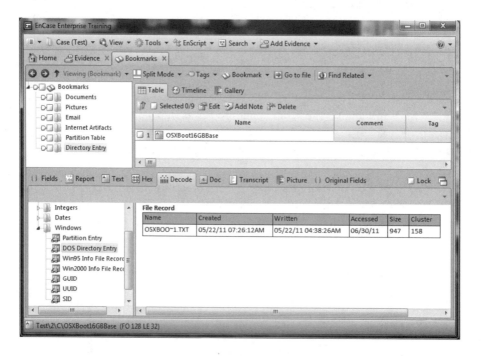

FIGURE 2.15   EnCase table view showing attributes from a directory entry that match information decoded in Figure 2.14

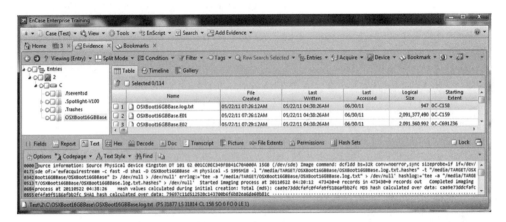

Viewing FAT Entries

In this exercise, I will show you how to locate and view FAT directory entries. All you need to follow along is any device formatted with FAT.

1. Preview a USB thumb drive (any FAT version) by turning on the write-protect switch and mounting it in Windows. (Write-protecting your media is always a best practice but is not necessary for this exercise! Since EnCase now has FastBloc Software Edition included, you can practice best practices by write blocking; we'll show you how.)

2. Launch EnCase (dongle required), and open a new case in EnCase, accepting the default values.

3. With a case open within EnCase Forensic (EnCase), select Tools ➢ FastBloc SE (see Step 26). Select your write block mode and insert your thumb drive into the USB port. Write Blocked is the default mode and caches the attempts to write to the drive. Write Protected does not cache the attempts to write to the drive. After the media is placed into the USB port and it is recognized by the operating system, a pop-up window will appear, indicating that the media is connected and the status of the device. Select Close.

4. Click Add Evidence; in the screen that follows, choose Add Local Device.

5. In the screen the follows, accept the defaults and click Next. Locate your USB drive, place a blue check next to it, click Next, and then click Finish. Your thumb drive should be visible in the left pane as a device. Make certain the file system is visible.

EXERCISE 2.1 *(continued)*

6. Find a file of interest in a folder somewhere. Note carefully this file's parent folder and path to that folder. You want to put the parent folder in the table pane. To do this, place the parent folder's parent in the tree pane. If its parent is the root, then place your focus on the root level in the tree pane. When you see the parent folder of your file in the table pane, place your cursor on that parent folder in the table pane. The data for that parent folder is now in the view pane. In the view pane, select the Text View tab. The data for this parent folder should be in red.

7. You'll see your data in red, but it is not formatted into nice 32-byte–wide entries. Let's fix that.

8. In the view pane, under the Text tab, you'll see Text Style with a black triangle, indicating a drop-down menu. From this drop-down menu, choose Text Styles.

9. From the resultant Edit Text Styles screen, choose New.

10. Use the same settings we used earlier in Figure 2.13 (Name: FAT Directory, Line Wrap: Max Size, and Wrap Length: 32) On the Code Page tab, use the ISO-6937 or its nearest equivalent.

11. Under View, choose Text Styles. In the left pane, right-click at the root level of the folders, and select New Folder.

12. Name the new folder **custom**.

13. Place your cursor on the custom folder, right-click, and choose New.

14. You are given a pane to create a new text style. Use the settings in Figure 2.13. On the Code Page tab, select Other, and select Latin 9 (ISO) for the code page.

15. When done, click OK.

16. From the Text Style drop-down menu, choose your newly created text style to apply it.

17. Go back to the table pane, and locate your parent folder in the right pane.

18. Click it in the table pane to view its contents in the view pane. Make sure you have the text view in the bottom pane. You should see your entries in nice 32-byte rows.

19. With your cursor, select the data for the 32-byte entry for your file of interest, as shown in Figure 2.12.

20. Right-click the selected 32-byte entry, choose Bookmark Data, and select the raw text as the type. If you like, you can create a new directory to contain this information, naming it something such as **Directory Entry**.

21. Under View, choose Bookmarks.

22. In the bottom section of View pane, go to the Decode tab.

23. In the left pane, you'll see View Types. Under Windows, choose DOS Directory Entry, and the results will be displayed in the right pane.

24. Use this technique to bookmark directory information for a directory entry whose starting cluster is overwritten and in use by another file.

25. After previewing or acquiring the USB device, it is necessary to remove the USB and then turn off the FastBloc SE. First, remove the USB device from the computer.

26. Turn off FastBloc SE as a running process by accessing Tools ➢ FastBloc SE. In the resulting menu, click Clear All. In the Plug and Play dialog box, it will ask, "Remove write-blocking for all devices on all channels?" Click Yes.

Another alternative for bookmarking directory entry information is to simply bookmark a file of interest and choose the various directory entry attributes to show in the resulting report, as shown in Figure 2.16.

FIGURE 2.16   Bookmark of file of interest with directory entry data showing in the report

	Name	Value
1	Name	OSXBoot16GBBase.log.txt
2	Tag	
3	File Ext	txt
4	Logical Size	947
5	Category	Document
6	Signature Analysis	
7	Signature	
8	Protected	
9	Protection complexity	
10	Last Accessed	06/30/11 12:00:00AM
11	File Created	05/22/11 07:26:12AM
12	Last Written	05/22/11 04:38:26AM
13	Is Picture	
14	Code Page	
15	MD5	
16	SHA1	
17	Item Path	2\NoName \OSXBoot16GBBase.log.txt
18	Description	File, Archive
19	Is Deleted	
20	Entry Modified	
21	File Deleted	
22	File Acquired	
23	Initialized Size	947
24	Physical Size	4,096
25	Starting Extent	0-C16321024

> Bookmarking the file and showing its directory attributes in the report is the method most commonly used to report this information. However, you can't use this method when the file has been deleted and its starting cluster is in use by another file. EnCase is showing you the directory entry for such a file, but has no data to go with it as it is in use by another file. Any attempt to bookmark such a file will actually bookmark the file that has overwritten the data. When you encounter such a situation, having the knowledge and skills to bookmark the "raw data" is most useful!

The Function of FAT

Thus far, we have thoroughly dissected the physical features of the FAT file systems and delineated its underlying structures. While examining these structures, some of the functions started to emerge. In the following sections, I'll describe how those structures function in detail as they interact with the operating system to read, write, and delete files.

From the previous discussions, you understand that the purpose of the FAT is twofold. First, whenever a file or directory's contents exceed one cluster, FAT tracks the sequence of clusters that constitute that file or directory. Second, FAT tracks which clusters are available to be used by the operating system, marking bad clusters so they won't be used, and ensuring that clusters allocated and in use by files and directories aren't overwritten.

How a File Is Stored

Also from the previous discussions, you understand that the purpose of the directory entry is to track every file and directory in a partition. It does so by storing its status, its name, its starting cluster, and its length in bytes, as well as other file metadata or attributes. Let's now examine how those functions interact with our operating system.

The first task is discovering what takes place during the simple act of reading a small file that is contained within one cluster. When the operating system calls for a file to be read, it is called by the filename and path. The path leads to the filename stored in the directory entry. It is the information stored in the directory entry that allows the operating system to begin to locate the data that constitutes this file. The filename for our example will be autorun.inf, which is located in a folder named New Report, which in turn is contained in the root directory of a FAT16 partition. The operating system looks in the parent folder and reads the directory information. Figure 2.17 shows the information contained in the directory entry.

According to the directory entry, autorun.inf starts in cluster 2065 and has a size of 65 bytes. The operating system goes to cluster 2065 and starts to read the data, knowing its length is 65 bytes. After reading 65 bytes of data it stops, because the end of the data for the file has been reached. Any other data in the cluster is ignored since it is not part of the file. The file's logical size is 65 bytes. A file will also have a physical size, which is the size of the clusters it occupies. Since it occupies one cluster (in this case a cluster contains only one sector), its physical size is 512 bytes.

Figure 2.18 shows the FAT entry for cluster 2065. (Each two-byte array represents one cluster in FAT16; thus, the two-byte array at file offset 4130 represents cluster 2065.) Its value is 0xFFFF, which for a FAT16 partition means that cluster is marked as end of file (EOF) since it is greater than 0xFFF8. This particular FAT16 partition uses one sector to constitute one cluster. One cluster will therefore hold 512 bytes of data before requiring an additional cluster, and thus 65 bytes fit easily in one cluster. Figure 2.19 shows cluster 2065, which contains the file's data with 65 bytes selected.

FIGURE 2.17   Directory information for the file to be located and read in the example

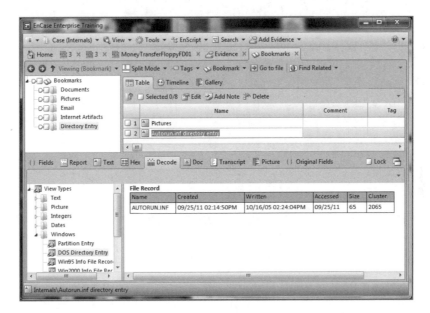

FIGURE 2.18   FAT entry for cluster 2065, showing the cluster marked as EOF

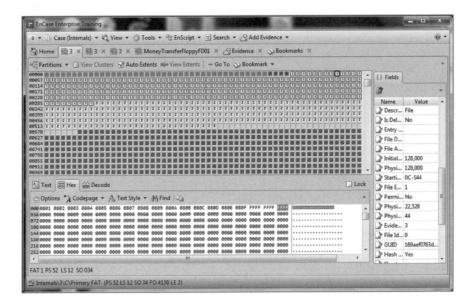

FIGURE 2.19   65 bytes of data found in cluster 2065 that constitute the file autorun.inf

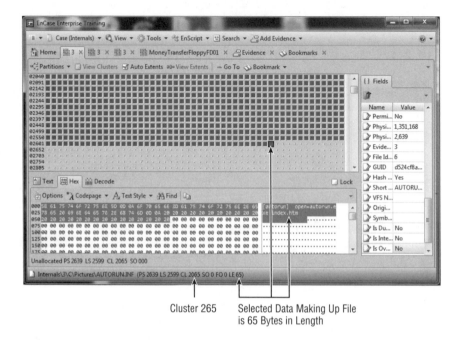

Cluster 265   Selected Data Making Up File
is 65 Bytes in Length

In the previous example, the data was contained in one cluster. In our next example, the data will not fit in one cluster and will span several clusters. When this happens, the FAT is necessary to link together the clusters. Let's see how it actually works with real data.

Figure 2.20 shows the file DSC00088.JPG having a starting cluster of 2 and a length of 512,848 bytes. You know that each cluster consists of one sector on this particular partition, and therefore one cluster can hold 512 bytes. To find out how many clusters a file will occupy, you divide the file size by the number of bytes in a cluster or, in this case, 512,848 bytes divided by 512 bytes per cluster, which equals 1,001.6 clusters (and some change). Since partial clusters are not allowed, this file will require 1,002 clusters to hold its data. You will expect the file to completely occupy all of the first 1,001 clusters (1,001 × 512 = 512,512 bytes) and the first 336 bytes of the last cluster in the chain (512,848 total bytes – 512,512 stored in first 1,001 clusters = 336 bytes). To check this reasoning and the math, EnCase has a File Extents tab. By selecting the file of interest in the table pane, details concerning this file are viewed in the bottom or view pane. Various tabs are available in the view pane, and one of them is the File Extents tab. Choose this tab, and the file extents for the selected file will display. Figure 2.21 shows the file extents for the file in our example, and when choosing the File Extents tab in the left pane, the right pane returns the File Extents information for the file.

FIGURE 2.20 File DSC00088.JPG has a starting cluster of 2 and a file length of 512,848 bytes.

	Name	File Created	Last Written	Starting Extent	Logical Size
2	DSC00088.JPG	09/25/11 12:55:26PM	10/18/04 04:35:38PM	0C-C2	512,848

FIGURE 2.21 The File Extents tab shows DSC00088.JPG starts at cluster 2 and occupies 1,002 clusters and the same number of sectors since one cluster in this case is one sector.

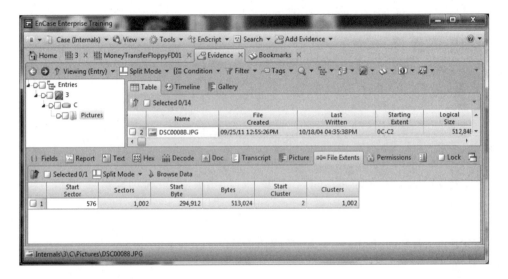

If you go to the FAT entry for cluster 2, since you know the file spans many contiguous clusters, you would expect cluster 2's entry to tell you where to find the next cluster for the file. Figure 2.22 shows the entry for cluster 2 as 0x0003, which is decimal value 3, meaning that cluster 3 is the next cluster in the chain. Looking at cluster 3, you can see it has a value of 0x00004 (decimal 4), meaning the next cluster in the chain is 4. Looking at cluster 4, you'll find it has a value of 0x0005 (decimal 5). Because this file occupies contiguous clusters (not fragmented), this pattern will persist until you reach the FAT entry for cluster 1,003, the last cluster in the chain. Figure 2.23 shows the FAT entry for this cluster. Looking at this entry, you'll find it has a value of 0xFFFF, meaning it is the EOF. Since this is the last cluster in the chain, you can expect the file to end there and to be marked as EOF. Table 2.7 reinforces and explains in chart form what you see in the raw data.

FIGURE 2.22 The FAT entry for cluster 2 shows a value that points to cluster 3, which is the next cluster in the run.

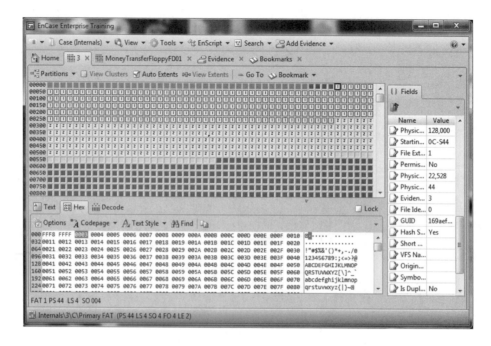

FIGURE 2.23 The FAT entry for cluster 1003 is highlighted. Its value indicates it is an end-of-file marker.

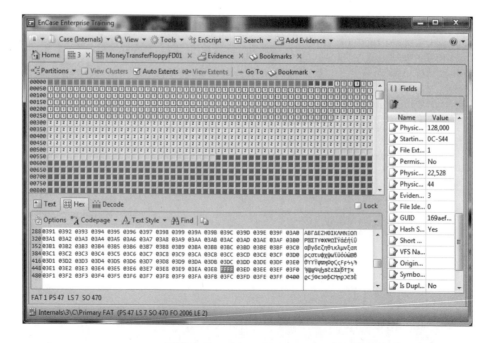

TABLE 2.7   FAT entries for file DSC00088.JPG

FAT cluster #	Value hex	Value decimal	Meaning	Bytes of file contained In cluster
2	0x0003	3	Next cluster holding file's data is cluster 3	512
3	0x0004	4	Next cluster holding file's data is cluster 5	512
4	0x0005	5	Next cluster holding file's data is cluster 5	512
Pattern repeats from cluster 5 to cluster 1,002 (998 clusters)				510,976
1,003	0xFFFF	65,535	Greater than 0xFFF8 (65,528), meaning it is EOF	336
				512,848 Total Bytes

Now that you understand how the directory entries work in conjunction with the FAT to read files and have analyzed this process using raw data in an actual FAT, writing a file is just an extension of what you already know. To get you started, you will use the values shown in Table 2.8 and Table 2.9 as your hypothetical FAT and directory entries to write a file.

TABLE 2.8   File Allocation Table (FAT16: 1 cluster = 8 sectors = 4,096 bytes)

0	1	2	3	4	5	6	7	8	9	10	11	12	13
**	**	E	4	E	E	8	E	E	0	B	0	0	0
14	**15**	**16**	**17**	**18**	**19**	**20**	**21**	**22**	**23**	**24**	**25**	**26**	**27**
0	0	0	0	0	0	0	B	0	0	0	0	0	0

Bold numbers indicate cluster numbers (they don't exist in a real FAT!)
E = End of file, 0 = Available, B = Bad cluster

Remember that the first addressable cluster is cluster 2, but the FAT array starts with entries for cluster 0 and cluster 1. The values for these two entries do not relate to cluster usage but are used for other "housekeeping" chores as already described.

TABLE 2.9 Table of directory entries

Filename	Extension	Created	Accessed	Written	Start cluster	Length
file1234	txt	6/5/2011 1745 hrs	6/5/2011	1745 hrs 6/5/2011	2	4,095
file5678	txt	6/5/2011 1756 hrs	6/5/2011	1756 hrs 6/5/2011	3	4,097
fileabcd	txt	6/5/2011 1800 hrs	6/5/2011	6/5/20111800 hrs	5	4,096
filewxyz	txt	6/5/2011 1815 hrs	6/5/2011	6/5/2011 1921 hrs	6	8,000
file8765	txt	6/5/2011 1820 hrs	6/5/2011	6/5/2011 1820 hrs	7	286

To summarize the FAT (Table 2.8) and its corresponding directory entries (Table 2.9), the following are true:

- file1234.txt is 4,095 bytes in length and starts with cluster 2. Because it fits within a cluster (a cluster holds 4,096 bytes), only one cluster is needed, and the entry in the FAT for cluster 2 is marked as EOF.

- file5678.txt is 4,097 bytes in length and starts with cluster 3. Because it exceeds one cluster by one byte, it requires a second cluster to hold its contents. The FAT entry for cluster 3 is 4, meaning that cluster 4 holds the one byte needed to hold the data. As the data ends in cluster 4, cluster 4 contains the EOF marker.

- fileabcd.txt is 4,096 bytes in length and starts in cluster 5. Because its contents fit exactly in one cluster, no other clusters are needed, and cluster 5 is marked as EOF.

- filewxyz.txt is 8,000 bytes in length and starts in cluster 6. Eight thousand bytes divided by 4,096 bytes (the bytes in one cluster) is 1.95, meaning this file will take two clusters to hold its data. You would expect the entry for cluster 6 to contain the value for the second and final cluster, which is cluster 8. The entry for cluster 8 is marked as EOF. This file is fragmented, meaning its data is not contained in contiguous clusters, since its data is contained in cluster 6 and 8. Cluster 7 holds data for another file.

- file8765.txt is 286 bytes and starts in cluster 7. Its contents fit easily in one cluster, and cluster 7 is marked as EOF.

To write a file on this FAT16 file system, the file is given a name either by an application or by the user. Say you create your first file and call it yourfile.txt. This file has a length of 7,580 bytes. You could write this file using Table 2.8 and Table 2.9 as the starting point. The changes resulting from adding the hypothetical file will be reflected in Table 2.10 and Table 2.11.

Say the operating system first seeks an available cluster to which to write the data. Cluster 9 is available and will be the starting cluster for our data. Because this file will require two clusters, the operating system seeks the next available cluster. Because cluster 10 is marked

Bad, cluster 11 is the next available. Thus, the operating system stores the data in clusters 9 and 11, marking the FAT entry for cluster 9 with the value for cluster 11, and cluster 11 is marked as EOF. See these entries in Table 2.10. A directory entry is written in the appropriate parent directory indicating the file's name, starting cluster, length, and other metadata or attributes. See Table 2.11 for this entry. Because this example file is contained in two noncontiguous clusters (9 and 11), it is a fragmented file.

TABLE 2.10   File Allocation Table (FAT16: 1 cluster = 8 sectors = 4,096 bytes)

0	1	2	3	4	5	6	7	8	9	10	11	12	13
**	**	E	4	E	E	8	E	E	11	B	E	0	0

14	15	16	17	18	19	20	21	22	23	24	25	26	27
0	0	0	0	0	0	0	B	0	0	0	0	0	0

TABLE 2.11   Table of Directory Entries

Filename	Extension	Created	Accessed	Written	Start Cluster	Length
file1234	txt	6/5/2011 1745 hrs	6/5/2011	6/5/2011, 1745 hrs	2	4,095
file5678	txt	6/5/2011 1756 hrs	6/5/2011	6/5/2011, 1756 hrs	3	4,097
fileabcd	txt	6/5/2011 1800 hrs	6/5/2011	6/5/2011, 1800 hrs	5	4,096
filewxyz	txt	6/5/2011 1815 hrs	6/5/2011	6/5/2011, 1921 hrs	6	8,000
file8765	txt	6/5/2011 1820 hrs	6/5/2011	6/5/2011, 1820 hrs	7	286
yourfile	txt	9/5/2011 1712 hrs	9/5/2011	9/5/2011, 1712 hrs	9	7,580

The first character of the file or directory name in a directory entry has a name and purpose. It is called the *status byte*. When in use by a file or directory, its purpose is somewhat obscured, because it is seen simply as part of the file or directory name. When a file or directory is deleted, its purpose becomes clear; the first character of the file or directory is changed to 0xE5 to signify to the operating system that the entry is deleted. This causes the OS to ignore the file and not display it to the user. Aside from making changes to the FAT to mark the clusters as unallocated, that is all there is to deleting a file. Let's delete a file in our FAT16 file system and see how it works.

The Effects of Deleting and Undeleting Files

Using Table 2.12 and Table 2.13, delete `file5678.txt`. To do so, simply change the first character of the filename in the directory entry to 0xE5. In the hypothetical table, the 0xE5 takes up four characters, but in a real system, 0xE5 is one byte, as was the character it replaced. In a real directory entry, *f*, which is 0x66, is replaced by 0xE5. To complete the deletion, go to the FAT entry of the file's starting cluster, which is cluster 3. Cluster 3 contains a value of 4, which is noted by the OS. Cluster 3 is marked with a 0, making it available for allocation. Cluster 4 contains an EOF, and the OS knows this is the end of the cluster sequence, so it marks it with a 0, making it available for allocation, and then stops. The file is deleted as far as the operating system is concerned. Aside from the first character of the directory, the remaining 31 bytes are untouched. The data in clusters 3 and 4 remain untouched. Because clusters 3 and 4 are marked with zeros, they are available to hold the contents of another file, and thus can be completely or partially overwritten. As they stand, however, they are easily and completely recoverable.

TABLE 2.12   File Allocation Table (FAT16: 1 cluster = 8 sectors = 4,096 bytes)

0	1	2	3	4	5	6	7	8	9	10	11	12	13
**	**	E	0	0	E	8	E	E	11	B	E	0	0

14	15	16	17	18	19	20	21	22	23	24	25	26	27
0	0	0	0	0	0	0	B	0	0	0	0	0	0

TABLE 2.13   Table of directory entries

Filename	Extension	Created	Accessed	Written	Start Cluster	Length
file1234	txt	6/5/2011 1745 hrs	6/5/2011	6/5/2011, 1745 hrs	2	4,095
0xE5ile5678	txt	6/5/2011 1756 hrs	6/5/2011	6/5/2011, 1756 hrs	3	4,097
fileabcd	txt	6/5/2011 1800 hrs	6/5/2011	6/5/2011, 1800 hrs	5	4,096
filewxyz	txt	6/5/2011 1815 hrs	6/5/2011	6/5/2011, 1921 hrs	6	8,000
file8765	txt	6/5/2011 1820 hrs	6/5/2011	6/5/2011, 1820 hrs	7	286
yourfile	txt	9/5/2011 1712 hrs	9/5/2011	9/5/2011, 1712 hrs	9	7,580

To undelete or recover a file, you simply reverse the process by which it was deleted. In Tables 2.14 and 2.15, undelete this file. You start the process by going to the directory entry. You change the 0xE5 to the original character if known or a best guess if unknown, or you use some standard character, such as an underscore. If the file has a long filename and its entries are intact, the original character can be derived from that source. In this example, change the first character to an underscore character (see Table 2.15).

The next step in the process is to go to the FAT entry for the starting cluster for this file (Table 2.14), which from the directory entry you know to be 3. This file uses two clusters, so the value that must be entered for cluster 3's entry must be the next cluster in the chain. The next available cluster after cluster 3 is cluster 4. Thus, a value of 4 is entered for cluster 3, and an EOF mark is made for cluster 4's entry. At this point, the file has been successfully recovered. This is the basic manner in which EnCase will recover files automatically for you.

TABLE 2.14   File Allocation Table (FAT16: 1 cluster = 8 sectors = 4,096 bytes)

0	1	2	3	4	5	6	7	8	9	10	11	12	13
**	**	E	4	E	E	8	E	E	11	B	E	0	0

14	15	16	17	18	19	20	21	22	23	24	25	26	27
0	0	0	0	0	0	0	B	0	0	0	0	0	0

TABLE 2.15   Table of directory entries

Filename	Extension	Created	Accessed	Written	Start Cluster	Length
file1234	txt	6/5/2011 1745 hrs	6/5/2011	6/5/2011, 1745 hrs	2	4,095
_ile5678	txt	6/5/2011 1756 hrs	6/5/2011	6/5/2011, 1756 hrs	3	4,097
fileabcd	txt	6/5/2011 1800 hrs	6/5/2011	6/5/2011, 1800 hrs	5	4,096
filewxyz	txt	6/5/2011 1815 hrs	6/5/2011	6/5/2011, 1921 hrs	6	8,000
file8765	txt	6/5/2011 1820 hrs	6/5/2011	6/5/2011, 1820 hrs	7	286
yourfile	txt	9/5/2011 1712 hrs	9/5/2011	9/5/2011, 1712 hrs	9	7,580

The undelete process is not perfect. The file filewxyz.txt is fragmented, occupying two noncontiguous clusters, which are clusters 6 and 8. This file has been deleted in Table 2.16 and Table 2.17. The first character of the name in its directory entry has been changed to

0xE5, and the FAT entries for clusters 6 and 8 have been changed to 0, making them available for allocation by the system.

The file file8765.txt occupies a single cluster, which is cluster 7. This file has also been deleted, and that deletion is reflected in Table 2.16 and Table 2.17. The first character of the name in its directory entry has been changed to 0xE5, and the FAT entry for cluster 7 has been changed to 0, marking it as available for allocation by the system.

TABLE 2.16   File Allocation Table (FAT16: 1 cluster = 8 sectors = 4,096 bytes)

0	1	2	3	4	5	6	7	8	9	10	11	12	13
**	**	E	4	E	E	0	0	0	11	B	E	0	0

14	15	16	17	18	19	20	21	22	23	24	25	26	27
0	0	0	0	0	0	0	B	0	0	0	0	0	0

TABLE 2.17   Table of directory entries

Filename	Extension	Created	Accessed	Written	Start Cluster	Length
file1234	txt	6/5/2011 1745 hrs	6/5/2011	6/5/2011, 1745 hrs	2	4,095
_ile5678	txt	6/5/2011 1756 hrs	6/5/2011	6/5/2011, 1756 hrs	3	4,097
fileabcd	txt	6/5/2011 1800 hrs	6/5/2011	6/5/2011, 1800 hrs	5	4,096
0xE5ilewxyz	txt	6/5/2011 1815 hrs	6/5/2011	6/5/2011, 1921 hrs	6	8,000
0xE5ile8765	txt	6/5/2011 1820 hrs	6/5/2011	6/5/2011, 1820 hrs	7	286
yourfile	txt	9/5/2011 1712 hrs	9/5/2011	9/5/2011, 1712 hrs	9	7,580

Clusters 6, 7, and 8 are marked with zeros, with 6 and 8 holding the data for what used to be filewxyz.txt and cluster 7 holding the data for what used to be file8765.txt. Directory entries for these two files have had their status bytes changed to 0xE5, telling the operating system that these files are deleted and to ignore them. The files are both deleted as far as the operating system is concerned.

As with any busy operating system, data is constantly changing, with data being overwritten nearly every time a new file or directory entry is written. If the directory entry for what used to be file8765.txt were overwritten, recovering filewxyz.txt could be problematic. Let's see why by looking at Table 2.18 and Table 2.19.

TABLE 2.18   File Allocation Table (FAT16: 1 cluster = 8 sectors = 4,096 bytes)

0	1	2	3	4	5	6	7	8	9	10	11	12	13
**	**	E	4	E	E	0	0	0	11	B	E	0	0

14	15	16	17	18	19	20	21	22	23	24	25	26	27
0	0	0	0	0	0	0	B	0	0	E	0	0	0

TABLE 2.19   Table of directory entries

Filename	Extension	Created	Accessed	Written	Start Cluster	Length
file1234	txt	6/5/2011 1745 hrs	6/5/2011	6/5/2011, 1745 hrs	2	4,095
_ile5678	txt	6/5/2011 1756 hrs	6/5/2011	6/5/2011, 1756 hrs	3	4,097
fileabcd	txt	6/5/2011 1800 hrs	6/5/2011	6/5/2011, 1800 hrs	5	4,096
0xE5ilewxyz	txt	6/5/2011 1815 hrs	6/5/2011	6/5/2011, 1921 hrs	6	8,000
coolfile	txt	9/5/2011 1820 hrs	6/5/2011	9/5/2011 1820 hrs	24	286
yourfile	txt	9/5/2011 1712 hrs	9/5/2011	9/5/2011, 1712 hrs	9	7,580

With the directory entry for file8765.txt overwritten, there's no way to tell that its former data was and still is in cluster 7. When it comes time to recover filewxyz.txt, you can restore the first character to an underscore and go to its starting cluster, which is cluster 6. You know it occupies two clusters, and without knowledge to the contrary, you can assume that the next available cluster is the next cluster in the series. Thus, when you recover the clusters, you are recovering clusters 6 and 7, not 6 and 8, which are the correct clusters. The data in cluster 6, the starting cluster, is correct, but the data in cluster 7 belongs to a different file. The entry, after recovery, for cluster 6, is 7, and cluster 7 contains the EOF marker. Table 2.20 and Table 2.21 show this erroneous recovery.

TABLE 2.20   File Allocation Table (FAT16: 1 cluster = 8 sectors = 4,096 bytes)

0	1	2	3	4	5	6	7	8	9	10	11	12	13
**	**	E	4	E	E	7	E	0	11	B	E	0	0

14	15	16	17	18	19	20	21	22	23	24	25	26	27
0	0	0	0	0	0	0	B	0	0	E	0	0	0

TABLE 2.21 Table of directory entries

Filename	Extension	Created	Accessed	Written	Start Cluster	Length
file1234	txt	6/5/2011 1745 hrs	6/5/2011	6/5/2011, 1745 hrs	2	4,095
_ile5678	txt	6/5/2011 1756 hrs	6/5/2011	6/5/2011, 1756 hrs	3	4,097
fileabcd	txt	6/5/2011 1800 hrs	6/5/2011	6/5/2011, 1800 hrs	5	4,096
_ilewxyz	txt	6/5/2011 1815 hrs	6/5/2011	6/5/2011, 1921 hrs	6	8,000
coolfile	txt	9/5/2011 1820 hrs	6/5/2011	9/5/2011 1820 hrs	24	286
yourfile	txt	9/5/2011 1712 hrs	9/5/2011	9/5/2011, 1712 hrs	9	7,580

The method of recovery you just employed manually is the same logic and method used by EnCase and other data recovery software. The directory entry gives only the starting cluster. The second cluster in the chain is assumed to be the next unallocated cluster after the starting cluster. The third is assumed to be the next unallocated cluster after that one, and so forth, until the number of clusters holding the data is reached. You can see the error that occurred with a two-cluster file. With extremely large files that become fragmented on busy systems, the potential for errors in recovering files is significant.

Your best chances for successful recovery will be when fragmentation is minimal and the deletion was recent. When you have an erroneous recovery, the error will usually stand out. If it is an image, chances are you'll see a partial picture. If it is a web page, you'll see it begin as HTML code and suddenly change to something else, typically binary data. When this occurs, you'll understand what has happened and can explain why. Partial recovery is better than no recovery!

When EnCase recovers a deleted file, it will check to see whether the deleted file's starting cluster is in use by another file. If not, it will recover the data by the previous method. If the starting cluster is in use by another file, it will report this as an "overwritten file." In the right pane, you are looking at the information contained in the deleted file's directory entry. The bottom pane contains the data for the file that overwrote the deleted file's starting cluster. As previously mentioned, an attempt to bookmark an overwritten file will result in bookmarking the file and data that overwrote that file. It may be possible to manually recover some data in the second and subsequent clusters of an overwritten file.

Slack Space

When I was discussing logical file size and physical file size, I mentioned that the operating system ignored the data in the cluster after the logical file. Forensically, however, you don't want to ignore that data because it can contain valuable evidence. The data between the end of the logical file to the end of the last cluster allocated to the file is called *slack space*.

Slack space will usually contain data from files that used this space before, making it a rich depository of evidence.

Slack space is actually composed of data from two different sources. When data is written to media, it is written in blocks of 512 bytes or one sector. If only one byte of actual file data is to be written, the system must also write another 511 bytes such that it writes 512 bytes. Before Windows 95B, the "extra" data or filler was randomly taken from slack and caused many security concerns. With Windows 95B, that filler data became zeros. Because of its history, the portion of the slack space from the end of the logical file to the end of the sector (not the cluster) was called *RAM slack*. More recently, the term *sector slack* is also applied, and both refer to the same portion of the slack space. The remainder of the slack, from the end of the last sector containing the logical file until the end of the cluster, is called *file slack*. The entire slack space, comprising both RAM or sector slack and file slack, is shown in the default color of red when viewed in EnCase.

In Figure 2.24, the data in the logical file appears in the default color of black. When the logical file ends, EnCase displays the rest of the characters in red. At the beginning of the red characters, you can see that they are all 0x00 (RAM or sector slack) until the sector boundary is reached, at sector #511. In this example, I have selected the entire range of RAM slack (363 bytes) to make it more visible. After the sector boundary, what's left is data remaining from files that were deleted, which is the file slack.

FIGURE 2.24   Slack space will appear in red. Windows Vista and Windows 7 still leave slack space evidence for the examiner!

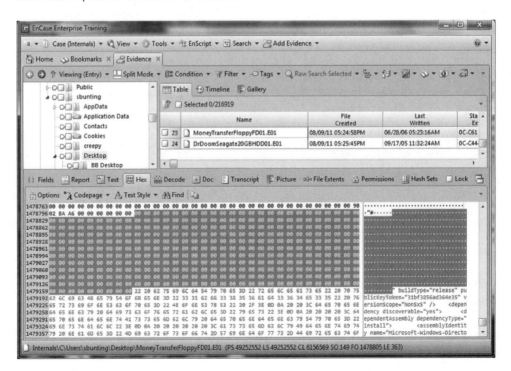

Directory Entry Status Byte

Before I conclude the discussion of FAT file systems, there's one more important point to cover. The directory entry status byte (the first byte of the 32-byte directory entry), as you have seen it used thus far, either has contained the first character of a valid file or directory name or has contained 0xE5 to indicate a deleted file or directory. It can contain a few other values that have special meaning.

Believe it or not, if you wanted to have the first character of a file as hex E5, you'd need the value 0x05. Also, if the first byte contained the value of 0x00, that means the entry is not used and entries beyond this point are not searched. However, the most important value for the forensics examiner, of the ones not yet covered, is that of 0x2E or 0x2E2E. Most may recall it more affectionately as the "dot double dot" signature for a directory, as shown in Figure 2.25.

FIGURE 2.25   Classic "dot double dot" directory signature

```
00000 .         ··ÄPYC2C2··ÇYC2sI····
00032 ..        ··ÄPYC2C2··ÇYC2·····
00064 Bp··ÿÿÿÿÿ··ñÿÿÿÿÿÿÿÿÿÿ··ÿÿÿÿ
00096 ·d·b·x·i·n···ñs·1·4·0·x···z·i
00128 DBXINS~1ZIP ·)ÇYC2C2··¨CO2tIç··
00160 B··m·s·i······ÿÿÿÿÿÿÿÿÿÿ··ÿÿÿÿ
00192 ·D·B·X·p·r···¨e·s·s·S·e·t···u·p·
00224 DBXPRE~1MSI ·CÇYC2C2··÷¨ÿOCI·R··
```

When the value of the first directory entry line begins with 0x2E, or "dot," it denotes that it is a directory entry and the "dot" points to itself. The second directory entry line that follows will begin with 0x2E2E, or "dot dot." This entry points to its parent directory. If you are at a command prompt and type **cd..**, you will change into the parent directory from where you were. In the "dot dot" line, the value contained in the "starting cluster" (byte offsets 26 and 27) will be that of the parent directory for the directory in which you currently are, as shown in Figure 2.26. If that value is 0x00, the parent directory is in the root directory, as shown in Figure 2.27.

FIGURE 2.26   Parent directory's starting cluster at byte offsets 26 and 27

```
00000 .         ··ÄPYC2C2··ÇYC2sI····
00032 ..        ··ÄPYC2C2··ÇYC2·██·····
00064 Bp··ÿÿÿÿÿ··ñÿÿÿÿÿÿÿÿÿÿ··ÿÿÿÿ
00096 ·d·b·x·i·n···ñs·1·4·0·x···z·i
00128 DBXINS~1ZIP ·)ÇYC2C2··¨CO2tIç··
00160 B··m·s·i······ÿÿÿÿÿÿÿÿÿÿ··ÿÿÿÿ
00192 ·D·B·X·p·r···¨e·s·s·S·e·t···u·p·
00224 DBXPRE~1MSI ·CÇYC2C2··÷¨ÿOCI·R··
```

FIGURE 2.27   Same value in hex as it is hex 00. The parent of this directory is in the root directory.

The importance of understanding the "dot double dot" directory signature is recognizing it when you see it but also understanding its structure. Not all deleted directories are going to be shown initially by EnCase. You can instruct EnCase to recover folders, at which time it will search for folders in the unallocated clusters of the partition looking for this signature, and will then recover anything that is recoverable. If you are asked questions on the exam about how directories are structured or recovered, understanding these concepts is extremely important to establishing your credibility as a forensics examiner.

NTFS Basics

Another file system used by the Windows operating system, starting with Windows NT, is New Technology File System (NTFS). NTFS, compared to the FAT file system, is more robust, providing stronger security, greater recoverability, and better performance with regard to read, write, and search capabilities. Among other features, it includes support for long filenames, a highly granular system of file permissions and access control, and compression of individual files and directories. Accordingly, it is a far more complex file system. Covering it with the level of detail I have afforded the FAT system would not be feasible. Therefore, our purpose here is to provide a brief overview.

NTFS (version 1.0, also dubbed NT3.1) first rolled out in August 1993 with Windows NT. It went through two more iterations up through 1996 (versions 1.1 and 1.2, also dubbed NT3.5, NT3.51, and NT4.0). Windows 2000 gave birth to version 3.0, also dubbed NTFS 5.0. With XP in the fall of 2001, version 3.1 was born and also dubbed NTFS 5.1. Still under version 3.1, Windows Server 2003 rolled out in 2003 with a NTFS 5.2; Windows Server 2008 and Windows Vista rolled out with NTFS 6.0. And finally Windows Server 2008 R2 and Windows 7 rolled out with NTFS 6.1.

Windows NT and 2000 provided NTFS as a formatting option, defaulting to FAT unless the user chose otherwise. Starting with Windows XP, the default format is NTFS. Thus, newer Windows systems will mostly use NTFS, but FAT will still continue to coexist with NTFS (it is used on other forms of media, as discussed earlier).

From the previous analysis of file systems, you know that, regardless of their name, they must perform certain basic functions for the system:

- Track the name of the file (or directory)
- Track the point where the file starts
- Track the length of the file along with other file metadata, such as date and time stamps
- Track the clusters used by the file (cluster runs)
- Track which allocations units (clusters) are allocated and which are not

NTFS does all these things and more. An NTFS partition is identified as such, initially at least, by an entry in the partition table of the MBR. From Chapter 1, "Computer Hardware," you know that Windows requires the partition to be properly identified in the partition table in order for Windows to mount it. When the NTFS partition is formatted, the VBR for NTFS is created and 16 sectors are reserved for its use, but typically only 8 are used for data. Bytes 3–6 of the first sector of the VBR will be "NTFS." Recall that FAT32 stored the backup of its VBR in the reserved area at the beginning of the volume. By contrast, NTFS stores its backup copy in the last sector of the partition.

In an NTFS partition, unlike FAT, all the important file system data is contained in actual files. NTFS uses many system files, but at the very heart of the NTFS system are $MFT (master file table) and $Bitmap. $MFT is similar to the directory entry in FAT, and the $Bitmap is similar to the FAT1 and FAT2 in FAT.

$Bitmap is a file that contains one bit for each cluster in the partition. It tracks allocation only and does not track cluster runs. If a cluster has a 0 in $Bitmap, that indicates it is available for use by the system. If a cluster has a 1, the cluster is allocated to a file. It is a simple system.

$MFT is a database with an entry for every file and directory in the partition, including an entry for itself. Each entry is fixed in length and is almost always 1,024 bytes. Each entry has a header (FILE0), which is followed by series of attributes. Everything about a file is an attribute, including the data itself. If a file is small, sometimes its data is stored within the $MFT and is called *resident data*. Cookie files are an excellent example of files that are almost always resident data. Typically the average maximum length for resident files is about 480 bytes. This varies with the type and length of the attributes in the $MFT. If a file can't be stored in the $MFT, then it is stored in a cluster, and in place of the resident data, the cluster runs are stored.

When a file is deleted on an NTFS partition, a flag in the $MFT is set, indicating the file is not in use, and the allocated clusters are marked with 0s in $Bitmap, which means they are unallocated. In addition, the index buffer entry for the logical folder is deleted. Because the $MFT record is otherwise untouched, an accurate record of cluster runs is usually intact, thus making recovery more reliable. The downside of recovering files in NTFS is that $MFT can grow but not shrink. As files are deleted, their $MFT records are efficiently and quickly overwritten, especially with XP.

Table 2.22 lists the major system files of the NTFS system along with a brief description of their functions.

TABLE 2.22   NTFS system files

MFT record #	Filename	Description
0	$MFT	Master file table; each MFT record is 1,024 bytes in length.
1	$MFTMirr	Contains a backup copy of the first four entries of the MFT.

TABLE 2.22 NTFS system files *(continued)*

MFT record #	Filename	Description
2	$LogFile	Journal file that contains file metadata transactions used for system recovery and file integrity.
3	$Volume	NTFS version and volume label and identifier.
4	$AttrDef	Attribute information.
5	$.	Root directory of the file system.
6	$Bitmap	Tracks the allocation status of all clusters in the partition.
7	$Boot	Contains partition boot sector and boot code.
8	$BadClus	Bad clusters on partition are tracked with this file.
9	$Secure	Contains file permissions and access control settings for file security.
10	$UpCase	Converts lowercase characters in Unicode by storing an uppercase version of all Unicode characters in this file.
11	$Extend	A directory reserved for options extensions.

New to NTFS, starting with Windows Vista, are Transactional NTFS and symbolic links. Transactional NTFS allows applications to group changes into a transaction. By making it a transaction, it is guaranteed that all the changes are made or none of them. Further, any applications outside the transactions will not see the changed data until it is committed. This process uses a Common Log File System (CLFS) to record the changes before they are committed, such that if a failure occurs, the system can be rolled back to a safe point. Symbolic links are often dubbed soft links. Symbolic links are resolved on the client side, not the server side. When symbolic links are shared, the target of the link is subjected to the same access controls as on the client. These links can be to files or directories.

🌐 Real World Scenario

"You Won't Find Anything Because I Wiped the Hard Drive"

The superintendent of a local school district called to report that child pornography had been found on one of their computers. The school board had assigned a computer to the foreperson of a contractor hired to renovate their school. After the contractor was terminated and the computer returned to the school board, they discovered the computer contained images of child pornography. Instead of notifying law enforcement, the superintendent turned the computer over to a school board member, who was employed as a computer system administrator. According to the superintendent, the board member printed the images and provided them to the school board attorney. I quickly made arrangements to retrieve the printed images from the school board attorney and informed her of the possible ramifications of possessing images of child pornography.

I met with the school board member (who still had possession of the computer) and advised him as well of the possible ramifications of his actions. When I asked for the computer, he said, "You won't find anything because I wiped the hard drive." He said his intentions were to remove any evidence of child pornography (since he had already preserved the photos in printed form) so the computer could be reused. When I asked what method he used to wipe the contents of the hard drive, he reminded me of his credentials and said he had used a wiping utility that he commonly uses at his job. Nonetheless, I received permission from the superintendent to examine the computer and took possession of it.

As I started the examination, I immediately observed that the hard drive did not contain a logical volume with a directory structure. However, I noticed actual data within the sectors, not just a repeat of some arbitrary hexadecimal value, which would indicate that the drive had indeed been wiped. I then pointed to physical sector 63 and observed the text "NTFS" in its complete context; in hexadecimal it was "EB 52 90 4E 54 46 53," which would indicate an NTFS partition. Why physical sector 63? At that time, I could not tell whether it was ingrained in me to automatically go to physical sector 63 or whether I actually knew that the first 63 sectors, physical sector 0–62, were reserved for the MBR and that the next sector contained information about the partition. Regardless, I pointed EnCase to physical sector 63, right-clicked, chose Add Partition, and selected the option to rebuild an NTFS partition. The Add Partition feature interprets the selected sector as the beginning of a VBR and rebuilds the previously removed partition based on the information contained within.

Upon a successful recovery of the partition, I was able to provide a detailed explanation of how and when the noted images were obtained.

With Windows 7, a regular format will wipe! For years, Windows did not truly wipe data during the format process. However with Windows 7, a regular format will wipe. Fortunately, the default format option is Quick Format, which does not wipe. Keep that in mind if you are told that Windows 7 was used to "format."

CD File Systems

When CDs first came out, as with many things, standards were lacking—and history has shown that a lack of standards can limit the growth of an industry or product. Several representatives of the CD industry and Microsoft met at the High Sierra Hotel in Lake Tahoe. The standard they published in 1986 for CD standards was aptly named High Sierra. Two years later in 1988 the International Organization for Standardization met and revised the High Sierra standard, calling it ISO 9660. ISO 9660 allowed for cross-platform capability for CDs between PCs, Unix, and Macintosh computers. Such universality wasn't without a price, and ISO 9660 CDs had the following limitations at the Level 1 implementation:

- Only uppercase characters (A–Z), numbers (0–9), and the underscore were permitted in the file name.
- Names used the 8 dot 3 file-naming convention.
- Directory names could not exceed 8 characters and could not have extensions.
- Nesting of subdirectories was limited—no deeper than 8 levels.
- Files had to be contiguous.

Minor improvements to this standard were implemented. Level 3 interchange rules allowed (using the previous rule set as a base) 30 characters in the filename. Level 3 implemented another improvement to the Level 2 rule set by not requiring files to be contiguous.

Microsoft developed the Joliet extension of ISO 9660 with the advent of Windows 95. Joliet offers significant improvements over its ISO 9660 predecessor. With Joliet, files or directories can be 64 characters long (Unicode support), directories can have extensions, the 8-levels-deep subdirectory barrier was removed, and multiple-session recording was supported.

When examining a CD that was created with Joliet, you will see an ISO 9660 directory and a Joliet directory, as shown in Figure 2.28 and Figure 2.29. This won't be visible in Windows, and can only be viewed on software designed to analyze CDs. With two separate directory structures pointing to the same data, operating systems that support Joliet can use that directory system and its features. Those that don't support Joliet use the ISO 9660 with its limitations.

FIGURE 2.28   CD with both ISO 9660 and Joliet directory structures. Note the Joliet directory names.

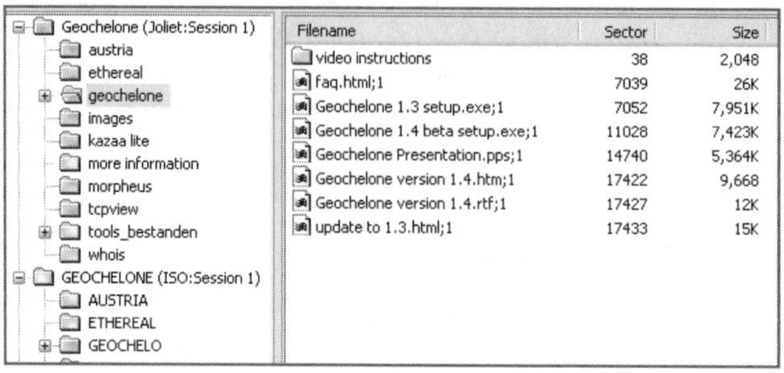

FIGURE 2.29   CD with both ISO 9660 and Joliet directory structures. Note the same directory names with ISO 9660 naming limitations.

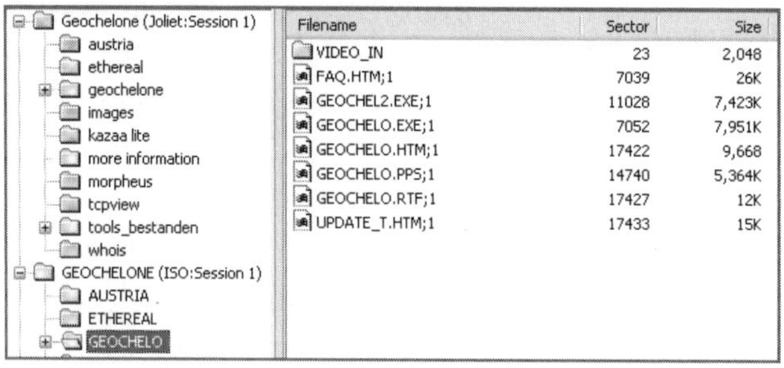

Universal Disk Format (UDF) is a relative newcomer to the CD scene. UDF uses a technique called *packet writing* to write data in increments to CD-R/RW disks. UDF allows for 255 characters per filename, which is a significant improvement over Joliet. Roxio DirectCD is an example of packet-writing software that writes using the UDF format. Unless you have the driver installed, you can't read a CD written with UDF, which often causes problems for examiners. Roxio provides a free driver at its website, which enables you to read a CD created in UDF. Another, less preferred option is to use DirectCD to close the session on a UDF CD. When this occurs, the filenames are converted to Joliet, and filenames that had a 255-character limit are truncated to 64.

Macintosh uses a native HFS format on its media and can use it on CDs, but HFS CDs can't be read by PCs. The hybrid disc is often used to overcome this issue, creating both an HFS directory and a Joliet directory, both pointing to the same set of data and readable by both the Macintosh and PCs.

Much like the Joliet extension, the Rock Ridge extension was created for Unix, which naturally supported Unix file-system features. Rock Ridge can't be read by PCs, but the basic ISO 9660 feature is present and read, and thus the Rock Ridge extensions are ignored when read by a PC.

Beginning with Version 5, EnCase supports CD images created by CD Inspector. You can use CD Inspector to examine CDs, including the "difficult" ones. CD Inspector provides an imaging utility that creates an image with a `.zip` extension. Those image files can be opened directly in EnCase. For this reason, many examiners prefer to use CD Inspector to examine and image problem CDs and rely on EnCase for analyzing the data.

exFAT

In 2006, Microsoft introduced the exFAT file system with Windows Embedded CE 6.0, and shortly thereafter it appeared in Windows Vista with Service Pack 1. It is a proprietary file system designed for flash media and is often dubbed FAT64. While it has many other new features, exFAT boasts a file size limit of 16 EiB (1 exbibyte = 2^{60} bytes = 1,152,921,504,606,846,976 bytes). For years, FAT32 had imposed a file size limit of 4 GB. This huge file size limit was welcome news for forensic examiners needing to store large files on a robust file system that is compatible with many operating systems.

The following operating systems support exFAT as well:

- Windows XP and Windows Server 2003, running Service Pack 2 and with a special patch (KB955704)
- Windows Vista with Service Pack 1
- Windows Server 2008
- Windows 7
- Later versions of OS X Snow Leopard (10.6.5)
- All versions of OS X Lion support exFAT. This OS X support includes not only read and write functions, but the ability to create exFAT partitions as well.
- As of this writing, the Linux kernel lacks support directly for exFAT; however, progress is underway.

There are four major areas or regions of exFAT:

- The main boot region
- The backup boot region
- The FAT region (normally only FAT1 is found unless TFAT is configured and then FAT2 will be found)
- The data region

EnCase supports exFAT partitions and has done so since midway through EnCase 6. Figure 2.30 depicts an exFAT partition in the disk view of EnCase 7. The focus is on the first sector (Logical Sector 0) of the partition known as the volume boot record (VBR). You should immediately note the file system name EXFAT highlighted in the view pane at offset 3 and running 8 bytes. The main boot region starts at Logical Sector 0 and runs for 12 sectors, ending at Logical Sector 11. The backup boot region immediately follows starting at Logical Sector 12 and again running for 12 sectors. After the backup boot region is an unused region, followed by FAT1. The offset to the beginning of and length in sectors of FAT1 is defined in the VBR at offsets 80 and 84 (4 bytes each). The data area will follow the FAT region and will also be defined in the VBR. Table 2.23 sets forth the various fields and offsets of the exFAT volume boot record.

FIGURE 2.30   Disk view of exFAT file system. The focus is on the VBR. Note the file system name highlighted in the view pane.

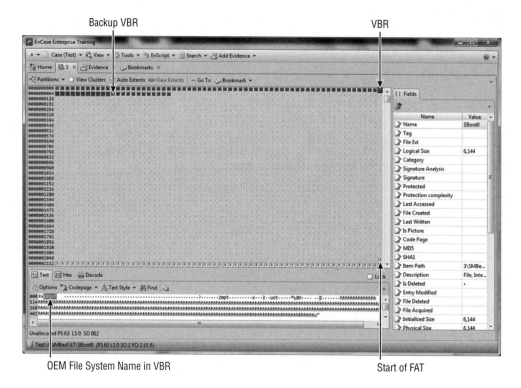

TABLE 2.23   Volume boot record: exFAT file system

Decimal offset	Length	Field description
0	3	Jump code
3	8	EXFAT: OEM file system ID

TABLE 2.23   Volume boot record: exFAT file system *(continued)*

Decimal offset	Length	Field description
11	53	Must be 0x00
64	8	Partition sector offset (will be zero for removable media)
72	8	Total sectors in the volume
80	4	Offset to beginning of FAT
84	4	Physical size of FAT in sectors
88	4	Offset to bitmap
92	4	Allocation units in the volume (bit count)
96	4	First cluster of the root directory
100	4	Volume serial number
104	2	File system revision number V.M (for example, 1.0)
106	1	Volume flags
107	1	Active FAT
108	1	Bytes per sector (power of 2 – 2^9 = 512)
109	1	Sectors per cluster (power of 2)
110	1	Number of FATs (1 or 2, and only 2 if TexFAT is configured and in use)
111	1	Used by INT 13
112	1	Percentage in use
113	7	Reserved
120	390	Boot program
510	2	VBR Signature 0xAA55

The exFAT file system will see expanded use over time, while currently it is not all that commonly encountered. The following is a list of important concepts pertaining to exFAT:

- The exFAT file system uses 32-bit arrays within the FAT to describe cluster numbers and has a limit of 4,294,967,285 (2^{32-11}) cluster addresses.

- exFAT uses free space bitmaps to reduce fragmentation, as well as allocation/detection issues.

- Each cluster is tracked in the bitmap, and a single bit is used to denote the status of each cluster (1 = allocated and 0 = unallocated).

- When a file is created in an exFAT file system, the sequence of events may differ from that which occurs in a FAT file system. If the file is fragmented, the exFAT and FAT function in the same manner. If, however, the file is not fragmented, the FAT is not updated.

- The exFAT file system uses the FAT (or a linked list) to document data file fragmentation. There will be a flag in one of the directory entry records to indicate whether the FAT is being used to document the fragmentation of the file.

- The FAT in an exFAT file system does *not* track whether clusters are unallocated or allocated as it does in a FAT file system. Rather, the exFAT FAT will contain data indicating one of three possible conditions: pointer to the next cluster or fragment, end of file (FF FF FF FF), or no fragmentation being tracked (00 00 00 00). Remember, the bitmap tracks allocation in exFAT!

- Within the directory entries of exFAT, there are multiple 32-byte records with at least three for each directory entry. Each of these records will have an identifier byte. They are as follows:

  - Directory Entry Record, which will have a Record ID of 0x85 and will contain attributes, the created timestamp, the last-accessed timestamp, and the last written timestamp.

  - Stream Extension Record, which will have a Record ID of 0xC0 and will contain the logical size, starting extent, size of filename, CRC of filename, and flag that determines whether the FAT is being used to track the clusters allocated to the file.

  - Filename Extension Record, which will have a Record ID of 0xC1 and will contain the filename in Unicode. Additional records will be added to accommodate longer filenames.

- When a file is deleted on an exFAT file system, regardless of fragmentation, the FAT is *not* zeroed out, because the FAT does not track allocation, since this function is carried out by the bitmap. The forensic import of this is that if the file was fragmented, the cluster runs are *not* destroyed upon deletion, which does occur with FAT file systems. Thus, fragmented files have a higher likelihood of successful recovery on exFAT file systems, so long as the clusters themselves have not be reused, which of course would result in overwriting FAT records.

- When a file is deleted on an exFAT file system, the first bit of the record identifier is changed from a 1 to a 0, which is strikingly similar to marking the first byte in a directory entry with 0xE5 on a FAT file system.

For those seeking an in-depth understanding of the exFAT file system, you should read the SANS paper entitled "Reverse Engineering the Microsoft Extended FAT File System (exFAT)" by Robert Shullich. You can find it at www.sans.org/reading_room/whitepapers/forensics/reverse-engineering-microsoft-exfat-file-system_33274.

Summary

This chapter explained the file systems used on Windows operating systems. Because the FAT file system is the most prevalent and has a long history, I covered its structure and function in great detail. The FAT file system works primarily with the directory entries and the FAT to read and write data on its partition. The FAT tracks cluster allocation and cluster runs in use by a file. The directory entries track the names of files and directories, along with their starting clusters and lengths. Using these basic features, files are read, written, and deleted. By reversing the deletion process, you learned how to recover deleted files.

I also covered the NTFS file system. At the heart of the NTFS file system are the master file table (MFT) and the bitmap ($Bitmap). The bitmap tracks only whether clusters are allocated. The MFT is similar to the directory entry in FAT, only much more robust. Everything about a file, including sometimes the data itself, is an attribute and stored in the MFT. If the data is small enough, it is stored as resident data in the MFT. If it is too large, it is stored in clusters, and the data runs are stored in the MFT.

You examined the various CD file systems and their history and features. ISO 9660 is the universal format that can be read by all platforms, but it has limitations. The Joliet extension of ISO 9660 contains expanded features for Microsoft platforms. Packet-writing software creates a UDF format that greatly enhances the length of filenames and allows for writing small amounts of data in increments. Its drawback is that it requires a driver to read on machines without the packet-writing software. To create universality, CDs are often written with multiple directory structures pointing to the same set of data. In this manner, an operating system can use the best directory it can support.

Finally, I covered Microsoft's new file system, exFAT. This file system was created for flash media and provides for a maximum file size of 16 EiB. This file system has four main regions, which are the boot region, the backup boot region, the FAT region, and the data region.

Exam Essentials

Know the physical features of the FAT file system.   Understand and locate the reserved area, the FAT, and the data area on FAT12/16/32 file systems. Understand how FAT12, FAT16, and FAT32 differ with regard to the physical features.

Be familiar with the volume boot record (boot sector).   Know how to locate the boot sector on FAT12/16 and FAT32 file systems. Understand the data contained therein and its importance, particularly in the event a partition must be restored.

Understand the FAT and the directory entry.   Be able to explain how files are read, written, and deleted using the FAT and directory entries. Know how files are recovered by reversing the process by which they were deleted and the limitations of that process.

Define the basics of the NTFS file system.   Explain how the bitmap is used only to track cluster allocation and how the MFT is used to store file attribute information, including filename, starting cluster, cluster runs, and data length, among other attributes.

Be familiar with the exFAT file system.   Know the maximum file size that is supported by this file system. Be able to name and locate the four major regions of this file system.

Review Questions

 The word "FAT" applies to FAT12, FAT16, and FAT32 file systems, unless exFAT is specifically mentioned.

1. On a FAT file system, FAT is defined as which of the following?

    A. A table consisting of master boot record and logical partitions

    B. A table created during the format that the operating system reads to locate data on a drive

    C. A table consisting of filenames and file attributes

    D. A table consisting of filenames, deleted filenames, and their attributes

2. How does a corrupted sector located in the data area of a hard drive affect the corresponding cluster number on a FAT in a FAT file system?

    A. It does not affect the corresponding cluster number on a FAT; therefore, the rest of the sectors associated with the assigned cluster can still be written to.

    B. It does not affect the corresponding cluster number on a FAT; only the corrupted portion of the sector is prevented from being written to.

    C. It does affect the FAT. The corresponding cluster number is marked as bad; however, only the corrupted sector within the cluster is prevented from being written to.

    D. It does affect the FAT. The corresponding cluster number is marked as bad, and the entire cluster is prevented from being written to.

3. Which of the following describes a partition table?

    A. It is located at cylinder 0, head 0, sector 1.

    B. Is located in the master boot record.

    C. It keeps track of the partitions on a hard drive.

    D. All of the above.

4. Which selection keeps track of a fragmented file in a FAT (not exFAT) file system?

    A. File Allocation Table

    B. Directory structure

    C. Volume boot record

    D. Master file table

5. If the FAT, in a FAT file system, lists cluster number 2749 with a value of 0, what does this mean about this specific cluster?

    A. It is blank and contains no data.

    B. It is marked as bad and cannot be written to.

    C. It is allocated to a file.

    D. It is unallocated and is available to store data.

6. Which of the following is true about a volume boot record?

    A. It is always located at the first sector of its logical partition.

    B. It immediately follows the master boot record.

    C. It contains BIOS parameter block and volume boot code.

    D. Both A and C.

7. The NTFS file system does which of the following?

    A. Supports long filenames

    B. Compresses individual files and directories

    C. Supports large file sizes in excess of 4 GB

    D. All of the above

8. How many clusters can a FAT32 file system manage?

    A. $2 \times 32 = 64$ clusters

    B. $2^{32} = 4{,}294{,}967{,}296$ clusters

    C. $2 \times 28 = 56$ clusters

    D. $2^{28} = 268{,}435{,}456$ clusters

9. In a FAT file system, the FAT tracks the _____ while the directory entry tracks the _____.

    A. The filename and file size

    B. The file's starting cluster and file's last cluster (EOF)

    C. The file's last cluster (EOF) and file's starting cluster

    D. The file size and file fragmentation

10. How many copies of the FAT does each FAT32 volume maintain in its default configuration?

    A. One

    B. Two

    C. Three

    D. Four

11. Which of the following is *not* true regarding the NTFS file system?

    A. Data for very small files can be stored in the MFT itself and is referred to as resident data.

    B. Cluster allocation is tracked in the $Bitmap file.

    C. Data that is stored in clusters is called nonresident data.

    D. Cluster allocation is tracked in the File Allocation Table (FAT).

12. A file's physical size is which of the following?

    A. Always greater than the file's logical size

    B. The number of bytes in the logical file plus all slack space from the end of the logical file to the end of the last cluster

    C. Both A and B

    D. None of the above

13. A directory entry in a FAT file system has a logical size of which of the following?

    A. 0 bytes

    B. 8 bytes

    C. 16 bytes

    D. One sector

14. Each directory entry in a FAT file system is ____ bytes in length.

    A. 0

    B. 8

    C. 16

    D. 32

15. By default, what color does EnCase use to display directory entries within a directory structure?

    A. Black

    B. Red

    C. Gray

    D. Yellow

16. What is the area between the end of a file's logical size and the file's physical size called?

    A. Unused disk area

    B. Unallocated clusters

    C. Unallocated sectors

    D. Slack space

17. What three things occur when a file is created in a FAT32 file system?

   A. The directory entry for the file is created, the FAT assigns the necessary clusters to the file, and the file's data is filled in to the assigned clusters.

   B. The filename is entered in to the FAT, the directory structure assigns the number of clusters, and the file's data is filled in to the assigned clusters.

   C. The directory entry for the file is created, the number of clusters is assigned by the directory structure, and the file's data is filled in to the FAT.

   D. The directory structure maintains the amount of clusters needed, the filename is recorded in the FAT, and the file's data is filled in to the assigned clusters.

18. How does EnCase recover a deleted file in a FAT file system?

   A. It reads the deleted filename in the FAT and searches for the file by its starting cluster number and logical size.

   B. It reads the deleted filename in the directory entry and searches for the corresponding filename in unallocated clusters.

   C. It obtains the deleted file's starting cluster number and size from the directory entry to obtain the data's starting location and number of clusters required.

   D. It obtains the deleted file's starting cluster number and size from the FAT to locate the starting location and amount of clusters needed.

19. What does EnCase do when a deleted file's starting cluster number is assigned to another file?

   A. EnCase reads the entire existing data as belonging to the deleted file.

   B. EnCase reads the amount of data only from the existing file that is associated with the deleted file.

   C. EnCase marks the deleted file as being overwritten.

   D. EnCase does not display a deleted filename when the data has been overwritten.

20. Which of the following is *not* true regarding the exFAT file system?

   A. Cluster allocation is tracked in the File Allocation Table (FAT).

   B. When a file is deleted, the corresponding entries in the File Allocation Table (FAT) are reset or zeroed out.

   C. Cluster allocation is tracked in an allocation bitmap.

   D. An entry in the FAT of 00 00 00 00 means that the FAT is not tracking allocation for this file.

Chapter

3

First Response

ENCE EXAM TOPICS COVERED IN THIS CHAPTER:

- ✓ **Incident response planning and preparation**
- ✓ **Handling evidence at the scene**

How we respond to an incident or crime involving computers is largely based on how well we plan and prepare for such a response. History has proven repeatedly that even a mediocre plan is better than no plan. That having been said, the importance of proper planning and preparation can't be emphasized enough.

Regardless of your response capacity, be it law enforcement officer, military personnel, civilian examiner, or member of an enterprise incident-response team, you will have certain issues and concerns in common with other forensics examiners. You will always need a plan. Because every incident is different, you will have to tailor your plan to fit the incident.

Once at a scene or incident, the number and types of systems you may encounter are vast and ever-changing. It is important for you to be able to identify the various platforms and properly handle each type of evidence so as to secure the evidence and yet not damage critical systems in the process. How evidence is handled at the scene is often far more important than the laboratory analysis work that is done later. Data recovery and analysis and subsequent prosecution depend on the proper seizure and handling of evidence at the scene.

Once the incident is over, an often-overlooked part of the process is that of debriefing. By critically analyzing what went well and what went wrong, you ensure that plans and procedures can be modified and improved so that future incidents are handled more effectively than the previous ones.

In this chapter, you will learn the basics of incident-response planning and preparation. We will discuss the various items and issues you should consider while making your plans and preparations. You will also learn the basic rules and procedures for handling computer evidence at the scene.

Planning and Preparation

Incident response does not exist in a vacuum. Its successful implementation rests on policies and procedures, plans, drills, staff training and experience, and proper equipment. Although this chapter will focus on the pragmatic aspects of planning and preparation, you should review and follow the policies and procedures unique to your organizational unit. Many organizations have well-developed incident-response plans and flowcharts that define various incident types, as well as types of response. Furthermore, you should strive to continually build your knowledge and skills as well as to obtain and use the best hardware and software your budget can support. Finally, even though we are all busy, you should take the time to test your plans and preparations by conducting practice drills. It is far better to make mistakes while practicing than to do so in the field. Practice drills provide the opportunity to build teamwork, improve techniques, and test your plan and your staff.

Responding to an incident or scene involving computers requires some specific considerations or protocols; however, in most respects, they are like any other response. You need to know beforehand, as much as possible, the who, what, when, where, why, and how. Every scene holds its share of unknowns, but the goal is to minimize the unknowns as much as possible before responding. The more you know in advance, the better and safer your response will be.

The Physical Location

Safety is the foremost consideration for all first responders, regardless of your response capacity. People who use computers to commit crimes can hurt you just as much and just as easily as people who don't use computers to commit crimes. When a person's livelihood is jeopardized (losing their job over computer misuse) or their freedom is at stake (going to jail for distributing child pornography with their computer), they can become unpredictable, desperate, or violent. This aspect of human behavior and its potential tragic consequences can never be overstated or underestimated and, therefore, must be considered in every response plan.

When you are assessing a physical location, one of your first considerations must be its physical address, its description, and the type of structure it is. Is the location residential or business? Is it a single-family residence or an apartment building? Is it one-story, two-story, or more? Is it a warehouse, laboratory, office building, strip mall, or office suite?

After determining the type of location, you must consider its size, scope, and other special characteristics. If it is a residence, what kind of neighborhood is it in? Does it have an alarm system? Is there a watchdog? Does your computer-assisted dispatch (CAD) show any calls for service at the location, and if so, what was their nature? Were weapons involved? If it is an apartment building, does the apartment complex management provide Internet access, and if so, where is the wiring closet, and who is the administrator? If it is in an office complex, does it cover one office on one floor, an entire floor, or multiple floors? Does it cover multiple buildings? Are some of the computers located with the suspected users, and are other involved computers, usually servers, located elsewhere, perhaps thousands of miles away in another jurisdiction?

Personnel

The personnel present at a scene affects safety and incident-response plans. To the greatest extent possible, you should attempt to determine as much as possible about the people expected to be present. Personnel records and criminal histories are possible sources for this information. Naturally, access to these records will vary in accordance with your jurisdiction, employment status, and so forth.

If the location is a business, you must determine its hours of operation. In some cases, it may be better to respond while employees are present. In this manner, a suspect can be placed physically at the computer, but it also poses the risk that the suspect may attempt to destroy data when first responders arrive. In other cases, an after-hours response may be preferred.

When accessing a business, determining the number and arrival pattern of employees is important, as well as how many employees are expected to be using computers when you arrive. When possible, it is advisable to identify a friendly system administrator on the inside. You must first, however, make certain the system administrator is not involved and is truly "friendly." This person is often helpful and can save you countless steps. He or she can often point you to sources of information you would probably have overlooked, particularly when it comes to logs, old backups, and so forth. System administrators are also an excellent source of determining the network topography, usernames, and passwords.

If is it a business and the suspect is known, you should gather as much information as possible about the suspect(s):

- Determine whether they work at a desk, on the road, in an office, in a lab, or in a warehouse.

- Determine whether they are physically located where they can observe arriving first responders.

- Determine in advance their username and email address.

- Determine their home address and phone number.

- Determine what kind of car they drive and its registration number and state.

- Determine their physical description, or, better yet, obtain a photograph.

- Determine whether they have a close friend in the office who may help them, tip them off, or be in collusion with them.

- Determine their "history" to the greatest extent possible, using the resources at your disposal, which vary according to your response capacity.

Computer Systems

Although accessing the physical layout and personnel involved may be routine for most incident responses of any nature, it is the computer systems involved and the associated specialized preplanning for them that makes computer incidents unique and challenging. The field of computer forensics is becoming increasingly specialized. There is simply too much out there for any one person to know it all. If you know you are going to be conducting a field acquisition of a live multi-terabyte server configured with RAID 5 and running Microsoft Exchange Server, you probably want to have someone on the team who is knowledgeable with those systems, and you want to have adequate resources to acquire an image from a live machine and store that image. Only by gathering information and planning can you be assured those resources will be available when needed.

Let's review a list of various questions or issues for you to consider that are specific to computer systems when they are subject to a first-response scenario. Although not every question or issue will be present in every scenario, it is nevertheless a good checklist to use as a baseline:

- What type of evidence is believed to be present? Are you searching for bootleg software on a company computer? Are you looking for child pornography? Are you looking for a set of "cooked books" in an embezzlement case?

- What will be the limit or scope of your search? Are you authorized to search only certain computers? Are you authorized to search only for specific files?

- How many computers will be at the location? Are those computers expected to be running, or does company policy dictate that they be turned off at night?

- If it is a business or government facility, is there a computer-use policy? What are its provisions? Do the employees have any expectation of privacy on company machines? Are there logon "banners" present? Have they consented to monitoring?

- Will people who present special privacy concerns be there? Examples include publishers, attorneys, physicians, and clergy. (If you expect to encounter data from any of these groups of people who are known to have privileged data, things can get incredibly complicated very quickly. You should consult counsel in advance in these situations.)

- What kinds of computers are present? Are they all new with 2TB drives in each machine, or are they older machines with 80GB drives? What kind of operating systems are in use?

- Is any form of encryption being used, such as Microsoft Encrypted File System (EFS) or BitLocker, PGPdisk, Jetico's BestCrypt, or others?

- Is a network present; if so, what kind? Is it wired, wireless, or both?

- Where are the servers, and what operating systems are they running?

- Is a map available showing the network topography? As importantly, can you have a copy?

- Where are the server backups located (both on-site and off-site, including the "cloud")?

- Where are the proxy server, router, firewall, web server, and other critical system logs stored?

- Is the network/IT function outsourced or in-house?

- Is the network administrator part of the problem or part of the solution?

- Who has the root or administrator passwords?

- Will the network or specific machines have to be shut down?

- Is a wireless network present, and if so, what are its type, scope, and other particulars? (I suggest carrying a pocket wireless detector to assist in this exploration. If a specialized detector is not available, a smartphone will work in a pinch.)

- Depending on the systems present and their use, will the computers be shut down if they are running? If so, at what point, how, and by whom?

- Because some people using computers may be innocent and others may be suspect, how will the incident-response team interact or direct the people using computers when they arrive? Will everyone be asked to step away from their computers, or only those who are suspects or targets?

- Who are the suspects or targets? How many are present, and where will they expected to be?

- Does the suspect or target use a laptop or other mobile computing device? Does the suspect or target use a thumb drive or similar portable storage device? If so, does the device belong to the company, and is it usually with the suspect when at work?

- Will all computers be seized or all imaged in place? Will some be seized for lab imaging and some be imaged in place? What will be the criteria to determine whether a machine is seized or imaged?

- If you have a requirement for previewing and searching for keywords prior to seizure, what keywords can be used to distinguish computers containing evidence from those that do not?

- Does the evidence sought involve images? What types of images are expected (stills or movies)? What is the expected image content?

- If this is a civilian response, does the suspected activity rise to the level where law enforcement involvement is going to be necessary? Child pornography is one example. If so, who is going to coordinate this with the chief executive officer (CEO), corporate counsel, and law enforcement? Are suspects going to be brought in initially, or only if illegal activity is discovered during your incident response?

- Are network connections, running processes, or other volatile data important to the investigation? If so, how is such going to be preserved and acquired?

- Where is the nearest computer-supply store? What are the address, phone number, store hours, and manager's name? You may need something you don't have with you, and a local computer store might be much closer than your lab.

What to Take with You Before You Leave

The best answer to this question is to pack everything imaginable and take at least two of everything! There is a basic rule in this business: cables will never fail in the lab when you have a spare on the shelf; they will, however, invariably fail in the field when you are miles from the lab, it's after-hours, and the computer stores are closed. With that in mind, let's go over some basic items for your field kit.

Checklists are an absolute necessity for fieldwork. Create them, customize them for various "jobs," and revise them as needed. Despite your best efforts, you will fail to include some much-needed item on your list. Make sure you update your lists as you find deficiencies.

Your goal in creating your list will be to replicate your lab function on a smaller scale for portability and field use. Here are some suggested items as a starting point for you to use to create your own lists:

- Toolkits. A computer field technician service kit is a nice start. Include cable ties. Consider also a set of the star head attachments for the hard-to-open devices and don't forget the new "pentalobe" screwdrivers for Apple devices!

- Portable lighting, flashlights, batteries, and a magnifying glass. (One of my favorites devices in the category is a lightweight headlamp. It frees both hands and puts the light right where you need it!)

- Latex gloves.

- Small first aid kit.

- PC reference guide.

- Digital camera to capture live data on screens and the state of the scene. Include a ruler!

- Extension cords, surge protectors, multistrip receptacles, and uninterruptible power supplies (UPSs). You take UPS power for granted in the lab, but when you must image in the field, the power will invariably fail near the end of the imaging job. Protect your data by packing a UPS or two.

- Hub or switch and network cables for setting up a small network in the field. You may want to create a small gigabit network if you have a team and are acquiring several systems in the field. You could send all your images to one large storage device, keeping all your images in one place and sharing other resources as needed.

- Network cross-over cables and spare network interface cards (NICs) for network cable acquisition or field intelligence module (FIM) acquisition.

- Spare internal floppy drive—if direct DOS acquisition must be made from a suspect computer using EnCase 6, it may or may not have a working floppy drive from which to boot.

- EnCase network bootable floppies (EnCase6 or older only) and CDs loaded with versions of Linux EnCase (linen) to match versions on portable acquisition computer(s). Have images of the same, and have extra blank floppies and CDs to make more in the field as needed.

- Forensically sound bootable Linux distributions such as Knoppix distributed by the EnCase Training Department or Raptor, which can create an EnCase evidence file and is useful for many imaging tasks.

- Storage hard drives on which to place images, wiped and formatted, along with USB to IDE/SATA adapters.

- EnCase Portable for triage searches and hard drive acquisitions.

- A supply of 4, 8, and 16 GB thumb drives that have been wiped and formatted and upon which you have placed WinEn and WinAcq. They are used, respectively, to image RAM on Windows machines and/or to do a live acquisition of running Windows machines. Both are command-line interfaces (CLIs).

- MacLockPick, which is a tool originally designed to collect volatile data from Macintosh systems but that can now do the same for both Windows and Linux systems.

- Faraday bags for shielding mobile devices from the network.

- Guidance Software's Tableau hardware write-blocking device. Include an IDE–SATA bridge for attaching SATA drives to Tableau as well as a 2.5-inch notebook hard drive adapter.

- Portable field imaging computer (laptop, custom briefcase model, small form factor unit, and so on). Include all adapter cards, cables, power supplies, peripherals, system disks, spare keyboard and mouse, and so forth, needed for your unit. Have all necessary software loaded and an updated OS with patches, updated antivirus protection, and sync time with the time standard before going in the field. Don't rely on one field-imaging computer. Carry a backup unit!

- EnCase manuals on disk; keep a current set of manuals downloaded and loaded on your field units.

- Cables, cables, and more cables! Pack power supply cables, IDE 80 wire cables, SCSI cables, SATA cables, molex power cables, floppy disk cable, and so forth. A good set of USB and FireWire cables with the "multiple personality" plugs for either end is a good thing to pack.

- Adapters: IDE to SATA, USB to SATA, SCSI 50-pin to 68-pin, SCSI 68-pin to 80-pin, Toshiba Protégé 1.8 drive to 3.5-inch IDE (Apple iPods), mini-SATA to SATA…and the list goes on.

- Tags, labels, bags, antistatic bags, evidence tape, and indelible ink markers.

- Field logbook or notebook, pens, and pencils.

- Anything special required for the upcoming job.

- Pack your dongles! Need I say more?

You'll see references to various types of acquisition methods and devices, such as network cable acquisition, direct DOS or Linux acquisition, and Tableau throughout this chapter. I'll cover those methods and devices in more depth in Chapter 4.

A useful tool to pack for the field—or to have in the lab, for that matter—is a bar code scanner. Serial numbers are becoming increasingly more complex and smaller. Seeing them and recording them accurately is always a challenge. You can purchase a simple USB bar code scanner for about $200. It's a simple matter to plug it in and let the drivers load. At this point, you need to merely open your favorite text editor and scan in serial numbers. If you work with a database or spreadsheet in the field or lab, this is great. Simply place your cursor in the appropriate field or cell and scan in the serial number. It will save you immeasurable time and aggravation. Furthermore, entry errors will approach zero. Once you start using one, you will wonder how you ever managed without one!

The more information you can acquire about the computer systems that you are about to search, the better you can pack for the job. The hardest jobs to pack for are the ones where you know next to nothing about what's there. When that occurs, you have to over-prepare in all regards, including equipment and staffing.

Regardless, have a plan, and work according to that plan. Create your packing list, use it, and modify it, keeping it current at all times. When you have to go out in the field, many times the response will be unexpected and with a sense of urgency. You will have many things on your mind, and the stress level is often elevated. It's a great comfort to be able to pull out a list, pack, and mark off the items, knowing you probably will have most of what you need, consistently and reliably. If you do a significant amount of fieldwork, it is advisable to have most of what you need packed in field cases and ready to go. Even so, before venturing out, check what you have packed against your list. Preparation is the key to success when it comes to fieldwork.

Search Authority

Regardless of your response capacity, your actions must be permitted by some authority. In a law enforcement setting, the authorization could be a search warrant, consent to search, or a call from a victim whose computer system is in some way involved in their victimization, as in a network-intrusion case. In a non–law-enforcement setting, the authorization to search for evidence may be a directive from corporate counsel, it may be authorized by policy pursuant to an incident-response activation, or it may be a court order to a special master for the court in a civil matter. Regardless, all responders are bound to certain limits imposed by your authorizing process.

In that regard, all first responders must be fully aware of the limits of that search authority as part of the preparation and planning phase. The limits may be specified computers, specified types of files, specified user files, or types of evidence. Each person conducting the search and seizure must limit the scope of their searches to stay within the boundaries of their authorized limits. Also, you need a plan in effect as to how to proceed if evidence is found in plain sight that exceeds the search authority. It happens often!

If, for example, you were investigating an embezzlement case, you would reasonably find yourself limited to searching for a set of "cooked books." If you find contraband images in the same folder as spreadsheets, with the latter being covered in your search authority, then the contraband images would be held to have been found in plain view while you were acting within the scope of your search authority or warrant and thus admissible as evidence. If you were to start searching for more contraband images, such an act would exceed the scope of your authority and subsequent images so would generally be inadmissible. The proper course of action in such circumstances is to stop searching for contraband images and seek authorization in the form of an additional search warrant. Only then can you legally search for more contraband images. Your planning process should account for these possibilities so you'll be prepared in the event they occur.

With regard to search warrants in general, the laws are much too variable to attempt any meaningful discussion as to form, substance, and specific procedures. Because computer search warrants can get rather complex, I strongly advise you to review your warrant with your prosecutor, who will be the one ultimately carrying the burden of introducing it into evidence. When the prosecutor is involved early in the process, things generally go better in court.

When you execute a search warrant, most jurisdictions require you to leave a copy of the warrant at the premises searched, but not the affidavit for probable cause. Also, you are usually required to leave behind a list of the items seized pursuant to the search warrant. I also strongly recommend that each member of the search team have a copy of the warrant in the preparation phase when possible. In this manner, everyone involved knows their boundaries, and misunderstandings are less likely to occur when you arrive on the scene.

 For additional legal information, you can download Guidance Software's *EnCase Legal Journal* from its website: www.guidancesoftware.com.

Handling Evidence at the Scene

In this section, I'll cover the various aspects of handling evidence at the scene. I'll begin with securing the scene. Once the scene is secured, you need to document everything in place. After documenting the scene, the next step is that of seizing various items, namely, computers. Before computers can be seized, they typically have to be shut down. I'll discuss the various issues associated with operating systems and system function as they relate to shutting down various systems. I'll end the discussion with the bagging-and-tagging process, transporting, and securing, all in support of the all-important chain of custody. Let's get started!

Securing the Scene

When you arrive at the scene, safety is the number-one priority. Regardless of your response capacity, those assigned to search and seize digital evidence need to be able to do so safely. Typically, two basic functions or teams are designated.

One team is the entry or security team. Their job is to establish perimeter control, make the initial entry, secure the area for the search team, and provide ongoing security and perimeter control throughout the search-and-seizure operation. The second team conducts the search operation.

Recording and Photographing the Scene

After the area is secure, the search team enters the area and begins their job. Before anything is touched or removed, the scene is recorded through a combination of field notes, sketches, video, or still images. Once the area has been recorded to show how things were initially found, the search team begin their methodical search-and-seizure process. Search teams are often responsible for the following functions:

Recorder   Takes detailed notes of everything seized.

Photographer   Photographs all items in place *before* they are seized.

Search-and-seizure specialist   Searches and seizes and then bags and tags traditional evidence (documents, pictures, drugs, weapons, and so on).

Digital evidence search-and-seizure specialist   Searches and seizes and then bags and tags digital evidence of all types.

Seizing Computer Evidence

Before seizing computer evidence, you must consider many issues. However, before considering those issues, stick to the basics. One of the most fundamental rules is that you should employ measures that avoid contaminating any evidence.

Physical Evidence

Computers may be subjected to computer forensic examinations, but they may also be subjected to other forms of analyses. Often fingerprints are lifted from computer components such as the mouse, DVDs, CDs, thumb drives, or perhaps even a hard drive. It is best in these circumstances that the prints lifted be those of the suspect and not yours.

Also, computers may contain hairs, fibers, or body tissues, depending on the incident or circumstances. When other examinations are to be conducted, coordinate your activities with others who will be conducting such examinations. In all cases, you must avoid commingling your fingerprints, hairs, fibers, and body tissues with those already present. At a bare minimum, you should use latex (or a nonallergenic substitute) gloves as a standard practice when handling computer evidence. If you follow this guideline as a matter of practice, it minimizes the concern of whether you did wear them in one case and not in another. If the other examinations are going to include hairs, fibers, and body tissues, a Tyvek suit or equivalent is recommended while handling computer evidence, both at the scene and in the lab. Your goal is to protect the evidence—both digital evidence and more traditional forms of evidence—from contamination.

Finally, some computer components are particularly unsanitary. Without going into great detail, suffice it to say that some computer components reflect the rather unsanitary habits and practices of their respective users. Gloves can serve as a barrier in these circumstances and help protect you from certain pathogens that can survive even when exposed to air. Because computers create an electrostatic field inside, they are magnets for dust, dirt, hair, fibers, and other airborne particles, aided by the fan that draws in outside air (and debris) for cooling. This collection of airborne debris has the potential to transmit disease, so many examiners opt to wear a breathing mask in addition to gloves when opening cases to remove hard drives.

Those Computers Don't Work Anymore!

A large safe was stolen during a burglary, and the case went cold. As luck would have it, the safe contained a wealth of credit card information, and six months later one of the credit card holders reported unauthorized activity on their card. I'm sure most would be shocked to learn that some of the online purchases were pornography!

Once we got over our shock, which lasted less than a nanosecond, we traced the IP address, captured during the online purchase of pornography, to a residence in an adjoining state. The son of the owners of the residence used to work for the establishment from which the safe was stolen. Within 36 hours, we greeted those occupying the residence at dawn with a search warrant in hand.

We started in the living room of the main house and saw two computers sitting in the middle of the living room floor. They were a matching pair with the only apparent difference being the serial numbers. When questioned about the computers, the suspect's mother replied, "Those computers don't work anymore. They are pieces of junk [referring to them by brand name], and I was getting ready to throw them away." We seized them nevertheless, along with other computers in the main residence.

As we continued the search, we were very careful what we touched and where we stepped. There were young teens sleeping on every available bed or sofa, in varying stages of alertness from the previous night's activities. Pets roamed rather freely and relieved themselves where convenient. At best, the last time this house had been cleaned was most likely the day they moved in, and that was years ago.

Our suspect, however, was not to be found. As the occupants started to wake up, information started flowing, and to our surprise, we found that our suspect did not live in the residence. He was, however, supposed to be living in the equipment shed in the backyard. As we later discovered, our suspect was, in addition to being a burglar, an electrician. He had trenched in electricity, telephone, and cable (including high-speed Internet) from the house to the equipment shed in which he had taken up residence.

When we looked at the shed, we were somewhat doubtful that anyone would be living inside. Nevertheless, when we hit the shed, our suspect was inside, asleep, and enjoying his air-conditioned abode. It was a two-room shed, and both rooms were full of stolen goods, including computers, credit cards, checks, and the safe he had stolen. He had since peeled it open and removed its contents, but he could not dispose of it since he had wrecked the truck he originally used to steal and transport it. We needed a truck to remove all of the stolen goods. We also learned that in some areas, an equipment shed is also a residence.

Back in the lab, it was time to pull the hard drives from the computers. When I carefully opened the two that did not work and were about to be discarded, I was shocked when I saw the motherboards, CPUs, and cooling fans. The CPU cooling fans were jammed with hair (human, pet, and other) and other chunks of dust and debris. They looked more like nests or termite mounds on the motherboard than they did a CPU and cooling fan. They made weird noises and barely turned when powered on to get the system time. The motherboards and all electrical components were likewise coated with the same collection of materials that, when combined, would make a "Hazmat Cocktail" like no other!

Rather than risk cooking the components to get the system time, I subjected both systems to a thorough cleaning, using appropriate environmental and personal protection safeguards. Once cleaned, the systems worked flawlessly. As it turned out, these two systems were not stolen or involved in any of the criminal activity and were later returned to the mother. She was told she wouldn't have to discard them because they had been fixed. Since she opened the door by asking what was wrong with them, the explanation involved a diplomatic lesson in cleanliness and housekeeping and how that might be more economical than discarding computers when they are less than a year old.

As an aside, one of my favorite findings in that case was from the laptop next to the suspect's bed in the room that adjoined the "peeled safe." Two Google searches were found:

```
www.google.com/search?sourceid=navclient&ie=UTF-8&oe=UTF-
8&q=how+to+crack+a+vault
```

```
www.google.com/search?sourceid=navclient&ie=UTF-8&oe=UTF-
8&q=how+to+crack+a+safe
```

And, yes, you can find plenty of information on "how to crack a safe" using Google!

Volatile Digital Evidence

Now that you have protected the traditional evidence as well as the examiner, it is time to turn your attention to protecting and capturing the digital evidence. Therefore, as one of the first things on your list, you should photograph the screen to capture the "state" of the system as you found it. If there's an instant messenger window open with a conversation recorded on the screen, this is likely your only chance to capture it because it is in RAM and will be gone upon shutdown (unless the user was logging their instant messenger traffic).

When photographing screens, a short desktop-style tripod is useful, coupled with a camera that affords macro focusing for getting close-ups of screen details in sharp focus. If you are not going to take these photographs yourself, you want to make sure, as diplomatically as possible, that the person taking photographs of the screen has some experience doing so and knows what they are doing. I prefer doing this myself; I get what I want, I have the resultant images in my possession throughout, and I can easily include them in my report without having to seek them elsewhere. Regardless, you don't want a picture of the screen; you want pictures of the details shown on the screen!

As alluded to in the previous paragraph, data contained in volatile RAM is gone upon shutdown, as are running processes, network connections, and other important data. With increasing frequency, investigations depend in varying degrees on the state of the system when it was live. For example, for a network-intrusion case in progress, the network connections, logged-in users, and running processes would be vital to the case. Shutting down a computer would effectively destroy some of your best evidence in the case.

Similarly, the live system state could be an issue in a child porn possession case if the defendant makes the claim they were hacked and not responsible for the content of the computer. In other words, the "Trojan Defense" is raised by the accused. Although an examiner could later restore an image to a drive and attempt to reconstruct the live state, you can only approximate it since the volatile RAM data disappeared the moment the system was shut down. In such circumstances, you use the best evidence you have available, which is the examination of the live restored system coupled with the forensic examination of the hard drive, along with antivirus and spyware scans.

Many cases, therefore, can benefit in various degrees by capturing live system state data before shutting down the computer. The nature of the case and your available resources (time, equipment, and staff) will determine whether you can capture live system state data. Although it is beyond the scope of this text to cover methods of capturing and analyzing system state data, it is worthwhile to note that EnCase Enterprise, Field Intelligence Model (FIM) 6, and EnCase Portable have the capability of capturing this data using the snapshot feature. The snapshot feature is also planned to be included in a future release of EnCase Forensic 7. As such, these versions of EnCase are tremendous tools by which to carry out the analysis and imaging of live systems.

EnCase, starting with version 6.11, ships with a commandline tool named WinEn, which is used to image RAM memory. It is located in the root directory of the EnCase program files and is named winen.exe or winen64.exe for the 64-bit version. It is best run from a USB drive and by placing the resultant image file on the same USB drive.

You want to launch a command-line interface (run as Administrator for Windows Vista, Windows Server 2008, or Windows 7) from which you'll launch the executable. As shown in Figure 3.1, you will be prompted for the various pieces of information required to complete the image. When done, you can use EnCase to examine the resultant image. You can also use EnCase Portable to image the RAM.

We have reached a point now where not imaging RAM and otherwise capturing volatile data is the exception instead of the norm. There is simply too much valuable information that is destroyed by not capturing it.

FIGURE 3.1   WinEn is being used to capture RAM. Note that this is the 64-bit version and that the user is prompted for the various input items. Just a helpful hint, Compress is either 0, 1, or 2 (no compression, good compression, or best compression)

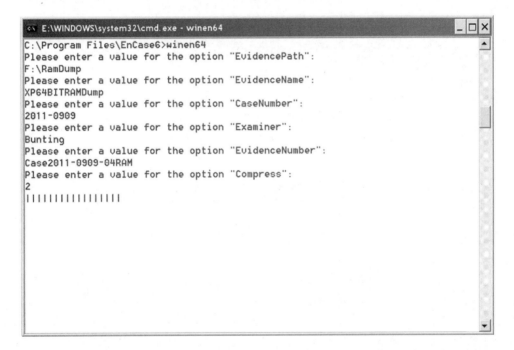

You can use the same versions (Enterprise and newer versions of EnCase Forensic) to image live systems via a network connection without shutting them down. This can be useful in a variety of circumstances. If you encounter a disk or volume encrypted with Windows BitLocker or with software such as BestCrypt or PGPdisk and the disk is mounted (you can see the unencrypted data), it can be imaged while mounted, allowing the data to be captured in an unencrypted state in the resultant image. But if the computer were shut down and then imaged, the image would be a stream of encrypted data. If you are tasked with imaging a production server that cannot be shut down without harming a business operation, EnCase Enterprise or EnCase Forensic 7 will again be your tool of choice for the job.

First responders should check any live machine for mounted encryption before deciding to "pull the plug." Failing to do so is asking for trouble, given the increasing prevalence of various encryption schemes, such as BitLocker, PGP, BestCrypt, TrueCrypt, and so forth. Fortunately, there are tools becoming available for this task, such as CryptHunter. It is a command-line tool that searches for characteristics known to be associated with various encryption schemes. Figure 3.2 shows how CryptHunter responds to the discovery of BitLocker.

FIGURE 3.2 CryptHunter has discovered the presence of BitLocker. Your choice now is to disable the protectors on BitLocker or image the mounted encryption while live and mounted. An even better choice would be to do both!

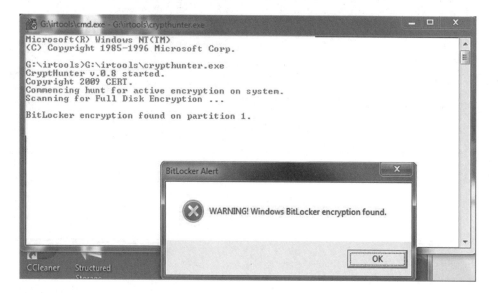

I just mentioned disabling the protectors on BitLocker. Without delving too deeply into BitLocker intricacies, suffice it to say that you can enter a command from the Windows CLI (running as administrator) that will disable the protectors on BitLocker by rendering the key into clear text into an unencrypted partition. During mounting of the BitLocker-encrypted volume, Windows will see this key, use it to mount the encrypted volume, and ignore other protectors that would normally be required. Enter the following command from the Windows CLI:

```
cscript manage-bde.wsf -protectors -disable c:
```

Before doing so in a live case, I suggest you test this procedure in the lab first!

To assist with imaging live systems, EnCase started shipping WinAcq with EnCase 6.16. It is a command-line tool with prompts given to provide the necessary information to complete the image. You can image a live physical drive or logical volume with this tool. As with WinEn, WinAcq is located in the root of the EnCase program files, is named `winacq.exe` (there is no 64-bit version currently) and needs to be run from the command line with administrator rights starting with Windows Vista.

 The EnCase FIM version was available only to law enforcement or government entities and was retired in version 6, with the incorporation of the functionality into EnCase Forensic in a later release of version 7. The Enterprise version has the same functionality and is available for corporate or civilian use. The differences between the two rest primarily with the Secure Authentication for EnCase (SAFE) configuration and licensing.

If the Enterprise, FIM 6, Portable, or Forensic 7 versions are not available to you and the live system-state data is critical to your investigation, you have a decision to make: either forgo the data or capture it by less-than-ideal means. If you must capture the data without Enterprise, FIM 6, Portable, Forensic 7, or some third-party tool, you are left with carefully navigating to the areas where your data is located, capturing it, and meticulously documenting your rationale, process, and findings. Examples of areas of interest might be using the `netstat.exe` command to capture network connections and porting the output to a USB drive. Another might be capturing running processes using Task Manager or doing so using a command-line interface, again porting the output to a floppy disk. Although that is not the best method to employ, if you can document the process and basis for doing so thoroughly, there's usually little difficulty resulting from this method. You must, however, understand that if a rootkit has been installed, nothing can be trusted as output from any Windows binary because it can be altered. Thus, you should bring your own trusted binaries when capturing volatile data by this method.

Clearly, live analysis is warranted in many cases. Depending on your operating environment, you may be involved almost exclusively in analyzing and imaging live systems. Such is the case with many corporate examinations using the EnCase Enterprise model. Quite by contrast, in a law enforcement setting, much of your work will likely be on systems that have been shut down and seized by field agents and delivered to you in the lab for analysis. Most of us find ourselves somewhere in between, with some of both. Regardless, your operating environment, resources, policies and procedures, and the nature of the case will combine to be the factors that decide whether the analysis and imaging will be done on a live system or one that has been shut down and imaged offline.

 Live analysis is clearly beyond the scope of this text. If you want more information on this topic, *Mastering Windows Network Forensics and Investigation* by Steve Anson and yours truly covers this topic in detail. The use of the EnCase FIM and Enterprise models as live-response tools is covered as well. The text is available from Wiley at www.wiley.com/WileyCDA/WileyTitle/productCd-0470097620.html.

Computer Shutdown Procedures

At this point in our discussion, I'm proceeding as though you've decided to shut down the computer and image it in the lab. The screen information has been photographed, and relevant information about its system state has been recorded to the greatest extent possible with the resources at hand. Before shutting down the computer, disconnect it from its network connection by removing the network cable. This prevents the possible remote destruction of data.

The manner in which a computer is shut down is very much dependent on the operating system and function. Most Windows workstation models can simply be shut down by pulling the power cord. By contrast, some Windows servers running high-end business databases are not very fault tolerant, and a power loss (pulling the plug) can corrupt the database—and with it comes potential liability for you. To preserve data, these systems require a normal system shutdown.

Since the decision of how to shut down a computer is operating system dependent, you must first determine what kind of operating system is running. Simplicity is often the best choice in this business, and in this case it means asking someone who likely knows. Usually the computer system owner or user knows what the operating system is. In an office, often the same operating system is deployed on all the workstations, and someone in the office usually knows which operating system is in use. The system administrator is most helpful in making these determinations, especially when your work involves the server room. Often your preplanning information gathering will include what operating systems are at your target location. Table 3.1 shows the recommended shutdown procedures for various operating systems commonly encountered. Figure 3.3 shows a Linux prompt where the user is changed to root and the shutdown command has been entered. You will note that the $ prompt changes to # when the user is changed to the root user.

FIGURE 3.3   A Unix/Linux prompt. You must be root to shut down most Linux/Unix systems. The su root com root mand logs in as root (a password is necessary). At the root prompt, the shutdown command sequence is entered.

```
stephen-buntings-ibook-g4:~ sbunting$ su root
Password:
stephen-buntings-ibook-g4:/Users/sbunting root# shutdown -h now
```

TABLE 3.1   Best shutdown procedures based on operating system in use

Operating System	Characteristics	Shutdown Procedures
DOS	Full-screen text on a solid background, usually black. Prompt includes drive letters, backslashes, and usually an >; for example, C:\DOS>.	Photograph the screen, and note any running programs, messages, and so on. Pull the plug from the rear of the computer.

TABLE 3.1 Best shutdown procedures based on operating system in use *(continued)*

Operating System	Characteristics	Shutdown Procedures
Windows 3.1	Program Manager instead of Windows Explorer. Colored tile bar. Standard menu.	Photograph the screen, and note any running programs, messages, and so on. Pull the plug from the rear of the computer.
Windows 95	Start button with Windows symbol.	Photograph the screen, and note any running programs, messages, and so on. Pull the plug from the rear of the computer.
Windows NT Workstation	Start button with Windows symbol.	Photograph the screen, and note any running programs, messages, and so on. Pull the plug from the rear of the computer.
Windows NT Server	Start button with Windows symbol.	Photograph the screen, and note any running programs, messages, and so on. Use normal shutdown procedure.
Windows 98/Me	Start button with Windows symbol.	Photograph the screen, and note any running programs, messages, and so on. Pull the plug from the rear of the computer.
Windows 2000 Professional	Start button with Windows symbol.	Photograph the screen, and note any running programs, messages, and so on. Pull the plug from the rear of the computer.
Windows 2000 Server	Start button with Windows symbol.	Photograph the screen, and note any running programs, messages, and so on. Use normal shutdown procedure.
Windows XP	Green Start button with Windows symbol.	Photograph the screen, and note any running programs, messages, and so on. Pull the plug from the rear of the computer.
Windows 2003 Server	Green Start button with Windows symbol.	Photograph the screen, and note any running programs, messages, and so on. Use normal shutdown procedure.

TABLE 3.1   Best shutdown procedures based on operating system in use *(continued)*

Operating System	Characteristics	Shutdown Procedures
Windows 2008 Server	Round Aero circle with Windows symbol in lower-left corner (default location)	Photograph the screen, and note any running programs, messages, and so on. Use normal shutdown procedure.
Windows Vista / Windows 7 / Windows 7 Enterprise	Round Aero circle with Windows symbol in lower-left corner (default location)	Photograph the screen, and note any running programs, messages, and so on. Pull the plug from the rear of the computer.
Linux/Unix	If GUI present, look to the Start button with the Unix/ Linux version symbol or icon, such as a red hat or fedora. If in console (no GUI), look to prompt for something like [root@localhost root]#[user@host dir]$.	Photograph the screen, and note any running programs, messages, and so on. Use normal shutdown procedure. In many cases, the user will need to log in as root to shut down the system. If GUI, right-click the desktop and select Console or Terminal from the context menu. At the resulting prompt, look for # at the right end. If not, type su root. You will be prompted for a password. If you have it, type it in. If you don't, you'll probably have no choice but to pull the power cord. When at root, note the # at the end of the prompt. When at root, type shutdown –h now, and the system should shut down. (For Irix or Solaris, you should use shutdown –i0 –g0 to achieve the same result.)
Macintosh	Apple symbol in top-left corner. Trash icon usually in lower right.	Photograph screen, and note any running programs, messages, and so on. Record time from the menu bar, and simultaneously record the known standard time. Pull the plug from the rear of the computer. Note: If Mac is running OS X, BSD (a Unix variant) is running as a subsystem process. Also, Macs can run as servers (web, database, email, and so on). If any of these conditions apply, a normal Mac shutdown is the safer course of action. For OS X, click the Apple icon, and choose Shut Down. You will be prompted to confirm (see Figure 3.4). For legacy Macs, click Special, and click Shut Down. When it is shut down, pull the power cord.

FIGURE 3.4   Max OS X shutdown. Note the Apple icon in the upper left. Click this icon, and you'll see the Shut Down menu option.

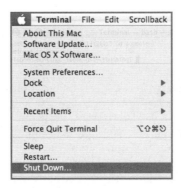

The characteristics noted in Table 3.1 are general guidelines to follow when you are completely in the dark and have no other information. Alternatively, you can interact with the system to attempt to determine the operating system. If this becomes necessary, use caution, and document, in detail, every step taken. Such cases are actually rare, and with experience, most examiners recognize most operating systems when they see them. What is tricky, however, is whether the operating system is a server variety or the computer needs to be treated as though it were a server. Sometimes a "workstation" flavor of an OS is used with a database server application. This rarely occurs in a home setting, but it is something to watch for in a business setting. When critical business applications are known to be running or you are in doubt, it pays to err on the side of a normal shutdown procedure.

If you are "pulling the plug" to shut down a system, you should pull the plug from the rear of the computer. If you get in the habit of pulling it from the wall, you may encounter a situation where a UPS might be in place, and pulling it from the wall under such conditions only triggers a power failure condition. If so configured, this information is recorded on the host computer, and sometimes emails or pages are sent, and the host may start into a normal shutdown. Instead of preserving data, your actions are now causing data to be written to the system, overwriting potential evidence in the process. Get into the habit of pulling the plug from the rear of the computer.

Similarly, if you are attempting to shut down a laptop and you pull the power from either the wall or the rear of the computer, most often the battery still remains, providing power to the laptop. You must remove the battery as well. Keep the battery and the power supply with the laptop when you seize them.

As a final note on shutting down computer systems, remember to document what procedure you used, when you did it, how you went about it in detail, and the rationale or reason why. For the purposes of this discussion, assume that you must shut down and seize a Windows 7 Enterprise system on which a large SQL-based business database application is running. Although you would ordinarily pull the plug on a Windows 7 Enterprise workstation, in this case there is a more compelling need to protect the database from being corrupted from a sudden power outage caused by pulling the plug. A normal shutdown is advised so that the SQL database can go through a normal shutdown before the OS shuts down.

By documenting what you did and why, you will probably avoid questions regarding why you shut down normally when most of the documentation calls for pulling the plug for a Windows 7 Enterprise workstation. If the question is still asked, you can refer to your report, which is already in opposing counsel's hands, to answer that question.

Bagging and Tagging

Once the computer is shut down, it is time—well, almost time—to treat it like most other forms of evidence, which involves subjecting it to the bagging-and-tagging process. Even if you are conducting a live acquisition and leaving the target computer in place when you leave, you will still want to document the cabling and physical configuration of that computer. You will also want to bag and tag the drive or media that contains the image that you obtained. Thus, *bagging and tagging* refers to either form of acquisition, with some variation in degree depending on whether you are physically removing the target computer.

Before bagging and tagging occurs, you need to make sure you label all the cables and photograph the rear of the computer with cables and tags in place. Since you should have already removed the network cable earlier, you should reconnect it for this process. If your photographer did not already photograph the rear of the computer, as they should have at the outset, have it done now before attaching labels so that the rear appears as you found it.

To label a cable and connection, attach a label to the cable near its terminal end, and place one next to its corresponding port on the computer. For each cable and port pair, mark the labels with a unique letter, starting with A and sequencing through the alphabet until you have all labeled and marked. In this manner, cable A goes with port A, cable B goes with port B, and so forth. Photograph the rear from different angles. When done, remove the cables, and you are ready for bagging and tagging. Using this method, you can show how the computer was configured and connected when you found it and provide for a means to reconstruct that configuration if necessary.

Bagging and tagging has a purpose, and it is not to bolster the revenues of the makers of such products. Bagging protects against contamination and tampering. Tagging provides a means of associating the attached and bagged evidence with a particular location, date, time, case, event, and seizing agent. Tagging also provides for a means of creating the first link in the *chain of custody* of the evidence. Chain of custody is a concept in jurisprudence that applies to the process by which evidence is handled to assure its integrity as proof of a fact in court. Practically speaking, it refers to the "paper trail" that tracks seizure, custody, control, transfer, analysis, and disposition of all evidence. Tagging can also serve as an integrity seal for the bag, part of the chain of custody, depending on the type of tag used.

Because evidence, including computer evidence, comes in all shapes and sizes, bagging can be challenging. Computer evidence also presents another complication in that it is subject to potential damage from static discharges. This occurs when objects of dissimilar electrical potential make contact. Accordingly, when bagging computer components, you must avoid using plastic bagging materials that do not possess antistatic properties. Large plastic antistatic bags can be purchased for this purpose; however, brown wrapping paper or paper bags are more economical alternatives.

When bagging smaller items such as hard drives, flash media, and the like, small antistatic bags are recommended because you can see the contents and have antistatic protection as well. These are often in surplus from component purchases and can be purchased quite inexpensively.

When completing information on the tag, don't skimp on details. If you get in a hurry and plan to do it "later," you may find that you forget to do it at all or complete it with incorrect information since the details are no longer fresh in your mind. Be thorough by recording the details at the time of the seizure event.

When transporting computer evidence from the scene to the lab, pack it carefully so that a bump or sudden deceleration doesn't cause it to shift and become damaged. Also, you want to keep it away from strong magnets such as the type that are often found on the "Kojak lights" of unmarked police vehicles, which are the style that are temporarily attached to the roof via a strong magnet in the base.

Don't Forget to Look Up!

Once while investigating the criminal activities of a "rogue" system administrator, I interviewed one of his associates. Apparently our suspect admitted to his associate that, while working for his previous employer, he had installed a "hidden" NT server above the drop ceiling of the computer room while working the night shift. He told his associate that he made frequent use of this "hidden" resource for a long time.

I called the head of the IT department for this institution and advised them of my apparent discovery. Two hours later, the IT manager called back. Upon removing the ceiling panels, they had found an NT server hidden in the ceiling, surreptitiously hard-wired into their main system. He commented that for more than a year he had system problems that defied resolution. Needless to say, another investigation commenced, with a clear suspect indicated.

When searching an area for computer evidence, look in unexpected or hidden areas. Especially nowadays, with ubiquitous wireless connectivity, it is easy to conceal a networked laptop or wireless router almost anywhere.

Over the years much has been said about keeping magnetic media away from the radio frequency (RF) energy emitted by police radio transmitters located in police cars. Theoretically, this is to avoid data corruption from the radio frequency energy. As yet, no one I know has confirmed such data corruption in actual practice. I have read accounts of people deliberately attempting to induce such a loss by exposing magnetic media to RF energy and failing to corrupt the data. It is hard to conceive of a burst of energy that would corrupt data in such a pattern as to create an image depicting child pornography where none previously existed! Nevertheless, it is probably still good practice to keep the media as far away from such sources as possible to minimize such claims.

Once the evidence arrives at the lab, just like traditional evidence, it should be logged into the master evidence log or database and secured in an environment or space that assures its evidentiary integrity. In this manner, it is safeguarded against claims of tampering, and the documentary trail secures the chain of custody for the evidence.

If at any point in the examination process the evidence is removed or the seal is broken, this should be recorded in the evidence log or database. Similarly, when evidence is resealed and returned to storage, it should be dutifully recorded in the log.

EXERCISE 3.1

First Response to a Computer Incident

The purpose of this exercise is to prepare you for the second part of your EnCE examination, which is the practical. After passing your written examination, you'll be given a CD with a case to work. Part of that process will be to document your first-response procedures for your report. To prepare for the phase, assume the following:

1. You are responding with others to the scene of a computer incident. You are the one responsible for the computers at the scene. The target system (only one) is in a business. The screen is locked, with the operating system logo displayed as Windows 2008 Server. The prompt explains that the computer is locked and that only the administrator can unlock it. The system administrator is available and is not the target of the investigation, and she is considered a person with high integrity who is willing to assist.

2. Describe in detail how you would take down this machine and take it to the lab for imaging if the Enterprise, FIM 6, Portable, or EnCase 7 version is not an option and if your directive is to seize it and take it to the lab.

3. Write your narrative as though it were going to be included in your report. Be sure to describe your shutdown methodology and reasoning. Include details sufficient to establish the complete chain of custody from the scene to the lab.

When all is said and done, the computer evidence has been preserved and secured in such a manner as to prevent contamination or tampering. Furthermore, its entire history of possession and processing has been documented in such a way as to maintain its chain of custody. Although questions can always be raised, it is the answers to the questions that are important. If you consistently treat evidence in the manner I've described, you'll always be in a position to answer the questions in a way that ensures your evidence will be introduced in court to the finder of the facts.

Summary

This chapter explained the fundamentals of the incident-response process. I discussed the importance of planning, with a focus on gathering information about the target of your incident response and on packing for the task at hand, thus ensuring you have the staff and equipment resources you need on-site.

Next, I discussed how to handle evidence at the scene, highlighting the importance of securing and then processing the scene. I explored the pros and cons of employing immediate shutdown vs. first capturing the volatile system-state data. I also covered the various shutdown methods based on the type of operating system in place and the function of the computer system. Finally, I discussed how to bag and tag computer evidence as a means of protecting it from contamination and tampering and thus assuring the chain of custody from the scene to the courtroom.

Exam Essentials

Know how to plan for an incident response.   Understand the planning and preparation process. Know what information to seek about the target location, specifically the type of facility, the personnel present, the suspect or target, and the computer systems expected to be present. Know how to prepare a detailed packing list for field equipment needed for an incident response.

Understand the importance of scene security and safety.   Understand that the safety of all people present is everyone's primary responsibility, and, simply because it is a computer incident, this responsibility is in no way lessened or diminished. Understand how the scene is secured initially and throughout the process, most often by people for whom scene safety and security is the primary function.

Know what data is lost when you shut down a computer.   Understand that volatile system-state data (network connections, running processes, logged-in users, and so on) is effectively gone when a system is shut down. Understand that encrypted volumes are often deployed and that pulling the plug effectively renders this data useless in most cases. Know your options for capturing volatile data if it is necessary to your investigation. Know how to identify encrypted volumes and to take steps to mitigate their impact and/or image them while live and mounted.

Know when to shut down normally and when to pull the plug.   Understand the risks involved when pulling the plug on certain computer systems. Know for which operating systems it is usually the best practice to pull the plug and for which operating systems it is usually the best practice to go through a normal shutdown sequence. Be able to list what the exceptions are and why they exist.

Understand the importance of bagging and tagging.   Understand the unique nature of computer evidence and how it must be carefully bagged so as to protect it from static discharges. Be able to explain how bagging and tagging protect the evidence from contamination and tampering and preserve the chain of custody. Be able to explain the phrase *chain of custody.*

Review Questions

1. What is the first consideration when responding to a scene?

   A. Your safety

   B. The safety of others

   C. The preservation of evidence

   D. Documentation

2. What are some variables regarding a facility that you should consider prior to responding to a scene?

   A. What type of structure is it?

   B. How large is the structure?

   C. What are the hours of operation?

   D. Is there a helpful person present to aid in your task?

   E. All of the above.

3. What are some variables regarding items to be seized that you should consider prior to responding to a scene?

   A. Location(s) of computers

   B. Type of operating system

   C. Workstations or mainframes

   D. System-critical or auxiliary machine

   E. All of the above

4. Generally speaking, if you encounter a desktop computer running Windows 7, how should you take down the machine?

   A. Shut down using Windows 7.

   B. Shut down by pulling the power cord from the outlet.

   C. Shut down by pulling the plug from the computer box.

   D. All of the above.

5. Generally speaking, if you encounter a computer running Windows 2008 Server, how should you take down the machine?

   A. Shut down using its operating system.

   B. Shut down by pulling the power cord from the outlet.

   C. Shut down by pulling the plug from the computer box.

   D. All of the above.

6. Generally speaking, if you encounter a Unix/Linux machine, how should you take down the machine?

    A. Shut down using its operating system.

    B. Shut down by pulling the power cord from the outlet.

    C. Shut down by pulling the plug from the computer box.

    D. All of the above.

7. When unplugging a desktop computer, from where is it best to pull the plug?

    A. The back of the computer

    B. The wall outlet

    C. A or B

8. What is the best method to shut down a notebook computer?

    A. Unplug from the back of the computer.

    B. Unplug from the wall.

    C. Remove the battery.

    D. Both A and C.

9. Generally speaking, if you encounter a Macintosh computer, how should you take down the machine?

    A. Shut down using the operating system.

    B. Shut down by pulling the power cord from the outlet.

    C. Shut down by pulling the plug from the computer box.

    D. All of the above.

10. Which selection displays the incorrect method for shutting down a computer?

    A. DOS: Pull the plug.

    B. Windows 7: Pull the plug.

    C. Windows XP: Pull the plug.

    D. Linux: Pull the plug.

11. When shutting down a computer, what information is typically lost?

    A. Data in RAM memory

    B. Running processes

    C. Current network connections

    D. Current logged-in users

    E. All of the above

12. Which of the following is not acceptable for "bagging" a computer workstation?

    A. Large paper bag.

    B. Brown wrapping paper.

    C. Plastic garbage bag.

    D. Large antistatic plastic bag.

    E. All of the above are acceptable for bagging a workstation.

13. In which circumstance is pulling the plug to shut down a computer system considered the best practice?

    A. When the OS is Linux/Unix

    B. When the OS is Windows 7 and known to be running a large business database application

    C. When the OS is Windows (NT/2000/2003/2008) Server

    D. When Mac OS X Server is running as a web server

    E. None of the above

14. How is the chain of custody maintained?

    A. By bagging evidence and sealing it to protect it from contamination or tampering

    B. By documenting what, when, where, how, and by whom evidence was seized

    C. By documenting in a log the circumstances under which evidence was removed from the evidence control room

    D. By documenting the circumstances under which evidence was subjected to analysis

    E. All of the above

15. It is always safe to pull the plug on a Windows 7 Enterprise operating system.

    A. True

    B. False

16. On a production Linux/Unix server, you must generally be which user to shut down the system?

    A. sysadmin

    B. administrator

    C. root

    D. system

17. When would it be acceptable to navigate through a live system?

    A. To observe the operating system to determine the proper shutdown process

    B. To document currently opened files (if Enterprise/FIM edition is not available)

    C. To detect mounted encryption

    D. To access virtual storage facility (if search warrant permits; some are very specific about physical location)

    E. All of the above

18. A console prompt that displayed backslashes (\) as part of its display would most likely be which of the following?

    A. Red Hat Linux operating system

    B. Unix operating system

    C. Linux or Unix operating system logged in as `root`

    D. MS-DOS

19. When called to a large office complex with numerous networked machines, it is *always* a good idea to request the assistance of the network administrator.

    A. True

    B. False

20. Subsequent to a search warrant where evidence is seized, what items should be left behind?

    A. Copy of the affidavit

    B. Copy of the search warrant

    C. List of items seized

    D. A and B

    E. B and C

Chapter

4

Acquiring Digital Evidence

ENCE EXAM TOPICS COVERED IN THIS CHAPTER:

- ✓ Creating EnCase DOS boot disks
- ✓ Booting computers using EnCase DOS boot disks
- ✓ Drive-to-drive acquisitions
- ✓ Network and parallel cable acquisitions
- ✓ FastBloc/Tableau acquisitions
- ✓ FastBloc SE acquisitions
- ✓ LinEn acquisitions
- ✓ Enterprise and FIM acquisitions
- ✓ EnCase Portable acquisitions

Following best forensics practices, I typically conduct examinations or analyses on copies of the original evidence. In this manner, I preserve the original, protecting it from alteration or corruption. The *copy* of the original evidence is more commonly called an *image*. For this image to be a copy and the legal equivalent of the original, it must represent a duplicate image of the original. Thus, every 1 and 0 on the original must be replicated on the copy or image. In this chapter, I'll discuss the various methods of acquiring the original evidence and rendering from it an image upon which you can conduct your forensic examinations.

In the previous chapter, I discussed first-response issues, from preparing yourself and equipment to processing the scene. During that discussion, I made several references to different methods of acquiring digital evidence, both in the field and at the lab. EnCase provides many options for acquiring digital evidence, some of which are available in all models of EnCase and some are available only in the Enterprise and FIM versions.

Each case is unique and presents its own set of challenges and obstacles. No doubt you will use one or two of your favorite acquisition methods for most of your casework. You should, however, be familiar with the other options or methods to use when circumstances force you to use another method to get that image.

I'll begin with the basics: creating boot disks in either floppy or CD format. Using those boot disks, you can boot a computer into a DOS mode that is forensically sound. From there you acquire media using the drive-to-drive, network cable, and parallel cable methods. While these are legacy methods, you can still encounter older systems where such techniques become the best option.

Beginning with EnCase version 5, a Linux-based utility has been included in the EnCase distribution. This utility is called Linux EnCase (LinEn). It provides similar functionality to the DOS boot; however, LinEn runs under Linux, which means that instead of a 16-bit operating system, as with DOS, you are running under a full 32-bit operating system. Thus, you have all the features of the traditional EnCase for DOS with the added bonus of the Linux command-line features and much faster performance.

Starting with EnCase 6, the DOS version of EnCase is no longer available (because floppy disks are going the way of the dinosaurs). Remaining in its place, however, is LinEn. Even though floppy disks are fading away, there are still plenty of legacy boxes out there for which a floppy boot disk may be needed (these systems were made in the era when CD-ROM drives were an expensive option). A good examiner should know how to create a floppy disk using EnCase version 7, but with an earlier DOS version of EnCase as the executable.

FastBloc is a hardware write-blocking device developed for use with EnCase. It has undergone an evolution that now encompasses several hardware models. FastBloc hardware devices are no longer available and have been replaced by the Tableau line of hardware write blockers, which came about when Guidance Software acquired the assets of Tableau, LLC. I'll discuss how it can be used to acquire hard drives in Window, DOS, and LinEn.

With EnCase 7, FastBloc Software Edition (dubbed FastBloc SE), formerly available as an added cost option, is now included as part of the basic software feature set. With FastBloc SE, you can write block Plug and Play USB, FireWire, and SCSI devices easily. These options appear in the Tools menu.

EnCase Portable is a relatively new tool that allows for the collection of data in the field. Among its collection tool sets is the ability to make acquisitions. We'll cover the acquisition capabilities of this tool.

Finally, I'll discuss the feature set of the Enterprise and FIM versions of EnCase, with their unique ability to acquire media over a network while maintaining an extremely secure environment known as SAFE (Secure Authentication for EnCase). As an added feature, these versions can capture volatile system-state data, thus making them valuable tools for live analysis and live acquisitions.

Creating EnCase Forensic Boot Disks

 Initially, I'll focus on creating EnCase DOS boot disks using EnCase 5 (or older). I'll switch to EnCase 7 when the new features of that version merge into the process.

The purpose of the forensic boot disk is to boot the computer and load an operating system in a forensically sound manner so that the evidentiary media is not changed. A normal DOS boot disk will make calls to the C: drive primarily via COMMAND.COM but also with IO.SYS. Figure 4.1 shows COMMAND.COM making a call to the C: drive. Also, it will attempt to load DRVSPACE.BIN (disk compression software) if present. An EnCase forensic boot disk will be modified so that any calls to the hard drive (C:) are redirected to the floppy drive (A:). EnCase accomplishes this by modifying the COMMAND.COM and IO.SYS files when creating or converting to forensic boot disks, as shown in Figure 4.2. If DRVSPACE.BIN is found, it will be deleted to prevent it from mounting the drive. In this manner, an EnCase forensic boot disk can boot a computer to a forensically sound, safe version of DOS.

FIGURE 4.1   Normal Windows start-up disk with COMMAND.COM making a call to the C:

```
  1    COMMAND.COM    UTOEXE.BAT   ŷ    Ûv  ÚA    PATH= C:\WINDOWS\COMMAND PROMP
```

FIGURE 4.2   Windows start-up disk modified by EnCase with COMMAND.COM making same call to A:

```
□ 1    COMMAND.COM   UTOEXE.BAT  ÿ    Ûv  ÚA    PATH= A:\WINDOWS\COMMAND PROMP
```

EnCase can update an existing boot disk running on Windows 2000/XP/2003/Vista/7. EnCase can convert an existing start-up disk to a forensic boot floppy (as shown in Figure 4.2) under those same versions of Windows. Under any version of Windows thus far referenced, it can create a boot disk from an evidence file or boot disk image. During this process, files such as the drivers or the updated version of EN.EXE can be added. Version 5 can also create a bootable CD from an ISO image with the same ability to add files as it is rendered to CD.

All this functionality is available by choosing Tools ➢ Create Boot Disk, as shown in Figure 4.3. In the resulting window, choose A to create a floppy, or choose ISO Image to create a CD (see Figure 4.4). If you select A, the next choices will be Update Existing Boot Floppy, Overwrite Diskette With A Boot Floppy Base Image, or Change From A System Diskette To A Boot Floppy, as shown in Figure 4.5.

FIGURE 4.3   Creating a boot disk using the Tools menu in EnCase 5

FIGURE 4.4   Choose a floppy (A) or CD (ISO image).

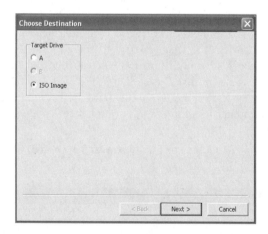

FIGURE 4.5   Forensic boot floppy formatting options

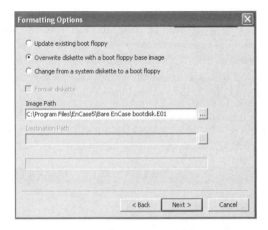

With the first option (Update Existing Boot Floppy), you are given the opportunity to add or replace files on an existing boot floppy, such as drivers or the latest version of EN.EXE. With the second option (Overwrite Diskette With A Boot Floppy Base Image), the floppy in your drive is overwritten with the boot floppy image of your choice. Many examiners keep custom boot floppy images on hand for a variety of specialized tasks. The third option (Change From A System Diskette To A Boot Floppy) allows the user to take a regular start-up floppy (one that is not forensically sound) and convert it to a forensic boot disk. The files (COMMAND.COM and IO.SYS) are modified (DRVSPACE.BIN, if found, is deleted) as described earlier and as shown in Figures 4.1 and 4.2. All three options provide, as a final step, the option to add or replace files (see Figure 4.6).

FIGURE 4.6   All three formatting options provide the option to add or replace files; in this example, EN.EXE is updated, and SCSI drivers are added.

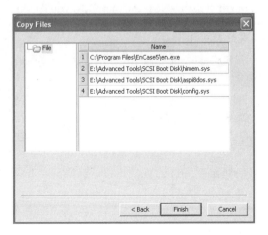

The foregoing steps were demonstrated using EnCase 5, which was the last version of EnCase to ship with en.exe, which is the DOS version of the EnCase acquisition tool. EnCase 6, and now EnCase 7, provides a similar mechanism for creating a boot floppy; however, en.exe will not be available in the program files that ship with EnCase, and thus you won't be able to use EnCase to update the en.exe file. With later versions of EnCase (after 5), you'll need to use an image of a boot floppy, available from Guidance Software's support portal in the Boot Disks section of the Downloads tab. Figure 4.7 shows this feature located on the EnCase 7 Tools drop-down menu.

FIGURE 4.7   The feature to create a boot floppy is found on the drop-down menu under Tools on the toolbar.

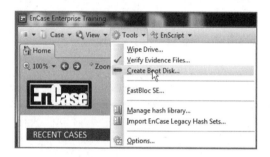

Booting a Computer Using the EnCase Boot Disk

Despite advances in technologies that allow acquisitions to occur in the Windows environment using FastBloc, Tableau, or other write-blocking methods, you'll sometimes still need a DOS boot. To make matters worse, you have to use the suspect machine to host the boot. The situations requiring this method include the following:

- Geometry mismatches between the host BIOS (legacy) and your exam machine BIOS (the latest and greatest)

- Suspect hard drive that is "married" to the host motherboard via a security scheme

- Hard drive that is part of a hardware RAID, particularly when reconstructing the RAID from individual hard drives, in which it is a RAID scheme that is not supported by EnCase

Seeing Invisible HPA and DCO Data

You may also encounter a *Host Protected Area* (HPA) or a *Device Configuration Overlay* (DCO). HPA was introduced with the ATA-4 standard. Its purpose is to create a place at the end of the drive for vendors to store information (recovery, security, registration, and so on) that is invisible to the BIOS and hence protected from user access or erasure (format, and so on). DCO was introduced with ATA-6 and was initially intended as a means of limiting the apparent capacity of a drive. DCO space also appears at the end of the drive and is not seen by the BIOS.

Because neither HPA nor DCO areas can be seen by the BIOS and both can contain hidden data, one way to access this data is via Direct ATA. This method is available using EnCase for DOS on a forensic boot disk. In Direct ATA mode, EnCase communicates directly with the ATA controller and is able to access all sectors, including HPA and DCO sectors that weren't seen or accessed by the BIOS.

HPA or DCO?

When trying to determine whether you are seeing all the sectors in a drive, you'll often look to the sectors reported by the manufacturer. In some cases, you can miss sectors this way. Recently while imaging a Western Digital WD800 80 GB drive, I noted that the manufacturer reported on the drive label that the drive contained 156,250,000 LBA sectors. While looking at the physical drive attached to FastBloc FE in Windows, EnCase was reporting all 156,250,000 sectors as seen by the BIOS, which matches the sectors reported by the manufacturer. Should I conclude that there is no HPA or DCO in place?

Your first clue to this problem typically occurs when you connect your target drive to FastBloc or Tableau in Windows and note that the total number of sectors on the drive, as reported by EnCase, is lower than the number of sectors known to be available on the drive (Total LBA Sectors). Instead of relying upon the hard drive label, you should consult the manufacturer's website for more accurate technical specifications for the hard drive. Because best forensic practices call for accounting for all sectors on a drive, this should be standard practice with all drives. When EnCase is reporting fewer sectors than the manufacturer, you should suspect HPA or DCO and investigate further. EnCase for DOS Direct ATA's access feature is one method to reconcile the difference and obtain all the sectors on the drive, albeit a legacy method.

You can use LinEn—EnCase running under Linux or the FastBloc SE module—in lieu of EnCase for DOS for detecting and accessing HPAs and DCOs. I'll cover its feature set later in this chapter.

Other Reasons for Using a DOS Boot

Sometimes, for other reasons (legacy equipment, HPA, DCO, and so on), you may opt for a DOS boot when the storage drive is on your examination machine. Because this is a known, safe, forensic environment, it is far better than using the suspect's computer. Even so, you still must control the boot process so that you boot from your forensic boot disk and not the target drive.

When booting with the suspect machine, there is always risk since it is an unknown environment. When you have no other good option, you must proceed carefully. If you make an error or omission along the way, you risk altering your evidence drive because of an accidental boot of that drive. Your goal is to control and test the boot process so that you can boot the machine with your known safe forensic boot disk, and at the same time ensure that your target evidence drive is safe from calls and writes during the boot.

Chapter 1 gave you a solid understanding of the boot process, and Chapter 3 explained when and how you shut down a system. It is now time to put that knowledge to work. The following steps provide a framework for safe forensic booting of the suspect machine. Keep in mind, however, that nothing is guaranteed. Even if you are DOS-booting from your examination machine, you should still follow the basic format: configure the boot process, test, confirm, and proceed carefully. Always be prepared for the unexpected by having your hand on the power cord, ready to pull it immediately if something goes wrong.

Steps for Using a DOS Boot

To use a DOS boot, follow these steps:

1. Make certain that the target computer is powered off. Refer to your own policies and the guidelines in Chapter 3 with regard to appropriate shutdown procedures, which depend on the operating system, applications, function, and environment.

2. Disconnect the power cord from the back of the computer, and open the case. Inspect the interior for hard drives and connections, noting in particular anything unusual. It is common to find disconnected hard drives inside as well as additional connected hard drives mounted in any available space.

3. Disconnect both the power cable and data cable from any connected hard drive. If more than one hard drive exists, label the data connections before disconnecting them so they are reconnected properly when the time comes to do so.

4. Insert the forensic boot disk into the drive. If you are booting with a CD, use a paper clip to open the drive tray first. If you're not familiar with this technique, there is a tiny hole in the face of most CD/DVD drives. Pressing a straightened paper clip into the hole opens the tray when the unit has no power.

5. With all hard drives disconnected and your boot disk inserted, reconnect the power cord, and start the computer. Immediately be prepared to enter the Setup routine, which occurs around the time you first see something on the screen. Typically you will see a message on the screen such as "To Enter Setup Press F2." Often the key you need to press to enter

Setup is displayed, but in some systems this is hidden from the user. When this happens, you can refer to the system manual, if available, or you can try the more common keys, which are as follows:

- F1 (for IBMs and many clones).

- F2, F12, or Delete (common with many Gateways, Dells, HPs, and other clones).

- F10 (common with Compaqs).

- Ctrl+Alt+Esc or Ctrl+Alt+Enter (if the previous keys don't work).

- Sometimes removing all bootable media, including your forensic boot disk, will force a system to enter Setup or provide a prompt that reveals the elusive key that accesses Setup.

6. Once inside Setup, locate the boot settings, specifically, the boot order. This is the process you seek to control! Before making changes, record the current order in your notes. Set the order so that your forensic boot disk device (floppy or CD) appears before the target hard drive.

7. Save your changes as you exit Setup. If you don't save the changes, the old settings will apply.

8. It is now time to test the boot environment to make certain the settings you configured work and that the forensic boot devices also work. At this point, your target hard drive(s) should still be disconnected. Start the computer, and make certain your boot device works. If so, power down the computer, and disconnect the power cord.

9. If you are going to be using a hard drive on the target machine to store the image, you should connect it and again test your boot environment to see whether the system attempts to boot to the hard drive. If all is well and your system boots to the forensic boot disk, again, power down your system and disconnect the power cord.

10. If all is safe at this stage, it is time to reconnect your target hard drive. Then double-check that your forensic boot disk is still inserted. Reconnect the power cord, and keep your hand on it where it connects to the case so you can abort the process if it fails. Start the system, and watch the boot process. If you followed the steps carefully and thoroughly tested your boot environment, it should boot to the forensic boot disk. If it does not, at the first sign of a problem immediately pull the power cord.

Before connecting this storage drive to your system, make sure of the following:

- The drive is formatted with FAT (DOS doesn't recognize NTFS)

- The drive has a unique volume label to identify it later

- A directory (use DOS naming conventions) exists to store your image

Drive-to-Drive DOS Acquisition

A drive-to-drive DOS acquisition takes place entirely in DOS, and the target drive and the image storage drive are attached to the same motherboard, which is why it's called *drive-to-drive*. It is a simple means of acquisition because you need to pack only an EnCase boot disk and a storage hard drive. No dongle is needed. Many examiners, having started forensics years ago when this was the standard acquisition method, still prefer it.

Drive-to-drive is a relatively fast acquisition. The speed limitation is usually imposed by the slowest component in the ATA subsystem, be it the controller, cable, configuration, or drive speed. The faster configuration will usually be master-to-master on different channels (primary and secondary) vs. master-to-slave on the same channel. If you're providing your own cable for your storage drive, make sure it is an 80-conductor IDE cable; shorter is better. The closer you get to the 18-inch maximum length for these cables, the greater the possibility of communications errors during acquisition.

Steps for Drive-to-Drive DOS Acquisition

When conducting a drive-to-drive DOS acquisition, you should follow these steps:

1. Make sure your system is configured, tested, and ready for a safe boot to a forensic boot disk as outlined in "Booting a Computer Using the EnCase Boot Disk" earlier.

2. If you are booting using the suspect's computer, install the storage drive on that system. If you are booting to your examination machine, install the suspect's hard drive on that system. When doing so, keep in mind the following:

   - Configure your drives so they are cabled and pinned as masters. Master-to-master data transfer will give you better performance.

   - EnCase for DOS can write only to a FAT-formatted drive, so format as FAT only.

   - Use a volume label name on the storage drive that uniquely identifies it in the EnCase for DOS environment. Doing so avoids confusion and mistakes that could result in imaging your storage drive onto your evidence or target drive.

   - The file directory path on the storage drive that will contain the image files must already exist. Create a directory after formatting and before attaching the evidence drive to the system. In this way, you avoid accidental writes to the evidence drive.

3. With the EnCase boot disk inserted and the target and storage drives properly attached, start the computer, and carefully monitor the boot; be in a position to pull the cord from the back of the machine immediately if things go wrong.

4. When DOS boots and the A prompt appears, type **en**, and press Enter. EnCase for DOS will start. On the left pane you will see physical devices, and on the right pane you will see logical devices. The logical devices will be color-coded to correspond with the color-coding on the physical devices on which they are installed.

5. If you have selected a DOS boot because all sectors were not accessible through Fast-Bloc in Windows, now is the time to change from BIOS access (default) to Direct ATA access. Do this by pressing M or by tabbing to the Mode tab. If you started with a

DOS boot for other reasons, check now to make certain the sectors reported by the BIOS access match those reported by the manufacturer. If they do, you can proceed to the next step. If they don't, as in Figure 4.8, you need to switch to the Direct ATA access using the Mode tab, as shown in Figure 4.9 and Figure 4.10.

FIGURE 4.8 Two Western Digital 30 GB drives. Western Digital reports these drives as having 58,633,344 LBA sectors. XBIOS is reporting only 58,621,185 sectors (see arrow). That means 12,159 sectors (6,225,408 bytes) are not being seen by the BIOS!

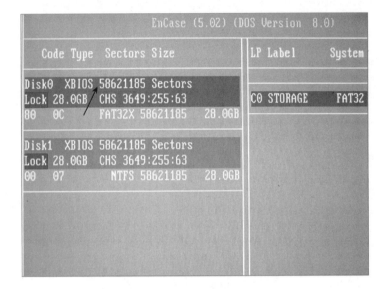

FIGURE 4.9 To access the hidden sectors, switch to Direct ATA access using the Mode tab.

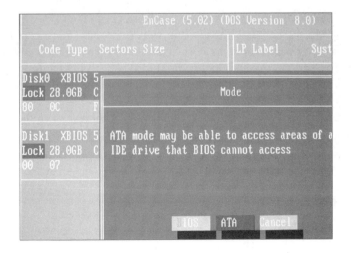

For a logical device to appear on the right pane, it must be a partition recognized by DOS, which means only FAT partitions appear. NTFS partitions, even though they are Microsoft partitions, do not show in the right pane! Similarly, don't expect to see Linux, Mac, or other non-DOS partitions here.

FIGURE 4.10   After switching to the Direct ATA access mode, all 58,633,344 sectors are visible (see arrow).

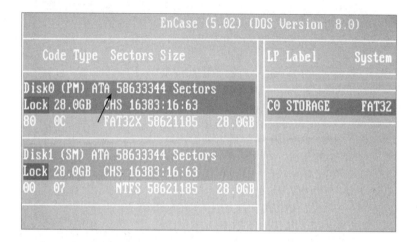

6. By default, EnCase for DOS implements a software write block on all devices, as indicated by the word *Lock* appearing in red next to each device. You will need to unlock your storage drive before EnCase can write to it. This is where it is important to have given a unique name to the volume so it can be unmistakably identified and unlocked. When you are certain you have identified your storage drive, unlock it by pressing L or by tabbing to the Lock tab and pressing Enter. You will be given a choice of drive letters and numbers to unlock. Once you choose your storage drive, the word *Lock* in red will no longer be next to your drive. Check and double-check before proceeding.

7. When you have unlocked the storage drive, press A to acquire. You will be given a choice of drives to acquire, both by letter (logical) and by number (physical). Usually you will want every sector on the drive and will choose the physical drive.

8. You will be prompted for the path on the storage drive on which to place the drive image. You must enter the path exactly as it exists on the storage drive along with the name of the file. As a safeguard, this path must already exist.

9. You are prompted for the case number; enter it, and continue to the next step.

10. You are prompted for the examiner's name; enter your name.

11. You are prompted for an evidence number. Many naming conventions are possible. Use your lab protocol, and enter the number.

12. You are next prompted for a brief description of the evidence; enter it, and continue to the next step.

13. The system date and time appears next. If correct, press Enter. If not, enter the correct date and time. Entering the correct date and time doesn't change your system time, but it does reflect in the acquisition information reported by EnCase as Reported Time and Actual Time.

14. The next prompt allows you to enter any notes you want.

15. You are then given the option to compress the evidence. Because compression saves you disk space (two to three times less space) but costs you more time to process the compression algorithm (up to five times as long), here is where you ask yourself whether you have more time or more disk space available to you. Because time seems to be the scarcer of the two, I rarely use compression.

16. You are next asked whether you want to generate an MD5 hash of the drive as it is acquired. It is by this process that the acquisition hash is generated that later allows you to verify that the copy you made is the same as the original. It is recommended that you always generate this value. At no time have I ever skipped this process, and I can't conceive of a situation where I would. Nevertheless, it is optional.

17. EnCase next prompts you to provide a password. Simply pressing Enter here negates applying a password—which I recommend you do unless you have a compelling need to include a password. Keep in mind that if you apply a password and then forget or lose it, the recovery is expensive. Passwords are useful in some applications. In special master situations, an examiner can acquire the evidence, but the special master applies the password. In this manner, the examiner can acquire and retain the image, but it can be read and examined only in the presence or with the permission of the special master who holds the password. This is often done in cases in which the image contains privileged information and special protective measures must be used.

18. Your next option will be that of determining the file segment size (chunk size) of the image file. Rather than creating one massive file, the files are created in segments, or what we commonly call *chunks*. The smallest size is 1 MB, and the largest size is 2,000 MB (2 GB). The default of 640 MB is recommended, because a file this size fits on a CD and seven "chunks" will fit nicely on a DVD (4.7 GB).

19. Your next choice is the number of sectors to acquire. This will default to the number present on the device you are acquiring, which is almost always what you want. Sometimes, naturally, you'll need a different number to acquire. Sometimes you have to acquire an image of a drive that has been restored onto another drive. As often happens, the drive receiving the restored image is larger than the drive image placed on it. When acquiring such a drive, you'll want to acquire only the number of sectors reported in the image restored and not the entire drive. If you restored a 20 GB drive onto a 30 GB drive, you'll want to acquire only the number of sectors comprising the 20 GB drive.

20. The next option was new with EnCase 5: the ability to vary the granularity of the acquisition. In prior versions, if EnCase discovered a sector with an error, the entire block of 64 sectors (32 K) was zeroed out. If only one sector was bad, 63 sectors of potentially valuable data was disregarded and counted as null. With versions 5 and 6, you can change the default of 64 sectors to 1, in powers of 2. Thus, settings can be 64, 32, 16, 8, 4, 2, or 1. If one sector is bad and the setting is 64, then all 64 sectors are zeroed out. If one sector is bad and the setting is 32, then 32 sectors are zeroed out. If one sector is bad and the setting is 1, only the bad sector is zeroed out, meaning no data is lost. It might seem that the best setting would be 1, but such granularity results in a performance hit, slowing down acquisition. Typically you use the default setting of 64 and lower it only if you encounter a drive with errors.

21. At this point, the acquisition will start. Depending on the system, the drive sizes, and the options selected, the process can take hours. A progress bar will appear, giving you a lapsed time and an approximation of the time remaining. EnCase will create files using the name you designated earlier and with extensions starting with .e01, .e02, and so on, until done. The files created will be in the chunk sizes you specified in the earlier setting, 640 MB by default. With large drives and no compression, the number of files can be significant. If 100 or more files are needed, after the .E99 extension is reached, the extension will change to .eaa, .eab, .eac, and so on. If the files needed to store the image exceed that on the current storage drive, you will be prompted for a location for additional storage. It is important to have adequate storage space formatted, ready, and mounted even if it is more than one storage drive so that it is available when EnCase needs it.

Supplemental Information About Drive-to-Drive DOS Acquisition

I cover FastBloc in detail later in this chapter. In the meantime, you need to know that Tableau bay-mounted forensics bridges can be used for drive-to-drive DOS acquisitions. The Tableau bridges all have IDE channel write-blocking function. The target or suspect hard drive can be connected to Tableau bridge and uses hardware write-blocking features to protect it from accidental writes in the event that the wrong drive is unlocked using the software write-blocking feature of EnCase for DOS. Aside from the initial connection, everything else is the same.

Thus far, the discussions have dealt with PC-based systems. If you encounter Mac hard drives, you can't boot them with an EnCase boot disk in their host systems. Rather, you usually need to move the drive to your examination machine and acquire it as another IDE drive. (But see the sidebar "Acquiring a Mac Drive Using FireWire" for another option.) The same goes for Unix and BSD; those drives will have to be transferred to the examination computer for imaging. None of these partitions will show as logical partitions in the right pane, because DOS does not recognize them. Nevertheless, their physical drives will populate the left pane, and they can be acquired as physical drives. Later when the images are brought into EnCase for Windows, their file structures can be interpreted, mounted, and processed as with any other partition.

Dead Hard Drives Are Not Always Dead!

After a domestic-violence incident and initiation of a divorce proceeding, the soon-to-be former spouse of a network administrator walked into the office of her soon-to-be ex-husband's supervisor. She told her husband's supervisor that he had "trojanized" the entire network—he had captured passwords and was eavesdropping on his boss's email account from his home machine. Among other things, she placed a hard drive on the supervisor's desk, claiming it had been in her husband's computer and that he had left it behind when he moved out.

The police were immediately notified, and I was called in to examine the machines in that network. I isolated the infected network segment and began the task of acquiring images of each machine for later examination. This occurred several years ago, and EnCase Enterprise and FIM as tools for capturing volatile data were not options at the time. The subsequent examination established that the various machines on that subnet either had Back Orifice currently installed or had them installed at one time. The Back Orifice server had been built on the network administrator's workstation and had been deployed in a "dancing cat" program popular with the staff. A list of staff passwords was found, as was a similar list from the network administrator's previous place of employment. Old habits seem to die hard!

The suspect's home hard drive was dead. It would not spin up, and it appeared that its only use was going to be as a "bithead" paperweight. The spouse indicated her husband would experiment with hard drives, attempting to "kill" them by zapping them with high voltages. She thought he had zapped that one and that was probably the reason he had left it behind. She commented that it was a shame because she was certain that drive was in his machine when he was getting into all those email accounts.

The drive sat around for a while until one day I decided to send it out to a clean room. Before I underwent that expense, I thought I would try replacing the circuit board on the drive. With a little bit of Googling I located two identical model drives and had them shipped overnight. I took the circuit board from one and placed it on the "dead" drive. When I connected it and powered it on, the drive spun up, and the acquisition was a success.

Needless to say, the drive was loaded with emails intercepted from his boss's account. The date and time stamps coincided with modem connection logs from the server that were tied to his telephone number.

We spent two days in court successfully defending against a motion to suppress the recovered hard drive evidence. Because it was marital property at the time, the spouse had a legal right to the hard drive and could turn it over to the police if she elected to do so. With that issue resolved, a guilty plea followed.

Even if a hard drive seems dead, there may be ways of bringing it back to life!

Acquiring a Mac Drive Using FireWire

Although you can't use an EnCase DOS boot disk to boot a Mac, you can sometimes avoid having to remove drives to image them on another system. This is especially useful on Mac laptops where disassembly is quite a chore. The trick to use is the Mac FireWire boot mode. When you turn on a Mac, hold down the T key until you see the FireWire icon the screen. At this point, connect the Mac to your Windows forensics box via a FireWire cable. Windows can't read the partition table and will see it only as a physical drive. EnCase, however, can see the physical drive and mount the file system. From there, it's a simple matter to acquire, and the speed is quite respectable.

The examiner should understand that this method is not a true write-block method and only depends on the inability of Windows to recognize the partitions used by the Mac. If a Mac is an Intel-based system and is configured in a dual-boot configuration using "Boot Camp," the Mac will have partitions that Windows will recognize and mount. In such a case, placing a Tableau FireWire write blocker between the Windows machine with EnCase and the Mac in Target mode is an option. Thus, before using a method such as described, you must be sure of what the platform is and its configuration. If in doubt, use another method.

In February 2011 Apple released Thunderbolt interface technology on all new releases of Macintosh computers. Without digressing into a technical discussion of the properties and uses of Thunderbolt, let's simply look at it as a potential acquisition method for a Mac. If you boot into the Target mode of a Thunderbolt-equipped Mac, you will see the Thunderbolt lightning bolt icon and also a FireWire icon, if equipped with FireWire in addition to Thunderbolt. Because there are no Thunderbolt hardware write blockers available as yet, the Thunderbolt port can be used to attach the Mac in Target mode, provided one write protects that connection via other means. The easiest way to do this is to attach the Mac in Target mode to another Mac via the Thunderbolt cable. Before making the attachment, the acquisition machine must first have disk arbitration disabled. With that done, the Mac in Target mode can be safely attached and imaged. Another option is to attach the target machine booted to Target Disk Mode to another machine booted to a Raptor boot disk. Using this method is yet another way to safely leverage the Target Disk Mode feature.

So far, I have discussed primarily IDE drives. If you encounter a SCSI drive, you can image it in its host computer in a drive-to-drive DOS acquisition as long as you load the SCSI drivers onto your EnCase boot disk. Figure 4.6 earlier in this chapter shows these being added within EnCase. You can image a SCSI drive in a like manner on your examination machine as long as you have an SCSI adapter expansion card or the same chipset on board.

Once you have acquired your drive, regardless of type, you need to power down, disconnect your target or suspect drive, and return it to secure storage, applying best practices throughout (documentation, antistatic bags, labeling, and so forth). At this point, make sure the image you acquired is a good one. To do so, boot to Windows, open EnCase, and open the image you just acquired. Make sure EnCase can read the file structure and that you successfully completed the verification process before you consider the imaging job complete.

Network Acquisitions

Another method of acquiring hard drives is via a network cable between a machine containing the target media, booted to EnCase for DOS or Linux (LinEn), and a second machine running EnCase in the Windows environment. It often provides the best of both worlds, allowing some of the advantages of a DOS boot (Direct ATA access) combined with the enhanced functionality of EnCase in Windows. Again, this technique is now regarded as a legacy technique, having been replaced by LinEn. If you find it necessary to use this method, you will find it best to run EnCase 5 under Windows XP for the examination machine.

Reasons to Use Network Acquisitions

Network acquisition methods are useful in a variety of situations. They include the following:

Acquiring Invisible HPA or DCO Data   If you encounter an HPA or DCO, you can place the drive in a safe lab machine and boot to EnCase for DOS while connected to your regular lab acquisition machine running EnCase in a Windows environment. Likewise, a network cable acquisition is useful for booting from the suspect's machine when encountering geometry mismatches between a legacy BIOS (usually the suspect's machine) and a new BIOS (usually your lab machine) or when encountering RAID configurations. A RAID can be booted to DOS using its native hardware configuration to mount the logical physical device. EnCase will see this RAID as a mounted physical device, enabling acquisition and preview via the network cable connection to EnCase in Windows.

Acquiring Data from a Laptop Hard Drive   Sometimes removing a hard drive from a laptop is problematic because of physical access or other concerns, such as proprietary security schemes marrying the hard drive to the motherboard. If you are able to access the BIOS and control the boot process, a network cable acquisition is a viable option as long as you use a great degree of care and prudence.

Acquiring Data Quickly   A network cable acquisition is also handy for "black bag" jobs where you have to quickly acquire a target hard drive when the owner or user of the target hard drive is not physically present. With little disturbance to the physical environment, you can connect your examination laptop to the target machine via a network cable, boot to EnCase for DOS or Linux, and preview or acquire if needed.

Previewing Data Before Acquiring   EnCase for DOS or Linux doesn't allow direct previewing of the data; however, when connected via network cable to EnCase for Windows, you can see the drive completely in the EnCase GUI environment. In circumstances where certain images or keywords must be present to warrant seizure, a network cable acquisition is useful. Thus, it is a great tool for a variety of field and lab situations. You can also use EnCase Portable for a quick preview.

Understanding Network Cables

Before starting a network acquisition, you must keep a few other considerations in mind. The first is the cable. I have been calling it simply a *network cable*, but the cable used is more specifically a *network crossover cable*. A yellow crossover cable ships with each version of EnCase.

 Yellow does not necessarily denote a crossover cable in the field. Twisted-pair cable comes in a variety of colors, and those colors can be used to denote cable for a room, subnet, or any other differentiating purpose. Sometimes there is no purpose—someone needed to make a cable and used whatever color was available. Often a crossover cable has a tag or label to denote it, but don't depend on it!

A crossover cable is a network cable used for special purposes, one of which is to enable two computers to have network connectivity by connecting directly to each other via a single network cable. A regular network cable will not work for this purpose. On a crossover cable, on one end only, the positive and negative "receive" pair are switched with the positive and negative "transmit" pair, respectively with regard to the positive and negative to maintain polarity. In this manner, the machines can "talk" to each other over the network crossover cable.

 When packing for the field, it is a good idea to pack an extra crossover cable. To avoid extra bulk, a nice alternative is to pack a crossover adapter, which allows you to use any network cable as a crossover cable. If you have to image several machines in a small area, using a crossover cable adapter allows you to situate your examination laptop in one spot and use a very long network cable to reach the various target machines. In a pinch, a network hub or switch can serve as a crossover adapter, enabling you to use regular network cables! A switch with full duplex will actually be faster than your crossover cable.

Now that you understand the need for a crossover cable, you must ensure a couple of other things. First, make sure the target machine is equipped with a network interface card (NIC). Second, make sure you have an EnCase boot disk or CD configured for network support, specifically a set of DOS packet drivers for the installed NIC card.

Not all NIC cards serve this purpose equally well. Some lack DOS driver support. Some have great features and very reliable DOS driver support. Others fall in the middle of these two extremes.

Preparing an EnCase Network Boot Disk

You could experiment with different NIC cards and drivers, or you could use the ENBD (EnCase Network Boot Disk) or the ENBCD (EnCase Network Boot CD). The ENBD/ENBCD was developed and is continually updated by the Ontario Province Police (OPP), and through OPP's generosity, this resource is available to all EnCase users via the Guidance Software website.

The ENBD.EXE file is a self-extracting floppy disk image, as shown in Figure 4.11. Since a floppy disk is a limited resource (1.44 MB), the amount of support you can pack on a floppy is limited. ENBD currently provides 29 different drivers supporting more than 190 device variants. The ENBD also comes in different flavors depending on the laptop PCMCIA NIC card it supports. These versions don't have the variety of support, but they occupy less floppy disk space, allowing room for other tools. After extracting the ENBD to the floppy, you must also copy the version of EN.EXE that came with the version of EnCase you are running on the Windows machine. You can manually copy EN.EXE onto the floppy or use the EnCase Update Existing Boot Floppy feature.

FIGURE 4.11   ENBD self-extracting to a floppy; when done, place EN.EXE on the floppy before use.

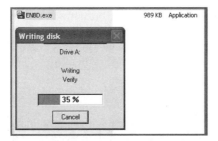

Version Note

EnCase version 5 is the last version that comes with EnCase for DOS (EN.EXE). Using an EnCase boot floppy will not work with version 6 or 7. Various boot floppy images are still available on the Guidance Software website. The ENBCD, as described next, is also available on the website but won't be updated for versions of EnCase newer than version 5.

Keep in mind, however, that a network cable preview and acquisition is available using Linux for EnCase (LinEn) in EnCase 6 and 7. I'll discuss this tool later in the chapter.

Preparing an EnCase Network Boot CD

The ENBCD currently is a CD mirror of the ENBD in its full version. Because a CD provides much more file space, it ultimately has the potential to offer much more support than its floppy counterpart. The ENBCD is under constant development; the devices it supports are listed on the Guidance Software website. A major difference between the two is that the ENBCD already contains the most current version of EN.EXE. The caveat here is that problems can occur if the EN.EXE version does not match the version in use on the Windows platform. Therefore, make sure you use the correct version of the ENBCD. The extension of each ENBCD file indicates the EnCase version it contains.

The ENBCD is a self-extracting file that creates an ISO file and launches a quick set of instructions describing how to burn the CD image (ISO file) using either Nero or Roxio. You are given a choice as to where the ISO will be extracted. Take careful note of the location so you can find it again later. Easier yet, use the browse feature to move the ISO to your desktop. With Roxio, you need only to insert a blank CD and double-click the ISO image on your desktop, and everything happens automatically, making it a simple process and circumventing the steps provided in the instructions. Either way, creating the ENBCD is a simple process.

If your target machine contains a NIC that is supported by the ENBD or ENBCD, you are set to go. If your target machine does not have a supported NIC, you'll need to install one in the target machine. You should choose one from the supported list of NIC cards and pack it, along with a spare, in your field kit.

The ideal configuration is to use a supported gigabit NIC in conjunction with a gigabit NIC in your examination machine. In that manner, you'll get gigabit transfer speed between the two machines, and the network connection will not be the limiting factor. If both the DOS and the Windows platforms are robust systems, you'll get extremely fast acquisitions.

Once you have a supported NIC in each machine connected via a crossover cable and you have created your EnCase network boot disk in either the floppy or CD version, you are ready to begin a network cable acquisition.

In lieu of ENBD/ENBCD, the machine containing the target drive can be booted with a forensically configured version of Linux. LinEn, which is EnCase for Linux, can be run in Linux in a manner akin to EnCase for DOS. A network crossover cable acquisition can be carried out in the same manner after LinEn is started. The Linux distribution will determine the level of support for NIC, SCSI, and USB devices.

Steps for Network Acquisition

When conducting a network cable acquisition, you should follow the steps discussed next.

Booting Up

The first part of the network acquisition process is safely booting up the target machine. Follow these steps:

1. With regard to the Windows machine, it is best to wait until the DOS machine is ready before starting EnCase in Windows. Simply run Windows with the crossover cable connected, don't start EnCase, and focus your attention first on the target machine.

2. With regard to the target machine, as with the DOS drive-to-drive acquisition, you need to control and test the boot process so that the target machine boots from your ENBD/ENBCD before it attempts to boot from the target hard drive. The safest configuration is to enable a boot only from the floppy or CD and to disable the hard drive boot by removing the hard drive from the boot order altogether. Follow the procedures outlined in "Drive-to-Drive DOS Acquisition" earlier in this chapter to make certain the target hard drive is disconnected while you configure and test the boot order in the Setup utility.

3. Once you are completely satisfied that the boot process is tested and under control, reconnect the target media drive, make certain the network crossover cable is connected between the two machines, make sure the ENBD/ENBCD is in the boot drive, and reconnect the power cable. Boot the target machine (suspect or lab machine) with your hand on the power cord at the rear of the machine. If the machine doesn't boot to the ENBD, disconnect the power at once.

4. Once the ENBD starts, a menu will appear with the following choices:

    *   *Network Support*: A second menu will launch providing various driver support installation options for network support. For network cable acquisitions, choose this option.

    *   *USB – Acquisition (no drive letter assigned)*: If you want to acquire a USB device, this option loads the USB drivers to enable acquisition of a USB-connected device.

    *   *USB – Destination (drive letter assigned)*: If you want to store an EnCase evidence file or other data to a USB-connected device, this option will load the drivers to allow you to mount a USB-connected device with a drive letter so that DOS can write to that drive. Since DOS is the operating system, it must be a FAT partition. After the ASPI USB Manager loads and configures your USB device, EnCase for DOS launches automatically. You have to look in EnCase for your drive letter. This is useful for drive-to-drive acquisitions when your storage drive is a USB-connected storage device.

    *   *Clean Boot*: As with a bare-bones floppy boot, you are presented with a DOS prompt from which you can carry out DOS tasks or launch EnCase for DOS (EN.EXE) without any of the ENBD supported features.

Setting Up Acquisition

The second part of the acquisition process involves loading drivers, setting up the access mode, choosing your connection type, and disabling firewalls:

1. You should choose #1, Network Support, to load network support options. You are next given a choice of several options. If SCSI devices are present, you should first load the SCSI drivers before the NIC drivers. The SCSI driver menu will offer an "autodetect" or manual select option. Autodetect usually works and is the recommended first choice. Once your SCSI drivers are loaded, if they were needed, you next load your NIC drivers. The recommended method is again the autodetect method. Manual selection and loading is usually necessary only if you encounter difficulty with the automated detection and installation methods. Once your NIC is detected and the DOS packet drivers are installed, ENBD launches EnCase for DOS preconfigured to run in the server mode. Note that the default mode is BIOS.

2. If you have chosen the ENBD because of HPA/DCO issues, you will have to press Esc and then click OK to temporarily shut down the server while you change the mode to Direct ATA access. Once that is done, press V or Tab to go to the Server to launch the Server panel. At this point, you have a choice to make between using a parallel port or a network connection. Choose Network, and you will be back where you were when EnCase started, with the program preconfigured to launch to this mode. At this point, EnCase for DOS is in the Server mode with a network connection listening for EnCase for Windows to connect. It is time to turn your attention to the Windows machine.

NOTE that one of your choices when starting the server (if you are using version 5 or earlier) is to use a parallel cable. Before network connectivity became available in EnCase, the parallel cable was the method of connecting two machines and pulling data from the target machine to the Windows examination machine. It still works, but it is horribly slow when you consider the size of modern hard drives. If no other options are available, this is still a choice. Instead of connecting the machines via network cable, connect them via a parallel cable. Instead of choosing Network on both the DOS and Windows machines, choose Parallel Cable. Aside from the speed difference, everything else is much the same. Parallel-cable acquisitions are not supported in EnCase version 6 and newer. If you think about it, it makes sense. Why support a feature that would take weeks or months to image today's hard drive sizes?

3. Before launching EnCase on the Windows machine, first consider firewall and other issues affecting connectivity. If you have your own firewall installed, you must configure it to allow EnCase to use a network connection. The numerous amount and types of firewalls prohibit a detailed explanation of how to do this. Suffice it to say that this approach won't work until you configure your firewall to allow the EnCase network connection to pass. The easiest solution is to turn off your firewall altogether for this operation, remembering

to enable it again when done. If you are using Windows XP Service Pack 2 or greater, a firewall is present. If it is present and enabled, it will prevent this connection until you disable it, as shown in Figure 4.12, or until you add ENCASE.EXE to the Exceptions tab. To access the Windows firewall options, choose Start ➢ Control Panel ➢ Windows Firewall. Alternatively, you can turn off the firewall altogether.

FIGURE 4.12   Windows XP Firewall options. Make sure Off is selected, or go to the Exceptions tab and add ENCASE.EXE as a program.

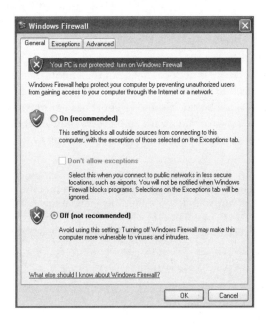

4. Usually you do not have to change anything on the Network Settings tab because EnCase usually works well and allows a connection without you altering anything. I recommend changing your network connections only if you have a problem. If you have difficulty achieving the network connection described in the next step, come back and adjust your network settings. Remember that when you are done, you'll need to restore your previous settings if you want to connect to your network again! Therefore, note your settings before changing them. To modify your network settings, click Start ➢ Control Panel ➢ Network Connections. Next, right-click Local Area Connection, and choose Properties. Then, double-click TCP/IP, and the Properties dialog box will launch. Configure the settings as follows:

    ▪ Change to a fixed IP, entering **10.0.0.50** in the IP Address box.

    ▪ For a subnet mask, enter **255.255.255.0**.

    ▪ Remove any DNS or WINS settings; they can prevent the crossover cable connection from taking place.

5. Once you are satisfied that a firewall won't stop the connection, you are ready to launch EnCase in Windows. Open your case, or start a new case. (If you aren't familiar with that process, refer to Chapter 6.) Click Add Device on the EnCase toolbar. In the resulting dialog box, place a blue check in the Network Crossover option in the right pane by simply clicking in the selection box. Click Next, and EnCase will poll the EnCase for DOS server for a list of the available devices. Select the device you want to examine, then click Next, and finally click Finish. EnCase for DOS will transmit the data to EnCase for Windows that allows you to view the file structure of the selected devices in the Windows version. This process may take a few minutes, depending on the network connection and the complexity of the device you selected. If you watch the EnCase for DOS server, the amount of data being transferred can be viewed in "real time."

6. In this manner, you can now preview the selected device in EnCase for Windows, as shown in Figure 4.13. There is no local image of the remote drive; therefore, the data is pulled over the wire as it is needed for the preview. There can be a lag time when viewing large files. You can create bookmarks and a report of your previewed data at this stage. You can also create a logical evidence file to preserve individual files or entire directories on the target drive—before, during, or after the acquisition of the entire physical disk.

FIGURE 4.13 A drive being previewed over a network cable. Note the lower right of the physical device icon has a little blue triangle, indicating that the device being viewed is a live device vs. an image. You should note that this view involves EnCase 5.

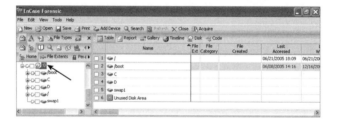

7. If your intent was to preview only, you are effectively done and can disconnect after you have finished with the report of your findings. If, however, your intent is to acquire an image of the selected device, you can do so at this time. Go on to the next section.

Specifying Data Acquisition Options

Once you've connected your machines and are previewing the data on the target machine, you need to make several choices about how to capture, verify, and store the data. Follow these steps:

1. To acquire a device that you are previewing, in the left pane right-click the device you want to acquire, usually the physical device, so you can acquire all the data. From the resulting context menu, click Acquire, as shown in Figure 4.14.

FIGURE 4.14   To acquire a device being previewed, right-click the device, and click Acquire.

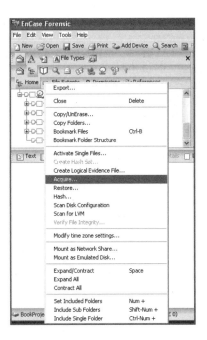

2.   You are presented with a dialog box that basically tells EnCase what to do with the image after the image is acquired, as shown in Figure 4.15.

FIGURE 4.15   In this dialog box, you tell EnCase what to do with the image after it is acquired.

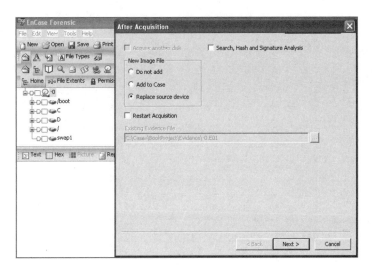

You can conduct a search, hash, and file signature analysis immediately following acquisition. If you are going to search, you must first have created and selected the keywords you intend to use. If you choose this option, you'll have the ability to run any or all of these tools against either the entire case or the newly acquired device, with the latter being the default. If you are imaging a floppy, you'll have the option to acquire another disk, and the next disk will sequence the number of the first disk by one to facilitate the imaging of a batch of floppies. With regard to the new image, you can choose whether to add it to the case. Another option is to replace the source drive that is already in the case with the image.

When the image is done, the image will replace the live device, and the little blue triangle will disappear. If you have previewed the drive, conducted searches, or made bookmarks, when the image replaces the source drive, those search hits and bookmarks will be resolved from the live device to the image.

A feature of EnCase 5 and newer versions is the ability to restart an acquisition in progress without starting over. For a host of reasons, an image can abort short of completion. With this option, you tell EnCase where the interrupted image file is located, and it picks up where it left off.

3. For the example's purposes, you are imaging a hard drive over a network cable and want to replace the source drive with the image, so select the Replace Source Drive option. Because you have no search defined, leave that option unchecked. Since you aren't restarting an image, you can leave that option deselected as well. At this point, you are ready for the next step. Click Next to see the wide range of acquisition options, as shown in Figure 4.16.

FIGURE 4.16   Acquisition options for EnCase 5 in Windows

4. When you did your imaging in EnCase for DOS, you were presented with a linear series of questions and options. In EnCase for Windows, those options plus added features are all presented in one dialog box. When you type in the name of the evidence, EnCase automatically adds this name in the Evidence Number text box and appends the name to the path of the Output Path at the bottom of the dialog box. You can change either or both (Evidence Number or the filename in the Output Path text box) later if you want, but usually the default is the better option. You may want to double-check your output path to be certain it is going where you intend. Other options are as follows:

- *Notes*: As with EnCase for DOS, enter whatever brief notes you want that can help link the evidence to the case.

- *File Segment Size*: As with EnCase for DOS, this is the "chunk size" option that determines the size of the EnCase evidence files. They can range from 1 MB (to fit on a floppy) up to 2 GB. Again, the default of 640 MB fits nicely on a CD, and seven evidence files of this size fit on a 4.7 GB DVD. The default is the recommended setting.

- *Compression*: As with EnCase for DOS, you can choose to compress. Because compression takes less disk space but more time, you have to decide which is the scarcer resource when you have to acquire. EnCase for Windows gives you the added choice of a middle ground, where you can choose "good" compression instead of "best." It's a good compromise when both time and disk space are concerns. When doing a network acquisition, the compression occurs on the server side and can result in a faster acquisition if your network connection is slow or if you are using parallel cable because you have less data to pass through the connection.

- *Start and Stop Sectors*: As with EnCase for DOS, the defaults represent the beginning and end of the selected device. Recall from "Drive-to-Drive DOS Acquisition" earlier in this chapter that you may need to change this setting if you are acquiring a device that was restored onto a larger device. You would want to acquire only the sectors associated with the original device, not the extra sectors at the end of the larger device.

- *Password*: There is no difference between a password applied within EnCase for DOS or Windows, which means everything from the discussion about this topic in EnCase for DOS applies. Just remember, if you apply a password, don't lose it!

- *Block Size*: This is a feature available in EnCase 5 and newer; it does not appear in EnCase for DOS. The block size refers to the size of the buffer used for acquiring data and computing the Cyclical Redundancy Check (CRC). DOS has an upper limit of 64 sectors, so this is not an option in DOS. With EnCase for Windows and LinEn, block sizes can range from 64 sectors to 32,768 sectors. I will discuss the EnCase evidence file in detail in Chapter 6, but for now you need to understand that EnCase normally writes a CRC for every 64 sectors of data. If you increase the block size, CRCs are written for larger blocks of data, thereby speeding up the acquisition process. If the block size is set to 256 sectors, for example, instead of writing a CRC for every 64 sectors, one will be written for every 256 sectors. You may be asking, why not make the setting 32,768 sectors every time and get the fastest possible acquisitions? As with many things in the computing world, performance gains often come with a trade-off. Every time that EnCase accesses data in the evidence file for processing, it first checks the integrity of that data by checking the CRC of the block in which the data resides. When accessing very small files, instead of checking the CRC of 64 sectors, EnCase must read and calculate the CRC of 32,768 sectors, which could slow down the program. Furthermore, if the evidence file contains a corrupted bit, EnCase knows only that the CRC for the block is bad and doesn't know which bit is corrupted. The larger the block size, the larger the amount of data affected by this error. Although such problems are rare, they can and do occur. The default block size of 64 sectors is a good compromise that I recommend. If you increase it, just understand its impact in other areas. There is also a relationship between this setting and the setting that follows, Error Granularity.

- *Error Granularity*: This feature set was first offered with EnCase 5 and is available in EnCase for Windows, DOS, and Linux. In versions of EnCase earlier than version 5, if an error was found in one sector, the remaining sectors in that block were zeroed out to increase the speed of the acquisition, meaning data was lost. Numerically, this means a block of data contains 64 sectors, or 32,768 bytes. If only one sector (512 bytes) were bad, 32,256 bytes of good data would have been zeroed out when brought into the evidence file. Needless to say, 32,236 bytes of data could contain valuable evidence of guilt or innocence. The data is still available through a network preview of the drive with errors, but this is a time-consuming, manual process. The default setting for error granularity is 64, and if left unchanged, EnCase will handle errors as it always has, which is in the manner just described. You should leave this option set at 64 unless you encounter errors, because lowering it slows down the acquisition proportionally to the degree of granularity. If you encounter errors, you can acquire the image again with a lower Error Granularity setting. You can lower Error Granularity from 64 in powers of two, down to one (64, 32, 16, 8, 4, 2, 1). With a setting of 1, if one sector is bad, no good data will be zeroed out.

Thus far, I have discussed lowering the Error Granularity setting to capture more data if errors occur. Using a lower Error Granularity setting slows down the acquisition, and increasing the setting speeds up the acquisition. The upper limit for the Error Granularity setting is the block size. Figure 4.17 shows Block Size and Error Granularity settings of 32,768 sectors. With this setting, a CRC is computed and written for every 32,768 sectors instead of every 64 sectors. This setting also increases the buffer size (memory) to hold this data. Both combine to give faster acquisitions. However, these very large settings are not very practical, because one bad sector would result in the loss of more than 16 MB of good data. Again, the defaults of 64 are recommended. Note in EnCase 7 the options for granularity are Standard and Exhaustive. Standard is the same as the block size and Exhaustive is a granularity of 1 sector.

FIGURE 4.17 The Maximum Error Granularity setting is determined by the Block Size setting. Here they are both set at their maximum value of 32,768 sectors. Again, since we are using a legacy acquisition method, EnCase 5 is in use.

- *Generate Image Hash*: By default, this setting is enabled, and an MD5 hash value is computed for the device being acquired; that value is stored in the evidence file as a means of verifying the authenticity of the original evidence stored in the evidence file. An MD5 hash is a 128-bit value that is calculated based on an algorithm developed by Rivest, Shamir, and Adleman (RSA). It is often called an *electronic fingerprint* because it uniquely identifies any stream of data or file. The odds of any two files having the same MD5 are 1 in 2^{128}, which is, more graphically, 1 in 340,282,366,920,938,000,000,000,000,000,000,000,000. Needless to say, when two files have matching MD5 values, there is an extremely high confidence factor in stating that the contents of the two files are identical. The MD5 algorithm, which is publicly available, is the industry standard in the computer forensics field. However, it does take time to calculate, so turning it off would speed up an acquisition. This might be of some value if you were testing or working on some data that was not of evidentiary value and time was critical. It is recommended that you always leave this feature enabled and that you generate an MD5 hash of all evidentiary data in accordance with best forensic practices.

- *Quick Reacquisition*: This feature was first offered in EnCase 5. It is an option only when you are acquiring an image from an EnCase evidence file. It is not available when acquiring a device. After you have acquired a device and created an image of it in the form of an evidence file, you may have occasion to acquire it again. The purpose behind doing so is to change certain limited properties of the evidence file. By reacquiring an evidence file, you can change its compression (adding or removing), you can add or remove a password, or you can change its file segment size (chunk size). Also, beginning with EnCase 5, you can adjust the block size or error granularity upon reacquisition.

Often you will acquire an image in the field without using any compression because that is the fastest way to acquire. You can also increase the Block Size and Error Granularity settings to further speed up the acquisition. When you get back in the lab and need to create your working copy of your evidence file, you can do so by reacquiring it with "best" compression. You may also change the Block Size and Error Granularity settings back to their defaults, increasing the integrity of the evidence file. You can then let the program run overnight, thus saving space on your lab drive, and store the uncompressed original separately when done. Reacquiring with or without compression does not in any way change the MD5 of the original data stream.

Adding or removing compression or changing the block size or error granularity requires a full reacquisition process and can't be accomplished via the Quick Reacquisition option. The other two properties, changing a password or changing the file segment size, can be achieved quickly using the Quick Reacquisition option. Thus, if you need only to add or remove a password or change the chunk size, use this option to save time on the reacquisition process.

It is important to understand that reacquiring the image does not change the MD5 value of the original data stream acquired from the device if you change any or all of these five properties (compression, password, file segment size, block size, or error granularity).

The start and stop sectors can also be changed during reacquisition, but this is rarely done. If you acquire a physical device and want to reacquire only a logical partition, you can do so with this feature. You enter the start sector at the first sector of the partition and the stop sector at the last sector of that partition. Because you are changing the size of the original image, your new acquisition hash will be different from your original acquisition hash; they now represent different data streams. The new verification hash will match your new acquisition hash, however, during the verification process.

- *Read Ahead*: If you are using the Enterprise or FIM version of EnCase 5 or 6, this option speeds up acquisitions through sector caching. If you are not using Enterprise or FIM, this box is grayed out.

- *Output Path*: As previously mentioned, this value defaults to the proper location, and the filename is generated from the value you entered when you completed Name. If all is correct and to your liking, you don't need to change it. If you want, simply browse to the desired location, also changing the filename if you prefer.

- *Alternate Path*: This feature is new to EnCase 6. If you are not sure your output path location will hold your intended image, you can specify an alternate path to hold the overflow. Although prior versions prompted you if you exceeded the capacity of your intended output, with the Alternate Path feature, it happens automatically without human intervention if you specify the alternate path.

5. When all acquisition options are set, click the Finish button, and EnCase will acquire the image according to the settings you entered.

The speed of your acquisition will vary depending on the size of your target drive, the speed of your network connections, the overall performance of your two machines, and the acquisition settings you specified. As EnCase acquires the data, it calculates the amount of data imaged as a function of the time required to do so. Based on the amount of data remaining to be imaged, EnCase gives you an approximation of the time required to complete the job. This data is displayed in the progress bar in the lower right. As the imaging progresses, the figure usually increasingly becomes more accurate.

If for any reason you need to stop the acquisition, you can do so by double-clicking the progress bar. A window will appear asking you whether you want to stop. Click OK, and the process will stop.

When the process has completed, an acquisition report window will appear that provides information about the acquisition. This information may be directed to the console for use by EnScript, to a note in your bookmarks, or to a log record, as depicted in Figure 4.18.

FIGURE 4.18   Acquisition completion report with options for directing the output to various locations

If you opted to have your image added to the case or to replace the source drive upon completion, a verification process starts immediately upon the image coming into the case. The verification process involves recalculating the CRC for each block in the data stream and recalculating the MD5 hash. All recalculations are compared with the original values, and all must match to successfully verify. The original hash value is called the *Acquisition Hash*, and the hash value calculated during verification is called the *Verification Hash*. To achieve a successful verification, all CRC acquisition values must match all CRC verification values, and the Acquisition Hash must match the Verification Hash.

Figure 4.19 shows the result of a successful verification where the verification process is reporting zero errors (all CRC values matched) and the Acquisition and Verification Hashes are showing identical MD5 values. The verification information is available on the Report tab for the selected device. Only when you have conducted a successful verification of your acquisition should you consider the job complete.

FIGURE 4.19   Verification shows zero errors (CRC values matched), and the Acquisition and Verification MD5 hashes are identical.

File Integrity:	Completely Verified, 0 Errors
Acquisition Hash:	fa1a32b57675a4a6e5466f8db8337e1f
Verify Hash:	fa1a32b57675a4a6e5466f8db8337e1f

At this point, we'll move away from legacy acquisition techniques and continue with our discussions of acquisitions using today's software and hardware. You must, however, remember that there may come a time when you have to regress and use legacy methods if you encounter some type of legacy gear, because it is still out there. The more acquisition skills and capabilities you have, the better job you can do when facing atypical acquisition challenges.

Real World Scenario

Technology Time Warp

In a homicide case, in which there were three mistrials, the defendant attempted to introduce a falsified email into evidence between the last two trials. The attempt was detected, and a separate investigation was undertaken to investigate this additional crime. During the course of this investigation, we executed one search warrant and two attorney general's subpoenas in the women's correctional facility wherein the defendant was incarcerated.

Computer networks for computers used by inmates are nearly nonexistent. Rather, networking relies upon the "sneaker net," which means placing data on floppies and moving data between computers in that fashion. And I did say floppies, not CDs and not USB devices. Most of the computers used by the inmates were donations, state surpluses, and the like. That said, legacy equipment was the norm, not the exception. And, media (floppies, and so on) are contraband and not to be kept in cell areas.

Few machines had CD drives, and USB ports were few and far between. Floppy diskette drives were present in every machine, and to say that the hardware and software was old was to understate the situation.

Since no Internet was present, no antivirus software was in use, and boot sector viruses were present on nearly every machine and floppy encountered. We imaged 30 computers and more than 150 floppies on three separate days. During the imaging of the 30 computers, we used a wide array of imaging techniques, including DOS boot floppies.

We rarely see today the boot sector viruses that permeated this environment. When taking the dd (Linux disk dump) images (the result of some of the imaging techniques used) back to the lab, they suddenly disappeared. Since they had boot sector viruses, the dd images were quickly picked off by the antivirus software on the lab machines and placed in quarantine. To get around this ongoing problem, all dd images had to be reacquired and placed in EnCase compressed images.

While such situations are uncommon, you never know when or where something like this could occur. Therefore, having legacy techniques available can save the day.

Accompanying me on this assignment was the lead homicide detective for the case, Detective Joseph Szczerba. As this very chapter was being written, on September 16, 2011, Joseph Szczerba was stabbed to death while subduing a violent offender. Lieutenant Szczerba was a cop's cop, one of New Castle County's best officers, and simply a great person. May his soul rest in peace.

FastBloc/Tableau Acquisitions

FastBloc was, initially, a hardware write-blocking device developed by Guidance Software to work in conjunction with EnCase, but it does not require EnCase. FastBloc write-blocking devices have been replaced by Tableau units. FastBloc or Tableau write blockers can function as a stand-alone write-blocking device in the Windows environment, allowing you to preview the data directly in the Windows Explorer interface. Additionally, you can run third-party tools such as antivirus or spyware detection software against the target drive with full write-block functionality. In fact, the hardware versions of FastBloc can be used on other operating systems.

With the release of EnCase 6 and continuing into EnCase 7, FastBloc comes in a software version as well, dubbed FastBloc SE (Software Edition). In fact, FastBloc SE was an added-cost option in EnCase 6, while, with EnCase 7, it is included as part of the basic software suite of tools. I cover this version in "FastBloc SE Acquisitions" later in the chapter.

Available FastBloc Models

FastBloc has truly undergone numerous model evolutions since its inception. All models provide write blocking for the target drive.

The original FastBloc is now called FastBloc Classic, which has a SCSI interface with the host computer. Although still supported, it is no longer available for purchase.

The second generation of FastBloc devices are the FastBloc LE (Lab Edition) and the FastBloc FE (Field Edition).

The FastBloc LE has an IDE interface with the host computer and is better suited for semipermanent installation on the host computer. With its IDE host interface, it can be used equally as well in a DOS or Windows environment.

The FastBloc FE was the first in the series to be designed for portability. It was designed for field use and has a flexible interface, allowing USB-2 or 1394a (FireWire) host interfaces. Although both interfaces are present, you are warned not use both at the same time!

The 1394a and 1394b protocols allow "daisy chaining" of FireWire devices, which means you can add one or more FireWire devices in a chain to the second FireWire FastBloc port, provided you have connected to the host computer via the other FireWire port rather than the USB port.

WARNING   The daisy-chained devices attached to FastBloc are turned on or off with the FastBloc power switch. Furthermore, write blocking by FastBloc occurs only to the 40-pin and 44-pin IDE interfaces. Daisy-chained devices are not afforded write-block protection.

Any of the FastBloc devices mentioned thus far have an IDE interface that is write-blocked. With the addition of an IDE-to-SATA bridge, FastBloc can be used with SATA drives as well, greatly adding to its functionality.

FastBloc 2 Features

During 2006, FastBloc 2 was released. Like its predecessor, it was offered in field and lab editions, with the former being dubbed FastBloc2 FE and the latter FastBloc2 LE. The field edition, according to the Guidance Software website, contains the following features:

- Write-blocked, which protects the drive's contents by preventing disk writes. Uses industry-proven WiebeTech write block firmware.
- Computer forensic software recognition, which is recognized and reported by EnCase software.
- Daisy-chained FireWire 800 ports for endless configuration capabilities.
- Individual OXUF922 bridge for perfect compatibility and fast performance.
- ATA-5 and ATA-6 compatibility. You can use your old drives and your new, big drives as well.
- Notebook drive capability with included 2.5-inch notebook drive adapter.
- SATA compatibility with included SATA adapter that expands the range of drives that can be attached and analyzed.
- Durable anodized aluminum construction, made with briefcase-tough aluminum.
- Self-aligning drive connector to easily attach and remove disk drives.
- LED status indicators that are power attached. On and access are discernible at a glance. Access LED is red for easy monitoring of drive activity. Other LEDs are green.
- 100–240 VAC power supply. It works anywhere.
- Plug and Play. No new drivers are necessary for using with Windows 2000, Windows XP, or Windows Vista; Mac OS 9.1, 9.2, or OS X; and Linux distributions that support FireWire.
- USB 2/USB support.
- Portable with Pelican carrying case.

This is clearly a major upgrade to the previous field edition version. Guidance Software partnered with WiebeTech to produce this version. Additionally, the FastBloc2 FE can be purchased with an adapter kit, which, per the Guidance Software website, contains the following:

- Adapter for Toshiba 1.8-inch drives (the type used in Apple iPods)
- Adapter for Hitachi 1.8-inch drives
- Adapter for microdrives (used in iPod Mini and in many digital cameras) or compact flash modules
- Adapter for PC Card drives, as used in PCMCIA slots

- 3.5-inch cable adapter (for accessing conventional IDE drives in hard-to-reach places in desktop computers)
- USB 2 cable

With the adapter kit, the FastBloc2 FE can be used to image the 1.8-inch drives found in iPods and some of the smaller laptops, as well as the new microdrives, making it much more versatile because it keeps pace with the new media being continually developed.

In 2010, Guidance Software acquired the assets of Tableau, LLC. In doing so, the FastBloc product line ended, and the Tableau product line took its place. Tableau manufactures a series of write-blocking forensic bridges in both field and lab or bay-mounted types, as shown in Figure 4.20. They work in much the same way as FastBloc products such that the directions and procedures for both products are quite similar. Even so, one should always review and follow the manufacturer's instructions and resolve any differences using the manufacturer's advice.

FIGURE 4.20 Tableau product line of write-blocking forensic bridges

As for which models one should have on hand, much will depend on what devices you typically encounter; however, sooner or later, you can count on encountering most of the mainstream devices, meaning you need several models in your toolkit. The T35es model will handle IDE and SATA drives and will be the workhorse in your kit. USB thumb drives and external drives are ubiquitous, and the Forensic USB Bridge (T8-R2) is great for acquiring those devices. The FireWire Bridge (T9) is great for acquiring Macintosh computers in the Target Disk Mode (TDM) on the FireWire channel. If you work with high-end computer systems found in data centers, having a bridge for SCSI and SAS drives is needed for those times when you have to pull drives out of servers.

If you image mostly in labs, there is a series of bay-mounted forensic bridges. Which one you choose will largely depend on your needs and, of course, your budget.

No acquisition kit is complete without a series of drive adapters to connect the various connector types that seem to evolve overnight. These adapters will be needed for both IDE and SATA connections. Figure 4.21 shows the various types of adapters available from Tableau as of press time.

FIGURE 4.21   IDE and SATA disk adapters available from Tableau

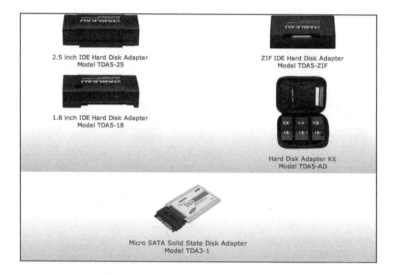

2.5 inch IDE Hard Disk Adapter
Model TDA5-25

ZIF IDE Hard Disk Adapter
Model TDA5-ZIF

1.8 inch IDE Hard Disk Adapter
Model TDA5-18

Hard Disk Adapter Kit
Model TDA5-AD

Micro SATA Solid State Disk Adapter
Model TDA3-1

Steps for Tableau (FastBloc) Acquisition

To conduct a FastBloc acquisition, you should follow these steps:

1. Connect your FastBloc to your host computer via either a USB or a 1394a/b connection (both are available on FastBloc2 FE), but not both. The host computer can be running when you make this connection, or you can make your connections while the computer is off and then boot the system.

2. Your target drive should be set for master or single if it is a Parallel ATA (PATA). Adjust the jumper accordingly. Western Digital drives can be a little persnickety and often work better with no pins at all. If your drive does not require configuration as to master/single and so forth, then disregard this step.

3. Connect the DC power from the FastBloc to the target hard drive. This applies only to 3.5-inch drives; 2.5-inch drives from laptops derive their power (5 volts only) directly through their 44-pin connection or through other connections for even smaller drives (1.8 inch drives, microdrives, and so forth).

4. Connect the IDE cable from FastBloc to the target hard drive. Most 3.5-inch hard drives should be connected using the 80-conductor cable. Some older drives, designed to operate with the 40-conductor cable specification, should use that cable. Laptop drives should be connected to the 44-pin connection. When connecting IDE connections, take care to attach the pin-1 connection to its corresponding pin-1 connection on the cable. If you are connecting the newer microdrives in their various sizes and flavors, you'll need to use an adapter that is provided with the FastBloc2 FE adapter kit to connect the target drive to FastBloc2 FE.

Most connectors are "keyed" with a notch to prevent incorrect connections. Believe it or not, with a little force you can bypass this protection, thus forcing the protruding notch to fit where it isn't supposed to fit, totally reversing all of the connections. The sidewall of the connection flexes and bulges outward to facilitate the notch. When IDE connectors get "worn," this is even more likely to occur. Just because it "fits" doesn't make it right! Pay careful attention to what you are doing, or you may see smoke where it shouldn't be. Also, take care if using longer IDE cables; the closer you get to the 18-inch maximum, the more likely communications errors will occur.

Flat-ribbon cables don't like being bent and twisted, especially repeatedly. They protest this treatment by failing when you least want them to fail! Invest in a few 6-inch and 12-inch-round shielded IDE cables with a single IDE 40-pin connection on each end. Use the 6-inch one when you have the hard drive detached, and use the 12-inch one when you have to "reach" a mounted hard drive in a case. The shielding in these cables guards against communications errors, facilitating fast, error-free acquisitions. The round cable design makes them flexible and impervious to wear and tear from the repeated use that is typical of forensics work.

5. Connect the power supply to FastBloc, and power on FastBloc. If the host computer is already running, Plug and Play (PnP) should recognize FastBloc and mount the attached hard drive.

6. If the host computer is not on, boot it up at this time. During start-up, PnP should recognize FastBloc and mount the attached drive.

7. You can confirm that FastBloc (or Tableau) was detected and mounted by opening the Device Manager (right-click My Computer, and choose Properties; on the Hardware tab, choose Device Manager). Under Disk Drives, you should see FastBloc listed, as shown in Figure 4.22. If Windows can recognize and successfully mount any of the partitions on the target drive, it will do so when FastBloc is mounted. When this is the case, you can preview the partitions with Windows Explorer. Sometimes partitions aren't mounted, but they are partitions that Windows should recognize and mount. Perhaps there is something about the partition that Windows finds problematic and won't mount. If the physical drive is mounted, EnCase will see the partitions when Windows refuses to do so.

FIGURE 4.22 When FastBloc is successfully detected and mounted by Windows PnP, FastBloc is listed under Disk Drives, as shown here in the Windows Device Manager.

8. Run EnCase in Windows on the host examination computer to which FastBloc is attached. Open a case, or start a new case. When a case (new or old) is open, you'll be on the case home page. Under the Evidence section, click Add Evidence.

9. On the screen that follows, since FastBloc mounts the drive locally, choose Add Local Device, as shown in Figure 4.23.

FIGURE 4.23 FastBloc is a mounted local device; therefore, you can click Add Local Device to access FastBloc.

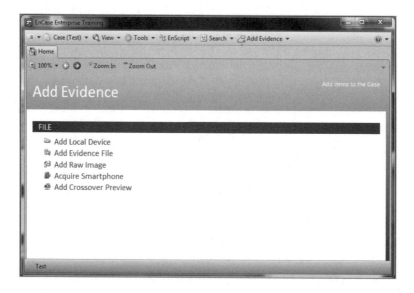

10. On the screen that follows, accept the defaults for now, unless you are using a legacy FastBloc, meaning one predating the Tableau units. If you are using a legacy FastBloc, check the box Detect Legacy FastBloc, as shown in Figure 4.24, and click Next. The Add Local Device screen appears next as a listing of all local devices (physical and logical), as shown in Figure 4.25. EnCase 7 shows volumes under and offset from their parent physical devices, making them much better to comprehend at a glance. Under Choose Devices, you see a listing of all local devices, both logical and physical.

Recall that the blue triangle at the lower-right corner of the icon denotes a live device. FastBloc doesn't have a blue triangle; instead, it has its own special icon, making it easy to identify the write-blocked target drive. The FastBloc icon is the device symbol with a square around it in (blue in EnCase 5 or green in EnCase 6 and 7). Additionally, in the Write Blocked column, you'll see an indicator in the column next to the FastBloc device. The indicator is a Boolean indicator for true, meaning the device is write-blocked. Sometimes this blue square or green square can be missing along with the Boolean indicator for true in the Write Blocked column. The cause is typically a cable issue or an improperly jumpered drive. Even if the blue or green square and the Boolean indicator for true are missing, the device attached to FastBloc is still write-protected. With a blue check, select the physical device that is indicated with the Fast-Bloc icon, as shown in Figure 4.25. Any mounted partitions on the device connected to FastBloc will also be displayed with a green square. Selecting the physical device gives you all the sectors on the physical device, whereas selecting the logical device gives you only the sectors within that partition. Almost always you will seek all the sectors and will select the physical device.

FIGURE 4.24 If using a legacy FastBloc (predating Tableau units), you must check this box for detection to occur.

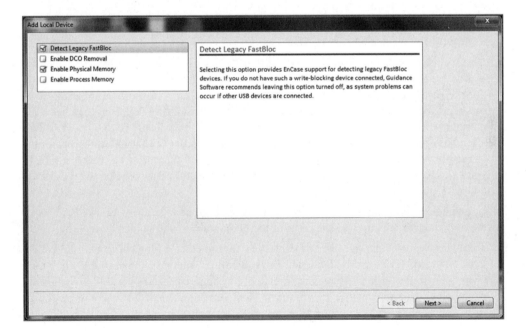

 The Boolean indicator for Show True is, by default, a dot. For Show False, the default indicator is nothing or null. Many examiners prefer to change this to Yes and No for added clarity. You can do this by choosing Tools ➢ Options ➢ Global. You can replace the dot for Show True with Yes and the null for Show False with No. Figure 4.25 reflects this change.

FIGURE 4.25   Choose Devices window. FastBloc devices are denoted with a blue square (EnCase 5) or a green square (EnCase 6 and 7) icon indicating their write-blocked status.

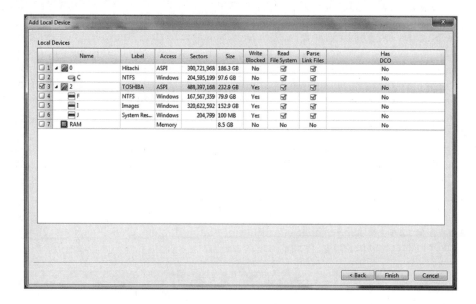

11. Before clicking Next to proceed, confirm that EnCase, through the BIOS interface in Windows, is able to see all the sectors on the drive as reported by the manufacturer. For the FastBloc physical device (not logical!), check to see that in the number of sectors reported by EnCase in the Sectors column (in this case 488,397,168) matches the number reported by the manufacturer for this drive on its website. Also, note that there is a column named Has DCO. If present, a Yes will appear. If a DCO is present, return to the previous screen, check Enable DCO Removal, and then proceed. Once satisfied, you can access all the sectors on your target drive, select the FastBloc physical device, and click Finish.

12. Upon clicking Finish, you'll see your evidence object appear as a row on the Evidence tab, which is immediately to the right of the Home tab, as shown in Figure 4.26.

13. To preview your evidence object or drive, you should place a blue check on it and click Load Selected Device on the Evidence Tab toolbar, or you can simply double-click the object. It will take a few minutes for the device to be parsed and viewable in the Tree pane, which will appear in a few minutes. Most veteran users of EnCase will recognize this view when it loads. Figure 4.27 shows the Tree pane.

FIGURE 4.26   Evidence object appearing as a row on the Evidence tab

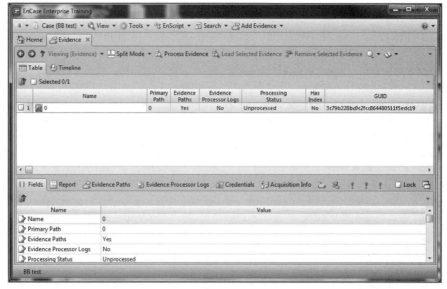

FIGURE 4.27   EnCase 7 Tree pane from which you can navigate the device. From this pane, you can also acquire the live device being previewed by placing the object to be acquired in the Table pane, selecting it, and clicking Acquire on the Evidence Tab toolbar.

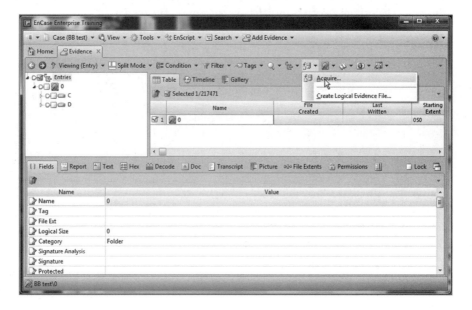

14. At this stage you can preview the drive, searching and bookmarking as is necessary. In Exercise 4.1, you will have the opportunity to preview your own hard drive, and you'll see how this works. You can also produce a report and print it directly or save it as a web document or as a Rich Text File (RTF)–formatted file, which is usable by most word processing software. If you create search hits, bookmarks, and so forth, and acquire the device (selecting the Replace Source Drive option), those search hits and bookmarks will transfer and resolve to the image, keeping your work intact.

15. If you opt to acquire the FastBloc/Tableau device, you can do so at this time. The acquisition will occur completely in the EnCase for Windows environment with full hardware write-block protection for the target drive. Veteran EnCase users are used to right-clicking and the device and choosing acquire, but EnCase 7 no longer provides that option. Acquisition is available by many means. If you chose to process the evidence object on the Evidence tab's Table pane, you could acquire it as a precursor to processing for evidence. From the Tree pane, where you currently are, you can also acquire. First, from the Tree pane, force the object to be acquired to appear in the Table pane. Place your cursor on that object in the Table pane. With the focus on the object to be acquired, click the Acquire icon on the Evidence tab's toolbar, which is shown in Figure 4.24. At the far right of the same toolbar is a drop-down menu from which acquisition is also available.

At this point, you will see the EnCase 7 acquisition options. Previous versions have placed this information on one busy menu screen, whereas EnCase 7 spreads them out over three tabs, which are Location, Format, and Advanced.

Figure 4.28 shows the Location tab where the name, evidence number, and notes are entered. In addition, the Mirror Acquisition, Restart Acquisition, and Remote Acquisition options are available. Finally, the output path can be selected as well as an alternate path in the event the primary path is insufficient to contain the data.

FIGURE 4.28 EnCase 7 acquisition options Location tab

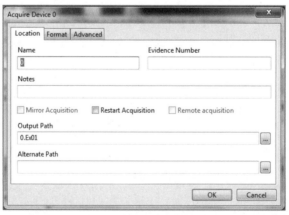

Figure 4.29 shows the Format tab where the evidence file format (Ex01 or E01) can be selected, as well as compression, hashing, and file segment size options. From this tab you can also apply encryption to the evidence file and set a password, although this is not normally recommended.

FIGURE 4.29   EnCase 7 Format options tab

Figure 4.30 shows the Advanced tab where the Block Size, Error Granularity, Start Sector, Stop Sector, Read Ahead, and thread options can be set.

FIGURE 4.30   EnCase 7 Advanced options tab

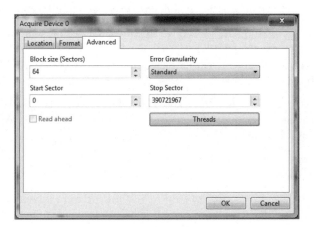

When your acquisition is done, on the Report tab for the imaged FastBloc device, a notation appears that the acquisition was completed using FastBloc, which documents the write-protected acquisition method.

Although you can use other hardware write-blocking devices in EnCase, only FastBloc or Tableau units will currently show with a blue square icon (Version 5) or a green square icon (Version 6 and 7) and the Boolean true for write-blocked. Also, only FastBloc or Tableau will show as write-protected in the device-acquisition report.

Windows 7 is currently recommended for running EnCase 7. The 64-bit version is much preferred over the 32-bit version because EnCase needs the resources and memory management provided by this platform.

EXERCISE 4.1

Previewing Your Own Hard Drive

Previewing your own hard drive using EnCase is an excellent technique for testing and research. You can also use it to study or familiarize yourself with various acquisition options.

You may also find it helpful to refer to Figures 4.22 through 4.30 if you need help or visual support.

1. Launch EnCase (*with dongle*), start a new case, and simply accept the defaults.

2. Click Add Evidence.

3. Click Add Local Device, accept the defaults on the screen that follows, and click Next.

4. Place a blue check next to your hard drive (the physical device; your boot or system hard drive will usually be drive 0), and click Next. Then click Finish on the next screen. EnCase should return you to the Evidence tab with your hard drive showing as an object in the Table pane.

5. To have EnCase parse your drive and show its objects, you must blue check (select) the drive and select Load Selected Evidence from the Evidence tab's toolbar or simply double-click the drive. It will take a few minutes to parse and load.

6. Once EnCase has parsed your drive, it will appear in the Tree pane. You can preview it at this point if you'd like.

7. In the Tree pane, place your cursor on Entries, at the top or root level. This will force your hard drive, the physical device, to appear in the Table pane. In the Table pane, place your cursor on this physical device. By placing your cursor (focus) on it, it becomes the object or your next action, which is acquisition. With your focus on your

drive, click the acquisition icon and drop-down menu on the Evidence tab's toolbar (refer to Figure 4.24 for help locating this icon). From this drop-down menu, choose Acquire.

8. From the Location tab, under Name, type a name, such as **HDD01**. Note how EnCase automatically inserts this name in one other location, which is in the filename portion of the Output Path entry. You can change this if you'd like.

9. From the Format tab, note that the default evidence file format is ex01, that compression is enabled by default, that the MD5 hash is the default, that the file segment size is 2048 MB (2 GB), and that no password / encryption is enabled. I suggest looking at the options for each of these settings.

10. From the Advanced tab, note that Block Size is set to 64 sectors. Note that Error Granularity, by default, is standard. With EnCase 7, Error Granularity is no longer an integer but rather either Standard (same number of sectors as the block size) or Exhaustive (one sector). Unless you have a reason to do otherwise, these default settings are recommended. Next, you can see your Start and Stop Sector defining the range of your acquisition. Normally you would not need to change these. Finally, you see that you can adjust the threads, both reader and worker threads.

11. Click Cancel, and you are back to your case.

12. From the Tree pane, click the back or left arrow (situated directly below the Home icon) to return to the Table pane of the Evidence tab. Place a blue check on your hard drive. On the Evidence tab's toolbar, click Remove Selected Evidence.

13. Close EnCase.

FastBloc SE Acquisitions

Beginning with EnCase 7, FastBloc SE is part of the basic feature set and is no longer an added-cost option.

About FastBloc SE

With this version of FastBloc, SE, you can use special drive controller software in EnCase to control reads and writes to attached evidentiary media. FastBloc SE can control writes to Plug and Play drives on USB, FireWire, and SCSI channels.

HPA and DCO

Earlier in this chapter, I discussed HPA and DCO, which are special protected areas of a hard drive that are ordinarily hidden from view. As you'll recall, to view them in EnCase for DOS, you had to use the direct access mode.

With FastBloc SE, HPA and DCO support is present as long as the controller card in the forensics machine is ATA-6 compliant. If only an HPA is present, the HPA settings are temporarily removed and later replaced. If a DCO is present, the DCO settings are permanently removed. If a DCO and an HPA are present, both the HPA and DCO settings are permanently removed.

These settings are stored in the onboard controller memory only. No changes are made to the data stored on the drive. Nevertheless, you should document this change when you encounter it.

Steps for FastBloc SE Acquisitions

To use the FastBloc SE to protect Plug and Play USB, FireWire, or SCSI devices from writes, first make sure no devices are attached. Once that is done, follow these steps:

1. Launch EnCase, and choose Tools ➤ FastBloc SE, as shown in Figure 4.31.

2. From the ensuing dialog box, choose Write Blocked, as shown in Figure 4.32. At this point, the EnCase software begins scanning the buses, watching for any device to be attached. When one is detected, EnCase imposes a write block on it and notifies you.

Test First!

Before acquiring real evidence, you should, according to best practices, test the hardware and software to make certain that write-blocking protection is being successfully implemented. To do so, mount a nonevidentiary drive, one that has been hashed first, in the write-protected configuration described previously. Although the drive is write-protected, you should attempt to alter data on the drive. When done, shut down the forensic computer, remove the test drive, and hash it again on a known platform or device. Both hashes should match, and if they don't, you have a problem with either hardware, software, or technique. You should repeat your test a few times and document the results. If at any point either the hardware or software changes, you should test and document again.

FIGURE 4.31   The FastBloc SE option on Tools menu

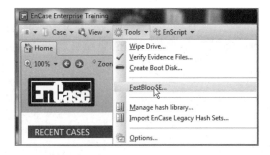

FIGURE 4.32   The FastBloc SE dialog box

3. Attach the PnP device to the system (USB, FireWire, or SCSI).

When the device appears in the list of volumes and you see Yes or a dot in the Write Blocked column, as shown in Figure 4.33, the attached device is write-blocked.

FIGURE 4.33 The FastBloc SE dialog box showing the device attached and its "write-blocked" status

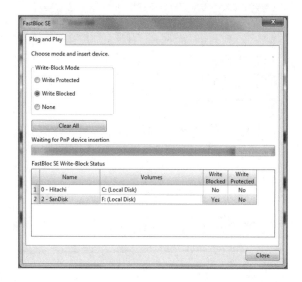

4. In EnCase, either create a new case or open an existing one.

5. On the case home page, click Add Evidence and then Add Local Device. On the page that follows, accept the defaults and click Next. On the screen that follows, shown in Figure 4.34, you will see a dot or Yes in the Write Blocked column, and the icon for the device will have a green box around it, both indicating a successful write block.

FIGURE 4.34 List of local devices showing that the device just added is write-blocked

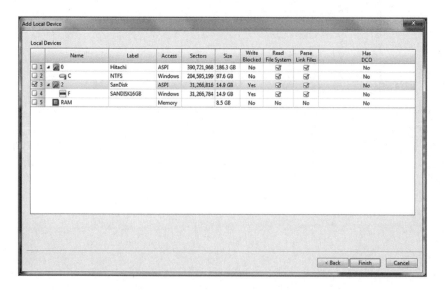

6. Select the write-blocked target device (blue check), and click Finish. The device will appear in EnCase in the Evidence tab's Table view. At this point, you can choose to process and acquire as part of the processing. Alternatively, you can double-click the evidence object, causing it to parse and be displayed in the Tree pane. From the Tree pane, you can preview and acquire in the customary manner.

Write Block or Write Protect?

With the FastBloc SE tool, you have the option of two different types of write blocking or protecting. For sure, both protect the device from writes. If you choose Write Block, writes are prevented but are cached locally to prevent Windows error messages. If you choose Write Protect, writes are prevented, nothing is cached locally, and Windows launches error messages when writes are attempted, which occurs upon mounting. Unless you enjoy Microsoft error messages, you will usually use the Write Block option. Some users, however, enjoy the reassurance of the error messages, because they know that write protection is at work.

When you are finished previewing/acquiring the write-blocked device, carry out the following steps to remove the device and the write-blocking feature:

1. Physically remove the device from host computer. You could attempt to eject it, but the system will see the device in use and not allow it to be stopped. Because it is write-blocked, physically removing it will not harm it.

2. Next, you need to stop the write-blocking software in EnCase. In EnCase, choose Tools ➢ FastBloc SE. Refer to Figure 4.33, and note that there is a Clear All button. Click this button, and you'll receive a Clear All confirmation window (Figure 4.35) asking whether you want to remove the write-blocking protection. Choose Yes, and you'll receive confirmation that it has been done and will take effect when the next device is plugged in, as shown in Figure 4.36. Next, close the FastBloc SE dialog box, and you are finished.

FIGURE 4.35   Confirm the All Clear window that removes write-blocking on all devices.

FIGURE 4.36   Confirmation that write blocking has been removed

FastBloc SE is a powerful and versatile set of various write-blocking utilities. The USB, FireWire, and SCSI write-blocking tools don't require any hardware, relying upon write blocking at the Plug and Play level, and make them quite handy for field work. Either way, examiners are given more options and tools to protect evidentiary media in a world of rapidly evolving media types.

LinEn Acquisitions

LinEn, or EnCase for Linux, is a new feature of EnCase 5 and newer versions. Since EnCase 6, the DOS version of EnCase (EN.EXE) is no longer provided, and you will have only LinEn available. LinEn is similar to EnCase for DOS, but it offers all the advantages of running under Linux. DOS is a legacy 16-bit operating system, whereas Linux, like Windows, is a 32-bit or 64-bit operating system. Thus, you get tremendous performance advantages using LinEn compared to EnCase for DOS.

Mounting a File System as Read-Only

Unlike DOS or Windows, Linux enables you to manually select whether you want to mount a file system as read-only. In doing so, you are able to manually mount target evidence media in a write-protected manner, protected by the operating system instead of other methods or devices. To achieve this, however, you'll need to turn off the automounting of file systems in Linux so that when it boots, file systems are not mounted. That enables you to mount devices manually, carefully controlling the process. To do this in SUSE and Red Hat, do the following:

- For SUSE, run Yast (Yet Another System Tool) by choosing Main Menu ➤ System ➤ Configuration. Open the Runlevel Editor, and disable the autofs feature.

- For Red Hat, run Services, which is located in Main Menu ➤ System Settings ➤ Server Settings. Disable the autofs feature.

Many people prefer to run LinEn from their favorite Linux distribution on a boot CD, such as Helix, Knoppix, SPADA, and so forth. Many of these security distributions of Linux already boot with the automounting of file systems disabled or mount systems read-only, depending on how they have been configured or reconfigured in some cases. You should test your version to see how it mounts file systems when it boots. You could remaster the boot CD to include LinEn, but that necessitates doing so each time LinEn is updated. Instead, place your updated copy of LinEn on your FAT32 storage volume or removable USB drive, and run LinEn from that location. This keeps your Linux boot CD clean with no need for constant updating and places the updated copy of LinEn on the writable storage volume, making for an efficient working platform or methodology.

LinEn Ships on Helix and Other Linux Security Boot Disks

Various versions of Helix (available from www.e-fense.com/helix/) actually include LinEn in their GUI under Forensics, making it easy to use. The latest version of Raptor now includes LinEn as well.

EnCase can update the Helix distribution with the latest version of LinEn. This does not replace the version of LinEn that ships with Helix. Rather, EnCase places the updated version in the root of the CD. If you run LinEn from the Helix GUI, you'll run the older version. To run the updated version, use the root console, making sure you are root (# in the prompt). At the command line, type the following, pressing Enter after each line:

```
cd /cdrom
./LinEn
```

The LinEn console will run, and you can acquire using the newest version of LinEn. Before you do this, however, you'll need to mount a read-write drive on which to place your image, or you'll need to prepare your network connections if you plan to do a network connection to make your acquisition. The instructions for these tasks follow. For now, I just wanted you to know about Helix and how to access the updated version of LinEn that EnCase can install onto Helix.

This version of Helix (free version) is no longer available as a free download. Paid users of Helix 3 have access to the last free version from the download area at www.e-fense.com. Because this distribution was widely used and circulated, it is very much still in use and popular, although its use will certainly begin to fade as the outdated Linux kernel starts to get long in the tooth and fails to support newer hardware. Meanwhile, for those still using it, the previous information very much still applies.

Updating a Linux Boot CD with the Latest Version of LinEn

To update a Linux boot CD, you'll first need to render the Linux boot CD into an ISO image. There are many tools to do this. I like to use WinISO for this purpose. Once this step is done, follow these steps:

1. Launch EnCase, and choose Tools ➢ Create Boot Disk. You'll see the dialog box shown in Figure 4.37.

2. Choose ISO Image, and click OK. You'll see the Formatting Options dialog box, as shown in Figure 4.38.

FIGURE 4.37   The Choose Destination dialog box

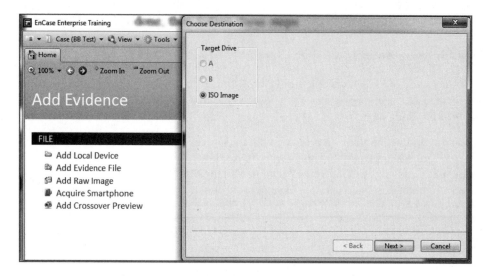

FIGURE 4.38   The Formatting Options dialog box

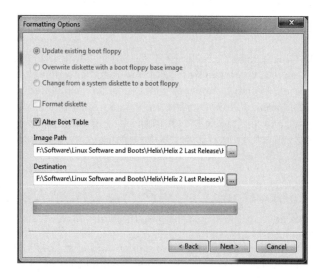

3. Choose Alter Boot Table check box, browse to the path containing the ISO file, and then browse to a path and filename for your modified ISO that EnCase will create.

When ready, click Next. The next dialog box, shown in Figure 4.39, allows you to add files to the ISO image.

FIGURE 4.39   The Copy Files dialog box

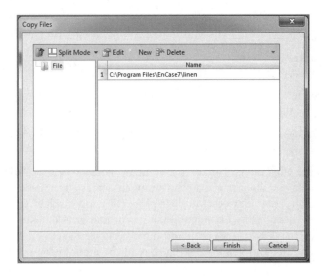

4. In the Copy Files dialog box, right-click in the right pane, and choose New. You will then be able to browse to the location of LinEn, which is in the root of the folder `Program Files\EnCase7`. When ready, click Finish, and EnCase will insert the updated version of LinEn in the root of the CD and will create the new ISO at that path you specified.

5. Your final step is to burn the ISO onto a CD using the burner of your choosing.

Running LinEn

When running LinEn, you must be running as `root` because you must be in total control of the system. Although LinEn will run in the Linux GUI, the GUI uses system resources and limits the resources available to LinEn. For best performance, run LinEn in the console mode.

 The next paragraph contains instructions for those running Linux from a hard drive installation. Changing the runlevel on a CD distribution is for advanced Linux users.

To configure Linux to boot in the console mode, you'll need to modify the boot runlevel, which is controlled by the file `inittab` located in the `/etc` folder. Edit the `inittab` file with your favorite text editor (vi is one such tool). Locate the line in the `inittab` file that reads `id:5:initdefault:`. The 5 tells Linux to boot to the GUI. Change the 5 to a 3, which will cause Linux to boot to the console mode. Remember to save your changes! When Linux reboots, it will start in console mode. You should leave your forensic Linux system set up to boot this way. You can always run the GUI by typing **startx**.

Before mounting drives and starting LinEn, you need to get used to a different way of looking at devices from what you might be accustomed to viewing in Windows. Linux will list IDE devices as follows:

hda: Primary Master
hdb: Primary Slave
hdc: Secondary Master
hdd: Secondary Slave

For partitions on a hard drive, Linux will append a partition number to the hard drive designator. Examples include the following:

hdc1: Secondary Master First Partition
hda3: Primary Master Third Partition

If you are not sure what devices are on a system, at the console type **fdisk -l**, and the devices will display. If you want to see all the mounted devices, type **mount** at the console, and press Enter. All mounted devices and their properties will display. To see more display options for either of these or any Linux command, type **man fdisk** at the console, and press Enter. Replace fdisk with the command of your choice to see others. The command man stands for "manual," and you are asking to read the manual for any command that follows man.

Before you start, have a storage volume ready to accept your EnCase evidence file. When creating any storage volume, it is recommended you employ best forensic practices and wipe the drive first. This avoids any claims of cross-contamination of evidence file data. Use a FAT32 volume with a unique volume label for this purpose. Although Linux can read NTFS, with the appropriate distribution or module, writes to NTFS are not stable enough for evidentiary work, with few drivers available for this purpose (and they are in beta at best). An EXT2/3-formatted partition can be used for faster evidence file writing in Linux; however, the evidence file segments must be moved to a FAT or NTFS partition prior to examination with EnCase Windows. Optionally, you could load a driver to allow Windows to mount EXT2/3 partitions, thereby allowing direct use of the EXT2/3 partitions. Given that, you should connect your storage volume to your Linux imaging platform.

Linux Writes to NTFS

Currently, most Linux distributions ship with the relatively new NTFS-3G driver, by which Linux can both read and write to NTFS partitions. In the event you are using an older distribution, you can download the driver. As with any change, you should test and validate before using it in a forensic setting.

At this point, you should be ready to begin. You should have done the following:

- Configured your Linux system so that the autofs (automounting of file systems) is off and file systems will not be mounted on boot.
- Configured your Linux system to boot into the console mode.
- Attached your target drive to the Linux imaging platform.
- Attached your storage drive (FAT32 with unique volume label) to the Linux imaging platform.
- Placed LinEn on either the Linux volume or the storage drive. Either way, it should be in a known location so you can easily find and execute it.

Steps for LinEn Acquisition

To conduct an acquisition using LinEn, you should follow these steps:

1. Boot your Linux machine to the console, and log in as root.

2. Check to see what file systems are mounted. Type **mount**, and press Enter. Your target drive should not be mounted.

3. Check to see what devices are available. Type **fdisk -l**, and press Enter. Locate your target drive and your storage drive. You should know how you connected them (primary master, and so on) and should be able to locate them using the Linux naming convention (hda for primary master, and so on).

4. Mount your storage drive. Create a directory by typing **mkdir /mnt/fat32**. Mount the storage volume on this mount point by typing **mount /dev/hda1 /mnt/fat32**. Remember that Linux is case sensitive and that FAT and fat are quite different in Linux. Remember also that hda1 means the first partition on the primary master. If you storage volume is elsewhere, adjust accordingly.

5. Check that your storage drive is mounted by again typing **mount** and pressing Enter. You should see your storage volume mounted.

6. If you have not yet done so, create the folder on your storage volume to hold the EnCase evidence file. (This location must already exist and will not be created by LinEn.) Do so by typing **cd /mnt/fat32**. You will be in the root of your mounted storage volume. Using the mkdir command, you can create a suitable directory, such as /cases/casename/evidence. It is best to do this when you format it and when you don't have evidence drives mounted. With that methodology, mistakes are less likely to occur.

7. Navigate to the location where LinEn is located. Assuming it is in /mnt/fat32/encase/LinEn, type **cd /mnt/fat32/encase**, and press Enter. Then type **ls -al**, and press Enter. You should see LinEn, but note that the default name is all lowercase, linen. Because Linux is case sensitive, you must type it as it appears! If you prefer it as LinEn, as it is often dubbed, just rename it.

8. Launch LinEn by typing **./LinEn** and pressing Enter. Unless the path where LinEn is located appears in your defined PATH, you'll need to prefix the command with **./**, which tells Linux to look in the current directory for the command that follows. There is no space between **./** and the command that follows, **LinEn**. If you insert a space, you'll get an error. If you get a Permission Denied error, you'll need to change the permissions on the file. Type **chmod 777 LinEn**, and it should work.

9. LinEn should launch, and you should see an interface that is similar to EnCase for DOS. Note that the Lock tab is missing; Linux is handling that function. Linux communicates directly with the hardware, which means the Mode tab is also not needed. You are left with Acquire, Hash, Server, and Quit, as shown in Figure 4.40.

FIGURE 4.40   LinEn as shown at start-up with options for Acquire, Hash, Server, and Quit

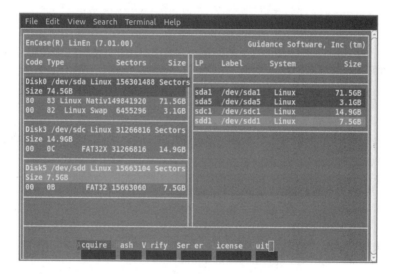

10. You can conduct an MD5 hash using the Hash tool. With this you can hash a physical drive or logical volume.

11. To acquire an image, press A or use the Tab key to go to Acquire and press Enter. What you see next is a choice of physical and logical devices available to image, as shown in Figure 4.41. However, they appear as Linux sees them. Therefore, you'll need to know how you connected your device and its properties such as its size, volume name, and so forth, to identify it. If you are accustomed to Linux, it's a snap. If you are accustomed to Windows, it will require some learning on your part. Select your device, and press Enter.

FIGURE 4.41 Choose a drive to acquire in LinEn, noting that devices use the Linux naming conventions.

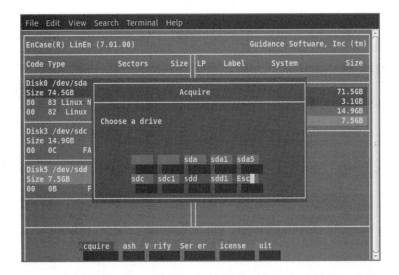

12. You are next prompted for the path for your evidence file. Although this prompt is the same as EnCase for DOS, the path you type must satisfy the Linux path requirements and must be case sensitive as well. Recall that you created a directory on your storage drive (FAT32) and called it /cases/casename/evidence. To address that in Linux, you need to prefix it with the path to the mount path; it would appear as /mnt/winfat/ cases/casename/evidence/*USBTD001*, with *USBTD001* representing the name of the evidence file you want to create.

13. From this point forward, all screens are the same as you found in EnCase for DOS with one exception. In EnCase for DOS, the block size was fixed at 64 sectors because of DOS limitations, and changing the block size was not an option. In Linux, however, it is an option. After you enter your Maximum File Size or file chunk size option, you will have the opportunity to adjust the block size. The same pros and cons previously discussed for block sizes apply; they apply equally to the Error Granularity setting, which immediately follows the Block Size option.

14. Once you've entered the Error Granularity setting, LinEn starts acquiring, providing you with the same acquisition status screen you saw in EnCase for DOS. When the image is complete, you get another window telling you it is done, the name and path of the file, and the time it took to acquire.

15. You have the option in LinEn to acquire via network cable. (Thankfully, there is no parallel cable option!) The physical setup is the same: you connect your Linux imaging machine (lab or suspect) to a Windows machine running EnCase using a network crossover cable. At this point, the process is the same as in EnCase for DOS. If you

can't make a connection, exit LinEn. To make things work, you may have to assign an IP address to the Linux platform and different host IP on the same logical network for the Windows machine. I covered the method of changing the Windows IP and network settings in "Steps for Network Acquisition" earlier in this chapter. Refer to that information, and set the Windows machine to 10.0.0.50 and a subnet mask of 255.0.0.0. For the Linux machine, do the following:

1. At the console command line, type **ifconfig eth0**.

2. If no IP is assigned or one is assigned that doesn't fall in the 10.0.0.*x* network, you need to assign one. Type **ifconfig eth0 10.0.0.1 netmask 255.0.0.0**, and press Enter.

3. Type **ifconfig eth0** again, and check to make sure your settings are there (if you belong to the doubtful lot, like many of are, who like to check and double-check). It's like a carpenter who measures three times and cuts once!

4. Restart LinEn, and start the server. Restart EnCase on Windows, and follow the steps for making a network cable acquisition. When you have to choose devices in EnCase for Windows, the list of available devices will again be as Linux sees them and names them. Everything else is the same.

HPA and DCO in LinEn

LinEn supports direct access mode if the underlying Linux distribution supports it. If it doesn't, you won't see it. Thus, whether HPA or DCO can be seen and acquired by LinEn depends on your Linux distribution.

Remember that what is supported in the way of attached devices (USB, FireWire, SCSI, and so forth) depends completely on the Linux distribution being used. For the best device support, use the most current distributions of Linux, and update them with the most current version of LinEn.

Enterprise and FIM Acquisitions

EnCase Forensic allows you to preview and acquire over a network crossover cable, with the length of the crossover cable setting the limit as to how far apart the machines can be. With the EnCase Enterprise (EE) and EnCase Field Intelligence Model (FIM; its end of life is with EnCase 6) editions of EnCase, the preview and acquisition occur over the network and can occur over thousands of miles if need be. In a later release of EnCase 7, EnCase Forensic will have the ability to preview and acquire one machine at a time over the network. The only practical limitation is the speed of the connection. This method of preview and acquisition cuts travel expenses drastically and enables incident-response time to be cut to near zero levels, if the systems are in place when the incident occurs.

Another distinction between the network cable preview and acquisition and one done with EE or FIM is that with EE and FIM, the target system is live and running its native operating system. As such, the target machine can be examined with or without the user's knowledge and the live system-state data (volatile data) can be previewed and captured. By capturing the volatile system-state data, examiners can analyze running processes, network connections, logged-in users, and much more. Such data is valuable when examining network intrusions, mounted encrypted volumes (if mounted, they can be previewed and acquired intact), cases where malicious code is running, and cases where covert analysis is warranted. The live system-state data is accessed by an optional feature called Snapshot, which is a sophisticated EnScript located, naturally, in the EnScript section.

This is not intended to be a tutorial on how to configure, administer, and use EE or FIM. That involves two weeks of training and is beyond the scope of this book. Rather, the intent here is to familiarize you with the function and features so you can understand them well enough to intelligently decide on their applicability in any given situation should the need arise to deploy them.

The major differences between the EE version and the FIM version are in licensing and configuration. The FIM version can be licensed only to law enforcement and military customers. The EE version is, essentially, for everyone else needing EE/FIM features. Additionally, the FIM was licensed for only one simultaneous connection, whereas EE starts at three connections and goes up depending on customer need and licensing agreements. The Snapshot feature that captures live system-state data is a separate license and is enabled for all connections when purchased.

To understand the configuration differences, you must first understand how EE is configured and functions; only then can you appreciate how FIM differs from EE. There are three major components of an EE/FIM system. As shown in Figure 4.42, those components are the examination machine, the servlet node (target machine), and the SAFE.

FIGURE 4.42 Schematic of EnCase Enterprise. Note the three components: the examination machine, the servlet node (target machine), and the SAFE.

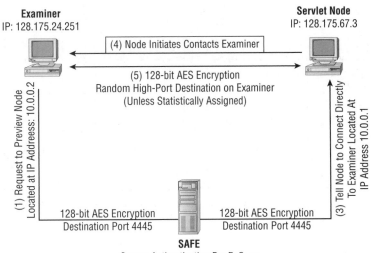

As the examiner, you have EE on your examination machine. Your target machine (servlet node), however many miles away, must have a servlet installed and running. A *servlet* is a small piece of code that places the target machine in a server mode listening on the network for a connection. The servlet is thus a server that will communicate with your examination machine, and it must also communicate with yet another machine called a SAFE. SAFE, as explained earlier, stands for Secure Authentication for EnCase. The SAFE is not technically necessary for a network forensic connection, but it is necessary to place a high-level of security and supervisory control over the entire process.

The function of the examination machine and the servlet node (target machine) are self-evident, because they are analogous to the two machines in the network cable acquisition model. What is slightly different, however, is the installation of the servlet. The servlet acts as a secure network connection to the examination machine, after first authenticating through the SAFE. The servlet allows EE to have physical access to the target computer at a level below the operating system. When installed, the servlet listens on port 4445, but you can configure it for other ports when you create and install it.

The servlet can be preinstalled by a variety of methods, or it can be installed when needed. You can be physically present for the installation, or you can deploy the servlet remotely by using one of many remote administration tools or "push technologies," such as Active Directory. It can be done manually or automated with scripts. To install the servlet on Windows systems, you must have administrator rights. On Linux/Unix, you must have root-level privileges. Guidance Software has published a small manual, available on its website, that deals strictly with deploying servlets.

The SAFE, the new piece in the model, is a stand-alone machine that stands between, initially, the examination machine and the servlet node. The SAFE is usually administered by, or at the direction of, a high-level person in the organization, typically at the level of the chief information officer or equivalent.

This SAFE administrator controls what servlet nodes the examiner can access and is dubbed the *keymaster*. The granularity of control is very coarse or very fine. The controls can determine the days and times an examiner can access a given node. Further, the controls can determine the level of functions permitted to the examiner. For example, an examiner can be limited to previewing only and not permitted to acquire or copy files.

Each examiner must be added to the list of examiners for each SAFE and is assigned keys for authentication and encryption. Before a node can be accessed by an examiner, the keymaster must log on to the SAFE and add the servlet node to the list of nodes the examiner may access, along with any limitations on that access. Furthermore, all traffic between any devices in the EE system is encrypted using 128-bit Advanced Encryption Standard (AES) encryption. Thus, the SAFE provides supervisory oversight, serves as an authentication gateway, and facilitates the encryption of the network connection.

When an examiner wants to connect to a target machine, the examiner communicates with the SAFE with a request to do so. If the requested connection and access is permitted by the established rules, the SAFE communicates with the target node. The SAFE tells the target node to communicate directly with the examination machine. The servlet node (target machine) then communicates directly with the examination machine, and the session takes place with whatever controls may be in place as directed by the SAFE. This connection is depicted in Figure 4.42.

Firewalls will have to be configured to enable this traffic to pass. Any host-based firewall on a servlet node will also have to be configured to allow the servlet connection to pass. As a fail-safe, if for any reason the servlet node can't connect directly to the examination machine, the connection may route to the examination machine through the SAFE. Although the connection will be somewhat slower, it will, nevertheless, occur. With EnCase 6, the servlet has the ability to initiate a timed, unsolicited, outbound connection to the SAFE for snapshot purposes. This is designed for users who are operating behind a firewall.

The FIM was basically an EE system with one slight configuration modification. With the FIM, the SAFE is located directly on the examiner's machine, usually a laptop, and the examiner and the keymaster are the same person. Because there is no third-party keymaster overseeing the connections, the FIM has become a very powerful tool. It was developed for law enforcement and military applications. EnCase Forensic 7.04 is planning to continue this functionality.

Figure 4.43 shows the FIM configuration. If you look carefully, the major difference is where the SAFE is located. In the EE, the SAFE is located on the SAFE administrator's PC. In the FIM, the SAFE is located on the examination machine, removing the third party altogether. Otherwise, they function in the same manner.

FIGURE 4.43   FIM schematic with SAFE located on examiner's machine. Compare this to EE schematic in Figure 4.42, where SAFE is a separate machine controlled by the SAFE administrator (keymaster).

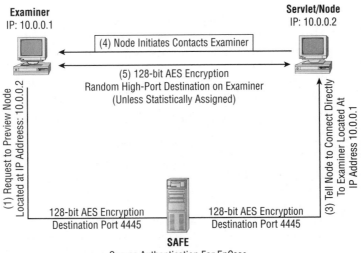

In law enforcement and military applications, the FIM is often connected to a target host (servlet node) directly with a crossover cable. Of course, this differs from the network cable acquisition since the target host is live and the servlet is installed directly by the examiner. Usually, with most home machines, the user has administrator rights and servlet deployment is a minor task. When the connection is made, the examiner has access to the storage media on the target host plus the live system-state data.

The FIM is not limited to a crossover cable connection and can also connect to any network machine on which the servlet is deployed. In law enforcement and military use, it is ideal for surreptitious remote previewing and acquisitions, with proper search authority having been secured.

Another extremely useful application of the FIM is when conducting previews or acquisitions on business servers that can't be shut down. It's a simple matter for the examiner to connect to the network on which the server resides. The examiner next deploys the servlet on the target server. With that done, the examiner logs in as keymaster and adds the IP address of the target server to the list of nodes the examiner can access. The examiner logs off as keymaster and then logs back into the SAFE as the examiner. At this point, the examiner can connect to the target server and conduct a preview or acquisition as needed. All storage media is available, as is the live system-state data. The examiner completes the job at his or her leisure, the server stays up, and business goes on as usual.

EE and FIM are very powerful and flexible tools. As live forensics has become mainstream, their value to the industry has been realized.

 With the release of EnCase 7, Guidance Software has discontinued the FIM product line. Current FIM users will be channeled into the EE product line, which effectively provides the same result with the same functionality. Therefore, EnCase 6 will be the last release that has the FIM module and therefore for which the foregoing discussion applies. Naturally, EnCase 7 Enterprise will continue to develop and offer new features. Guidance Software will develop EnCase 7 such that a future release of EnCase 7 (expected for 7.04) will have provide FIM-like functionality as a standard feature!

EnCase Portable

While EnCase Portable has many features, I am not going to attempt to cover them all but will instead cover its acquisition features. I'll cover the use of it to acquire from EnCase Portable as a boot device. With that knowledge, using it to make a live acquisition is a mere subset of doing so from boot.

I'll assume you have EnCase Portable installed and otherwise ready to use. If you are going to use EnCase Portable to acquire a hard drive or sizeable device, one of the first considerations is to have media prepared to receive or store the image. With EnCase Portable, there is one added step, which is to prepare that device to work with EnCase Portable.

The EnCase Portable model is a triage and evidence collection tool that is currently in its version 3 release. EnCase Portable serves many useful functions. It can function in a live mode where it can be used to collect data from live Windows machines. That data can be files, volatile data (snapshot), RAM image, or a live drive. It can also be used to boot from USB (when supported) or from a CD. When used as a boot device, it can be used to acquire logical or physical devices. In the latter mode, it can also boot Macintosh systems, including those hard-to-image MacBook Air models. In most cases, the Macintosh systems will have to be booted with the CD and not the USB, but it can be done very nicely.

When using a CD to boot a MacBook Air, you'll find that not just any external CD drive will work. Rather, you'll need the one made by Apple for the MacBook Air in order to boot from a CD. Apple likes to give its hardware a lobotomy, at times, when it comes to working with non-Apple hardware.

To prepare the media, you'll need to attach the sterile media to the Windows system onto which EnCase Portable has been installed. Next, you start EnCase and open your case. The next step is to open the EnScript menu and run the Portable Management EnScript, as shown in Figure 4.44. When the Portable Management menu opens, go to the Storage tab. In that tab, you should see, perhaps among others, the sterile media that you attached. Select that device, right-click it, and click Prepare, which is shown in Figure 4.45. EnCase Portable will quickly prepare the drive, and you will see a Boolean dot in the Prepared column, as shown in Figure 4.46.

FIGURE 4.44   Portable Management EnScript

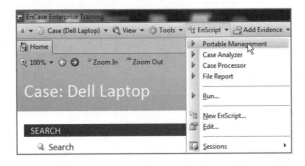

FIGURE 4.45   Select drive, right-click, and click Prepare

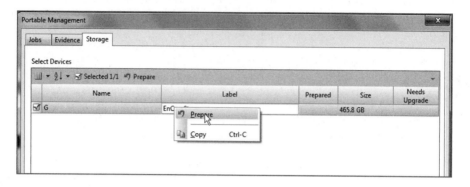

FIGURE 4.46   Drive prepared to receive evidence from EnCase Portable

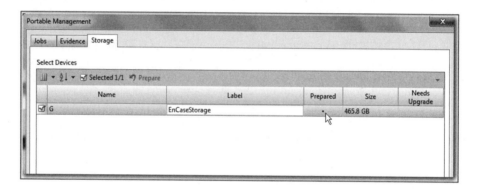

With the drive prepared to receive evidence from EnCase Portable, you should next simply exit the Portable Management tool, exit EnCase, and remove the drive. Next, you will boot the suspect computer with either the EnCase Portable Codemeter USB device or the CD. If you use the latter, you must also have the Codemeter attached for the license to be available; otherwise, EnCase Portable won't run. By now, you know the precautions and steps involved in booting a suspect machine using forensic boot media (CD or USB), so I won't revisit those steps other than to say that you must address the boot order and take control of the process to ensure booting from your media.

In this example, I'll use a USB bootable machine and insert the Codemeter USB and start the machine. You should not have any other USB devices inserted when booting from the USB dongle. Once the boot starts from the USB, you see the Windows splash screen appear. As long as you have taken the proper steps and are actually booting from the USB device, don't be alarmed as EnCase Portable is booting under Windows "BARTPE." Next, you'll see the EnCase Portable desktop background and messages from EnCase while it searches for devices and reports to you, as shown in Figures 4.47 and 4.48. As EnCase begins its search for drives, connect your target media that is prepared to receive evidence from EnCase Portable.

FIGURE 4.47   EnCase Portable searching for devices after Windows boot

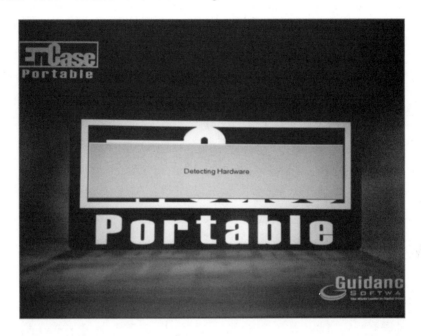

FIGURE 4.48   EnCase Portable allowing only EnCase-specific write-protected drives

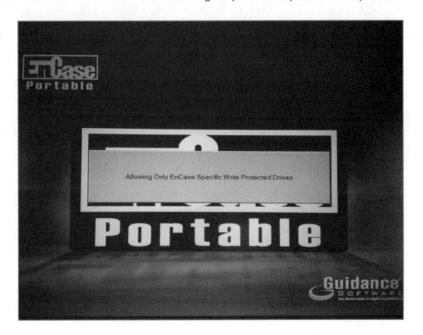

Once EnCase Portable has polled the devices, it loads, and you are presented with a menu of tasks. You can choose from among prepared jobs or create your own. In this example, I'm simply going to choose Create A Copy Of Drive Or Memory and click Run Job, as shown in Figure 4.49.

FIGURE 4.49   EnCase Portable menu from which you choose a task and run it

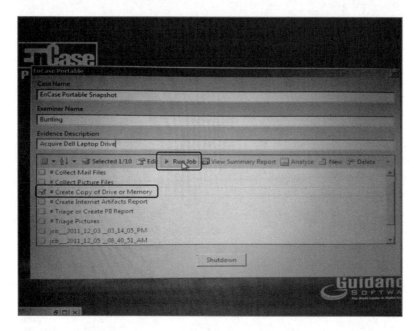

As the task runs, you'll receive a message that EnCase Portable is searching for drives. When it is complete, you will see the Acquisition menu listing the available drives to acquire. You should not see your target media in this list. In this example, shown in Figure 4.50, select the logical C volume with a blue check, select Verify Acquisition (on by default), and click OK to start. Since you prepared and attached your target drive that is intended to receive the image, EnCase detects this drive in the background and, upon starting the acquisition, places the image on that drive automatically without any prompting. In Figure 4.50, you can see at the top (I've circled it) that EnCase Portable has detected and is reporting the amount of storage available for my collection, which in this case is 465 GB.

When the acquisition task has completed, you'll see the status change in the Status menu, as shown in Figure 4.51. To exit EnCase Portable at this juncture, close the Status menu, which will leave you viewing the EnCase Portable main menu, as shown in Figure 4.52. At the bottom of this menu, click Shutdown, which is circled, and EnCase Portable and Windows will shut down completely.

FIGURE 4.50 EnCase Portable Acquisition menu from which you select the devices to acquire. Note the amount of storage drive free space that is being reported.

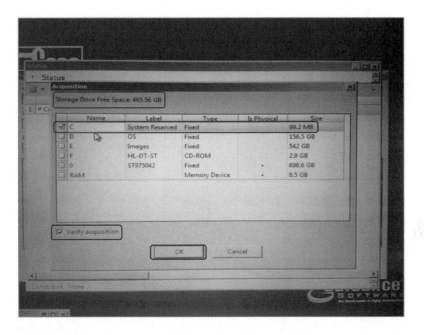

FIGURE 4.51 Status menu reporting that the acquisition has completed

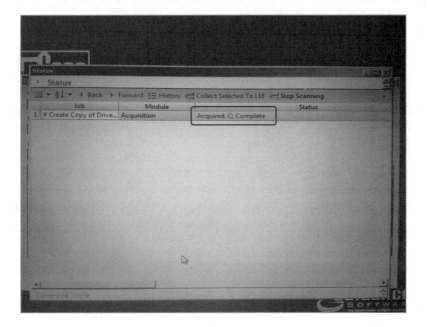

FIGURE 4.52   Shutting down EnCase Portable and Windows from the EnCase Portable main menu

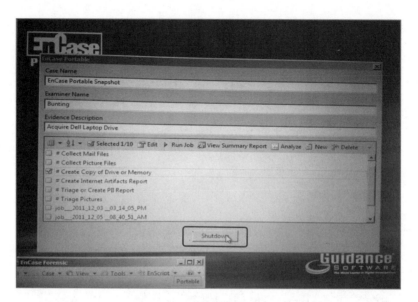

At this point, your suspect machine has been shut down, and you can remove your EnCase Portable Codemeter device and the storage media containing the image you collected. The image can be transferred manually to your EnCase examination machine, or you can use the Portable Management EnScript to handle the task. To use the latter method, connect your EnCase Portable storage drive (containing acquisition image), start EnCase, open your case, and run the Portable Management EnScript, as shown previously in Figure 4.44.

When the Portable Management menu displays, switch to the Evidence tab, which is displayed in Figure 4.53. The Portable Management EnScript will have polled for EnCase Portable storage devices and will display them on the Select Device drop-down menu. Since, in this example, I had only one connected, it was already being displayed along with the name of the task I ran to collect the evidence, which is Create Copy Of Drive Or Memory (circled). With this task selected in the left pane, the evidence files associated with that task are displayed in the right pane.

In this example, I'm selecting the acquired image in the right pane (circled and selected with a blue check) to be copied into the case. At the bottom, you define the path to copy the evidence to with the Copy Evidence To dialog box (circled). Also in the bottom section, there are two copy options. You can delete the evidence on your storage drive after it is copied to your examination machine. In this example, I'm not selecting this option because best practices call for examining a copy and storing the original in a secure location. I am, however, selecting the other copy option, which is to add the evidence to the case. When you have selected all the options you deem appropriate, you click Copy (circled) on the Collected Evidence toolbar to initiate the action. When the copy task completes, the completed job details are displayed in a status report, as shown in Figure 4.54.

FIGURE 4.53   Portable Management dialog Evidence tab from which evidence is copied into your open case

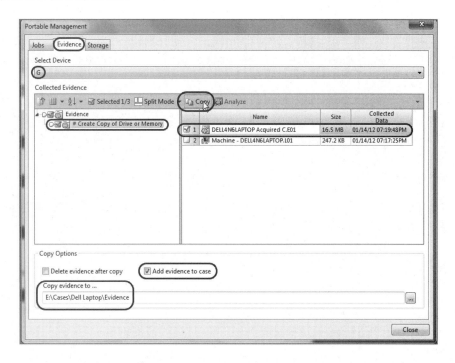

FIGURE 4.54   EnCase Portable status report

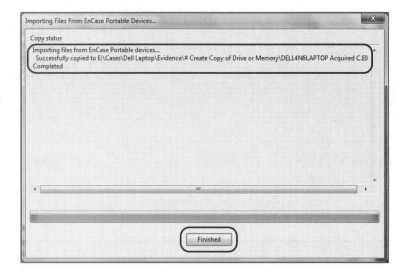

When done, click Finish to close the status report, and click Close to close the Portable Management EnScript. If you browse the evidence in your case, you will see the evidence item already added to the case, since we selected that option, which saved us many steps. Figure 4.55 shows the image after being added to the case and opened.

FIGURE 4.55 Image acquired with EnCase Portable being displayed in EnCase after being added to a case using the Portable Management tool

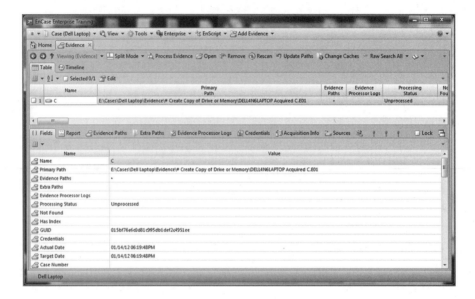

 EnCase Portable can extend the reach of your expertise into the field. You can direct nonexpert field personnel to act on your behalf using this tool with minimal instruction, since the tasks are canned or prepared in advance in the lab. In this manner, forensic examiners can focus on examination and analysis and less on collection tasks, making best use of scarce and valuable resources.

Helpful Hints

As you encounter various devices, here are some suggested acquisition solutions:

- If you encounter a floppy disk, flip the write-protect notch to read-only and acquire in EnCase for Windows on a system where the floppy drive has been tested for its ability to write protect. Alternatively, you could do a DOS acquisition, but there's usually no need.

- If you encounter a Zip or Jaz disk, use an IDE Zip or Jaz drive, and acquire in EnCase for DOS. You will need the GUEST.EXE file to mount the Iomega drivers. The easiest solution is to download the Zip-booter boot disk image from the Guidance Software website, update it with the latest EN.EXE, and you are set.

- If you encounter a CD/DVD, you can safely image it in Windows. You may encounter difficulties with some CD/DVD file systems. An alternative in these cases is to use CD Inspector, create a Zip image file, and bring the Zip file into the EnCase environment. This functionality is new starting with EnCase 5.

- If you encounter USB Flash media, you can usually image it in Windows by flipping the write-protect switch and doing so in combination with the registry setting that makes USB devices read-only. This setting is available only in Windows XP SP2 or newer. If neither of these write-protect features is an option, the ENBD/ENBCD has a feature to load DOS USB drivers. EnCase for DOS can then be used. Another option is to use LinEn on a version of Linux that has support for your USB devices, making sure you first disable automounting of the file system as previously discussed. Another option is to use the FastBloc SE. Using this module, USB, FireWire, and SCSI devices can be quite easily acquired in a forensically sound manner.

Summary

This chapter covered the many facets of acquiring digital evidence. I covered the process by which you control the boot process by modifying the boot order in Setup and modifying boot disks so that any calls made to the hard drive are redirected to the boot disk. You examined three methods of creating EnCase boot disks within EnCase.

After understanding the process and making EnCase boot disks, I discussed the reasons why EnCase boot disks are needed despite advances in write-blocking technology allowing acquisitions in Windows. For example, you may encounter geometry mismatches between legacy and modern BIOS code. You may encounter proprietary security schemes that marry hard drives to chips on the motherboard. You may also encounter HPA or DCO areas of the drive that can't be seen by the BIOS in Windows. Any of these conditions warrant booting with EnCase for DOS or LinEn in Linux to be able to access the drive directly through the ATA controller.

I detailed the process of booting a computer with EnCase boot disks using a carefully controlled sequence. Before connecting the target drive, you must configure the system to boot from the EnCase boot disk and make certain it works before reconnecting the target drive.

Drive-to-drive acquisitions occur when the storage media and the target media are mounted on the same machine. I detailed how to use EnCase for DOS for these acquisitions, based on the foundation I laid for creating EnCase boot disks and booting from them. I discussed the importance of preparing storage media formatted to FAT32, with a unique volume label and with a preconfigured directory path for the EnCase evidence files. I showed how to account for all sectors on a drive and how to switch to the Direct ATA mode when encountering HPA or DCO areas, usually indicated when all sectors can't be seen by the BIOS.

Network cable acquisitions occur between two machines connected by a network crossover cable. One machine is running EnCase for Windows, while the other machine is running EnCase for DOS or LinEn under Linux. The target host machine runs EnCase (DOS) or LinEn in a server mode first. Once that machine is waiting to connect, the EnCase for Windows machine is started. When choosing the devices to acquire, the network crossover option is selected, which then connects with the waiting server, and a network connection is established over which previewing or acquisition occurs.

Network cable acquisitions can be used to overcome HPA or DCO issues. They are relatively fast acquisition methods and even faster using gigabit NIC cards on both ends and LinEn as the tool. In lieu of a network cable, a parallel cable connection can be substituted. Parallel cable transmission rates are horribly slow, and network cable is much faster and preferred. Parallel cable acquisitions aren't available in LinEn and therefore are available only through EnCase 5.

While discussing network cable acquisitions, I detailed the many acquisition options in EnCase for Windows. You examined the pros and cons of adjusting block sizes and error granularity, both of which are new starting with EnCase 5. You can increase block sizes and make error granularity less coarse and increase acquisition speeds. The downside is possible data loss when encountering errors during acquisition or later if data becomes corrupt in the evidence file.

FastBloc/Tableau units are hardware write-blocking devices that block writes to IDE drives or SATA drives if connected via an IDE/SATA bridge. Models are also available to write-block SCSI and SAS drives. You examined how FastBloc/Tableau integrates with EnCase or as a stand-alone device within Windows.

FastBloc has been available in five hardware models and is still used extensively in the field and in labs:

- FastBloc Classic has a SCSI interface with the host.

- FastBloc LE has an IDE interface with the host.

- FastBloc FE has a USB or 1394a interface with the host.

- FastBloc2 FE has a USB or 1394b interface with the host and interfaces with the target using a series of adapters for the various types of media that are rapidly evolving.

- FastBloc2 LE, the laboratory version of the FE, is intended to be mounted in the host computer forensic computer. The FastBloc shows as a special icon with a blue (EnCase 5) or green square (EnCase 6 & 7) around the physical device. It also shows as Write Blocked with a Boolean indicator for true. FastBloc also is reported in the acquisition details listed on the Report tab for the acquired image.

- With the acquisition of the Tableau company by Guidance Software, the FastBloc product line was discontinued and in its place are several field and laboratory (bay-mounted) models

LinEn is EnCase for Linux, which is new beginning with EnCase 5. Linux affords many advantages over DOS because Linux is a 32-bit OS (optionally 64-bit), while DOS is a 16-bit OS. Linux controls how devices are mounted and whether file systems are mounted; if file systems are mounted, they can be mounted as read-only. I detailed how to configure mainstream Linux not to automount file systems and how to change the runlevel so that Linux starts in the console mode and not the GUI mode. Using the fdisk -l command, you can see what devices are available; using the mount command, you can see what file systems are mounted and how. Using the Linux naming conventions, hda2 is the second partition on the primary master, while hdd1 is the first partition on the secondary slave. When running LinEn, you can acquire, hash, or run in the server mode for network cable acquisition with nearly the same interface options as EnCase for DOS.

EnCase Enterprise and EnCase FIM can preview and acquire target systems (servlet nodes) over a network connection with no limitations on distance. If the Internet can reach the target, you can reach it with EE or FIM. FIM is for law enforcement or military customers, and EE is for all others. The three components of the EE or FIM system are the examiner machine, the servlet node (target host), and the SAFE. The SAFE authenticates the connection, acts to limit and supervise the process, and facilitates the encrypted connection. With EE, the SAFE is on a separate PC administered by a SAFE administrator known as the *keymaster*. With FIM, the SAFE resides on the same PC as the examination machine, making the examiner and keymaster the same person. In addition to previewing and acquiring a live host, EE or FIM can capture live system-state data using the Snapshot feature.

EnCase Portable is a field device consisting of a bootable USB Codemeter/storage device, additional USB storage media, a USB hub, an installation DVD, a bootable CD, and a carrying case. EnCase Portable is used for triage and collection of evidence and can be used by nonexpert field personnel. Among the many collection tasks available, EnCase Portable can acquire hard drives at either logical or physical levels. These acquisitions can be carried out against lives devices or by booting suspect machines using either USB or CD boot devices. If booting from the CD, the USB Codemeter must also be attached. Before media can be used for storage by EnCase Portable, it must first be prepared using the Portable Management tool.

The EnCE test under EnCase 6 will contain questions pertaining to EnCase DOS boot disks. Beginning with the EnCase 7 EnCE test, examiners will no longer be tested on EnCase DOS boot disks and related concepts.

Exam Essentials

Know how use the LinEn for Linux tool.   Be able to explain the various conditions that would warrant a LinEn acquisition. Explain the importance of modifying Linux to disable the automatic mounting of the file system upon boot. Explain why it is important to boot Linux to the console mode and how to configure this change. Explain what acquisition options are available in LinEn. Understand how Linux names devices and partitions.

Understand why and how an EnCase boot disk is made.   Know where the tools are located to create an EnCase boot disk. Be able to explain the steps involved in creating an EnCase boot disk and also how to update an EnCase boot disk with an updated version of LinEn. Explain how Linux achieves write blocking and the importance of using forensically sound distributions of Linux for this purpose.

Understand how to boot a computer with an EnCase boot disk.   Be able to explain the various conditions that would warrant booting a computer with an EnCase boot disk. Explain the process of preparing the target host computer for a safe boot using the EnCase boot disk. Know how to change the boot order in Setup and why this step is important. Describe each step in booting the computer using an EnCase boot disk and the importance of each step.

Know how to do a disk-to-disk acquisition.   Be able to explain the various conditions that would warrant a disk-to-disk acquisition. Be able to explain the difference between the BIOS and Direct ATA modes, how to switch between them, and why this would be necessary. Know how to adjust the Error Granularity setting and be able to explain the effects of changing the setting. Be able to explain the connections and steps necessary to conduct a disk-to-disk acquisition using EnCase for DOS.

Know how to conduct a network cable acquisition.   Be able to explain the various conditions that would warrant a network cable acquisition. Know what kind of cable is required for this acquisition, and explain the difference between this cable and a regular network cable. Explain the importance of controlling the boot process on the target host. Explain the steps involved in booting the target host and making the connection to EnCase for Windows. Describe the various acquisition options. Understand how to adjust the block size, and explain the pros and cons of changing it. Understand which evidence file properties you can change by reacquiring. Explain why the MD5 hash does not change when you reacquire and change any of these properties, unless you change the number of sectors.

Know how to conduct a Tableau acquisition.   Know the different Tableau models, and explain how their host connections are different. Explain how to connect the FastBloc to the host and to the target drive. Describe the process by which Tableau is powered on and its attached drive is mounted in Windows. Know what the Tableau icon looks like and where and how its "write-block" status is reported or indicated in EnCase. Describe how Tableau can be used as a stand-alone write-blocking device by which to use third-party tools to examine the drive in Windows without EnCase. Understand the disk-caching problems associated with using FastBloc with Windows 98/Me.

Understand EE and FIM configuration and capabilities.   Know the three components in EE or FIM systems, and explain how they function. Understand under what circumstances an EE or FIM would be valuable to an investigation. Understand what types of data that EE or FIM can capture that other EnCase models can't. Explain volatile system-state data and its importance to an investigation. Explain how EE and FIM differ.

Understand EnCase Portable configuration and capabilities.   Know how to prepare storage media using the Portable Management tool. Describe how to boot a suspect machine using a USB or CD device to boot the EnCase Portable software. Describe how to acquire a device and subsequently transfer the acquired image to an open case. Understand how EnCase Portable can be used by nonexpert field personnel under the direction of an examiner to triage and collect evidence in the field.

Review Questions

1. When acquiring a hard drive using a Linux boot disk with LinEn, what would be the cause of EnCase (LinEn) not detecting partition information?

   A. The drive has been FDisked and the partition(s) removed.

   B. The partition(s) are not recognized by Linux.

   C. Both A and B.

   D. None of the above.

2. LinEn contains a write blocker that protects the target media from being altered.

   A. True

   B. False

3. As a good forensic practice, why would it be a good idea to wipe a forensic drive before reusing it?

   A. Chain-of-custody

   B. Cross-contamination

   C. Different file and operating systems

   D. Chain of evidence

   E. No need to wipe

4. If the number of sectors reported by EnCase does not match the number reported by the manufacturer for the drive, what should you do?

   A. Suspect HPA.

   B. Suspect DCO.

   C. Use Tableau or FastBloc SE to access the sectors protected by HPA or DCO.

   D. Boot with LinEn in Linux.

   E. All of the above.

5. When acquiring digital evidence, why shouldn't the evidence be left unattended in an unsecured location?

   A. Cross-contamination

   B. Storage

   C. Chain-of-custody

   D. Not an issue

6. Which describes an HPA? (Choose all that apply.)

   A. Stands for Host Protected Area

   B. Is not normally seen by the BIOS

   C. Is not normally seen through Direct ATA access

   D. Was introduced in the ATA-6 specification

7. Which describes a DCO?

   A. Was introduced in the ATA-6 specification.

   B. Stands for Device Configuration Overlay.

   C. Is not normally seen by the BIOS.

   D. It may contain hidden data, which can be seen by switching to the Direct ATA mode in EnCase for DOS.

   E. All of the above.

8. At which user level must the examiner function when using LinEn?

   A. Administrator

   B. Admin

   C. Root

   D. Any user

   E. None of the above

9. Reacquiring an image and adding compression will change the MD5 value of the acquisition hash.

   A. True

   B. False

10. When reacquiring an image, you can change the name of the evidence.

   A. True

   B. False

11. Which of the following should you do when creating a storage volume to hold an EnCase evidence file that will be created with LinEn? (Choose all that apply.)

   A. Format the volume with the FAT file system.

   B. Give the volume a unique label to identify it.

   C. Wipe the volume before formatting to conform to best practices, and avoid claims of cross-contamination.

   D. Create a directory to contain the evidence file.

   E. Format the volume with the NTFS file system.

   F. All of the above.

12. In Linux, what describes hdb2? (Choose all that apply.)

   A. Refers to the primary master

   B. Refers to the primary slave

   C. Refers to hard drive number 2

   D. Refers to the second partition

   E. Refers to the secondary master

13. In Linux, what describes sdb? (Choose all that apply.)

   A. Refers to an IDE device

   B. Refers to a SCSI device

   C. Refers to a USB device

   D. Refers to a FireWire device

14. When acquiring USB flash memory, you could write-protect it by doing what?

   A. Engaging the write-protect switch, if equipped

   B. Modifying the registry in Windows XP SP2 (or higher) to make USB read-only

   C. Using ENBD/ENBCD USB DOS drivers and having EnCase for DOS "lock" the Flash media

   D. Using LinEn in Linux with automount of file system disabled

   E. Using FastBloc SE to write block USB, FireWire, SCSI drives

   F. All of the above

15. Which are true with regard to EnCase Portable? (Choose all that apply.)

   A. Storage media must be prepared using the Portable Management tool before it can be used by EnCase Portable.

   B. If booting using the EnCase Portable Boot CD to boot, the EnCase Portable dongle must also be connected so that the license can be accessed.

   C. The EnCase Portable can triage and collect evidence in a forensically sound manner from live machines or to do so in a boot mode.

   D. The EnCase Portable can be configured with custom tasks created by the examiner using the Portable Management tool.

16. LinEn can be run under both Windows and DOS operating systems.

   A. True

   B. False

17. When using LinEn, the level of support for USB, FireWire, and SCSI devices is determined by what?

   A. The drivers built into LinEn

   B. The drivers provided with the ENBCD

   C. The distribution of Linux being used

   D. A and B

   E. None of the above

18. How should CDs be acquired using EnCase?

   A. DOS

   B. Windows

19. Select all that are true about EE and FIM.

   A. They can acquire or preview a system live without shutting it down.

   B. They can capture live system-state volatile data using the Snapshot feature.

   C. With EE, the SAFE is on a separate PC, administered by the keymaster.

   D. With FIM, the SAFE is on the examiner's PC and the keymaster and the examiner are the same person.

   E. FIM can be licensed to private individuals.

20. Which of the following are true? (Choose all that apply.)

   A. LinEn contains no write-blocking capability. Rather, write blocking is achieved by disabling the automount feature within the host Linux operating system.

   B. LinEn contains its own onboard write-blocking drivers and therefore can be safely run on any version of Linux.

   C. LinEn can format drives to both NTFS and FAT formats.

   D. Before using a target drive onto which to write evidence files, LinEn must be used to unlock the target drive and render it writable.

   E. LinEn can format drives to EXT2 or EXT3 format.

Chapter

5

EnCase Concepts

This book has made numerous references to the EnCase evidence file. I've talked about many of its properties, such as compression, file chunk size, protection via password, MD5 hash, and CRC frequency. In this chapter, I'll closely examine the evidence file. I'll describe its major components and its various properties in detail. The evidence file, as you'll see, is constructed to maintain the authenticity and integrity of the original evidence, both of which are crucial in maintaining the chain of custody.

It is important that you understand how EnCase works with the evidence file "under the hood" so you can explain or demonstrate why or how the evidence is preserved and unaltered in the EnCase environment. To that end, you'll use evidence files included on the online resource page (www.sybex.com/go/ence3e) for this book in an exercise that demonstrates what happens when the evidence file is corrupted or subjected to deliberate tampering. When you finish this chapter, you'll thoroughly understand the EnCase evidence file and have a high degree of confidence in the integrity of the data under examination.

Examples are included on the online resource page and in Exercise 5.1.

EnCase Evidence File Format

The EnCase evidence file is often called the *image file*. This is a carryover from the original imaging methods that had their roots in the Unix dd command. In Linux or Unix, everything is a file. Thus, a device, such as a hard drive, can be addressed as a file. Using the dd command, you can copy one hard drive onto another hard drive with the apparent ease of copying a file, although the process certainly takes longer. The copy produced can be a stream of data sent from the original drive to the copy drive, with the end result being two identical drives, assuming the copy drive contained the same number of sectors. Alternatively, you could direct the copy to an actual file instead of a device. The end result of this process is a large file whose contents are a bit-by-bit copy of the original device. This image file is often given the extension .img to denote it as such.

Regardless of its name, the primary purpose of an EnCase evidence file is to preserve an exact bit-for-bit copy of the target media. Unlike a Linux dd image, which contains only the bit-for-bit copy, the EnCase evidence file contains the bit-for-bit copy plus other information that serves to "bag-and-tag" the evidence file to preserve the chain of custody. Achieving this same bag-and-tag effect in Linux would require several separate steps. Even then, the bag-and-tag items are still separate items and not integrated into the image. With EnCase, by contrast, this bag-and-tag information is created automatically and integrated into the evidence file while it is created. By doing so in one automated step, you ensure that the evidence is placed in a sealed, self-authenticating evidence container, thus preserving the integrity of the evidence.

CRC, MD5, and SHA-1

Throughout this book, I have mentioned the CRC and the MD5. During the discussion of acquisitions, I described MD5 in detail. For purposes of understanding the file integrity component or function of the EnCase evidence file, I need to digress at this point to review and expand your understanding of the CRC and MD5. In this manner, you can better appreciate what these values mean and how they contribute to the file integrity measures employed by EnCase.

You may recall from the previous discussions that an MD5 (Message Digest 5) is an algorithm or calculation applied to streams of data (files, devices, and so on). The result of this calculation is a 128-bit hexadecimal value (32 characters with each character or byte containing 8 bits each). The number of possible values for this hexadecimal number is 2^{128}. Thus, the odds of any two files having the same MD5 value are 1 in 2^{128}. In tangible terms (to the extent that such numbers are tangible), that is one in approximately 340 billion billion billion billion. Because the odds are so remote of two files having the same hash value, one can statistically infer, with an extremely high degree of confidence, that two files having the same hash value have the same file contents. The reverse can also be inferred: if two files have different hash values, their contents are different. For this reason, the MD5 is an industry standard in the computer forensics field for verifying the integrity of files and data streams.

A Cyclical Redundancy Check (CRC) is similar in function and purpose to the MD5. The CRC algorithm results in a 32-bit hexadecimal value. The number of possible values for a 32-bit hexadecimal value is 2^{32}, and the odds of any two numbers having the same CRC is one in 2^{32}. Translated, this means that the odds of any two files having the same CRC are 1 in 4,294,967,296 (4 billion and some change!). Although the odds associated with a CRC hardly approach those offered by the MD5, 1 in 4 billion is still a statistically strong validation.

The MD5 requires more calculations than the CRC, and hence more time and system resources are required to generate an MD5. Because the CRC is faster to generate and uses fewer system resources, it has value in that regard and is used frequently for maintaining data integrity in a variety of applications. It is a good compromise solution for providing data integrity checking when performance is an issue. As you'll come to appreciate, EnCase makes frequent use of the CRC during its program operations and uses both the CRC and the MD5 when validating the entire evidence file. Combined, the CRC and MD5 provide powerful data integrity tests throughout the entire acquisition and examination process.

With the release of EnCase 6, support for SHA-1 was added. SHA-1 is another cryptographic hashing algorithm that was designed by the U.S. National Security Agency (NSA) and released in 1995. Whereas the MD5 produces a 128-bit value, SHA-1 produces a 160-bit value. By providing a greater number of potential outcomes, hash collisions are reduced by this more robust algorithm. EnCase supports both MD5 and SHA-1, allowing either or both to be calculated.

Evidence File Components and Function

An EnCase evidence file has three major components: the header, the data blocks, and the file integrity component (CRC and MD5/SHA-1). The header will appear on the front end of the evidence file, and the data blocks follow the header. The file integrity component exists throughout and provides redundant levels of file integrity.

Each compartment has its own integrity *seal*, and the header is *sealed* with its own CRC. Each data block is verified with its own CRC. The entire data block section is subjected to an MD5/SHA-1 hash, called an *acquisition hash*, which is appended after the data blocks. The header and all CRCs are not included in this MD5/SHA-1 hash. It is important to understand that the MD5/SHA-1 hash is calculated only on the data.

Although the header and the data blocks are clearly separate data areas, the file integrity component is interwoven throughout. It can be viewed abstractly as a separate component, but when viewed in its physical form, it is ubiquitous throughout the evidence file, as you can see in Figure 5.1.

FIGURE 5.1   Physical layout of the EnCase evidence file. The header appears at the front of the file, followed by the data blocks. Note that the file integrity components (CRCs and MD5/SHA-1) are interwoven throughout.

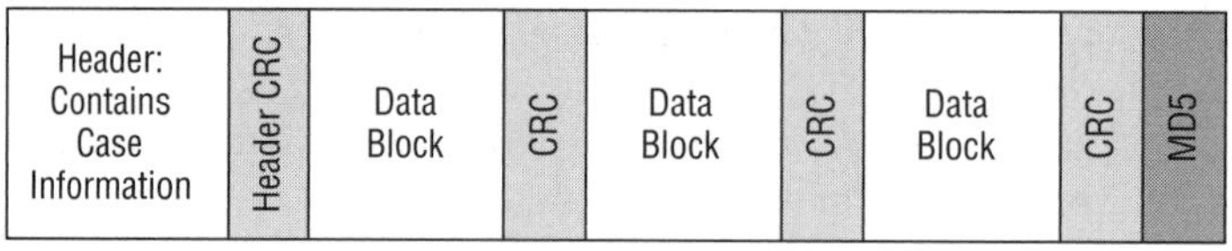

Header: Contains Case Information	Header CRC	Data Block	CRC	Data Block	CRC	Data Block	CRC	MD5

The above physical layout in Figure 5.1, and subsequent discussion, applies to evidence files that are not compressed. When compression is applied, there are no CRC's following Data Blocks. Rather, the compression/decompression process contains its own validation process.

Now that you have an overall understanding of the construction of the evidence file, I'll show how one is created, starting with the header. The header contains much of the case information that you entered at the Options screen during acquisition, along with other information. You may expect the following, among other data, to be contained within the header:

- Evidence name
- Evidence number
- Notes
- Date/time of acquisition
- Version of EnCase used for acquisition
- Operating system under which acquisition took place

Once the acquisition options (name, number, notes, and so on) have been entered and the system information has been gathered, this information is placed in the header. The header is subjected to a CRC and compressed. The header is always subjected to compression even when the data is not. Compressing it saves space and removes the ability to alter clear-text data. In this manner, the documentary information concerning the evidence is sealed for integrity. This component, the header, and its CRC are placed on the front of the evidence file.

Immediately following the header are the blocks of data. Before EnCase 5, these data blocks were always 64 sectors (32 KB), except for the last data block, which was almost always less than 64 sectors. Starting with EnCase 5 in Windows and LinEn in Linux, the block sizes can be changed up to 32,768 sectors (16 MB). The default size is still 64 sectors. In the discussions that follow, you must understand that changing the block size when you acquire data will affect the block sizes in the evidence file and, with that, change the frequency of the CRC values. For example, changing the block size to 128 sectors will mean that a CRC will be written for every 128 sectors instead of the default size of every 64 sectors.

For now, let's assume that the block size is unchanged and remains the default size of 64 sectors. With this default setting, the buffer or memory size is set at 64 sectors. This means data will be read into memory in blocks of 64 sectors. Once this data is in memory, a CRC is computed for this block of 64 sectors. Additionally, this block is computed into the cumulative MD5 hash that is being calculated over the entire set of data from the first sector to the last sector acquired. If you opt for no compression, the data block and its CRC are appended to the evidence file. If you select compression, the block of data and its CRC are compressed and appended to the data file.

EnCase uses industry-standard compression algorithms when compressing its evidence files. The amount of compression you will achieve will vary, depending on the type of data on your drive. Drives with lots of zeros in the unallocated space compress very well. By contrast, if the unallocated space contains lots of data of types that don't compress well, you'll obviously achieve less overall compression. On the average, using compression enabled, you'll see average compression rates approaching 50 percent. Compression comes with a cost, which is increased acquisition time. Acquisition times with compression can approach three times the amount that no compression requires. Also, as previously noted, when compression is applied, the compression / decompression algorithm verifies the data in lieu of CRC's for each data block as used with uncompressed evidence files.

When the last block of data in the target device is reached, it will rarely be exactly 64 sectors—it is usually smaller than 64 sectors. That block of data is written to the evidence file along with its CRC. At this point, there is no more data to process, and the acquisition hash (MD5/SHA-1 value) is complete and is written in the section, which is then appended to the end of the evidence file. In addition to the MD5/SHA-1 acquisition hash, you will find other data in this area. This data area is the last segment of the evidence file. It is approximately 3 KB in size and contains metadata that describes various properties of the evidence file, such as offsets for start and stop points for header, data area, and so forth. The MD5/SHA-1 is part of the metadata contained in this final segment.

If the target media will not fit in one evidence file, as defined in the file segment size (file chunk size) setting, it will span as many evidence files as are needed to contain it. The first evidence file created will contain the header at its beginning, followed by as many data blocks as will fit based on the file segment size and the degree of compression selected. When more than one evidence file is required, the MD5/SHA-1 can't be completed and written until the last block of data is read. Therefore, no MD5/SHA-1 will be written to the first evidence file when multiple files are required.

 When creating file segment sizes, EnCase 7 has new minimums and maximums for file segment sizes. The minimum file segment size is 30 MB, and the maximum file segment size is 8,796,093,018,112 MB. Naturally, the file system being used for storage must be able to support file sizes this large.

Since the header is contained in the first evidence file, it is not necessary for the header to be written again. This means all subsequent evidence files will have no header section. The MD5/SHA-1 value can't be completely calculated and written until the last data block is processed, so only the last evidence file in the series will contain the MD5/SHA-1 value and metadata appended to the end.

Figure 5.2 shows how evidence files are constructed when multiple evidence files are required. Any evidence file that is neither the first nor the last will contain only data blocks and CRC values for each block. In Figure 5.2, the diagram in the middle, between the first and last blocks, depicts evidence files that are neither first nor last. In most cases, evidence file segments looks like the middle one in Figure 5.2, because most cases involve relatively large devices that result in a large number of evidence files when the image is acquired.

When the first evidence file is written, the filename is the one you designated when selecting the acquisition options. The extension for the first file is .e01; the extension for the second file is .e02, and so on, until evidence file numbers reach 100. The extension for evidence file 100 is .eaa. The extension for evidence file 101 is .eab, which continues until evidence file number 126 (.eaz). The file extension for evidence file 127 is .eba. The sequencing continues as needed until the last evidence file is created. If you are using the new evidence file format, which we'll cover momentarily, the extension will be .ex01, .ex02, and so on.

FIGURE 5.2   Evidence file format when multiple evidence files are required

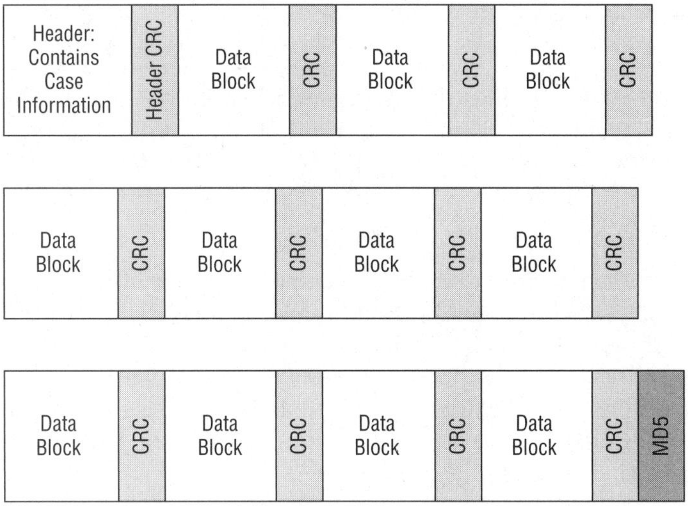

Header: Contains Case Information	Header CRC	Data Block	CRC	Data Block	CRC	Data Block	CRC

Data Block	CRC	Data Block	CRC	Data Block	CRC	Data Block	CRC

Data Block	CRC	Data Block	CRC	Data Block	CRC	Data Block	CRC	MD5

The above physical layout in Figure 5.2 applies to evidence files that are not compressed. When compression is applied, there are no CRC's following Data Blocks. Rather, the compression / decompression process contains its own validation process.

When selecting a source drive to hold your evidence files, it's best to try to contain your files on one drive. Thus, the size of the source drive should be adequate to hold all the data from the target drive. If you are imaging an 80 GB drive with no compression, logic might lead you to think you can contain the image on an 80 GB drive. But, assuming the two 80 GB drives contain the same number of sectors, this will not be the case because an evidence file contains some data overhead in addition to the actual data. The header takes some space, the MD5/SHA-1 area takes some space, and the CRC values require 4 bytes per block of data. The overhead is small, but it is enough that you can't put the uncompressed image of a drive on a drive of equal size.

If you make this mistake, EnCase will warn you when your source drive is full and will prompt you for a path to continue the acquisition. In such a case, you could finish the acquisition by placing the small amount remaining on your system drive. The data must be placed on a drive that is currently mounted on your system. If you need to image a drive that was 100 GB and you have only two 60 GB drives, you should mount them both before starting your acquisition. When the first one fills, EnCase will prompt you for a path to continue, at which point you would point EnCase to your second source drive.

If you span your acquisition over two or more drives, when you add your image to EnCase, it will eventually prompt you for the location of the rest of the evidence files as it loads the image. The capability to span drives when acquiring is a nice feature. There have been many times when this feature has saved my day.

If you'll recall from Chapter 4, EnCase includes an option in the Acquisition Options menu called Alternate Path. If you provide an alternate path for your evidence file output, EnCase will automatically switch over to the alternate path if the primary path fills, writing the remainder of the evidence files to that location.

When choosing a source drive to contain a compressed target image, you can expect to achieve a nearly 50 percent compression factor using compression. You can't count on that factor, however; it is only an average, and your actual results will depend on the type of data on the target drive. It is best to always have extra room for storage beyond what you expect. As a general rule, when using compression, I prefer to have 75 GB available on a source drive to image a 100 GB device. Even then, you should still have some reserve space mounted and ready in the event your storage drive fills.

New Evidence File Format

With EnCase 7, a new evidence file format emerged, dubbed the Ex01 format. Following suit, a new logical evidence file format also emerged, dubbed the Lx01 format. This new format allows for encryption and extensibility. Originally, the compression format changed to BZIP, which is better for compressing files, but is also slower. Therefore, for performance issues, the LZ compression format was reinstituted with EnCase 7.02. The same information stored in the E01 format is stored in the Ex01 format; however, additional information is present, and the data format has been restructured, as shown in Figure 5.3.

When you acquire in EnCase 7, the default evidence file format will be the new format (Ex01 or Lx01 in the case of a logical acquisition). You still have the option in EnCase 7 to create the legacy format (E01 or L01). EnCase 7 will open the legacy format as well. With time, you can expect to see a phasing out of the legacy format which will be replaced by the new format altogether.

I just mentioned that the new evidence file format restructured how data was stored. Figures 5.1 and 5.2 show the CRC values stored at the end of each data block that they represent. In the new format, they are now stored in a table in the Link Record area.

FIGURE 5.3 New EnCase evidence file format

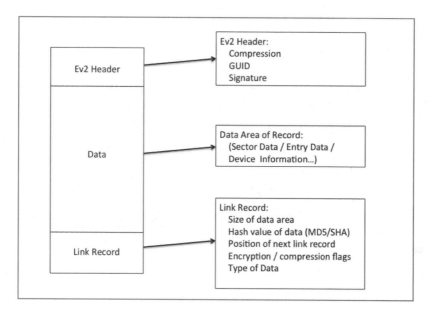

Evidence File Verification

At this point, you know that when EnCase creates an evidence file, it calculates CRC values for its header and each block of data. Additionally, it calculates an MD5/SHA-1 value for the data only. No other data (header, CRC, metadata, and so on) is included in this MD5/SHA-1 hash. If you were to use a third-party tool to calculate an MD5 and/or SHA-1 hash of the device imaged by EnCase, the MD5 and/or SHA-1 hashes should match. If EnCase included data other than the target drive in the hash, those values would not match. Thus, it's important to understand that EnCase calculates the MD5/SHA-1 value from the data contained in the target device only.

The acquisition hash (MD5 or SHA-1) is calculated on the original subject media. The verification hash (MD5 or SHA-1) is calculated on the data only portion of the evidence file.

After a device is imaged, its image file is brought into EnCase automatically. Whenever an evidence file is added to an open case, a file verification process automatically occurs. When an evidence file is being verified, as shown in Figure 5.4, there is a progress bar indicator in the lower-right corner of the EnCase window. If the evidence file is small, as in the case of a small USB drive, the verification occurs so quickly that the progress bar isn't seen.

FIGURE 5.4   File verification progress bar shown in lower-right corner of EnCase window

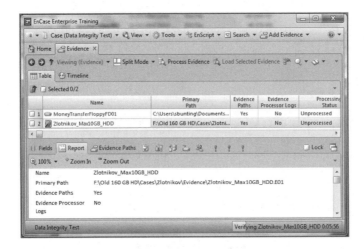

If for any reason you want to cancel the verification process, double-click this progress bar, and you will be provided with a prompt that lets you terminate the verification process.

If you look at the Report tab for a device that is currently being verified, such as the one shown in Figure 5.5, you'll note the absence of a verification hash, and the File Integrity field will indicate that the file is verifying. Figure 5.6 shows the same report after the verification process has completed. The verification hash value is included in the report and should match the acquisition hash. Additionally, the File Integrity field should report that the file verified with zero errors.

The fact that the image file verified is reassuring; however, you should understand what happens "under the hood" when this process occurs. By understanding that process, you'll feel even better about the results. Furthermore, you'll be in a position to explain the process to a court or jury if the authenticity of the evidence is challenged. A solid explanation can thwart defense challenges regarding the authenticity of the evidence and bolster your image as a competent examiner.

The verification process is actually simple. Each block of data in the evidence file is subjected to a verification CRC calculation. For a block of data to pass the test, its verification CRC must match the CRC value calculated when it was acquired and stored in the evidence file with the block of data. If a CRC for a block of data does not match its stored acquisition value, an error is reported for that block of data. This CRC recalculation and verification occurs for each block of data in the evidence file.

FIGURE 5.5   Report view for a device in which verification is underway. Note the absence of a verification hash.

FIGURE 5.6   Report view for a device after verification has completed. Note that the verification hash is present and matches the acquisition hash. Note also that the File Integrity field reports that the file verified with zero errors.

In addition to the CRC verifications, the blocks of data are subjected to a recalculation of the MD5/SHA-1 hash. The resultant value is called the *verification hash value*. The verification hash value and the acquisition hash value are compared and should match. To achieve successful file verification, the verification CRC values for all blocks of data must match their acquisition values, and the verification MD5/SHA-1 hash must match the acquisition MD5/SHA-1 hash. As you can see, the verification process is redundant, with one (CRC) cross-validating the other (MD5/SHA-1), thus providing an extremely strong mechanism for ensuring the integrity of the digital evidence within the EnCase environment.

Much has been written about MD5 hash collisions. A hash collision occurs when two dissimilar data streams have the same hash value. As previously stated, the odds are remote (2^{128}), but they can occur. Some have criticized the continued use of the MD5 because of this. Keep in mind that EnCase is *not* relying on just the MD5. Rather, EnCase uses both a CRC and an MD5 to validate data. I am unaware of any reports of an MD5 hash collision with a simultaneous CRC collision!

Additionally, EnCase allows you to choose a SHA-1 hash instead of an MD5 hash, or, for those wanting both, you can choose an MD5 and a SHA-1 hash.

The verification process occurs automatically whenever an evidence file is added to a case. At times you should reverify an evidence file. If you have copied the evidence file to another drive, you may want to check that the file did not get corrupted in the process. Also, as a best practice, you should check it one more time at the conclusion of a case and also before going to court. Whatever the reason, there is a mechanism for doing this.

To verify an evidence item, go to the Evidence tab and view the evidence items in the Table tab. Place your focus (cursor) on the evidence item you want to verify, and then go to the Evidence tab's drop-down menu at the extreme right and choose Verify File Integrity, as shown in Figure 5.7. You will be prompted to confirm. When you click Yes, you will see the verification progress bar in the lower-right corner. When the reverification is complete, you won't see a report of the results, unless there is a verification failure, at which time you will receive a pop-up error message. To view the results, simply place your cursor on the evidence item in the Table tab of the Evidence tab. In the view or bottom pane, go to the Report tab, and the results will be among those items reported for the device. Specifically, look for File Integrity, Acquisition MD5/SHA-1, Verification MD5/SHA-1, and CRC errors. If errors are present, which is rare, you will find the sector groups in which the CRC errors were found at the bottom of the report.

To demonstrate how a corrupted evidence file would appear upon verifying file integrity, a 4 in an evidence file was altered to a 5 with a hex editor. This effectively changes only one bit in the evidence file (0000-0100 is changed to 0000-0101). After verifying the evidence file, Figure 5.8 shows the results in the Report tab for the selected device.

FIGURE 5.7　To verify the integrity of an evidence file, place your focus (cursor) on the device, open the drop-down menu at the far right, and select Verify File Integrity.

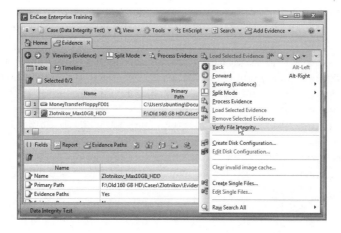

FIGURE 5.8　Report view for device with corrupted data. Note that changing one bit from a 0 to a 1 (changing a 4 to a 5) produces a drastic change in the verification hash (MD5 value) when compared to the acquisition hash. If there are errors, the impacted sector groups will be reported at the end of the report, which is shown in the inset in the lower right.

The File Integrity field indicates that the verification completed and found one error, meaning the CRC for one block failed to match its stored acquisition value. The one block of data could have one or many errors. All that EnCase can determine is that the CRC values for one block (64 sectors by default) do not match, which is reported as one error. If another block of data also contained one or many errors, then EnCase would report two errors.

Next, you can see that the verification hash does not match the acquisition hash and that the difference is drastic despite that only one bit changed. If you look further down the report, you can see the details of the errors, which is shown in the inset of Figure 5.8. The block of data containing the CRC error begins at sector 0 and ends with sector 63. Since the block size is 64, the block covers sectors 0 through 63, which is a range of 64 sectors.

With earlier versions of EnCase (up through and including version 4), if a block of data contained an error, you could not view any of the data in that block. An error of this type would be that the data block's CRC value, when read by EnCase, did not match its acquisition value. Such an error could occur if the evidence file were corrupted or altered. Since a block of data, by default, is 64 sectors, one corrupted bit could preclude the examiner from viewing otherwise good and valuable evidence contained in that block. Therefore, the ability to see or work with data in a corrupted block was enabled beginning with EnCase 5.

With this added feature, I can't overstate the importance of verifying an evidence file at the conclusion of a case. For certain, you must be assured that your evidence file is verified at the conclusion of your work so you can affirmatively state that the evidence file's integrity was maintained throughout. This is a simple matter of reverifying the various evidence files in the case, which I've already described.

In addition to reverifying, you may also need to hash the various devices, because the resultant bookmark will contain a time stamp for the calculation as well as the hash value, as shown in Figure 5.9. Because the verification report lacks a time stamp, this extra step is highly recommended. I describe the process of hashing a device later in the chapter.

FIGURE 5.9   Results of hashing a device. Note the time stamp and the hash value are contained in this report, which can be stored as a notes bookmark.

Best practices call for making an evidence file image and creating a copy on which to work. If you found that your working copy of your evidence had been corrupted, such as that shown in Figure 5.8, you would immediately make another working copy from your original image and reverify your work in the case.

As you begin to grasp the inner workings of EnCase, you will appreciate the work that has gone into the program to ensure data integrity at every step of the process. Also, you will learn the importance of the relationship between acquisition block sizes and the corresponding frequency of the CRC values.

Increasing the block size can have an adverse effect if corruption occurs in a block of data, because the block of data protected by the CRC is larger. If the block size is changed from the default size of 64 sectors to 128 sectors to speed up the acquisition, the downside is that a CRC value will be written for every 128 sectors instead of every 64 sectors. If the evidence file later developed a corrupted block, the affected block size would be 128 sectors instead of 64 sectors, and more data would be unavailable to the examiner. If you must increase the block size to speed up an acquisition, it is recommended that you reacquire it with a default setting of 64 sectors when time permits. In that way, you enjoy the faster acquisition when you need it, and you can later restore your data integrity protection to a more acceptable level.

EXERCISE 5.1

Understanding How EnCase Maintains Data Integrity

In this exercise, you will create a case and add to it an evidence file. That evidence file will verify correctly. You'll then save the case and exit EnCase. Next you'll substitute your verified evidence file with another one of the same name that is identical in all respects except that one bit has been changed. This change could simulate unintentional data corruption, or it could simulate intentional alteration of evidence. Regardless of how or why the evidence file changed, EnCase cares not. You'll reopen the case with the altered evidence file, and you'll see EnCase's file integrity protection features at work. When you are done, you'll be able to affirmatively assert and testify as to what happens if original evidence has been altered in the EnCase environment. You can also use these files to test versions of EnCase as they are released. Let's get started!

1. Open EnCase 7, create a new case named Data Integrity Test, and accept all the default path locations.

2. By using the default paths, you should have a folder named Data Integrity Test located in the path Documents\EnCase\Cases\Data Integrity Test. Create a sub-folder named **Evidence** under the folder Data Integrity Test. You should note while in the root of Data Integrity Test that EnCase has already created and saved the case file for you!

3. On the online resource web page is a folder named DataIntegrityTest. Under that folder are two subfolders: Normal and Corrupted. In each of these subfolders is one evidence file: MoneyTransferFloppyFD01.e01. From outward appearances, the files seem identical; however, their parent folder names (Normal and Corrupted) are

indicative of their true contents. Copy the evidence file from the Normal folder to the Evidence folder you just created.

4. Go back to EnCase; from the Home tab, click Add Evidence and then Add Evidence File. Browse to the file MoneyTransferFloppyFD01.e01 that you just placed in the Evidence folder and click Open.

5. EnCase will display the new piece of evidence in the Table tab of the Evidence tab. When a new evidence file is added to EnCase, it will automatically begin verifying the integrity of that evidence file. Since this was a floppy image, it happened nearly instantaneously. Let's see whether the file verified. You should be in the Evidence tab with only one evidence item showing in the Table tab. Place your cursor on that evidence item and click the Report tab in the view or bottom pane. Scroll down the report, and note that the file verified successfully and that the verification and acquisition hashes match.

6. Double-click the evidence item in the Table tab, and the evidence item will load, parse, and display in the Viewing tab of the Evidence tab. In the Tree pane, place your cursor on the floppy device, and the root-level directory structure will appear in the Table pane. Examine the contents of the only intact file in the root directory, which is a text file (MoneyTransfer.txt) containing information about a money transfer. Note carefully the account numbers because the next time you see these numbers, one digit will have changed!

7. Save your case, and exit EnCase.

8. On the online resource web page, locate the folder DataIntegrityTest\Corrupted\. Copy the evidence file in this folder into your Evidence folder. When asked if you want to overwrite the existing evidence file by the same name, select Yes. You now have a file by the same name and attributes as your previously verified evidence file. The only difference between the files is that someone has altered your evidence file by one bit when they changed one digit in an account number.

9. Start EnCase, and open your previously saved case. EnCase thinks that it has already verified this evidence file, so no file integrity check will occur. Check the contents of the text file in the root directory. You should note that the last digit of the account number has been changed.

10. To view the contents of the text file, you are in the Viewing tab of the Evidence tab. Click the green left-arrow (Back) to go back to the Table tab under the Evidence tab. Place your cursor on your evidence item, and at the far right of the Evidence tab, click the triangle for the drop-down menu and select Verify File Integrity (as depicted earlier in Figure 5.7). This process should take a matter of seconds because the evidence file is very small. Because there is an error, you should receive a pop-up warning indicating a file integrity check error. Click OK on the error message, and repeat the

process for checking the results on the Report tab for the floppy device. You should see that the verification completed with an error. You should see that the hashes do not match, and you should see a notation that sectors 0–63 could not be verified, meaning the error is contained in one 64 sector block of data starting at sector 0. If you go back to text file containing the account number, you'll note that this data is found in physical sector 33, which is in the unverified block.

11. You should now have an appreciation for the importance of post-case verification. If this had been a real-world case, you would replace the corrupted evidence file with another copy made from the original evidence file image.

12. Close EnCase without saving.

EnCase provides a tool that allows the examiner to verify individual evidence file segments. The need for this arises when evidence files are archived onto CDs and DVDs. You can access this feature by choosing Tools ➢ Verify Evidence Files. The MD5/SHA-1 hash can't be checked with this feature; however, EnCase verifies the CRC values for each block of data in a single evidence file.

Hashing Disks and Volumes

At this stage you understand that when EnCase acquires data, it calculates and writes CRC values for each block of data and then computes an MD5 hash (alternatively a SHA-1 or both) for the entire device or stream of data acquired. Whenever the resultant evidence file is added to a case, it is automatically verified. Every block of data is subjected to CRC reverification, and the entire device is subjected to a reverification of the MD5 hash (alternatively a SHA-1 or both). You can also reverify an evidence file manually at any time and should always do so at the conclusion of a case. Thus, EnCase was built with data integrity at its very core, and by understanding how it functions, you can better appreciate its built-in protections and be in a better position to explain them.

In addition to the protections and integrity checks discussed thus far, you can employ yet another integrity check by manually hashing a disk or volume that has been acquired. The hash feature will calculate an MD5 hash (alternatively a SHA-1 or both) for the selected physical or logical device. You can compare this value to the acquisition hash in the Report view. To hash a device, go to the Viewing tab. In the Tree pane, place your cursor at the root level, forcing the devices to be viewed in the Table pane. In the Table pane, place your cursor on the device to be hashed. On the Evidence tab, go to the Device Functions drop-down menu and choose Hash, as shown in Figure 5.10. You are next asked for the range of sectors to hash. Usually you will select the defaults—which is the entire device, as shown in Figure 5.11. Also, you can choose which hash algorithm you want to use, MD5, SHA-1, or both.

FIGURE 5.10   To hash a device, place your cursor on it in the Table pane, go to the Device Functions drop-down menu, and choose Hash.

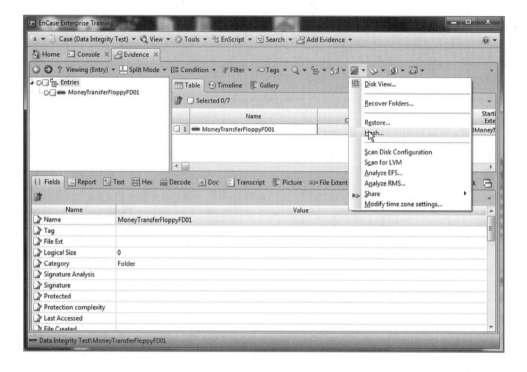

FIGURE 5.11   Before hashing, you are given an option to choose a start and stop sector. Usually, you'll choose the default, which is the entire device.

After the hash is done, you can compare this value to the acquisition hash, and they should match. The nice part about this feature is that you will be presented with a report, as shown in Figure 5.12, which contains the date, time, evidence name, sectors hashed, and hash value. You can include this report in your overall report as a note bookmark by selecting the Note check box. As I mentioned earlier in this chapter, since the Verify File Integrity function does not date/time stamp its results, you can include this hash report to reinforce your report.

FIGURE 5.12 Results of hashing a physical device. All the details displayed can be bookmarked and included in a "note bookmark."

 The Verify File Integrity function can be run only at the level of the acquired device. If you acquired a physical device, you can use the Verify File Integrity feature at the physical level only, and not at the volume level. If you acquired a physical device, you can hash it at either the physical level or the volume level. If you are using the hash feature to check the integrity of your acquired physical device, make sure you conduct your hash of the physical device. If you hash the volume instead, the results will differ as you are hashing a different set of sectors. In short, make sure you are comparing apples to apples, not apples to oranges!

EnCase Case Files

A *case* file is created when you first create a case in EnCase 7. Prior to EnCase 7, you had to manually create the various folders needed for EnCase to store various case-specific files. Starting with EnCase 7, you need only to accept the default base case folder or point to another location. EnCase 7 then creates the various subfolders as shown in Figure 5.13. Figure 5.14 shows the screen that opens when you tell EnCase to create a new case. You can see the default base case folder. Since I named this case BrandNewCase, you can see that it creates a folder by that name under the base case folder, as shown in the full case path entry. Also, if you look in Figure 5.13, you will see that EnCase now creates the case file for you initially and stores it in the root of the case name folder.

FIGURE 5.13   Various subfolders automatically created by EnCase under main case folder

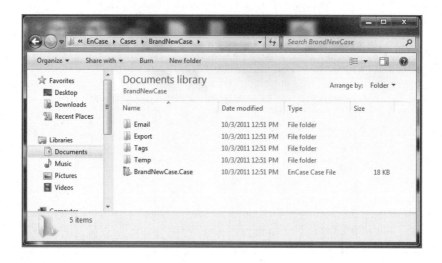

FIGURE 5.14   When you click Create New Case, the Case Options dialog appears, and you can set the Base Case folder and Case Name, as well as other parameters.

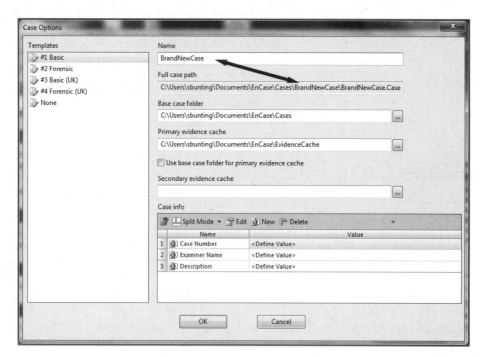

The case file is a plain-text file, mostly in Unicode, that contains pointers to the evidence file and case-specific information. Because the evidence file itself never changes, all search hits, bookmarks, notes, sorts, hash analysis, file verification information, and so forth, are stored in the case file with pointers to the evidence file. When you recover a partition, there is no partition inserted into the original evidence file. Rather, the partition is virtually reconstructed with data and pointers in the case file.

With time and analysis work, in prior versions of EnCase, these case files could get quite large and take some time to load. EnCase 7 changes this by saving compound (compressed archive files such as .zip and .rar), email archive files (.pst, .ost, .nsf, and so on) and other such files to disk as devices. They are accessed as needed for analysis and allow the case file to open almost instantly. The case file represents all your work in a case, so maintaining its integrity is important. You should frequently save your work by clicking Save as you complete a process or are about to start another step of the analysis. It takes only one unexpected crash and the loss of significant work to make this habit second nature.

Backing up the case file is also an important function. EnCase creates a backup automatically, as you'll see in the next section, but it is important to back up the case file at various points in your case, preferably daily. If a case file develops a problem, the backup can also be corrupted. Keeping daily backups of your case file in appropriately named folders gives you the Windows 7 equivalent of restore points. Figure 5.15 shows how you can organize such a daily case-file backup system. It takes only a few seconds to copy your case file to a backup folder, and if faithfully carried out, this process can save you a full day of work at some future point.

FIGURE 5.15   Folder naming and organizational structure to contain daily backups of your case file

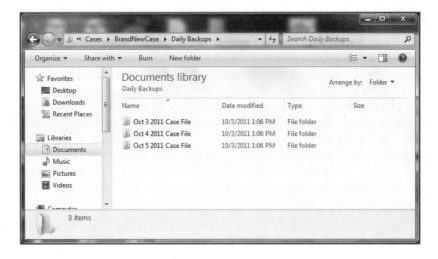

EnCase Backup Utility

The EnCase backup utility made its debut in EnCase 7.04 in May 2012. With its release, you can forget about .cbak files and the old way of backing up EnCase case files. In its place is a robust backup engine that will back up the following:

- Case file
- The contents of your case file, *except* for the following:
  - Temp folder
  - Export folder
  - Evidence files (.e01, .ex01, .l01, and .lx01)
- Primary evidence cache (only those cache files referenced in the case being backed up)
- Secondary evidence cache (only those cache files referenced in the case being backed up)
- Metadata for all files in backup (timestamps, file sizes, and so on), which are stored, among other data, in a SQLite database situated in the root of the backup path.

Before creating a case and defining the path for the case backup, you should first give careful consideration to where this backup will be stored. By default, the backup will be stored on the operating system drive, specifically in your user space. For some examiners, this may be acceptable; however, for most it will likely not be acceptable. If you've optimized your system and are running your OS on a relatively small SSD, you will not want to use the default location. In keeping with best practices, your backup should not be on your local system but should be safe on yet another attached system or perhaps a SAN or NAS.

You will select the path for the backup location when you create a new case, as shown in Figure 5.16. You have a choice of having a backup occur every 30 minutes or not at all, by selecting or deselecting the Backup Every 30 Minutes option. Future releases may allow adjusting this interval from within the new case Options menu. Clearly, turning this backup off is not a very good practice, because you will not have any backup at all.

From the Options menu in Figure 5.16, you may choose the maximum size for your case size backup in gigabytes. Currently the default size with version 7.04 is only 30 gigabytes, which I find to be far too small. You don't know what size your evidence cache will be until you process it. If this setting is too low, your initial backup, regardless of size, will complete. However, no subsequent backup will occur until you adjust this setting upward. You will see warnings occur on the bottom of the EnCase window. If so, change this setting at once so that your system can properly continue to back up critical files. I recommend setting this figure high at first and then later evaluating the size of your backup and how large you want it to be. You can then lower this setting if you'd like.

FIGURE 5.16   The new case Options menu contains basic backup configuration settings.

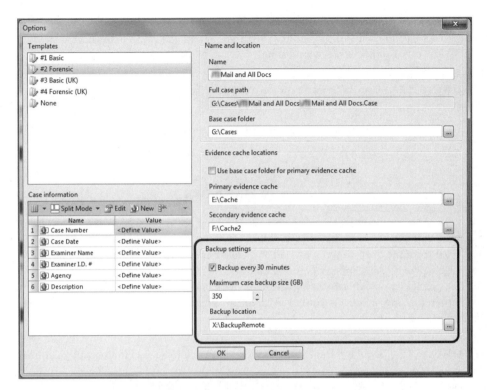

Once you create your case with the proper backup settings in place, the process will run as a background task. When it runs, every 30 minutes, you will see a green progress bar in the lower right, labeled Case Backup, as shown in Figure 5.17. There are a few pointers you should know about your backup feature in addition to knowing the contents it protects.

- By default a schedule backup will occur on 30-minute intervals, normally starting 30 minutes after the previous one completed (not started!).

- If you need to stop the backup, double-click the thread in the progress window in the lower right.

- The backup will stop when you close the case.

- When the backup runs, it disables the automatic timer, thus making sure the 30-minute interval is based on when the previous backup completes.

- When EEP runs, the backup stops as EEP creates and modifies a large number of files that the backup is trying to back up as they are being added or modified, which is not a good thing to have occur.

• When EEP completes, the backup process will start shortly thereafter and usually will run for a long time because of the amount of new data in the evidence cache. While work can be done while the backup is running, it is a good practice to let this backup occur uninterrupted, because you want to get your evidence cache backed up for the first time. You may want to think of this first backup as just an extension of the EEP process in terms of workflow and time.

FIGURE 5.17   Backup thread running as shown in progress bar in the lower-right corner

It will be rare that you will need to recover from the backup. If, however, you need to do so, you will need to first close the case that you want to back up. You access the backup dashboard from the drop-down menu on the Case tab, as shown in Figure 5.18. From there, Use Current Case, Specify Case File, or Specify Backup Location will all eventually take you to backup dashboard. In Figure 5.18, there is no current case open (Use Current Case is therefore grayed out) because I'm about to show you the basics of restoring a case. Thus, I'll specify a case file for the case I want to restore.

FIGURE 5.18   Click the Case tab's drop-down menu to access the backup dashboard.

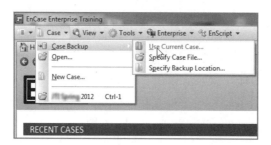

Once you select the case file for the case you want to back up, you'll next see the backup dashboard, as shown in Figure 5.19. Before you can see any backup dates and times, you must first place your cursor on the Scheduled folder in the left, or Tree, pane. Only then do you see in the Table pane the list of dates and times for the various backups that have been created. Figure 5.19 shows one backup having been selected from which to restore. With one selected, the next step is to click Restore, which is found on the toolbar and is one of the items circled in Figure 5.19.

FIGURE 5.19   Backup dashboard showing available "restore points" based on scheduled backups that have been made

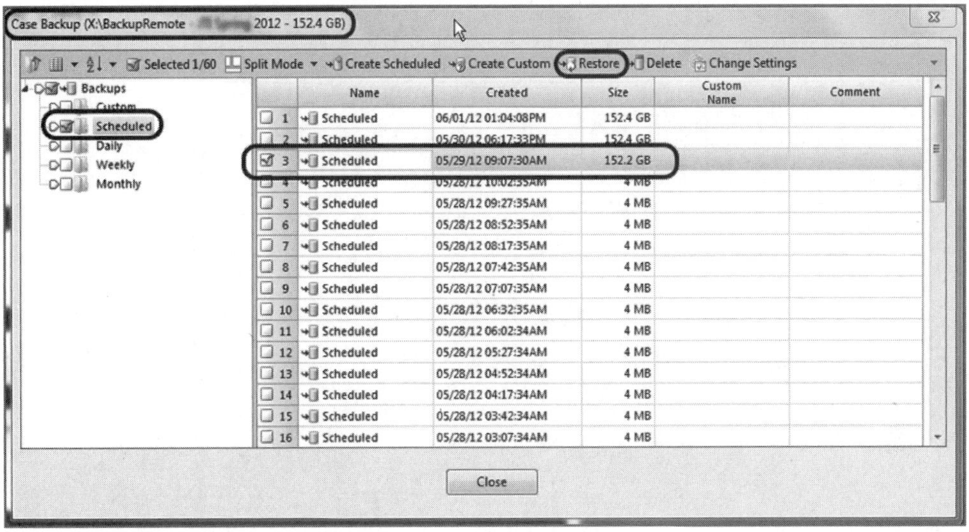

Clicking Restore will launch yet another menu, which will force you to make a decision to restore your case to its current location or to a new location, as shown in Figure 5.20. Whatever you do, do not rush through this process simply accepting the defaults, because the default here is to restore to the same location. By all means, give this some thought. If you accept the default, EnCase will write over your evidence cache and your case folder, except for the Temp and Export folders and evidence files. If you overwrite existing files and folders, even with those exceptions, you could, potentially, make your problem worse. Just keep in mind that the default option will overwrite the current state of your case. Before doing so, make sure this is what you want to do. I would suggest, before restoring to the original location, that you copy your case folder and evidence cache elsewhere, just in case.

The first time I attempted to restore to the original location, a path error message occurred. After clicking through the error, my next choice was that of reopening the case. When I did so, a message appeared that my case file was corrupt. When I went to examine my case file, I found it was missing. I had to recover my case file before I could continue. From that experience I learned a valuable lesson, and it is one that forms the basis of my recommendation to make a copies of evidence cache and your case folder before restoring to the original location.

FIGURE 5.20   When restoring, you must choose between the original case location or a new location.

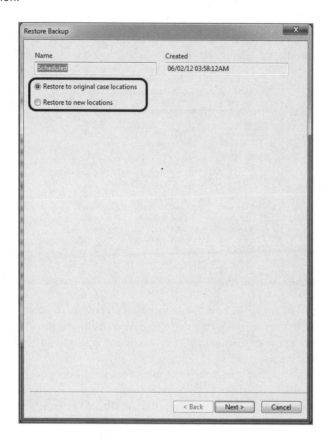

If you decide to restore to a new location, you'll be prompted for a location for both your case and your evidence cache. If you've opted to restore to the original location, you will see a screen similar to that in Figure 5.21, with all the original path settings in place, except grayed out because they are locked in as everything is configured to be restored in its original place. If you opt for a new location, you'll see the screen as in Figure 5.21 in which all the path locations are configurable. You could, as I have done in this example, restore your evidence cache to its original location and restore the case file to a new location. Once you have selected your options, click Finish, and the restoration will start. As is often the case, there is considerable data to be written, and restoring will take a commensurate amount of time. When the task is completed, you can reopen your case, and you will be at the point in time you selected from your list of backups.

FIGURE 5.21   Restore Backup dialog on which you may configure new paths and from which you launch the restoration task

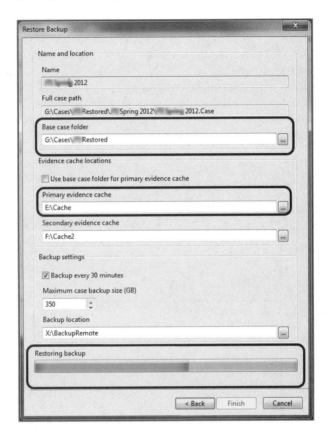

If you look carefully at Figure 5.21, you will note that the case file (and with it the evidence files) are on drive letter G. The primary evidence cache is on yet another drive letter, which is E. The secondary evidence cache is on yet another drive letter, which is F. The backup location is on yet another drive, which is X and is a mapped drive. Notice that none of these storage locations is found on drive letter C, which is the operating system. Drive G (primary evidence cache) is a RAID 0 array of SSD drives, thus optimized for high throughput reads and writes. Drive F (secondary evidence cache) is also SSD storage. Drive C (the O/S) is also SSD storage. Drive G (case and evidence files) is a high-performance RAID 5 with platter-based storage.

This configuration reflects the author's recommended hardware configuration for running EnCase 7. If you missed those recommendations, they are at the beginning of the book at the very end of the foreword. Providing EnCase with adequate resources that are properly configured is essential for having EnCase 7 perform the way it was designed. You will not regret following these recommendations!

Before we conclude our discussion of the EnCase Backup utility, you may have noted the presence of daily, weekly, and monthly backups on the backup dashboard. For example, Figure 5.22 shows daily backups. These are not special backups created daily but rather the first backup (not the last!) that occurs on each day the case is open. It is simply dubbed or virtually established as a daily backup. For each daily backup listed, you'll find a scheduled backup for that precise time. Much the same can be said for the weekly and monthly backups. They are organizational constructs, if you will, created out of the scheduled backups. You can recover or restore from any of them, just as I demonstrated with the scheduled backups.

FIGURE 5.22   Daily backups shown in the backup dashboard

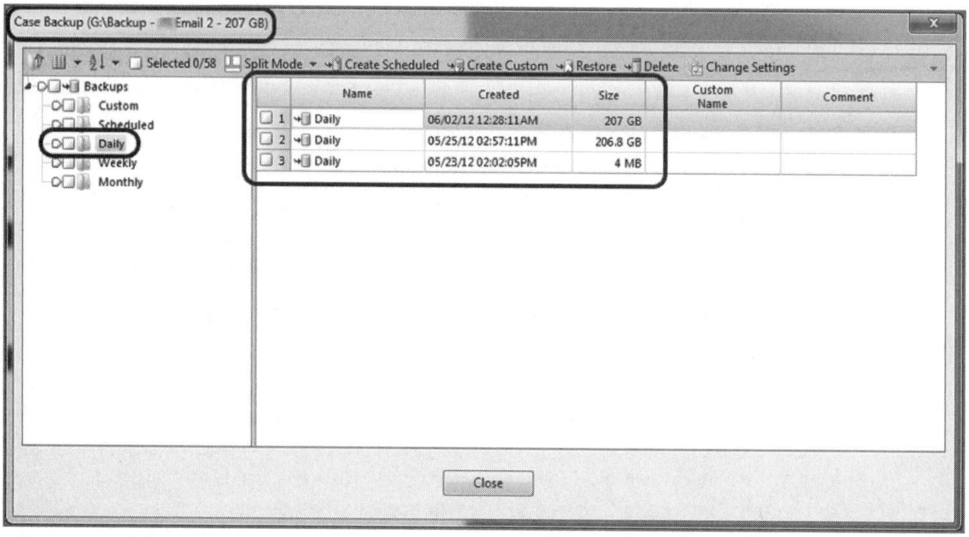

You will also note that you can create custom backups, create additional scheduled backups, delete backups, and change settings from the toolbar menu. While the default backup settings I have discussed will more than suffice for most examiners, you can embark on a much more customized backup program. The release notes for EnCase 7.04 and subsequent user manuals do a very nice job of discussing these custom options, including describing size and frequency limitations. If you are interested in further customizing the backup process, you should read this material first.

NOTE If you need to, you can change the logical name of the evidence file. This does not change the contents of the evidence file, and the evidence file will still verify. For example, you can change SuspectFloppy01.e01 to SuspectFloppyFD01.e01. You can also move the evidence file to another path or drive. When EnCase opens a case and the evidence file is not where EnCase last recorded it, it will prompt you for the new path. Changing the evidence filename or its location does not affect file integrity or the verification process at all. Changing the evidence file's logical name on the examiner hard drive will not change the unique name of the evidence file displayed in the EnCase case file and report. That name is included in the header of the evidence file and is protected by a CRC. To change the unique name of an evidence file, the original evidence must be reimaged, thus creating a new evidence file with the new name.

EnCase Configuration Files

Prior to EnCase 7, global configuration settings for EnCase were stored in a series of initialization files (dubbed ini files after their file extension). By default they were all stored in \Program Files\Encase#\Config, and they were all applied globally to every instance of EnCase, regardless of the user on the system.

EnCase 7 has certainly undergone a significant change in the way configuration files are stored. Starting with Windows Vista, Microsoft became more security conscious and encouraged programmers to separate program data from user data because of security permissions for the different data types. Also, the user could go to one general area for user files and thereby stay away from critical program and configuration data.

With EnCase 7, Guidance Software designed its program to adhere to these data storage recommendations. An added benefit to this scheme is that by separating program data from user data, global configuration files could be updated without overwriting custom user settings. For example, if you created custom text styles, upgrading EnCase could result in the loss of those custom settings. Under the new storage scheme, the default text styles that ship with EnCase can be updated when the program is updated. The user-created text styles are stored with user data and are untouched by these changes. This is a most welcome change.

The following are the storage paths used by EnCase to store configuration data, along with a brief description of the files stored therein:

- User data (C:\Users\UserName\Documents\EnCase): You may expect to find files created by the user in this folder, which will, in turn, contain many subfolders for organizational purposes, as shown in Figure 5.23. The default location for the base case folder is in this folder.

- User application data (C:\Users\UserName\AppData\Roaming\EnCase7-1\Config): These are files that are configuration files, along with some temporary files that are user-specific. As such, other users of EnCase on this system will not be affected by these settings. Figure 5.24 shows a typical set of files found in this folder. Veteran users of EnCase will recognize some of these filenames. The viewer configuration file (viewers.ini) is where file viewers configured by the user are stored. The file local.ini is a familiar file, but its use has been greatly expanded under EnCase 7. It traditionally held recently opened cases and other historical information but now holds, for example, user-defined text styles. In this fashion, you can have global text styles and user text styles combined, and updating one doesn't impact the other. You should note that this folder (EnCase7-1) and the one that follows under Global Application Data are version-specific, and the suffix following EnCase will change as EnCase is updated.

- Global application data (C:\Users\Default\AppData\Roaming\EnCase7-1\Config): This folder contains global configuration settings for all users on this machine and typically contains the NAS settings.

FIGURE 5.23   Subfolders organized under the folder reserved for user data

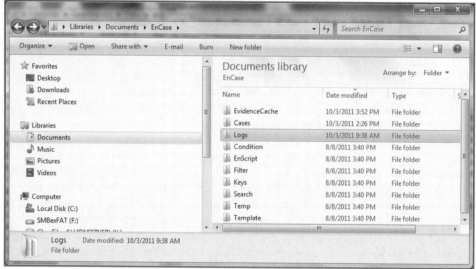

 With Windows Vista and Windows 7 came a new folder structure under the user's root folder. The folder named My Documents in Windows XP and earlier was renamed Documents, or at least that is what is shown by EnCase. However, when you see the Documents folder in Windows Explorer, you'll see it as My Documents in some views and as Documents in other views. It is seen as My Documents because of a hidden file located in the Documents folder that points to a registry location that defines how the file is supposed to appear, regardless of its real name.

FIGURE 5.24   Files typically found in the folder reserved for user application data

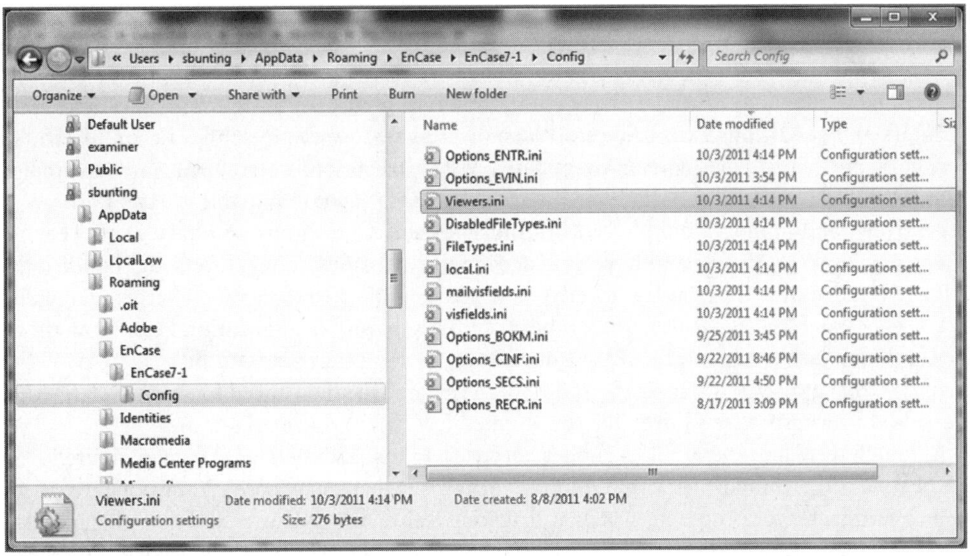

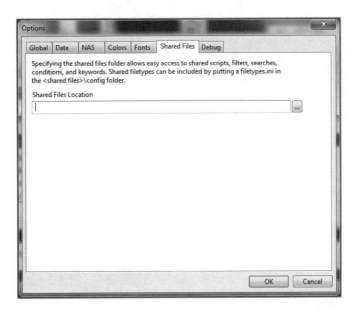

In addition to the previous configuration file locations, you can also define a shared location to keep various settings such that they can be shared by other users in your lab group. Settings that can be shared are, for example, Keys, Text Styles, File Types, Conditions, Searches, and EnScript modules. Figure 5.25 shows the Shared Files tab under Tools ➢ Options where this location is configured.

FIGURE 5.25   Shared Files tab where shared configuration files can be stored for group access

EnScripts can be stored in two or sometimes three locations now. The `EnScripts` folder under `\Program Files\EnCase 7` is where veteran EnCase users would expect to find it, and it is one of the locations. The user can now have their own EnScript folder located at `\Users\UserName\Documents\EnCase\EnScript`. In the previous paragraph, we learned that we could share EnScripts under the Shared Files tab. Therefore, if configured, the third location would be defined under that tab, as shown in Figure 5.25.

Filters and conditions used to be stored en masse within a single configuration file and were constantly being overwritten by updates, which frustrated users. Now, user-created conditions and filters will be stored in the user data area (`Condition` and `Filter` folders, respectively) and in individual files within those folders. Conditions will have `.Enfilter` extensions, and conditions will have `.EnCondition` extensions. Thus, filters and conditions will become separate files, easily stored, easily shared, and therefore much better managed.

File types and file signatures used to be stored in separate configuration files. Now they are combined into a single table (`FileTypes.ini`), except that there will be at least two such files (one global and one user), and perhaps even three if a shared location is defined. Individual user settings will override the shipped (global) and shared settings.

Although there are several folders under `\Program Files\Encase 7`, as shown in Figure 5.26, one of considerable import for configuration purposes is the `certs` folder. Your dongle may require certificates for proper licensing. When you receive your software and licensing information from myaccount@guidancesoftware.com, any certificates that are needed will be provided via download links. Place these certificates in this folder for proper licensing and function of your software, as shown in Figure 5.27. You should note that the `pcert` and `scert` files are installed as part of EnCase. In this case, the `EnCase.cert` file is required for this particular dongle to have EnCase 7 functionality. There are other cert files that may be required to be placed here depending on your version of EnCase and licensing methods in use.

FIGURE 5.26 Folders under EnCase 7

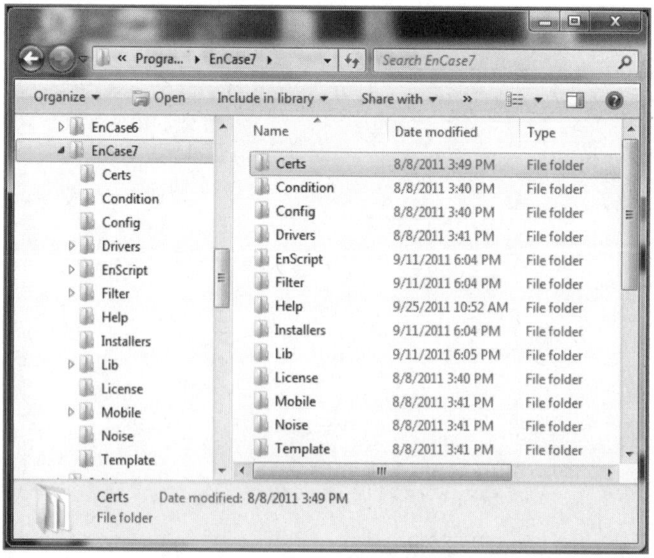

FIGURE 5.27   Licensing files (.cert extension) in the Certs folder

Evidence Cache Folder

The evidence cache folder is a container folder for a variety of files associated with the parsing of the evidence file when it is first loaded and also the subsequent processing by the EnCase evidence processor. At a minimum, it will contain the device caches, device index, and keyword search results. The location of this folder is defined when you first create a new case, as shown in Figure 5.14 in the entry named Primary Evidence Cache. Each device in the case has a GUID, as shown in the report area for the device in Figure 5.28. If this same file were to be reacquired, it would be assigned a new GUID even though the hashes would be identical. When the evidence cache is created for a device in a case, the folder containing the evidence cache information will be assigned a folder name bearing that GUID, as shown in Figure 5.29. Figure 5.29 also shows the various files stored in the evidence cache folder.

FIGURE 5.28 GUID for device that is unique to each acquisition

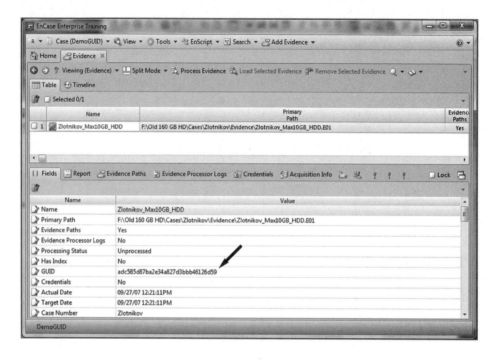

FIGURE 5.29 GUID-named folder in evidence cache folder bearing same GUID assigned in Figure 5.28

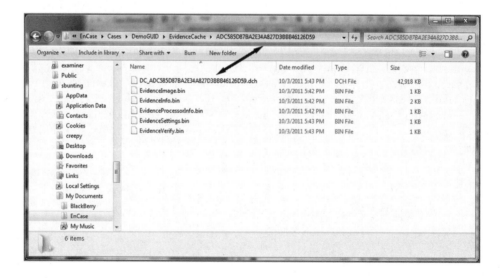

Terminology Is Important!

It seems each time I attend a computer forensics course, I am told to rephrase the wording of how I acquire a forensic copy of digital evidence. Terms such as *mirror*, *bit-by-bit*, *bitstream*, and *image* have been used at one time or another to describe a forensic acquisition of digital evidence. With regard to acquiring evidence using EnCase, I use the phrase "an exact copy to an EnCase evidence file."

Defense attorneys have asserted that the EnCase evidence file is not an exact duplicate of the original evidence. Some savvy ones try to prove their point by mentioning that the MD5/SHA-1 hash value of the original evidence does not match that of an EnCase evidence file—and they are correct. Forensic examiners have commonly used the previous terms to describe how they acquired evidence using EnCase because that is what they were taught. Now that you have a better understanding of the EnCase process, you can explain that an EnCase evidence file does contain an exact copy of the original evidence in the data blocks. The matching acquisition and verification hashes are derived from original evidence and the data blocks. In addition, an EnCase evidence file contains additional data such as case information, CRC checks, and MD5/SHA-1 hash values of the original evidence outside the data blocks.

So, when someone challenges an EnCase evidence file claiming it is not an exact duplicate of the original evidence because of different MD5/SHA-1 hash values, you can argue that an EnCase evidence file does contain an exact duplicate of the original evidence along with additional information. As to whether an EnCase evidence file has the same MD5/SHA-1 hash value as the original evidence—of course it doesn't, because of the additional information contained within the evidence file. However, EnCase will only verify and generate an MD5/SHA-1 hash value of the information contained within the data blocks of an evidence file, which is then compared to the MD5/SHA-1 hash value of the original evidence obtained during the acquisition.

Summary

This chapter covered the EnCase evidence file. This file has three essential parts: the header, the data blocks, and the file integrity components.

The header contains the case information. It appears at the front of the evidence file and is subjected to its own CRC calculation to ensure its integrity. It is always compressed.

The data blocks contain, by default, 64 sectors (32 K) of data. The block size can be adjusted upward, starting with EnCase 5, to speed acquisitions. Each block of data contains its own CRC value, and each block is included in the overall MD5 calculation (alternatively SHA-1 or both) for the entire device being imaged. If compression is chosen, the block of data and its CRC are compressed.

The file integrity components are the CRC values and the MD5 hash (alternatively SHA-1 or both). CRC values are calculated and stored for the header and all data blocks.

The MD5 hash is calculated against the data only and does not include the header or any CRCs. The CRC values are stored with each block of data. The MD5 is stored at the end of the file in an appendix containing the MD5 along with other evidence file metadata.

EnCase 7 introduces a new evidence file format, dubbed ex01 and 1x01. This new format changes the storage structure somewhat and allows for encryption and a new compression format (bzip2). The new format contains three major sections or parts within the file(s), which are Ev2 Header, Data, and Link Record.

Whenever an evidence file is added to a case in EnCase, it undergoes a file integrity check. The CRC for each block of data is recalculated and compared to the stored acquisition CRC value. The MD5 (alternatively SHA-1 or both) for the entire device is recalculated, resulting in a verification hash, which is then compared to the acquisition hash. For a file to be successfully verified, all CRC values must match, and the verification and acquisition hashes must match. A reverification can be run at any time to reaffirm a file's integrity.

A CRC is an algorithm that results in a 32-bit value. The odds of any two files having the same CRC value are roughly 1 in 4 billion. An MD5 is an algorithm that results in a 128-bit value. The odds of any two files having the same MD5 value are roughly 1 in 340 billion billion billion billion.

EnCase has a feature that allows you to hash a physical device or volume. This feature generates an MD5 (alternatively SHA-1 or both) hash in a report that is date/time stamped. This can be included in your report to reinforce EnCase's file integrity features.

The EnCase case file stores information about the evidence file in the form of data and pointers to the evidence file. In this way, search hits, bookmarks, notes, file signature analyses, and so forth, are contained in a file separate from the evidence file yet "married" to it through metadata and pointers. The case file is saved when you exit EnCase or click the Save button. It is usually stored in the root of the case name folder.

The EnCase backup files are created automatically by EnCase. The files backed up by this process are the evidence cache and the case folder, except for the Temp and Export folders and EnCase evidence files. They are stored separately from the case files and are stored, by default, in a folder located in the user space on the operating system drive. In most cases, this default location is not recommended and should be configured elsewhere in a safe location, suitable for critical backup data. By default the backup process runs every 30 minutes after the previous backup completes. Backup options are set when a new case is created or can be modified from the backup dashboard. The backup dashboard is accessed from the Case tab's drop-down menu. The backup dashboard, among other things, lists the various backups that have been created. The EnCase backup dashboard enables you to select any backup point and restore your case to that point in time, either overwriting your original data folder paths or creating new ones.

EnCase stores its configuration settings in INI files. There are, starting with EnCase 7, both global and user configuration files. Global configuration files are stored in Program Files\EnCase 7\Config and Users\Default\AppData\Roaming\EnCase7-1\Config. Configuration files specific to the user are stored in Users\UserName\AppData\Roaming\EnCase7-1\Config and Users\UserName\Documents\EnCase. The storage paths for various configuration files can be configured to a shared location so that examiners in a multiuser lab can share configuration files and work under one standardized EnCase environment.

Exam Essentials

Understand the components and function of the EnCase evidence file.   Be able to name and describe the three major components of an EnCase evidence file, in both the legacy and new formats. Understand and be able to explain the mechanisms by which data integrity is maintained in the evidence file. Describe how an EnCase evidence file is created. Explain how changing the block size changes the frequency of CRC values.

Know how the file verification process works.   Know under what circumstances the verification process occurs. Understand and be able to explain what takes place during the file verification process and what conditions must be met for a successful evidence file verification. Be able to conduct a manual file verification. Know where to find the results of the file verification process, and be able to describe the results and their meaning to the file integrity process.

Know how to hash a physical device or a volume.   Understand and be able to explain the MD5 and SHA-1 hash. Describe how to hash a physical device or a volume and bookmark the results. Understand how to compare the results of these hash values with the acquisition and verification hashes. If hashing to verify an acquisition value, explain the importance of hashing the correct device (physical or logical).

Understand the content and function of the EnCase case file.   Explain the purpose of the EnCase case file. Be able to explain in general terms the kind of information contained in the file. Explain when and how the file is named, its extension, when it is saved, and where it should normally be stored.

Understand the function of the EnCase backup process.   Explain the purpose and features of the EnCase backup dashboard. Be able to explain which files and folders are backed and which are not. Know how often the default backup process occurs. Explain how the path for the backup is established as well as where this path should be located. Describe the process by which the backup dashboard is used to restore a case to a given point in time.

Understand how and where EnCase stores its configuration settings.   Know where both the global and user configuration files are stored. Explain how to configure a shared location such that various configuration files can be shared in a lab group. Explain what kind of data is stored in the common configuration files.

Review Questions

1. The EnCase evidence file is best described as follows:

    A. A mirror image of the source device written to a hard drive

    B. A sector-by-sector image of the source device written to corresponding sectors of a secondary hard drive

    C. A bitstream image of a source device written to the corresponding sectors of a secondary hard drive

    D. A bitstream image of a source device written to a file or several file segments

2. How does EnCase verify the contents of an evidence file, using the default settings?

    A. EnCase writes an MD5 and/or SHA-1 hash value for every 32 sectors copied.

    B. EnCase writes an MD5 and/or SHA-1 value for every 64 sectors copied.

    C. EnCase writes a CRC value for every 32 sectors copied.

    D. EnCase writes a CRC value for every 64 sectors copied.

3. What is the smallest file size that an EnCase evidence file can be saved as?

    A. 64 sectors

    B. 512 sectors

    C. 1 MB

    D. 30 MB

    E. 640 MB

4. What is the largest file segment size that an EnCase evidence file can be saved as?

    A. 640 MB

    B. 1 GB

    C. 2 GB

    D. 8,796,093,018,112 MB

    E. No maximum limit

5. How does EnCase verify that the evidence file contains an exact copy of the source device?

    A. By comparing the MD5 hash value (alternatively SHA-1 or both) of the source device to the MD5 hash value (alternatively SHA-1 or both) of the data stored in the evidence file

    B. By comparing the CRC value of the source device to the CRC of the data stored in the evidence file

    C. By comparing the MD5 hash value (alternatively SHA-1 or both) of the source device to the MD5 hash value (alternatively SHA-1 or both) of the entire evidence file

    D. By comparing the CRC value of the source device to the CRC value of the entire evidence file

6. How does EnCase verify that the case information—such as case number, evidence number, notes, and so on—in an evidence file has not been damaged or altered after the evidence file has been written?

   A. The case file writes a CRC value for the case information and verifies it when the case is opened.

   B. EnCase does not verify the case information, because it can be changed at any time.

   C. EnCase writes a CRC value for the case information and verifies the CRC value when the evidence is added to a case.

   D. EnCase writes an MD5 value of the case information and verifies the MD5 value when the evidence is added to a case.

7. For an EnCase evidence file to successfully pass the file verification process, which of the following must be true?

   A. The MD5 hash value (alternatively SHA-1 or both) must verify.

   B. The CRC values and the MD5 hash value (alternatively SHA-1 or both) both must verify.

   C. Either the CRC or MD5 hash values (alternatively SHA-1 or both) must verify.

   D. The CRC values must verify.

8. The MD5 hash algorithm produces a _____ value.

   A. 32-bit

   B. 64-bit

   C. 128-bit

   D. 256-bit

9. Regarding the EnCase backup process (EnCase 7.04 and newer), which are the following are true?

   A. The case file backup is stored with a .cbak extension.

   B. By default, the backup frequency is every 30 minutes after completion of the previous backup.

   C. The evidence cache and the case folder are backed up, except for EnCase evidence files and the Temp and Export folders.

   D. All of the above are correct.

   E. Only B and C are correct.

10. If an evidence file has been added to a case and completely verified, what happens if the data area within the evidence file is later altered?

   A. EnCase will detect the error when that area of the evidence file is accessed by the user.

   B. EnCase will detect the error only if the evidence file is manually reverified.

   C. EnCase will allow the examiner to continue to access the rest of the evidence file that has not been changed, but will not allow access to the corrupted or changed block.

   D. All of the above.

11. Which of the following aspects of the EnCase evidence file can be changed during a reacquisition of the evidence file?

    A. Investigator's name

    B. Evidence number

    C. Notes

    D. Evidence file size

    E. All of the above

12. An evidence file was archived onto five CD-ROMs with the third file segment on disc 3. Can the contents of the third file segment be verified by itself while still on the CD-ROM?

    A. No. All evidence file segments must be put back together.

    B. Yes. Any evidence file segment can be verified independently by comparing the CRC values.

13. Will EnCase allow a user to write data into an acquired evidence file?

    A. Yes, when adding notes or comments to bookmarks.

    B. Yes, when adding search results.

    C. A and B.

    D. No, data cannot be added to the evidence file after the acquisition is made.

14. All investigators using EnCase should run tests on the evidence file acquisition and verification process to do which of the following?

    A. To further the investigator's understanding of the evidence file

    B. To give more weight to the investigator's testimony in court

    C. To verify that all hardware and software is functioning properly

    D. All of the above

15. When a noncompressed evidence file is reacquired with compression, the acquisition and verification hash values for the evidence file will remain the same for both files.

    A. True

    B. False

16. The Ex01 evidence file format consists of three parts, which are the Ev2 Header, Data, and CRC record block.

    A. True

    B. False

17. The EnCase evidence file's logical filename can be changed without affecting the verification of the acquired evidence.

    A. True

    B. False

18. An evidence file can be moved to another directory without changing the file verification.

    A. True

    B. False

19. What happens when EnCase attempts to reopen a case once the evidence file has been moved?

    A. EnCase reports that the file's integrity has been compromised and renders the file useless.

    B. EnCase reports a different hash value for the evidence file.

    C. EnCase prompts for the location of the evidence file.

    D. EnCase opens the case, excluding the moved evidence file.

20. During reacquisition, you can change which of the following? (Choose all that apply.)

    A. Block size and error granularity

    B. Add or remove a password

    C. Investigator's name

    D. Compression

    E. File segment size

Chapter

6

EnCase Environment

In this chapter, you will explore the many views and features of EnCase. Each version of EnCase has introduced new features, resulting in additional interfaces or views. Screen real estate is always a scarce resource, and the arrangement and placement of features will always be a programming challenge. EnCase 7 changes the viewing landscape significantly when compared to previous versions. Veteran users, myself included, grumbled when they first experienced the changes; however, once you take the time to learn the new interface, you'll find that it is logically arranged and easy to use. The best way to learn the new interface is to use it, so, with that being said, let's get started.

Home Screen

When you launch EnCase 7, you will see the Home screen, as shown in Figure 6.1. From this screen, aside from what is available on the various toolbar menus, you can open a case, create a new case, choose options, view paths, or access the help screens. If you have recently opened cases, they will also be available to you under the Recent Cases section, as shown in Figure 6.1.

From the Home screen shown in Figure 6.1, I opted to open an existing case, which was called bbtest. Soon, I'll go into creating a new case, but for now I simply want to show the EnCase landscape. Upon opening the existing case, you can see many options still on the Home screen pertaining to the open case, as shown in Figure 6.2.

In the Evidence category, you can add evidence or process evidence. In the Search category, you can search the case or view the results of a search. In the Browse category, you can view evidence or view records, such as email or Internet artifacts. In the Report category, you can go to the reports created thus far, go to the bookmarks view, or work with report templates. In the Case category, you can view case information, modify options, modify hash library settings, or save the case.

So that you can see how EnCase 7 displays information, let's choose to browse evidence (click Evidence in the Browse section). This will open the Evidence tab, and in the Table tab of the Evidence tab you will see, in table and row format, the various evidence items in the case, as shown in Figure 6.3.

FIGURE 6.1   EnCase 7 Home screen, from which you can open cases, create a new case, select options, view current paths, or access help

FIGURE 6.2   After opening an existing case, the Home screen provides the examiner with many options pertaining to the case.

FIGURE 6.3   Upon choosing to browse evidence, the examiner is taken to a tab displaying the evidence items currently in the case.

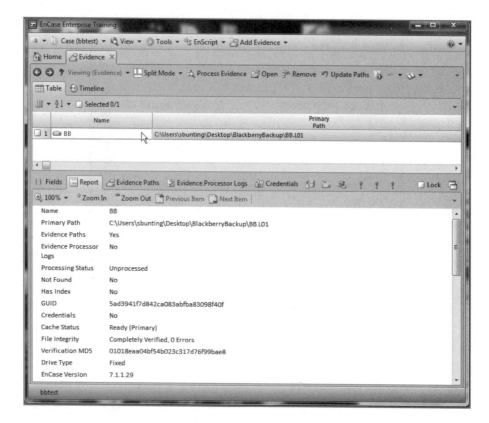

At this point, EnCase is displaying only a list of evidence items in the case and no data. To view a particular evidence item, you need only double-click it in the Table tab, which will parse and load into a Viewing tab. If you've already viewed it before, the data will be read from the evidence cache, and the results will be displayed quickly. If it is the first time viewing an evidence item, it must first be parsed and the evidence cache created, which may take a few minutes depending on the size and complexity of the evidence being loaded.

Of course, there are few times when you have multiple evidence items and want to see only one item. Usually, you want to browse them all. Many veteran users of EnCase miss a step here that enables them to browse multiple items, and thus they get frustrated. It is very simple to do but often overlooked. To load and view multiple evidence items, simply select them with blue check marks. As soon as you select one item, the Load Selected Evidence toolbar option (on the Evidence tab) becomes active (no longer grayed out). Select the evidence items you want to load and view and click Open, as shown in Figure 6.4.

FIGURE 6.4   To load and view multiple evidence items, select them (the blue check mark) and click Open on the Evidence tab toolbar.

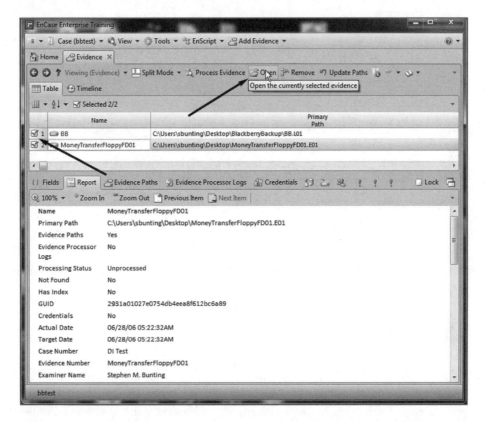

Once your evidence item loads, you'll see the results displayed in the Viewing Entry tab under the Evidence tab. For veteran EnCase users, this view will be quite familiar, as shown in Figure 6.5.

FIGURE 6.5   Evidence loaded and ready for viewing

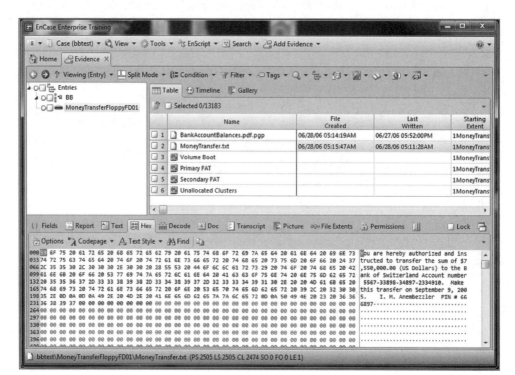

EnCase Layout

Once you've loaded the evidence, EnCase provides you with, by default, a Tree-Table view from the Evidence tab. As just stated, this view is quite familiar to veteran EnCase users and will probably be the view most often used, but it is not the only view, which I'll discuss shortly.

In the Entries Tree-Table view, EnCase divides its screen real estate into three windows that are named for their primary examination function: the Tree pane (formerly the Left pane), the Table pane (formerly the Right pane), and the View pane (formerly the Bottom pane), as shown in Figure 6.6. Granularity or detail increases as you move through the primary panes from the Tree pane to the Table pane and finally to the View pane. If you want details about an object (physical device, volume, or folder), place the cursor focus on it (in other words, highlight it) in the Tree pane, and the Table pane will display the details about that object. If you want more details about an object in the Table pane, highlight it in the Table pane, and the details will appear in the View pane. Once you get down to the data level of granularity in the View pane, you can view or interpret that data in several ways, effectively getting still more information or granularity from the View pane.

EnCase uses what amounts to a tabbed viewing environment. The tabs have labels that describe the view available under that tab. In this book and in the formal documentation, we'll refer to the various views by the view offered by the tab, such as Report view, Hex view, and so forth. Many examiners, however, refer to the views as tabs, such as Report tab, Hex tab, and so forth. There is really no difference, so don't be confused. The tab gives you access to the view, and it becomes, to many, a matter of preference how they name it when talking about it.

FIGURE 6.6   EnCase divides its screen real estate into the Tree, Table, and View panes.

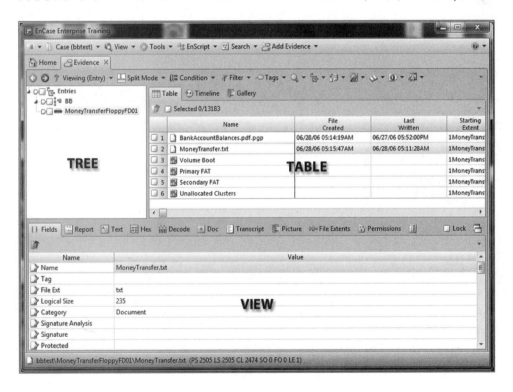

In addition to case Entries view, EnCase offers many other views or features that function in the same manner, providing more granularity as you move through the viewing panes. EnCase 7 uses tab views. As you open other views (Bookmarks, Secure Storage, or Records, for example), tabs will appear for each view. In Figure 6.7, I simply went to the View menu and opened Bookmarks, Secure Storage, and Records, which caused each to launch in its own tab. Once you take a few minutes to familiarize yourself with how it works, it is easy to find your way around.

FIGURE 6.7   Arrows point to various tabs.

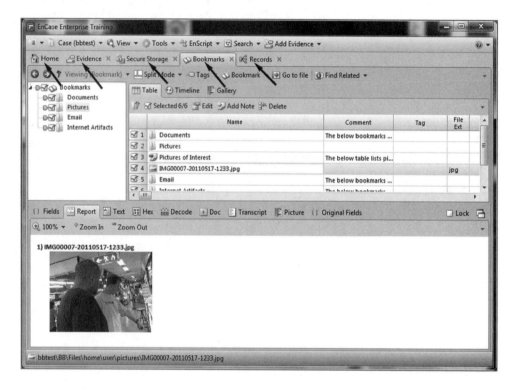

I cover many of these other views or features later in this chapter. For now, I'll focus on showing how to create a case and work in the Entries Tree-Table view. The option to work with the cases appears on the Home screen and also on the case drop-down menu on the application toolbar. Which you decide to use is often a matter of personal preference. For now, let's use the Home screen and open its tab, which is the leftmost tab, as shown in Figure 6.7 (note the house icon next to it). Another reason for working from the Home screen is because you will see this screen by default whenever you open EnCase. Thus, it is from here that you will start your exploration of EnCase's environment and features.

Creating a Case

The Tree pane is the starting point for the detail that follows in the other two panes and the location from where you will do much of your work in EnCase. However, before you can work with the Tree pane, or any pane for that matter, you need to have a case open. And before you can have a case open, you need to create a case. When EnCase starts, it opens by default to the Home screen. From the Home screen, you create a case by clicking New Case in the case file section. Alternatively, you can select Case ➢ New Case from the application toolbar. After you click New Case, you are presented with the dialog box shown in Figure 6.8. I have sectioned this box into four major areas to assist with the discussion. Those areas are the templates area (A), case name area (B), path area (C), and the Case Info area (D). I discussed this dialog box to some degree in Chapter 5 when I covered the paths and storage locations of EnCase files.

FIGURE 6.8   The Case Options dialog box

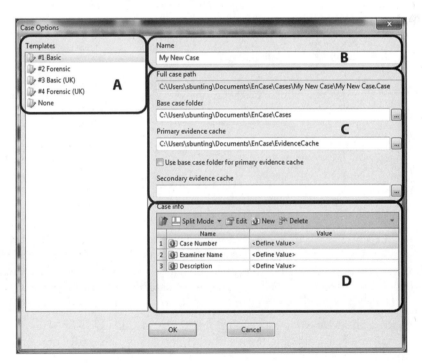

Templates   Templates, section A, are new in EnCase 7. A template has an extension of .CaseTemplate and is stored in the Users\<Username>\Documents\EnCase\Templates folder. EnCase ships with predefined templates, and the user can create more if needed. Templates save time, and you are encouraged to use them. Each template contains a uniquely defined set of case template information for the following:

- Case information items with default values
- Bookmark folders and notes
- Tag names
- Report template
- User-defined report styles

Many users prefer their own template. This is very simple to do as you create a case using a template. Once you create the various customized items you want to save, such as the examiner name or bookmark folders, simply go to the Case drop-down menu on the application toolbar and choose Save As Template. When you do, you will see a dialog box, as shown in Figure 6.9, in which you can choose a name and path, as well as whether you want to include hash library path(s) or bookmark notes to the template.

FIGURE 6.9   Save As Template dialog box

Name   In the section labeled B, there is a field in which to enter the case name. Enter a descriptive name for your case, which may include a case or complaint number. The text you enter here will also populate the full case path immediately below, in which the containing folder will bear the case name as will the name of the case file. When you have many cases to manage, being very descriptive and detailed, while still being brief, is quite helpful.

Full Case Path   The first field in the section labeled C is the full case path. This field is grayed out, and you can write to it directly. Rather, its data is a derivative of the base case folder (immediately below) and the case name (immediately above).

Base Case Folder   The base case folder is the second field in the section labeled C. By default, your cases will be stored in your Documents or My Documents folder. It is usually better to have this location on a drive other than your system drive and to store your evidence and evidence cache with your case files.

Primary Evidence Cache   The primary evidence cache path is the third field in the section labeled C. When EnCase loads an evidence item for viewing, it parses and stores metadata associated with that evidence item. Each acquired evidence item is assigned a GUID, and a folder by that GUID name will contain the cached data associated with that evidence item. When the evidence processor runs, it likewise stores data in this folder. Naturally the purpose of caching this data and storing it separately for each evidence item is increased performance as well as increased scalability across large evidence sets. By selecting the box under this field, you can assign this path to the base case folder.

Secondary Evidence Cache   The secondary evidence cache path is the last field in the section labeled C. This location is for previously created caches, and you can store them in this location. EnCase will only read previously stored caches from this location. All new caches will be written to the primary cache folder.

Case Info   In the section labeled D in Figure 6.8, you will see several fields into which you can or should enter data pertaining to the case. Of course, the fields will vary according to the template you select in the section labeled A. Minimally you should enter your name as the examiner, along with a case number and description. Some fields will not change from case to case (your name, for example), and thus a custom template could save you time, if you take the time to create one. In the past, EnCase required you to at least enter your name to proceed; however, this is no longer required.

Case file organization and management are extremely important skills for an examiner to acquire. When computer forensics was in its infancy, best practices and technology at the time called for storing only one case image per drive to prevent comingling or cross-contamination of data. As caseloads grew and technology evolved, best practices have been modified accordingly. Because EnCase encapsulates a device image into an evidence file that has powerful and redundant internal integrity checks, cross-contamination of image files is not the issue it was in the past. In that regard and in many other areas, EnCase has changed the face of computer forensics and, with it, best practices.

Many labs have massive storage servers that hold EnCase evidence and case files. Instead of segregating storage in separate physical devices, as in the past, storage today is often networked and segregated using distinctive folder-naming conventions that are consistent with best practices for case management. In this manner, several examiners can access the same evidence files concurrently and work on different facets of the same case as a team. What used to be physical separation of cases is now facilitated by logical or virtual separation.

EnCase also allows the examiner to open multiple cases at the same time and to conduct concurrent analyses on them. Sometimes cases are created separately and are found later to be related. In these instances, EnCase facilitates examining them as separate yet related cases. Or, if the cases are separate, the examiner can multitask, working manually on one case while another case is being subjected to simultaneous automated processing.

Regardless of how you use EnCase, file management and organization are critical components for keeping case evidence and information segregated. Guidance Software recommends case folder–naming conventions that follow along the lines of those shown in Figure 6.10. In this manner, all cases are contained in the folder Cases and yet are separated by distinct subfolder names. With prior versions of EnCase, the examiner had to create this folder structure; however, with EnCase 7, the structure is automatically created when you create a new case. You need only identify the base path. EnCase creates subfolders called Email, Export, Tags, and Temp. Figure 6.10 contains these folders and two more, which are Evidence and EvidenceCache. You can place these folders anywhere you like. I like to keep them all in one place. For performance, you should consider keeping all of them off the system drive. You could place the Evidence and EvidenceCache folders on separate drives as well to, again, enhance performance. If you do, however, you add to the complexity of your configuration with more locations to track. As soon as you have created your case, EnCase 7 will automatically save the case in the root of the case folder using the case name you assigned. As you go along and do work, you should save using the Ctrl+S key combination, or you can do so from the Case drop-down menu.

It is a good practice to have the case, the case file, and the case folder all named the same, and EnCase 7 does all of that for you. It's also wise to incorporate the case filename as part of the evidence filename. When they are all named consistently, errors and confusion are less likely to occur. Table 6.1 shows an example of a good file- and folder-naming practice. If the files are misplaced, the naming convention alone can associate them with their lost relatives.

TABLE 6.1   Examples of good file and folder naming conventions

Description	Name
Case name entered in Case Options dialog box	ABCStockFraud_39_05_003487
Case folder name under Cases folder (automatic with EnCase 7)	\Cases\ ABCStockFraud_39_05_003487
Case file name (automatic with EnCase 7)	\Cases\ ABCStockFraud_39_05_003487\ ABCStockFraud_39_05_003487.case
Hard drive evidence file	\Cases\ ABCStockFraud_39_05_003487\Evidence\ ABCStockFraud_39_05_003487_40GBWDHDD01
USB thumb drive evidence file	\Cases\ ABCStockFraud_39_05_003487\Evidence\ ABCStockFraud_39_05_003487_1GBUSBTD01

FIGURE 6.10 Multiple cases stored in a single Cases folder

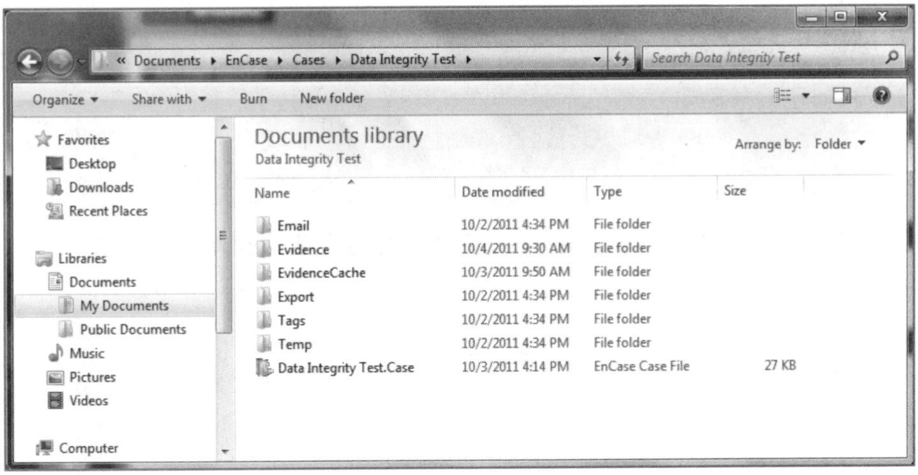
« Documents ▸ EnCase ▸ Cases ▸ Data Integrity Test ▸
Search Data Integrity Test
Organize ▾
Share with ▾
Burn
New folder
Favorites
Desktop
Downloads
Recent Places
Libraries
Documents
My Documents
Public Documents
Music
Pictures
Videos
Computer
Documents library
Data Integrity Test
Arrange by: Folder ▾
Name
Date modified
Type
Size
Email 10/2/2011 4:34 PM File folder
Evidence 10/4/2011 9:30 AM File folder
EvidenceCache 10/3/2011 9:50 AM File folder
Export 10/2/2011 4:34 PM File folder
Tags 10/2/2011 4:34 PM File folder
Temp 10/2/2011 4:34 PM File folder
Data Integrity Test.Case 10/3/2011 4:14 PM EnCase Case File 27 KB

NOTE Remember that, by default, the backup case file (`.cbak`) is located in `\Users\UserName\Documents\EnCase\Cases\Backup.` `\EnCase*\Backup`. This location places the backup files in very close proximity to the case files and on the same drive. By default, they had to be configured somewhere and to a location that exists. It is wise to place your backups on a drive that is separate from your case files. Also, remember that, starting with EnCase 6, multiple backup files are maintained (the frequency and number of backup files retained is configurable).

After you have created a case and it is automatically saved with first created, it is time to add evidence to that case. To do so, click Add Evidence, which is located on the Home screen. (This option is not available until you either create or open a case.) At this stage, you add a local device, add an evidence file, add a raw image, acquire a smartphone, or add a crossover preview, as shown in Figure 6.11. If you are operating in the enterprise or FIM environment, you can connect to a network device that is running the servlet. I covered adding a local device and acquiring it in Chapter 4, so now I'll simply add an evidence file by choosing Add Evidence File and browsing to its location, as shown in Figure 6.12. Once you have added evidence to your case, save your case.

FIGURE 6.11   Add Evidence screen

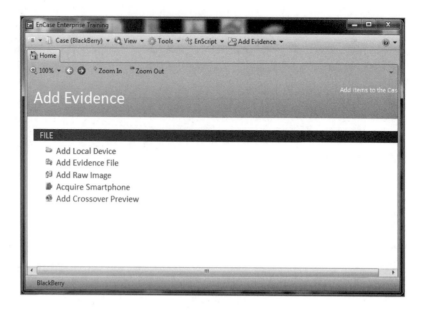

FIGURE 6.12   Browsing to an evidence file

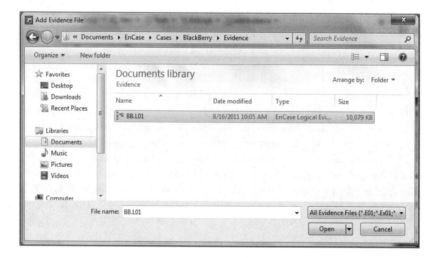

There is a saying that has its roots in Chicago: "Vote early and vote often." In forensics, you should apply similar logic by saving early and saving often. Get into the habit of clicking the Save button (easier yet is the Ctrl+S key combination) when you have completed significant work and when you are about to embark on a new task or process. An even better practice is to use the File ➤ Save All command!

Tree Pane Navigation

Let's navigate within the EnCase environment. In the previous section, you created a case and added a device (I added an evidence file, but you can add your own local hard drive). If you use your own drive, you'll find that it is an excellent place to explore and to conduct research. Before you can work in the Tree pane, you have to open your evidence item. As you'll recall, you can double-click the evidence item or select it and click Open on the Evidence tab toolbar. Now you are in the case Entries view, in which the Tree pane displays the devices in your case along with their hierarchical structure down to the folder level. Files contained at any level will be displayed in the Table pane along with any folders at that same level as the displayed files.

Figure 6.13 shows the EnCase case Entries view with the local hard drive added to the case along with a BlackBerry backup logical evidence file, a Mac OS X evidence file, a Linux evidence file, and three hardware RAID 5 evidence files configured and mounted as a logical RAID within EnCase. When you look at the Tree pane, you can see all the devices in the case along with their associated icons. EnCase uses a vast number of icons in its environment. You can find a complete listing for the last three versions on this page `https://support.guidancesoftware.com/node/`.

FIGURE 6.13   EnCase supports many different file systems, which can be mounted in the same case and searched simultaneously.

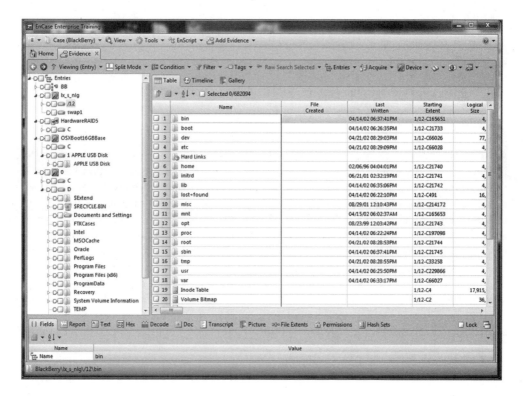

Figure 6.14 shows a physical device (live in this case, with a blue triangle in the lower right) and its associated volume. The physical device icon is a depiction of a hard drive with the arm and heads spanning the platter. It takes some imagination, but that's what it is. The volume icon is a gray 3D box of some sort.

FIGURE 6.14   A live physical device and its associated volume. Note the icon for the physical device has a blue triangle in the lower right, indicating it is a live device.

Figure 6.15 shows an OS X (Macintosh) image file mounted in EnCase. Because there is no blue triangle in the lower-right corner, you know you are not looking at a live device but rather an evidence file. The icon is the same except for the absence of the blue icon in the lower-right corner.

FIGURE 6.15   An OS X evidence file physical disk icon that does not have a blue triangle in the lower right, indicating it is not a live device

EnCase offers another type of live device view: a remote preview carried out over the network using the Enterprise of FIM models of EnCase. In this case, the blue triangle would be a red triangle.

Figure 6.16 shows three devices that have no volumes because they are three physical devices imaged from a hardware RAID 5 system. As such, all you see are three physical device icons. Well, that's not entirely true, because you do see icons for volumes, but there's nothing under them because there are no black triangles. What happens is that, on Drive 0, the beginning data is present (MBR, VBR, and start of FAT1), but because the next stripe of data (in this case 64 KB) goes to the next drive, there is nothing to support the remaining structure, and you get an empty volume icon. In this case, the second 64 KB, which goes on Drive 1, is all zeros, which rarely happens except in a controlled data set such as this one. The first parity stripe, an XOR of the first 64 KB on Drives 0 and 1, goes onto the first 64 KB of Drive 2, making it a mirror of Drive 0. Anything XOR'd with all zeros is a mirror of itself, in essence. Since you've probably heard more than you wanted to know about a RAID at this point, we'll move on.

Anyway, within EnCase, these devices have been manually configured to form a logical RAID 5 device, shown by a special icon. This icon in EnCase 7 appears as two gold cylinders, spanned with black arrows. This logical physical RAID 5 device has a logical partition in it, labeled Raid 5 64K Stripe Size. This volume has been renamed using a feature available in EnCase 7. When you right-click a volume, one of the options is Rename, which has been selected in this case both to demonstrate the feature and to describe the properties of the RAID.

FIGURE 6.16   Three physical devices from a hardware RAID 5 configured and mounted as a logical RAID 5 within EnCase

If you turn your attention back to the physical device named 0 in Figure 6.14, you will note that next to the device icon is a black triangle pointing downward. Immediately below the physical icon, you see a volume icon labeled C. To the far left of the volume icon you see a clear triangle pointing to the right; it indicates that the object is collapsed and that there are more objects under it. You can view these additional items by clicking the clear triangle and thus expanding the object to reveal its contents, as shown in Figure 6.17. If you contrast the physical device named 0 with those associated with the hardware RAID in Figure 6.16, you'll note that one of the physical drives in the RAID does not have a clear triangle, which is the one labeled HDR5SCI1.

FIGURE 6.17   Clicking the clear triangle next to an object expands that object one level below the level of the object.

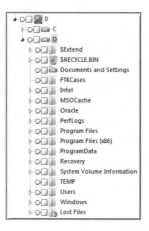

Figure 6.17 depicts the new folder structure that earmarks it, at a glance, as Windows 7 (Server 2008 and Vista also). One of the most significant changes from its predecessors in this structure is the relocation of user profiles from `Documents and Settings` to `Users`. You should note the special icon for `Documents and Settings`, which denotes a link. Whenever you have a link, look in the column in the table viewed named Symbolic Link, and you will find the location to which the link points, which in this case is the folder Users.

At times, you will drill down so deep into the hierarchical structure that you can't see the forest for the trees. Rather than reverse your way back to the top by clicking triangles until you have a bad case of carpal tunnel, you can right-click any object and contract everything below it by selecting Collapse All, as shown in Figure 6.18. By choosing this option at the level of the physical device, you can contract the device completely. Conversely, you can right-click and choose Expand All at any level you choose. You will find the former far more useful than the latter.

FIGURE 6.18   You can expand all or collapse all by right-clicking an object in the Tree pane.

Between the triangle collapse or contract signs and the device icon are two other boxes. One is a square, and the other is five-sided and shaped like the home plate on a baseball field. The square box is for selecting objects for subsequent action or processing. When objects are selected, a blue check appears in the box next to the object. Selecting an object in the Tree pane selects that object and all child objects. Selecting an object in the Table pane selects only that object.

As objects are selected, a cumulative count of selected objects appears in the Dixon box, named after the examiner who suggested this feature. This box has moved from its location on legacy versions of EnCase and is now located below and just to the right of the table tab itself and above the first column in the table, as shown in Figure 6.19. The count tells how many objects are selected out of the number of objects in the case. Before choosing an action to perform on selected files, it pays to check the Dixon box to make sure the count of selected files accurately reflects your intentions. If you really wanted to copy/unerase six files but instead had accidentally selected 200,000-plus files, it's better to catch it before you click OK than after.

By clicking directly in the Dixon box, you can select or deselect all objects in the case.

FIGURE 6.19   The Dixon box shows the number of selected objects (217,054) out of the number of objects in the case (682,112).

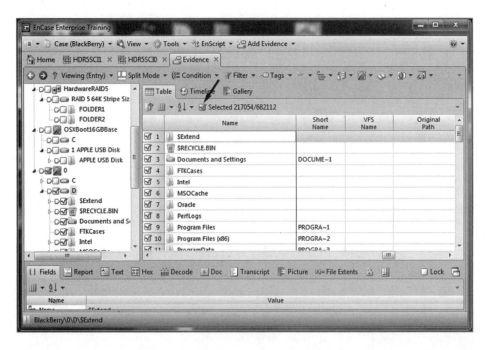

The interface element that looks like a five-sided home plate box has been called many things (see the sidebar "What Do You Call That Thing?"). In this book I call it by its official name, the Set Included Folders trigger or button. When this box is enabled, all files and objects at that level and below are shown in the Table pane. The Set Included Folders trigger remains at the level and location activated until you toggle it off or on at another location, as shown in Figure 6.20. Optionally, you can hold down the Ctrl key and selectively set included folders at different locations, as shown in Figure 6.21.

FIGURE 6.20 The Set Included Folders trigger activated at the Content.IE5 folder level, showing all child objects in the Table pane

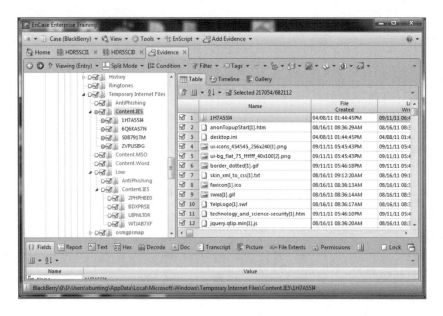

FIGURE 6.21 In addition to having Set Included Folders activated at the Content. IE5 folder, you can hold down the Ctrl key and activate it at multiple locations; in this case, it is activated at the Content.IE5 level for the Low folder also, which allows you to see the Internet cache files from both locations combined.

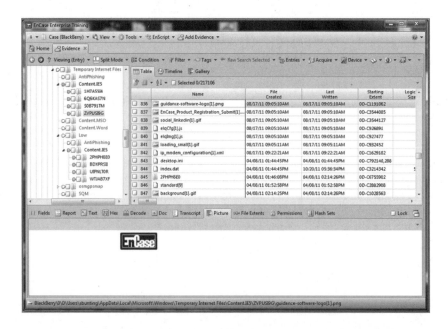

What Do You Call That Thing?

You'll also see the following names used in the field for the Set Included Folders trigger:

- Green box

- Home plate (the name most often used in the field by examiners)

- Show-all button

- Set-Include Switch

- Set-Include Button

- Set Included Option

While in the Tree pane, EnCase 7 gives you new views or modes, which effectively provide choices over how you split the Tree pane or whether you want to see the Tree pane at all. The default view is the Tree-Table view, which is the traditional Tree in the left pane, Table in the right, and View in the bottom pane view by which examiners have viewed EnCase since the beginning of time. To change from the default view, the Tree-Table view, click the Split Mode drop-down menu, which is located on the Evidence tab toolbar immediately to the left of the Condition menu, as shown in Figure 6.22.

FIGURE 6.22   Split Mode menu from which the examiner can choose between Table, Tree-Table, Traeble, and Tree modes of views

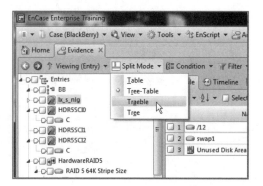

If you opt for the Table view, you will have no Tree view, only the table. The Tree-Table view is the default, which probably needs no further explanation because you have been working in this view from the outset. You may opt for the Traeble view, which offers a unique view in that the tree is brought into the Name column of the Table view. The Tree view is gone, and you have only the Table and View panes (top and bottom). From the Name column you can start with a device and drill down to a volume and from there to a folder and finally down to a file, all in the Name column. The details of each item selected in the Name column will appear in the View pane, as shown in Figure 6.23. The final option is the Tree view, in which the Table view is gone and the tree is in the left pane and the View pane in the right. From the Tree pane, you can drill all the way down to the file level, meaning you can select files in the Tree pane and view the data in the View pane, as shown in Figure 6.24. In both figures, the same file is being viewed, which is 1.txt.

Before we move to the Table pane, let's look at various functions you can perform from the Table pane and how that is achieved in the new EnCase 7 interface. In past versions of EnCase, most of the functionality of EnCase was on the right-click context mouse button. While the menu under the right-click button wasn't always well-organized, it was very functional once you knew what was there and the lay of the land, so to speak. EnCase 7 has taken most of the right-click functionality and organized it over a series of menus along the Evidence tab toolbar, as shown in Figure 6.25.

As you can see, they are grouped by various categories or functions. For example, in Figure 6.26, you can see the various functions or operations under the device menu. In our example, you can see that the VFS (Virtual File System) and PDE (Physical Disk Emulator) functions are under the Device menu, off the Share submenu, and are listed as Mount As Network Share and Mount As Emulated Disk, respectively.

FIGURE 6.23   Traeble view

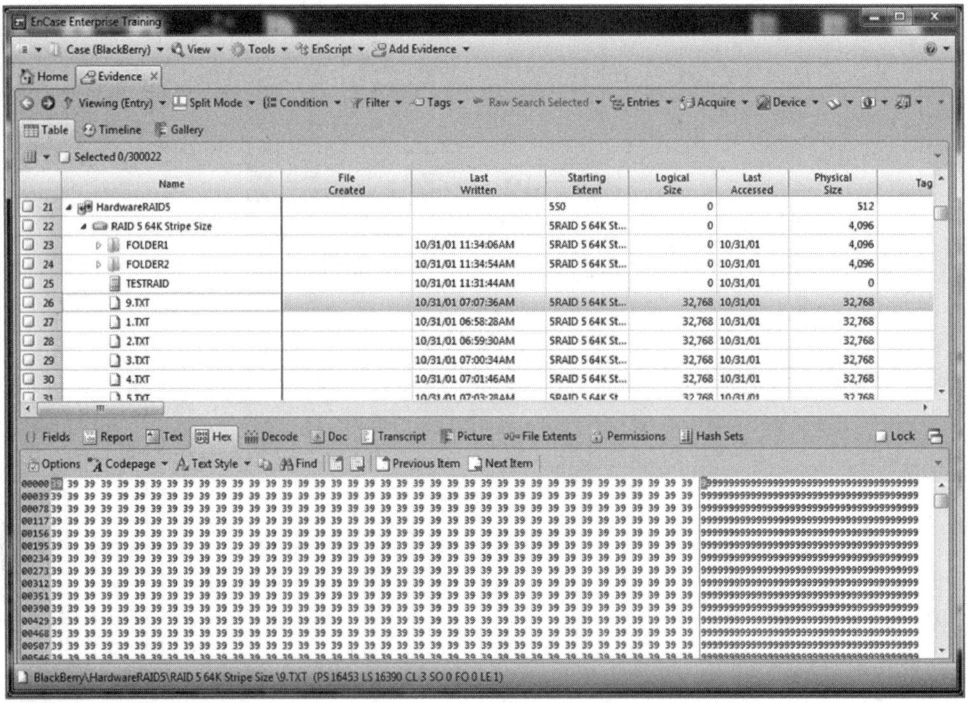

FIGURE 6.24   Tree view

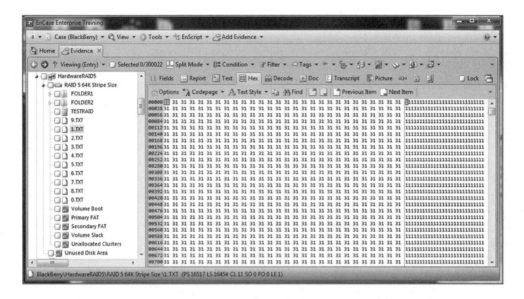

FIGURE 6.25   Evidence-level menus located along the Evidence tab's toolbar

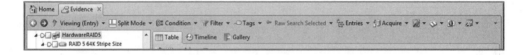

FIGURE 6.26   Various functions available from the Device menu, specifically showing VFS and PDE

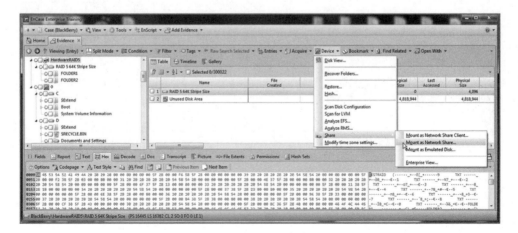

At first, admittedly, this can be a bit confusing to find features in the various menus, especially for those who have become used to these features being on a right-click menu. However, the right-click menu functions can be a bit daunting to a new EnCase user as well. As more and more features are added to EnCase, there's a limit to what can be reasonably added to a right-click menu, and thus the decision was reached to create menus for these function instead of overloading an already crowded right-click menu. That being said, with improvements and new features come change, and we all have to adjust and learn new methods and workflows.

However, for those veteran "right-clickers," there is a right-click equivalent menu system, although it is not so obvious. This system of menus is officially called the *right-side menu*, but many have unofficially dubbed it the "super secret menu." One may forget about something called a right-side menu, but something called a "super secret menu" is something one remembers. I'll call this menu, going forward, the right-side menu, but don't forget its unofficial name! Figure 6.27 shows the Evidence tab's right-side menu, specifically showing accessing the same features shown in Figure 6.26.

In 7.03, there is now the availability through a right-click of the Entries, Acquire and Device submenus through a right-click.

FIGURE 6.27 The right-side menu contains a collection of the menus found individually along the Evidence tab toolbar.

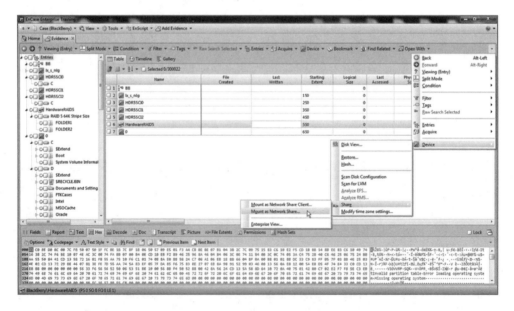

The Evidence tab is not the only pane or toolbar with a right-side menu. Figure 6.28 shows an open right-side menu for the Table pane. The arrows show the other available right-side menus. You should explore their contents and then decide whether you prefer one menu for everything or specific menus. It is largely a personal choice.

Finally, evidence is not the only thing that can be viewed in the Tree view. If you click View, as shown in Figure 6.29, you can open tabs for many other purposes. If, for example, you were to open bookmarks or records, they would open in a tab in the Tree-Table view. While the default view, you could also open bookmarks, records, or others in the Table, Traeble, or Tree mode.

FIGURE 6.28 Another open right-side menu with arrows pointing to other right-side menus

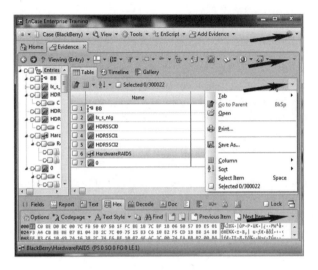

FIGURE 6.29 Views or tabs available from the View menu on the application toolbar

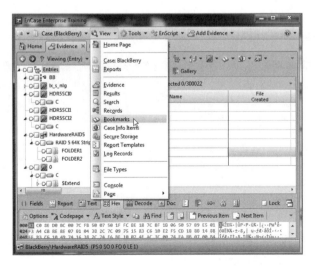

Table Pane Navigation

Now that I've covered most of the case Entries view features in the Tree pane, I'll focus on the features of the Table pane. To simplify things for now, I have not covered the various tab views in the Tree pane. I'll return to them later. The Table pane has several tabs, but the default tab is Table View, in which the objects appear in a spreadsheet view, with the various attributes or properties of the objects appearing in columns.

Table View

From the Table view, you can sort, hide, move, lock, and otherwise configure columns to streamline your examination. There are more columns than you can see at once unless you have multiple monitors configured to accommodate such a view. Except for those lucky enough to have dual- or triple-monitor configurations, most of us need to arrange the columns so that we can view meaningful and related information.

One of the most useful features is the ability to lock a column, which is most often applied to the Name column. In fact, the Name column is locked by default in EnCase 7. When the Name column is locked, you can scroll through the columns, and the object name remains visible throughout the process. If you wanted to lock a column other than Name, or perhaps lock the first two columns including Name, you must first unlock the Name column. To do so, place your cursor in the Name column. Next, open the right-side menu for the table, as shown in Figure 6.30. On the right-side menu, open the Column submenu and choose Unlock.

You can also use the Column drop down menu above.

FIGURE 6.30   Unlock a column by clicking in a locked column, opening the right-side menu, choosing Column, and then choosing Unlock.

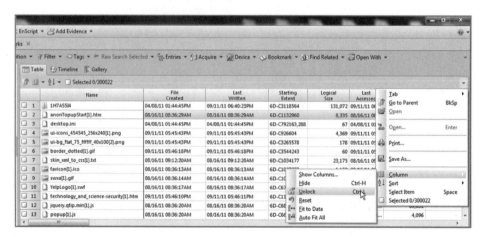

To lock a column, you simply repeat the steps, except that you lock instead of unlock. First decide which column you are going to lock. In my example, my columns are in the default configuration, with the Name column first and the Tag column second. I have decided to lock the Tag column such that I can always see both the Name and Tag columns as I scroll across the Table view. First I place my cursor focus in the Tag column. Next I go to the right-side menu, open the Column submenu, and click Set Lock. A dark line appears on the right side of the locked Tag column indicating the location of the locked column. As shown in Figure 6.31, when you scroll across the columns, both the Name and Tag columns remain visible.

FIGURE 6.31   A dark line marks the right edge of the locked column. The column(s) to the left of the dark line will remain locked while those to the right of it will scroll by.

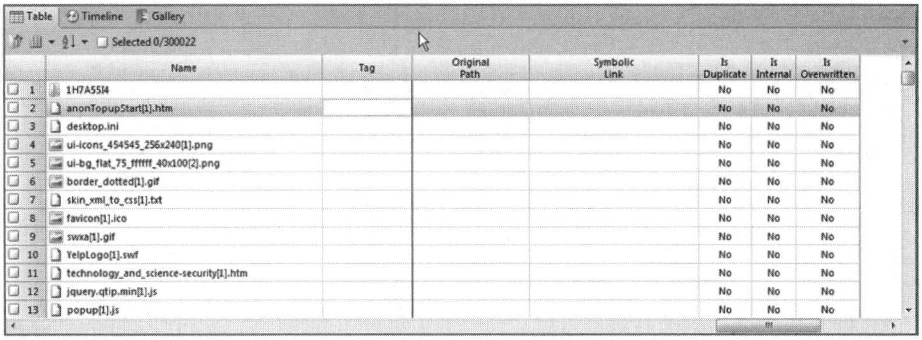

Sorting columns is an excellent analysis tool. With EnCase you can apply up to six sort levels, although three levels are the most you will typically ever require.

To sort a column, you can do one of the following:

- Place your cursor in the column, and open the Sort menu from the Table toolbar, as shown in Figure 6.32. Next, pick your option from among those offered.

- Double-click the header of the column you want to sort. Double-click it again to reverse the sort order.

FIGURE 6.32   The Sort menu allows various sorting options for columns.

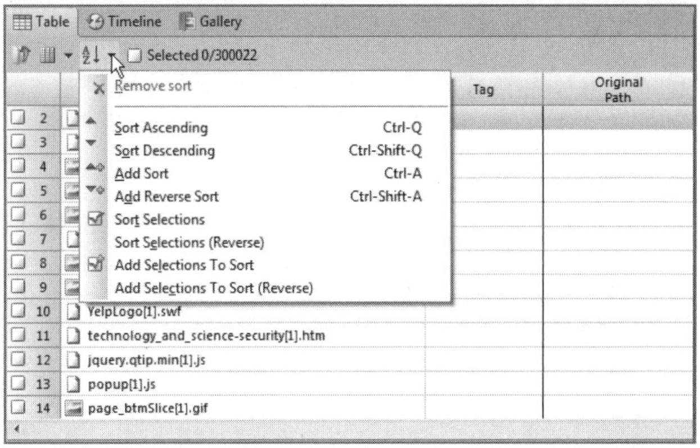

In Figure 6.33, I've applied a sort just to the File Ext column. The little red triangle indicates the direction of the sort. I've also applied a second sort to the Name column (see two triangles on that column) such that all files are sorted first by file extension and second by name. If you want to apply a second sort, simply hold down the Shift key, and double-click the column header. You can also place your cursor in the second column to be sorted and choose among the options under the Sort menu.

FIGURE 6.33   A second sort has been applied, shown by the two triangles on the Name column.

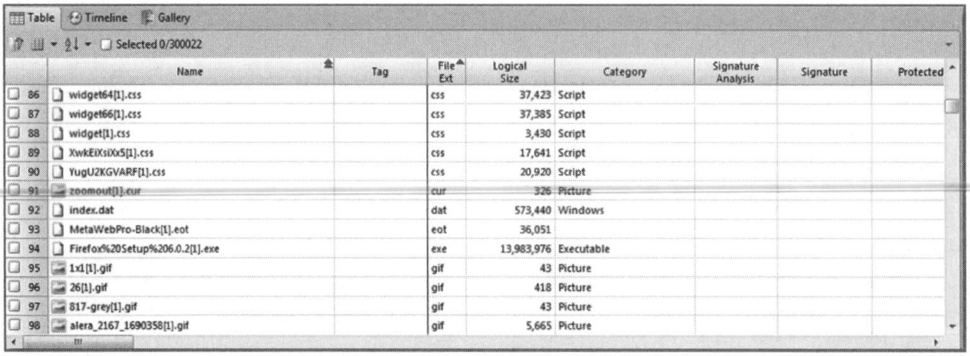

If you want to sort in the opposite direction, hold down the Ctrl key while double-clicking the column header. If applying a second sort, hold down both Ctrl and Shift (in other words, press Ctrl+Shift) while double-clicking the column header.

If you prefer using menus, select a column to see a variety of sort options in the Sort menu.

To remove a sort, double-click the column header. Without the Shift key, this action replaces the old sort with your new sort.

To return all columns to their unsorted state, select any column anywhere in the table, and choose Remove Sort in the Sort menu.

EnCase features a very useful sort that is not obvious. You can sort on the very first column (which has no name). When you have items "blue checked" and selected, a simple double-click to this column brings all your selected items to the top; that is, EnCase sorts selected items from unselected items. Once you have your files selected and sorted on the "blue check mark" column, you can add a second sort to put your selected files in chronological order. In Figure 6.34, several files of interest were selected from several hundred in the sample. Once selected with blue check marks, they were sorted by the unnamed column containing the blue check marks. They were subjected to a second sort based on time, creating a chronological listing of the files selected.

Columns can be hidden or displayed easily. This allows you to remove irrelevant data and focus on what's important to your case. The quick way to hide a column is to place your cursor on it and press Ctrl+H. Pressing Ctrl+H again hides another column—the one your cursor moves to after you hide the first column.

FIGURE 6.34   An undocumented but extremely useful sort occurs when you select files and sort on the unnamed column header above the blue checked boxes. EnCase sorts between those selected and those not selected.

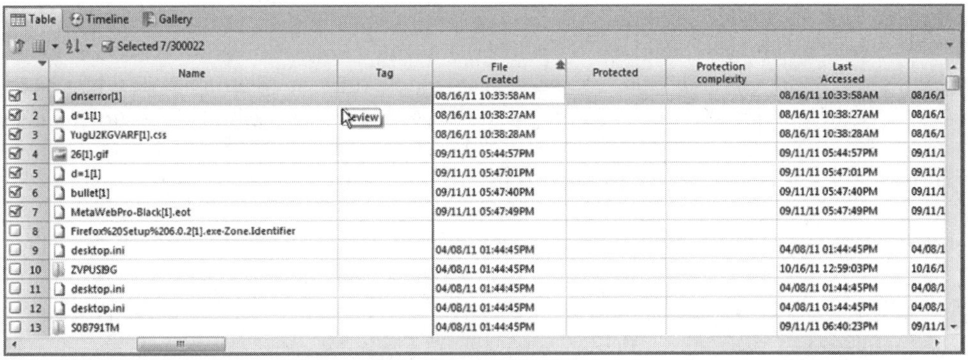

You can show a hidden column in two ways. To show, or hide, specific columns, open the Table right-side menu, open the Column submenu, and choose Show Columns, as shown in Figure 6.35. Any box that is hidden or deactivated will not have a blue check. You can place blue checks in these boxes and click OK to restore them. With this feature, you can be precise in selecting which columns to display. To restore all columns to their default view, open the Table right-side menu, open the Columns submenu, and then select Reset. This restores the window to the default settings.

FIGURE 6.35   Show Columns gives you precise control over which columns are displayed. Access this menu from the Table right-side menu, under the Column submenu.

Of all the tasks you can perform on columns, perhaps the most useful is the ability to pick them up and move them around. In this manner, you can compare relevant data within the context of other relevant data. It is handy to have that data next to the comparison data rather than somewhere off the screen where you can't see it.

To move a column, click and drag the column header to where you want it moved. When you release the mouse button, the column moves to its new location. You can even replace a locked column by dragging a new column onto the locked column. If you ever get your columns hopelessly rearranged, hidden, and otherwise not to your liking, use the Reset command (see the earlier discussion of Reset) to restore the default settings.

While working in the Table pane, invariably there will be times when the data in a column exceeds the column width. You can always go to the top where the column name is, hover your mouse over the column separator, and drag it to the desired width, as shown in Figure 6.36. A faster option is to simply place your cursor over the data you want to view; a floating box will appear that displays all data for that particular entry, as shown in Figure 6.37.

FIGURE 6.36   Adjusting column width

		Name	Item Path	Size column	Tag
□	1	1H7A55I4	0\D\Users\sbunting\AppData\Local\Microsoft\Windo		
□	2	anonTopupStart[1].htm	0\D\Users\sbunting\AppData\Local\Microsoft\Windows\T...		
□	3	desktop.ini	0\D\Users\sbunting\AppData\Local\Microsoft\Windows\T...		

FIGURE 6.37   Floating box reveals data too large to display in column

		Name	Item Path	Tag	File Ext	Logical Size	Category
□	1	1H7A55I4	0\D\Users\sbunting\AppData\Local\Microsoft\Windows\Temporary Internet Files\Content.IE5\1H7A55I4				Folder
□	2	anonTopupStart[1].htm	0\D\Users\sbunting\AppData\Local\Microsoft\Windows\T...		htm	8,335	Email
□	3	desktop.ini	0\D\Users\sbunting\AppData\Local\Microsoft\Windows\T...		ini	67	Windows
□	4	ui-icons_454545_256x240[1].png	0\D\Users\sbunting\AppData\Local\Microsoft\Windows\T...		png	4,369	Picture
□	5	ui-bg_flat_75_ffffff_40x100[2].png	0\D\Users\sbunting\AppData\Local\Microsoft\Windows\T...		png	178	Picture
□	6	border_dotted[1].gif	0\D\Users\sbunting\AppData\Local\Microsoft\Windows\T...		gif	60	Picture
□	7	skin_xml_to_css[1].txt	0\D\Users\sbunting\AppData\Local\Microsoft\Windows\T...		txt	23,175	Document
□	8	favicon[1].ico	0\D\Users\sbunting\AppData\Local\Microsoft\Windows\T...		ico	1,150	Picture
□	9	swxa[1].gif	0\D\Users\sbunting\AppData\Local\Microsoft\Windows\T...		gif	5,223	Picture
□	10	YelpLogo[1].swf	0\D\Users\sbunting\AppData\Local\Microsoft\Windows\T...		swf	1,311	Multimedia - Video
□	11	technology_and_science-security[1].htm	0\D\Users\sbunting\AppData\Local\Microsoft\Windows\T...		htm	64,713	Email
□	12	jquery.qtip.min[1].js	0\D\Users\sbunting\AppData\Local\Microsoft\Windows\T...		js	67,184	Script
□	13	popup[1].js	0\D\Users\sbunting\AppData\Local\Microsoft\Windows\T...		js	782	Script

If at any point while working in the Table view you see data that you want to copy, place your cursor on the data, right-click, and choose Copy. Your data is now stored in your clipboard and can be pasted anywhere that is enabled within the Windows environment. This is most useful when need to copy a long filename, hash value, path, or the like.

Just before press time, EnCase 7.04 was released and with it came some changes. One that was nearly overlooked was the changing of the column names Signature and Signature Tag to File Type and File Type Tag. This began as a change late in EnCase 6.19, changing the column name from Signature to File Type. To be consistent, EnCase 7.04 carried through this change, extending it to include the change from Signature Tag to File Type Tag.

The column names describe the property or attribute of the objects; Table 6.2 lists the column names.

TABLE 6.2 Column names explained (column order is default for EnCase 7.02—use Reset in Column submenu)

Column header name	Description
Name	This column identifies the object as a file, folder, or volume. It is sometimes preceded by an icon that indicates the object's status.
Tag	This will display any tags you placed on an entry.
File Ext	This column displays the file's extension if it has one. Windows uses file extensions to determine which application to use to open it, while other OSs instead use headers or other metadata information in addition to file extensions to do so. EnCase reports the actual extension used by the file. If it has been changed, the real extension remains an unknown until a file signature analysis is run.
Logical Size	This column specifies the actual size of data in a file from first byte to last byte, reported in bytes.
Category	The file category is pulled from the File Types table and is a general category, such as documents or images.
Signature Analysis	Returns the results of the file signature analysis.
File Type	This column is populated after a file signature analysis and returns the result of that process. Thus, the File Type column returns the identifier of the header or signature of the object that has been identified within the File Types table. (See Chapter 8 for more information.)
Item Type	An item type describes the type of evidence, be it an entry (file or folder), email, record, or document.
Protected	This field will be populated after evidence processing has occurred and will indicate whether it's encrypted or password-protected.
Protection Complexity	Tied to Protected and indicates details found regarding file's protection.
Last Accessed	This column indicates the date/time a file was last accessed. The file does not have to change but be accessed only. Programs vary in the way they touch this time stamp. It may or may not reflect user activity. Some hex editors allow data to be altered, and no date/time stamps are changed.

TABLE 6.2   (continued)

Column header name	Description
File Created	This column indicates the date/time a file was created in that particular location. You can edit a file after it was originally written, giving it a last-written date/time later than originally written (created) date/time. If you move it to a new location, the file will take on a new creation date/time for when and where it was moved, making it "appear" to have been created after it was last written. This concept confuses many, but the key is understanding that the creation date/time typically indicates when it was created in its current location and that files can be moved around after they were last written.
Last Written	This column displays the date/time that a file was opened, the data was changed, and the file was saved. If the file is opened and the data isn't changed, there shouldn't be a change in the last-written date/time.
Is Picture	If the file is an image, this will display a Boolean for true, and how this is displayed will be based on the settings in the Tools ➢ Options ➢ Global menu.
Code Page	This is the character encoding table upon which the file is based.
MD5	This is the MD5 hash value of each file that is displayed after hash analysis processing is completed.
SHA1	This is the MD5 hash value of each file that is displayed after hash analysis processing is completed.
Item Path	This displays the full path to the file, including the evidence filename.
Description	This column briefly describes the object (file, folder, volume), some of its attributes, and what the icon means that sometimes accompanies the object name. Here is an example: File, Hidden, System, Archive, Not Indexed.
Is Deleted	This column displays a Boolean true or false value* indicating whether the file has been deleted.
Entry Modified	This column indicates the date/time a file or folder's file system record entry was changed. This pertains to NTFS and Linux file systems. For example, in an NTFS file system, if an entry in the MFT changed, then this time stamp will reflect that. Even in the case of resident data, if so much as a single byte is modified, regardless of whether the size of the data changes, the MFT is altered, and this is reflected in the entry modified time stamp.
File Deleted	This column reports the date/time of file deletion according to a Windows Recycle Bin INFO2 database.

TABLE 6.2 (continued)

Column header name	Description
File Acquired	This column reports the date/time the evidence file in which object resides was acquired.
Initialized Size	Initialized Size pertains to NTFS file systems only, and it is the size of the file when it is opened. Windows can preallocate space for a file such that the amount of data written to the file can be less than the allocated or logical size. For example, let's say Windows allocates 1 MB for a file but writes only 100 bytes of data to it. The initialized size of this file is 100 bytes, and its logical size is 1 MB. On a standard search, the entire logical file is searched. But the data beyond the 100 bytes written could be residual from previous writes. The Initialized Size option specifies that you want to search only the data written and not the entire space allocated.
Physical Size	This column specifies the actual size of the file plus slack space. This figure reflects the number of clusters occupied by the file in bytes. If a cluster is two sectors (2 n 512), that cluster is 1,024 bytes. If a file is 2 bytes and contained within one cluster, then that file has a logical size of 2 bytes and a physical size of 1,024 bytes.
Starting Extent	This is the starting cluster for a file in the format Evidence File Number (order within the case)	Logical Drive Letter	Starting Cluster Number; in the case of resident data in a master file table (MFT), the starting cluster will be followed by a comma and the byte offset from the beginning of the cluster to the beginning of the data.
File Extents	This column lists the number of data runs or extents for a file. If a file has one extent, then the clusters are contiguous and it is not fragmented. If a file has two or more, the file is fragmented
Permissions	This displays a Boolean true or false value* stating whether security settings have been applied to the object. If true, security settings apply, and details are available in the Permissions tab in the View pane. Windows and Unix permissions are detailed in the resulting window.
Physical Location	The physical location is the number of bytes into the device that a file begins. In the case of unallocated clusters (UC), EnCase reads the UC as one virtual file based on reading the FAT (FAT System) or $Bitmap (NTFS). In the case of UC, the physical location will be the number of bytes into the device that UC begins, which is the byte offset to the first unallocated cluster on the device.
Physical Sector	This is the starting sector where a file starts.
Evidence File	This displays the evidence file in which object resides.

TABLE 6.2 (continued)

Column header name	Description
File Identifier	This is the file table index number. In NTFS, this is the record number in the MFT. For ext2/3/4 and Reiser (Linux) and UFS (Unix), this is the inode number; for HFS/HFS+ (Macintosh), this is the catalog number.
GUID	Global Unique Identifier. Entry-specific GUID assigned to enable tracking throughout the examination process.
Short Name	This displays the DOS 8.3 filename. A file named LongFileName.txt would appear here as LONGFI~1.TXT.
VFS Name	This displays the filename for files as they are mounted in Windows Explorer after EnCase Virtual File System is activated and the device is mounted. This column was formerly called Unique Name, alluding to the purpose, which was to prevent conflicts in displaying the files with the exact name in the same folder in Windows Explorer.
Original Path	If the file is an allocated, nondeleted file, this column is blank. If the file is deleted and has been overwritten, this column will show which file has overwritten the original file. If the file is in the Recycle Bin, this column shows the original location of the file when it was deleted. Also, you'll see an entry here if the file is hard-linked, showing the other path(s) pointing to this file.
Symbolic Link	Windows (especially Windows Vista/7) and Unix (including Linux and AIX) use symbolic or soft links, which are files similar to the link files in Windows. They contain no data about the file that is pointed to, only the path to it; their value lies mostly in pointing to resources on other systems.
Hash Set	This displays the hash set a file belongs to if it matches a known value in the hash library. If it doesn't match or no library has been defined, nothing appears in this column. This column displays only after the hash analysis has run and a file is found belonging to one or more hash sets.
Is Duplicate	This displays true if the file displayed is a duplicate of another file.
Is Internal	This denotes hidden files that are used by the operating system internally and are hidden from the user. An example would be the $MFT or $Bitmap files on and NTFS file system or the inode table on an EXT3 file system.
Is Overwritten	This displays true if the original file is deleted and its space is currently occupied by another file.

*For a Boolean true or false, EnCase by default displays a dot for true and nothing for false. This display is user configurable in the Tools ➤ Options ➤ Global menu. For example, you could enter Yes instead of a dot or No instead of nothing.

Gallery View

Thus far, we have been working with the default tab or view in the Table pane, which is the Table view. Another view is the Gallery view, which is one of the three tabs located in the Table pane, as shown in Figure 6.38. From this view, you can see images in the case at whatever level you choose, from one folder to the entire case. Using the Set Include Folders button in the Tree pane, you can direct the content of the Table pane.

FIGURE 6.38   Three tabs available from the Table pane

		Name	Tag	Is Duplicate	Is Internal	Is Overwritten
☐	1	lx_s_nlg		No	No	No
☐	2	HDR5SCI0		No	No	No
☐	3	HDR5SCI1		No	No	No
☐	4	HDR5SCI2		No	No	No
☐	5	HardwareRAID5		No	No	No
☐	6	0		No	No	No
☐	7	BB		No	No	No

Table | Timeline | Gallery
Selected 0/300022

Until a file signature analysis has been done, which is a built-in function within the EnCase evidence processor and can also be run separately on selected files, EnCase displays images based on the file extension. After the file signature analysis has been completed, the files will display based on their file header information. Firefox and other browsers rename cached files and remove their extensions. Without a file signature analysis, the temporary Internet files stored by Firefox are not visible as images within EnCase. When certain peer-to-peer programs start a download, the filename has a .dat extension and remains that way until the download completes. Many files exist as partial downloads that are images but won't display until a file signature analysis is completed. In addition to programs altering file extensions, some users may attempt to obscure files by changing their file extensions. While this may hide a file from the casual user, it is no match for forensic software. I'll discuss how it is done in Chapter 8, but it is an important step (running the EnCase evidence processor) if you want to see all images in the Gallery view.

While in the Gallery view, you can select image files, bookmark image files, or copy/unerase image files, individually or in groups. Figure 6.39 shows the EnCase Gallery view. You can change the size of the image thumbnails by right-clicking in the Table pane and selecting Fewer Columns, More Columns, Fewer Rows, or More Rows, as shown in Figure 6.40.

In the past, corrupted images have caused system crashes; however, starting with EnCase 5, EnCase has built-in crash protection. When corrupted images are detected, they are cached, and EnCase does not present them again. In the Tools ➢ Options ➢ Global menu, you can change the maximum amount of time that EnCase tries to read an invalid image before it times out and caches it. This setting defaults to 12 seconds, as shown in Figure 6.41.

FIGURE 6.39 EnCase Gallery view showing all images in an Internet cache by using the Set Included Folders feature

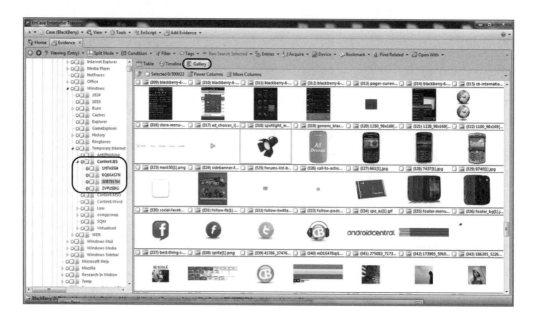

FIGURE 6.40 You can change the size of the Gallery view thumbnails by right-clicking and choosing more or fewer columns or rows.

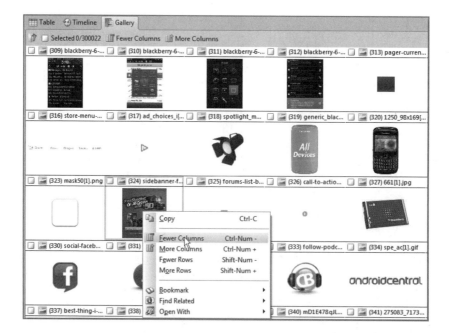

EnCase supports America Online (AOL) .art files (files with an .art file extension). AOL uses a proprietary form of compression known as Johnson-Grace compression, named after the company that developed it. As a bandwidth-saving measure, AOL converts other image types to .art files, which produces an extremely high compression rate. By default, rendering AOL .art files is enabled but can be disabled by the user. If you look in the image options in Figure 6.41, you can see the box to disable rendering these files.

FIGURE 6.41   In the Tools ➢ Options ➢ Global menu, you can change the timeout period EnCase waits before caching an invalid image.

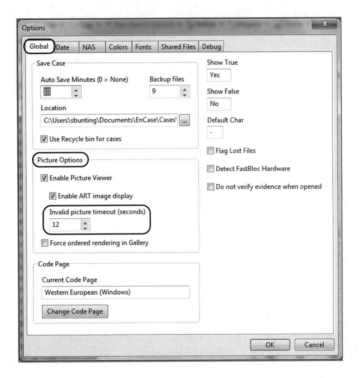

Timeline View

The Timeline view enables you to review chronological activity in a graphical view. By default, all dates and times are enabled and appear in the view. On the Timeline tab toolbar, there is a menu named Date Type from which you can enable or disable the various time stamps. In the Tree pane, by using the green Set Included Folders trigger, you can select the level of Table pane content, ranging from single folders to multiple folders, volumes, devices, or even the entire case.

A particularly interesting view is often simply that of looking at deleted files only. If a person knew on a given date they were the target of an investigation, such a view often reveals file-deletion activity shortly thereafter. In the Timeline view, you can see this easily and visually. Figure 6.42 shows a Timeline view where the only dates and times are for file deletions. Each square represents one file, and when the number of files gets too large to show individual squares, the number of files is used instead. In Figure 6.42, you can see six files were deleted on October 18, 2011, during the hour starting at 1900.

FIGURE 6.42 EnCase Timeline view showing only dates and times for file deletions. Such a focused view can be quite revealing when depicted visually.

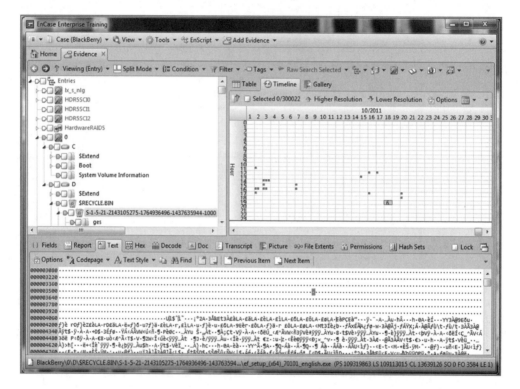

Sometimes you need to drill down and get more detail. You can double-click in numbered boxes and drill down or click Higher Resolution or Lower Resolution on the Timeline tab toolbar. Alternatively, you can use the plus and minus keys on the number pad and achieve the same result. Figure 6.43 shows drilling down to get more detail. When you place your cursor and click a square representing a file in the timeline, the contents of that file will appear in the View pane, its location is highlighted in the tree, and the full path appears at the bottom in the GPS area.

FIGURE 6.43   Drilling down and achieving higher resolution in the Timeline view. Each tiny red square represents a file, and placing your cursor on it displays its contents in the View pane, its location in the tree, and its path in the GPS.

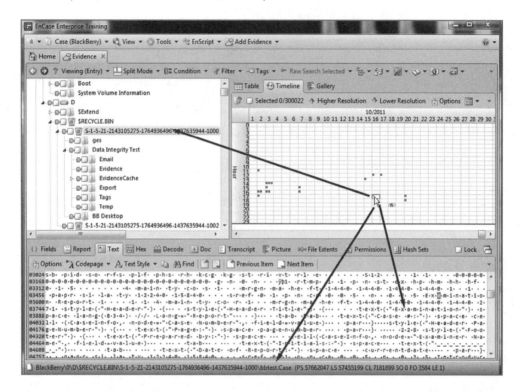

Each of the different date and time stamps is separately color-coded. Toggling each one on and off is a quick way to check which color is coming and going as you toggle. You should note that on the Timeline tab toolbar, there is an Options menu. Clicking Options provides you with the color codes, as shown in Figure 6.44, along with the ability to change them if you like. Another option is the ability to manually specify a range for the Timeline view, which is nice if you are looking at a precise period and want to exclude all other data. I encourage you to use this date range filtering tool because you will find it simply works better once you have a range on which to focus your attention.

There is no reporting or printing feature for the Timeline view. The best way to use it is to take screenshots. Those images can be included in Microsoft PowerPoint presentations or placed in your final report, be it web or print based. They can make a powerful addition as a link in a web-based report.

FIGURE 6.44   Color codes are available by opening the Options menu on the Timeline tab toolbar. From this dialog box, you can change the colors or manually specify a time range.

Disk View

Maybe I need a life, but I make frequent use of the Disk view. Typically, this is one of the first views I go to when I first preview a device. At a glance, the topography of the drive is at your fingertips. It is no longer available as a Table view tab, but it is nearby. To use it, place the device or object you want to view in the Table pane by placing your cursor on its parent in the Tree pane. Since I want to see the device "physical disk 0" in the disk view, I place my cursor on the root of the entries in the Tree pane, and the various devices appear in the Table pane. I then place my cursor on physical drive 0 in the Table pane and click once to highlight it and make it the target for my Disk view, as shown in Figure 6.45. Let me emphasize again that the target is based only on the focus of your cursor and that blue checks don't work for this purpose! Once you have your target in the Table pane and highlighted with your cursor, open the Device menu on the Evidence tab toolbar and choose Disk View, as shown in Figure 6.46. For those of you who have been paying attention and remember the super-secret menu (officially the right-side menu), you can also access this feature from the Evidence tab toolbar right-side menu if you drill down into the Device submenu.

By default, you see a series of colored square blocks, each representing one sector. If you would prefer that each block represent a cluster, simply click the check box next to View Clusters on the toolbar for this view. I have circled that option in Figure 6.47. The blocks are color-coded as to their function. Former versions had a legend for these color codes, but the early releases of EnCase 7 do not. There are plans to restore the legend, so you'll have to await for the return of that feature. Blue blocks are allocated sectors or clusters. The gray blocks with the raised bump in the center are unallocated sectors or clusters. There are many others.

FIGURE 6.45   The target for Disk view is in the Table pane and highlighted with the cursor.

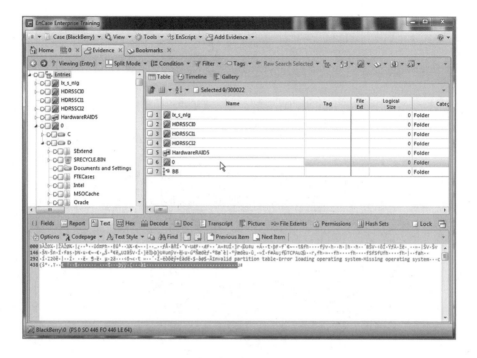

FIGURE 6.46   Selecting Disk View from the Device menu

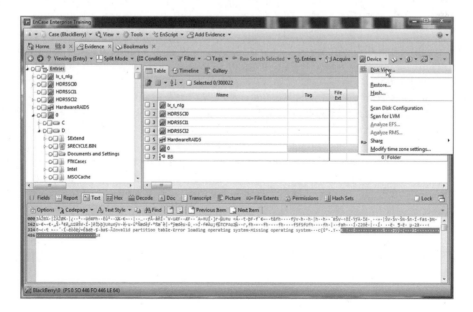

When you are in the Cluster view, remember that clusters are logical units that exist within a partition. You won't see sectors that exist outside the partition because they aren't clusters!

I have opened disk 0 into the Disk view and have navigated to physical sector 5,466,336 (circled also in Figure 6.47), which happens to be the beginning location of a program called EnCase. Upon placing my cursor on that sector, as shown in Figure 6.47, all sectors in that set of extents become highlighted, by default. The feature is called Auto Extents and may be toggled on and off on the Disk View toolbar (also circled in Figure 6.47).

FIGURE 6.47   Disk view with focus on starting sector of the EnCase program file

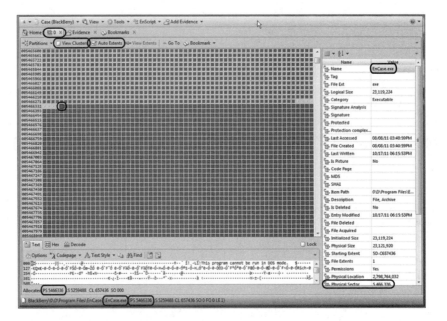

If you right-click in the disk area, you can go to a sector by typing in the sector number. You can also use the Go To feature from its menu on the Disk View toolbar, which is shown in Figure 6.48.

Also available from the right-click menu is the ability to add or delete partitions, which is quite helpful if someone FDISKed their drive. To add a partition, you must first locate the beginning of the partition and place your cursor in that location. Once you are at the beginning, you open the Partitions menu and choose to add a partition, as shown in Figure 6.49. In many cases, EnCase will read the partition information in the selected sector and the information needed to create the partition will be already in the window that follows, but sometimes you will need to make adjustments, which requires further knowledge. We'll cover recovering partitions in depth in Chapter 10. Figure 6.50 shows a partition about to be recovered at physical sector 2048, which is where Windows 7 now starts its first NTFS partition on a new installation. EnCase has read the data in the volume boot record (sector 2048) and knows the partition information (type, sectors per cluster, sectors in partition, and so forth).

FIGURE 6.48   The Go To function is available three ways: via the toolbar menu, right-click, and Ctrl+G.

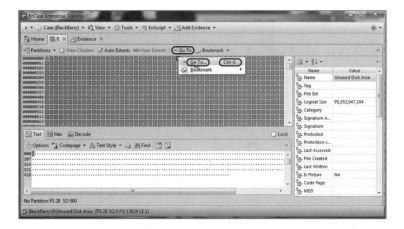

FIGURE 6.49   Partition menu options

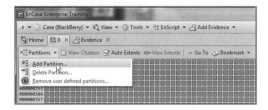

FIGURE 6.50   An NTFS partition about to be recovered at physical sector 2048

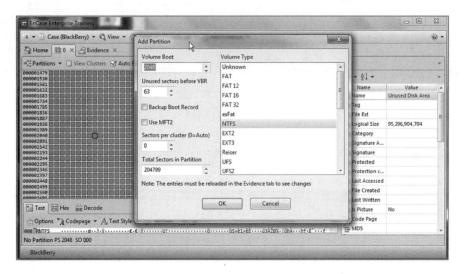

One final function you can carry out from the Disk view is that of bookmarking. I'll get into bookmarking in Chapter 7, but for now, just remember that you can create bookmarks while in the Disk view.

View Pane Navigation

The View pane is where the data is found. The functionality of the View pane is driven by the content of the Table pane but could be otherwise if you are using the Traeble or Tree viewing mode. When you are in the Entries view, there will be various tabs in the View pane that will enable you to see multidimensional data. These options enable different ways to view data, as shown in Figure 6.51. The method you choose will depend on your preferences and the task you are performing. If your data is ASCII text, nothing beats the Text view for simplicity and formatting options.

FIGURE 6.51   View Pane viewing tabs

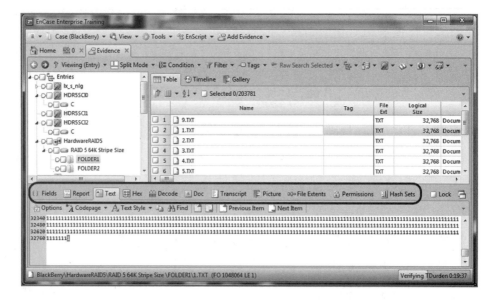

Text View

In the Text view, like all the other views in the View pane, the content is driven by the object selected in the Table pane. The format of the output is determined by the current text style as specified in the Text Style menu located on the Text tab toolbar. You can fine-tune your text style without changing your views. You can even add new styles or edit existing ones all from the Text Style menu. Figure 6.52 shows the Text view with the Text Style menu choices.

FIGURE 6.52   Text view with the Text Style menu open

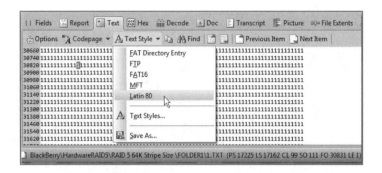

Rather than choose a text style, because first you'd have to create one, you can use the Options menu in conjunction with the adjoining Codepage menu to achieve the same effect dynamically. Essentially, these two menus are the two tabs that make up the New Text Style menu. By simply making these adjustments dynamically with these two menus, you can do most of your work in this fashion, saving text styles for the more complicated configurations for custom text styles that you save and reuse. Figure 6.53 shows the two tabs (Options and Code Page) for the New Text Style menu. Figure 6.54 shows the Options menu from the toolbar. Figure 6.55 shows the Codepage menu from the toolbar. Now that you've seen how it all works, you probably do as I do, which is to leave the Codepage menu set for Western European Windows and simply adjust the line wrap and length settings under Options as needed.

FIGURE 6.53   New Text Style menu with Options tab and Code Page tab

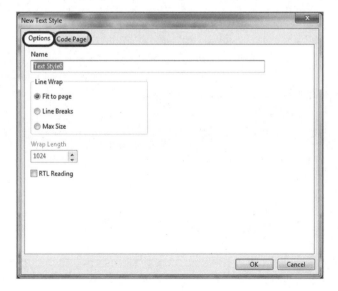

FIGURE 6.54   The line wrap and length can be set from the Options menu.

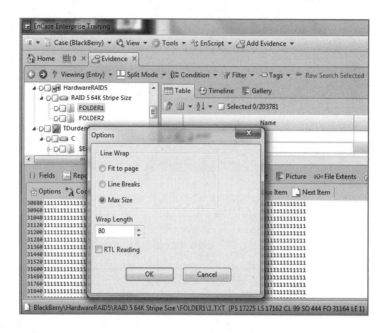

FIGURE 6.55   The code page for viewing text can be chosen from the Codepage menu.

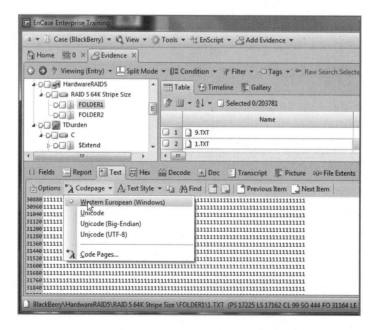

While in the Text view, you can sweep data by clicking and dragging it to select it. From there you can bookmark, export, or copy/paste data as needed.

Hex View

Another way to view data is in the Hex view. As shown in Figure 6.56, in this view each byte is shown in hexadecimal notation on the left side and is also represented in a Text view in the inset to the right of the Hex view. Hex is the pure raw data (binary data expressed in hexadecimal notation), whereas the text displayed is interpreted or influenced by code pages. When you need to see raw data, use the Hex view.

FIGURE 6.56 The Hex view of a JPG file. Note the Text view inset to the right, and the Options, Codepage, and Text Style menus are along the Hex tab toolbar at the far left.

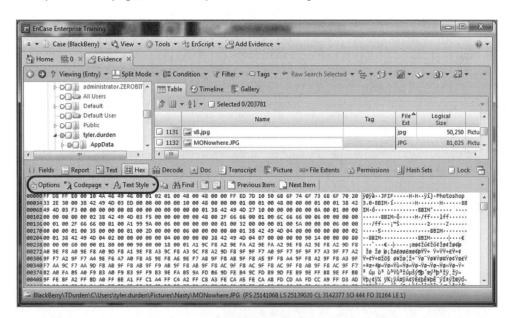

Like the Text view, the Hex view lets you select data and do many things with it, such as bookmarking, exporting, copying/pasting, and so forth. You will see in Chapter 7 that you can bookmark this data and view it in many different ways. You can view it as text, integer values, date/time stamps, partition tables, or DOS directory entries, just to name a few. You can pass this data to third-party decoding tools as well. When you get into advanced analysis or research and testing, you will spend considerable time in the Hex view.

Picture View

If EnCase detects that the file selected in the Table pane is an image, it will attempt to view the image using the Picture view in the View pane. If the file is not detected as an image, the image box will be unavailable. EnCase determines the file type based on extension until a file signature analysis has been completed, at which point the program determines the file type based on the file's signature instead of its extension. As you'll recall, the file signature analysis occurs as an automatic feature when the EnCase evidence processor runs. I'll cover file signature analysis in detail in Chapter 8.

Figure 6.57 shows a file as an image. This file is from a user's picture folder. Because this file was a picture and had a proper file extension, EnCase detected it by its signature and displayed it automatically in the Picture tab of the View pane.

FIGURE 6.57   A file shown as an image automatically in the Picture tab of the View pane

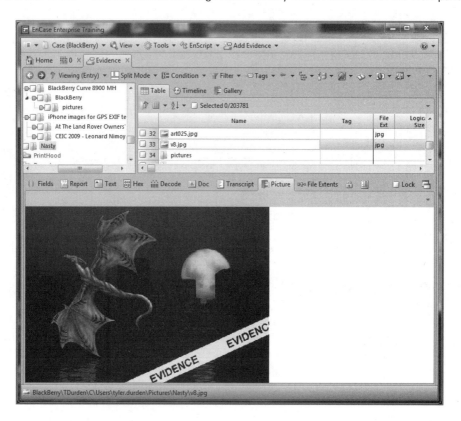

Report View

The Report view is a detailed report of the properties of the object selected in the Table pane. You will see all the attributes and properties of the object in this view, and if file permissions are in effect, they will be detailed as well. It is a quick way to obtain focused information on an object. You can right-click the report and export it as a web page or as a document. Sometimes you need lots of details about a couple of files. Here is the place to come to view that information and create a quick report.

Doc View

The Doc view is the integration of Stellent Inc.'s Outside In Technology into EnCase. In essence, this means that many common file formats, such as Microsoft Word, Microsoft Excel, Adobe PDF, and others can be viewed the way they would look in the native application. Printing and bookmarking are also available within the Doc view. Figure 6.58 shows a Microsoft Word document being viewed and an excerpt from that document being bookmarked.

FIGURE 6.58   Doc view in which many common file formats can be viewed as though shown in their native applications

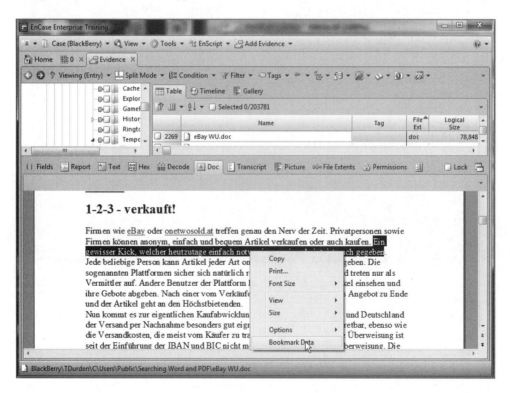

Transcript View

The Transcript view is also an integration of Stellent Inc.'s Outside In Technology. This view suppresses file noise, such as formatting and metadata. The text displayed within this view is text that is typically indexed for search by the indexing engine. Any search hit or bookmark will appear in both the Doc and Transcripts views. Figure 6.59 shows the Transcript view of the same document shown in Figure 6.58.

FIGURE 6.59   Transcript view of the document shown in Figure 6.58

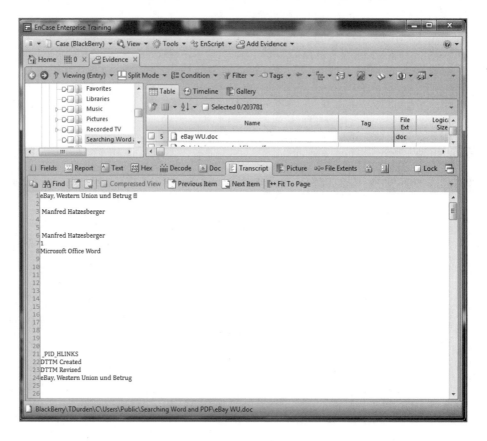

File Extents View

The File Extents view provides details about the cluster runs for any file. Figure 6.60 shows the File Extents view for the pagefile.sys file, which is the paging file for memory. Such files are large and can be very fragmented, such as this one.

FIGURE 6.60 File Extents view showing highly fragmented pagefile.sys file

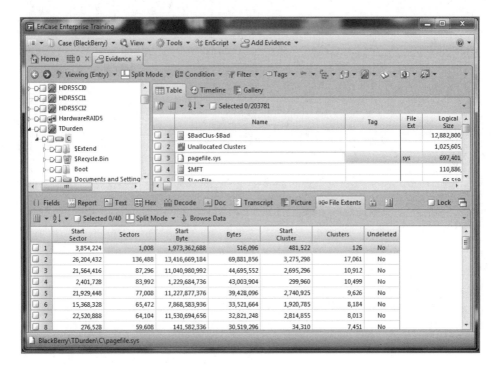

Permissions View

The Permissions view provides detailed security permissions for a file, including the owner, the security ID number (SID on Windows), read, write, execute, and so forth. Figure 6.61 shows a file found in a Windows Recycle Bin. Because Recycle Bins have SID-named folders, it is often difficult to determine which Recycle Bin belongs to which user when there are many users. Looking at the permissions of files in a Recycle Bin will tell you who owns the file and their SID, which you can in turn match with their SID-named Recycle Bin folders.

FIGURE 6.61 Permissions view for a file found in a Recycle Bin

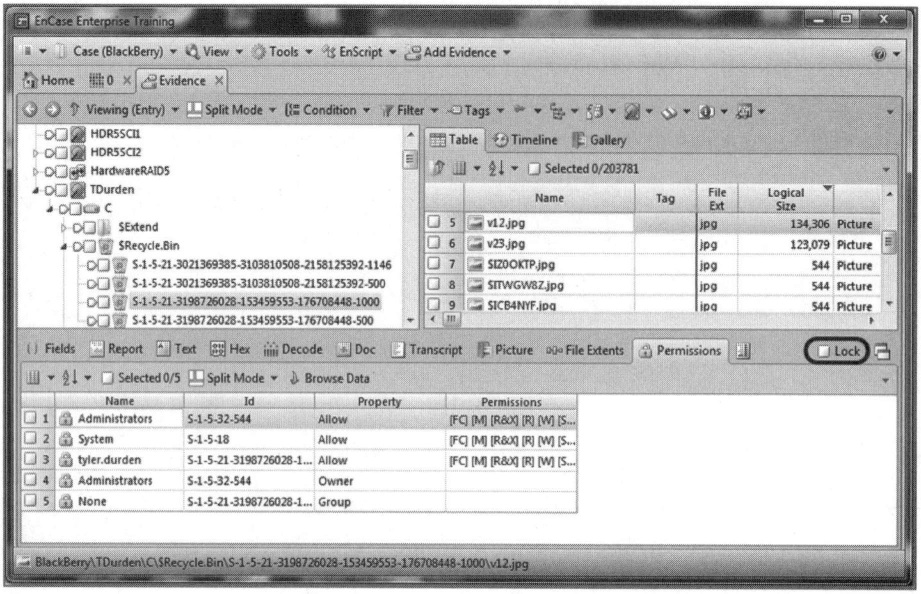

Decode View

In legacy versions of EnCase, you had to bookmark, or at least start to bookmark, to decode certain data types and strings, such as time stamps, directory entries, integers, and so forth. EnCase 7 provides a tab for decoding, making the process much easier once you've figured out how it works and gotten accustomed to using it.

To decode data, first locate the data in either the Text or Hex tab and select it. Next, click the Decode viewtab and select the decoding type you want to apply, and it's done. That was simple enough, so I will demonstrate the process to decode the partition table located in the master boot record. I like working on such data from the Disk view, so I first launched the Disk view for the physical drive. Since the MBR is located at sector 0, I put my cursor on the first sector, and that data is then displayed in the View pane below. I opted to view the data in the Hex view. I located the partition table starting at file offset 446 and ending on offset 509, for a total of 64 bytes. I selected that data, as shown in Figure 6.62.

With the data selected, move to the Decode view. In the left pane of the Decode view, select the appropriate view type, which in this case is Windows ➢ Partition Entry. As soon as you select it, the data is visible in the right pane, as shown in Figure 6.63.

FIGURE 6.62   Partition table selected in Hex view

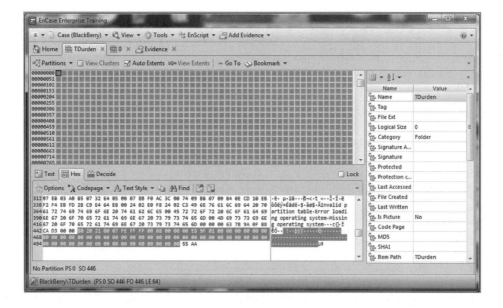

FIGURE 6.63   Decode view from which the view type is selected and displayed

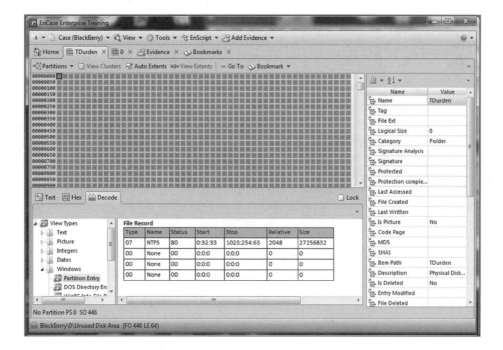

Field View

The Field view is new to EnCase 7, but there's nothing complicated about it. It's nothing more than the fields displayed in the Table view displayed in the bottom pane for the times you are in the Table view and need to see the metadata contained in the various fields. For example, if you are in the Gallery view and want to know the information about a particular file, you can switch to the Field view in the View pane and see this data quickly.

Lock Option

The user can "lock" a view type for the View pane. When the lock is on, EnCase will display data in the View pane that you have locked until you toggle the lock off. This is often useful when you want to see all data in hex, including pictures. EnCase, without the lock on hex, would view an image in the Picture view. The lock is a simple toggle feature; just check the box to the right of the hash sets view. If you refer to Figure 6.61, you'll see that I placed a circle around it.

Dixon Box

I covered the function and purpose of the Dixon box earlier in this chapter and showed you where it was located in Figure 6.19. It is located immediately to the right of the Sort menu on the Table tab toolbar. The Dixon box indicates the number of selected objects in the case and the total number of objects in the case. If no objects are selected, clicking the box selects all objects in the case. If objects are selected, clicking the box deselects all currently selected objects.

You should develop a habit of keeping a close watch on the Dixon box when selecting objects for an action. It can save you considerable time by preventing unintended copy/unerase or other actions. Suppose you select Unallocated Clusters for a search and then forget to clear the selection when you are done. Next, you locate a couple of files that you want to copy. You select those two files and choose to copy the selected files. If you glance at the Dixon box, you should see three selected instead of two, which should prompt you to modify your selection before proceeding. If you didn't bother to check first, you better have lots of space and time—EnCase will do as you directed and copy the entire unallocated space, along with the two files you really wanted to copy.

If you start an action and it seems to be taking longer than it should and you realize you have subjected more files than you intended to the operation, you can usually abort the process by double-clicking the progress bar in the lower-right corner. You will be prompted to confirm your decision to cancel the process underway.

Depending on what you are doing, aborting in this way is not always an option. Sending a "search hit" in the unallocated clusters to a third-party viewer is one such example. Once that process starts, the only way to stop it is to stop EnCase. EnCase is a powerful tool and will caution you or prevent you from making poor or destructive choices. But as I mentioned earlier, it doesn't stop or caution you from making choices that are not particularly smart ones. EnCase is quite accustomed to carrying out laborious tasks that can take hours or days.

The Dixon box is a valuable indicator and tool that helps you make good decisions and also allows you to select or deselect globally quickly. You should utilize it to its fullest extent—it can save you considerable time as you process cases.

You will often select many files in varied locations for later action. Before proceeding with a desired action, check to see which files you have selected. The Dixon box can tell you how many but not which ones. There are two quick methods of seeing all your selected files together. First, you can apply the green Set Included Folders trigger at the case level and sort on the column containing the selection boxes. Double-click the nameless column header (above the check boxes) that contains the blue check marks, and all selected files will be at the top of your sort.

Navigation Data (GPS)

Starting with EnCase 5, EnCase displays your precise location in the evidence file at the bottom of the screen on the status bar, as indicated in Figure 6.64. Prior versions displayed it in the bar separating the View pane from the Tree and Table panes. This is real-time information and is updated whenever you change the data being viewed. Although its official title is *navigation data*, most examiners simply call it the GPS, after the Global Positioning System that provides precise information on your exact position on Earth. In EnCase, the navigation data at the bottom of the screen tells you where you are in an evidence file with the same relative precision as GPS.

FIGURE 6.64   Navigation data (GPS) is displayed in the bottom of the screen on the status bar. This information indicates your precise position in the evidence file.

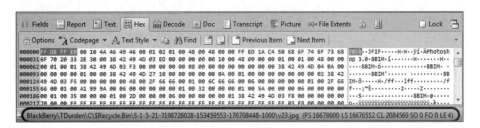

The information displayed is quite detailed. As shown in Figure 6.64, the information reads from left to right. Table 6.3 explains the format.

TABLE 6.3   Navigation data explained

Name	Indicator	Description
Full Path Name		Standard path-naming convention starting with the case filename, followed by the device name, followed by the complete path to the file currently being accessed.
Physical Sector Number	PS	Physical sector number of the data currently being accessed. Each device starts at sector 0 and ends with a number based on the number of sectors in that device, minus one (1,000 sectors are numbered 0 through 999).
Logical Sector Number	LS	The logical sector number relative to the partition you are in. Each partition is numbered with sectors starting at 0 and ending on a number based on the number of sectors in the partition minus one.
Cluster Number	CL	The cluster number for the data being accessed. Remember that clusters are logical constructs within a partition. If you are outside a partition, in the MBR for example, don't expect to see a cluster number!
Sector Offset	SO	The byte offset value within the sector where the data currently accessed resides. With 512 bytes per sector, expect these values to range from 0 to 511.
File Offset	FO	The byte offset value within the file currently being accessed. Values will range from 0 to the number of bytes in the file minus one. If you are sitting on the first byte in a file, the FO is 0. If you are sitting on the last byte of a 123-byte file, the FO is 122 (123 – 1 = 122).
Length	LE	The length of bytes currently highlighted/selected. It defaults to 1 until you select data by clicking and dragging to select data. This indicator is useful when selecting ranges of data for analysis, bookmarking, or exporting.

The GPS indicator is an extremely valuable tool. You should familiarize yourself with its format and make frequent reference to it. It is great tool for teaching and data research. With some research tasks, you can't function without it. Regardless of your purpose, using it and understanding this indicator will make you a better examiner.

Find Feature

EnCase is, by far, one of the most user-driven products I have ever used. I can't recall ever sending a suggestion to Microsoft and later seeing it in one of its products. By contrast, I have seen several suggestions sent by users to Guidance Software appear later as features in EnCase.

The Find feature is an example of a user-suggested feature and is quite useful. It's not one that jumps out at you, but once you discover where it is and what it can do, you'll use this feature frequently.

When you are in the Text or Hex view, the Find feature is available to search the data in that view. It is also available in the Console and EnScript Code views for use in programming or searching results sent to the console. You can right-click in the data area and choose Find. You can also use the shortcut Ctrl+F or open the Find menu located on the toolbar for the view you are in (Text or Hex).

The Find dialog box is straightforward in appearance and function, as shown in Figure 6.65. Before activating the feature, you can select text or data from the data present in Text or Hex view, and that data will autofill into the Expression text box, saving you time and preventing typing errors. Once the dialog box is open, you can choose regular text or GREP search options (I'll cover GREP in Chapter 7). You can search the entire document—from the cursor to the end of the file or document or within the area of data that you have currently selected. After the first hit, you can scroll to the next hit by pressing the F3 function key.

FIGURE 6.65   The Find dialog box is accessed from the data area of the View pane or from the Find menu on the view toolbar. It has powerful search features and can save you time when you want to search for an expression in a file.

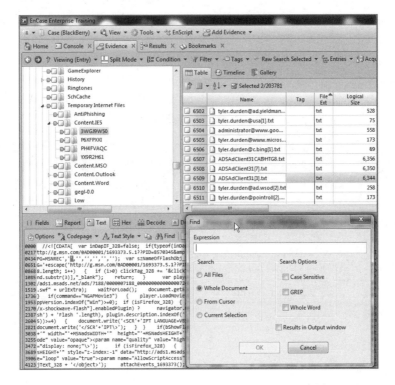

Other Views and Tools

Prior to EnCase 7, recent versions of EnCase offered a filter pane in the lower-right corner. However, with EnCase 7, that pane is no longer present. The various tools in the pane have now been moved to locations consistent with their function and have been absorbed into the new menu system. I will discuss those tools now for those used to accessing them in that location.

Conditions and Filters

Queries are no longer used in EnCase 7, and conditions and filters are located now on the toolbars for the various views and tools for which they are applicable. Figure 6.66 shows the location of the Condition and Filter menus on the Evidence Entry view , with the Filter menu open. With legacy versions of EnCase, the results of all conditions and queries were immediately viewable in the Entries view, but EnCase 7 now sends all condition and filter runs to the Results view, the tab for which is also shown in Figure 6.66. To see the results of your conditions or filters, you'll need to open the Results tab.

FIGURE 6.66 The Condition and Filter menus now appear on the toolbars for the various views for which they are applicable. Open the Results view to see filter and condition results.

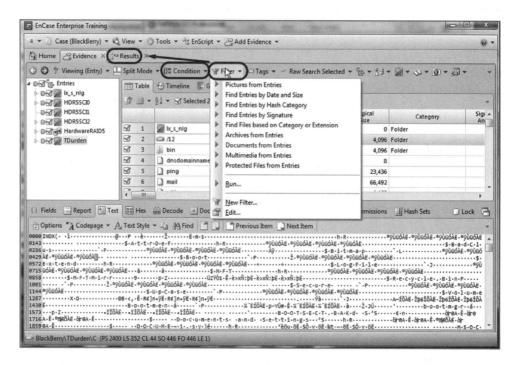

EnScript

EnScript now appears prominently on the application toolbar, as shown in Figure 6.67. You can run EnScripts from this drop-down menu or create or edit your own.

FIGURE 6.67   EnScript menu on application toolbar

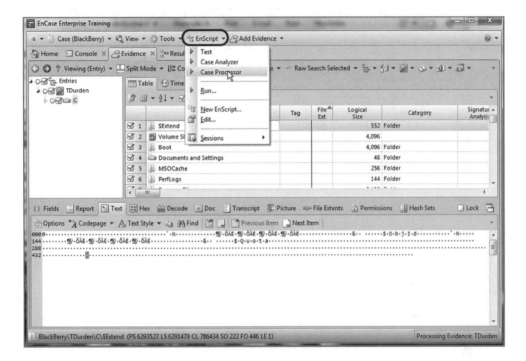

Text Styles

Text styles are located on the toolbars for the various views for which they are applicable. We covered how to use them earlier in this chapter as well as how you can use Options and Codepage menus to make dynamic adjustments to text views and thereby avoid having to create and apply text styles. Figure 6.68 shows the Text Style menu on the Text view toolbar. Note that the Options and Codepage menus appear immediately to the left of the Text Style menu.

FIGURE 6.68   Text Style menu on the Text view toolbar

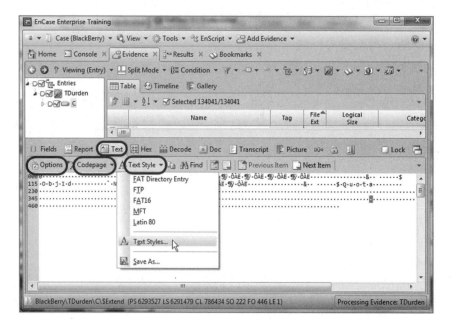

Adjusting Panes

In Exercise 6.1, you'll navigate around the EnCase environment. Before you do so, let's look at one more nice EnCase feature, which is adjusting the viewing panes. You can adjust the various panes to suit your viewing preferences. Between the Tree and Table panes and between the View pane and the two upper panes, you will see vertical and horizontal separator bars. If you place your cursor over these bars, as shown in Figure 6.69, the cursor changes to a horizontal or vertical sizing indicator, allowing you to click and drag the bar to the desired location.

EnCase views can be greatly enhanced by working in a multiple-monitor environment. You can spread your EnCase view over however many monitors your budget will support and greatly increase your viewing ease and efficiency. Giving EnCase plenty of screen real estate allows you to spread your view according to your particular viewing needs and do so on the fly when needed. Also, you can undock or detach the View pane to create some truly customized screen configurations. You undock the View pane by clicking the Undock icon in the upper-right corner of the View pane, as shown in Figure 6.70. To return the View pane to the main body of EnCase, simply click the red Close icon in the upper-right corner of the View pane, as shown in Figure 6.71. The View pane will simply snap back to its original location.

FIGURE 6.69 Placing your cursor on the horizontal or vertical separator bar causes the cursor to change to a sizing indicator, indicated by an arrow, that you can click and drag to adjust pane sizes.

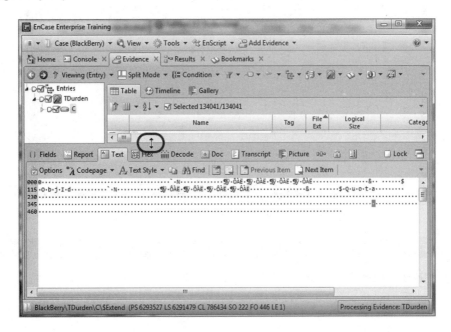

FIGURE 6.70 Click the undocking icon to undock View pane.

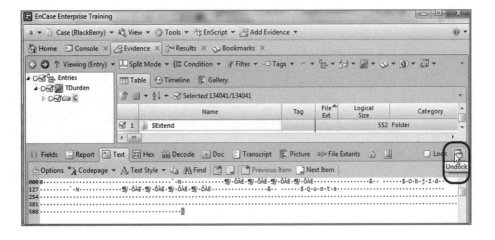

FIGURE 6.71   Click Close to return the docked View pane to its original location.

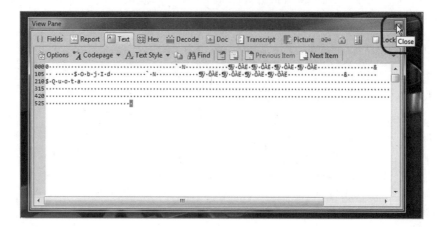

EXERCISE 6.1

Navigating EnCase

In this exercise, you'll create a new case, add an evidence file, and explore the many features and interfaces of EnCase 7.

1. On the website for this book (www.sybex.com/go/ence3e), locate a folder named Navigation, and copy its single evidence file (Navigation.E01) onto your examination computer.

2. Start EnCase, create a new case, and name it **Navigation**. Accept the default path locations.

3. Go to the location of your case files and open the Navigation folder, which was created by EnCase. If you are using Windows 7 and accepted the defaults, the path would be C:\Users\YourUserName\Documents\EnCase\Cases\Navigation. You should take note that EnCase created four folders (Email, Export, Tags, and Temp) and saved your case already, which is named Navigation.Case and stored in the root of your current folder.

4. In the folder Navigation, create a subfolder named **evidence** and place the evidence file from step 1 into this folder.

5. From the EnCase Home screen, you should see your open case named Navigation and have several options. Click Add Evidence, and on the screen that follows, click Add Evidence File. Browse to the evidence file you just placed in the new subfolder. Select it and open it. When the file loads, EnCase will open the Evidence view, and you'll see the evidence item; however, you'll see its name as FileSigAnalysis. I've renamed an evidence file's name to match the chapter's content. You'll use this same evidence file for a later chapter for dealing with file signature analysis, so don't worry too much about the name. Just have fun navigating and exploring EnCase views and features.

6. Before doing any work, save your case again now that you have added evidence.

7. This is a very small evidence file, and it should have verified almost immediately. Unless there was a problem, you won't even know it happened, but let's be sure it verified correctly. While still in the Evidence tab Table view, highlight your evidence item and then open the Report view in the View pane.

8. From the Report view, answer the following: did your evidence file properly verify? (Answer: it should be completely verified with 0 errors.) On what date was it acquired? (Answer: 8/12/2003.) Which version of EnCase was used to acquire this file? (Answer: 4.14.)

9. Go back to the Table pane and double-click your evidence item to open it in the Entries view. In the Tree pane, place your cursor on the root of the tree on the word *entries*. In the Table view, highlight the evidence item. In the View pane, switch to the Report view. What file system is on this evidence item? (Answer: FAT12.) How many sectors are on this device? (Answer: 2,880.) Can you again confirm that your evidence verified correctly? Again, it should have done so.

10. Return to the Tree pane and place your cursor on the floppy icon. In the Table pane, you see five objects, one of which is a folder named FileSignatureAnalysis. Place your cursor on that folder in the Table pane. In the View pane, open the Text view. What color is the data? (Answer: Red.) In this case, what does this color indicate? (Answer: Directory data.)

11. In the exercise in Chapter 2, you should have created a text style for viewing FAT directory entries. If so, from the Text Style menu on the Text view toolbar, locate your 32-byte-wide FAT directory text style, and select it. Your data should snap into place, revealing each 32-byte directory entry on a separate line. If you did not create one, don't worry, because you can apply the same view on the fly. Open the Options menu on the Text view toolbar. Select Max Size, set the wrap length to 32, and click OK. Immediately everything should fall in place, and now you should see the value of working with the Options menu.

12. In the Tree pane, place your cursor on the folder FileSignatureAnalysis. You should see 10 files in the Tree pane. In the Table pane, place your cursor on the file jpeg image.jpg. In the View pane, you should see the image appear. In the View pane, switch to the Hex view by clicking its tab. You are now seeing the hexadecimal notation for binary data. Note the first four bytes of the JPEG file, which are FF D8 FF E0. This is one of several JPEG headers. I'll get into that more in a later chapter, but you should get used to seeing it and recognizing right away.

13. Return to the Table pane, where 10 files are listed, and click the Gallery view. Only two images are showing (a third is trying to display but doesn't). At this point, EnCase is looking to file extensions for file types since you have not yet run a file signature analysis (which you will do in Chapter 8). Even though other images are present in this list, only two are legitimate JPEG images with .jpg extensions, and they are shown by EnCase.

14. Return to the Table view in the Table pane. Locate and highlight the file named jpeg image.jpg. The picture should resolve and appear in the View pane. If not, switch to the Picture view, and the image will appear. In the View pane, place a check in the Lock box. This should lock the View pane in the Picture view.

15. Go to the top of the list in the Table pane. Examine each of the 10 files by highlighting them, which forces them to resolve as pictures in the View pane as you do.

16. As you locate files that are images, select them. You can do this by clicking in the square box to the left and adjacent to each file, or you can press the spacebar, which places a blue check and advances down the list by one. When done, you should have selected two files. Check the Dixon box, and it should confirm 2 out of 16 selected.

17. At the top of the Table pane, double-click in the nameless column header above the blue check boxes. You have sorted those selected from those not selected, forcing all your selections to the top of the list. You can sort in only one direction with this particular column. By default, it is a reverse sort and places the selected items at the top. Although this is a short list, imagine the usefulness of doing this at the case level with thousands of files.

18. Add a secondary sort to this sort. Go to the File Created column. Hold down the Shift key, and double-click the File Created header at the top of this column. You are now looking at your selected files in chronological order based on when they were created. They were all created on the same date, with just a few seconds separating each of them. Note that they all have last-written dates that predate their file creation, which makes it appear they were last written before they were even created. In fact, they were, because they were really created elsewhere, modified elsewhere, and moved to their present location. As you'll recall, the created date reflects when they were moved or created at their present location.

19. In the Table pane, click the Timeline view. Uncheck all boxes except File Created Date. You should see the number 10 in the Timeline area, indicating 10 files with file creation dates. Double-click 10 until it resolves to squares for each file. Click different squares and see the data for each appear in the View pane. In the View pane, switch to the Fields or Report view and see the metadata appear for each square or file that you click.

20. In the Tree pane, click the Set Included Folders trigger at the case level. If you click in the polygon-shaped box, it should turn green. When you do so, note that all objects

in the case now appear in the Table pane. Even so, all selected files are still together at the top of the list since the previously defined sorts are applied to the new data brought into this view when you applied the Set Included Folders trigger. Turn off the Set Included Folders trigger by clicking it again.

21. In the Tree pane, highlight root or entries, which forces the evidence item to appear in the Table pane. Place your cursor on the evidence item (FileSigAnalysis), and on the Evidence toolbar, open the Device menu and select Disk view. In the View pane, click the Hex view. You have both the Disk view and Hex view now. In the Disk view, note the various colored squares. You are looking at a floppy. It is a volume device and does not have an MBR. What occupies its first sector, however, is a VBR. After the VBR, you see FAT1 and FAT2. Following the FAT is the root directory, shown in green. Immediately following the root directory is the first cluster that can hold data for files. Place your cursor on the first blue square.

22. Look at the GPS in the bottom of the screen. You should be on PS33 LS33 CL02. Recall that on FAT usable clusters start at 02 and that the first two FAT entries (00 and 01) hold other metadata. With a floppy, the volume starts with the first sector, and thus the physical sector and the logical sector offsets are the same, which is something you won't often see. Move your cursor one blue box to the right of your present location. You should be on PS34 LS34 CL03. Note that you have moved one box, and the cluster number and the sector numbers both advanced by one. With a floppy there is one sector per cluster, and therefore one sector equals one cluster. If you look at the toolbar, you will note that View Clusters is grayed out. Because you are looking at a floppy with one sector equaling one cluster, the Sector view and the Cluster view are one in the same.

23. Right-click in the data area, and choose Go To. Type **2879**, and click OK. You are now sitting on sector 2879. Because there are 2,880 sectors on this floppy (0–2879), you are sitting on the last sector of this device. Click the X in the Disk view to exit the Disk view.

24. In the Tree pane, highlight the folder FileSignatureAnalysis. In the Table pane, highlight the file named no header in table and matches no other header MATCHES.txt. In the View pane, click the Text view. You should see some text in this file. The fifth word in this file is the word *file*. With your cursor, click and drag over this word to select it. Note in your GPS that the LE is 4, indicating the length in bytes of the selected data. With the Word file selected, press Ctrl+F, or right-click and choose Find. Accept the default, which is Whole Document. Click OK, and the first search hit should be the text you selected. Press F3 to find the next search hit, and it should find the second and final search hit. You can press F3 until you hear the error beep, indicating there are no more matching search hits.

25. Save your case, and exit EnCase.

Other Views

Thus far, I have covered most, not all, of the EnCase views that are specific to a case. There are some more views, but they will be more meaningful to cover as you start processing evidence using the EnCase evidence processor. For example, the Records view is where you can find considerable data that is derived from the EnCase evidence processor. Figure 6.72 shows email details as they appear on the Records view. Some of the views I have referenced already as well as others will be covered in more detail in later chapters.

Global Views and Settings

EnCase has several views or settings that affect the EnCase environment and are thus considered global. Let's start with the File Types view. In legacy EnCase versions, there were separate views for file types, file signatures, and file viewers, all of which are interrelated. EnCase 7 combines those views into one File Types view. You access this view through the View menu on the application toolbar, as shown in Figure 6.73.

FIGURE 6.72 Email is viewed on the Records view after running the EnCase evidence processor.

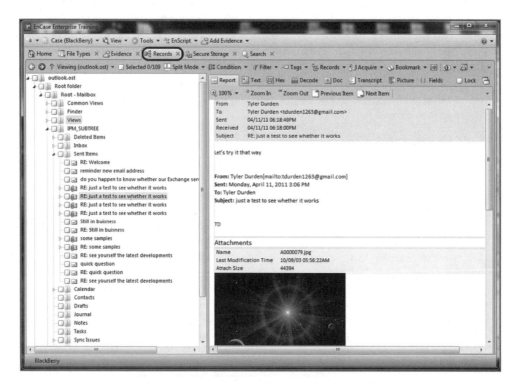

FIGURE 6.73   Accessing the File Types view from the application toolbar View menu

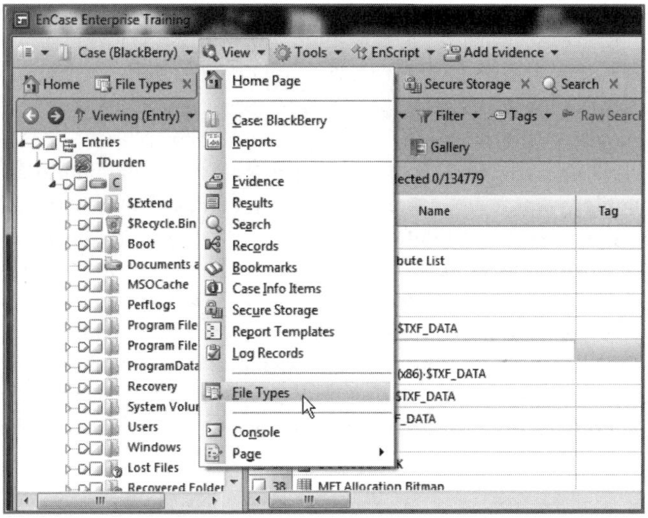

Once you open the File Types view, you will see, if you scroll to the bottom, that there are more than 800 entries or file types that are defined in this table. Figure 6.74 shows the File Types view and specifically the more significant entries for the standard JPEG image file type. You can see how the signature, file type, and viewers are combined into this one view.

FIGURE 6.74   File Types view highlighting a JPEG Image Standard file type

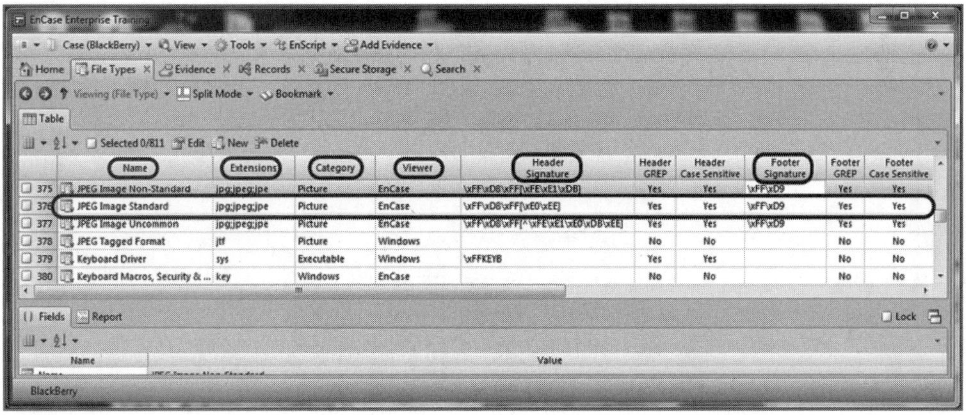

From the File Types view, you can delete, modify, or create new file types entries. On the toolbar, you'll see the icons to do any one of the three. If, for example, you want to create a new one, simply click New, and you will be able to provide the necessary information in the New File Type dialog box, as shown in Figure 6.75. The team at Guidance Software does an excellent job of keeping up-to-date on file types but can't possibly include them all.

If you encounter new file types, you have the ability to add them. If you add one, it will be stored separately in the user's AppData area and not in the global settings. In this manner, when Guidance Software updates its file types data, it does not overwrite ones you created.

What Happens When I Double-click a File in EnCase?

When you double-click a file in EnCase, it looks to the file types data (stored in the filetypes.ini file) for what to do. If the file type is set for internal viewing, it will have EnCase as the file viewer, and EnCase will tell you it is set for internal viewing. If the file type is set for Windows to handle the viewing, based on whatever is set in the Windows registry for that file extension, it will have Windows as the file viewer. In that case, EnCase creates a temporary file (placing it in the temp directory of the case folder) and then passes it to Windows for viewing. If the file viewer is set for an installed viewer, one you have configured, then that viewer will be listed as the viewer. Again, EnCase will create a temporary file and pass it to that specific viewer for viewing in the Windows environment.

FIGURE 6.75   New File Type dialog box

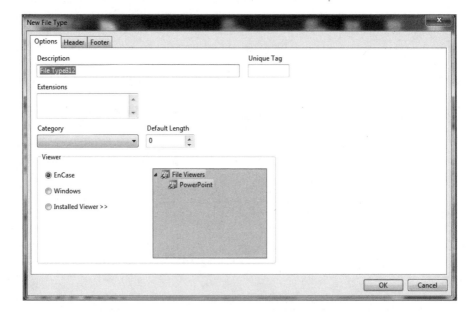

While many files can be viewed successfully within the EnCase environment, there are times when external viewers aren't just better, they are necessary. To configure an external viewer in legacy versions of EnCase, there was a separate view, but EnCase 7 simply provides the option to do so at the point where you use one, as shown in Figure 6.76. In this case, I decided that I wanted to open this image with an external viewer. To do so, I right-clicked the file in the Table view and selected the Open With submenu. My only choice for an external viewer, as shown here, is PowerPoint. Since that is not the viewer I'd prefer to use for images, I decided to add one, which in this case is Quick View Plus. To add a viewer, simply select File Viewers, and you will see the Edit File Viewers dialog box. Click New, and you will have the ability to name the viewer and provide the path to its executable file by which it launches, as shown in Figure 6.77. Once configured, the next time you right-click and choose Open With, your newly installed viewer is available, as shown in Figure 6.78.

FIGURE 6.76 Using an external viewer to view a file in EnCase

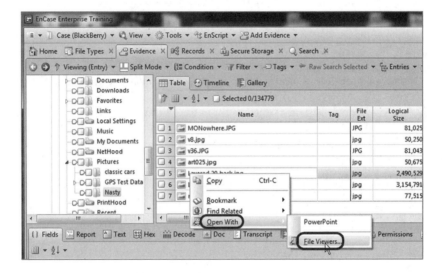

FIGURE 6.77 Adding a new external file viewer

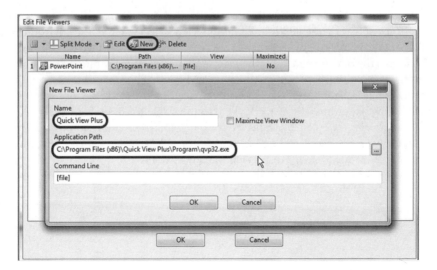

FIGURE 6.78   Newly configured external viewer now available

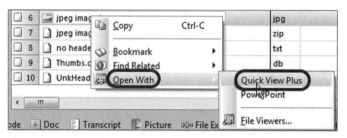

EnCase Options

EnCase provides an interface that allows the user to change many of the EnCase environment properties. This interface is available in the Tools ➢ Options menu.

The Global view contains several options that affect EnCase globally. I have mentioned that EnCase, by default, uses a dot to indicate a Boolean true condition and null (nothing) to indicate a Boolean false condition. Many of the columns in the Table view contain dots or nulls to indicate the presence (or absence) of a condition or property. Figure 6.79 shows the default global values, including the dot and null, under Show True and Show False, respectively. Figure 6.80 demonstrates how this configuration displays for the Is Picture column in the Table view. As you can see, dots and blanks aren't always the best way to communicate a clear meaning. To change this to a more meaningful value, many examiners replace the dot with Yes and the null with No, as shown in Figure 6.81. After making the changes, Figure 6.82 shows the effects of this change, with Yes and No showing now instead of dots and blanks.

You should note in Figures 6.79 and 6.82 that there are other options on the Global view. As previously mentioned, you can change the backup settings regarding frequency, number of files, location, and whether or not to use the Recycle Bin. I also discussed some of the picture options. You can also change the global code page as well as other settings.

Several other options presented in the Options view affect the EnCase environment. As needs arise, just remembering where they are accessed is usually sufficient. You can make a useful change to the date format from the Date view in the Global options that will cause the day of the week to be displayed in all date/time values. This change is not documented in the manuals but is a great time-saver when you need to know the day of the week, which is often quite important in analysis work. The default value for dates is *MM/DD/YY*, which returns, for example, *10/24/11*. By changing the value to Other and customizing the string to *ddd MM/dd/yy*, you ensure that it will return *Mon 10/24/11*, as shown in Figure 6.83. This is usually quite adequate for displaying the day of the week.

FIGURE 6.79 Global options showing the default values. Note that Show True is populated with a dot and Show False is populated with a null.

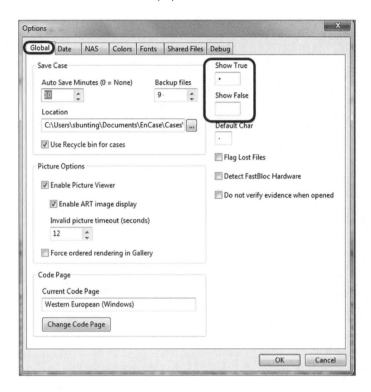

FIGURE 6.80 The Is Picture column populated with dots and blanks

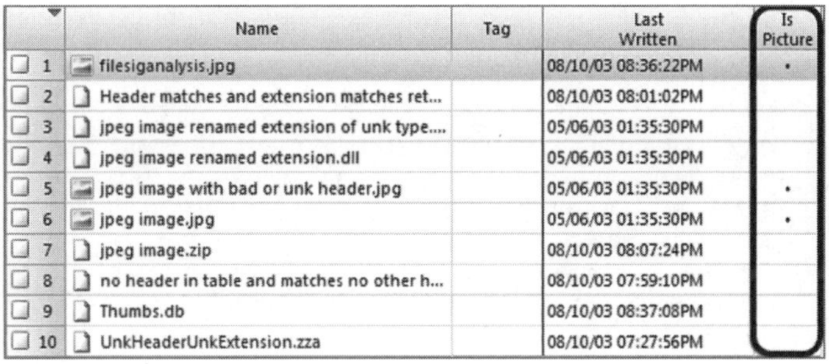

		Name	Tag	Last Written	Is Picture
☐	1	filesignanalysis.jpg		08/10/03 08:36:22PM	•
☐	2	Header matches and extension matches ret...		08/10/03 08:01:02PM	
☐	3	jpeg image renamed extension of unk type....		05/06/03 01:35:30PM	
☐	4	jpeg image renamed extension.dll		05/06/03 01:35:30PM	
☐	5	jpeg image with bad or unk header.jpg		05/06/03 01:35:30PM	•
☐	6	jpeg image.jpg		05/06/03 01:35:30PM	•
☐	7	jpeg image.zip		08/10/03 08:07:24PM	
☐	8	no header in table and matches no other h...		08/10/03 07:59:10PM	
☐	9	Thumbs.db		08/10/03 08:37:08PM	
☐	10	UnkHeaderUnkExtension.zza		08/10/03 07:27:56PM	

FIGURE 6.81   Boolean Show True is replaced with Yes, and Show False is replaced with No. These values are more meaningful when displayed in context.

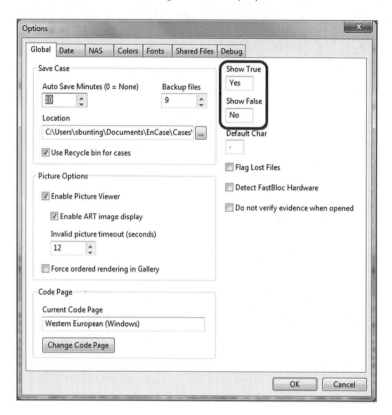

FIGURE 6.82   The Is Picture column populated with Yes and No instead of dots and blanks

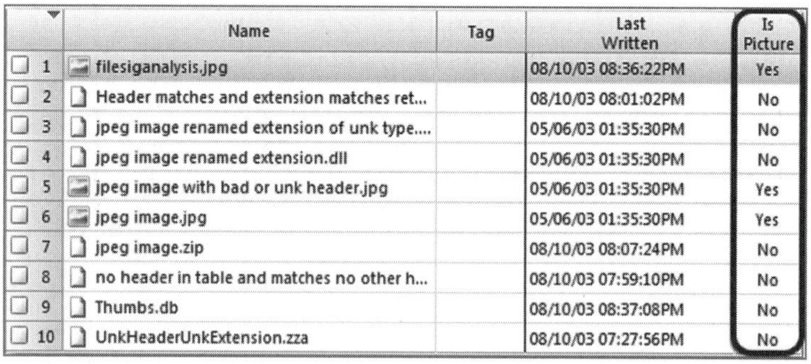

		Name	Tag	Last Written	Is Picture
☐	1	filesiganalysis.jpg		08/10/03 08:36:22PM	Yes
☐	2	Header matches and extension matches ret...		08/10/03 08:01:02PM	No
☐	3	jpeg image renamed extension of unk type....		05/06/03 01:35:30PM	No
☐	4	jpeg image renamed extension.dll		05/06/03 01:35:30PM	No
☐	5	jpeg image with bad or unk header.jpg		05/06/03 01:35:30PM	Yes
☐	6	jpeg image.jpg		05/06/03 01:35:30PM	Yes
☐	7	jpeg image.zip		08/10/03 08:07:24PM	No
☐	8	no header in table and matches no other h...		08/10/03 07:59:10PM	No
☐	9	Thumbs.db		08/10/03 08:37:08PM	No
☐	10	UnkHeaderUnkExtension.zza		08/10/03 07:27:56PM	No

FIGURE 6.83   Changing the date format to show the day of week

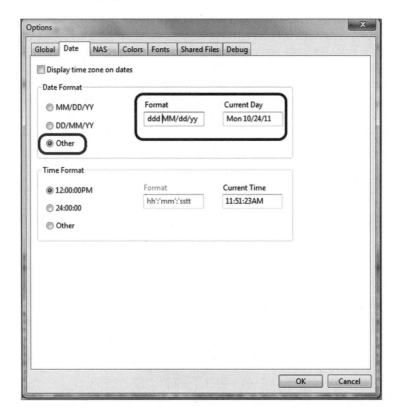

You can, however, be very elaborate with your customization. Changing the string to *dddd MM/dd/yy* will return *Monday, 10/24/11*, and changing it to *dddd MMM dd, yyyy* will return *Monday, Oct 24, 2011.*

When you enter the custom string, it is case-sensitive, so pay close attention to details. You may encounter a legacy EnScript that works only with the default date time format and usually involves prompts for the user to input date and time ranges. If you experience EnScript difficulties in that regard and those are truly rare encounters, switch back to the default to run that EnScript. You can restore your customized string when you finish.

As you can see from the various tabs or views, you can change many options as needed. If you work with foreign languages, you'll need to work with the Fonts view. Detailed instructions are available on the Guidance Software website. If you work in a networked lab and have one central source for your EnCase environment files, you can map those paths on the Shared Files view.

One final view, the Colors view, deserves your attention. Examiners often find it necessary to modify slightly some of the default colors. You can radically change the EnCase color palette from this view. We recommend you make small incremental changes. In this fashion, you change one feature's color palette and examine its impact throughout the EnCase environment before making additional changes.

A color that is often changed or tweaked is the Search Hit color, since the default may not view well in certain viewing and lighting conditions, especially if you are projecting your EnCase view, which is sometimes necessary. If you open the Colors tab and locate Bookmark, you will see the foreground and background colors for this feature. If you want to change the background, double-click the background, and you are presented with the color palette. Initially, you should probably stick with the same basic color, but choose one that is more or less saturated and visible, based on your tastes and viewing environment, as shown in Figure 6.84. The color palette options are endless, but you should proceed cautiously, making small incremental changes and evaluating before making more changes.

FIGURE 6.84   You can change the color palette for the Bookmarks background by going to the Tools ➢ Options ➢ Colors view.

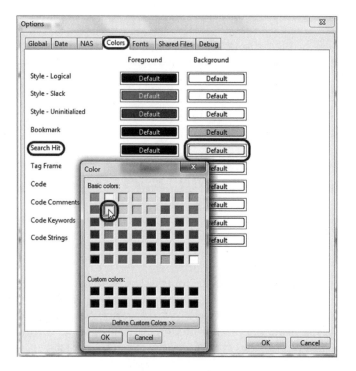

Before we leave the global options, there are two other tabs that need your attention. If you are in a lab environment that uses a network authentication server or if you are using EnCase Enterprise, the NAS tab is where you configure paths to these resources. Finally, the Debug tab, shown in Figure 6.85, provides system cache settings that can be adjusted, but usually the defaults are just fine. If you are experiencing issues with EnCase, technical support may direct you to send them a stack or heap log. To do this, you have to enable that logging on the Debug view. Ideally, you'll never have to do this, but things do happen, and this tool can assist greatly in solving your problem.

FIGURE 6.85   Debug tab from which debug logging and system cache can be configured

Thinking Outside the Box

You just spent an entire chapter dealing with the EnCase interface. Sometimes it is good to get out of that frame of reference for a while so you can truly think outside the box! With that in mind, let's digress by jumping into the Macintosh environment, which is more like culture shock than a digression.

This case eventually resulted in an employment termination. Naturally, it is necessary to protect identities, and therefore certain case details must remain purposefully vague.

The target of this investigation is a scientist who stood accused of manipulating research data to apply for and receive government research grants. This was ongoing research spanning many years as well as previous employers, and it involved significant funds, to say the least. It was the government research integrity office that initially discovered the altered data and initiated the investigation, which later broadened.

I was tasked with seizing and imaging all the computer systems used by this scientist, which was a daunting task since there was no cooperation from the scientist and little information. My directive was simple, or so it seemed: get it all! The systems covered the gamut and included Windows, Solaris, and Macintosh boxes, some of which were actively connected to scientific instrumentation.

At some point later in the process, months down the road, certain data files were identified as being relevant. They were on a Mac G4 system. These files were among hundreds of like files covering the research life of this scientist, with data ranging back to the early 1980s. Recall that some operating systems—including Mac operating systems prior to OS X—don't use extensions to identify and associate files to applications. Examining these files in the EnCase environment provided no information as to which scientific application created the files, and cooperation was not forthcoming.

We typically think of Tableau as a hardware write-blocking device that we use in Windows. We can use it with EnCase, or we can use it within Windows with the Explorer interface or with other third-party tools. What we often don't think of are the uses that are beyond the norm or the out-of-the-box applications of Tableau.

In the case at hand, I used EnCase to restore the Mac image onto a drive of identical make, model, and geometry. I attached the restored drive to my Tableau unit. I connected the Tableau to my lab Mac via a 1394 cable and booted the system. Upon boot, the questioned hard drive was mounted, read-only, and sitting on my Mac desktop awaiting my perusal. My first thought was that this was far too easy. I was right!

My first task was to run an MD5 of the mounted physical drive using the Mac Terminal application. This interface provides a Unix command line, and, being Unix, MD5 comes with the package. After about 90 minutes or so, the hash was completed, and the value matched the acquisition hash reported by EnCase. This was great—I had established that the drive under examination was identical to the one acquired, and nothing had changed when it was mounted in the Mac environment.

Based on my discoveries using EnCase, I knew the identity and exact location of the files in question. Using the Mac equivalent of Windows Explorer, which is called Finder, I navigated to the files in question. Mac stores information about files in metadata that is viewable via a Get Info command, similar to the Properties command in Windows. There are at least three ways to access this command:

- If you select a file and press Command+I, you get it immediately.

- A second way is via a right-click menu option called Get Info.

  Since Apple likes to hobble its users by providing only a one-button mouse (or to this day by disabling right-click functionality by default on its Magic Mouse or trackpads), you have to hold down the Control key while clicking the one-button mouse to access the right-click options. If you want to use a Mac to its fullest potential, use a mouse that has two-buttons or its equivalent and enable the secondary click in the system preferences. Then you are an instant Mac power user!

- The third way is under Finder. Select the file, and from the File menu on the tool-bar, choose Get Info.

The Get Info results for the files in question immediately revealed the identity of the scientific analysis program that created the files. Armed with that information, I was then in a position to read the data for the first time in this investigation.

Mac, unlike Windows, does not use a registry to store installation information for programs. When programs are installed on a Mac, the installation information is usually stored with the program files or in plist files in various standard locations. What this means for the forensics examiner is that you can run just about any program that is on the read-only target drive, and it will run flawlessly (see the note regarding licensing at the end of this sidebar). If you have any difficulties because of the read-only status, just drag the application to your Applications folder on your system drive, and you are back in business.

When I attempted to run the relevant scientific application to read the data, I encountered yet another issue. This was a legacy program and wouldn't run under Mac OS X, requiring instead the Mac Classic environment. As it turns out, Mac ships Classic support with most versions of OS X. Although not a clearly marked road to follow, it is on the install disk labeled Additional Software. Pop in the CD, follow the prompts, and five minutes later I had support for legacy programs running under Mac Classic.

When Lion (OS X 10.7.X in July 2011) joined the line of Macintosh "cat" operating systems, legacy program support (Classic) ended. Nevertheless, as examiners, we are always encountering legacy computing equipment and software, which means we have to maintain some older gear for those nostalgic ventures we often encounter. In short, keep an older Wintel box and an older Mac box in your inventory!

After a seemingly long journey, I was able to run the scientific applications, read all the data, and export it in several formats readable by the investigators. When done, I ran another MD5 of the target drive. After all that activity, reading data and running programs directly from that drive, not one bit had changed, and the MD5 hashes were all alike.

The Tableau write-blocker is a truly versatile device, and it does block all writes regardless of the environment in which it is run. Don't be afraid to think out of the box and use it in nontraditional ways, documenting and testing along the way to assure the integrity of your processes and analyses.

Note: In this case, to avoid legal issues over licensing, I purchased a license for the latest version of the involved software. Even though licensed for the latest and greatest, I used the older version on the target drive as well so as to see the data using the same version of the software (as did the accused party).

Summary

This chapter covered the EnCase environment and its features and functions. It covered how EnCase organizes its views into increasingly granular content, starting with the Tree pane, moving to the Table pane, and ending with the View pane. What is displayed in any given pane depends on the object highlighted in the pane before it in the hierarchy.

The chapter also covered how to create a case within EnCase from the Home screen and to subsequently add evidence to that case. I discussed how EnCase automatically creates a folder structure to contain the various case files when a new case is created and how to modify the paths for those case and evidence files.

While in the Evidence tab Entries view, the Table pane offers the Table, Gallery, and Timeline views. From the Table view, you can see all the case objects, folders, and files. Their properties are listed in columns. You can move, sort, or hide columns from view. The Timeline view offers a chronological view of data in a graphical environment. The Gallery view shows all images based on file extension. If a file signature analysis has been run, as an integral part of the EnCase evidence processor, the Gallery view will be based on the file signature data.

The Disk view, accessed from the Evidence tab toolbar Device menu, displays a device according to a color-coded legend. It defaults to Sector view, which can be changed to Cluster view. As each sector is highlighted, its data is shown in the View pane. From the Disk view, the examiner can navigate with the Go To feature, bookmark data, or create/delete partitions.

The View pane offers the Text, Hex, Doc, Transcript, Picture, Report, Fields, File Extents, Permissions, and Hash Sets views. The Text view shows plain text, while the Hex view shows both hexadecimal notation and a text view. The Doc view allows common file formats to be viewed as though in their native application. The Transcripts panel is similar to the Doc view, but it filters noise and metadata from the view, displaying the extracted text without formatting. The Picture view shows images. The Report view shows case object properties in a ready-to-export format. The file can be exported in RTF, HTML, TXT, XML, or PDF format. The Fields view is a listing of the same properties found in the Table view. File Extents lists the details for the cluster runs for any selected file. Permissions will list the security permissions for the selected file, including the owner, SID, groups, read/write/execute permissions, and so forth. The Hash Sets view will list the hash sets to which the file belongs, if any, along with their properties. EnCase offers several views or case-processing features. They can be accessed from the View menu or, if open, by clicking their tab. Some views are launched by virtue of starting a task. For example, when you add evidence to a case, the result is that the Evidence view opens and lists the evidence items in the case. The Home screen is the default screen when opening EnCase. This view allows you to open cases, create new cases, and access options. When a case is opened, the Home screen allows you the options of searching, reviewing search results, adding evidence, processing evidence, browsing evidence or records, creating reports, browsing bookmarks, and accessing options.

The Evidence tab entries view provides the examiner with a view of all devices, folders, and files in the selected case that have been parsed and loaded. Along the Evidence tab toolbar you can find several menus from which additional views or tools can be launched. At the far right end of each toolbar, and there are several, is the right-side menu, which is a collection of all the menus located on that toolbar. It is similar to the former right-click context menu in content and function.

The Bookmarks view holds all of your case bookmarks and is the point from which your final report is generated. After running the EnCase evidence processor, which I'll cover in detail later, many of the results are available on the Records tab, some of which are email, thumbnail, and archived or compressed files. From this view, you can analyze, bookmark, and report your results. From the Device menu (located on the evidence tab toolbar), you can launch the Disk view, recover folders, restore, hash, scan disk configurations, scan for LVM, analyze EFS, analyze RMS, share (VFS and PDE), and modify time zone settings.

Examiners with programming skills can create and modify EnScripts from the EnScript menu located on the application toolbar. You can also run EnScripts from this location. The console, to which considerable output is directed by various tools and EnScripts, is located on the View menu, which is found on the application toolbar.

At the global level, the examiner can configure various options. The File Types view (available from the application toolbar View menu) combines file types, file signatures, and file viewers into one view or interface. You can modify, delete, or add entries. If you add entries to this database, they will be stored in the App Data area and thus are separate from the main file types database.

You can add external file viewers at the various points where you can view a file and send its contents to an external viewer. For example, in the Evidence tab entries view, you can right-click a file in the Table view and select Open With. At this point, you can send the file to an already configured external viewer or configure and add a viewer from the same menu.

Finally, EnCase has an Options menu, which is accessed from the Tools menu on the application toolbar. From the Global tab, you can configure backup options, picture-viewing options, default code page, and settings pertaining to Boolean viewing. On the Date tab, you can configure the formats for date and time separately. From the NAS tab, you can set paths for the NAS key path and Enterprise safe key and address. You can adjust various colors from the Color tab. From the Fonts tab, you can configure fonts for the EnCase environment, which will be required when working with many foreign languages. In a multiuser lab environment, shared settings, keywords, and the like can be configured on the Shared Files tab. The Debug tab is the location to go for adjusting the system cache or enabling debugging logs (stack or heap).

Exam Essentials

Understand how EnCase organizes its workspace.   Understand the Home screen and explain how to open and create cases. Explain how to add evidence or browse evidence from the Home screen. Understand the Evidence tab entries view. Explain the Tree pane, Table pane, and View pane as to what data is displayed in each and how they interact. Describe the Table, Gallery, and Timeline views from the Table pane. Explain how to launch the Disk view and explain its purpose and features. Explain the concept of multidimensional data and how it can be viewed in the View pane. Be able to list which tabs are found in the View pane.

Understand how EnCase stores configuration and case data.   Explain how and where EnCase creates paths and filenames for the various case-related files. Understand where EnCase stores both its global and user configuration files and what types of data are stored in each of the various configuration files.

Understand how to navigate within EnCase.   Understand the hierarchical tree structure displayed in the Tree pane. Know the function of the Set Included Folders trigger and the file selection functions. Understand and be able to explain how they differ. Know how to move, sort, hide, and lock columns in the Table view. Understand what information is provided in the Report view and how it can be used. Explain the Gallery view and what information will be displayed and under what conditions. Explain the function and importance of the Timeline view. Know the function and purpose of the Disk view and be able to explain the meaning of the various color-coded elements.

Understand and explain the differences between the Text and Hex views.   Describe the purpose of and know how to create and select a text style. Explain how to use the Options and Codepage menus to create dynamic text styles. Also describe the purpose of the Report view in the View pane. Explain the purpose and function of the Permissions tab. Explain the purpose and function of the File Extents tab.

Explain the Docs view and how the Transcripts view is both similar and dissimilar. Describe how the Pictures tab on the View pane functions. Explain the purpose and function of the Lock button. Understand and be able to explain the Dixon box and how it assists the examiner.

Understand the EnCase menu system.   Be able to locate and describe the various toolbars that are in the various EnCase views. For any given menu on the Evidence toolbar, be able to describe the various functions available. Explain the function and contents of the right-side menu and how it relates to the other menus on the same toolbar.

Review Questions

1. In the EnCase Windows environment, must an examiner first create a new case before adding a device to examine?

   A. Yes

   B. No

2. When EnCase 7 is used to create a new case, which files are created automatically in the case folder under the folder bearing the name of the case?

   A. `Evidence`, `Export`, `Temp`, and `Index` folders

   B. `Export`, `Temp`, and `Index` folders

   C. `Email`, `Export`, `Tags`, and `Temp`

   D. `Evidence`, `Email`, `Tags`, and `Temp`

3. From the EnCase 7 Home screen, which of the following *cannot* be carried out?

   A. Opening a case

   B. Creating a new case

   C. Opening options

   D. Generating a encryption key

   E. None of the above

4. When creating a new case, the Case Options dialog box prompts for which of the following?

   A. Name (case name)

   B. Examiner name

   C. Base case folder path

   D. Primary evidence cache path

   E. All of the above

5. What determines the action that will result when a user double-clicks a file within EnCase?

   A. The settings in the `TEXTSTYLES.INI` file

   B. The settings in the `FILETYPES.INI` file

   C. The settings in the `FILESIGNATURES.INI` file

   D. The settings in the `VIEWERS.INI` file

6. In the EnCase environment, the term *external viewers* is best described as which of the following?

   A. Internal programs that are copied out of an evidence file

   B. External programs loaded in the evidence file to open specific file types

   C. External programs that are associated with EnCase to open specific file types

   D. External viewers used to open a file that has been copied out of an evidence file

7. Where is the list of external viewers kept within EnCase?

   A. The settings in the `TEXTSTYLES.INI` file

   B. The settings in the `FILETYPES.INI` file

   C. The settings in the `EXTERNALVIEWERS.CFG` file

   D. The settings in the `VIEWERS.INI` file

8. When EnCase sends a file to an external viewer, to which folder does it send the file?

   A. Scratch

   B. Export

   C. Temp

   D. None of the above

9. How is the Disk view launched?

   A. By simply switching to the Disk view tab on the Table pane

   B. By launching it from the Device menu

   C. By right-clicking the device and choosing Open With Disk Viewer

   D. None of the above

10. Which of the following is true about the Gallery view?

   A. Files that are determined to be images by their file extension will be displayed.

   B. Files that are determined to be images based on file signature analysis will be displayed after the EnCase evidence processor has been run.

   C. Files displayed in the Gallery view are determined by where you place the focus in the Tree pane or where you activate the Set-Included Folders feature.

   D. All of the above.

11. True or false? The right-side menu is a collection of the menus and tools found on its toolbar.

   A. True

   B. False

12. True or false? The results of conditions and filters are seen immediately in the Table pane of the Evidence tab Entries view.

   A. True

   B. False

13. How do you access the setting to adjust how often a backup file (`.cbak`) is saved?

   A. Select Tools ➤ Options ➤ Case Options.

   B. Select View ➤ Options ➤ Case Options.

   C. Select Tools ➤ Options ➤ Global.

   D. Select View ➤ Options ➤ Global.

14. What is the maximum number of columns that can be sorted simultaneously in the Table view tab?

    A. Two

    B. Three

    C. Six

    D. 28 (maximum number of tabs)

15. How would a user reverse-sort on a column in the Table view?

    A. Hold down the Ctrl key, and double-click the selected column header.

    B. Right-click the selected column, select Sort, and select either Sort Ascending or Sort Descending.

    C. Both A and B.

16. How can you hide a column in the Table view?

    A. Place the cursor on the selected column, and press Ctrl+H.

    B. Place cursor on the selected column, open Columns menu on the toolbar, and select Hide.

    C. Place cursor on the selected column, open the right-side menu, open the Columns submenu, and select Hide.

    D. Open the right-side menu, open the Columns submenu, select Show Columns, and uncheck the desired fields to be hidden.

    E. All of the above.

17. What does the Gallery view tab use to determine graphics files?

    A. Header or file signature

    B. File extension

    C. Filename

    D. File size

18. Will the EnCase Gallery view display a .jpeg file if its file extension was renamed to .txt?

    A. No, because EnCase will treat it as a text file

    B. Yes, because the Gallery view looks at a file's header information and not the file extension

    C. Yes, but only if a signature analysis is performed to correct the File Category to Picture based on its file header information

    D. Yes, but only after a hash analysis is performed to determine the file's true identity

19. How would a user change the default colors and text fonts within EnCase?

    A. The user cannot change the default colors and fonts settings.

    B. The user can change the default colors and fonts settings by right-clicking the selected items and scrolling down to Change Colors and Fonts.

    C. The user can change the default colors and fonts settings by clicking the View tab on the menu bar and selecting the Colors tab or Fonts tab.

    D. The user can change default colors and fonts settings by clicking the Tools tab on the menu bar, selecting Options, and selecting the Colors tab or Fonts tab.

20. An EnCase user will always know the exact location of the selected data in the evidence file by looking at which of the following?

    A. Navigation Data on status bar

    B. Dixon box

    C. Disk view

    D. Hex view

Chapter 7

Understanding, Searching For, and Bookmarking Data

ENCE EXAM TOPICS COVERED IN THIS CHAPTER:

- ✓ Understanding data
- ✓ EnCase Evidence Processor
- ✓ Conducting basic searches
- ✓ Conducting advanced GREP searches
- ✓ Bookmarking your findings
- ✓ Organizing your bookmarks and creating reports
- ✓ Indexed searches

We've heard it said, and we'll hear it said again: "It's all about the 1s and the 0s." Computers store or transmit data as strings of 1s and 0s in the form of positive and negative states or pulses. From that we get characters and numbers, all of which make up the data we find on computer systems. This chapter will begin with a review of binary numbers and their hexadecimal representations.

Once you understand how data is stored, you'll then want to begin processing it. To help you do so, this chapter will cover the basics of the EnCase Evidence Processor, which is a new feature beginning with EnCase 7. It is, perhaps, more than just a feature; it's a collection of case-preprocessing tools that will change your forensic workflow. Among those tools you will find the ability to index your data for later lightning-fast searches, plus the ability to conduct the more conventional raw searches using keywords.

Once you have a firm grasp of how data is stored and how to run the EnCase Evidence processor, the chapter will describe how to perform simple basic searches for that data. Then, you'll step into the more advanced searching techniques known as GREP. GREP is a powerful search tool and one you need to master both for the examination and for everyday forensics.

Understanding data and locating it would not be beneficial if there were not some way of marking those findings and rendering them into some organized format that would later be generated into a report. EnCase has a powerful and, equally as important, flexible bookmarking and reporting utility.

The first aspect of your talent that your client or the prosecutor will see is your report. It needs to present well and read well. It will form the first, and maybe the last, impression they will have of your work and your capabilities. You can be the world's sharpest and brightest forensics examiner, but if you can't render your findings into an organized report that is easy to navigate, read, and understand, you will not do well in most aspects of this field.

More than a few times I've heard the comment that EnCase doesn't have a very good reporting feature. I'm always taken aback by that remark. EnCase has, in my opinion, an excellent report-generating utility at several levels. Furthermore, the bookmark view provides many ways to organize and customize the report, which is probably the most flexible and customizable in the industry. Finally, you are given the option, at all levels of reporting, of generating an Rich Text Format (RTF) or web document.

In all fairness to that criticism, I am convinced, based on many ensuing discussions that followed this criticism, that the remark has its roots in lack of awareness of and training in using EnCase's reporting utilities. It is time to close that knowledge gap. Because reporting your findings is a critical element to your success as a forensics examiner, Appendix A is devoted to that topic. In addition, the online resource that accompanies this book contains a downloadable sample report that you can use as a template or front end for your EnCase-generated report. This chapter also covers the basics of bookmark organization. Appendix A will pick it up from there and take you through the steps of creating a top-quality report.

This chapter concludes by covering indexed searching. This feature is new, starting with EnCase 6, and allows near-instantaneous search results once the index has been created. Creating the index will take time, but once done, the results will be worth the wait.

Understanding Data

In the following sections, I'll cover binary data first, which is how 1s and 0s are rendered into human-readable characters and numbers. Following that discussion, I'll cover the hexadecimal representation of binary data. Because 1s and 0s aren't very readable or workable in their raw form, programmers have developed an overlay by which binary data can be viewed and worked with that's much easier. It's simply called *hex*.

I'll wrap up the discussion of data with the ASCII table and how each character or decimal number therein is represented by a binary and hexadecimal value. Because computing has become global, the limits of the ASCII table mean that not all the world's languages can be represented by 1 byte or 256 different characters. Accordingly, Unicode was born; 2 bytes are allotted for each character, making possible 65,536 different characters in a language. Therefore, I'll also present an overview of Unicode.

Binary Numbers

Computers store, transmit, manipulate, and calculate data using the binary numbering system, which consists purely of 1s and 0s. As you may know, 1s and 0s are represented in many forms as positive or negative magnetic states or pulses. They can be lands or pits, light passing or not, pulses of light, pulses of electricity, electricity passing through a gate or not, and so forth. When you think about it, there are seemingly endless conditions where you can create a yes or no condition that can be in turn interpreted as a 1 or 0. Binary is absolute; it is a 1 or a 0. It is a yes or no condition without any maybes, although you can assemble a sufficient number of 1s and 0s arranged to spell "maybe!"

Binary numbers are arranged in organizational units. The smallest unit is a bit. A *bit* is a 1 or a 0 and is capable therefore of having only two possible outcomes. Two bits can have four possible outcomes, which are 00, 01, 10, or 11. Three bits can have eight possible outcomes, while 4 bits can have 16. Four bits is also the next unit and is called a *nibble*. Table 7.1 shows the possible number of outcomes, for up to 4 bits.

TABLE 7.1   Number of outcomes from 1 to 4 bits

Number of bits	Number of outcomes	Binary number
1 (bit)	2	0 or 1
2	4	00 01 10 11
3	8	000 001 010 011 100 101 110 111
4 (nibble)	16	0000 0001 0010 0011 0100 0101 0110 0111 1000 1001 1010 1011 1100 1101 1110 1111

If I continued this table, I'd quickly fill the rest of the book—for every bit you add, you double the possible number of outcomes over the previous number. Mathematically, you are working with exponents or powers of 2, which are written as $2^0 = 1$, $2^1 = 2$, $2^2 = 4$, $2^3 = 8$, $2^4 = 16$, and so on. The powers of 2, as previously noted, add up quickly, as shown in Table 7.2.

TABLE 7.2   Base-2 raised to powers from 0 to 128

Base number	Power	Decimal value
2	0	1
2	1	2
2	2	4
2	3	8
2	4	16
2	5	32
2	6	64
2	7	128
2	8	256 (8 bits)
2	9	512

TABLE 7.2   Base-2 raised to powers from 0 to 128 *(continued)*

Base number	Power	Decimal value
2	10	1,024 (1 kilobyte)
2	11	2,048
2	12	4,096
2	13	8,192
2	14	16,384
2	15	32,768
2	16	65,536 (16 bits)
2	17	131,072
2	18	262,144
2	19	524,288
2	20	1,048,576 (1 megabyte)
2	21	2,097,152
2	22	4,194,304
2	23	8,388,608
2	24	16,777,216
2	25	33,554,432
2	26	67,108,864
2	27	134,217,728
2	28	268,435,456
2	29	536,870,912
2	30	1,073,741,824 (1 gigabyte)

TABLE 7.2   Base-2 raised to powers from 0 to 128 *(continued)*

Base number	Power	Decimal value
2	31	2,147,483,648
2	32	4,294,967,296 (32 bits, number of possible outcomes with CRC)
2	40	1,099,511,627,776 (1 terabyte)
2	50	1,125,899,906,842,620 (1 exabyte)
2	64	18,446,744,073,709,600,000 (64 bits)
2	128	340,282,366,920,938,000,000,000,000,000,000,000,000 (128 bits, number of possible outcomes with MD5)

Did you ever wonder why a hard drive is rated by the manufacturer as 30 GB and yet when you put it in your computer, it is only 27.9 GB? Many people think they have been shorted 2.1 GB and call tech support. It may also be raised as a question by opposing counsel wanting to know why EnCase didn't see all of the drive. The answer could rest with an HPA or DCO, as previously discussed in Chapter 4. If, however, you are seeing all the sectors on the drive, an HPA or DCO is not the answer. The answer is, in part, found in Table 7.2. Note that the terms *kilobytes, megabytes, gigabytes, terabytes,* and *exabytes* were inserted at their respective locations. If a drive contains 58,605,120 sectors, it contains 30,005,821,440 bytes (multiply the number of sectors times 512 bytes per sector). A manufacturer, because it wants to paint its drive in the best possible light, uses base-10 gigabytes (1,000,000,000). The manufacturer simply moves the decimal point over nine places and rounds it off, calling it a 30 GB drive. Computers don't care about marketing at all and work with a binary system, wherein 1 GB is 1,073,741,824 bytes (2^{30}). If you divide 30,005,821,440 by 1,073,741,824, you'll find the answer is 27.94 and some change. Thus, your computer sees a drive with 30,005,821,440 bytes as having a capacity of 27.9 GB. EnCase reports the drive as having 27.9 GB as well. If opposing counsel asks where the missing 2.1 GB went, you can now explain it!

So far, I've covered a bit and a nibble (4 bits). The next organizational unit or group of bits is called a *byte*, which consists of 8 bits and is a well-known term. A byte also contains two 4-bit nibbles, called the *left nibble* and the *right nibble*. A byte can be combined with other bytes to create larger organizational units or groups of bits. Two bytes is called a *word*; 4 bytes is called a *Dword* (double word).

Dwords are used frequently throughout computing. The Windows registry, which will be covered in a later chapter, is full of Dword values. Because a Dword consists of 32 bits (4 bytes with each byte containing 8 bits), it is used frequently as a 32-bit integer. You'll see plenty of Dwords in this business.

Larger than a Dword is the Qword or Quad word, which, as you might have guessed, consists of four words. Because a word is 2 bytes, four words consist of 8 bytes. Because a byte consists of 8 bits, 8 bytes (Qword) contains 64 bits. You'll encounter more Dwords than Qwords, but Qwords are out there, and you need to be at least familiar with the term and its meaning.

Table 7.3 shows these various bit groupings and their properties. These are terms you should understand well because they are part of the core competencies that an examiner should possess. Advanced computer forensics deals with data at the bit level. Before attending advanced training, it is a good idea to review these concepts so they don't hold you back and, better yet, so you can move forward with a firm grasp of the subject matter.

TABLE 7.3 Names of bit groupings and their properties

Name	Bits	Binary
Bit	1	0
Nibble	4	0000
Byte	8	0000-0000 (left and right nibbles)
Word	16	0000-0000 0000-0000
Dword (Double Word)	32	0000-0000 0000-0000 0000-0000 0000-0000
Qword (Quad Word)	64	0000-0000 0000-0000 0000-0000 0000-0000 0000-0000 0000-0000 0000-0000 0000-0000

The byte is a basic data unit, and understanding how it is constructed and evaluated is an important concept. From the previous discussion, you know that it consists of 8 bits and that it has two 4-bit nibbles, which are the left nibble and the right nibble. Figure 7.1 shows the basic byte, with a left and right nibble each consisting of 4 bits, for a total of 8 bits.

FIGURE 7.1   A byte consists of 8 bits subdivided into two nibbles, each containing 4 bits; they are known as the left and right nibbles.

Left Nibble				Right Nibble			
2^7	2^6	2^5	2^4	2^3	2^2	2^1	2^0
128	64	32	16	8	4	2	1
0	0	0	0	0	0	0	0

Recall that there are 256 possible outcomes for 8 bits or 1 byte. Thus, when a byte is being used to represent an integer, 1 byte can represent a range of decimal integers from 0 to 255, or 256 different outcomes or numbers.

If you look at Figure 7.1, you see that each of the eight positions (8 bits) has a value in powers of 2. Also shown is their decimal value. The least significant bit is at the far right and has a decimal value of 1. The most significant bit is at the far left and has a value of 128. If you add all the decimal numbers, you find they have a value of 255. By turning the bits on (1) or off (0) in each of these positions, the byte can be evaluated and rendered into a decimal integer value ranging from 0 to 255.

To demonstrate how this works, Figure 7.2 shows how this evaluation is carried out for the decimal integer 0. For the values represented by each bit position to equal 0, all must be 0, and all bits are set for 0. This is fairly simple to grasp and is, therefore, a good place to start.

FIGURE 7.2   All bits are set to 0. All decimal values are 0 and add up to 0.

Left Nibble					Right Nibble				
2^7	2^6	2^5	2^4		2^3	2^2	2^1	2^0	◄-- Power of 2
128	64	32	16		8	4	2	1	◄-- Decimal Equivalent
0	0	0	0	-	0	0	0	0	◄-- Binary Code
0	0	0	0		0	0	0	0	0+0+0+0+0+0+0+0=0

At the other extreme is 255. When you add all the decimal numbers, their total was 255. Thus, to represent the decimal integer 255, all bits must be on, or 1. Figure 7.3 shows a binary code for a byte with all bits on. When you add the numbers in each position where the bit is on, the total is 255.

FIGURE 7.3   All bits are on, or set to 1. Each bit position's decimal value is added, and since all are on, the value is 255.

Left Nibble					Right Nibble				
2^7	2^6	2^5	2^4		2^3	2^2	2^1	2^0	◄-- Power of 2
128	64	32	16		8	4	2	1	◄-- Decimal Equivalent
1	1	1	1	-	1	1	1	1	◄-- Binary Code
128	64	32	16		8	4	2	1	128+64+32+16+8+4+2+1=255

Since you've visited the two extremes, let's see what happens somewhere in between. If you evaluate the binary code 0110-0011, as shown in Figure 7.4, you see that the bits are on for bit positions representing 64, 32, 2, and 1. The others are off and return a 0 value. If you add these numbers in the positions where the bits are on, you find that this binary code represents the decimal integer 99.

FIGURE 7.4   Evaluating binary code 0110-0011, we find bits on for bit positions 64, 32, 2, and 1. Adding those numbers returns a decimal integer value of 99.

Left Nibble					Right Nibble				
2^7	2^6	2^5	2^4		2^3	2^2	2^1	2^0	◄-- Power of 2
128	64	32	16		8	4	2	1	◄-- Decimal Equivalent
0	1	1	0	-	0	0	1	1	◄-- Binary Code
0	64	32	0		0	0	2	1	0+64+32+0+0+0+2+1=99

The system is fairly simple once you understand the concept and therefore demystify it. Using this analysis method, you can determine the decimal integer value for any byte value. Admittedly, a scientific calculator is much faster, but you will eventually encounter analysis work where you must work at the bit level, and understanding what is occurring in the background is essential for this work.

Hexadecimal

Working with binary numbers is, with practice, fairly simple. You can see, however, that the numbers in the left nibble are a little too large to easily add in your head. Back in the beginning of computing, programmers apparently felt the same way, so they developed a shorthand method of representing and working with long binary numbers. This system is called *hexadecimal* (most people simply call it *hex*). You've no doubt heard of or used hex editors. EnCase has a hex view for viewing raw data, and as a competent examiner, you need to be well versed in hex.

A hexadecimal number is base-16 encoding scheme. Base-16 stems from the number of possible outcomes for a nibble, which is 16. Hex values will usually be written in pairs, with the left value representing the left nibble and right value representing the right nibble. Each nibble, evaluated independently, can have 16 possible outcomes and can therefore represent two separate numbers ranging from 0 to 15. To represent these decimal values with a one-character limit, the coding scheme shown in Table 7.4 was developed and standardized.

TABLE 7.4   Hexadecimal values and their corresponding decimal values

Decimal	Hexadecimal
0	0
1	1

TABLE 7.4   Hexadecimal values and their corresponding decimal values *(continued)*

Decimal	Hexadecimal
2	2
3	3
4	4
5	5
6	6
7	7
8	8
9	9
10	A
11	B
12	C
13	D
14	E
15	F

Using this system of encoding, you can express the decimal values from 0 to 15 (16 different numbers or outcomes) using only one character. Because each nibble evaluated alone can have a maximum decimal value of 15, you have a system where you can have one character to represent the decimal value of each nibble. Figure 7.5 shows how this works when each nibble is evaluated independently using the hex encoding scheme. In the figure, a hex value of 98 means the left nibble has a decimal value of 9 and the right nibble has a decimal value of 8.

Using this system, you have a shortcut method for expressing the binary code 1001-1000, which is hexadecimal 98. This is usually written as 98h to differentiate it from the decimal number 98. Using the previous method of evaluating the decimal value of this same byte, as shown in Figure 7.6, we determine that the bits are on for bit positions 128, 16, and 8. Adding these together, you find that the decimal value for this same binary coding is 152. Thus, 98h, decimal 152, and binary 1001-1000 are all equal values, just expressed differently (base-16, base-10, and base-2).

FIGURE 7.5   The hexadecimal encoding scheme at work. The left nibble has bits on for 8 and 1 and has a value of 9. The right nibble has bits on for 8 only and has a value of 8. Thus, this binary coding (1001-1000) would be expressed in hexadecimal format as 98, or 98h.

Left Nibble					Right Nibble			
2^3	2^2	2^1	2^0		2^3	2^2	2^1	2^0
8	4	2	1		8	4	2	1
1	0	0	1	-	1	0	0	0
8	0	0	1		8	0	0	0
8+0+0+1=9					8+0+0+0=8			
			9	8				

FIGURE 7.6   The same binary coding shown in the previous figure evaluated as a decimal value. The bits are on for bit positions 128, 16, and 8, which total 152 for the decimal value.

Left Nibble					Right Nibble				
2^7	2^6	2^5	2^4		2^3	2^2	2^1	2^0	◄-- Power of 2
128	64	32	16		8	4	2	1	◄-- Decimal Equivalent
1	0	0	1	-	1	0	0	0	◄-- Binary Code
128	0	0	16		8	0	0	0	128+0+0+16+8+0+0+0=152

> You may also see hex denoted another way, which is with 0x preceding it. For example, 98h could also be written as 0x98. This method finds its roots in some programming languages (C, C++, Java, and others), where the leading 0 tells the parser to expect a number and the *x* defines the number that follows as hexadecimal. So, to keep things simple, I'll use the suffix *h* to denote hex, but you will see it in other publications using the other method.

To test your understanding of hexadecimal encoding, let's try a couple more examples using simple logic and not diagrams. At the very outset, you saw the example, in Figure 7.3, of all bits being on, meaning you add all the bit position decimal values and arrive at a decimal value of 255. Without resorting to diagramming, you can easily convert this to a hexadecimal value just using some logic. With all 8 bits on (1), each nibble's 4 bits are likewise on when you evaluate them independently. When a nibble's bits are all on, all the nibble's bit positions are totaled and they equal 15. Thus, each nibble's decimal value is 15. The hex encoding for decimal 15, according to Table 7.4, is F. So, each nibble's hex value is F, and, combined, they are FF.

Figure 7.7 shows an EnCase hex view in which FFh has been bookmarked and viewed as an 8-bit integer. Its binary coding (1111-1111) is shown as well as its decimal value of 255 and its hex value of FF. Not yet discussed is another interpretation of this data, which is as a signed integer with a value of -1. Further, this value has a character represented by it as well, which is ÿ (y with two dots over it). We will cover the ASCII table in the next section, and the character issue will make better sense.

Let's take that logic one step further to arrive at a hex value for the decimal value 254. That is, in simple terms, 255 minus 1! If all bits are on for 255, to get 254 you need to turn off the bit for the bit position value of 1, which is in the rightmost position. Thus, 255 is binary 1111-1111, and 254 is 1111-1110. To convert this to hex, at a glance, you know the left nibble is still F because nothing changed there. The right nibble is 1 less than before and should be decimal 14 (8 + 4 + 2 + 0). From Table 7.4, you know the hexadecimal value of decimal 14 is E. Thus, the hexadecimal value for decimal 254 is FEh.

FIGURE 7.7 EnCase hex view of FF bookmarked and viewed as an 8-bit integer. Note the various interpretations of this data that are possible.

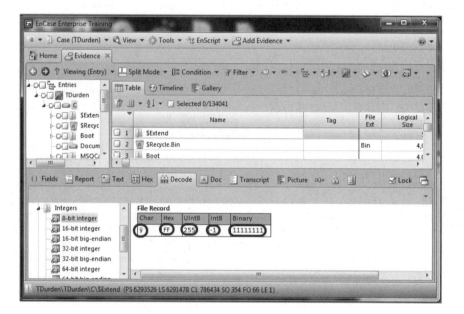

Characters

I mentioned that FFh, in addition to representing a decimal integer value of 255, could also represent a character, which in this case was ÿ (y with two dots over it). When data is stored or used by a program, the program defines the type of data it is. Without getting too involved in programming terminology, data can be text, integers, decimals, and so forth. Let's focus on text data.

ASCII

If the data is in a text format, the characters to be displayed are derived from a standard chart called the *ASCII chart*. This stands for the American Standard Code for Information Interchange and was created by Robert W. Bemer in 1965 to create a standard for interchange between the emerging data-processing technologies.

In the simplest of terms, the chart maps characters and escape codes to binary or hexadecimal values. If everyone uses the same mapping scheme, then when the text letter *A* is needed, 41h is used, and everyone with the same mapping system can read the letter *A* correctly since they are all using the same character mapping scheme.

Using this system, 7 of the 8 bits are used to create a table of 128 letters, numbers, punctuation, and special codes. Seven bits provides for 128 different outcomes or characters. This portion of the table (0–127) is called the *ASCII table*. It is sometimes called *low* or *low-bit* ASCII.

As much of this data is transmitted, the eighth bit is a parity bit and is used for error checking to determine whether an odd or even number of binary 1 bits were sent in the remaining 7 bits. The sending and receiving units have to "agree" or be in sync with the same odd or even parity scheme. When that is established, the sender sends a parity bit, and the receiver uses the sent parity bit to validate the received data. However, it is rarely used anymore because other, more reliable and sophisticated error checking systems have evolved. Besides that, we needed to use that extra bit for more characters!

As computing evolved and encompassed more disciplines and languages, additional characters were needed. When the PC was born in the early 1980s, IBM introduced the extended ASCII character set. IBM did away with the parity bit and extended the code to 8 bits, which provided twice the number of characters previously allowed with the 7-bit system. The new character set therefore provided 128 additional characters to the basic set. Most of these characters are mathematical, graphics, and foreign-language characters. This character set is also called the *high-bit* ASCII set.

You can find the complete set of ASCII character codes (low-bit and high-bit) on many websites, such as the following:

www.cpptutor.com/ascii.htm

If you will look over the entries, you will see them displayed in ascending decimal value order. Each line or item in this 256-character list has a decimal value, a hexadecimal value, and a character code. Since everything is stored in binary, as 1s and 0s, the list includes each character's binary coding as well.

Before moving away from the ASCII character codes, I'll touch upon a couple of the finer points that can help if well understood and possibly impede if not understood. The first point is that uppercase and lowercase letters are represented by entirely different code. An uppercase *E* is 45h, while a lowercase *e* is 65h. When I start covering searching for data, the concept of case-sensitive searching will emerge, where searching for 45h is different from searching for 65h. I'll get into that in detail soon enough. For now, just recognize that the two are different.

Understanding that upper- and lowercase letters are different is easy. What may be confusing are numbers. If I type the number 8 and it is stored as *text*, then 8 will be represented as 38h. But if the *integer value* of 8 is being stored for some math function, then it is likely stored as 08h since its data type is no longer text. Conversely, sometimes you will see what appear to be characters in the middle of gibberish when you are viewing binary data in text view. In these cases, EnCase is looking at binary data through the ASCII character set, and when hex values correspond with printable ASCII characters, they are rendered as such even though they really aren't text.

If numbers aren't confusing enough, sometimes you will find numbers stored as ASCII characters, while those same numbers are stored elsewhere as integers. A good example of this would be IP addresses. Sometimes the program will store an IP address as 128.175.24.251, which is pure human-readable ASCII text. Another program may store this IP in its integer form, which is the way the computer actually uses it. This same IP would read 80 AF 19 FB. In this method, each of the four octets of an IP address is represented by a single byte or 8-bit integer. Using the previous plain-text IP address, decimal 128 is 80h, decimal 175 is AFh, decimal 24 is 19h, and decimal 251 is FBh. Other programs, such as KaZaA, iMesh, and Grokster, sometimes store this same IP as FB 19 AF 80, which is the reverse order (little endian).

To summarize, the hex string 54 45 58 54 could be interpreted in several ways, depending on the context in which it is used and stored on the computer. As a 32-bit integer, it would represent a value of 1,413,830,740. As four separate 8-bit integers (as an IP address could be stored), it would stand for the IP address 84.69.88.84. If this string were found in KaZaA data, it would represent the IP address 84.88.69.84. Finally, if it were found in the middle of a string of text, it would stand for the word *TEXT*, spelled in all uppercase letters.

As you progress in the field, interpreting text and hex values will become second nature. Text will usually quite obviously be text when you see it. When you have to interpret integers, you'll usually be following an analysis guideline that describes where and how a certain piece of data is stored. You may, however, be conducting research in which you are reverse-engineering a data storage process. Under those conditions, you are flying blind, using trial and error to determine how data is stored and what it means forensically. For now, just remember that data can be interpreted in different ways, depending on the program and the context in which it is being used.

Unicode

As computing became global and the limits imposed by a 256-character code set could not accommodate all the characters in some languages, a new standard had to emerge. Unicode was the answer to this challenge. Unicode is a worldwide standard for processing, displaying, and interchanging all types of language texts. This includes character sets previously covered by the ASCII set (mostly the Western European languages). Unicode characters also allow for languages that use pictographs instead of letters, which are primarily the Eastern country languages, such as Chinese, Japanese, and Korean.

To encompass such a broad set of characters, Unicode uses 2 bytes per character instead of 1 byte. Unicode was introduced into EnCase version 4 and allows processing of any language for which there is an established code page or character set, which covers most of the world's written languages.

Although many languages don't require Unicode to render their character sets, many store text in Unicode. Sometimes they store the same text in ASCII and in Unicode simultaneously. The letter *A* in ASCII, as you'll recall, is 41h. The letter *A* in Unicode is 4100h. Searching for 41h is different from searching for 4100h. When I begin the discussion on searching, you'll want to remember the differences between ASCII and Unicode. Because considerable data is stored in Unicode, unless you have a good reason not to, you'll want to search for your data in both formats, ASCII and Unicode. Figure 7.8 is an EnCase view showing a string of text that is stored in a Unicode format.

FIGURE 7.8   Text string stored in Unicode. Note the 00 after each character.

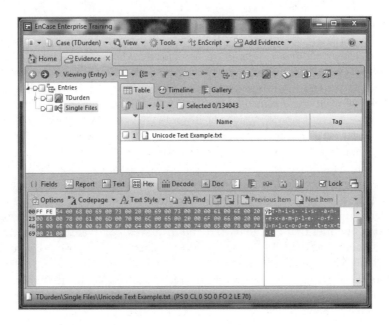

EnCase Evidence Processor

The EnCase Evidence Processor is a collection of tools that carry a series of routines necessary to the proper examination of evidence. It is best described as a highly configurable preprocessing tool. Before we start using this tool, we must first make certain we have followed several steps that constitute best practices, namely:

1. Allow EnCase to complete the evidence verification process.

2. Check the verification report to ensure that the verification completed with zero errors and that the acquisition and verification hashes match.

3. Determine the time zone settings for the various evidence items.

4. Adjust EnCase to reflect the time zone offsets as needed; otherwise, EnCase, by default, will assign the time zone offset of the examination workstation.

> **NOTE** If there are deleted partitions, you'll want to recover them before running the EnCase Evidence Processor.

I previously discussed evidence verification and how to check for successful verification. If you are unsure, you can review the material on this topic in Chapter 5.

As most file systems store data in GMT and display it in local time, it is usually a better practice to display and report time in the local offset. There are, of course, exceptions. A good example would be examining several devices in the same case that were in different time zones. In those cases, it is better to view them all in one time zone. Regardless, you need to know which time zone offset is configured for each device. In Windows, this information is stored in the registry, specifically at HKLM\System\ControlSet001\Control\TimeZoneInformation\TimeZoneKeyName. You should take note that the current control set will vary and that "001" will not always be the current set. We'll show you how that determination is made as well.

Before we examine the registry, we first have to navigate to the registry hive file in question, which is located at \Windows\System32\config\SYSTEM. There are other hive files in this folder, but for now we are concerned only with this particular one. Registry hive files are compound files that can be parsed and displayed in a hierarchical format, which is also called *mounting the file* in EnCase. To do so, place your cursor on the parent folder in the Tree pane, which forces the child objects to display in the Table pane, as shown in Figure 7.9. In the Table pane, you highlight the registry hive file named SYSTEM. On the Evidence tab toolbar, open the Entries menu and select View File Structure. You will next see a dialog box, as shown in Figure 7.10. Accept the defaults and click OK.

EnCase will take a few minutes to parse the hive file and display the results. You can see the progress bar in the lower-right corner. When done, you will notice that the hive file has turned blue, indicating it is now hyperlinked and also has a plus sign on it, as shown in Figure 7.11.

FIGURE 7.9 Parent folder is selected in the Tree pane. The hive file is highlighted in the Table pane. The View File Structure tool is then selected from the Entries menu.

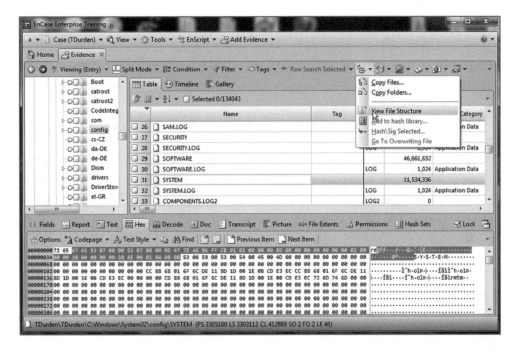

FIGURE 7.10 View File Structure dialog box from which options can be selected. The defaults are fine for getting the time zone offset.

FIGURE 7.11 SYSTEM hive is blue (hyperlinked) and has a plus sign on the icon, both of which indicate it has been mounted and can be viewed.

Since the SYSTEM hive file is now hyperlinked, simply click it, and it will open into its own viewing pane, as shown in Figure 7.12. To determine which control set is the current control set, we must look to the Select key and the value Current, both of which are circled in Figure 7.12. By highlighting Current in the Table pane, we can view its value in the View pane below, which can best be viewed in the Hex tab. Its value, in this case, is 01, which means ControlSet001 is the current control set.

FIGURE 7.12   Select key is showing the Current Control Set to be number 01.

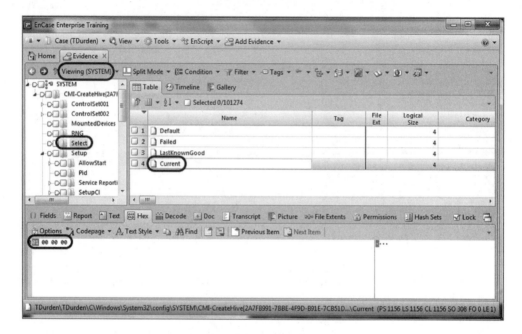

Knowing that, in this case, ControlSet001 is the current control set, we next drill down into this key until we locate the value TimeZoneKeyName, as shown in Figure 7.13. In this case, we see that the time offset is Pacific Standard Time (PST). Before we leave this key (TimeZoneInformation), we need to make certain that the Dynamic Daylight Time disable function hasn't been activated. This value is located under the TimeZoneInformation key and is named DynamicDaylightTimeDisabled. Normally, the Dynamic Daylight Time adjustment is enabled such that when daylight saving time is in effect, the time automatically adjusts. The registry is loaded with double negatives, which in this case disabled with a zero value means enabled, which is the default value and is shown in Figure 7.14.

At this point, we know how to determine the current control set, the time zone name, and whether the Dynamic Daylight Time adjustment is enabled or not. In our case, Pacific

Standard Time is the offset, and automatic adjustment occurs for daylight saving time. Let's put this information into EnCase for the device in question. To do so, we go back to the Entries view and in the Tree pane, highlight the root, forcing the device to appear in the Table pane, where we highlight it, as shown in Figure 7.15.

FIGURE 7.13   TimeZoneKeyName value indicates Pacific Standard Time.

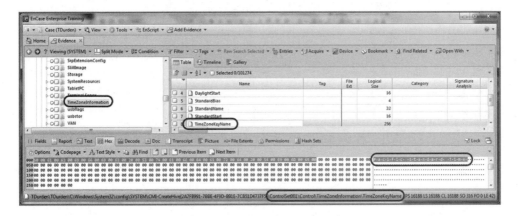

FIGURE 7.14   DynamicDaylightTimeDisabled is zero, meaning that the Dynamic Daylight Time adjustment is enabled.

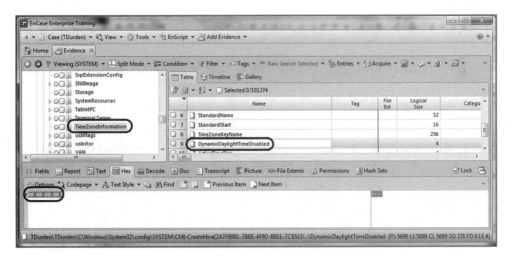

FIGURE 7.15 Modifying time zone settings

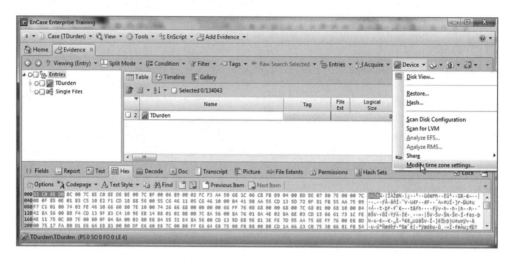

With the device highlighted in the Table pane, open the Device menu on the Evidence tab toolbar and select Modify Time Zone Settings, as shown in Figure 7.15. Because my examination machine was currently in the Central time zone, the default offset is Central Standard Time (CST). Since the evidence device was set to PST, we need to make an adjustment and change the offset to PST, as shown in Figure 7.16. When the correct time zone is selected, click OK, and the change is applied right away.

FIGURE 7.16 Changing time zone offset to Pacific Standard Time

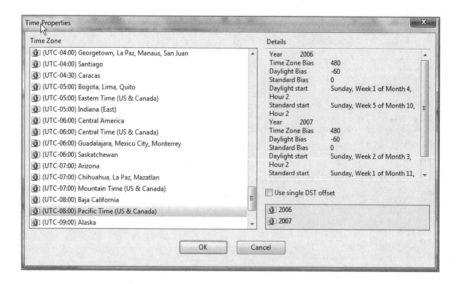

At this point, you have carried out your best practices by verifying your evidence acquisition and setting the proper time zone offset to your evidence. You are now set to run the EnCase Evidence Processor. In essence, there are two basic requirements, which are that there must be evidence in your case to process, which stands to reason. If you are previewing a device, you'll need to either acquire it first or make the acquisition a part of the evidence processing, which you'll soon see. Later versions of EnCase 7 are planned to allow for select processing of previewed evidence, such as running modules we will cover shortly. For the full power of processing, including indexing, you will want to acquire the evidence first.

Beginning with EnCase 7.03, the EnCase Evidence Processor may be run on previewed devices.

The EnCase Evidence Processor can be run from the Home screen or from the Evidence tab. We'll run it from the Evidence tab because that will likely be the most convenient location from which to run the tool. From the Evidence tab, select the evidence items you want to process and launch the EnCase Evidence Processor from the Evidence tab toolbar, as shown in Figure 7.17.

FIGURE 7.17   Running the EnCase Evidence Processor from the Evidence tab toolbar

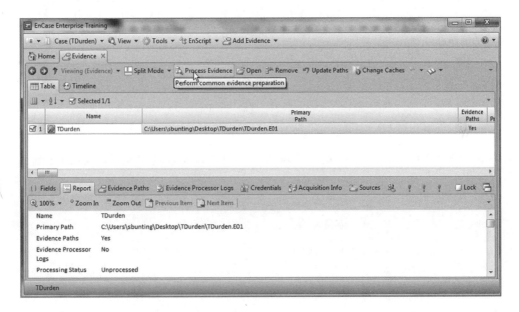

Once the EnCase Evidence Processor loads, the interface will appear, and you can change many options, as shown in Figure 7.18. As mentioned earlier, you can acquire as part of the processing. In the upper pane, the evidence in the case is shown. For each evidence item, you can choose to acquire and/or process. If you select to acquire an item, you'll be presented with device acquisition menu that should look very familiar, as shown in Figure 7.19.

FIGURE 7.18   The EnCase Evidence Processor menu showing various options for processing

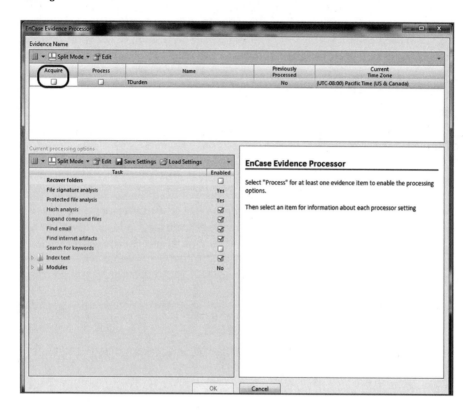

FIGURE 7.19   Upon choosing to acquire, you are immediately provided with a quite familiar menu.

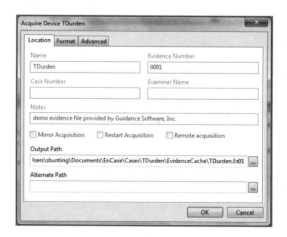

You will note that until you select the Process check box, the processing options are not available; they are grayed out. Upon selecting Process, the options become available, as shown in Figure 7.20. You should make a careful observation of the red flags in Figure 7.20. Any item with a red flag must be run the first time the evidence processor is run and can't be run in any subsequent runs. Any item without a red flag can be run during any subsequent runs of the processor.

FIGURE 7.20 Processing options become available when the Process check box is selected. Red flag items can be run only during the first run of the processor. Protected file analysis is now optional and may be activated or not.

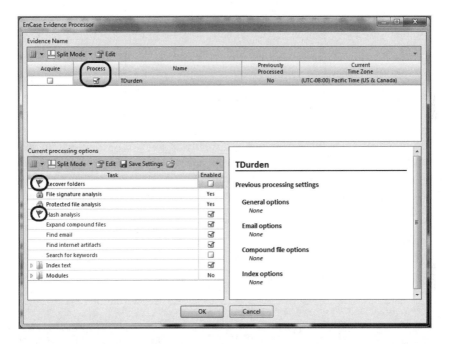

Recover Folders functions only for FAT and NTFS file systems. It is an option but has a red flag, meaning if you want to run it, you have to do so on the first run of the processor. Recover Folders is highly recommended, so you should run it unless you have a compelling reason not to, especially when you have only one chance to do so. File Signature Analysis and Protected File Analysis are locked and will run always. We'll talk more about the results of these two items in later chapters.

Hash Analysis also has a red flag and must be run on the first run or not at all. Any item that turns blue (hyperlinked) when checked has options. The hash analysis options are MD5, SHA-1, or both. Expand Compound Files, because it lacks a red flag, can be run at any time. Their options are also very simple, which is only archives at the current time.

Email can be run at any time also. Options for email are many but are still rather simple, since you are only selecting the various types of email for EnCase to search. Figure 7.21

shows the various types of email that EnCase can find and parse. You can expect this list to expand as EnCase adds support for additional or new email types.

FIGURE 7.21 Find Email options

EnCase can find Internet history for the various common browser types. It can also be run during any subsequent run of the processor. Your only option will be to search unallocated spaces. The default is no unallocated search, so you'll need to enable it for a comprehensive search.

Searching for keywords can now be done as part of the case processor. Checking its box and opening the options provides a menu that veteran EnCase users will find quite familiar, as shown in Figure 7.22. In the next section, I cover the various types of keywords searches and their options.

FIGURE 7.22 Keywords menu options

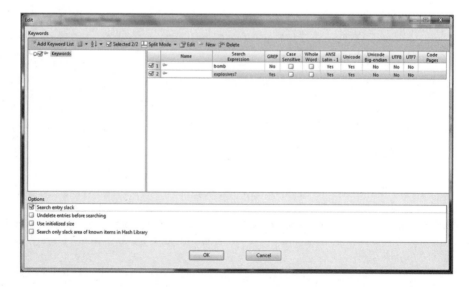

The next processing option is that of text indexing. This step requires considerable time to run, but the payoff is lightning-fast searches of the index later. Figure 7.23 shows the options for indexing. You can select a Noise File if you have one created. Its purpose is to eliminate certain common short words from index, thereby saving time and space. You can choose the minimum word length. Usually three letters is an ideal setting for words. Any fewer is simply bloat for the index. You have the option of skipping known items in the hash library, all items in the hash library, or neither. Finally, if East Asian languages are involved, you'll need to select the option to include support for those languages.

FIGURE 7.23   Index text options

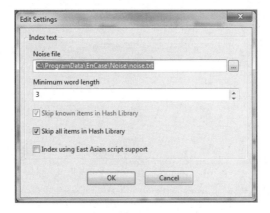

Under the text indexing option, there is an option for extracting personal information. The options are many, as shown in Figure 7.24, but are also quite self-explanatory. These include credit cards, phone number, email addresses, and Social Security numbers. You can also edit and create conditions to work with these options.

Several modules are available, and more will no doubt be added as this tool is enhanced. Figure 7.25 shows the various options currently available. All have extensive options available, and I suggest visiting each module's option set to become familiar with the various features and capabilities. One of particular interest is the File Carver option, shown in Figure 7.26. The tool uses the data in the File Types database to facilitate file carving. In essence, any file type in the database can be carved, albeit some more successfully than others. You have the option to search all files, unallocated spaces, and/or file slack. You can also opt to carve HTML files and webmail files as a separate option outside the file types.

FIGURE 7.24   Personal information options

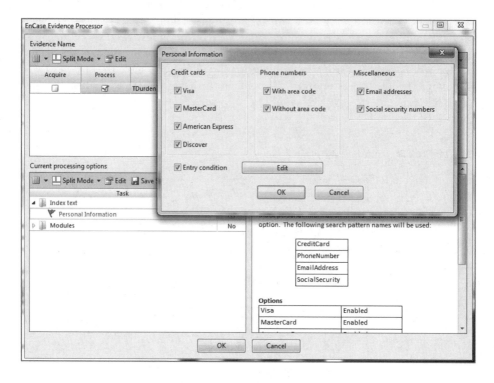

FIGURE 7.25   Processing modules available

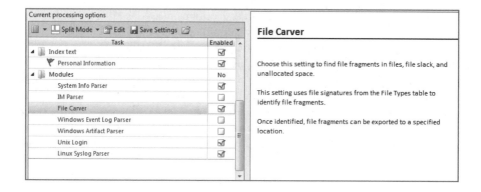

FIGURE 7.26   File carver options

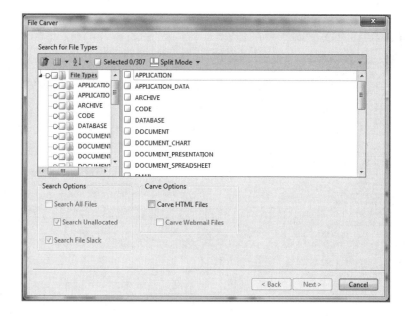

Once you have selected your options, you can click OK to run, as shown in Figure 7.27. If you prefer to save your evidence processor settings so that you don't have to configure them each time or would prefer to at least have a base set, you can do so. At the top of the processing options there is a toolbar with menus, including Save Settings and Load Settings. As the names imply, you can save and load settings using this feature. Once the processor starts running, it will take hours, perhaps days, depending on the amount of data involved and the options selected.

We are often faced with too much data and too little time, in which there are demands for answers right away. Such situations require you to triage and make decisions about which data to process now and which data to process later. Clearly, you need to run the red flag items during the first run. You also need to determine what your case is all about and which items to process to give you the answer sooner rather than later. If your case is all about email, run your red flag items and Find Email (see Figure 7.20) during the first run. You can then start your analysis work on the initial results, and you can perform another subject processor run in the background while working.

When your case processor finishes, the results of the processing appear in many places. Some items appear on the Records tab while others appear in the Entries view of the Evidence tab. As I cover the various topics, I include in those discussions the results of the Evidence Processor. For now, it's time to discuss keyword searching in depth.

FIGURE 7.27   Options selected and ready to run. Note the Save Settings and Load Settings options.

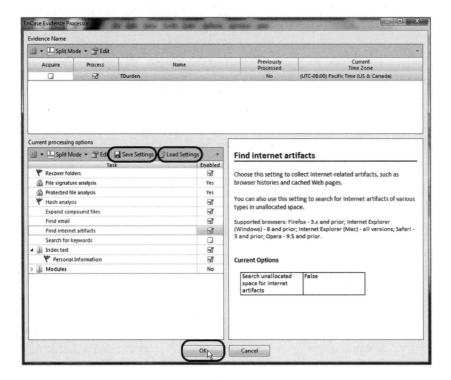

Searching for Data

EnCase provides for two basic methods for searching for data. One approach is that of using an indexed search. To do so, one must first create an index using the EnCase Evidence Processor, which we just covered. Searches are then conducted against the index, and results are nearly instantaneous. The other method of searching is that of raw searching, whereby keywords are created, and the entire stream of selected data is searched for strings matching those keywords. A related search method is the ability to search smaller sets of data while in the View pane. Each method has its time and place, with each having advantages and disadvantages. Indexed searching takes significant time to build an index but pays it back later with lightning-fast searches, including proximity searches, Boolean searches, and the like. Raw searches take time for each search, yet can be extremely precise or highly flexible when using GREP expressions. With experience, you know when to use which type.

As data sets have grown tremendously, indexed searching technologies have advanced to keep pace, to the point where indexed searching is usually the better choice. Further, many data types are compressed or otherwise obfuscated, such as PDF files, Office 2007, and newer formats (.docx, .xlsx, .pptx, and so on). Raw text searches against these file types are nearly useless. The index search in EnCase uses Outside In to extract the transcript text from the files, and this text is used in the index. Thus, indexed searching enables searching of files that would otherwise not yield fruit with traditional raw searches, and allows rapid searches across large sets of data. Also, to search many file types, such as Microsoft Office 2007 (and newer) files, PDFs, and the like, you must do so with an indexed search. For such file types, there is no searchable raw text. Rather, the text must first be extracted into transcript text and subsequently indexed. In short, unless you do an indexed search of Office 2007, newer file types (.docx, .xlsx, .pptx, and so on), and PDFs, you are going to miss data with your search.

In this chapter, I'll discuss raw searches in EnCase. Using EnCase's Raw Search All tool, you can search for keywords anywhere on the physical drive. You can search the entire case (all devices in the case) at once or any subset of data within the case, down to a single file. There is even a tool called Find that allows you to search within a block of selected text. This tool is covered in Chapter 6 and is available by selecting a right-click option, by choosing a menu, or by pressing Ctrl+F in the View pane while in the Text or Hex view.

Next, I'll cover how to create keywords. I'll discuss your options when conducting a search. Then I'll discuss GREP, which means "Globally search for the Regular Expression and Print." This tool comes from the Unix domain and is powerful for constructing searches. It allows you to be extremely focused or very broad, as the situation warrants.

Creating Keywords

You can't conduct a search without first creating a string of characters for the search engine to find. In EnCase, those search strings are called *keywords*.

Keywords and Keyword Files

Keywords, once created, are stored in a file for later use. Up through and including EnCase 3, keywords were stored in the case file and were case specific (unless exported and transferred manually to another case). With EnCase 4, keywords became a global resource and were stored separately in a global KEYWORDS.INI file. Starting with EnCase 5, the best of both worlds were combined, and keywords can be either global (stored in the KEYWORDS.INI file) or case specific (stored in the case file).

The concept of local and global keywords disappears somewhat with EnCase 7, at least within the interface. First, you must consider that you can, as you recall, run a raw keyword search from within the EnCase Evidence Processor. If you do so, the keywords will be stored within the device's cache files and can be used whenever the device is searched.

The other method or location of invoking the raw keyword search is from the toolbar of either the Evidence tab's Table tab or its Entries tab. If the former (Table tab), you will be raw searching all evidence devices. If the latter (Entries tab), you will be raw-searching based on the selections made in the Tree pane. When you conduct a raw search from the Evidence tab toolbar, the keywords are either loaded from or saved to a file. This file will contain keyword sets for your given search and are stored in files with the extension .keyword. Where you opt to store them is the only indicator of whether they are local or global. You create a keyword or keywords and then name the file in which they will be stored. In this manner, keywords can be grouped in as many files as you deem appropriate and are likewise stored where you deem appropriate. Once we start creating keywords, you will see how this works. For now, let's get started by creating keywords for a raw search.

Creating Keywords

To create a raw search keyword, you must first decide at which level you will conduct your search. If you are going to search all evidence devices, you can launch the search from the Table tab of the Entries view of the Evidence tab. In fact, from this location, you can only search everything. If you want to search a limited set of data, go to the Entries tab of the Evidence tab and select the items to search from the Tree and Table panes. From this location, you can also select all by placing a blue check mark at the root of the case in the Tree pane. If you are going to use blue check marks to select a limited data set for searching, it is a best practice to first check the Dixon box and reset it to zero (click in it once) before making selections. Otherwise, your search selection will be in addition to that which was previously selected. Figure 7.28 shows that two sets of user files have been selected in the Tree pane, with the Dixon box reflecting 3,623 files selected.

FIGURE 7.28 Files selected for search

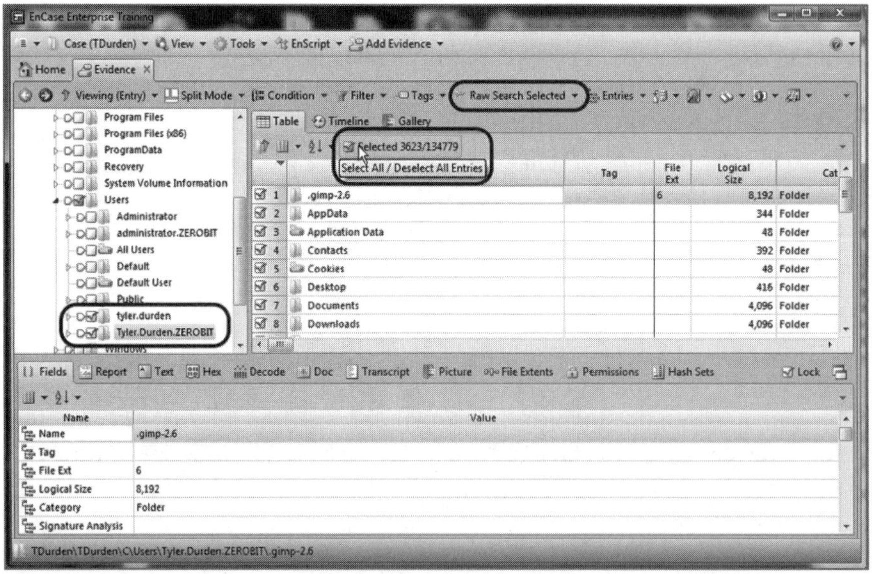

TDurden\TDurden\C\Users\Tyler.Durden.ZEROBIT\.gimp-2.6

Thus far, we've selected the files that we want to search. Now it's time to create a keyword, configure the various search options, and then launch the search. In Figure 7.28, you can see that the Raw Search Selected menu on the toolbar has been circled. Click on this menu, and choose New Raw Search Selected, as shown in Figure 7.29.

FIGURE 7.29   Raw Search Selected menu options

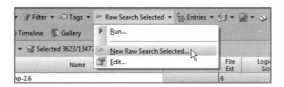

The New Raw Search Selected dialog box will appear next. Veteran EnCase users will be familiar with most of the menu features, as shown in Figure 7.30. It is important to note that this menu both creates or loads the keyboards and also launches the search when you click OK. You can see many options relating to the search, such as Search Entry Slack, User Initialized Size, and so on, appearing in the top section. Conducting a raw search always involved two menus in the past, one to create the keywords and another to configure and launch the search. With EnCase 7, it all takes place within one menu, making it more efficient and more intuitive for the new user.

FIGURE 7.30   New Raw Search Selected menu options

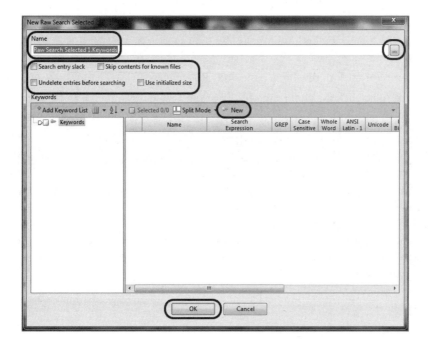

In the Tree pane, choose the folder you want to hold the keyword by highlighting it. If no folder exists, such as the case with Figure 7.30, you can simply allow your keywords to be stored in the root, or you can create one by right-clicking the root of the Keyword tree in the tree and choosing New Folder, as shown in Figure 7.31.

FIGURE 7.31 Creating a folder to contain and organize keywords

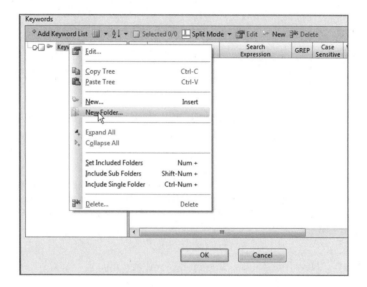

Now that you have a folder in which to contain your keyword, in the Tree pane, highlight this folder. Once you highlight the folder, you can launch the New Keyword dialog box in several ways:

- You can right-click in the Table pane and choose New.
- You can right-click the containing folder in the Tree pane and choose New.
- You can choose Edit ➢ New.
- You can press Insert on the keyboard.

Regardless of the launch method, you are presented with the New Keyword dialog box shown in Figure 7.32.

The dialog box provides numerous options or controls. We'll begin with the Search Expression box, because it is the core component of your search. In this box, you enter your search string. At this point, you should keep your search simple. Because you are working with the case from the previous chapter, search for two keywords associated with a message about a money pickup, or so you surmise. Enter the search expression **steg**, as shown in Figure 7.32.

FIGURE 7.32 In the New Keyword dialog box, you create keywords and assign search options to go with it. By default, searches are not case sensitive, meaning EnCase searches for uppercase and lowercase hex values for your keyword, as shown in the Unicode View box.

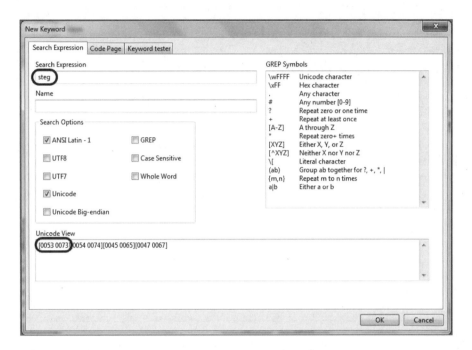

If you look in the gray box labeled Unicode View in Figure 7.32, you see the hex values for the characters you entered in brackets in both their uppercase and lowercase values. There are two hex values for each character because, by default, your search is not case sensitive and because EnCase will look for both uppercase and lowercase letters of the search expression you entered. I have circled the character(s) as it appears in uppercase and lowercase in hex. Most times, you probably should accept this default setting to find your search string in its varied renditions of all caps, no caps, or mixed caps.

Searching for both uppercase and lowercase characters increases search time compared to a case-sensitive search. If you know your search term appears in a certain format, you can select a case-sensitive search to save time and reduce the number of false positives. When you do, only the hex values for the exact characters you have entered for your search expression appear in the Unicode view, as shown in Figure 7.33. Remember from the previous section where I said that searching for an uppercase letter is different from searching for the lowercase of the same letter because they are both represented by different hex values in the ASCII table.

FIGURE 7.33 When making the search Case Sensitive, only the hex values for the keyword exactly as you typed it appear. Compare this to Figure 7.22, where the search was not case sensitive, and hex values for both uppercase and lowercase were present.

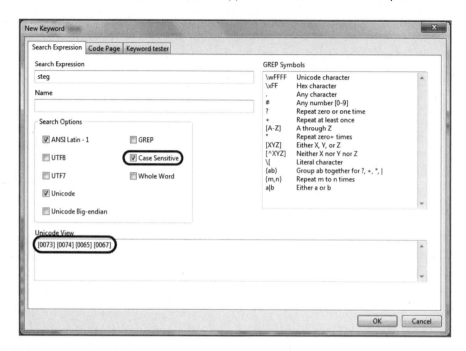

For purposes of this search, don't use any other search options. You have, however, many other search options to choose from for a variety of searching needs, as described in Table 7.5.

TABLE 7.5 Keyword search options

Tab	Name	Description
Search Expression	Search Expression	The actual search string or expression is typed into this field.
Search Expression	Name	Giving your keyword a descriptive name can be helpful. This "label" appears with the keyword in the Search Hits view. Some keywords are obvious and may not need a name. But when you have complex GREP expressions, account numbers, non-English words, or the like, naming is very important.

TABLE 7.5   Keyword search options *(continued)*

Tab	Name	Description
Search Expression	Case Sensitive	This option turns on or off the case sensitivity of your search. With it on, the search will be done exactly according to the case you specified.
Search Expression	GREP	With this option, you can use the standard GREP input symbols and characters to create custom searches that can range from extremely focused to very broad, depending on your search needs. (See "Conducting advanced GREP searches" later in this chapter.)
Search Expression	ANSI Latin - 1	This specifies ANSI Latin - 1 as the default code page for the search. If you deselect it, you need to specify a code page on the Code Page tab.
Search Expression	Unicode	Unicode, as previously discussed, uses 2 bytes (16 bits) for each character compared to 7 bits for low ASCII and 8 bits for high ASCII. If this option is off, searches will not find your expression if it appears in Unicode. When this option is on, searches will find your expression in both ASCII and Unicode formats. Unless you specifically don't want to find your search term in Unicode, you should turn this option on if you want to conduct a thorough search.
Search Expression	Unicode big-endian	PC-based Intel processors process data in a little-endian format, meaning the least significant bits are read first. Non-Intel processors are used in some Unix and Mac systems, and those processors work in the reverse order from the Intel. This is big endian. The most significant bits are read first. When searching for data stored in this format, select this option. Apple switched over to Intel-based processors for its Mac OS computers in 2006. It is now important to know from which system Mac OS data originated.
Search Expression	UTF-8	This is an encoding scheme defined by the Unicode standard in which each character is represented as a sequence of up to 4 bytes. The first byte tells how many bytes follow in the multibyte sequence. It is commonly used in on the Internet and in Web content.

TABLE 7.5 Keyword search options *(continued)*

Tab	Name	Description
Search Expression	UTF-7	This is an older encoding scheme that is mostly obsolete. It uses octets with the high bit clear, which are the 7-bit ASCII values. It is used for mail encoding, but it is a legacy scheme.
Code Page	Code Page	Using the code pages in this list, EnCase can display and search for non-English languages. See Chapter 20 of the EnCase user manual.
Keyword Tester	Keyword Tester	With this feature, you can test keywords on sample data files before running them against your case. This can save you hours of run time, particularly when you are testing new GREP expressions. When you switch to the Keyword Tester tab, your keyword carries over. Browse to the file containing your test data, and click Load. The results are displayed in the View pane in both hex and text. If you need to tweak your keyword, do so in the keyword box, and the results in the View pane are displayed in real time, making it very handy for fixing keywords.

Managing Keyword Files and Folders

When you begin to create keywords, it is best to get organized from the beginning. You can create and store related keywords in files (with a .keyword extension) and use files to organize. Within .keyword files, you can also create folders to further organize keywords. Figure 7.34 shows how you can use folders to organize keywords. At any level that you want to create a folder, place your cursor on that level, right-click, and select New Folder. You can name the folder at the time of creation or rename it later by right-clicking or by selecting the folder and pressing F2.

Normally, you start a search by clicking Raw Search Selected Or All, but the search runs only if a keyword is selected. Once you create a keyword and run it, you can then edit the keyword file later, adding keywords, organizing, expanding, and so on. If you don't select any keyword, the search doesn't run and you can save it only, which becomes a handy way to organize and manage your collection of keywords that you will reuse. Also, with the Raw Search menu open, you can import keywords. For example, you can export keywords from legacy EnCase versions and import them into EnCase 7.

FIGURE 7.34   Keywords can be organized into folders. Right-click at the desired folder level, and choose New Folder. This set was imported from EnCase 6 and has more than 21,000 keywords.

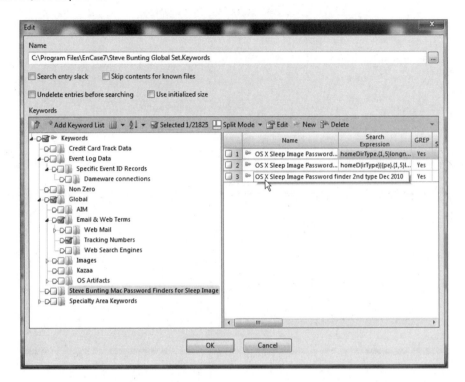

Additionally, you can delete a folder by selecting it and pressing the Delete key or by right-clicking and choosing Delete. You can move a folder from one location to another by simply by dragging it and dropping it in the new location within the Tree pane. You can rearrange the order of folders at a given level by highlighting their parent folder in the Tree pane. The child folders will appear in the Table pane. The folders in the Table pane have "handles"—the number box at the left side of the Table view for each row or folder. You can drag the folder up or down in the order by dragging and dropping the folder row by its handle.

If you use folders to organize keywords, you can view, add, or modify those keywords by selecting that folder in the Tree pane, as shown in Figure 7.34. The same Set Included Folders trigger used in the Case view (see Chapter 6) also works here and in other views. By turning on the Set Included Folders trigger in the Tree pane, you can work with keywords from that level down in the Table pane, as shown in Figure 7.35.

FIGURE 7.35   The Set Included Folders trigger is turned on at the top level, placing all keywords in all folders in the Table pane.

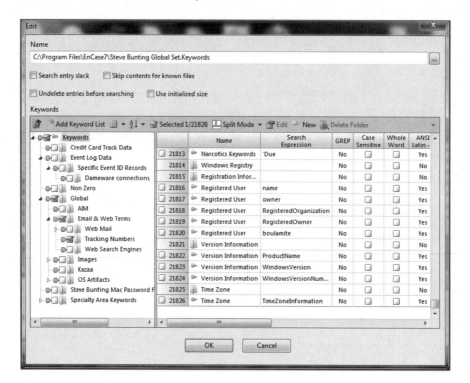

Adding Sets of Keywords

Before you actually conduct a search, you need to consider two other methods of bringing keywords into EnCase: importing or adding keyword lists. Before you can import, you must know how to export, because importing uses a previously exported keyword list.

Importing and Exporting Keywords

To export a keyword list, with all search properties intact, the best way is to organize the keywords into a folder. You can right-click keywords in the Table pane and drag them to a Tree pane folder. Upon releasing the mouse, you can Move or Copy them. Choose Copy. When you are done, you have the keywords you want to export in one folder. Alternatively, you can export the entire list by starting your export at the root level of the keyword list in the Tree pane. To export, in the Tree pane right-click the folder level at which you want to export, and choose Export. Figure 7.36 shows the resulting dialog box. Simply browse to a suitable location for your export file, and click OK to finish.

FIGURE 7.36   The Export dialog box for exporting a keyword list for importing. Browse to a suitable location, and click OK to finish.

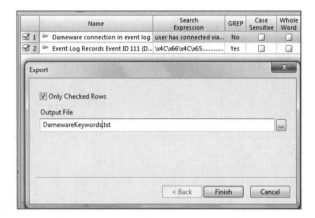

To import an exported keyword file, choose the level or folder in the Tree pane for your import location, and right-click. Choose the Import option, and you will be prompted for the path to the import file. Once that file is located, click OK, and the entire folder structure is imported in the same tree structure it had when you exported it.

Adding Keyword Lists

Another method of adding keywords is to add keyword lists. Choose the location for your keyword list. You can select a folder in the Tree pane or add it to a folder's list of keywords in the Table pane. Once you've selected the placement of your keywords, locate the Add Keyword List menu on the toolbar and click it, as shown in Figure 7.37. The Add Keyword List menu opens, as shown in Figure 7.38.

FIGURE 7.37   Add Keyword List button on toolbar

FIGURE 7.38 The Add Keyword List dialog box. Keywords can be typed or pasted in from other lists.

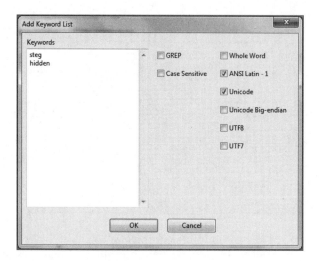

Keywords can be typed into this dialog box or pasted in after being copied from other lists. The various search options selected apply to all keywords in the list. When you have finished adding to your list, click OK, and the new keywords will be added at your selected location. If you don't want the same options for all keywords, you can change them after they have been added as a group.

GREP Keywords

One of your keyword options in Table 7.5 was that of a GREP search. GREP is a powerful search tool derived from the Unix domain, and as explained earlier, it means "Globally search for the Regular Expression and Print." In the various *nix operating systems, GREP is a command that recognizes a series of characters that are included in search strings, greatly adding to the versatility of string searches. EnCase embodies many of those GREP characters in its search engine, giving you pretty much the same search utility in EnCase as a search done with GREP in Unix.

The sheer power and flexibility of using GREP expressions over a regular search strings is phenomenal. Clearly, GREP expressions are tools a competent examiner must know well. It is also a topic to which considerable attention is given in the certification examination. Tests aside, GREP expressions are fun to work with and can really save you time and allow you to search for information you couldn't find any other way.

Introduction to GREP Symbols

Table 7.6 lists the various GREP characters supported by the EnCase search engine. As you go through the list and see the examples, you'll begin to appreciate their utility. Next, we'll work with some examples that will help you with practical applications of GREP expressions in real-world searches.

TABLE 7.6 Syntax for GREP characters or symbols

GREP symbol	Meaning
.	A period is a wildcard and matches any character.
\255	This is a decimal character (period).
\x	This is a character represented by its hex value. For example, \x42 is the uppercase B. Rather than searching for B, you can search instead for \x42.
?	A question mark after a character or set means that the character or set can be present one time or not at all. An example is kills?, which finds both kill and kills.
*	An asterisk after a character matches any number of occurrences of that character, including zero. This one is similar to a question mark, but instead of one time or not at all, it means one time, not at all, or many times. An example is sam_*jones, which finds samjones, sam_jones, or sam____jones.
+	A plus sign following a character matches any number of occurrences of that character, except for zero. Again, this one is similar to its cousins (? and *), except that the character preceding it must be there at least once. It can be present once or many times, but it must be present to match. An example is sam_+jones, which finds sam_jones or sam____jones. It does not find samjones because at least one underscore must be present.
#	A pound sign matches a numeric character, which is zero through nine (0–9). For example, #### finds 1234, 5678, or 9999, but it does not find a123 or 123b, and so on.
[ABC]	Any character in the square brackets matches one character. For example re[ea]d will find read or reed but will not find red.
[^ABC]	A circumflex preceding a string in brackets means those characters are not allowed to match one character. For example, re[^a]d finds reed but does not find read since a is not allowed to match.
[A-C]	A dash within the square brackets defines a range of characters or numbers. For example, [0-5] finds 5 but does not find 6.

TABLE 7.6   Syntax for GREP characters or symbols *(continued)*

GREP symbol	Meaning
\	A backslash preceding a character means that character is a literal character and not a GREP symbol or character. For example, *##\+##* finds *34+89* or *56+57* but does not find *566+57*. Preceding the + with a \ tells EnCase that the + is not to be treated as a GREP character but merely as a plus sign.
{X,Y}	The character preceding a pair of numbers inside curly brackets may repeat *X* to *Y* times. *{2,4}* would repeat two to four times. For example, *a{2,4}* finds *aa* or *aaa* or *aaaa*. It does not find *a*.
(ab)	Parentheses group characters for use with the symbols + (plus), * (asterisk), and	(pipe). See the next symbol for an example.
a | b	The pipe symbol acts as a logical OR, and *a|b* finds *a* or *b* but not *c*, *d*, and so on. To combine the previous symbol (parentheses) with this one for a more meaningful example, *encase\.(com)|(net)* finds *encase.com* and *encase.net* but does not find *encase.org* or *encase.gov*.
\w1234	This allows searching for Unicode code, where 1234 is four integers for Unicode code from the Unicode chart.

Creating Simple GREP Expressions

Now that you know the syntax for GREP, you can use a little creativity along with what you have learned thus far to create some useful GREP expressions. While you are doing it, you'll see how GREP works, and it will become second nature after a while. As an added bonus, you'll get to see EnCase's Keyword Tester in action, which will prompt you to use it quite often; it is a great way to test keywords and will save you loads of time.

You'll often be faced with finding a set of numbers, where you don't know what the numbers are but do know the format in which they should appear. In a corporate environment, you might want to know whether employees are storing Social Security numbers in plain text on their workstations. Such a practice may violate company policy or worse (if employees are stealing the numbers). In a criminal investigation, you may want to search for Social Security numbers that a suspect may have stolen, but you won't know the numbers. In either setting, you are looking for unknown Social Security numbers and want them all if they are present.

You know that Social Security numbers are nine digits and that sometimes those numbers are separated by spaces, such as 123 45 6789, or by dashes, such as 123-45-6789. Sometimes there are no spaces or dashes, such as 123456789. Thus, you want one GREP expression that will find nine digits stored in any of the three formats.

As the starting point, you need to find nine numeric characters, so you need #########. Next, you need to allow for separators consisting of a space or a hyphen, but you also need to allow for no separator at all. The GREP expression [\-]? means you will allow the characters in the brackets to appear either one time or not at all. Within the brackets is a space or a literal hyphen. (Because a hyphen is also a special GREP symbol, you need to use the backslash to indicate that you're looking for a literal hyphen, not using a symbol.) You will allow one to appear either once or not at all. If you inserted the [\-]? between the third and fourth numeric characters and again between fifth and sixth numeric characters, you'd have the expression you need: ###[\-]?##[\-]?####. Note, do not include the period (.) at the end of the sentence in your GREP expression, because in GREP it means "any character." This would be OK in most instances. However, it takes extra searching time, and if the Social Security number was at the end of a text file, it would not find the number, because there would be no character following the number.

Testing GREP Expressions

If you were to test this GREP expression, it would find each of the previous examples and in all three formats. At first glance you might be satisfied with the expression, but the moment you tested it on a real case, you would be overwhelmed by the number of false positives returned. In Figure 7.39 I used Keyword Tester in EnCase to illustrate this point. The GREP expression is inserted as the keyword, and GREP is enabled. I created a text file with three different Social Security number formats along with a string of 10 numbers. Using the Keyword Tester, I browsed to the test file and then clicked Load. The search engine looks for the keyword in the test data and returns the results.

FIGURE 7.39 The Keyword Tester tests a GREP expression against a small text file containing sample text to search.

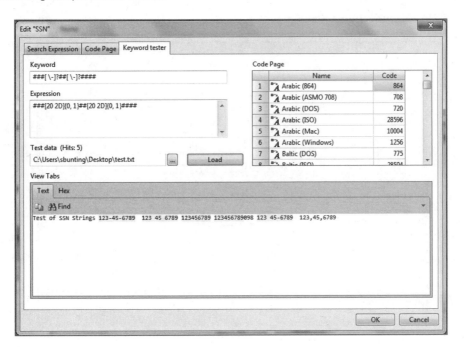

As you can see, this expression finds the occurrence of any nine numbers grouped together. The first three are SSN examples, and it finds them, but it also finds the next two. The fifth hit is an odd example of a Social Security number with a space and a dash used as breaks. Our GREP string will find this one as well. The fourth one is a string of 12 numbers. You would want nine numbers and no more. The way you have this GREP string constructed, it will find nine numbers among 10, 11, 12, 13, 14, or more numbers. Arrays of more than nine numbers are quite common, and finding them all is clearly not in your best interest. You want nine and no more.

If you were to take the expression and apply some logic and then some GREP characters, you could remedy the situation. Let's first apply the logic.

To find nine numbers standing alone instead of nine numbers in a string of more than nine numbers, you could apply a rule of sorts to the expression. You could say that the character preceding or following nine numbers can be anything except a number. Such a condition finds nine numbers standing alone, which is what you want. You now have the logic in place.

Next, you need to express the logic in a GREP expression. To create such a condition using a GREP expression, you use the square brackets and the circumflex to specify what you do not want. Thus, the expression [^#] says that the character can't be a number. Anything else will match, but not a number. If you append this to the front and back of the string, it looks like [^#]###[\-]?##[\-]?####[^#]. Again, do not include the period (.) in the GREP expression. Figure 7.40 shows this revised GREP string being tested against the test data file. It finds nine-number strings in any of our Social Security number formats, but it does not find ten-number strings. It works—and you are done.

FIGURE 7.40 I've used the EnCase Keyword Tester to test the revised GREP expression. By adding to the beginning and end, it finds only nine-digit SSN strings and not strings of ten or more digits.

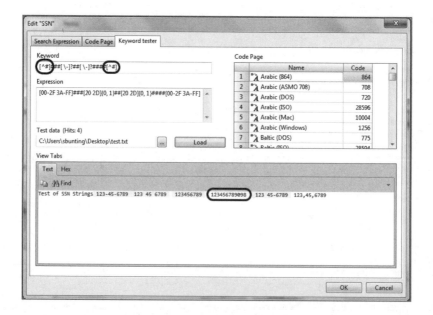

Sometimes you need to locate webmail addresses from one of the major ISPs that allow anonymous free accounts (such as Hotmail, Yahoo!, and Netscape). There are others for sure, but these three ISPs account for most you will encounter and are a good starting point for this example. You can modify your search as your needs dictate. You could create three separate keywords (@hotmail.com, @gmail.com, and @yahoo.net), or you could use one GREP keyword to find all three.

There is usually more than one way to create a workable GREP expression, but typically one way is cleaner or easier to work with. To solve the problem, let's use the parentheses and pipe (logical OR) expressions. So that you find email addresses and not Uniform Resource Locators (URLs, better known as *web addresses*), begin with the @ symbol. Because any one of the three services can match, place each within parentheses and separate them with an OR, or pipe symbol. The expression thus starts as @(hotmail)|(gmail)| (yahoo). This means that any string beginning with the @ symbol followed by hotmail *or* gmail *or* yahoo will match and be found.

From a practical sense, you could probably stop there and find what you are seeking, but since you want to learn more about GREP, let's continue the exercise. To find .com or .net on the end of this string, you need to add some more GREP characters. The period, or dot, is easy, but you need to make it a "literal period" because a period without the literal symbol is a wildcard character in GREP. You can represent it as \., which means a literal period.

To find .com or .net, you can use the same method you used in the preceding paragraph to find the mail services: the string in parentheses separated by logical OR (pipe symbol). The final GREP expression is @(hotmail)|(gmail)|(yahoo)\.(com)|(net). When you test it, as shown in Figure 7.41, it finds the webmail services you are seeking and does not find the others, which was the intent.

FIGURE 7.41   I've used the Keyword Tester again to test the expression, which finds email addresses for any of the three webmail services I was seeking.

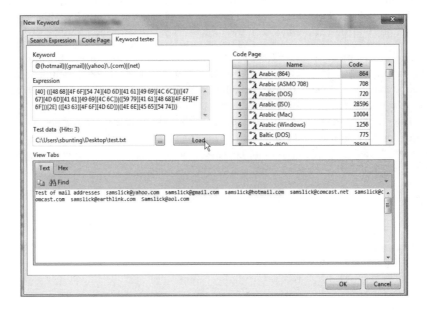

Real World Scenario

Tracking Numbers and Drug Runners with Brown Shorts

A mailing service had been receiving regular packages from a young man for several months. Each time he declared the contents as videotapes. One day the young man dropped off a package and promptly left after paying the fee. On this occasion he had failed to package it properly. The clerk had to repackage the parcel when he left. Instead of a videotape, as declared, the package contained a large bottle of Percocet. The clerk promptly called the police, who began an investigation.

The intended recipient of the Percocet found it in her best interest to cooperate because she happened to be an employee of a law enforcement agency in another jurisdiction. As it turned out, the young man sold a variety of painkillers via email, which was arranged by "referral" by a trusted third party. The sting was set up using the soon-to-be-former law enforcement employee, and the young man was arrested when he attempted to mail the next parcel at the mailing service counter. His pocket change at the time of his arrest was almost $10,000.

A search of his apartment revealed no details regarding his operation, and I was asked to examine the computers he used at his place of employment. It turns out he was a chemist and accessed several computers as he moved about his lab. The involved systems were imaged, and the details started to unfold.

The defendant was a member of a website that offered six levels of password-protected forums for its members. The forum topic at all levels was strictly devoted to the use of drugs, with an occasional referral for sales. Our defendant had two identities, one as a user and one as a dealer. When folks wanted to know where the user obtained his painkillers, he'd refer them to himself under his other identity. The recommendation and referral was always with the highest regard, naturally.

The operation was simple. All sales were paid using Western Union money transfers. All amounts were sent in increments that were less than $1,000 so that no identification was required to send or receive funds. A challenge question and answer was all that was required, which was all sent in an email. All used the various anonymous webmail services, especially "hushmail," to disguise their identities. All used abbreviated and altered code words for the drugs to avoid detection by company web or email content filters. For example, "o*y" was used for oxycodone. There was quite a list, and all users of this website used it religiously in their web posts and in their emails.

All shipments were sent via United Parcel Service (UPS) because they preferred to use couriers with "brown shorts" for whatever reason. As soon as the money was received, the drugs were sent via UPS, and the defendant sent an email to his customers along with the UPS tracking number. The defendant tracked the various shipments using the UPS web-tracking service to assure delivery. While conducting the forensics examination, it became apparent to me that UPS tracking numbers were the common link because they appeared in cached web pages and email correspondence between the defendant and his customers. If all UPS tracking numbers could be located, it would link deliveries, email addresses, quantities, payments, real names, real addresses, and dates and times.

I contacted UPS, and it provided information about the numbers and letters in its 18-character tracking number sufficient to build a GREP expression that would find all UPS tracking numbers in their various formats. With that search term in place, I located all UPS tracking numbers.

Identical tracking numbers were grouped together, and all information relating to that number and its drug sale was linked. Using this method, I identified all of his customers (more than 20 scattered around the country) by their real names and physical addresses. With this information, it was easy to build a spreadsheet that accurately depicted his sales to each customer. Because he was selling thousands of dollars worth of illegal pain killers each week, it was easy to understand why he walked around with $10,000 in cash in his pocket.

In the final analysis, it was by dumb luck that he was caught originally, but it was computer forensics alone that revealed the depth and details of his operation. It was a GREP expression that located UPS tracking numbers that greatly facilitated the latter. When the details of his operation were fully delineated, a guilty plea swiftly followed.

Useful GREP Expressions

For those who may want to use the UPS-tracking-number GREP expression (see the "Tracking Numbers and Drug Runners with Brown Shorts" sidebar) in their investigations, it is included along with a few others in Table 7.7. The publisher's website for this book has a GREP_Expressions folder that holds a file by the same name. The GREP expressions in Table 7.7 are contained in this file so that you can copy them directly to avoid making typographical errors. One tiny error can make a huge difference in the outcome. These GREP expressions were working at press time, but any vendor or programmer can make a change that could alter the results in the future. You should test them periodically with "known data" to be sure they are current.

TABLE 7.7 Some useful GREP expressions

GREP Expression	Description
1Z[ ]?[a-z0-9][a-z0-9][a-z0-9][ ]?[a-z0-9][a-z0-9][a-z0-9][ ]?[a-z0-9]#[ ]?####[ ]?###[ ]?#	Finds UPS tracking numbers. This number is an 18-character string, which is unique. To date, no false positive has been found. Figure 7.42 shows this GREP expression being tested in the Keyword Tester.
[a-z][a-z]#########us	Finds U.S. Postal Service Express Mail tracking numbers.
value="###########">	Finds FedEx tracking numbers as they appear in a web form. Too many false positives occur with the raw number, so this expression finds it in a web form. It doesn't eliminate false positives altogether, but it does reduce them tremendously. When a number is located in a web form, a second search for the specific number often turns it up in other locations.
<title>(MSN)?Hotmail	Locates web page title used by both old and new Hotmail web pages.
\x2E\x20\x20\x20\x20\x20\x20\x20\x20\x20\x20....................\x2E\x2E	Locates "dot double dot" signature for FAT directory entries.
(http)|(ftp)|(https)://[a-z#_\-]+\.[a-z#_\-\.]+	Finds URL addresses starting with, of course, http, ftp, or https.
<!\-\- ##:##:##\-[a-z0-9][a-z0-9][a-z0-9][a-z0-9][a-z0-9][a-z0-9] \-\->	Locates header for AIM Plus history files. If AIM Plus is installed, these files contain IM content. When they "roll off" or are deleted, this expression finds them in unallocated clusters as well.

Creating GREP expressions is both challenging and fun. When you create ones that can be used in future cases, be sure to place them in your Global Keywords view. The Keyword Tester is a handy utility to test GREP expressions. Without it, you pretty much have to test expressions against your case data, which is time-consuming. GREP expressions will greatly assist you with your cases, and you should take the time necessary to become adept at creating and using them.

FIGURE 7.42   A GREP expression that locates UPS tracking numbers is tested against a known tracking number in EnCase's Keyword Tester.

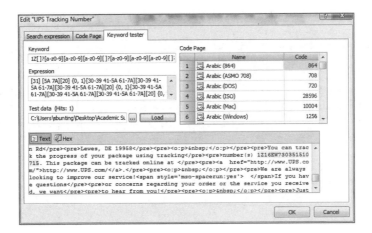

Starting a Search

Now that you have created keywords, it is time to use them to conduct searches. Before we created the keywords, we already selected the files we planned to search. In our case, we were searching all files for two users. In addition to selecting the files you want to search, you must select the search strings or keywords by which to conduct your search. By default, a keyword has a blue check mark when it is created. You can create as many as you want for any given search run and turn as many as you want on or off, but you'll need at least one checked before a search can be run. If you reuse sets of keywords, especially larger sets, you'll often need to select a few of many by selecting them. Once you have selected the keywords for which you want to search, you can begin your search by clicking Raw Search Select on the toolbar and clicking OK. However, there are a few search options you need to first consider. With legacy EnCase versions there was both a Keyword menu and a Search menu. Accordingly, the array of options was extensive, especially as many other processing options cluttered the Search menu. With there now being just one menu to create or edit keywords and to run the search from the same menu, the options are fewer and greatly simplified. Figure 7.43 shows the search options on the Raw Search menu, and Table 7.8 describes in detail those options.

When you conduct a raw search from the EnCase Evidence Processor, the menu is nearly the same, as shown in Figure 7.44, except that the four search options are at the bottom instead of the top. Also, the item that was dubbed "Skip contents for known files" in Figure 7.43 is dubbed "Search only slack area of known items in Hash Library" in Figure 7.44. While labeled differently, they perform the same function. You will also note in Figure 7.44 that there's no ability to save the keywords in a file. Rather, they are saved in the evidence cache of the device to which the search is applied. After making your selections, you can start the search by clicking OK.

FIGURE 7.43 The New Raw Search Selected dialog box from the Raw Search menu with the various search options circled

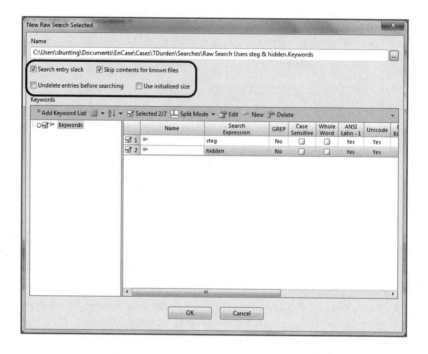

FIGURE 7.44 The Edit dialog box when launched from within the EnCase Evidence Processor

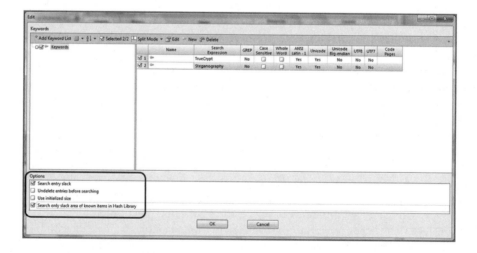

The Search Options may undergo some minor changes as EnCase 7 evolves and improves.

TABLE 7.8   Options in the Edit dialog box

Option	Description
Search Entry Slack	If you choose this option, EnCase searches the space between the end of the logical file and the last byte of the last cluster allocated to the file. This option must be selected to find data located in FAT32 directory entries.
Use Initialized Size	EnCase will search only the initialized size on an entry, which pertains to NTFS file systems only. When an NTFS file is opened and its initialized size is smaller than its logical size, the file space after the initialized size is zeroed out. In essence, a search of initialized size searches the data a user would see in a file.
Undelete Entries Before Searching	If you choose this option, EnCase will logically "undelete" files before searching the data. This will find keywords in those rare cases where a keyword spans the starting cluster and the next unallocated cluster. The next unallocated cluster may or may not belong to the file, but for the purposes of this search, the assumption that it does belong is forced on the search criteria.
Skip contents for known files or Search Only Slack Area of Files in Hash Library	To use this option, a previous hash analysis must have been done, or one must be done in conjunction with this search. If a file exists in the hash library, regardless of category (notable or known), the logical file is not searched. This feature can save time because known files are excluded from search while their slack areas are still searched. If this feature is turned off, a file selected for search will be completely searched (both logical file and slack) even if it exists in the hash library.

Webmail is often sought by examiners. The manner by which this has been carried out and the location of the tool have varied with various EnCase versions. Formerly webmail was parsed with an EnScript found among the Forensic EnScripts. EnCase 7 now includes this tool in the EnCase Evidence Processor as a special carve option under the File Carver. Ideally, this will save you a few steps when you need it!

Viewing Search Hits and Bookmarking Your Findings

EnCase 7 puts all search results under the Search tab, consolidating it for the first time. Past versions of EnCase had search results in different locations, depending on whether it was a raw search or indexed search. To open the Search pane, simply go to the View menu and choose Search. The Search tab contains subtabs, with one for Index, Tags, and Keyword hits. The subtab that opens is typically the last one used. Click the tab with the key icon, and the Keyword hits tab opens, as shown in Figure 7.45.

FIGURE 7.45   Keyword hits tab where the results of raw searches are located

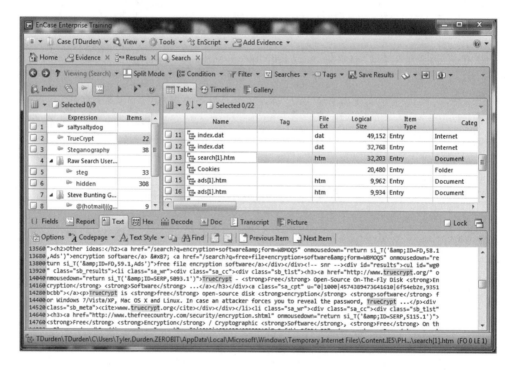

As of EnCase 7.04, a Raw Search of selected items will send the results of the search to the Results view, however those same results are also available in the Search view on a tab labeled "Keywords".

Figure 7.45 reveals lots of information about the new keyword search hit interface. In the left pane or Tree pane, if a raw search was conducted from the Evidence toolbar, there will be a folder bearing the name of the file in which it was stored. In that folder will be the various keywords. The keywords expression column will contain the search expression unless it was given a name, in which case the given name will supersede the expression. You should get in the habit of naming keyword expressions that aren't self-evident as to their meaning. Months can go by, and what made sense the day it was created often becomes obscure with the passage of time. You can do much analysis work directly from the Search tab. When viewing keyword search hits, some viewing options are available. The default view is the Table view, which is shown in Figure 7.45. You can view the files in which the keyword search hits appear in the Timeline and Gallery tabs or views. These are the same tabs or views you are accustomed to using in the Evidence tab, so there is not much further explanation needed.

Regardless of how you choose to group and view your search hits, you have many tools and options available from the Table pane when accessing the right-click menu. These tools and options are described in Table 7.9.

TABLE 7.9   Right-click menu options in Table pane of the search hits view

Menu name	Description of function
Copy	Copies the data in the table field in which the cursor is placed to the clipboard, which is good for copying file names, hashes, full path, and so on.
Save Results	Saves results of search to a file.
Bookmark	Launches the window by which search hits may be bookmarked. This will be covered in detail in the next section.
Go to file	Launches an entries viewing tab within the Search tab and places the focus on the selected file in the Table view pane within the context of its path in the Tree pane to its left.
Find Related	Finds files related by filename or by time.

Bookmarking

Bookmarks are references to specific files or data. Also, they can be notes inserted into the bookmark structure to provide additional information. Bookmarks can be created nearly anywhere that data is located, including the Search Keywords view, often called the search hits view. By having all bookmarks available in a single view—the Bookmarks view or subtab—the bookmarks can be organized into a hierarchical tree that is subsequently rendered as a report of your findings and analysis.

As previously emphasized, creating a well-written, meaningful report that also presents well is a critical skill for competent examiners to develop. Because bookmarks are the foundation of your report, bookmarking is likewise a critical skill.

Some bookmarks, such as the search summary and the case time settings, are created by EnCase as background logging functions, but most are created directly by the user. In the following sections, I'll cover the various types of bookmarks and how to create them. I'll also show you the basics of arranging and organizing your bookmarks, which will pave the way for the report-writing session in Appendix A.

Highlighted Data Bookmark

One of the most common bookmark types is the Highlighted Data bookmark. It is often called a *sweeping bookmark* or a *text fragment bookmark*. To create such a bookmark, you locate the data of interest in the View pane and select the text or data using a click-and-drag technique, with the starting point being the first byte in the data of interest. When the last byte is selected, release the left mouse button, and the text or data is selected and shaded or marked in dark blue. Place the cursor in the highlighted area, right-click, and choose Bookmark. Upon choosing Bookmark, you will have three options or types to choose, as shown in Figure 7.46.

FIGURE 7.46   A Highlighted Data, or sweeping, bookmark is created by selecting the text or data of interest, right-clicking the highlighted area, and choosing Bookmark, at which point three types are available. For a highlighted data bookmark, choose Raw Text.

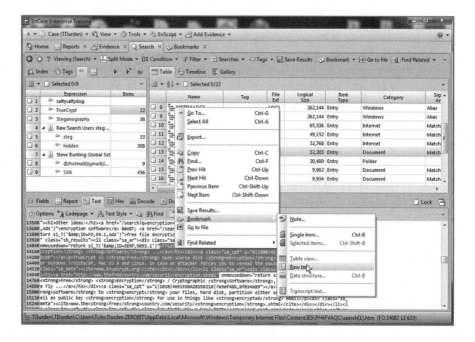

 Starting with EnCase 6, in addition to the text and hex views, bookmarks can be made in the Docs and Transcripts views.

Once presented with the Bookmark Data dialog box, you can enter comments concerning the data or choose a location in the bookmark tree for your bookmark, as shown in Figures 7.47 and 7.48. Creating a comment is very straightforward. You can type a comment or paste one in if you prefer. The maximum length for a comment is 1,000 characters.

FIGURE 7.47   A sweeping data bookmark can be given a comment by the examiner.

FIGURE 7.48   A sweeping data bookmark is placed in an appropriate folder, which in this case is an Internet artifact and from Internet Explorer.

In the Destination Folder pane of the Bookmark Data dialog box, you select the folder into which the bookmark will be placed. You can also create a folder at any location you want by placing your cursor on the location and typing the folder name into the field labeled New Folder, as shown in Figure 7.49.

FIGURE 7.49   Creating a new folder in the bookmark destination folder tree

Creating folders with meaningful names and doing so in a logical outline or tree format is essential for generating good reports. The folder names act as headings and subheadings in your report outline. It is easier to add this structure as you go along when things are fresh in your mind and therefore easily and accurately labeled.

When you bookmark raw text, that is exactly how the data will appear, unless you take the added step to decode it first. What decoded means is viewing the data through one of various data-interpretive layers. It can be decoded as HTML, integers, timestamps, and so on. Figure 7.50 shows how the data we just bookmarked appears as raw text. We get to the bookmark view by simply opening the View menu on the application toolbar and selecting Bookmarks.

When we look at this data, we realize that it is HTML format as it is from a web page. EnCase can decode this data and render it into text that appears as the computer user saw it. Let's go back to the Keyword tab under the Search tab again. With the same data highlighted in the Text tab of the View pane, and shown in Figure 7.51, simply switch to the Decode tab, located two tabs to the right of the Text tab. In the left pane of the Decode tab, you will find the various view types displayed in a tree view in five categories, which are Text, Picture, Integers, Dates, and Windows. Since our data is HTML, we will find it in the text category. Therefore, click on the text category and choose HTML from among the various text types. The data decoded as HTML will be seen in the right pane, as shown in Figure 7.52.

FIGURE 7.50   Data viewed as raw text

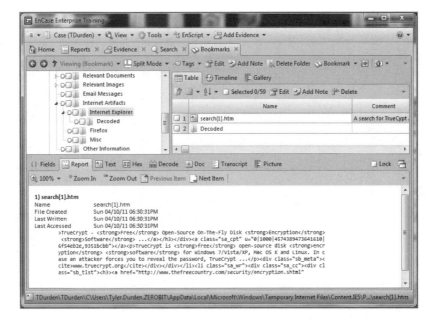

FIGURE 7.51   The raw text data is highlighted.

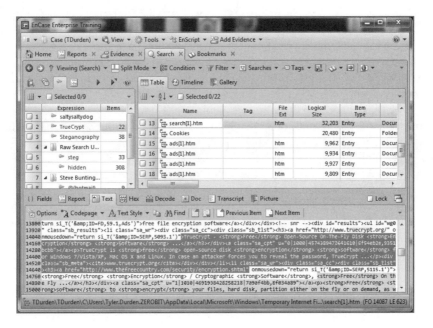

FIGURE 7.52   The Decode tab is used to render HTML code into text as shown in a web page.

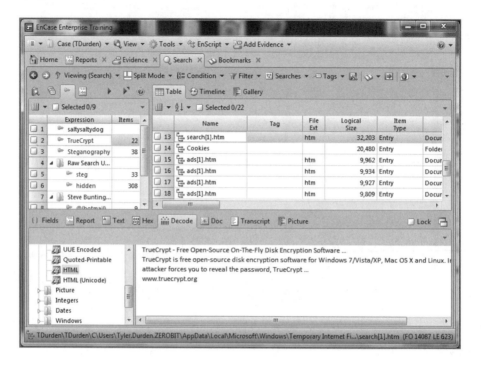

Of course, it is nice to decode and view the data, but that isn't always that useful. You want your reader to be able to see it decoded in your report as well. To make this happen, you can also bookmark the decoded data either in addition to or instead of the raw text format. In the right pane where the decoded data appears, right-click and select Bookmark. You will be given several types from which to choose; we want to choose Data Structure for this situation. Figure 7.53 shows the menus for creating a data structure bookmark. You'll next have the typical bookmarking options, which are Comments and Destination Folder. Once you are done, go to the Bookmarks tab and view the resulting data structure bookmark, as shown in Figure 7.54. You should note that the bookmark icon in Figure 7.53 (circled) is the same type of bookmark icon in Figure 7.54 (circled). As you see later, this decoded view will appear in the report, which is exactly what we want.

The data types from which to choose for viewing your data make bookmarking a most powerful feature. The types range from simple ASCII views to partition entries, dates, images, and various text styles for foreign languages and other special views. Table 7.10 lists the various data types along with a brief description of each type.

FIGURE 7.53   Bookmarking data structure of decoded data

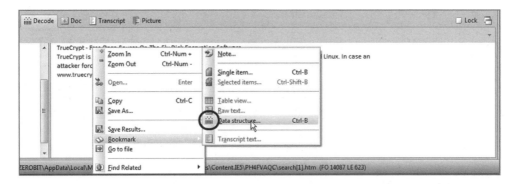

FIGURE 7.54   Completed data structure bookmark showing decoded data

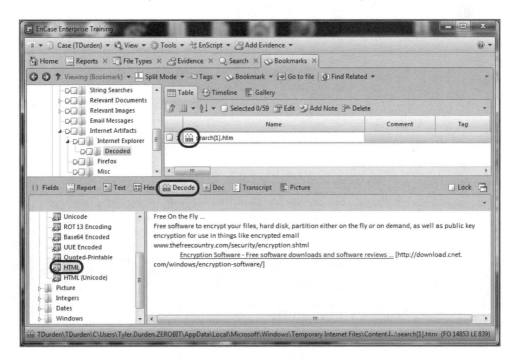

TABLE 7.10 Bookmark data types

Group	Data type	Description
Text	High ASCII	High ASCII includes all characters in the full ASCII table (256 characters).
	Low ASCII	Low ASCII consists of the first 128 ASCII characters only, which are mostly the alphabetic and numeric characters along with the common punctuation marks.
	Hex	Displays values in their hexadecimal representation, a base-16 numbering system (discussed in the beginning of this chapter).
	Unicode	Displays Unicode text in a normal format instead of "A.B.C." as it would appear in ASCII. Unicode uses two bytes per character instead of the one-byte ASCII system.
	ROT-13	ROT-13 encoding is simple ASCII text rotated 13 characters so as to appear encrypted. ROT-13 makes text obscure, not secure, and is often used in newsgroups. Microsoft also uses it extensively throughout the Windows registry. Numbers and special characters do not change. Only the alphabetic characters rotate, which makes this encoding scheme easy to recognize. You will use this data type when we cover Windows OS artifacts in Chapter 9.
	Base64 Encoded	Decodes Base64 encoded text into ASCII text.
	UUE Encoded	Encoding scheme for mail transport.
	Quoted Printable	An encoding scheme that uses printable ASCII characters and the equal sign to transmit 8-bit data over a 7-bit data path.
	HTML	Renders HTML code into a text view. HTML is the language of the Web. Thus, this view is extremely useful in bookmarking web page fragments.
	HTML (Unicode)	Unicode HTML.
Picture	Picture	EnCase's built-in viewer will display the following image types: JPG, GIF, EMF, TIFF, BMP, ART (AOL Johnson-Grace), and PSD (Adobe Photoshop).

TABLE 7.10   Bookmark data types *(continued)*

Group	Data type	Description
	Base64 Encoded Picture	Base64 is a type of encoding used for email attachments whereby high-bit ASCII characters are encoded using low-bit ASCII characters. This causes file sizes to grow by about 30 percent.
Integers	8-bit, 16-bit, 16-bit big-endian, 32-bit, 32-bit big-endian	Displays data in an integer format in either 8-, 16-, or 32-bit arrays. If big-endian, the most significant bit is stored and read first.
Dates	DOS	Packed 16-bit value used by DOS to store month, day, year, and time.
	DOS Date (GMT)	Displays data as a DOS date and converts to GMT.
	Unix Date	The number of seconds that have lapsed since "epoch," which is January 1, 1970, at 00:00 GMT (32-bit hexadecimal value).
	Unix Date big-endian	Same as previous, except in big-endian.
	Unix Text Date	The same base reference as Unix Date, except that the number of seconds since epoch is a 10-digit number instead of a 32-bit hexadecimal value.
	HFS Date	Macintosh file system numeric value representing month, day, year, and time.
	HFS Plus Date	Macintosh file system numeric value representing month, day, year, and time.
	Windows Date/Time	64-bit hexadecimal value for Windows date/time.
	Windows Date/Time (Local)	Same as Windows Date/Time, but for decoding 64-bit time stamps when expressed in local time.
	OLE Time	Resolves OLE container time stamp.
	Lotus Date	Date value for Lotus Notes database file.

TABLE 7.10   Bookmark data types *(continued)*

Group	Data type	Description
Windows	Partition Entry	Interprets 64-byte partition table values.
	DOS Directory Entry	Interprets 32-byte DOS directory entries.
	Windows 95 Info File Record	Interprets data from Windows 9*x* INFO files, which are the Recycle Bin database files.
	Windows 2000 Info File Record	Interprets data from Windows 2000, XP, and 2003 INFO2 files, which are Recycle Bin database files.
	GUID	Resolves and displays strings that conform to the Windows Globally Unique Identifier (GUID) format.
	UUID	Universally unique identifier resolver.
	SID	Resolves and displays strings in the Security Identifier (SID) format.

After you have entered your comment and selected a destination folder, click OK. If you want to have your data decoded, you can display it in the Decode tab and bookmark its data structure, thereby rendering the decoded view in the Bookmarks section. You may want to preview each bookmark as it is created to make sure you created what you intended, and that you placed it correctly in the intended location. It is a good practice to save after each bookmark. It takes only a second or two to press Ctrl+S. The practice creates a good habit that can translate into saved data and work when bad things happen to good people, good software, and good computers.

Notes Bookmark

A notes bookmark is versatile and can hold notes, comments, or any text format you can paste into it. It enhances or further explains information in your report. The limit is 1,000 characters, and there is a built-in formatting tool for changing font size, bolding, italicizing, and setting indentations.

To create a notes bookmark, right-click at the location where you want to insert the bookmark (or within the Tree pane, Table pane, or Bookmark Data dialog box in the Destination Folder pane), and choose Add Note. Alternatively, pressing the Insert key gives the same result.

Once you are viewing the Add Note Bookmark dialog box, as shown in Figure 7.55, you can type or paste in your text. The formatting options are straightforward. The check box labeled Show in Report is selected by default. This means your notes bookmark will appear in the Report view, which is typically the result you desire. The note will be appended to the end of the bookmarks in the selected folder as somewhat of an "end note." If you prefer it at the top, or anywhere else, you can go to the Table pane and click and drag it by its handle to the desired location.

FIGURE 7.55   Add Note Bookmark dialog box in which text can be typed or pasted. Limited formatting options are also available.

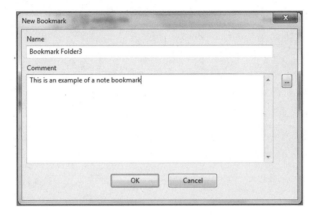

Notable File Bookmark

A notable file bookmark inserts a bookmark or reference to a file that contains information significant to your case. When you create a highlighted data bookmark, the data is shown in the bookmark and report. When you create a notable file bookmark, the data is not bookmarked. The bookmark contains the attributes or properties of the file.

To create a notable file bookmark, right-click the file from the Table view of the Entries view from the Evidence tab. Choose the Bookmark ➢ Single Item option, as shown in Figure 7.56, and you will be presented with the dialog box shown in Figures 7.57 and 7.58.

FIGURE 7.56   Bookmarking a single item

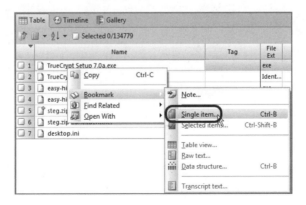

FIGURE 7.57   Bookmark Single Item dialog box from which you can add comments

FIGURE 7.58   Bookmark Single Item dialog box from which you choose the Destination Folder and from which you can also create a New Folder

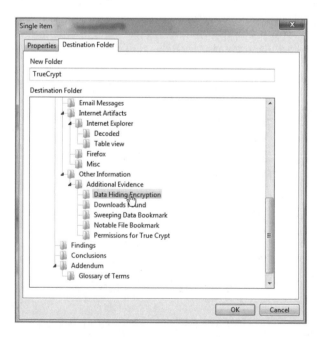

The choices are relatively simple. You choose a Destination Folder; once again, creating well-named folders is important. You can create a folder within the destination folder by simply providing the name of the folder. You can add a Comment specific to this bookmark if you want. Figure 7.59 shows the Report view created by this bookmark.

FIGURE 7.59   This is the Report view of notable file bookmark in the Bookmarks tab.

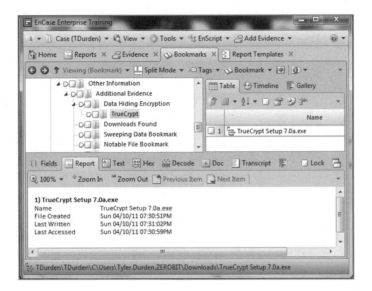

In past versions of EnCase, the metadata shown in Figure 7.59 was what appeared in your report. You could change it by editing the parent folder properties in the Tree pane and thereby customize the metadata fields that would appear in the report. EnCase 7 introduces a new way of reporting, which is greatly improved but does come with a learning curve. We'll explore some of those features later in this chapter.

Bookmarking Selected Items

Notable file bookmarks can be created from selected items. To do so, simply select the items you want to bookmark as a group with blue checks. When you right-click and choose Bookmark, you now have the option to choose Selected Items, as shown in Figure 7.60. Next, you select a destination folder as you did for a single notable file bookmark. It is a good practice to have a folder for each group of related files. You can let the folder name describe the contents of the group of bookmarks. Additionally, you can always create a notes bookmark to further describe bookmarked findings.

WARNING Before you begin creating file group bookmarks, get in the practice of checking the Dixon check box to make sure it is deselected. It wouldn't be the first time an examiner created thousands of file group bookmarks when they intended to create only a few! Also, you can create a single item notable-file bookmark using the shortcut keys Ctrl+B and selected items notable-file bookmarks with Ctrl+Shift+B.

FIGURE 7.60 Bookmarking a group of selected files

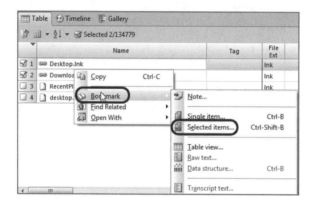

Other Bookmarks

When running various analysis routines, threads, or EnScripts, the results are often displayed with an option to bookmark the results. If the option is selected, the results are automatically pasted into a notes bookmark that is sent to the Bookmark view. Notes bookmarks are very versatile. You can click and drag the resulting bookmark to a folder of your choice for inclusion in your report. You can copy and paste data from third-party tools, Internet research, or most text data into a notes bookmark and thereby include it in your findings.

EnCase also uses another type of bookmark that is called a *log record bookmark*. It is most often encountered when an EnScript runs and parses data from entries. The data is written to a log record bookmark, and there is no pointer to the data. This is important when parsing the registry. Without this type of bookmark, a pointer would have to be used, and that would require leaving the registry hive files mounted, greatly increasing the case loading time.

To view log records, go to the View menu on the application toolbar and click Log Records. The log records will open in their own tab. Figure 7.61 shows the log records in a case. In this example, you will note that file verification has been run three times. The report view for the device doesn't show this at all, only that it has been run and verified but doesn't say when. Because we want to follow best practices and document that we verified the integrity of the acquired evidence both after acquisition and then again at the end, after all the processing is done, to demonstrate that the data was not changed or corrupted in the process, we can do so by bookmarking log records and including them in our final report.

FIGURE 7.61   Log records being viewed

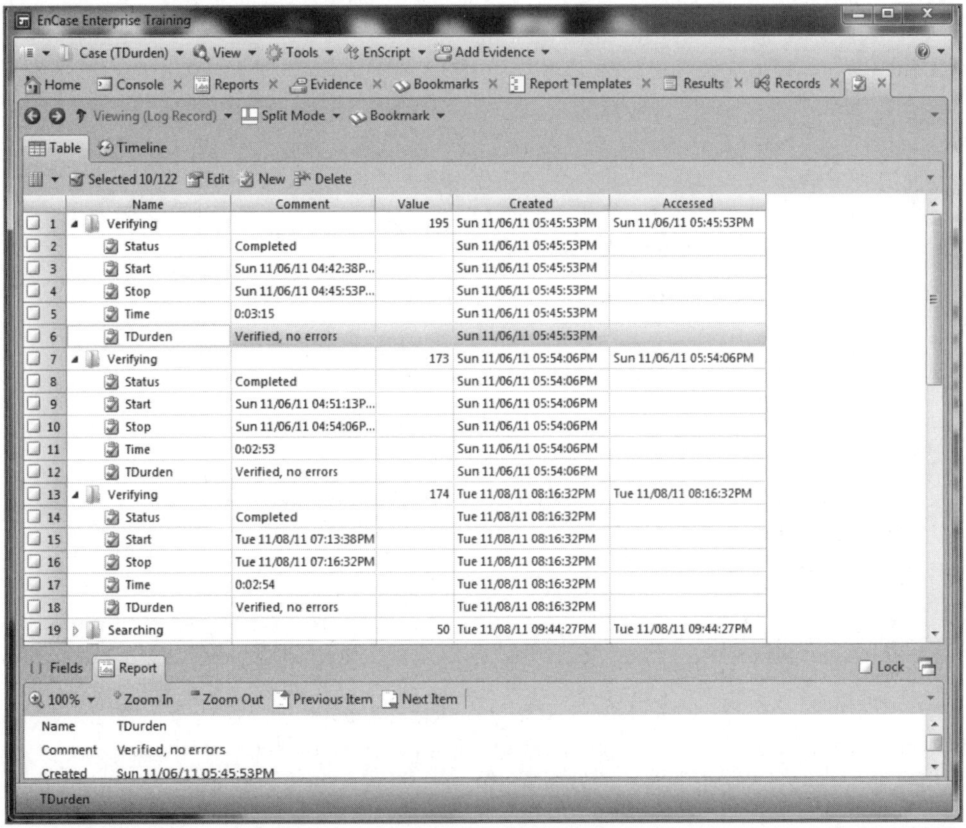

To bookmark a record log, a Table view bookmark is used, which is a new bookmark type released with EnCase 7. The Table view bookmark has many uses and is very versatile. Let's bookmark our file integrity verifications. In our example, Figure 7.61, I want to verify my first and last verifications. I am therefore going to place blue check marks for each of the table entries associated with these two verifications, as shown in Figure 7.62. You should note that a Table View bookmark is, by definition, one that will bookmark Table view entries and that to do so, we must have at least one such entry selected before this option is an available bookmark.

FIGURE 7.62   Entries selected in Log Record view

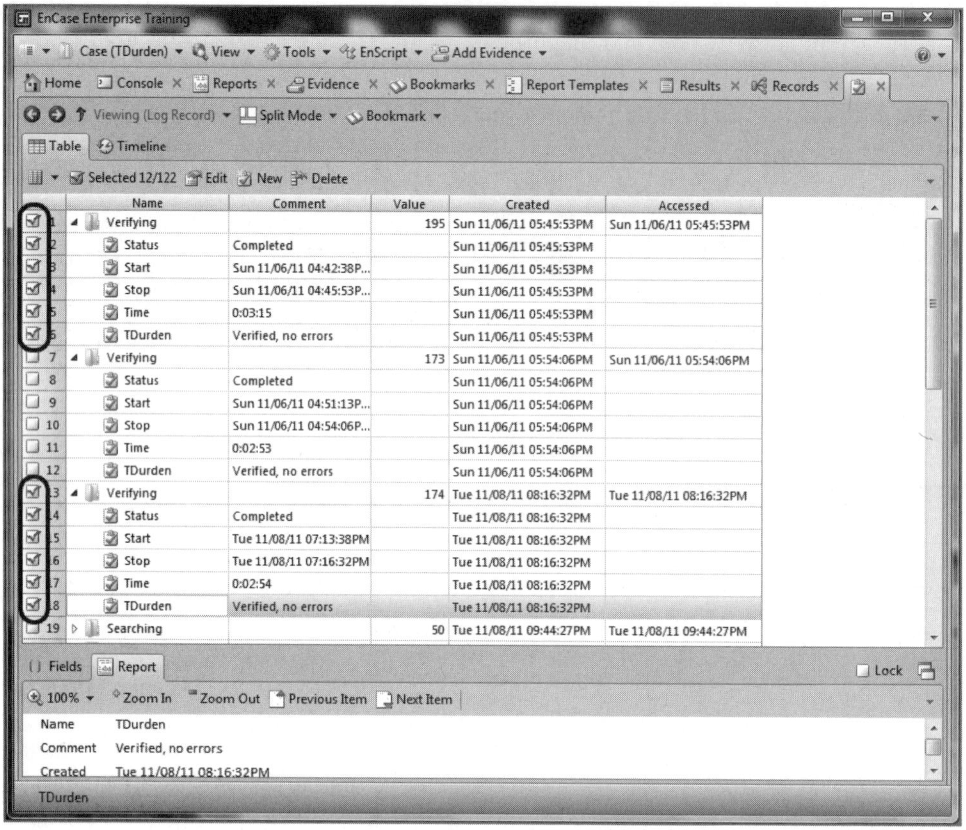

With entries in the table view selected, right-click and choose Bookmark ➢ Table View, as shown in Figure 7.63. In the screen that follows, you give it a Name and optionally include any comments, as shown in Figure 7.64. When you click Next, you are prompted for a destination folder within your bookmark folder structure, which is in turn linked to your report layout but may not be depending on your configurations in your report template. If a bookmark is not showing in your report, the problem can almost always be resolved in the report template settings. We'll get into that later, but it can be an issue and is worth mentioning now. In addition to selecting a Destination Folder, you can also add a New Folder, as shown in Figure 7.65. After a destination folder is selected, the final step in creating the bookmark is choosing which columns in the table view to appear in the bookmark. In this case, we'll select all of the columns, as shown in Figure 7.66. Select Finish and the Table view bookmark is complete and may viewed in the Bookmark tab, as shown in Figure 7.67. My report template is configured such that this table will appear in my report and will appear as shown in Figure 7.67.

FIGURE 7.63   Bookmarking a Table view

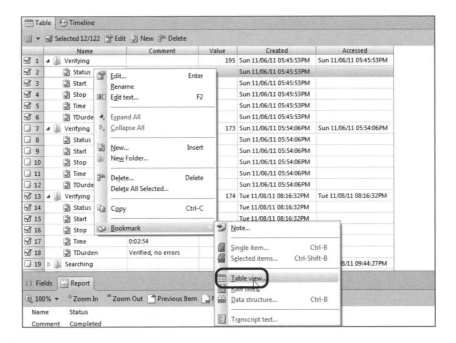

FIGURE 7.64   Naming the bookmark and adding comments

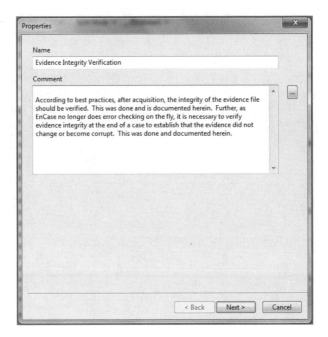

FIGURE 7.65   Selecting a Destination Folder and creating a New Folder

FIGURE 7.66   Selecting which Columns in Table view will appear in bookmark

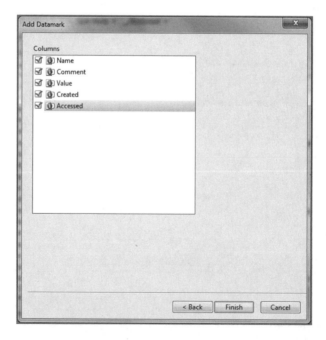

FIGURE 7.67 Completed Table view bookmark in Bookmarks tab

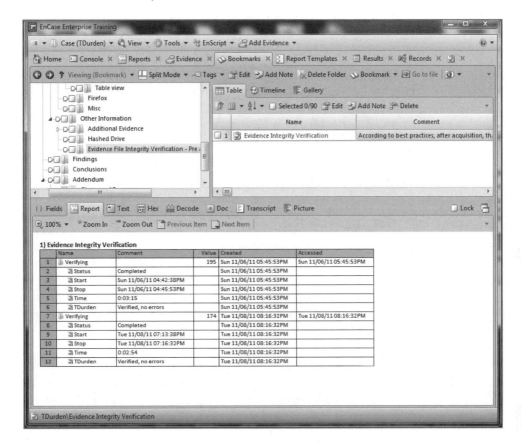

WARNING

When you add a new destination folder, make sure to place it in a destination folder for which the "recursive" feature has been enabled in the report template. If not, your new folder and bookmark will not be visible in the report. This is not just for Table view bookmarks but for any bookmark type for which you choose to create a new folder. We'll cover this feature when we discuss reports and the report template.

I've stated already that the Table view bookmark is very versatile. Many veteran EnCase users have no doubt seen entries in the Table view for deleted files that were overwritten. When such an entry is found and one attempts to create a notable file bookmark showing the entry for the deleted file, what you get is a bookmark for the file that overwrote the deleted entry and not the data in the Table view that you wanted to bookmark. It was out of the need to bookmark such entries that the new Table view entry bookmark was created. Now when you see a deleted file that is overwritten, you can easily bookmark that data with the Table view bookmark. Anything that appears in EnCase in a Table view can be bookmarked with this feature.

EnCase 7 tends toward fewer bookmark notes for various EnScripts and processing routines and instead sends output to log records and to the console. Veteran EnCase users who are used to finding bookmark notes for such things as hashing drives, searching, and the like will need to look to log records for the results. If you want a bookmark of such data, you now know how to create it with a Table view bookmark. In addition, output is often sent to the console. Figure 7.68 shows the output of hashing the device. You can copy the results in the Console tab and paste them elsewhere, such as a notes bookmark.

FIGURE 7.68   Console tab showing results of various processing tasks, with the last one being hashing of the device, which is highlighted

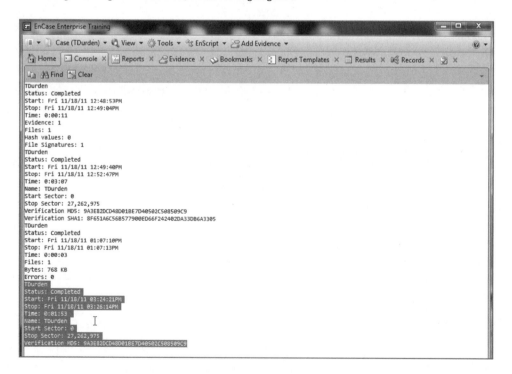

Some EnScripts will write their results to the console as part of their output. You should be cautious of this approach because anything already in the console can be overwritten. At best, anything written to the console will persist only until EnCase closes or the case is closed.

Organizing Bookmarks and Creating Reports

From the Table view pane and the Tree view pane, you have the ability to organize your findings. In the Tree view pane, you can add, delete, and move folders around. You can change the order of any folder's contents by selecting the container or parent folder in the Tree view pane, forcing its contents into the Table view pane. From the Table view pane, any item can be moved by clicking and dragging its handle. You can drag an item in the Table view pane to another folder in the Tree view pane by the same click-and-drag method. Right-clicking and dragging provides even more in the way of granular Copy Here, Move Here, Move Selected Items Here, or Copy Selected Items Here menu options, as shown in Figure 7.69.

FIGURE 7.69   Right-click, drag, and drop options

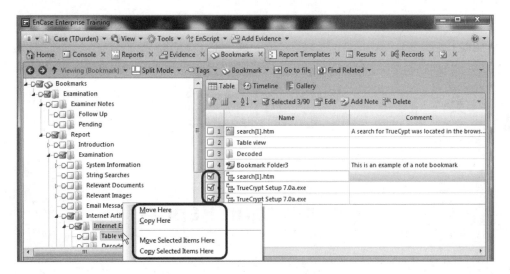

Bookmarks in the Table view have many right-click menu options. Probably the most used of these are the Delete, Delete Selected, Add Note, and Go To File options. Just remember that when you delete a bookmark, it is deleted.

Bookmark creation and organization combine to form the substance and layout of your report and thus become very critical to your final output. It pays to understand and modify the various elements because how your report appears reflects on your reputation as an examiner. For most of us, that should serve as sufficient motivation to roll up our sleeves and really understand bookmarks and how they link to reports.

In previous versions of EnCase, the Table pane included a Report tab from which the report was generated. You could preview it and eventually export it from that tab. EnCase 7 has done away with the Report tab on the Bookmarks tab. Rather, Reports has its own tab, and the configuration options for that report are done in the Report Templates tab.

As we have been creating bookmarks in this discussion, those bookmarks have been placed in the bookmark tree that was determined by the template we chose when we created our case. As I created the case with the forensic template, that template dictates the initial bookmarks and associated report template. You can create other templates or customize this one to suit your needs. As it stands, I can create a report, or at least a limited report, based on the bookmarks thus far created. To view this report, simply go to the application toolbar and choose View ➢ Reports. The Reports tab will open, and in it you will see the report as it currently stands with your various bookmarks there. Figure 7.70 shows the Reports tab and the default report heading.

FIGURE 7.70   Reports tab and default report header

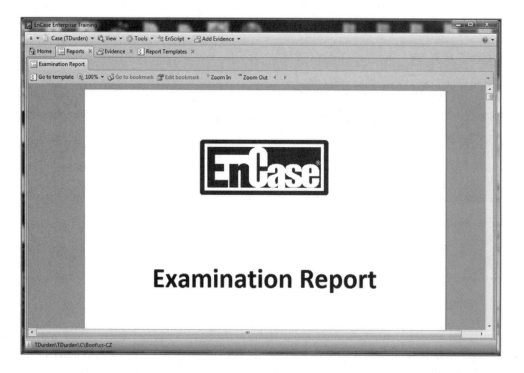

At this point, to export it for further editing and enhancement, merely right-click anywhere in the body of the report and choose Save As, as shown in Figure 7.71. You will next be presented with a variety of file formats that can be used to save the file, as shown in Figure 7.72. Additionally, you need to create a path and filename by which to save your report. A useful option, depicted in Figure 7.72, is the Open File check box. When checked, the saved report will open in the native application that is designated to open the saved file type. As HTML was selected, this report will open with the default browser, as shown in Figure 7.73.

FIGURE 7.71   Right-click in the report body and choose Save As.

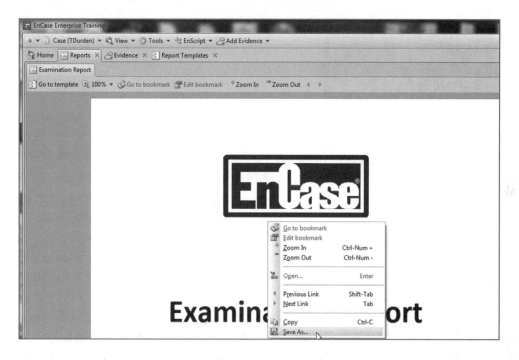

FIGURE 7.72   Different file format options for saving report, along with filename and path options

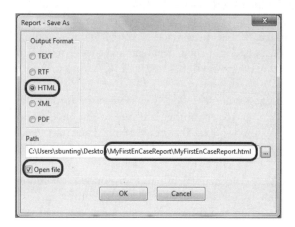

FIGURE 7.73 If the Open File option is selected, the report opens in the native application.

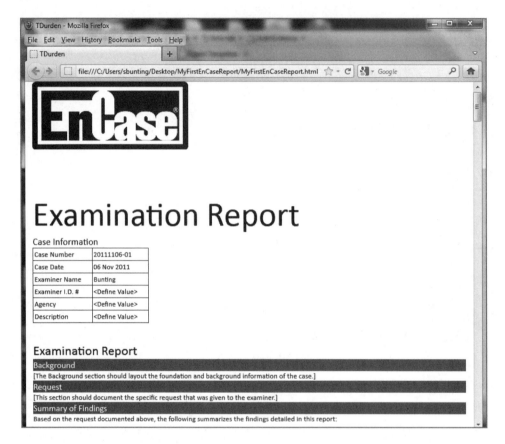

We could end our discussion of reports here, but that wouldn't do justice to the features found in the Report Templates tab. From the Report Templates tab, you can format the report, add sections, link bookmark folders to report sections, and much more. Finally, when you have a template that is customized to your agency or company, you can save your work as a template. Then, each time you create a new case, you use this template instead of the default set. When you do, you will have everything set up for you the way you customized it.

Before starting, I suggest you create a new case with the forensic template, or one that closely suits your needs. Once open, immediately go to the Bookmark tab. In the Tree pane, under Bookmarks, drill down to Examination\Report\Examination\Other Information. At that level (Other Information), create a new folder named **Additional Evidence**, as shown in Figure 7.74.

If you were to now go to the Reports tab and scroll down the report, you would find that your new folder does not appear under the section Other Information, as you might expect. Figure 7.75 shows this section and the absence of your newly created folder.

FIGURE 7.74   Create a new folder under Other Information.

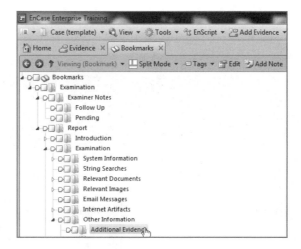

FIGURE 7.75   The Reports tab does not yet show your new folder.

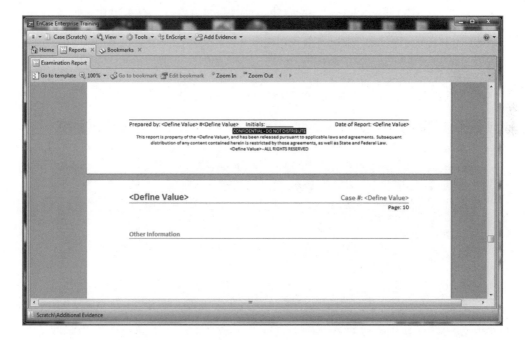

Your new folder does not yet show in the report because no link has been created between your bookmark and your report. This is a concept or feature that is new with EnCase 7. You create links between bookmarks and the report through the interface on the Report

Templates tab. You can access the template from the View menu on the Application toolbar; or, if you have the Reports tab open, there is a Go To Template tool button on the Report menu bar, as shown in Figure 7.76.

FIGURE 7.76   Go To Template button

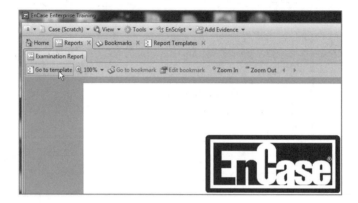

The Report Templates tab should open in the Traeble mode by default. If it doesn't, you may want to switch to it, because it seems the better choice for working in this tab. Next, locate the Other Information section, which is in the report body and is shown in Figure 7.77. To help you see the changes you will be making, it is suggested that you switch to the Report tab in the lower View pane, also shown in Figure 7.77.

FIGURE 7.77   Other Information section selected and viewed in the Report tab

The next step is to edit the section Other Information, which is done by simply double-clicking that item. You can also right-click it and choose Edit. When you do so, you will see the Edit "Other Information" dialog box, with three tabs, as shown in Figure 7.78. It will open to the Options tab, but we want to do our work on the Body Text tab, so switch to that tab, which is shown in Figure 7.79.

FIGURE 7.78   Edit "Other Information" dialog box, showing Options tab

FIGURE 7.79   Edit "Other Information" dialog box showing Body Text tab

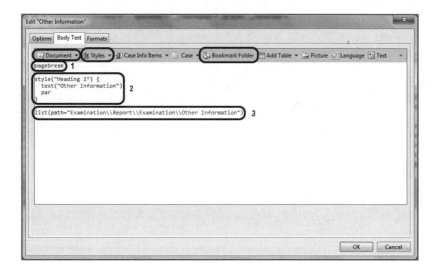

Before we start changing things, let's get an understanding of the information we see in the body text. I have circled the three separate items in Figure 7.79 that currently exist so we can isolate and understand them. Number 1 (pagebreak) does nothing more than force a new page for this item and is generated from choosing it from the document menu, which is also circled and is immediately above it in this case. Item 2 defines a text style for the text *Other Information* on the report page. It is generated by choosing it from the Styles drop-down menu, which is also circled. Once inserted, the cursor will appear where you start typing text.

Item 3 is the link to the bookmark. Without this link, nothing placed in the Other Information bookmark folder would appear in the report. All that would show would be the words "Other Information." Right now, it does not contain the recursive option, and therefore no folders placed therein show in the report, which is precisely why our folder doesn't show. It would, however, show any bookmark placed in the root of the folder Other Information but not subfolders or the contents of any subfolders. There are two ways of fixing this: One is to add the recursive option to the existing link, and the other is to create a link for our folder and make it recursive so that all folders placed therein will appear without having to edit the template. So that we can see the difference between the two links when we are done, we are going to use the second option, which is to insert a link to our new folder and make it recursive.

Place your cursor in the whitespace under item 3 in the body text, because this will cause the next item to be inserted at this point. Next, click the Bookmark Folder menu, which will provide a listing of bookmark folders that are available to link to the report, which is shown in Figure 7.80. Select the new folder that we just created, which is Additional Evidence. Before clicking OK to create the linkage, note the two options in the upper left. I have circled them to draw your attention to them. By default, they are *not* enabled. Show Folders causing the name of the folder (in our case Additional Evidence) to show or not show as a header or subtitle in the report. I prefer to have it show and name my folders accordingly. Recursive causes any folders and their subfolders to appear in the report. This option was not selected for the parent folder Other Information and is the reason our new folder does not appear in the report. Again, I prefer all folders to appear in the report, which is why I create them in the first place. So, enable both of these options, and then click OK to complete the link.

Once you click OK, you are returned to the body text, as shown in Figure 7.81. You can see the link to the new folder with the two options included, which are SHOWFOLDERS and RECURSIVE. You should immediately see that the link to the parent folder did not include these options. If it contained the recursive option, what we are doing now would not have been necessary.

FIGURE 7.80   Menu to link bookmarks to show in report

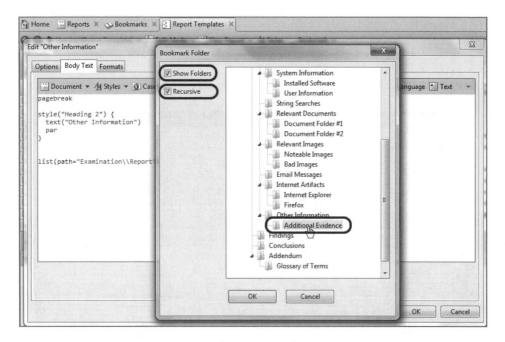

FIGURE 7.81   New bookmark link inserted with Recursive and Show Folders options in place

From the Edit "Other Information" dialog box, click OK to finish the work and apply it to the template. In the Report tab at the bottom, you will see the changes immediately as the newly created folder now appears in the report, as shown in Figure 7.82. You can, if you like, add a bookmark to this new folder and then check the report to make sure it appears.

FIGURE 7.82 New folder now appearing in report

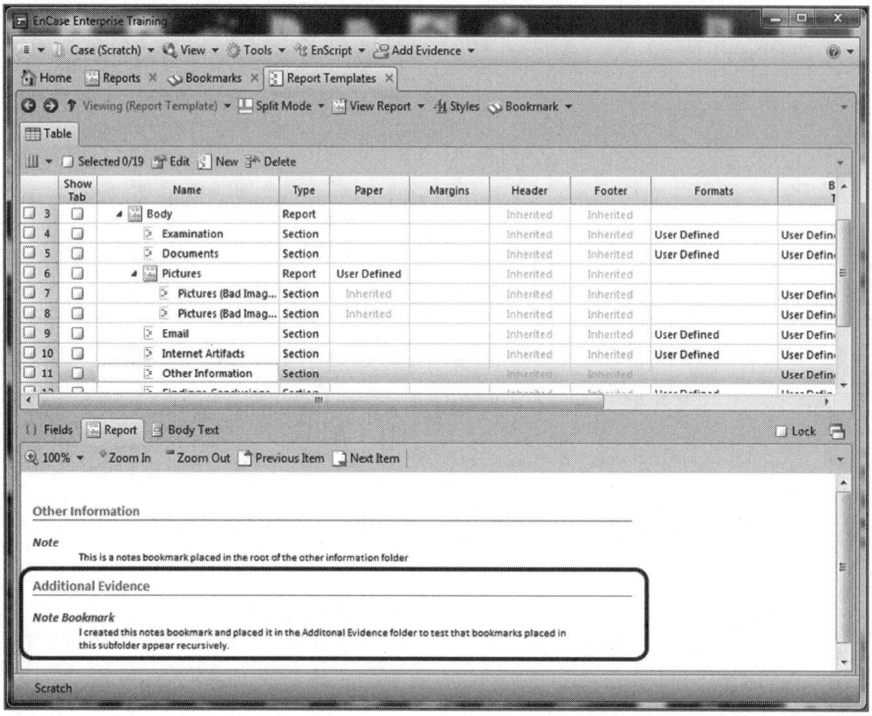

While we are working in the report template, there's another editing option that you should be able to do, which is modify the metadata that is shown in the report. The default is to show a file's name and MAC times (modified, accessed, and created). For some the default is sufficient, and for others it's just the opposite. I happen to fall into the latter category, so let's discuss how we change these settings. I have created a notable file bookmark in the new folder that we just created. If I view the report to see how this bookmark appears, I see it in the new folder (Additional Evidence), and I see the default metadata fields (name and MAC times), as shown in Figure 7.83.

FIGURE 7.83   Notable file bookmark with default metadata (name and MAC times)

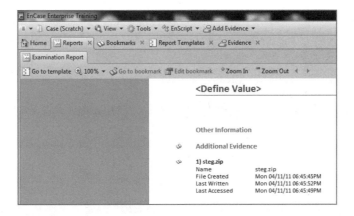

To change how metadata appears, we have to use the report template editor to edit the section where the bookmark appears. To fix this particular one, go the Report Templates tab and edit the section named Other Information, just as we did to link the bookmark to the report. This time, when the Edit "Other Information" dialog box opens, we are going to switch to the Formats tab, as shown in Figure 7.84. Among other objects that can be formatted, you will find formatting options for the various bookmark types. Our bookmark is a notable file bookmark, and you simply double-click that object to edit it. Figure 7.85 shows the open editor and the default code. I have circled the code that defines the metadata for clarity. This is the code that we need to edit.

FIGURE 7.84   Edit "Other Information" dialog box Formats tab

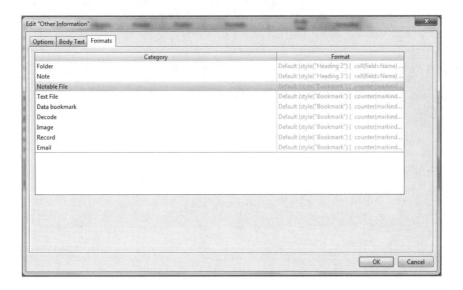

FIGURE 7.85   Code pertaining to metadata is circled

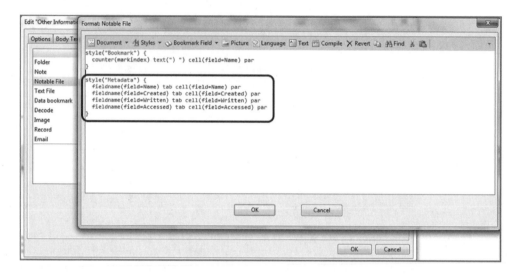

The field names that we'll be inserting will be generated from the Bookmark Field menu. In our example, I want to insert the full path immediately following the name field. First, we have to place our cursor at the insertion point. That also means we have to insert a carriage return to achieve the proper insertion point, as shown in Figure 7.86.

FIGURE 7.86   Insertion point for inserting a field following the Name field

With our cursor at the insertion point, click the Bookmark Field drop-down menu and choose Item Path, as shown in Figure 7.87. The end result is the insertion of that field into the code at the insertion point, as shown in Figure 7.88. The insertion places a carriage return at the end of the code, but not the beginning, such that you could continue inserting addition fields if you'd like. What the field insertion process fails to do, and understandably so, is to place the code at the end that triggers, effectively, a carriage return; this is the par code, which is the abbreviation for paragraph. Thus, you must manually insert the par at the end of the inserted field code. To tidy things up further, I removed the carriage return, although it would not appear as such in the report. Figure 7.89 shows how the finished insertion should appear.

FIGURE 7.87   Inserting Item Path from Bookmark Field drop-down menu

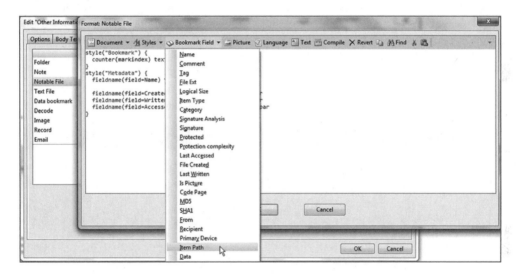

FIGURE 7.88   Line of code inserted without par at end and with extra carriage return

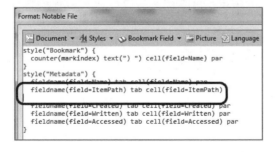

FIGURE 7.89 Shows finished insertion of code, which is how it should appear when done

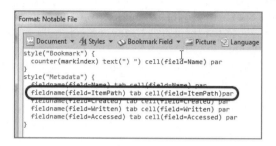

At this point, you have successfully inserted a line of code necessary to modify the file metadata that involves a notable file bookmark in this section (Other Information) of your report. Click OK in the Format: Notable File window, and click OK in the Edit Other Information window. When you do, you should see the changes appear on the Report tab for the Other Information section, as shown in Figure 7.90.

FIGURE 7.90 Report tab view showing Item Path field added to bookmark metadata

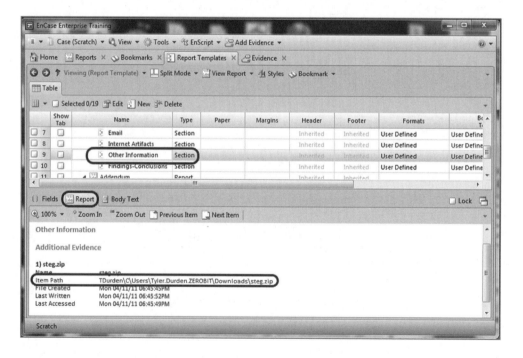

If you were reading carefully, you noted that I said that we added this field to the Notable Files bookmark for this section only. We did not insert this field for other bookmark types or in other sections. You could make changes at parent levels and have the changes inherited to the children, or you could make the changes at lower levels as preferred. Regardless of which you decide, make gradual changes and test the desired result with data as you go.

While this may seem a lot of work, once you get the hang of it, you can create the metadata fields to your liking for one bookmark type in one section and then copy and paste the code to other bookmark types and in other sections. There is more good news in that you need to do this only once, because you'll save your work in a template and reuse it hundreds of times. Thus, it is worth the one-time effort to develop a customized template that reflects favorably upon your work. Let's save our template and show you how to reuse it.

Let's assume you've changed the metadata for your various bookmark types in the different sections according to your preferences or those of your lab. You can and should make other changes, such as the logo, lab name, and address on the title page, as well as the examination tools. The latter (examination tools) are not changed in the template but rather in the bookmarks themselves. You'll find them appearing as notes bookmarks under the bookmark folder Examination Tools.

When all changes are completed, you simply go to the application toolbar and choose Save As Template on the Case drop-down menu, as shown in Figure 7.91. In the resulting dialog box, name your template something meaningful and clear. As shown in Figure 7.92, there are other options that can be saved in the template. The first two are paths to the evidence cache and the hash library. For now, we won't select them. The third option, circled in Figure 7.92, is what we want to select. By saving bookmark notes, we are saving the changes we made to items such as the Examination Tools notes bookmarks that we just took the time to modify from their default data. When done, click OK to save.

FIGURE 7.91   Save As Template option

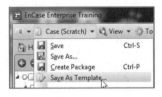

FIGURE 7.92   Save As Template dialog box by which to name the template and save your bookmark notes

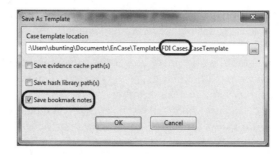

To see the fruits of your labor, create a new case, and you will see the name of the template you just created in the list of templates. Choose that template, and note that information appears in the Case Info section, as shown in Figure 7.93. You can give your case a name and click OK. You can go to your Report tab and see some of the changes made right away. Figure 7.94 shows the title page as customized. It had to be done only once and now appears with each new case. As you add bookmarks, all the customization you made will appear. From time to time you'll make added changes and tweak your template, making it look better and more professional each time.

FIGURE 7.93   New Case Options dialog box with the saved template appearing in left pane

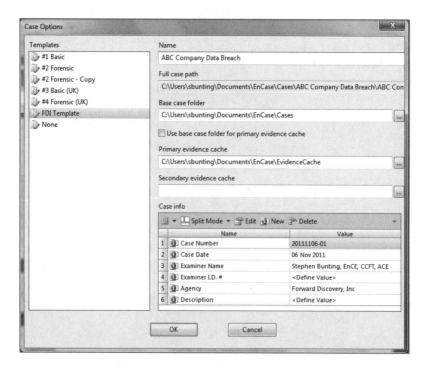

EnCase's bookmarks and the resultant reports, to which they are linked, are very powerful and very flexible features. The addition of the report template editor makes them even more customizable. The report template, at first glance, is intimidating, but once you roll up your sleeves and make a few changes, you get used to its function and features very quickly. In a very short time, you'll be an EnCase report power user!

FIGURE 7.94   A custom report is now available from the saved template and will be available for all cases going forward.

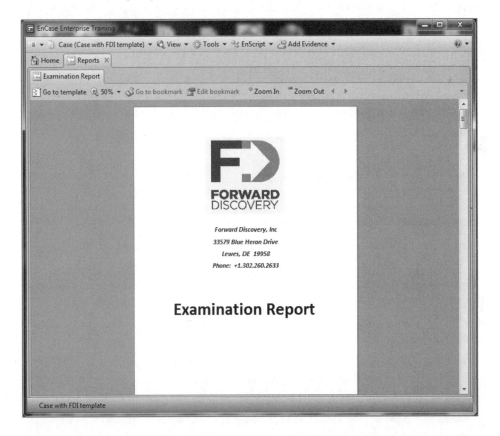

Examiners are encouraged to take the time to work with each of the features. In this manner, you can learn to quickly and easily create bookmarks that will be used to generate professional reports that convey your hard work and findings in a clear and meaningful way. In Appendix A, I will cover extensively how to work with your bookmarks to generate such reports.

EXERCISE 7.1

Searching for Data and Bookmarking the Results

In this exercise, you'll import keywords and conduct a GREP keyword search of your case for data, matching your keyword. When the word is found, you'll examine the search results, bookmarking the results using various data views. To complete the process, you'll create a paperless report, showing the results of your work. Let's get started.

1. Open EnCase, and from the Home tab, create a new case. Use your custom template or the forensic template. Name your case OnlineDrugSales. Accept the other defaults, and click OK.

2. From the publisher's website for this book, download the file DefFrostyUSB16MB_TD01 .E01. Go to the folder created for this case (\Users\UserName\Documents\EnCase\ Cases\OnlineDrugSales). In the root of this folder, create a folder named Evidence, and place this evidence file in that folder.

3. From the EnCase Home tab, select Add Evidence and choose Add Evidence File. Browse to the evidence file just added to this case, and click OK.

4. Let's follow best practices and check to make certain the evidence file is verified. From the Evidence tab (now open), select the evidence file in the Table pane. In the View pane, at the bottom, switch to the Report tab. Scroll down and check that the evidence file verified with no errors.

5. From the publisher's website for this book, download the file Keywords_For_Import .txt and place it somewhere convenient, which is most likely your desktop.

6. From the Evidence tab, double-click the evidence file to have it parsed and mounted in the Entries view.

7. In the Tree pane, place a blue check mark at the device level and note the Dixon box. It should say 526/526 selected.

8. On the Evidence toolbar, click Raw Search Selected and choose New Raw Search Selected. In the right-side menu (the super-secret menu), choose Import ➤ Open. Browse to the file we just downloaded, wherever you save it, and click OK.

9. You should have several GREP expressions in the resulting window, which are the ones mentioned earlier in this chapter. Browse to the keyword in the Tracking Numbers folder, and place a blue check mark for UPS Tracking Number. Browse to the Windows Artifacts folder, and place a blue check mark for the "dot double dot" directory. You should have selected two keywords for your search.

10. Give this search a name and save your search (and keywords). Choose an appropriate path for future use. Under search options, check Search Entry Slack and Skip Contents For Known Files. Click OK, and the search will run.

11. From the View menu, choose search and switch to the keywords tab. In the Tree pane, locate the keyword UPS Tracking Number and select it. Note that there is one search hit in the Table pane. Select that one search hit and switch to the Text tab in the View pane.

12. Select the text data in the Text view, which covers from the first byte to the *y* in *Frosty*. Check the length of the selected text in the GPS area; it should be 495 bytes. Right-click in the selected text, and choose Bookmark ➢ Raw Text. Place the bookmark in the folder named String Searches, and click OK.

13. Go to the View menu and click Reports. Scroll down and see that your bookmark appears under String Searches.

14. Go back to the Search tab/Keywords tab. In the Table pane, place your cursor on the file named Reply to August 20 2005 order.txt. Right-click the file and choose Go To File. The file will open in its own tab but still within the Search tab.

15. You should note that there are two other files in the same folder with this file. Place your cursor on the file Original Order with Address.txt and view its contents in the Text tab of the View pane. You should find the text rather unusual. With experience, you'll recognize this as ROT13 encoding. It is used in many places to obscure text, including the Windows registry in the UserAssist key. From the first byte, select all of the text present, which should be 260 bytes. With it selected, switch to the Decode tab.

16. In the Decode tab, locate ROT13 Encoding under View Types text views. When you select it, the text in the right pane is decoded, and you see clearly what is taking place!

17. In the right pane of the Decode tab, right-click and choose Bookmark ➢ Data Structure. Place the bookmark also in the String Searches folder.

18. Go to the Reports tab and locate your data structure bookmark.

19. Right-click anywhere in the body of the report, and choose Save As. Save your report in a web page format (HTML) and review.

20. Save your case and exit Encase.

Indexed Searches

Starting with EnCase 6, indexed searching was a search option. As with any new technology, it had its limitations and issues. EnCase 7 has a much improved, very robust indexing engine that makes indexed searching the preferred method to search a case going forward.

Considering the size of today's media and the time required for individual raw searches, it only makes sense.

As with any indexed search engine, an index must first be created from the data you want to search. The subsequent search is carried out against the index, not the data, and the result is near-instantaneous search results. Creating an index can take considerable time, but once done, the time savings are tremendous.

If you recall our earlier discussion in this chapter about the EnCase Evidence Processor, we covered the index text feature, which builds the index during the case processing phase. Thus, once your case processor has completed, you can search the index. Figure 7.95 shows the index text options in the case processor. You might want to go back to the section earlier in the chapter in which these options are discussed.

FIGURE 7.95   Index Text options in EnCase Evidence Processor

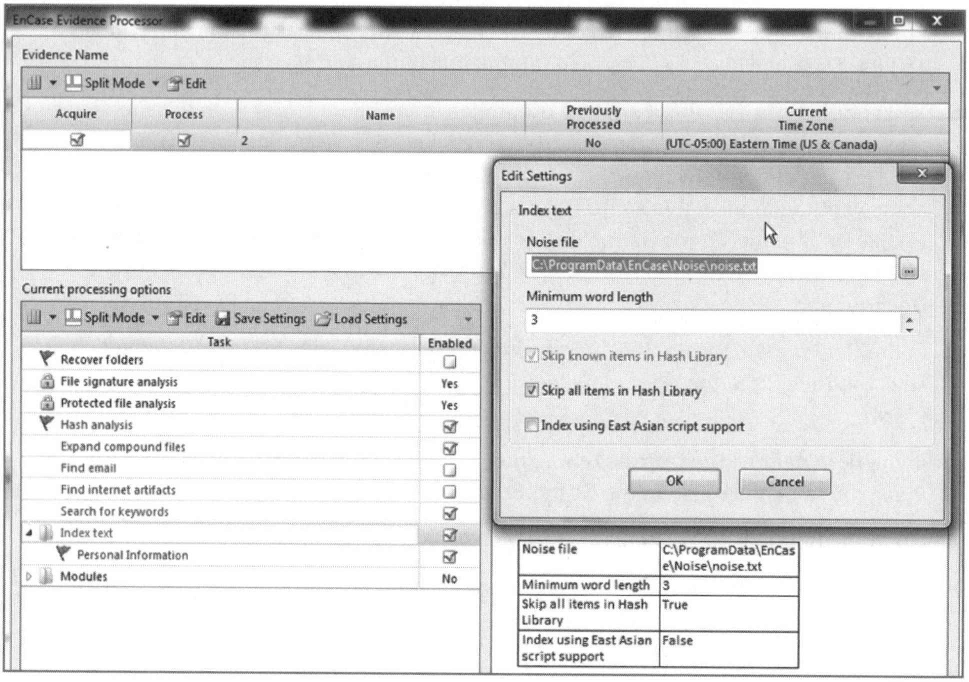

To search the index, you simply go to the Search tab and begin your search. The Search tab, as you recall, can be accessed from the View menu on the application toolbar. The default tab for the Search tab will be, normally, the last tab you used. So, if the Index tab is not the active tab, switch to the Index tab, and your screen should appear as in Figure 7.96.

FIGURE 7.96   Search tab with Index tab selected

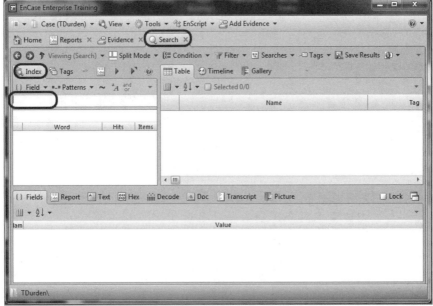

To begin a search, you need only type the keyword into the search string field where, by default, the cursor is located. As type in the keyword, the area below the keyword is dynamically populated with various iterations of the keyword, the number of objects in which it exists, and the total number of hits. For example, as I typed in **steganography**, EnCase reports the various hits in which steganography is the root of the string, as shown in Figure 7.97.

FIGURE 7.97   As a keyword is entered, a dynamic list of hits and items is created below.

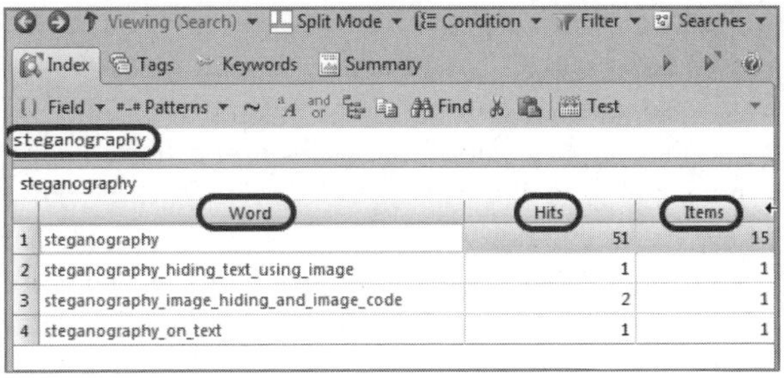

Once you are satisfied with your keyword, you run the query by clicking the play icon on the toolbar, which is circled in Figure 7.98, and the results are displayed in the Table view pane to the right. The Table pane lists the various items in which the keyword appears. You can easily browse the list, selecting various items and viewing the contents below in the various View pane tabs.

FIGURE 7.98 To run the query, click the Play icon, which is circled.

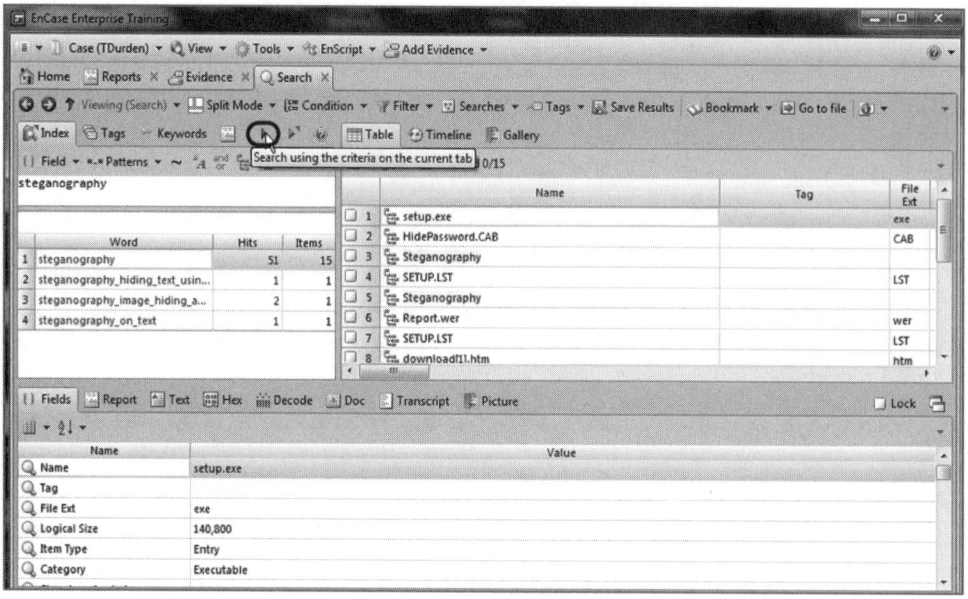

From the View pane, you have many viewing options, which include Text, Hex, Decode, Doc, Transcript, and Picture. Which view will be dictated by user preferences and viewing needs. To navigate between search hits, there are two icons immediately to the right of the Find Next icon. As shown in Figure 7.99, they enable you to sequence between search hits in either direction. To the right of these two buttons are two icons that are labeled Previous Item and Next Item. As the name implies, you can sequence through the items in the Table view pane with these two navigational aids. Finally, don't forget that you can use the Find and Find Next features to search within the text or beyond, including GREP searches.

As with keyword searches, you can bookmark raw text or notable files from the Search tab panes. Also, if you need to, you can use the Go To File feature. This is a very handy feature for viewing the file in a Tree pane. While in the Search tab Table pane, right-click a file of interest, and choose Go To File, as shown in Figure 7.100. When you do, the chosen file will open in its own Entries tab within the Search tab. To return to the Index tab, use the green left-arrow at the far-left side of the toolbar under the Home icon.

FIGURE 7.99   Next Hit and Previous Hit buttons enable quick sequencing between search hits.

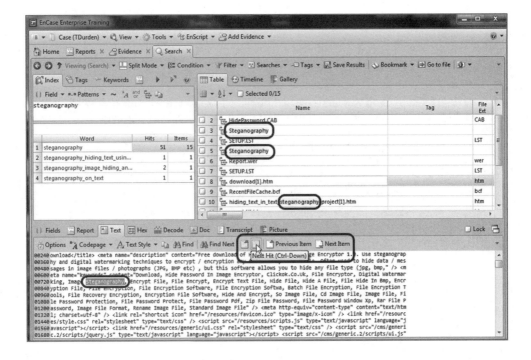

FIGURE 7.100   Go To File feature

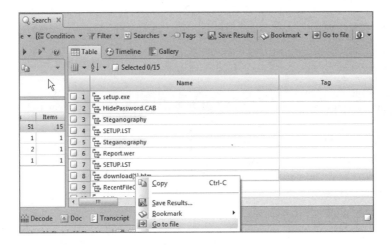

You are not limited to simple keywords with index searches. You can combine keywords with AND or OR logic. You can simply type **AND** or **OR** between the keywords, and it will turn blue, indicating it is being recognized as a Boolean logic operator, as shown in Figure 7.101. There is also an AND/OR button on the toolbar that will autofill either of those two words in the event you forget how to spell them. With AND logic, the query will return items that have both keywords, whereas with OR logic, the query will return items with either keyword.

FIGURE 7.101   Using Boolean AND/OR logic with keywords. In this case, AND logic required both keywords to be present in an item to return a successful query.

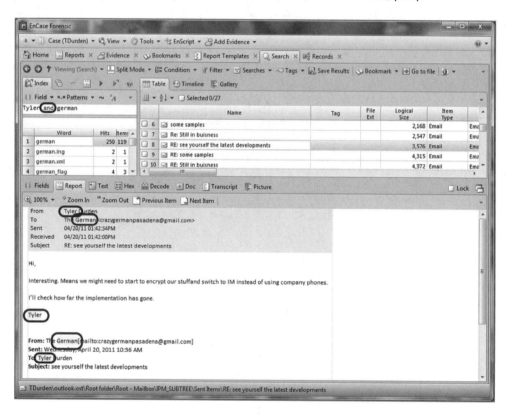

In addition to Boolean search operators, EnCase 7 has many other search operators. Proximity searches are very useful where you are trying to find one keyword near another keyword. The w/# operator is used to find one keyword within a specified number of words from another. For example, steve w/3 bunting will find items in which *steve* is within three words of *bunting*, no matter what order.

You can force ordering, however, by using a "one word before the other" operator. For example, steve pre/3 bunting would find items in which *steve* appeared before *bunting* and within three words, but it would not find *bunting* preceding *steve* by three words.

Instead of finding words close to one another, we can also go in the other direction, using a "keywords apart from each other" operator. Thus, we specify that keywords can't be within a specified number of words from each other. For example, `steve nw/3 bunting` would find only items in which *steve* and *bunting* existed more than three words from one another. If ordering were desired, `steve npre/3 bunting` would force the same conditions, but *steve* would have to precede *bunting* and be more than three words apart.

You may have noted that I spelled my name with all lowercase letters in the previous examples because case does not matter with index searches, unless you force the condition. On the toolbar, immediately to the left of the AND/OR logic button, you will find an a/A button. Clicking it will alternately insert a case-sensitive `<c>` or case-insensitive operator `<c->` into the search string, as shown below in Figure 7.102. When the case sensitive operator is used, the search string must match both the string and case, as also shown in Figure 7.102.

FIGURE 7.102   Case sensitivity operator in use

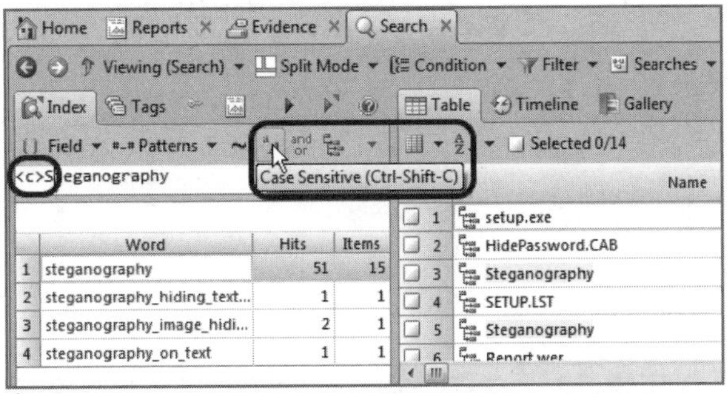

There are many more search operators that apply to index searches, and they change as improvements are made and capabilities enhanced. I suggest visiting the EnCase help feature, as shown in Figure 7.103; on the Contents tab, see Searching Through Evidence ➢ Searching Indexed Data ➢ Search Operators for a listing of the various operators along with helpful examples.

There are times when saving a search is desired, which usually means you want to run the search again in the future and don't want to take the time to re-create the search terms and logic. Also, you may be operating under strict searching guidelines that were crafted by attorneys arguing for days at their billable rates. In those cases, you want to apply the exact agreed-upon search criteria repeatedly and to have a record of that search in the event the search criteria is later questioned. Regardless of your underlying reasons for doing so, EnCase provides the mechanism. To save your search, go to the Searches menu on the Search tab and choose Save As, as shown in Figure 7.104. The default location will be `Documents\EnCase\Search`, which is a global location. If you would prefer to store them with the case, simply change the path. You should give the search file a name that describes the search and click Save. Any time in the future that you want to recall this search, simply go to this same menu and choose Open instead.

FIGURE 7.103   EnCase help feature with listing of available Search Operators with examples

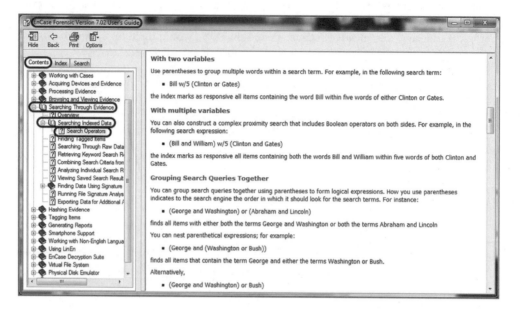

FIGURE 7.104   Saving a search for later use

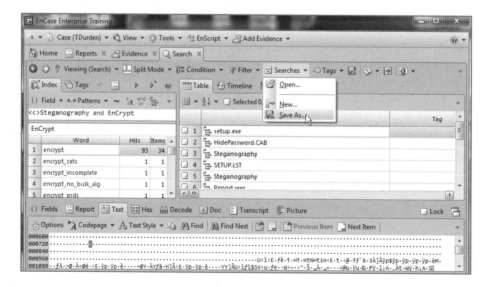

Tags

Thus far, I have not discussed tags. I did not see the point in tags, initially, until I realized that you can search for them, and then their true potential became visible. So, this seems to most appropriate point at which to discuss them. You can apply tags, both default and user-created ones, to items in EnCase and then later search for them from the Search tab. Very quickly, let's apply a tag and then search for it. Locate any item in the Table view and then locate the Tag column. I would suggest widening the Tags column for reasons that will quickly become obvious. Hold your cursor over the Tag column for any particular item, and you will see the various tags that are available appear as you move your cursor from left to right (or vice versa) within the Tag field, as shown in Figure 7.105. You need only click the desired tag, and the item is so tagged, as shown in Figure 7.106. You can add multiple tags, and you can toggle tags on and off. The Tags menu appears on various toolbars, and you can manage your tags from there, deleting, changing, and creating them as you see fit. I would suggest not having too many because they become rather cumbersome when you do.

FIGURE 7.105   Passing cursor over Tag field reveals available tags

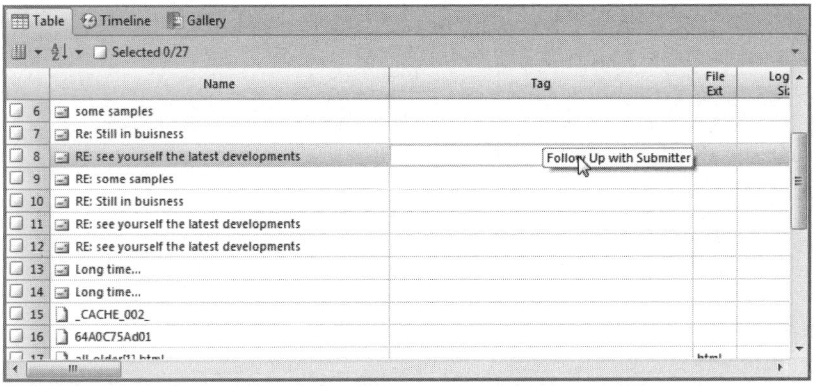

FIGURE 7.106   An item tagged for "Follow Up"

Now you can tag! I mentioned that you can search for them, so let's switch to the Tags tab in the Search tab. You should immediately see your tag names listed in the left pane. The total number of tagged items for each tag will reflect in the Count column for that particular tag. If the number is zero it is black. If it is other than zero, it will be blue. Since the blue indicates a hyperlink, you need only to click that link to have the items revealed in the Table View pane, as shown in Figure 7.107. Alternatively, you can place a blue check box in the tag's box and click the Play button. Either method will run the query. You can see in Figure 7.107 that the only item matching my query was the item I just tagged in Figure 7.106.

FIGURE 7.107   Query returned for tagged items

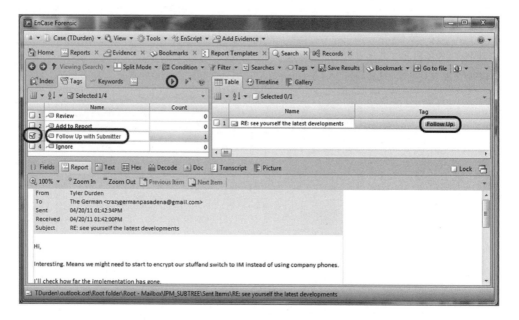

Before we conclude searching, let's cover two quick items. First is the Results tab. Whenever you run a query, we've seen that the results are sent to the Table pane to the right in the Index, Tags, or Keywords tabs, all within the Search tab. Simultaneously, they are also sent to the Results tab, which can be viewed from the View menu. You have a less cluttered interface to work with the results of the query, as shown in Figure 7.108. Some prefer it, and others do not.

Sometimes you may encounter a situation in which you may want to combine an index query with a keyword query or perhaps even a tag query. If you wanted to do so, you could place a blue check mark for the query criteria in each of the tabs (Index, Tags, and/or Keywords) and then activate the query across all tabs with selected items. The button to activate this special query is immediately to the right of the play button and is shown in

Figure 7.109. The results will be sent to both the Table pane and the Results tab, as previously mentioned.

FIGURE 7.108   Queries are also sent to Results tab, which offers a less-cluttered interface for working with search hits.

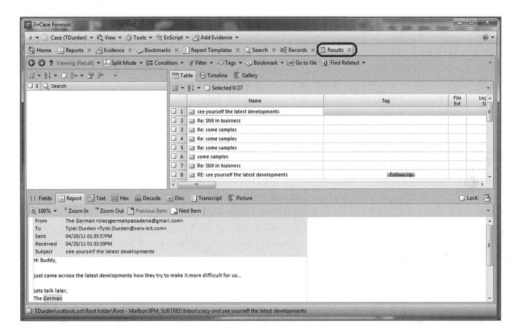

FIGURE 7.109   Search using combined criteria from all tabs

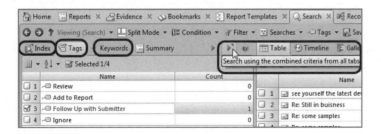

Do not search for words included in the noise file. If the word *the* appears in the noise file and you search for *the book*, EnCase will not return a hit for *the book* no matter how many times it exists.

Summary

This chapter covered data in its binary and hexadecimal formats. You learned that various storage devices have physical, optical, or electrical states of positive or negative, yes or no, on or off, and so on, that are rendered into 1s and 0s. Binary (base-2) is a system based strictly on 1s and 0s and is the system used by computers to store and transmit data.

A bit is the smallest unit and can have two outcomes, 1 or 0. A byte consists of 8 bits and can have 256 possible outcomes. A byte consists of two 4-bit nibbles. Of those two nibbles, there is a left nibble and a right nibble. Each nibble can have 16 possible outcomes.

Two bytes combined is called a *word*, which is 16 bits. Four bytes combined is called a *Dword*, which is 32 bits. Larger still is a *Qword*, which is four words and 64 bits.

Hexadecimal is a programmer's shortcut for expressing binary numbers. Each nibble of the byte is evaluated separately. Because each nibble can have 16 possible outcomes, those integer values are represented by a single character ranging from 0 to F (0, 1, 2, 3, 4, 5, 6, 7, 8, 9, A, B, C, D, E, F), which represents the integers 0–16, respectively. Each nibble is represented by a single character, and the two characters are combined to represent the entire byte.

ASCII was originally a 7-bit character set consisting of 128 of the common numbers, characters, and special characters. It is also called *low-bit ASCII*. To include some foreign languages, graphics, and math symbols, this character set was expanded to an extended 8-bit character chart. It consists of 256 characters and is often called *high-bit ASCII*.

As computing became global, the world's varied languages could not be expressed in a 256-character set. Unicode evolved to remedy this situation, allowing 2 bytes per character.

Best practices call for evidence file verification and adjustment of time zone offsets as the first steps after adding evidence to a case. The next step in the process, normally, is to run the EnCase Evidence Processor, which carries out many essential preprocessing tasks, such as recovering folders, analyzing file signatures, analyzing hashes, building a text index, and other tasks.

EnCase 7 has a powerful indexing engine for carrying out index searches, by which you can conduct searches against an index for near-instantaneous search results. Before you can do such a search, you must first create the index. The index is created when you run the EnCase Evidence Processor, which is new to EnCase 7.

EnCase uses keywords as search stings by which to conduct searches. Keywords can be created individually or in groups using keyword lists. Keywords can be imported from EnCase keywords that were exported.

When searching, you create and select keywords by which to search. You also select the data on which the search is to be conducted. You have various options when searching, such as case-sensitive searches, Unicode searches, and others. You can create specialized code pages for foreign-language searches.

Another type of search option is a GREP search. GREP searches allow special characters to be used to construct search terms that can greatly enhance your searching capabilities.

Keyword searches are carried out from the Raw Search menu or can be carried out from the EnCase Evidence Processor. Index searches are carried out from the Index tab of the Search tab.

Once a raw search has been conducted, the results are sent to the Table pane of the Keywords tab and to the Results tab. Search hits can be sorted in the Table view pane.

Files containing search hits can be tagged for further analysis in the Case view. Files containing search hits can be bookmarked from the Search Hits view.

Files or items can be tagged using default tags or user-created tags. Once tagged, items can be searched by those tags on the Search tab.

There are several types of bookmarks. One of the most common and feature-rich bookmarks is the highlighted data bookmark. Using this bookmark, data can be viewed in vast array of formats. The destination folder can be selected, created, or rearranged.

Files can be bookmarked individually as notable file bookmarks or in groups of files that have been selected. Table views can be bookmark using a special bookmark type, named a Table view bookmark. If data is viewed using the Decode tab, the results of the decoding process can be bookmarked using the Data Structure bookmark. Bookmarks are linked to the EnCase report; however, the link may not be automatic, depending on where the bookmark is placed. If a new folder or subfolder is created, the examiner may have to go to the Reports Template and edit the section to link the bookmark folder to a particular section in the report. Metadata for bookmarked files in reports can also be modified in the Reports Template, specifically in a particular section's formatting options for each bookmark type.

Bookmarks can be moved, deleted, or rearranged. Bookmarks are the foundation from which reports are generated. Creating a well-organized tree of bookmarks with meaningful folder names is essential to creating a good report. When a report is customized, it can be saved as a template, and future cases can benefit from less input during case setup and later with a customized professionally appearing report.

Examiners should take the time necessary to learn to create well-designed and well-organized bookmarks because they translate into well-designed and well-organized reports.

Exam Essentials

Understand binary data concepts.   Understand and explain how binary data is stored and translated into human-readable text and numbers. Be able to interpret a binary byte into its hexadecimal format. Understand hexadecimal representation and be able to convert between binary, hexadecimal, and decimal formats. Be able to interpret a binary byte into its integer or ASCII value.

Know and understand the ASCII and Unicode character sets.   Explain what the 7-bit low-bit ASCII character set is. Explain what the 8-bit high-bit extended ASCII character set is and how it evolved. Explain how a given hex value could be a character in one context but an integer in another context. Understand and explain the difference between 09h (decimal integer 9) and 39h (printed character 9).

Understand how Unicode evolved and how many bytes are used to represent one character. Know how many characters can be represented by Unicode.

Understand keywords and their implementation into the search process.   Explain how to create keywords. Understand and be able to explain how keyword searches can be saved. Be able to export and import keywords. Understand the importance of naming keywords.

Understand GREP search expressions.   Know and be able to explain what GREP means. Be able to create GREP expressions to search for specified search strings. Given a GREP expression, be able to determine which strings will match and which strings will not match. Know the purpose and function of the keyword tester.

Know and understand how to conduct searches.   Understand and be able to explain how to conduct a raw search in EnCase. Know what search options are available from the Raw Search menu and how they affect the search results.

Understand the Search Tab and the various tabs thereunder.   Understand and explain the features and functions available in the Search Tab view. Explain the various tabs in this view and their purpose. Explain how files containing search hits are bookmarked or tagged.

Know and understand how to create bookmarks.   Understand and be able to describe what a bookmark is and how to create each bookmark type. Understand how to decode data from a highlighted data bookmark and what the various view types are. Explain how to select destination folders. Explain the importance of organizing folders into a meaningful hierarchical format with folder names that describe their contents. Explain how to move folders and bookmarks. Describe how a report is generated and how bookmarks are linked to reports. Explain the purpose of the report template and some of the functions that can be carried out in that view. Understand the various formats by which reports can be exported or saved. Explain the process of generating a paperless report.

Know and understand how to run the EnCase Evidence Processor.   Understand and be able to describe how to launch the EnCase Evidence Processor. Explain the function and importance of processing items with a red flag. Describe the various functions and features of the processing options available in this interface. Explain how to acquire while running the EnCase Evidence Processor.

Know and understand how to conduct an index search.   Understand and be able to describe how to create an index and explain the options for creating the index. Know where the index file is stored and how its location is configured. Describe how to query an index from the Index tab. Explain the various search operators and know the syntax for the common types. Explain a noise file. Explain the function and features of the Results tab.

Review Questions

1. Computers use a numbering system with only two digits, 0 and 1. This system is referred to as which of the following?

   A. Hexadecimal

   B. ASCII

   C. Binary

   D. FAT

2. A bit can have a binary value of which of the following?

   A. 0 or 1

   B. 0–9

   C. 0–9 and A–F

   D. On or Off

3. A byte consists of ___ bits.

   A. 2

   B. 4

   C. 8

   D. 16

4. If 1 bit can have two unique possibilities, 2 bits can have four unique possibilities, and 3 bits can have eight unique possibilities. This is known as the power of 2. How many unique possibilities are there in 8 bits (2^8)?

   A. 16

   B. 64

   C. 128

   D. 256

5. When the letter *A* is represented as 41h, it is displayed in which of the following?

   A. Hexadecimal

   B. ASCII

   C. Binary

   D. Decimal

6. What is the decimal integer value for the binary code 0000-1001?

   A. 7

   B. 9

   C. 11

   D. 1001

7. Select all of the following that depict a Dword value.

    A. 0000 0001

    B. 0001

    C. FF 00 10 AF

    D. 0000 0000 0000 0000 0000 0000 0000 0001

8. How many characters can be addressed by the 7-bit ASCII character table? 16-bit Unicode?

    A. 64 and 256

    B. 128 and 256

    C. 64 and 65,536

    D. 128 and 65,536

9. Which of the following are untrue with regard to the EnCase Evidence Processor?

    A. A device must be acquired first before processing or be acquired as a requisite first step within the EnCase Evidence Processor.

    B. A live device can be subjected to normal processing by the EnCase Evidence Processor and does not have to be acquired first.

    C. Items marked with red flags denote items that are not applicable to the file system being processed.

    D. Items marked with red flags denote items that must be run during the first or initial run of the EnCase Evidence Processor and can't be run in any subsequent run thereafter.

    E. A raw keyword search can be conducted during processing by the EnCase Evidence Processor.

10. When performing a keyword search in Windows, EnCase searches which of the following?

    A. The logical files

    B. The physical disk in unallocated clusters and other unused disk areas

    C. Both A and B

    D. None of the above

11. By default, search terms are case sensitive.

    A. True

    B. False

12. By selecting the Unicode box for a raw search, EnCase searches for both ASCII and Unicode formats.

    A. True

    B. False

13. With regard to a search using EnCase in the Windows environment, can EnCase find a word or phrase that is fragmented or spans in noncontiguous clusters?

A. No, because the letters are located in noncontiguous clusters.

B. No, EnCase performs a physical search only.

C. No, unless the File Slack option is deselected in the dialog box before the search.

D. Yes, EnCase performs both physical and logical searches.

14. Which of the following would be a raw search hit for the *His* keyword?

A. this

B. His

C. history

D. Bill_Chisholm@gmail.com

E. All of the above

15. Which of the following would be a search hit for the following GREP expression?

`[^a-z]Liz[^a-z]`

A. Elizabeth

B. Lizzy

C. Liz1

D. None of the above

16. Which of the following would be a search hit for the following GREP expression?

`[\x00-\x07]\x00\x00\x00...`

A. 00 00 00 01 A0 EE F1

B. 06 00 00 00 A0 EE F1

C. 0A 00 00 00 A0 EE F1

D. 08 00 00 00 A0 EE F1

17. Which of the following would be a search hit for the following index search expression?

`<c>Saddam npre/3 Hussein`

A. Saddam Alfonso Adolph Cano Hitler Hussein

B. saddam alfonso adolph cano hitler hussein

C. Saddam Alfonso Hussein Adolph Cano Hitler

D. saddam alfonso hussein adolph cano hitler

E. Hussein Hitler Cano Adolph Alfonso Saddam

F. None of the above

18. Which of the following will *not* be a search hit for the following GREP expression?

[^#]123[\-]45[\-]6789[^#]

   A. A1234567890

   B. A123 45-6789

   C. A123-45-6789

   D. A123 45 6789

19. A sweep or highlight of a specific range of text is referred to as which of the following?

   A. Table view bookmark

   B. Single item bookmark

   C. Highlighted data bookmark

   D. Notable file bookmark

   E. Notes bookmark

20. Which of the following is *not* correct regarding EnCase 7 index searches?

   A. Before searching, the index must first be created using the Create Index EnScript.

   B. Before searching, the index must first be created using the EnCase Evidence Processor.

   C. All queries are case insensitive regardless of any switches or settings, because that is the nature of all indexed searches.

   D. By default, queries are case insensitive but can be configured to be case sensitive.

   E. A query for any word in the noise file will not return any items as all words in the noise file are ignored and excluded from the index.

Chapter 8

File Signature Analysis and Hash Analysis

ENCE EXAM TOPICS COVERED IN THIS CHAPTER:

- ✓ File signatures and extensions

- ✓ Adding file signatures to EnCase

- ✓ Conducting a file signature analysis and evaluating the results

- ✓ Understanding the MD5 hash

- ✓ Creating hash sets and libraries

- ✓ Importing hash sets

- ✓ Conducting a hash analysis and evaluating the results

This chapter will cover two data analysis techniques that are core skill sets for competent examiners because they are used in most examinations. You should, therefore, strive to master these techniques and their associated concepts.

The first technique is the file signature analysis. Most files have a unique signature or header that can be used by the operating system or application program to identify a file. Often, files have filename extensions to identify them as well, particularly in a Windows operating system. The file extensions and headers should, in most cases, match, although there are a variety of exceptions and circumstances where there is a mismatch, no match, unknown information, or anomalous results. A file signature analysis will compare files, their extensions, and their headers to a known database of file signatures and extensions and report the results.

The second technique is the hash analysis. You have used the MD5 and/or SHA1 hash to verify acquisitions of digital evidence, such as hard drives or removable media. You'll use that same MD5 and/or SHA1 hash to derive hash values of individual files and compare them to known databases of hash values. In this manner, you can identify known files by their MD5 and/or SHA1 hash. If they are known safe files, such as program files, they can be eliminated from further analysis. If they are known contraband files, they can be quickly identified and bookmarked.

Both techniques are important tools for forensics examiners to use when analyzing data. I'll begin the discussion with the file signature analysis.

File Signature Analysis

As you can imagine, the number of different file types that currently exist in the computing world is staggering—and climbing daily. Many, certainly not all, have been standardized and have unique file signatures or headers that precede their data. The two bodies that have undertaken this standardization are the International Organization for Standardization and the International Telecommunications Union Telecommunications Standardization Sector (ITU-T). When standardized headers are present, programs can recognize files by their header data. Also, many standardized files have unique extensions that are associated with the file's unique header.

Understanding Application Binding

The process by which an operating system knows how to open a particular file type with a given application is called *application binding*. There are many methods employed by various operating systems, and it is beyond the scope of this book to enter this realm too deeply, but you must at least give it some consideration so you can understand the topic at hand.

Windows, for example, uses file extensions to associate or bind specific file types with specific applications. File extensions are the letters that follow the last "dot" in a filename. Under this system, a file with the extension of .pdf will typically be opened by Adobe Reader. Windows cares only about the extension and nothing about the header. If you take a .jpg file and change its extension to .pdf, Windows will pass it along to Adobe Reader to open. Adobe Reader will report an error or problem with the file, and the file will fail to open.

Windows stores its application binding information in the registry. Because this setting can vary between users, it is stored in the user's registry file, which is ntuser.dat. The key where this information is found is \Software\Microsoft\Windows\CurrentVersion\Explorer\FileExts. Each registered extension will have its own key. Each of those keys has two subkeys: OpenWithList and OpenWithProgids. The information directing which program to open the extension is in these two subkeys.

The fact that Windows uses file extensions and not headers gives rise to a data-hiding technique in which the user changes the extension of the file to obscure its contents. If a file named MyContrabandImage.jpg was changed to lansys32.dll and moved to the system32 folder, the casual observer would probably never find it. Even a systems administrator would probably miss it. Even if someone noticed the file, an attempt to open it in Windows would fail.

EnCase would not, however, miss its contents once a file signature analysis had been conducted, which you'll soon understand as you progress through this chapter.

Other operating systems such as Unix (including Linux) use header information to bind file types to specific applications. Those systems are, therefore, not dependent on file extensions. You will find that many files on those operating systems do not have file extensions.

Mac operating systems use a combination of methods to bind files to applications. Macintosh uses the Hierarchical File System Plus (HFS+) on its current operating system, which is OS X. Macintosh legacy systems used an older version of this file system known as HFS. As part of the file system metadata, a Mac stores a 32-bit value called a *file type code* and another 32-bit value called a *creator code*. File type codes are 4-byte codes describing the various file types. Creator codes are 4-byte values assigned to various programs that create files. As of about 2003, there were more than 58,000 different file type and creator codes available in a third-party database for use in analyzing these codes. Legacy Mac operating systems use this metadata (file type code and creator code) to bind files with applications.

This system allows considerable flexibility, much to the delight of Mac users. One JPEG image can be opened by one program, while another JPEG image can be opened by another program based on the application that created the file rather than on its extension.

The Internet is changing the way the Mac operates, because cross-platform file exchanges are a way of life. When OS X arrived on the scene, application developers were asked to add file extensions as programs created files. Mac users protested, but the protests fell on deaf ears because Apple still insists on extensions for new Mac applications.

Mac OS X uses a list of seven rules of precedence for application binding. The first priority goes to "user defined," meaning that if a user chooses to open a specific file with a specific application, this setting will override all other settings. The second priority goes to the creator code, meaning that the application that created the file will open it as long as there is no overriding "user defined" setting. The third priority is that of file extension, which is new to the Mac world with the advent of OS X. If there is no "user defined" setting and no creator code, Mac OS X will use the file extension as the means to bind the file to an application. The last four rules of precedence are rather complex and go beyond the scope of this discussion. If the topic interests you, search `www.apple.com/search/` for the phrase *application binding*.

In Mac OS X version 10.7 (nicknamed Lion), if a Mac file lacks a "user defined" setting and lacks a creator code, the operating system looks next to the file extension to determine which application to use to open that file. If that file extension has been renamed to hide the file's true nature, the file does not open or opens with the application bound to that extension, which usually means it can't be properly viewed. Thus, as file extension application binding finds its way into the Mac operating systems, it creates another method for obscuring data on those systems. You can expect to see more filename extensions in the future when you examine Mac systems because application developers, despite protests, are being instructed to use filename extensions when they create applications. Following that trend, you may expect the use of file extension changes to hide data on Mac systems to rise commensurately.

Creating a New File Signature

When conducting a file signature analysis, EnCase compares a file's header, if one is present, with its extension, if one is present. This information is compared to a file types database of known file signatures and extensions that is maintained within EnCase and stored in the `FileTypes.ini` file. In EnCase 7, the signature data in the former `FileSignatures.ini` file was merged into the `FileTypes.ini` file.

To better understand the information stored in the file types database, let's examine the information in this database and create a new file signature. First you must go to the File Types view, which is located at View ➤ File Types, as shown in Figure 8.1.

The File Types view is a table or database of file extensions, categories, names, headers, footers, viewers, and other metadata. Any item selected in the Table pane can be viewed in the View pane from either the fields or report pane, which is the same data visible in the Table view except in a report format instead of in a tabular format. Figure 8.2 shows a standard `.jpg` file type in both the tabular and report views.

FIGURE 8.1   The file types database is accessed from the View menu on the application toolbar.

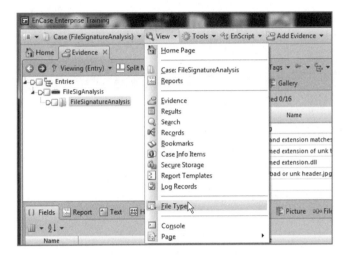

FIGURE 8.2   File Types view provides an interface to a database of file signatures from which you can add, modify, or delete file signature records.

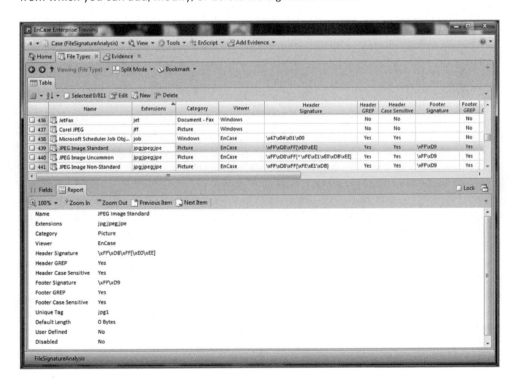

To add a record, click New on the File Types table toolbar. You will be presented with the New File Type dialog box, as shown in Figure 8.3.

FIGURE 8.3   The New File Type dialog box lets you enter Description, Extensions, file Category, Viewer, header, and footer strings. There are three tabs: Options, Header, and Footer.

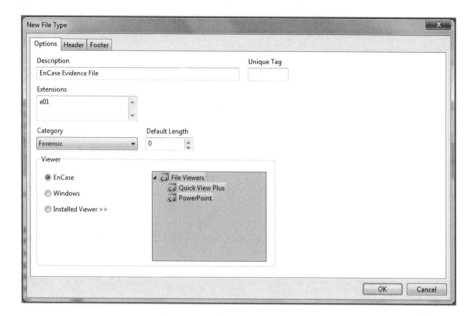

Deleting a record is as simple as right-clicking a particular record and choosing Delete. You can also, of course, choose a record and then click Delete on the File Types toolbar.

In this example, I added an EnCase Evidence File signature and placed it in the Forensic category. After entering the hex string, I selected the GREP check box. (See Figure 8.4.) For the extension, I entered **e01**, as shown in Figure 8.3. When done, I clicked OK, and the new signature was added to the database. This point is a good time to select File ➢ Save All.

Let's modify a record. You can double-click a file type record to open its properties, or you can select the file type, right-click, and choose Edit to open the same properties screen. Finally, you can choose a record and click Edit in the File Types toolbar. In this example, I'm choosing the file record named Outlook Express Email Storage File. From my analysis work, I have determined that this file signature is used not only by Outlook Express but also by MSN Mail for its local storage. The former has a file extension of .dbx and is already entered in the Extensions tab. There is no extension listed for the MSN Mail extension, which is .MailDB. You'll modify the name to include MSN mail and add the MSN mail extension, so double-click the file type Outlook Express Email Storage File, and you'll see the dialog box shown in Figure 8.5, which also reflects a name change for the file signature.

FIGURE 8.4   Header tab of the New File Type dialog box into which I've placed the header string for an E01 EnCase Evidence File type, choosing the GREP option

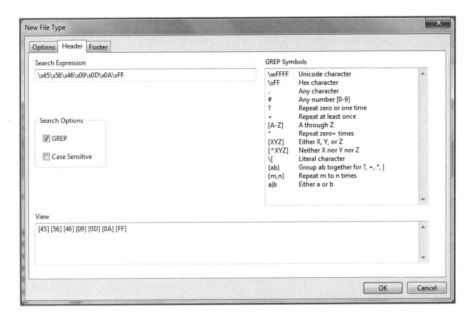

FIGURE 8.5   Options tab for editing a file type record. In this example, I have added "& MSN Mail" to the description and added an extension, delimited by a semicolon.

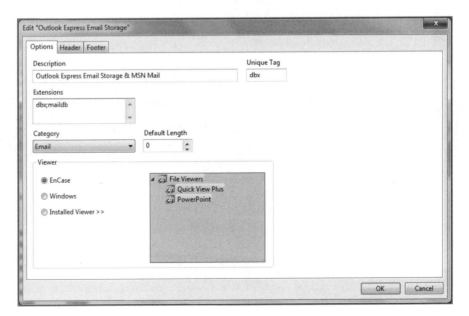

After changing the name to something that reflects its dual role, you next go to the Extensions field. Multiple extensions are separated by a semicolon as a delimiter. No spaces are used, only the delimiter. In this case, you're adding the extension `.maildb`, as shown in Figure 8.5. When done, click OK to change the record.

Conducting a File Signature Analysis

Now that you have an understanding of the information in the database, you can use that information to carry out a file signature analysis. From the File Signatures view, switch back to the Case Entries view. When running a file signature analysis, typically you want to run it over all the files in the case so that EnCase can rely on the true file type for all files instead of their extensions. With legacy versions of EnCase, you had to select files and run a file signature analysis on those selected files as an option from the search dialog box. Starting with EnCase 7, a file signature analysis is built into the Encase Evidence Processor. When you run the EnCase Evidence Processor, a file signature analysis is automatically run as a normal task during the first run.

To run a file signature analysis, simply launch the EnCase Evidence Processor and choose any set of options. You have no choice regarding choosing a file signature analysis because it is a locked option and will run always, as shown in Figure 8.6. When your processing options are selected, click OK to start processing.

FIGURE 8.6   File Signature Analysis is a locked option, meaning it will always run during the first run of the EnCase Evidence Processor.

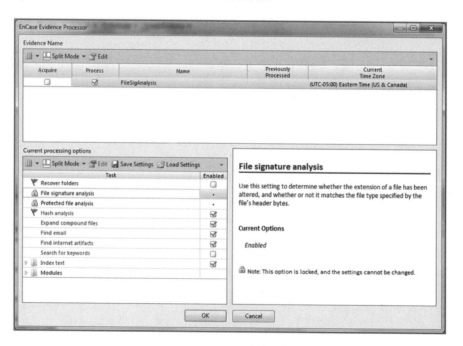

During a file signature analysis, EnCase examines every file on the device selected for processing and looks at its header to see whether there's a matching header in the database. If it finds one, then the header is known. EnCase next looks at the file's extension and compares it with the extension listed in the database for that known header. If the header is known and the extension matches, EnCase reports a match. If there is no extension for a given header in the file signature table, EnCase will report a match for any extension as long as the file's extension doesn't match any other header listed in the file extension table.

If EnCase can't find the file's header in the file signature database and it also can't find the file's extension in the database, EnCase reports the status of this file as unknown.

If EnCase locates a file's header in the file signature database, the header is known. If the extension that should correspond with the file's header is missing or incorrect, the header information is presumed correct and prevails. In such cases, EnCase reports the alias for this file and its proper signature.

Figure 8.7 shows a single file from a Mac OS X system. The filename is background. Note that the file, like many on Mac systems, is missing a file extension. Because no file signature analysis has yet occurred, EnCase is relying on file extensions to determine file type. Because there is no extension, EnCase does not show this file as an image. If you look at the data in the Hex view, however, you can see that its header is FF D8 FF E0, which with time you will immediately recognize as a JPEG image. Note that the Table view columns have been optimally arranged for file signature analysis; they are, from left to right, Name, File Ext, Signature, Signature Analysis, and File Category.

FIGURE 8.7   Image file from a Mac system. This file has no file extension. Since no file signature analysis has yet been run, EnCase does not yet recognize this file as an image.

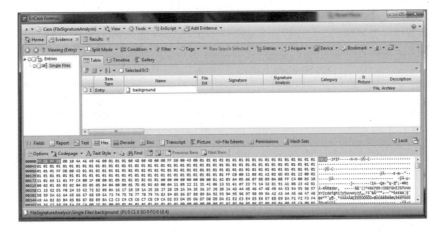

When a file signature analysis has been conducted and a file with a known header has a missing or incorrect extension, its *alias* is reported based on the file header information. Figure 8.8 shows the same image file after the file signature analysis has been run. Under Signature, EnCase reports JPEG Image Standard and notes an alias in the Signature Analysis column. Because EnCase now knows this file is a picture, the Picture view is enabled in the View pane, and the image appears there. Additionally, you will note that the category is now Picture and that the Is Picture column now has a positive Boolean value (a dot) in it.

FIGURE 8.8 The same picture files after a file signature analysis has been conducted. Note the alias is reported in the Signature Analysis column and that JPEG Image Standard appears in the Signature column.

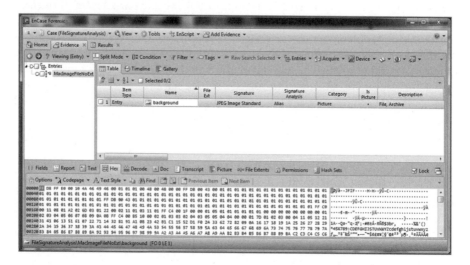

Another set of conditions often occurs during file signature analysis that is known as a *bad file signature*. When EnCase discovers a file that has a known extension and that extension has a known header but the file's header does not match that header or any other header in the database, the file status shows Bad Signature in the Signature Analysis column. Table 8.1 summaries the file signature status types reported by EnCase.

TABLE 8.1 Summary of file signature analysis status report

Filename	Header	Header in table	Extension	Signature	Signature analysis
picture.jpg	FF D8 FF E0	Known	Known and matches	JPEG Image Standard	Match
picture.dll	FF D8 FF E0	Known	Known and incorrect	JPEG Image Standard	Alias
anyfile.zza	FF D6 FE FF	Unknown	Unknown		Unknown
picture.jpg	D8 D8 FF E0	Unknown	Known and doesn't match		Bad Signature

Although it is rare, you can sometimes encounter an anomaly in which a file header matches a known header and the extension is in the table but has no header. In this case, EnCase believes the header information and reports the file with an alias for the header even though the file extension is correct. This sounds a bit confusing until you see an example, and then it makes perfect sense.

If EnCase were to encounter a text file during a file signature analysis and the first two letters of the text file were someone's initials, such as PK, you would encounter this anomaly. This is because a text file can start with anything, so it has no header. EnCase would identify the initials as a known header for a ZIP file. EnCase expects to see a .zip extension with a ZIP header. EnCase resolves conflicts using the header information, which means the file would be reported with an alias for a ZIP file even though it was a bona fide text file. These encounters are rare, but should they occur, you will recognize them for what they are based on your understanding of the file signature process and the rules for evaluating and reporting the results.

Just before press time, EnCase 7.04 was released and with it came some changes. One that was nearly overlooked was the changing of the column names Signature and Signature Tag to File Type and File Type Tag. This began as a change late in EnCase 6.19, changing the column name from Signature to File Type. To be consistent, EnCase 7.04 carried through this change, extending it to include the change from Signature Tag to File Type Tag. The text and figures in this section will reflect EnCase 7.03, but you should note the change going forward with EnCase 7.04.

File signatures are an important part of the examination process and are now built into the Evidence Processor. File signature analysis is done at the beginning of your processing so both you and EnCase are seeing files for what they really are. To make sure you understand this important tool, you'll run a file signature analysis in Exercise 8.1.

EXERCISE 8.1

Performing a File Signature Analysis

In this exercise, you'll run a file signature analysis on a small evidence file that contains a concise example of all the various file signature analysis results you will typically encounter. The filenames depict their file signature conditions and are intended to help you understand the results. It is a good exercise to do shortly before your examination to help solidify the file signature analysis concepts. Let's begin.

1. Start a new case in EnCase 7, naming it **FileSigAnalysis**. In the folder structure created by EnCase 7 for this case, create an additional folder named **Evidence**. Download the file FileSigAnalysis.E01 from the publisher's site for this book and place this file in the newly created folder.

2. From the Home screen, choose Add Evidence ➤ Add Evidence File. Browse to the Evidence folder, select the evidence file you just downloaded, and add it to the case.

3. From the Evidence tab, select the newly added evidence file. In the View pane, choose either the Field or Report tab. Check to see that the evidence file verified. Since this is a small evidence file, the verification process occurs very quickly, and no progress will have been seen.

4. Return to the Tree view pane, and in the table, double-click the evidence file to cause it to parse and load. You will now be viewing the entry after it loads. In the Tree pane, open the file structure. It should contain one folder, named FileSignatureAnalysis. Select that folder, and the 10 files in that folder should appear in the Table view pane. Arrange your columns to optimize them for file signature analysis. Arrange them, from left to right, as follows: Name, File Ext, Signature, Signature Analysis, Category, Is Picture, and Description (you may want to refer to Figure 8.7).

5. In the Table Pane, switch to the Gallery view. EnCase sees three files with extensions that indicate they are pictures and attempts to show all three, but only two are visible. Switch back to the Table view.

6. On the Evidence tab, just under the Home icon, click the green left arrow. On the Evidence toolbar, click Process Evidence. Place a check mark under Process for the FileSigAnalysis device. Accept all default settings, which will include File Signature Analysis because it is locked. Click OK, and the process should complete in less than a minute.

7. From the Evidence tab's Table view, double-click the evidence item FileSigAnalysis again to cause it to parse and load with the case processor information included. You will be taken to the viewing entry screen. With the focus in the Tree pane on the folder FileSignatureAnalysis, go to the Table view. Sort the Signature column by double-clicking the column head. Add a secondary sort on the File Ext column by holding down the Shift key and double-clicking its column head.

8. The first file in the list should be a JPEG file with a bad or corrupted header. If you look at the data in the Hex view, you'll see that the header does not match that of a JPEG header. Since it matches nothing else either, it is reported as Bad Signature. The filename clearly spells out its contents.

9. The second file has both an unknown header and an unknown extension and is reported as Unknown.

10. The third file in the list is a Thumbs.db file, which is created when a user opts for the thumbnail view in Windows Explorer.

11. The fourth file in the list is a JPEG image file with its extension renamed to .dll. In the Signature column, EnCase is now showing this file as *JPEG Image Standard. Furthermore, it is treating the file as a picture and is displaying it as such. The same holds true for the seventh file, which is an image file with its extension renamed to .zza.

12. Files 5 and 6 are examples of various files that match.

13. Figures 8 and 9 are examples of text files. The `.txt` extension is known, but since a text file can start with anything, they report as matches. Some legacy versions of EnCase will report entry 8 as a ZIP file if still using an older header definition ("PK" for the header), which then makes it an anomaly, as previously mentioned.

14. Switch to the Gallery view in the Table Pane. EnCase reports five files now as pictures and attempts to display them correctly. One fails to display as its header is corrupted, leaving four actual pictures that display. EnCase is now displaying images it did not display before the file signature analysis.

15. Save your case, and exit. You may use this evidence and case file at any time you need to quickly review the file signature analysis and reporting.

You've looked at a file signature analysis at the micro level to understand it, which is great for that purpose. It does, however, not lend itself very well to real-world cases in which there are hundreds of thousands of data sets. If you want to see the results of a file signature analysis by renamed extension, bad signature, or unknown, you can do so using a filter. From the Evidence tab, you can click Filter on the Evidence toolbar. Under Filter, choose Find Entries By Signature, as shown in Figure 8.9. The filter menu process will start to run, as shown in Figure 8.10. Note the options, and accept the defaults by clicking OK. Figure 8.11 shows the next set of options, which are the various signature conditions. In this example, I have selected Renamed Extensions. Click OK to apply the filter.

Veteran EnCase users would normally expect to see the filter applied to the evidence items on the Evidence tab, but such is not the case with EnCase 7. To see the filtered results, go to the Results view, as shown in Figure 8.12. From this view, you can bookmark, view, decode, or perform most any other analysis function that you could employ on the Evidence tab. It allows you to keep your various sets of results and view them instantly, making it a much-improved workflow and workspace when compared to legacy versions.

FIGURE 8.9   File signatures filter

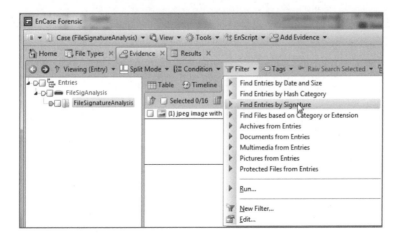

FIGURE 8.10   Run menu for the file signatures filter with some options

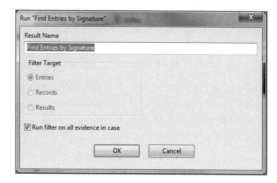

FIGURE 8.11   Options for different signatures from which you can choose any or all

FIGURE 8.12   Results of the file signature filter are viewable only in the Results view.

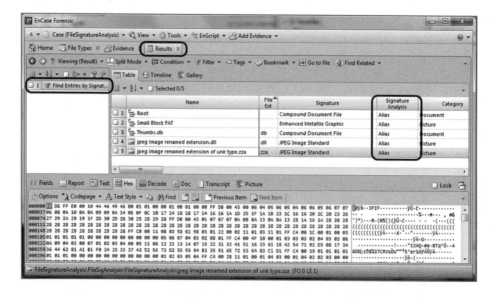

Hash Analysis

When I discussed acquisitions and verifications in Chapter 4, I covered the concept of hashing using the MD5 and SHA1 algorithms. An MD5 or SHA1 hashing algorithm, like other hashing algorithms, can be applied to any stream of data. All that is needed is a starting point and an ending point. In the context of acquisitions, the hashes were of volume and physical devices. In the following sections, I take a more granular approach and show how to conduct your hashing at the file level.

MD5 Hash

As you recall, an MD5 hash is an algorithm that is calculated against a stream of data with the end result being a 128-bit value that is unique to that stream of data, be it a device, a volume, a file, or a stream of network data. The odds of any two dissimilar files having the same MD5, better known as a *hash collision*, is one in 2^{128}, which is 340 billion billion billion billion and some change. The resultant statistical value is such that you can safely assume that the only file that will produce the same hash value is an exact duplicate of that file. Said another way, if two files have the same hash value, you can safely assume that the two files are identical in content. The inverse of this is also true, in that if two files produce different hash values, those files do not have the same content. (The names of the two files don't matter, because the hash calculation is conducted on the data contained in the file only and the file's name is stored elsewhere.) These concepts form the basis of hash analysis.

For those curious types who are wondering about the odds for an SHA1 hash collision, because the SHA1 algorithm produces a 120-bit value, there are 2^{160} possible outcomes. Expressed using scientific notation, the MD5 has 3.402823669209387e+38 possible outcomes, and the SHA1 has 1.461501637330904e+48 possible outcomes. To wrap your head around such numbers, take the astronomical figures produced by the MD5 hash and add another 10 zeros!

Hash Sets and Hash Libraries

When a file is hashed, the result is one hash value of one file. A hash set is a collection of one or more hash values that are grouped together because of common characteristics. The hash set may be a collection of hash values from a hacking tool such as SubSeven. In such a case, the hash values for that program are calculated and then gathered into a group of values and given a label, for example, SubSeven. Hash set examples could be Windows 7 program files, case "xyz contraband files," and the like. Hash libraries are collections of hash sets, which is concept you may want to remember!

EnCase has a feature that allows you to import hash sets from external sources. EnCase also lets you create custom hash sets at your discretion.

Before you can create any hash sets from within EnCase, you must first create a hash library container, which is a folder containing a series of file-based, database-like structures into which EnCase will store hash sets. To do this, I first created a folder in the EnCase 7 program files and named it Hash Libraries. I created two subfolders, one named Hash Library #1 and the other named NSRL, as shown in Figure 8.13.

FIGURE 8.13   Folder and subfolders created to contain Hash Libraries

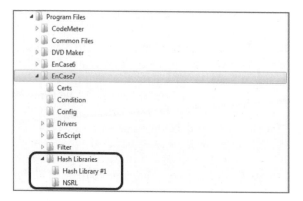

The latter subfolder (NSRL) came about by means of decompressing the NSRL files that are available when you register your dongle with Guidance Software, as shown in Figure 8.14. You need only register your dongle, download the compressed NSRL hashes, place the self-extracting file in the Hash Libraries folder, and extract. When you are done, you'll have folder named NSRL containing an EnCase 7 hash library, as shown in Figure 8.15.

FIGURE 8.14   Email link to latest NSRL hash sets received after registering your dongle

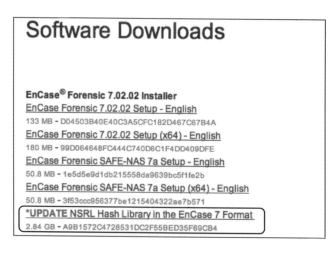

FIGURE 8.15   NSRL hashes in EnCase 7 hash library after downloading and decompressing

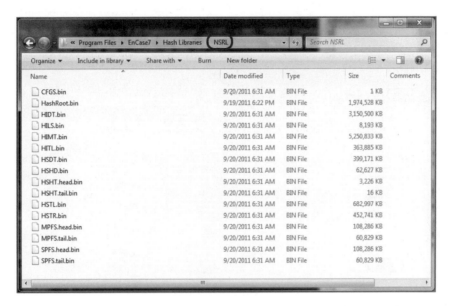

Now that you've created a folder structure to contain your custom hash sets and also created an NSRL hash library, the next step is to manage your hash sets. From here, you can create, open, edit, import, or export hash libraries and sets. To open the hash library manager, go to the Tools menu on the application toolbar and choose Manage Hash Library, as shown in Figure 8.16

FIGURE 8.16   Hash library manager on Tools menu

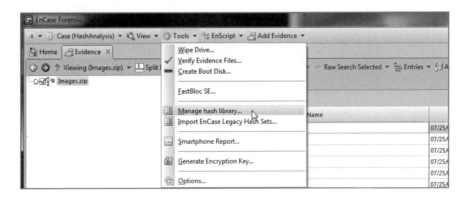

The first step is to open the NSRL hash library you just added. To do so, click Open Hash Library from the toolbar, and browse to the NSRL folder just created, as shown in Figure 8.17. Once it's open, you'll see the list of NSRL hash sets in this open library, as shown in Figure 8.18.

FIGURE 8.17 Opening a hash library

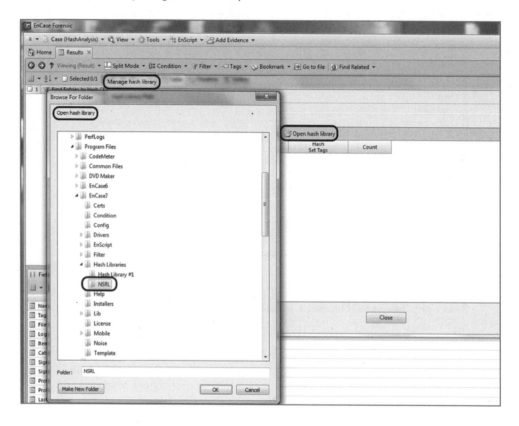

FIGURE 8.18 NSRL hash library open

		Name	Category	Hash Set Tags	Count
☐	1	Canvas			10,938
☐	2	Gallery			200,229
☐	3	Decimals Made Easy			122
☐	4	Microsoft Office XP Small Business			8,485
☐	5	Microsoft Office XP			6,972
☐	6	Microsoft Office XP			6,362
☐	7	Microsoft Licensing			9,555
☐	8	Office XP			7,828
☐	9	Publisher Deluxe with Photo Editing			13,533
☐	10	Office XP - for Students and Teachers			8,585
☐	11	Office XP			10,964
☐	12	Office XP 2002			6,356
☐	13	Office XP			9,904
☐	14	Office XP Small Business			8,458
☐	15	Applications Microsoft Office Family			8,855
☐	16	Linux Developers Resource			8,321

Now that you've opened an existing hash library, let's next create a new hash library in the contained folder you created, named Hash Library #1. From the Hash library manager, click New Hash Library and browse to the folder you created a few moment ago, as shown in Figure 8.19. Once you've directed EnCase to the path of your container folder (the new hash library), click OK. EnCase informs you that a hash library has been created at that location, as shown in Figure 8.20. If you look at the contents of that once empty container folder, you'll find that it has just been populated with the hash library database files, even though it's currently void of any hash sets, as shown in Figure 8.21. If you take note of your hash library manager, you'll see that the hash library you just created is open, but that it is also empty, with no hash sets yet in the newly created database, as shown in Figure 8.22.

FIGURE 8.19   Creating a new hash library

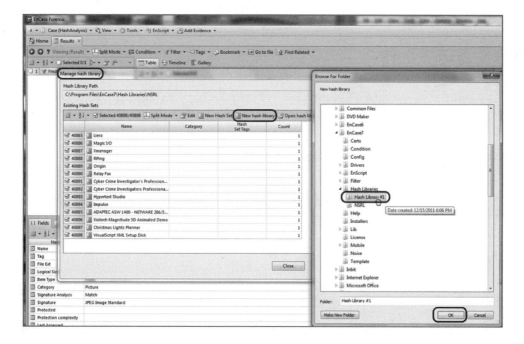

FIGURE 8.20   Message indicating successful creation of new hash library with path

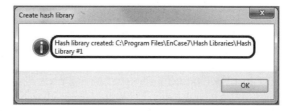

FIGURE 8.21 Hash library database files just created

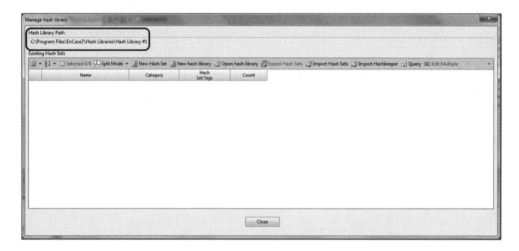

FIGURE 8.22 The new hash library is open, but it doesn't contain any hash sets at this point.

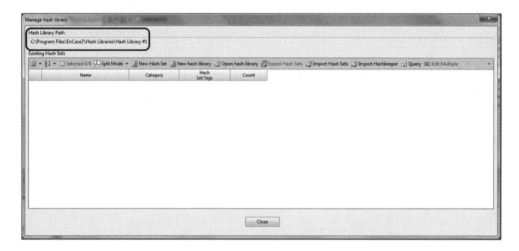

You may have collected large volumes of hash sets over your forensic careers using EnCase. As you've now surmised, EnCase 7 uses a much different format, and you are probably thinking you've lost your valued hash sets, but don't worry—EnCase 7 has a tool to import legacy hash sets quickly and easily. If you look immediately under Manage Hash Library in the Tools menu, you'll find another tool named Import EnCase Legacy Hash

Sets, shown in Figure 8.16. Click that menu item, and you'll see a dialog box as shown in Figure 8.23. You need to provide the path to your target hash library and to your legacy or source path containing your old or legacy hash sets. Make sure to place a check mark in the box directing EnCase to append the hash sets to the existing hash library. Click OK, and the process should be very quick.

FIGURE 8.23   Importing legacy hash sets into EnCase 7

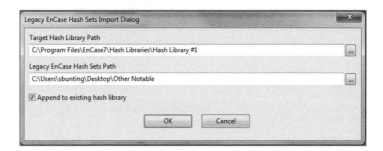

At this point, you can open the hash library manager to which you imported and view your legacy hash sets now in Encase 7, as shown in Figure 8.24. You will note that Notable was in the legacy hash sets and imported into the Category column. The Hash Set Tags column is new, and I edited that column according to the various types of hash sets.

FIGURE 8.24   Legacy hash sets imported into EnCase 7 hash library

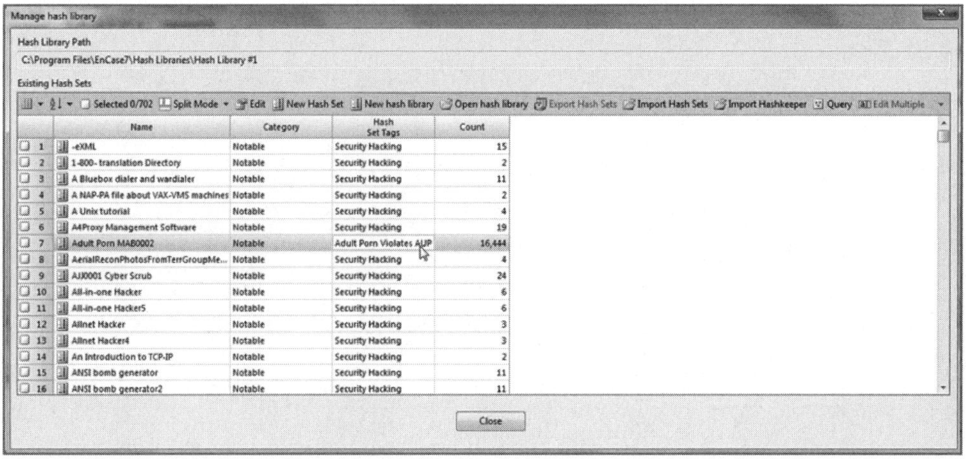

From the hash library manager interface, you can export selected hash sets, import hash sets, import Hashkeeper hash sets, and run queries against the open hash library database. Most of these are fairly straightforward operations; however, the ability to conduct queries is new to EnCase 7 and can be a very useful utility. Sometimes you have a file and its hash, or sometimes just a hash, and want to see whether it is known to your hash collection without subjecting the entire set of evidence files to processing just to find out.

To make a query, simply copy the file's hash value (MD5 or SHA1). Then, from within the hash library manager, launch the query from the toolbar and paste the hash value in the window so labeled. Next, click the query button; if the value is present, you'll see the results, as shown in Figure 8.25. By default, the view will be of the metadata, as shown in Figure 8.25. Figure 8.26 shows the other view, which is of the hash sets. If no hash set is found in the database, you will see nothing returned. You can query only the open database, so if you have multiple hash libraries, you'd need to open each one and make the query.

FIGURE 8.25 Querying the open hash library for an MD5 hash

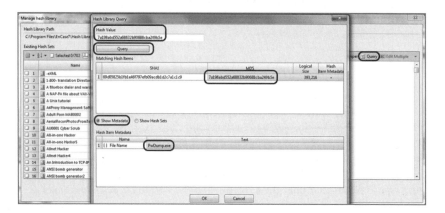

FIGURE 8.26 Alternate view showing hash sets instead of metadata

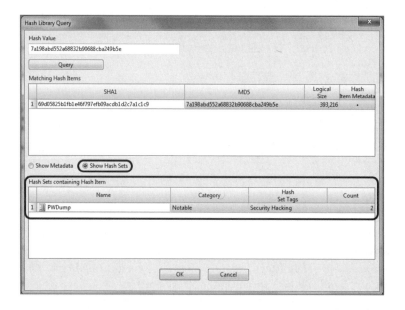

At this point, you've used the hash library to create hash libraries, import legacy data into hash libraries, and create an NSRL hash library. You've also seen how to query the hash library. Let's suppose you want to create a hash set and add it to one of your libraries. First, you must have a set of files that have hashes. Hashes are created when running the EnCase Evidence Processor, which is one way of generating hashes. However, there can be times when you want to create a hash set very quickly. There is a way of hashing selected files. In fact, the same tool allows you to just as quickly and easily run file signatures.

To do so, select (blue check mark) the files you want to hash. In my example, I have dragged and dropped a folder containing malware into EnCase, and the Single Files container automatically launches and contains these files. I have selected them so that I can act upon that selection. Next, I open the Entries menu on the Evidence toolbar and select Hash\Sig Selected, as shown in Figure 8.27. In the resulting dialog box, you can choose MD5, SHA1, and/or Verify File Signatures, as shown in Figure 8.28. I have chosen all three options in our example and clicked OK to finish.

FIGURE 8.27   Hashing or running file signatures on selected files

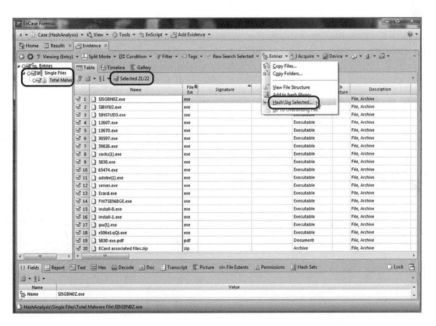

FIGURE 8.28   Options for hashing and file signatures

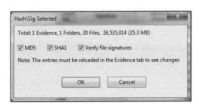

The hash values will not populate in the current view without additional user action. Click the green back button to go back to the Evidence Table tab, and double-click the evidence item to reopen it such that you are viewing the entries again, however this time with the updated hash information populated, as shown in Figure 8.29. You can see that both MD5 and SHA1 hashes were generated. Now that you have hash values for your files, you can create a hash set.

To create a hash set, you must select the files to be included in the set with blue check marks. Figure 8.29 shows that selection having been made. Next, click the Entries again, and this time select Add To Hash Library, which you will observe in Figure 8.27 to be directly above the Hash/Sig Selected tool. Next you will see the Add To Hash Library dialog box shown in Figure 8.30. At the top, you need to choose which hash library will contain the set. I have selected my secondary hash library.

On the right side, you can choose the metadata to include with each record in the hash set. The default selections (Name, Logical Size, MD5, and SHA1) are almost always adequate. The final decision is picking which hash set to place the new hashes. You can select an existing hash set with a blue check mark, or you can create a new one into which you can place the hashes. To create a new hash set, right-click anywhere in the Existing Hash Sets table area and choose New Hash Set, as shown in Figure 8.31. In the Create Hash Set dialog box, shown in Figure 8.32, give it a Hash Set Name, a Hash Set Category, and any Hash Set Tags to describe the contents. Click OK to create new set, and a message indicating successful completion should appear, as shown in Figure 8.33.

FIGURE 8.29   MD5 and SHA1 hashes created

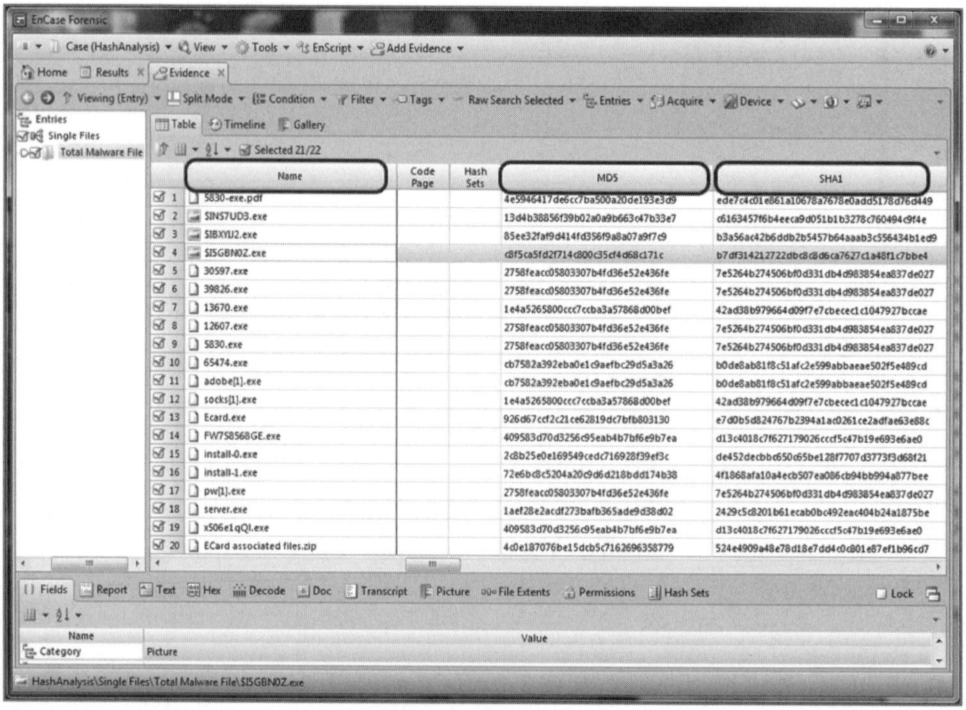

FIGURE 8.30   Add To Hash Library dialog box

FIGURE 8.31   Creating a new hash set

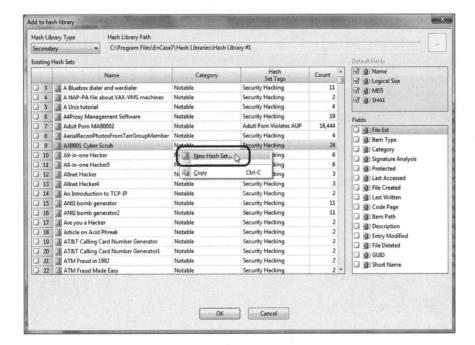

FIGURE 8.32   Providing new hash set with name, category, and hash set tags

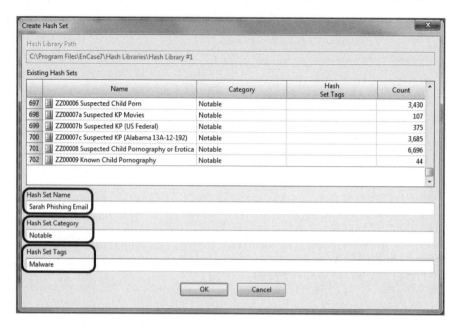

FIGURE 8.33   Successful creation of new hash set

Once the new set is created, select the new set to contain the new hash sets, and click OK, as shown in Figure 8.34. When you do, the dialog box will disappear as the new hash set is created. Of course, some of us, including me, like to know that the set was created. To do so, simply open the hash library manager and check the hash library to make sure, as shown in Figure 8.35.

FIGURE 8.34   New hash set selected to receive new hash set

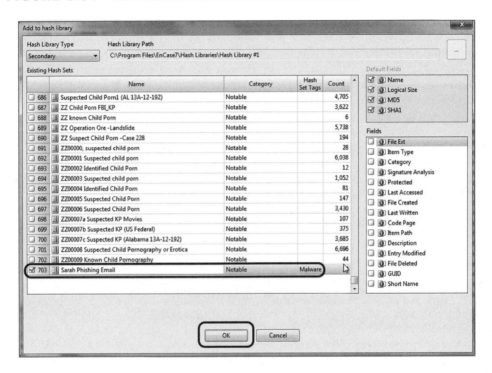

FIGURE 8.35   Verifying new hash set in hash library manager

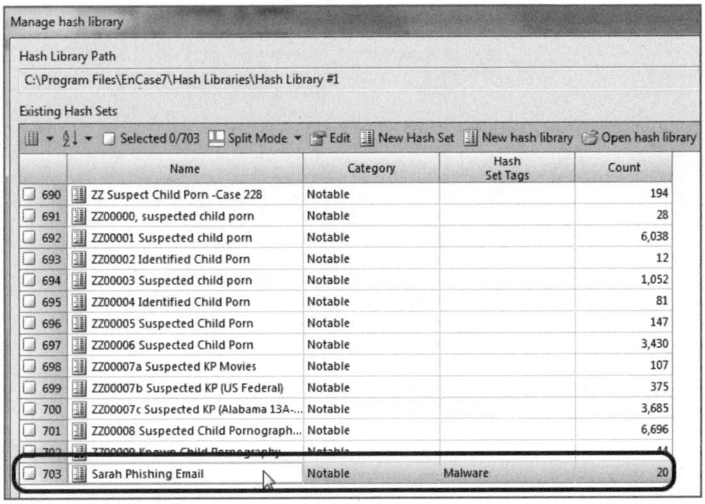

Hash Analysis

So far, you have created hash libraries and created hash sets, but you have as yet to apply given hash libraries and hash sets to a particular case. Until you do, there are no comparisons being made between hash values of files in your evidence with hash values found in your libraries. You apply the hash libraries from the Home screen for the particular case. In this example, I have a case named HashAnalysis open, and on the Home screen for this case, there is an option named Hash Libraries, as shown in Figure 8.36.

The resulting Hash Libraries option is the location by which you identify and select up to two hash libraries to apply to your case. The first time you use EnCase, you have to use Change Hash Library to identify the path to your two libraries (or just one if you so choose). Once you select the paths, you need to enable them with a blue check. Finally, you'll need to select which hash sets within the libraries to include. If you right-click within the "existing hash sets" table area, you'll get a menu that allows you to select all items, among other options, as circled and shown in Figure 8.36. When you are satisfied with your choices, click OK to apply the hash libraries to your case.

FIGURE 8.36   Hash Libraries option on Home screen of open case

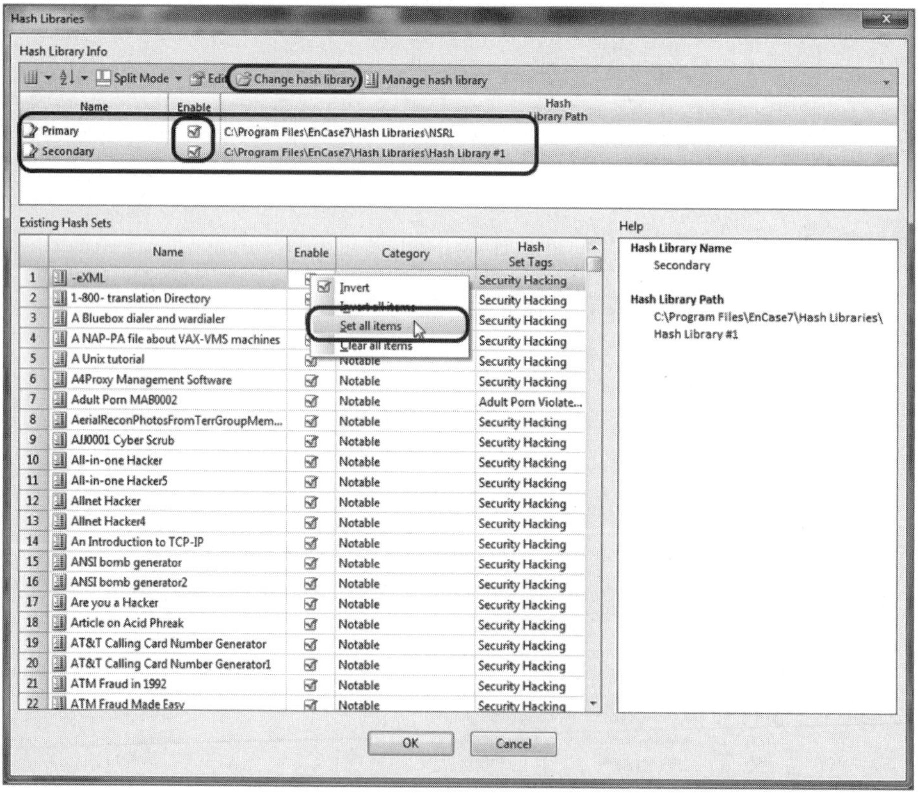

Before you can benefit from hashes and hash libraries, you must first hash the files in your case. As you should recall, there are two methods to hash your files. One is using the Evidence Processor, as shown in Figure 8.6, and the other is to select files and to choose Hash/Sig Selected, as shown in Figure 8.27. Once the hashing is complete, you can analyze the results by one of several methods.

You may recall during your search options that you can save time by opting to not search in the file content areas of files that were found in the hash libraries. This is a great "under-the-hood" benefit derived from hashing your files and maintaining extensive hash libraries.

With your hashing completed and your libraries applied to your case, you are now able to view the results of your hash analysis. At the most basic analysis level, any file that has a hash value appearing in the active hash libraries will have a positive Boolean value in the Hash Set column, as shown in Figure 8.37. In this example, an executable file named Ecard.exe was downloaded while following a link in a phishing email. It is malware and has been identified as such in my hash set; because it is malware, I have placed it in a Notable category, on which I can later filter. When a file's hash appears in the hash library, the information regarding its hash set is available on the Hash Set tab of the View pane. From this view, you can see the properties of the hash set.

FIGURE 8.37 View of file with hash value in hash library, including the Hash Sets tab in View pane

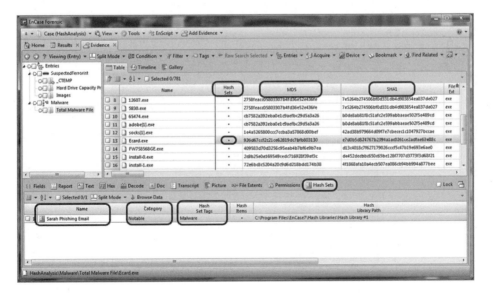

EnCase has a filtering tool that enables you to filter on hash categories. From the Evidence tab toolbar, open the Filter drop-down menu and choose Find Entries By Hash Category, as shown in Figure 8.38. In the screen that follows, accept the defaults, including the Run Filter On All Evidence In Case option, and click OK. In the screen that follows (Find Entries By Hash Category), you will find a listing of all available categories. In my example, I have located the Notable category, selected it, as shown in Figure 8.39, and finally I will click OK to apply the filter.

FIGURE 8.38   Running the Find Entries By Hash Category filter

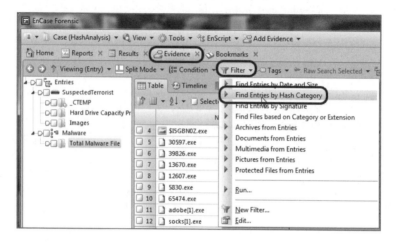

FIGURE 8.39   Selecting Notable hash category

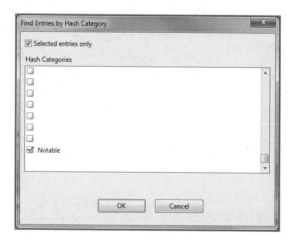

Once the filter has been applied, you will be taken to the results tab where you can work with the filtered set of files in much the same manner as you can on the Evidence tab.

Legacy versions of EnCase built a hash library from selected hash sets and, in doing so, deduplicated hash sets as they were added. Thus, if a hash appeared in multiple hash sets, only the first one added would be included in the hash library. This was done for performance but excluded potentially important information. For example, if a hash appearing as known in an NSRL hash set were added first, a subsequent identical hash value listing the hash as notable would be excluded. Thus, you had to be careful about the order in which hash sets were added to the hash library. With EnCase 7, if a hash value appears in multiple hash sets, you will see a report that indicates every hash set in which the hash appears. EnCase 7's improved database structure affords a much higher performance level along with greater extensibility and information.

When you select hash sets for inclusion in the hash library and you subsequently conduct an analysis using those hash values, you are locating files meeting criteria contained in those hash values. Thus, you are imposing a search on the files in the case. When selecting hash sets for inclusion in your hash library, make certain you are within the scope of your search authority, whatever that may be in your particular case. Let's assume your search authority in a case was limited to evidence relating to embezzlement. If you included known child pornography hash sets in your hash library and located child pornography using hash analysis, you have most likely exceeded the scope of your search authority in most jurisdictions. Make sure hash sets that are in your hash library are included or covered within the scope of your search authority!

You can use the EnCase filter for various hash categories, including queries on Known and Notable (or any other category you create). For these conditions to produce accurate results, be sure to exercise care with case and spelling when creating and importing hash sets. More than once, I've seen these categories incorrectly spelled while importing hash sets from examiners who are super folks and willing to share their work, but unfortunately there is no spell checker within most forensic tools.

Hash analysis can help you cut down on searches by eliminating known files. It can also assist you in rapidly locating files that can be identified from databases of known contraband or inappropriate content files, such as child pornography, adult pornography, hacking tools, and the like. Keep your hash sets up-to-date and share them when you develop unique sets. You should conduct your hash analysis early on in your case so the benefits can be realized from that point forward in your examination.

Summary

In this chapter, I covered file signature analysis and hash analysis. File signature analysis is a tool or process used within EnCase to identify a file by its header information, if it exists, rather than by the default method, which is file extension. File header and extension information is stored in a database in the file FileTypes.ini. File signature information can be added, deleted, or modified in the File Types view, which is a global view.

Until a file signature analysis is run, which occurs by default when the EnCase Evidence Processor runs, EnCase relies on a file's extension to determine its file type, which will in turn determine the viewer used to display the data. Once a file signature analysis is run, EnCase will view files based on file header information and not based on file extension. This is critical for viewing files whose extensions are missing or have been changed.

After a file signature analysis has been run, EnCase reports the results in the Signature and Signature Analysis columns. If a file's header and extension information are correct and match the information in the database, EnCase will report a match. If there is no matching header for a file and no matching extension, EnCase will report the file as Unknown. If a file's extension is in the database, the file's header does not match the header in the database for the file's extension, and further does not match any other header in the database, EnCase will report the file as having a Bad Signature. Finally, if a file's header is in the database and the extension is missing or doesn't match for the header, the signature has precedence in determining file type, and the file's true signature is reported in the Signature column with the word *Alias* appearing in the Signature Analysis column.

File hashing and analysis, within EnCase, are based on the MD5 hashing algorithm in addition to the SHA1 hashing algorithm. When a file is hashed using the MD5, the result is a 128-bit value. The odds of any two dissimilar files having the same MD5 hash is one in 2^{128}, or approximately one in 340 billion billion billion billion. Using this method, you can safely statistically infer the file content will be the same for files that have identical hash values, and the file content will differ for files that do not have identical hash values.

The MD5 or SHA1 hash thus forms a unique electronic fingerprint by which files can be identified. Using this method, files are hashed and collected in sets for files having similar characteristics. These groupings of hash values are called *hash sets*. Each set is given a name describing the group of files represented by the hash values. Furthermore, each hash set is assigned to a hash category, usually Known or Notable. A hash library contains a series of hash sets.

Files are hashed from within the EnCase Evidence Processor or from the Evidence tab's Entries menu tool named Hash\Sig Selected. Once files have been hashed and have hash values, you can create hash sets by selecting files and choosing Add To Hash Library from the Entries menu on the Evidence tab toolbar. Hash sets are stored in the databases of the EnCase hash libraries.

Hash sets are managed from the hash library manager. Hash sets can be added and edited from within this management tool. Also from this tool, hash sets can be imported from NSRL or Hashkeeper hash databases. From this view, selected hash sets are placed into the hash library, which is a collection of hash sets. Hash libraries are applied to a case from the Home screen for any given open case. Up to two libraries can be used with any case. From within the Hash Libraries dialog box, individual hash sets within hash libraries can be enabled or not.

Once files have been hashed, each file's hash value is listed. If, during the comparison process, the hash value matches any value in the hash library, a positive result will appear in the Hash Sets tab in the bottom pane, with the properties of the hash set(s) in which the value is included. Using this hash analysis, you can identify known files of various types. Known system and program files can be eliminated from further examination and searching, thereby saving time. Files that are notable for various reasons (hacking tools, contraband files, and so on) can be identified, and the appropriate action can be taken.

Hash analysis and file signature analysis both should be carried out at the beginning of your examination so that their benefits can be utilized at the outset, and they are included in the Evidence Processor for this reason. Reporting or output from the file signature can be analyzed by sorting on appropriate columns. In addition, various filters are available to assist with both file signature analysis and hash analysis. Both tools provide information to EnCase internally and to the examiner that greatly assists in the speed and accuracy of the examination process.

Exam Essentials

Know and understand the file signature process.   Understand and explain what a file header is. Be able to explain what a file extension is and how it is used in a Windows environment. Understand how a file type and category are determined before and after the file signature analysis process. Understand how EnCase views files and the importance of the file signature analysis to the proper viewing of file types.

Understand the purpose and function of the File Types view.   Know where the file types database is stored (FileTypes.ini). Explain how a file signature is created, modified, or deleted. Be able to explain what information is stored in a file signature record.

Understand and interpret the results of the file signature analysis.   Know and understand what constitutes a file signature match, a bad signature, an unknown signature, and a file signature alias. Explain how to use EnCase's column sorting features or file signature filter to analyze or view the results of the file signature analysis.

Know and understand file hashing and analysis.   Understand and be able to explain the MD5 and SHA1 algorithm. Know the length of an MD5 hash and the approximate odds of any two dissimilar files having the same MD5 hash value. Explain the significance of files having the same or different hash values. Explain the concept of an MD5 hash being an electronic fingerprint.

Know and understand what constitutes a hash set.   Explain how to hash a file. Explain what a hash set is and how it is created. Understand and be able to describe the process of naming and categorizing hash sets. Know where hash sets are stored and be able to explain their filenaming convention.

Understand the purpose and function of the hash library manager.   Explain what tasks can be carried out in the hash library manager. Understand and be able to explain the difference between hash sets and hash libraries. Explain the purpose of the hash library and how one is created.

Understand and interpret the results of a hash analysis.   Be able to explain what it means when a file has a hash value that returns a Notable value. Explain the importance of hash analysis in reducing search times. Explain how to use a filter to locate files with a Notable hash category.

Review Questions

1. When running a signature analysis, EnCase will do which of the following?

   A. Compare a file's header to its hash value.

   B. Compare a file's header to its file signature.

   C. Compare a file's hash value to its file extension.

   D. Compare a file's header to its file extension.

2. A file header is which of the following?

   A. A unique set of characters at the beginning of a file that identifies the file type.

   B. A unique set of characters following the filename that identifies the file type.

   C. A 128-bit value that is unique to a specific file based on its data.

   D. Synonymous with file extension.

3. The Windows operating system uses a filename's _____ to associate files with the proper applications.

   A. signature

   B. MD5 hash value

   C. extension

   D. metadata

4. Unix (including Linux) operating systems use a file's _____ to associate file types to specific applications.

   A. metadata

   B. header

   C. extension

   D. hash value

5. The Mac OS X operating system uses which of the following file information to associate a file to a specific application?

   A. The "user defined" setting

   B. Filename extension

   C. Metadata (creator code)

   D. All of the above

6. Information regarding a file's header information and extension is saved by EnCase 7 in the _____ file.

   A. `FileTypes.ini`

   B. `FileExtensions.ini`

   C. `FileInformation.ini`

   D. `FileHeader.ini`

7. When a file's signature is unknown and a valid file extension exists, EnCase will display the following result after a signature analysis is performed.

   A. Alias (Signature Mismatch)

   B. Bad Signature

   C. Unknown

   D. Match

8. When a file's signature is known and the file extension does not match, EnCase will display the following result after a signature analysis is performed.

   A. Alias (Signature Mismatch)

   B. Bad Signature

   C. Unknown

   D. Match

9. When a file's signature is known and the file extension matches, EnCase will display the following result after a signature analysis is performed.

   A. Alias (Signature Mismatch)

   B. Bad Signature

   C. Unknown

   D. Match

10. When a file's signature and extension are not recognized, EnCase will display the following result after a signature analysis is performed.

    A. Alias (Signature Mismatch)

    B. Bad Signature

    C. Unknown

    D. Match

11. Can a file with a unique header share multiple file extensions?

    A. Yes

    B. No

12. A user can manually add new file headers and extensions by doing which of the following?

    A. Manually inputting the data in the `FileSignatures.ini` file

    B. Right-clicking the file and choosing Add File Signature

    C. Choosing the File Types view, right-clicking, and selecting New in the appropriate folder

    D. Adding a new file header and extension and then choosing Create Hash Set

13. Select the correct answer that completes the following statement: An MD5 hash
_____.

    A. is a 128-bit value

    B. has odds of one in 2^{128} that two dissimilar files will share the same value

    C. is not determined by the filename

    D. All of the above

14. EnCase can create a hash value for the following.

    A. Physical devices

    B. Logical volumes

    C. Files or groups of files

    D. All of the above

15. With EnCase 7, how many hash libraries can be applied at one time to any case?

    A. One

    B. Two

    C. Three

    D. No limit to the number that can be applied

16. Will changing a file's name affect the file's MD5 or SHA1 hash value?

    A. Yes

    B. No

17. Usually a hash value found in a hash set named Windows 7 would be reported in the Hash
Category column as which of the following?

    A. Known

    B. Notable

    C. Evidentiary

    D. Nonevidentiary

18. With regard to hash categories, evidentiary files or files of interest are categorized as which
of the following?

    A. Known

    B. Notable

    C. Evidentiary

    D. Nonevidentiary

19. An MD5 or SHA1 hash of a specific media generated by EnCase will yield the same hash value as an independent third-party MD5 or SHA1 hashing utility.

    A. True

    B. False

20. A hash _____ is comprised of hash _____, which is comprised of hash _____.

    A. set(s), library(ies), value(s)

    B. value(s), sets(s), library(ies)

    C. library(ies), set(s), value(s)

    D. set(s), values(s), library(ies)

Chapter

9

Windows Operating System Artifacts

ENCE EXAM TOPICS COVERED IN THIS CHAPTER:

✓ Windows dates and times

✓ Adjusting for time zone offsets

✓ Recycle Bin and INFO records

✓ Windows Recycle Bin

✓ Link files

✓ Windows folders

✓ Recent folder

✓ Desktop folder

✓ My Documents folder

✓ Send To folder

✓ Temp folders

✓ Favorites folder

✓ Windows Low folders

✓ Cookies folder

✓ History folder

✓ Temporary Internet files

✓ Swap file

✓ Hibernation file

✓ Printing artifacts

✓ Windows volume shadow copy

✓ Windows event logs

Not many years ago, when Microsoft was announcing the release of Windows XP, many examiners were proclaiming the end of computer forensics. They claimed that the new security features of Windows XP were going to virtually eliminate all forms of artifacts and other evidence. Of the folks making these dire warnings, some were among the "who's who" of computer forensics. Windows XP arrived, and just like its predecessor (Windows 2000), it offered more operating system artifacts than did any release of Windows to date.

Even as XP artifacts were still being discovered, Microsoft released Windows XP's replacement, which was Windows Vista. Because Vista was not exactly well received, it was eventually replaced by Windows 7. Although Windows Vista and 7 changed some parts of the forensic landscape, others remain unchanged. Just as with all releases of Windows, Windows Vista and 7 have provided their fair share of new artifacts, and others will no doubt be discovered incrementally over the next few years as examiners test, probe, hack, reverse engineer, and so forth.

Because the term *artifacts* may not be a familiar term for some, here's what they are in a nutshell. As operating systems grew more complex, they simply stored more data. As operating systems evolved, paradoxically their user interface had to simplify so that computers could be used easily by users with few or no computer skills. To facilitate this interface and its ease of use, the operating system had to store even more information about the user, such as their actions, preferences, and credentials. The result of such data storage is an environment that is loaded with artifacts, which take the form of logs, files, lists, passwords, caches, history, recently-used lists, and other data. Some is in plain text, some is obscured, and some is encrypted (albeit weak encryption in far too many cases). As a general category or label, you refer to this type of data or information as *operating system artifacts*. Most important, you can use this data as evidence to identify users and their computing activities.

The subject of Windows operating system artifacts could well fill several books. Clearly such an endeavor is well beyond the intent and purpose of this guide. In this chapter, the focus is on developing a solid understanding of the more common operating system artifacts rather than trying to cover them all.

Dates and Times

It is difficult to approach any Windows operating system artifact without some prior appreciation for how Windows stores and uses dates and times. Dates and times are ubiquitous on any modern operating system. Their uses are countless, and their storage formats vary. Sometimes they are stored in local time and sometimes in Greenwich mean time (GMT, also known as Universal Time or Zulu Time). Sometimes, usually involving Internet-related data, the times are local to the time zone where they were generated and not necessarily local to the host computer. If there was ever a topic that will cause you to pause and scratch your head in this business, the time issue is at or near the top of the list.

You need only look at the forensic list serves and message boards to see the questions related to date and time stamps. Although it is great to pose questions and have them answered by other examiners, there is no substitute for research and testing by the individual examiner. Once you have tested and validated your findings, only then will you have a true understanding and firsthand knowledge because, until then, it is only hearsay!

Time Zones

Before attempting to understand how time is stored and interpreted, you must first understand the context in which it is being interpreted. By *context*, I'm referring to the time zone reference in which the time was stored. Because the world is divided into time zones and computers must keep track of time relative to those time zones, the various operating systems must implement methods to account for time zone differences. In order to accurately interpret date and time stamps, you must understand how operating systems and EnCase resolve these differences. Although each operating system has its own method, I'll limit this discussion to the Windows operating systems.

For Windows file-attribute dates and times (modified, accessed, and created, which are often called MAC times) the file system in use determines whether the date and time is stored in local time or in GMT.

When date and time stamps are recorded in a FAT file system, they are stored in the 32-byte DOS directory entry in local time, which is the time for the time zone for which the computer is configured. This system was developed when computing was more local and less global.

As computing became more global and the Internet evolved, Microsoft developed the NTFS file system and with it implemented a more elaborate and yet more logical time storage scheme. Dates and times stored for file creation, last written, last accessed, and last entry modified are stored in GMT using a 64-bit Windows date and time stamp. The operating system displays dates and times to the user based on the local time zone offset, which is normally set when the system is first configured but can be adjusted at any time.

Just because a computer was seized in a particular time zone does not mean it is configured for that time zone. Figure 9.1 shows the Windows dialog box in which the time zone is set. Because computers can be moved from one zone to another, incorrectly configured, or deliberately altered, the time and time zone offset may not be accurate. To resolve these issues, you need to know the machine's BIOS time and the time zone offset for which it is configured so you can apply the correct time zone offset to your case.

FIGURE 9.1   Windows 7 Time Zone Settings dialog box showing the Time Zone drop-down on which the user sets the local time zone

Prior to EnCase 4, you had to change the time zone offset of your examination machine (using the dialog box such as that shown in Figure 9.1) to match the time zone of your evidence. Starting with EnCase 4, there is an interface by which the examiner can set a time zone offset at the case or device level so all devices in a case are in proper time zone synchronization.

Aside from MAC times, as a general rule, you will find that today's Windows operating systems store most, not all, dates and times in GMT. These include dates and times stored in the registry, Internet history databases, and other operating system artifacts. Generally, you'll be looking to a published source to make such determinations. At other times, you'll be on your own to test and validate the data to make the determination.

Windows 64-Bit Time Stamp

Before I cover determining time zones and actually making adjustments, let's first examine the Windows 64-bit date and time stamp. This time stamp is one you'll learn to spot at a glance as you gain experience. Figure 9.2 shows a 64-bit Windows time stamp. It is an 8-byte string (64 bits), and its most significant value is 01h, which is located at the far right of the string because it is stored in little endian. As you'll recall, little endian values are calculated from right to left; thus, the most significant byte is on the right. This is the first value entered and calculated.

Now that you understand what the time stamp looks like, I'll discuss how it tracks time. I'll start with a concept I've already covered. If you'll recall, a Unix time stamp is a 32-bit integer value that represents the number of seconds that have lapsed since *epoch*, which is January 1, 1970, 00:00:00 GMT. It's an incredibly simple concept, and with a little math, you can figure out that the most number of seconds that can be represented by this value is 2^{32}, which is the integer value 4,294,967,296.

FIGURE 9.2   The Windows 64-bit time stamp with the most significant bit (01h) stored to the far right of the 8-byte string

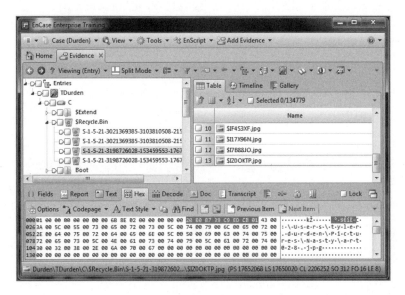

On Monday, December 2, 2030, at 19:42:58 GMT, 4,294,967,296 seconds will have lapsed since epoch, and the Unix time stamp will no longer be able to track time. No doubt a new time scheme will replace it, but with everything in computing, legacy issues seem to always persist and cause problems in unanticipated ways. As that time draws near, approximately 23 years from now, you can probably expect another event similar to Y2K.

Just because the Unix time stamp uses the label *Unix*, do not think this date format is limited to Unix machines. The Unix time stamp is used on many platforms and is used heavily on the Internet. You should expect to find the Unix time stamp frequently on Windows-based machines.

With that understanding of the Unix time stamp, let's look next at the Windows 64-bit time stamp. Instead of a 32-bit integer used by Unix, Windows uses a 64-bit integer. Rather than tracking seconds like Unix, Windows tracks the number of 100-nanosecond intervals (10-millionth of a second intervals). And finally, instead of starting on January 1, 1970, 00:00:00 GMT like Unix, Windows starts on January 1, 1601, at 00:00:00 GMT.

Some basic math tells you that 2^{64} (64-bit value) can represent a maximum integer value of 18,446,744,073,709,500,000. If you divide this number by the number of 100-nanosecond intervals that tick by in a year (which is a paltry figure at 315,576,000,000,000), you find that this time stamp can address a date range of 58,000 plus years starting at 1601. It is clear that Microsoft was looking to the future when it created this one!

To show this at work, consider the two Windows 64-bit date stamps shown in Figure 9.3. The first one (80 22 07 E3 B0 CB CC 01) is selected, and the second one, which follows immediately (72 C8 E6 CB DA CB CC 01), is circled. These are time stamps appearing in an index.dat file for the daily Internet history. In this particular file, the two time stamps are identical (URL Last Visited times) except that the first date is stored in local time and the second date is stored in GMT. This is one of those cases where Windows deviates from the norm and stores a time in local time. Because the local time offset for this host computer is Eastern (GMT -0500), you would expect the times to differ by exactly five hours if both were normalized and viewed in GMT.

FIGURE 9.3 Two similar Windows 64-bit time stamps, one stored in local time (first one selected) and the other (second one circled) stored in GMT. Because local time is EST (GMT -0500), the raw time difference between these two time stamps should be exactly five hours.

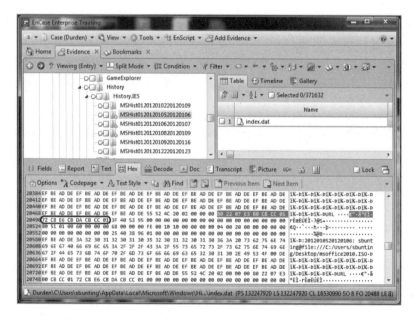

In Figure 9.4, the EnCase Decode feature is used on the selected data. (To use it, select the eight bytes in the Hex view and switch to the Decode view.) When the data is viewed as a Windows date and time, specifically using the local time option, the 64-bit value is resolved to the date and time January 5, 2012, 01:49:47 PM. Users of early versions of EnCase will note that, starting with EnCase 5, EnCase provides for a Windows local time option that was not available in previous versions. The local time option resolves time exactly as it is stored and does not apply the offset from GMT, thus rendering accurately any time stored as Local.

In Figure 9.5, the second time stamp is selected and viewed in the Decode view as a regular Windows date and time. Because this value is stored in GMT, you do not use the local time view. This value correctly resolves to the same date and time as the first date. EnCase applies the local time offset (GMT -0500) to the GMT time that is stored, and both time stamps can be resolved accurately.

FIGURE 9.4   First time viewed in Decode view as Windows Date/Time (Localtime)

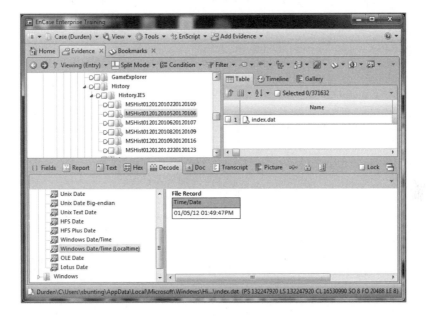

FIGURE 9.5   Second time viewed in Decode view as Windows Date/Time

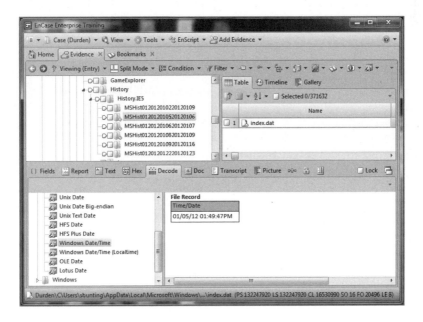

Let's carry this one step further and look at the exact values that are stored. The first date is the hex string 80 22 07 E3 B0 CB CC 01. EnCase 7 allows you to view this string as a 64-bit integer (via the Decode view). When you do, you will see this value resolve as 129,702,449,870,480,000. You can also enter the value into a calculator (scientific or programming modes). This value is stored in little endian, so if you are using a scientific calculator, you must enter the string in the reverse order, or 01 CC CB B0 E3 07 22 80, as shown in Figure 9.6. After the string is entered in the hex mode (base 16), switching to decimal mode (base 10) or mode converts the hex string to an integer value, which is 129,702,449,870,480,000. If you apply the same methodology to the second date hex string, reversing from little endian to read: 01 CC CB DA CB E6 C8 72) you find that it resolves to an integer value of 129,702,629,871,110,258. These two integer values represent the number of 100-nanosecond intervals since January 1, 1601, 00:00:00 GMT. If you are using EnCase 7, you need only view it as a 64-bit little endian integer in the Decode view.

FIGURE 9.6   The Windows 64-bit time stamp is entered in a scientific/programming calculator in reverse order because it is stored in little endian format. The left view is the Hex (base 16) view, and the right is the Decimal (base 10) view.

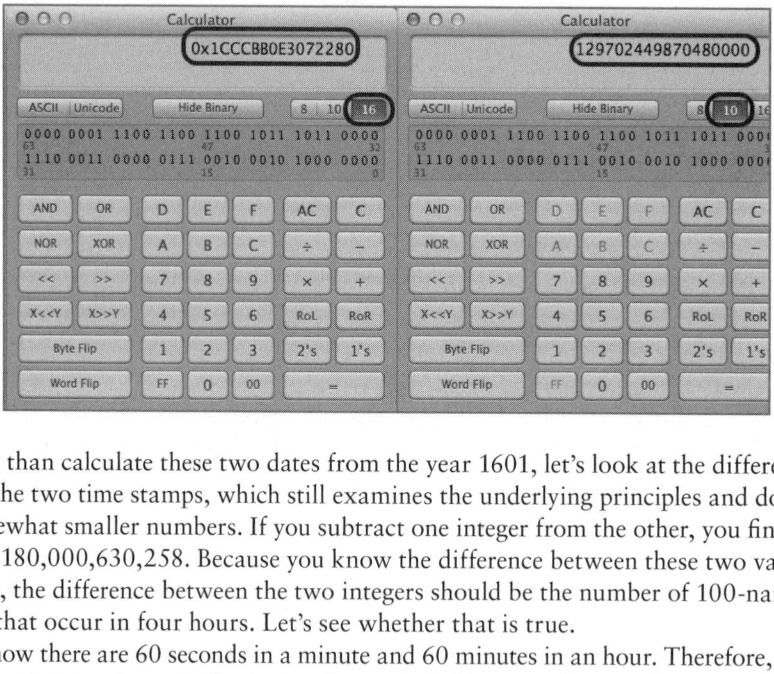

Rather than calculate these two dates from the year 1601, let's look at the difference between the two time stamps, which still examines the underlying principles and does so with somewhat smaller numbers. If you subtract one integer from the other, you find the difference is 180,000,630,258. Because you know the difference between these two values is five hours, the difference between the two integers should be the number of 100-nanosecond intervals that occur in four hours. Let's see whether that is true.

You know there are 60 seconds in a minute and 60 minutes in an hour. Therefore, there are 3,600 seconds in one hour. In five hours, there are 18,000 seconds. Because a 100-nanosecond interval is one 10-millionth of a second, you multiply 18,000 seconds by 10,000,000 to convert seconds to 10-millionth seconds. The result is 180,000,000,000 and matches (or nearly so) the difference (180,000,630,258) between the two integers that you know are separated by five hours. The difference is miniscule, measured in nanoseconds, and is caused by the difference in time the system takes to record these two times.

To show that these two hex values differ by five hours (and a few nanoseconds), I have placed both values in a tool named DCode (available free from www.digital-detective.co.uk/freetools/decode.asp) and resolved them both to UTC to normalize them. I would expect them to differ by five hours, and they do, as shown in Figure 9.7. You will note that the few nanoseconds by which they differ do not come into play at this level of granularity. You also know that EnCase is properly interpreting the time stamps and offsets, thus validating the tool.

FIGURE 9.7 DCode is used to show that raw data timestamps differ by five hours when both viewed as UTC.

Manually calculating Windows 64-bit time stamps is not something most examiners want to do with any degree of frequency, if at all. Fortunately, EnCase provides tools to convert these values for you. There is merit, however, in understanding how such dates are generated and stored. You may be asked some day in court, or you may need to engage in research and validation of data or tools. In either event, you'll be better prepared if you understand how the calculations are done.

Adjusting for Time Zone Offsets

By now you have an understanding of how Windows stores time stamps, and you also understand the importance of time zone offsets in determining accurate times. It is now time to determine the time zone offset for a system and how to adjust the EnCase environment so it will display properly.

With Windows, the time zone offset is stored in the registry. The registry is a large database of system configuration settings. It is stored in several files and is viewed and manipulated with a registry editor such as regedit, which is a built-in Windows utility. In Chapter 10, I'll cover the registry in more detail. If you are comfortable mounting and navigating the registry or you want to jump ahead to Chapter 10, you can ascertain the time zone offset manually in the following manner:

1. Determine which control set is the current control set.

    Mount the system registry file (SYSTEM) as you would other compound files by highlighting the file and choosing View File Structure from the Entries drop-down menu. Then navigate to System\NTRegistry\Select\Current. View this value as a 32-bit integer value. The value stored here (*n*) determines which control set is current.

In Windows NT/2000, the system registry key can be found by default in C:\Winnt\ System32\Config.

For Windows XP/Windows Server 2003 and 2008/Windows Vista/Windows 7, the system registry key can be found by default in C:\Windows\System32\Config.

2. In the system key, navigate to the control set matching the value found earlier (*n*), which is the current control set.

3. Under that control set, navigate to System\NTRegistry\ControlSet00n\ Control\TimeZoneInformation.

Under that key, there are several values used to establish the local time zone offset. Table 9.1 lists those values and how they are used to determine the time zone offset.

TABLE 9.1 TimeZoneInformation key values and their meanings

Value name	Data type	Description
ActiveTimeBias	32-bit integer	The number of minutes offset from GMT for the current system time.
Bias	32-bit integer	Based on the time zone setting, the number of minutes offset from GMT for that time zone.
DaylightBias	32-bit integer	Based on the time zone setting, the number of minutes offset from GMT for that time zone when daylight saving time is in effect.
DaylightName	Unicode text string	The name of the time zone for daylight saving time setting.
DaylightStart	Binary (four 2-byte sets; ignore last 8 bytes)	Date and time daylight saving time starts in this format: Day | Month | Week | Hour. Day: First two bytes or 16 bits. Evaluate as 16-bit integer. The seven days of the week are numbered 0–6, starting with Sunday (0). Month: Second two bytes. Evaluate as 16-bit integer with months numbered 1–12 (January being 1). Week: Third two bytes. Evaluate as 16-bit integer with weeks numbered starting with 1. Hour: Fourth two bytes. Evaluate as 16-bit integer with hour of the day being when the time will change, based on a 24-hour clock. For an example, see the StandardStart row of this table.

TABLE 9.1   `TimeZoneInformation` key values and their meanings *(continued)*

Value name	Data type	Description
StandardBias	32-bit integer	Based on the time zone setting, the number of minutes offset from GMT for that time zone, when standard time is in effect.
StandardName	Unicode text string	The name of the time zone for standard time setting.
StandardStart	Binary (four 2-byte sets; ignore last 8 bytes)	Date and time standard time starts in the format: Day | Month | Week | Hour All values evaluated as in DaylightStart value. A typical StandardStart value would appear as 00 00 | 0A 00 | 05 00 | 02 00 Day = 00 00 = 0 = Sunday Month = 0A 00 = 10 = October Week = 05 00 = 5 = 5th week Hour = 02 00 = 2 = 0200 hrs.

The `ActiveTimeBias` indicates, in minutes, the current offset from GMT. If you are in a time zone that uses daylight saving time and `ActiveTimeBias` equals the `StandardBias`, the computer is set for standard time. If the `ActiveTimeBias` equals the `DaylightBias`, the computer is set for daylight saving time. The `StandardName` will indicate the time zone setting for the host computer under examination.

An easier way to derive this information is through the use of the EnCase Evidence Processor and subsequently the Case Analyzer EnScript, in which you can choose to have this information summarized in a concise and informative report. In Chapter 10, I'll cover EnScripts in more detail. When you run the Case Evidence Processor, make sure to select System Info Parser module. When the EnCase Evidence Processor has completed, you can run the Case Analyzer EnScript, which will pull the information together from the Evidence Processor results and allow you to view it or create reports. After you have run the Case Analyzer EnScript, the time zone information that you extract will appear as shown in Figure 9.8. While this information is nice to have in this format, you must also keep in mind that best practices call for determining this information and modifying time zone settings before running the case processor. Thus, knowing how to obtain this information from the raw registry is important. The Case Analyzer Report for the time zone information is good to include showing what the settings are in report format and to validate your earlier time zone offset analysis.

FIGURE 9.8 Time Zone Artifacts extracted by the EnCase Evidence Processor and analyzed using the Case Analyzer EnScript. The active time bias is GMT (UTC) -7 hours (circled).

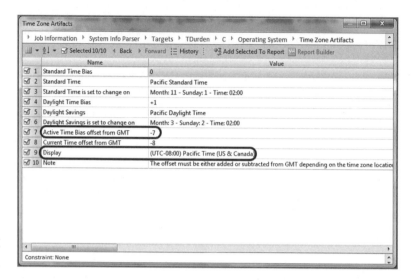

Thus, for our example as shown in Figure 9.8, the evidence item shown in the report was using Pacific time settings. During standard time, the offset from GMT is -8 hours for Pacific time. As the active offset for this device is -7 hours, we know that daylight savings time was in effect when seized. It is a good idea to validate this analysis and thinking by checking the most recent last-written timestamp on the device in question. In this case, the most recent timestamp was April 20, 2011, and thus daylight savings time was clearly in place. Thus, for this device, we'll have to adjust our time zone settings for this device to Pacific time so that the timestamps can be viewed in the time zone in which they were created. You now have two methods by which to determine the time zone offset for which the host computer is configured. Once that offset is known, the next step is to apply that offset to the case or individual devices if they have differing offsets. When done, all devices will be in sync with regard to time zone, and you can examine dates and times accurately.

WARNING

Because this step is critical to an accurate examination when dates and times are at issue, it should be done at the outset of your examination. Accordingly, you should include this step in your case-processing checklist and place it at the beginning as a standard mandatory step in the process.

Many functions in the Evidence Processor rely on the time zone settings to accurately process and display the Windows dates and times, so the time zone must be checked in the registry and set for the case or devices before running the core Evidence Processor functions, such as Index Text, Find Internet Artifacts, Find Email, and so on.

To adjust for the time zone offset, go the Evidence tab's Entries view, and in the Tree pane, place the focus at the top or Entries level, forcing the various devices into the Table pane. Highlight the device for which you want to modify the time zone settings in the Table pane. Having highlighted the device, select Modify Time Zone Settings from the Device drop-down menu, as shown in Figure 9.9. From the Time Properties dialog box, select the correct time zone offset based on your earlier analysis of the time zone settings for your device. In our example, we found it was set for Pacific time. Figure 9.10 shows the time properties being adjusted for UTC-08:00 Pacific time.

FIGURE 9.9   To adjust for time zone offset, highlight the device in the Table pane and choose Modify Time Zone Settings from the Device drop-down menu.

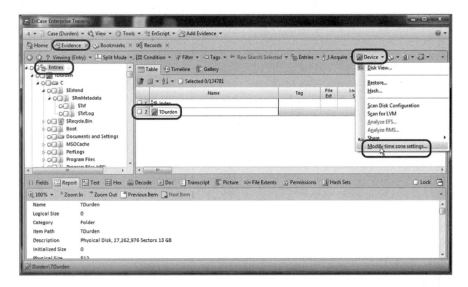

FIGURE 9.10   Time Properties dialog box from which the corrected time zone settings are chosen

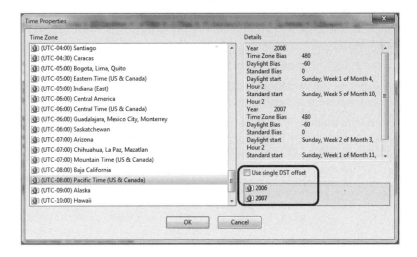

Once you have selected your settings, click OK, and the proper time zone offset will be applied at the case or device level you chose at the outset.

Because of the change to daylight start/stop times that occurred in 2007, EnCase now allows the examiner to adjust for unpatched systems that may need to be examined. If the examiner's machine is properly patched for the update to daylight saving time (KB931836), then EnCase will offer the option to use a single DST offset (circled in Figure 9.10) for the selected device. This allows the examiner to have EnCase employ the prior daylight start/stop times for evidence that it either is unpatched or was put in service after the change occurred. Using dual offsets (*not* selecting Use Single DST Offset) allows EnCase to adjust for daylight saving time based upon the date of activity—files accessed during the last week of March 2007 would, on a properly patched machine, be in daylight saving time, while other files accessed during the final week of March 2006 would not have been time stamped under DST.

At this point, your device or case will display the time stored in GMT to the accurate local time zone offset. So that you understand how all this ties together, let's examine how the entire process works by looking at a date and time stamp from its point of origin to its interpretation by EnCase.

In this hypothetical example, a suspect is using a computer in Oregon that is running Windows XP and formatted using NTFS. The time zone offset is configured for the Pacific time zone (GMT -0800) and is configured to automatically adjust for daylight saving time. The date and time is Sunday, October 12, 2003, 16:01:22 PDT. Daylight saving time is in effect, and thus the current offset is GMT -0700. At this point in time, your suspect writes a file to his system that ultimately becomes a file of interest in your case. Here is what happens from the time it is written until you view it in EnCase:

1. The precise time the file was written, in local time, was Sunday, October 12, 2003, 16:01:22 PDT.

2. Because this system is NTFS, the operating system converts the local time to GMT before storing it. The OS adds seven hours (current offset) to the time, making it Sunday, October 12, 2003, 23:01:22 PDT.

3. The OS stores this date in the following 64-bit hex string: 2A 42 17 C1 14 91 C3 01.

4. We know this string can be converted to a little endian 64-bit integer that would represent the number of 100-nanosecond intervals from January 1, 1601, 00:00:00 GMT.

5. The following day, the suspect's computer is seized for later forensic examination.

6. The date and time is now Monday, September 5, 2005, at 11:44:00 EDT, and the forensic examination is occurring in the Eastern time zone.

7. Because our examination machine is configured for Eastern time (GMT -0500) and daylight saving time is in effect, your current offset is Eastern daylight saving time (GMT -0400), and EnCase will default to the local offset for viewing time stamps unless told otherwise.

8. EnCase first determines that the NTFS file system is in place and decodes the time stamp in GMT as Sunday, October 12, 2003 23:01:22. Next EnCase looks to the offset applied and decides whether daylight saving time was in effect.

9. If you did not account for the offset in the evidence file, EnCase would subtract the default local offset and apply daylight saving time (GMT -0400) from the time stored in GMT and show the file as having been created on Sunday, October 12, 2003 at 19:01:22.

10. However, you follow the correct practices and determine the time zone offset in the evidence file, finding that it is PST (GMT -0800) and that daylight saving was in effect (GMT -0700). When you apply this time zone setting to your device, when EnCase reads the time stamp, it converts the date to PDT (GMT -0700) by subtracting seven hours from the time stamp as stored in GMT. It therefore correctly displays the time stamp as Sunday, October 12, 2003 16:01:22, which matches the date and time the file was written in its local time zone.

It is important to note that had this same scenario involved a FAT system, no adjustments would have been required because the time would have been stored in local time. Of course, the MS-DOS time stamp used in FAT systems, while simple, is also limiting.

The MS-DOS time stamp lacks seconds for last-accessed times because the 2 bytes that would record this information are used in FAT 32-file systems to describe starting clusters when they exceed 65,536 clusters. Also, the MS-DOS time stamp allows only 5 bits to describe seconds. Because 2^5 (5 bits) provides only 32 outcomes, this falls short of the 60 seconds in a minute. Thus, the stored seconds go only as high as 30 (actually 0–29) and are multiplied by 2 to achieve a time in seconds. 1×2 shows as 2 seconds, 2×2 shows as 4 seconds, and so forth. You won't see an MS-DOS time with an odd number of seconds. You will see only even numbers for seconds for MAC times in FAT file systems.

The Windows 64-bit time stamp used to track MAC times in NTFS is, by contrast, a much more robust and accurate means of tracking time. With complexity, however, comes the need for a deeper understanding of the underlying principles and more sophisticated analysis tools.

Now that you understand times and time zones, you can apply this knowledge as you examine other operating system artifacts, because time stamps are found throughout them.

Recycle Bin

By default, when a user deletes a file in Windows, the file is placed in the Recycle Bin. To bypass the Recycle Bin, the user must hold down the Shift key while pressing Delete. Because few users are aware of this option, most deleted files pass through the Recycle Bin on most systems.

When a file is in the Recycle Bin, the user has the option of restoring the file to its original location. A user can also select an individual file or files and delete them from the

Recycle Bin. The final option for the Recycle Bin is to empty it, which deletes all the files in the Recycle Bin.

With that, I have described the basic operation of the Recycle Bin as the user sees it. To enable this functionality, much is taking place under the hood. As an examiner, you need to understand the fine details of the Recycle Bin process so you can competently examine and later explain the evidence found therein. With that in mind, let's examine the underlying activity for each of the Recycle Bin's basic functions.

 Windows Vista, Windows Server 2008, and Windows 7 use the Recycle Bin, but the manner in which files are renamed once placed in the Recycle Bin is different from previous versions. Furthermore, there is no longer an INFO or INFO2 file. I'll discuss the new Windows Recycle Bin function later in this chapter, after I cover all Windows versions up to Windows Vista.

Details of Recycle Bin Operation

When a file is deleted and sent to the Recycle Bin, the directory or MFT entry for the file is deleted. Simultaneously, a directory entry or MFT entry is made for the file in the Recycle Bin. The new filename bears no resemblance to the original filename, however, because a special naming convention is applied to files placed in the Recycle Bin. The naming convention follows this format:

D[*original drive letter of file*][*index number*].[*original file extension*]

The *D* stands for *deleted*. If, for example, the file C:\My Files\letter.doc were deleted and sent to the Recycle Bin, its new filename in the Recycle Bin would be DC1.doc if it was the first file sent to the Recycle Bin (or the first file sent since the Recycle Bin was last emptied).

For earlier versions of Windows, the index numbers start at 0 for the first file sent to the Recycle Bin and increase by 1 for each file added. However, Windows XP starts its index numbers at 1 instead of 0. If the index number for whatever reason becomes an issue in your case, it is good practice to test and verify the results on a test box using the same version and service pack of Windows that is in question.

The INFO2 File

When you view a file in the Recycle Bin, you see the file's original name and path along with other information. Because the deleted file no longer bears its original filename, the displayed information must be stored somewhere, and that storage location is a hidden file named INFO2. Thus, when a deleted file receives a new name in the Recycle Bin, an entry is also made in the INFO2 file for the deleted file.

The INFO2 file is a database containing information about the files in the Recycle Bin. When you look at files in the Recycle Bin, you are actually viewing the contents of the

`INFO2` file. Therefore, when a file is sent to the Recycle Bin, the following information is placed in the Recycle Bin:

- The file's original filename and path (entered twice, once in ASCII and again in Unicode)
- The date and time of deletion
- The index number

The index number is the link between the new filename and the `INFO2` record because it is common to both. In Figure 9.11, the folder `Digital Camera` has been deleted. Because the data did not move and a new filename was created for this data in the Recycle Bin, the icon for `DualMonitorStation.JPG` has a red circular arrow icon in the lower right indicating the folder is overwritten because the starting cluster is in use by another folder or file. When a folder or file is overwritten, the Original Path column and the GPS locator (both circled) will indicate the path of the overwriting object, which is in this case a folder by the same name located in the Recycle Bin (`D\Recycled`). You should also note that the Description column also indicates that the entry is overwritten, which is again circled in Figure 9.11.

FIGURE 9.11 A folder is deleted and sent to the Recycle Bin. EnCase reports the original folder as overwritten because the starting cluster is in use by the new folder name created in the Recycle Bin.

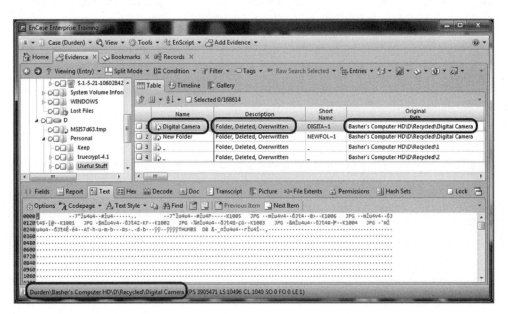

When you view the Recycle Bin, you find that the folder is present, as shown in Figure 9.12. EnCase reads the `INFO2` file and reports its former name as it was in its original location as `Digital Camera` and further reports its original path, which is `D:\Personal\Useful Stuff\Digital Camera`. When you are working in the Recycle Bin, the Short Name column lists the actual filename as stored in the Recycle bin folder, which in this case is DD4. The first *D* means deleted; the second *D* means the volume on which is was stored, and the 4 is the index record number in the INFO2 file. Since this is a folder, there is no extension. If it were to have been a file, the file extension would appear here, unchanged.

FIGURE 9.12 When file is sent to the Recycle Bin, it is renamed, and an entry is made in the INFO2 database.

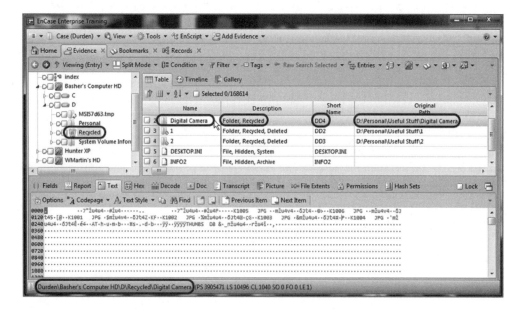

 In current versions of EnCase (version 6 and newer), the original filename of a deleted file is in the Name column, and the Recycle Bin name is in the Short File Name column. This will be the case only if the deleted file is listed in the INFO2 file. If it is no longer present in the INFO2 file, EnCase can't report the original filename and will display only the filename as it is found in the Recycle Bin.

Each record in an INFO2 database has a fixed length that varies according to the Windows version that created it. Table 9.2 shows the various pre–Windows Vista Windows operating systems and the length of their INFO2 database records. Interestingly, the name of the Recycle Bin varies also with the Windows version, and those names are likewise listed in the table.

TABLE 9.2   Comparison of Recycle Bins between Windows versions*

Operating system	Recycle Bin folder name	INF02 record length
Windows 9/Me	Recycled	280 bytes
Windows NT	Recycler	800 bytes
Windows 2000	Recycler	800 bytes
Windows XP/2003	Recycler	800 bytes

* Windows Vista, Windows 7, and Windows Server 2008 do not use an INF02 file so are not listed.

The length of each record is important because EnCase provides a bookmark-viewing tool that decodes the fields in the INF02 records, allowing you to include this information in a sweeping data bookmark. To use this bookmarking tool, you must know both the starting point and the record length. If you look at the Options dialog box in the View pane, you can set the correct record length. When you display the records in this manner, the starting point is easy to identify, and it also greatly facilitates accurate sweeping or highlighting of the data. I covered how to use the Options feature in Chapter 7, so I'll simply show the correct settings for a Windows NT–Windows Server 2003 series of INF02 records in Figure 9.13. Once you have highlighted the INF02 record in the Table view, its data is viewable in the View pane. It is at this point that you apply the Options settings. When the correct settings have been applied, the records will align in somewhat of a column, as shown and circled in Figure 9.13.

FIGURE 9.13   Options are set for a wrap length of 800 bytes, causing the INFO2 records to "align."

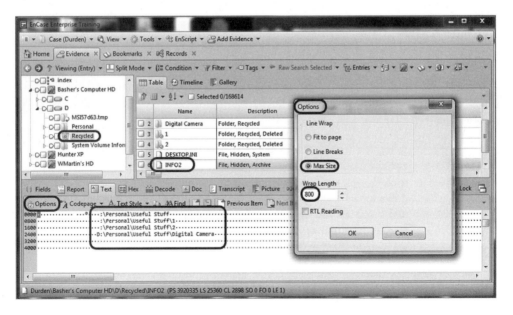

Note in Figure 9.14 that the data has been selected starting with the drive letter, which is the first character or byte of each record in the database. Remember this byte because it will have significance later. The selection will end on the row following the record, one space short of where the drive letter of the following record starts (or would have started were there another record). For clarity, I have selected only one of several records. Note also the length of our selection is shown at the bottom of the window (circled in the GPS section), which is 800 bytes.

FIGURE 9.14   One INFO2 record index, 800 bytes in length, has been selected.

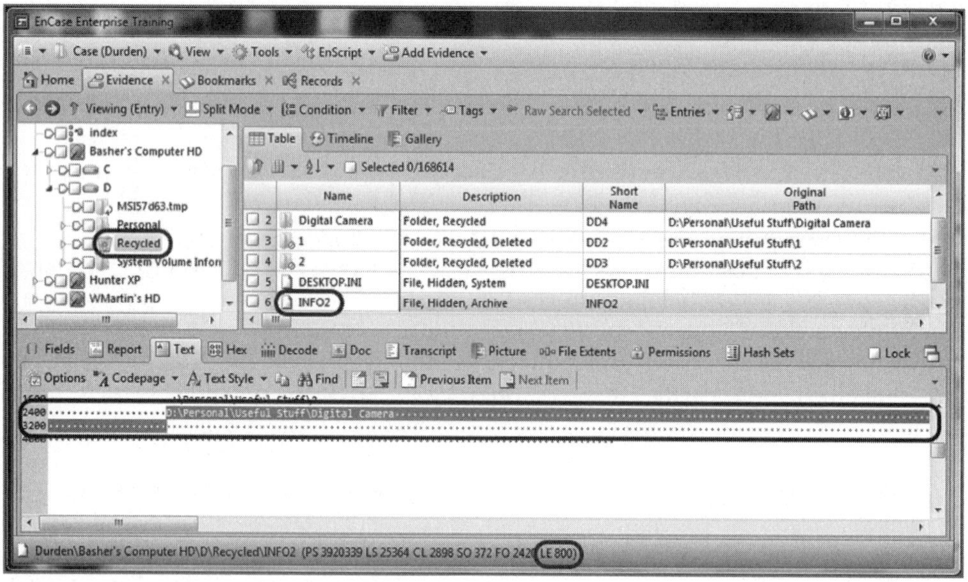

With the INFO2 record selected, to have EnCase parse it and display it, you need only switch to the Decode tab and select the correct View type in the left pane, which in our example is Windows Win2000 Info File record, as shown in Figure 9.15. The right pane will display the index number, the deleted date, and the complete path of the deleted file or folder. If you want to have this information in your report, you need only bookmark the information in the Decode tab.

EnCase uses the Decode View Type Win2000 Info File Record for INFO2 records that are 800 bytes in length (Windows NT, Windows 2000, Windows XP, and Windows Server 2003) and uses Win95 Info File Record for those that are 280 bytes in length from the Win9x legacy Windows systems. Neither type will work for the new format used starting with Vista. Again, we'll cover that issue separately.

FIGURE 9.15   INFO2 record decoded

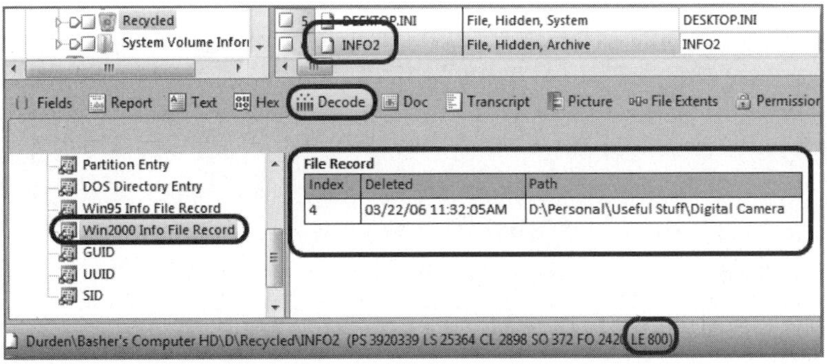

Determining the Owner of Files in the Recycle Bin

With Windows NT, Windows Server 2000, Windows XP, and Windows Server 2003, an added artifact appears in the Recycle Bin. When a user first deletes a file, a folder bearing the user's security ID (SID) number appears. Each user on the host system is assigned a SID, which is a globally unique identification number (GUID). Anything the user deletes goes into that uniquely named folder. From a forensic point of view, this is the real-world equivalent of throwing away trash with your name and Social Security number stamped all over it. Deleted files can be traced back to their owner through the SID.

The process of manually resolving the SID involves mounting the Security Accounts Manager (SAM) registry file, reconstructing the SID from the data therein, and linking it to a username. EnCase spares you that agony by scanning the SAM hive when loading your evidence files, thereby resolving SID numbers to locally authenticated users on the fly.

You can determine the user associated with a SID in several ways. In the case of files in the Recycle Bin, simply highlight the Recycle Bin in the Tree pane. In the Table view pane, place your focus on the folder bearing the name of the SID that is the focus of your inquiry. In the View pane, switch to the Permissions view (padlock icon), and the NTFS permissions will appear. To determine the owner, simply scroll down to the owner to determine the user associated with that SID, as shown in Figure 9.16.

This process works for local logon accounts where the host computer's SAM stores the SID and other credentials.

When the user logs onto a Windows domain, however, the SID information is not stored on the local host but rather on the domain controller (server). In that case, EnCase can't obtain the SID numbers by scanning the SAM hive on the local machine (they aren't there). Thus, usernames will not be resolvable under these conditions. Therefore, when domain logons are occurring, you will need to obtain the username for the SID in question and manually enter the SID and username in the Secure Storage view. After that, EnCase will remember that SID and username combination and resolve it for you.

FIGURE 9.16   Recycle Bin with folders bearing SID numbers for names. You can find the SID owner by switching to the Permissions view.

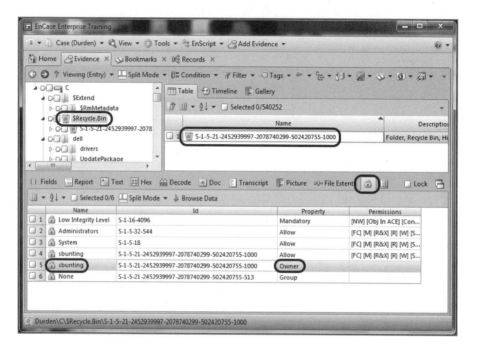

If a user attempts a domain logon and the domain controller is not available, the user can often log on anyway because, by default, the last 10 domain logons are cached locally. The EnCase EDS module included with version 7 processes these cached domain accounts with the Analyze Encrypted Files System (EFS) function. To use Analyze EFS, force the volume to appear in the Table view pane of the Evidence tab and place your cursor on it to highlight it. Next, choose Analyze EFS from the Device drop-down menu. Thus, by running Analyze EFS, any cached logons will be analyzed, and the resultant user names and SID numbers will be available to the examiner.

Files Restored or Deleted from the Recycle Bin

When the user empties the entire Recycle Bin, the directory entries (if FAT) or the MFT entries (if NTFS) for all files in the Recycle Bin are marked as deleted. The INFO2 database is adjusted to its default or empty size of 20 bytes (Windows XP/2003), thereby removing any INFO2 records from the active Recycle Bin database. If, however, you examine the file slack that immediately follows the 20-byte empty bin header, you'll see many of the INFO2 records that were in the Recycle Bin before it was emptied.

You may encounter a circumstance in which a user restores a file from the Recycle Bin. There is little in the way of documentation on this condition, and the results from it may confuse you when you view an INFO2 record in which this has occurred. When a file is restored, a record is created in the directory or MFT for the folder where the file was originally located when it was deleted. The entry for the file in the directory or MFT of the Recycle Bin is marked as deleted. So far, this is fairly logical and straightforward.

What happens next, however, is a little less than intuitive. The entry in the INFO2 record is not deleted. Rather, the first character of that record, which would ordinarily be the drive letter from which the file was deleted, is changed to 00h, as shown in Figure 9.17. This process is analogous to that of deleting a file or folder in a FAT volume where the first byte of the 32-byte entry is changed to E5h. Just as Windows Explorer ignores any entry beginning with E5h, the Recycle Bin interface ignores any record beginning with 00h.

FIGURE 9.17   When a file in the Recycle Bin is restored to its original path, the first character of its INFO2 record is changed to 00h.

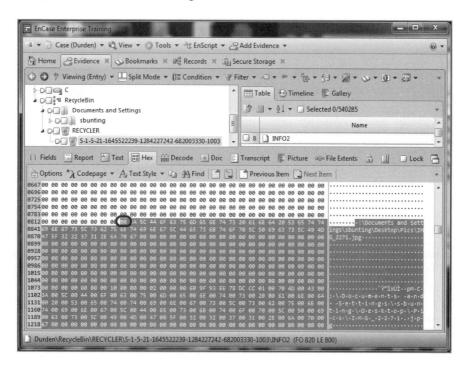

Although it isn't commonly done, a user can delete individual files from the Recycle Bin instead of emptying the entire Recycle Bin. From within the Recycle Bin, you can delete a selected individual file or groups of files by pressing the Delete button, right-clicking and choosing Delete, or choosing Delete from the File menu. Windows handles INFO2 records for files deleted from the Recycle Bin the same as files restored from the Recycle Bin—the directory or MFT entries are marked as deleted, and the first characters of the files' INFO2 records are changed to 00h.

The index numbers of these deleted/restored files will be reused the next time a file is deleted and placed in the Recycle Bin. Therefore, when the INFO2 database is processed by EnCase, the records for files restored or deleted from the Recycle Bin, and those subsequently added to the Recycle Bin will display with the same index number, as shown in Figure 9.18. EnCase does not make any distinction between active Recycle Bin records and null Recycle Bin records. It processes and reports both types of records. The information displayed is accurate, but it may not be the complete story if files were restored or deleted from the Recycle Bin.

FIGURE 9.18   The first record has been restored and has the same index number (1) as the fifth record, which has been subsequently deleted and added to the Recycle Bin.

Using an EnCase Evidence Processor to Determine the Status of Recycle Bin Files

If artifacts in the Recycle Bin are critical elements in your case and you need to determine whether files have been restored or deleted from the Recycle Bin, search the INFO2 records for the hex string 00 3A 5C. This string looks for :\ preceded by 00h and would indicate records in the INFO2 database for files that were restored or deleted from the Recycle Bin. With that information, you can further examine original paths for restorations and examine directory or MFT entries for filenames, starting clusters, and so forth. From that information, you may be able to determine what actually occurred to a file after it "left" the Recycle Bin.

Although understanding the function of the Recycle Bin is critical and the ability to manually process it is a necessary skill, automated processing saves you time so you can process your backlog of cases. To that end, the Windows Artifact Parser is an available module in the EnCase Evidence Processor, which, among other tasks, processes INFO2 records, both intact and fragmentary.

To use this module, first launch the EnCase Evidence Processor and open the Modules at the bottom, as shown in Figure 9.19. If you double-click the Windows Artifact Parser, you will see that you have three different types of artifacts from which to choose, of which Recycle Bin Files is one; make sure it is selected, as shown in Figure 9.20. You should note that an option is available in this menu to search for artifacts in unallocated clusters. If you opt to do so, keep in mind that this will add significantly to your processing time.

After you run the EnCase Evidence Processor, you can review the results of this module by running the Case Analyzer from the EnScript menu. The Case Analyzer will run and then provide you with an interface where you can drill down and review the various artifacts recovered. Figure 9.21 shows the Recycle Bin results. From here, you can select any item or all items for inclusion in a report.

FIGURE 9.19   The Windows Artifact Parser module in the EnCase Evidence Processor

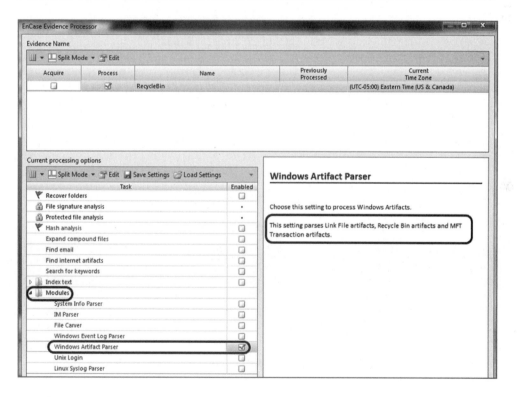

FIGURE 9.20   Options within the Windows Artifact Parser

FIGURE 9.21   Using Case Analyzer EnScript to view Recycle Bin results from the EnCase Evidence Processor.

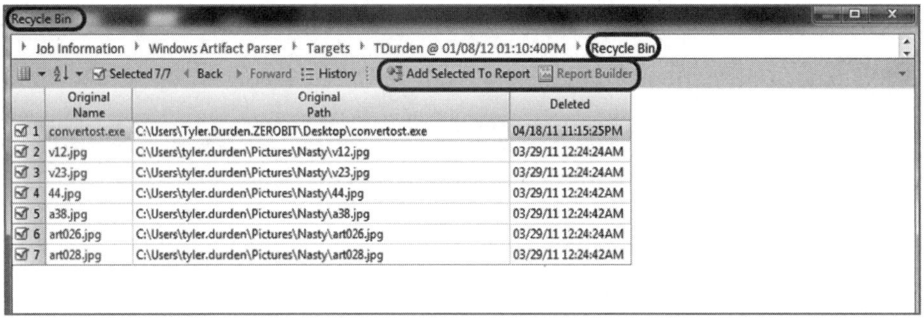

	Original Name	Original Path	Deleted
1	convertost.exe	C:\Users\Tyler.Durden.ZEROBIT\Desktop\convertost.exe	04/18/11 11:15:25PM
2	v12.jpg	C:\Users\tyler.durden\Pictures\Nasty\v12.jpg	03/29/11 12:24:24AM
3	v23.jpg	C:\Users\tyler.durden\Pictures\Nasty\v23.jpg	03/29/11 12:24:24AM
4	44.jpg	C:\Users\tyler.durden\Pictures\Nasty\44.jpg	03/29/11 12:24:42AM
5	a38.jpg	C:\Users\tyler.durden\Pictures\Nasty\a38.jpg	03/29/11 12:24:42AM
6	art026.jpg	C:\Users\tyler.durden\Pictures\Nasty\art026.jpg	03/29/11 12:24:24AM
7	art028.jpg	C:\Users\tyler.durden\Pictures\Nasty\art028.jpg	03/29/11 12:24:42AM

Recycle Bin Bypass

I cannot complete a discussion of the Recycle Bin without covering what happens when the Recycle Bin is configured to be bypassed altogether. The obvious consequence is that files are deleted from their original locations and are not sent to the Recycle Bin at all, making processing the INFO2 records a moot point.

Fortunately for forensics examiners, such a configuration is not the default, and making the changes is anything but obvious or intuitive. In fact, most users are not aware that it is an option. Nevertheless, security-conscious individuals or those wanting to cover their tracks may configure their systems to bypass the Recycle Bin when deleting files.

To configure your system to bypass the Recycle Bin, you must change the properties of the Recycle Bin. Right-click the Recycle Bin icon, from either the desktop or Explorer, and select Properties. Your choices are displayed in the Recycle Bin Properties dialog box shown in Figure 9.22. If you have more than one hard drive, you have the choice of creating the options globally or setting the options on a per-drive basis. In Figure 9.22 the option Do Not Move Files to the Recycle Bin has been selected. This option is being applied on the

Global tab, thereby overriding any individual drive options. With this setting selected, any file deleted will be erased immediately and not sent to the Recycle Bin.

FIGURE 9.22 The Recycle Bin Properties dialog box provides the option to bypass the Recycle Bin globally to both hard drives on this system.

This setting, when applied, is implemented by means of values stored in the registry. This feature is represented by the NukeOnDelete registry value set to 01h, which is found in the full registry path: HKEY_LOCAL_MACHINE\SOFTWARE\Microsoft\Windows\CurrentVersion\ Explorer\BitBucket. This setting is shown in the regedit interface in Figure 9.23. If this same setting were not globally applied but rather applied to a specific drive, the same value would appear in a subkey of this registry key named after the drive letter to which it applied. You can also see the two subkeys (c and e) of the BitBucket key in Figure 9.23.

FIGURE 9.23 Registry settings for bypassing the Recycle Bin globally for all attached drives

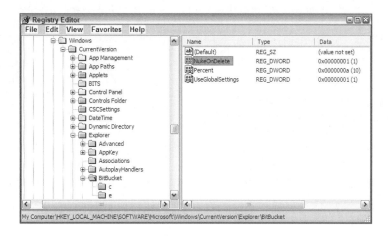

Applying this setting does not remove the `Recycle Bin` folder once it has been created, and it doesn't remove whatever contents may be in the Recycle Bin when the setting is applied. Once this setting is applied, whenever a file is deleted, the option of sending it to the Recycle Bin is no longer available.

If you are processing a case and you see a lot of deleted user files and find little or nothing in the `INFO2` record artifacts, you should suspect that the Recycle Bin has been bypassed. To confirm this suspicion, mount the registry, and examine this registry value.

I'll cover the registry in detail in Chapter 10, after which you may want to revisit this section. This text is also quite modularized, so you may want to jump ahead now.

Windows Vista/Windows 7 Recycle Bin

Just when forensic examiners had it all figured out with regard to the `INFO2` file databases, leave it to the engineers at Microsoft to change things. With the release of Windows Vista, the `INFO2` file disappeared, as did the file/folder renaming convention. Microsoft also renamed the containing folder for the Recycle Bin to `$Recycle.Bin`. Although the renaming of the containing folder is hardly an issue, the replacement of the `INFO2` database and the new renaming convention do change the landscape somewhat.

Even with the aforementioned changes, you should fear not. Instead of retaining the deleted file database information in one `INFO2` file, Windows Vista keeps this information in individual index files in the Recycle Bin that begin with `$I`. The remainder of the filename is an abbreviated GUID of sorts, and the file extension remains unchanged. The deleted filename, when placed in the Recycle Bin, is changed to a name that begins with `$R`. The remainder of the renamed deleted file (or folder) is also a GUID that matches that of its corresponding index file, and its file extension also remains unchanged.

Figure 9.24 shows the pairing of an index file, containing the deleted file information, and its corresponding deleted file. The file was originally `C:\Users\sbunting\Desktop\EventLogs.txt`, as shown in the index file named `$IHLR8PV.txt`. The deleted file is renamed `$RHLR8PV.txt`. The filenames differ only at the second filename character, with the index file having an *I* and the deleted file having an *R* at that location.

FIGURE 9.24 Windows 7 Recycle Bin with a pairing of index and deleted files

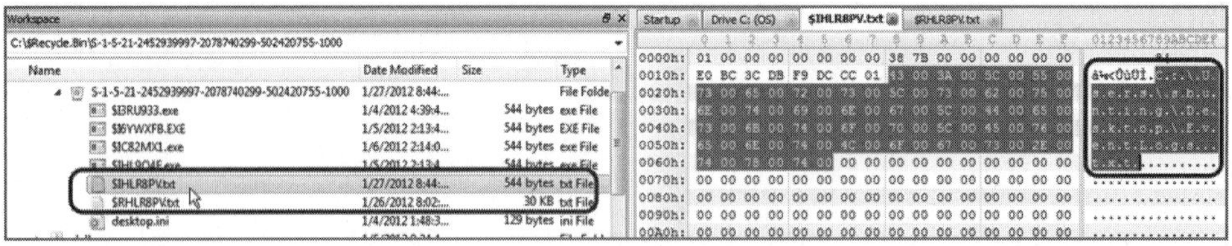

You will note that we are using a hex editor to show the raw filenames in Figure 9.24. When EnCase is used to view the same data, it will read the data in the index file and show the filename as it was before deleted. You can, however, see the raw filename in EnCase if you look in the Short Name column, as shown in Figure 9.25.

FIGURE 9.25   EnCase view of data shown in Figure 9.24. Note that EnCase resolves the name to the filename before it was deleted.

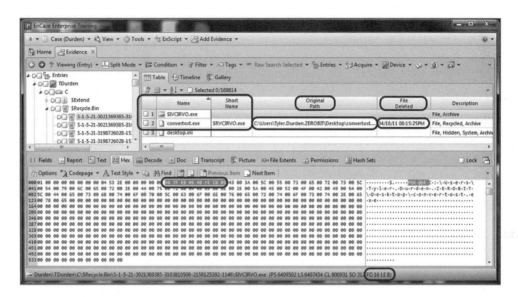

Within the index file, you can see (highlighted and circled in Figure 9.24) that the full path to the deleted file (or folder) begins at byte offset 24. This would be denoted in the GPS area as FO 24. Another important piece of metadata—the time stamp for when the file was deleted—immediately precedes the path name. This time stamp is a 64-bit Windows time stamp and is stored at byte offsets 16–23, as shown highlighted and circled in Figure 9.25. You can see (circled) in the GPS in the lower right that the highlighted area of the time stamp starts as byte offset 16 (FO 16) and is 8 bytes (64 bits) as denoted by the length (LE 8).

If you closely at Figure 9.26, you can see that the file creation date of the index file ($IHLR8PV.txt) was April 18, 2011, at 8:15:25 p.m. You would expect this index file to have been created in the Recycle Bin at the time the file was deleted. Therefore, the meta-data in the index file that shows when the file was deleted (Decoded in Figure 9.26) should match the file creation date of the index file. In addition to seeing this timestamp decoded, it also appears in the File Deleted column. In Figure 9.23, you can see that these three time stamps (Decoded timestamp in View pane, File Deleted timestamp, and File Created time-stamp for index file) do in fact match.

The index file has one other piece of metadata within it that can be of forensic interest, which is the file size of the deleted file. Since you have this information already in the prop-erties of the deleted file, this usually is of little added value. The deleted file size is stored as a Dword value at offsets 8–11. When the deleted object is a folder with child objects (files and subfolders), this value appears to represent the total logical size of the folder and its child objects.

You will find that when a folder and its child objects (files and subfolders) have been deleted, only the parent folder will be renamed to match the GUID portion of the index file. Its subfolders and files (children) will not be renamed. Figure 9.27 shows a parent folder named Logs deleted and renamed $RK2V8CK. Its corresponding index filename is $IK2V8CK (see Short Name column in Figure 9.27).

FIGURE 9.26 File deletion timestamp decoded and matches File Deleted timestamp and File Created timestamp for index file

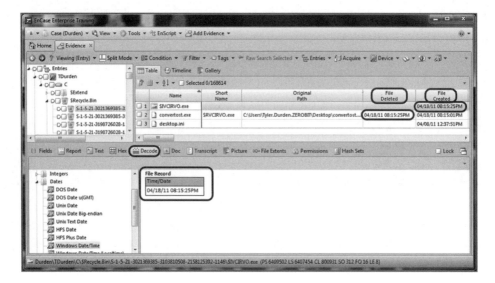

FIGURE 9.27 Folder named Logs has been deleted and has a raw filename (see Short Name) of $RK2V8CK.

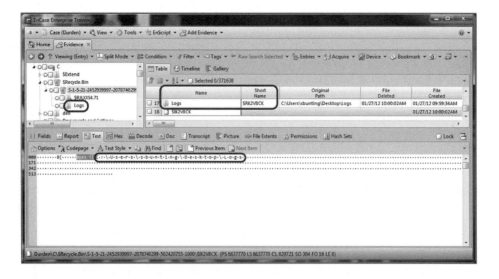

If we examine the contents of the Logs folder, we find that it contains a file named EventLogs.txt. If we look at the Short Name value for this file, we note that it has not a file beginning with $R, but rather its true short name, as shown in Figure 9.28. The user can't see the contents of a deleted folder in the Windows Explorer interface; however, we can with EnCase.

FIGURE 9.28   Child object of a deleted folder. You should note that these objects are not renamed when they are placed in the Recycle Bin.

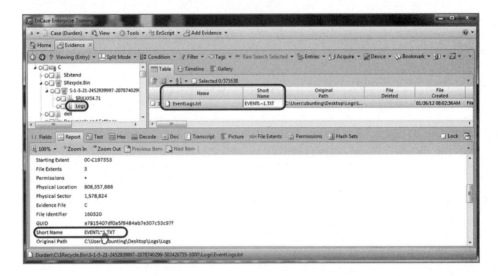

 Windows Vista and 7 can provide examiners with yet another forensic nugget in the updated Recycle Bin, which is the ability to identify files placed in the Recycle Bin from mapped drives. Thus, when a file from a mapped drive is deleted via the Recycle Bin, the Windows Vista/7 Recycle Bin stores it just as another file and tracks its network drive location, or at least this is supposed to be how it works. In practice, however, it does require tweaking to get it to work. Thus, it is possible for a user to force this behavior to occur, but I would expect to see this only on a more experienced user's computer. If it is present, it is much better for the examiner. If you want to enable it on your machine, see http://answers.microsoft.com/en-us/windows/forum/windows_7-files/windows-7-recycle-mapped-drives/95751679-428c-44b0-a8db-1783df9b5e13.

Link Files

Link files are also known as *shortcuts* and have the file extension .lnk. Link files refer to, or link to, target files. These target files can be applications, directories, documents, or data files. They can also be non-file-system objects such as printers or various management consoles. Clicking a shortcut causes the target file to run. If it is an application, the application is launched. If it is a document, the registered application runs and opens the document.

Link files are ubiquitous through Windows. Later in this chapter, I'll cover the Recent, Start, Desktop, and Send To folders, which consist, for the most part, of link or shortcut files. As you will come to appreciate, they are one of the fundamental pieces of the GUI point-and-click environment.

Changing the Properties of a Shortcut

Shortcuts have associated icons (little pictures) that display in the Windows Explorer interface or on the desktop if a shortcut is present there. These icons are predefined but can be changed by the user. To change a shortcut's icon, right-click the shortcut, and choose the Properties command. Then choose the Shortcut tab, shown in Figure 9.29.

FIGURE 9.29   Shortcut tab of the Properties dialog box for a shortcut or link file

In addition to being able to change the icon, you can change other properties of the shortcut, including its target file, from this interface. To change its icon, click the Change Icon button to open the dialog box shown in Figure 9.30. Other icons are usually available with the default one. The user can browse and use other "canned" ones. There are tools that let you create your own.

FIGURE 9.30   The Change Icon dialog box allows the user to change a link or shortcut file's icon.

Forensic Importance of Link Files

The forensic importance of link files lies in their properties, their contents, and the specifics surrounding their creation. Let's examine these various aspects so that you can better understand their function and hence their forensic use. Let's first look at how they are created.

Link files are ubiquitous. There are few places you can't find them. They are created by the operating system upon installation and by applications with which they are installed. They are created by user activity without the user's knowledge. Finally, they can be created deliberately by the user. Each category of link file creation has its own significance.

The operating system creates many link files by default when you install a particular version and service pack of Windows. The desktop is one place you will see default installation icons. The Recycle Bin is a typical default desktop link file. There are others in other locations that I'll cover.

When applications are installed, link files are placed in various locations, some optionally and some automatically. These link files provide the user the ability to launch the newly installed application. By default, a link file is almost always created in the appropriate program folder that appears on the Start menu. Usually as an option, link files can be created on the desktop or on the Quick Launch taskbar.

Certain actions by the user create link files without their knowledge. Because the user is creating virtual "tracks in the snow," such files are of particular forensic interest. Specifically, when a user opens a document, a link file is created in the Recent folder, in the root of the folder with the user's logon name (starting with Vista, this folder is located at Users\UserName\AppData\Roaming\Microsoft\Windows\Recent). The link files in this folder serve as a record of the documents opened by the user.

Users can create link files or move them or copy them to other locations. When a user wants frequent access to a program, file, folder, network resource, or other non-file-system resource (printer, and so on), they can create a shortcut (link file) in an easy-to-access location, most often the desktop. To create a desktop shortcut, the user right-clicks the desktop and chooses New ➢ Shortcut. The Create Shortcut Wizard appears, as shown in Figure 9.31, and guides the user through the process of selecting a target and giving the shortcut a name. A shortcut or link file to a folder named My Hacking Tools, Second Set of Books, Underage Cuties, or SSNs for Salewould have obvious evidentiary value.

FIGURE 9.31   The Create Shortcut Wizard allows the user to create shortcuts, which are actually link files.

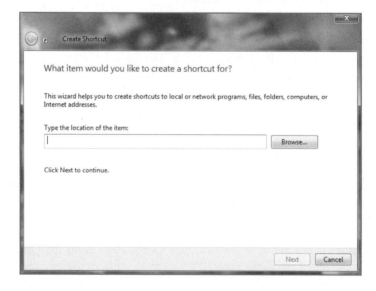

Link files, like any other file, have MAC time stamps that can be significant. If a program was installed on one date and a link file was created later, it can reveal that the user was not only aware that the program existed but went out of their way to create easy access to it. Each time a link file is "used," knowingly or unknowingly, information about the target file is updated in the contents of the link file; thus, the link file itself is modified each time it is used if the target contents have changed, which they nearly always do. When you understand the contents of the link file, why this occurs will become clear. To that end, let's examine the contents of a link file.

The data contained inside a link file describes the various attributes of the target file. It should be obvious that the complete path to the target file would be contained therein. In addition, various other attributes of the target file are recorded:

- Volume serial number on which the target file or folder exists. This can be useful for connecting a file to a unique volume.

- File's size in bytes. This can be of use to the examiner.

- MAC time stamps of the target file. This second set of MAC times for the target file can prove quite valuable in an examination.

MAC times are listed in the following order: created, last accessed, and last written. They are located in the link file at byte offsets 28, 36, and 44, respectively. Byte offsets start at 0 and can be identified easily on the GPS under FO, which stands for *file offset*. Figure 9.32 shows the cursor on byte offset 28, which can be verified by looking at the file offset (circled) in the GPS.

FIGURE 9.32   The cursor is on byte offset 28 of a link file. Starting at this byte and for the next 23 bytes (24 total), three 64-bit Windows time stamps show the created, last accessed, and last written times for the target file.

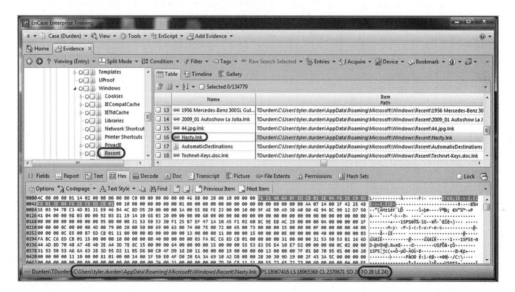

I often use the simple acronym CAW, as in the call of a crow, to help me remember the order these time stamps appear. *C* is for created, *A* is for last accessed, and *W* is for last written.

Careful observers may note that the path (circled) to the Recent folder shown in Figure 9.32 is not where it used to be! Figure 9.32 shows the Recent folder in Windows 7. Yes, our friends in Redmond moved it, and we'll cover that later in this chapter. For now, just concentrate on link file concepts.

To decode the MAC time stamps, start at byte offset 28 and sweep a total of 24 bytes (the LE indicator [circled] in GPS shows length or number of selected bytes). This selects the three Windows 64-bit time stamps for created, last accessed, and last written times for the target file. Once the data containing the time stamps is selected, simply switch to the Decode view. Under View Types, choosing Dates ➤ Windows Data/Time displays all three dates in their respective order (created, last accessed, and last written), as shown in Figure 9.33.

FIGURE 9.33 Created, last accessed, and last written times for a target file in a link file are decoded.

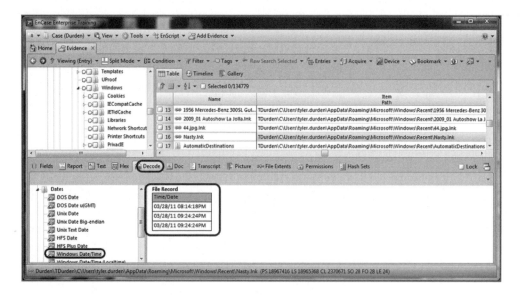

Link files, like many files, have a unique file header. The hex string \x4C\x00\x00\x00\x01\x14\x02 is used to verify file signatures. This string can also be used for finding link files anywhere they may exist.

> ### Windows Vista, Server 2008, and Windows 7 Last Accessed Time Stamp Disabled
>
> When the operating system is Windows Vista or newer, be careful when evaluating the last accessed time stamp. By default, in Windows Vista, a file's last accessed time stamp is disabled and is not therefore tracked. It would be nice if there were no value stored in the space allocated in the MFT for the last-accessed time stamp, but such is not the case. Windows Vista stores the file creation date and time in this space. Thus, EnCase will report what is stored in the MFT for this value, which is in reality the file or folder's creation time and not its last accessed time. Likewise, when link files are created in Windows Vista, the last accessed time stamp found in the link file will also be that of the creation date and time.
>
> Microsoft states that it did this for system performance improvement. This setting is stored in the registry at HKEY_LOCAL_MACHINE\SYSTEM\CurrentControlSet\Control\ FileSystem. In this key, the value NtfsDisableLastAccessUpdate will normally be 1, meaning Windows Vista, by default, is not tracking the last accessed time. If it is 0, the user has changed it, and Windows Vista will then accurately track the last accessed time. If you need more information about the registry, see Chapter 10. Although this value is certainly worth checking, don't expect to find too many home users caring enough to change this setting. In enterprise environments, the case may be different if the systems are managed by smart administrators who change this setting globally using group policy.

Using the Link File Parser

Link files have a complex structure, and decoding each field or piece of data within link files is beyond the scope of this text. Like for many tedious tasks facing the examiner, EnCase provides an automated method for decoding these files using an EnScript. Prior to EnCase 7, the link parsing tool was found within the Case Processor EnScript. Starting with EnCase 7, this same tool is now found within the EnCase Evidence Processor, specifically in the modules section as part of the Windows Artifact Parser. As you'll recall, the same parse options menu for the Recycle Bin files contained link files as well. Figure 9.34 shows the parsing options for the Windows Artifact Parser. Thus, parsing link files is as simple selecting this option and running the EnCase Evidence Processor.

When the EnCase Evidence Processor (EEP) completes, run the Case Analyzer. The Case Analyzer parses information found by the EEP and presents it to you in an interface that enables hierarchical navigation. To view the results, follow the navigation to the Windows Artifact Parser and downward from there to the link file. Figure 9.35 displays the results.

FIGURE 9.34 The link file parser is found in the EnCase Evidence Processor Windows Artifact Parser.

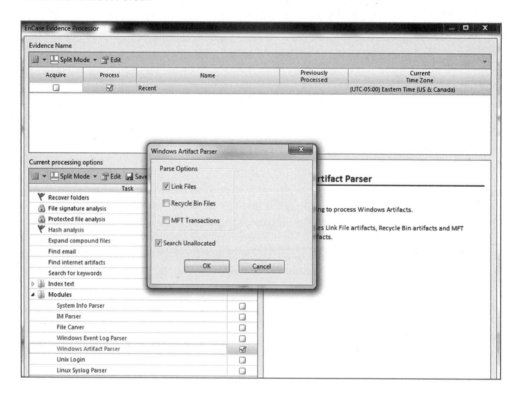

FIGURE 9.35 Link file parser results viewed through Case Analyzer interface. Note the hyperlink navigation bar that is circled.

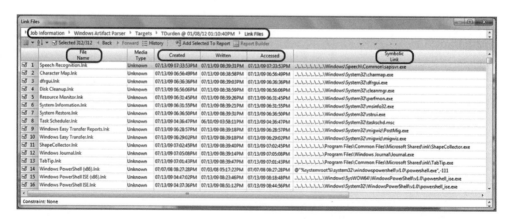

Note that link file data can be found almost anywhere. As link files are processed, they are stored in RAM memory, which is volatile data. As often happens, the operating system writes volatile data that is not currently in use to the swap file (`pagefile.sys`) to temporarily hold it there while it makes room in volatile RAM for a current task. The swap file, by default, is configured to adjust in size. While this adjustment occurs, clusters that were formerly allocated to the swap file find themselves in unallocated space, thereby placing link files in the unallocated space along with other data. Therefore, to be thorough, you should parse for link files in the unallocated spaces. You may recall this parsing option from Figure 9.34.

With Windows XP/Vista/7, if the system is placed into hibernation or hybrid sleep, the contents of RAM are written to the `hiberfil.sys` file. As the result of this process, link files, not to mention other data, can be found in this file.

As you have seen, link files provide significant information to the examiner. We'll cover in detail several folders in which link files are found, because their significance varies based on where they are found. Before delving into those specific folders, let's examine the general directory structure created on current versions of Windows (2000, XP, Server 2003, Vista, Server 2008, and Windows 7) because the directory structure itself is forensically significant in the information it offers.

Often, you'll need answers quickly and don't have time to run the EnCase Evidence Processor over an entire device or case. If you need, for example, just the link files in the Recent folder, create a logical evidence file (LEF) from the Recent folder and simply run the EnCase Evidence Processor Windows Artifact Parser (Link files selected) against that single LEF. You'll get your information returned quickly without having to wait for unnecessary information to process.

Windows Folders

Each version of Windows has its own unique directory structure and file and folder naming conventions that differentiate that version from the other versions. With experience, the examiner can usually have a good idea which version of Windows is installed by looking at the directory structure for certain telltale file and folder names. Despite how convincing these naming and structure conventions may appear, these normal conventions are not cast in granite. The final determination of what operating system is installed is derived from the registry, which I'll cover in Chapter 10.

Nevertheless, the examiner should be familiar with the directory structures and file and folder naming conventions that are normally used by the various versions of Windows. With that knowledge and familiarity, navigating and locating operating system artifacts is greatly facilitated along with an understanding of their significance as they relate to a particular version of Windows.

The folder name that contains the Windows system files has varied with Windows versions. With Windows 9x versions, the system files were contained in the Windows folder. System files were stored in the WINNT folder with Windows NT and 2000. Just when you thought there was some discernible logic in their naming conventions, Windows XP came out and reverted to storing the system files in the Windows folder. Even with Windows Vista and beyond, the Windows folder remained the same. That seems straightforward enough, but things can deviate from this convention if an upgrade from one version of Windows to another occurred or if the user engaged in customization. Table 9.3 shows the system folder and user profile folder conventions for various versions of Windows. The naming conventions are for default new installations and do not apply to upgrades.

TABLE 9.3   Default new-installation system folder and user profile folder names for versions of Windows

Operating system	User profile folders	Default system folder
Windows 9x/Me	No Documents and Settings folder	C:\Windows
Windows NT	C:\WINNT\Profiles	C:\WINNT
Windows 2000	C:\Documents and Settings	C:\WINNT
Windows XP/2003	C:\Documents and Settings	C:\Windows
Windows Vista/2008/7	C:\Users	C:\Windows

All versions of Windows NT (NT, 2000 XP, 2003, Vista, 2008, 7) create a unique artifact when the user first logs onto the system. A folder is created that bears the name of the logged-on user. This folder will appear in Documents and Settings for Windows 2000, XP, and 2003; in Users for Windows Vista and beyond; or in WINNT\Profiles for Windows NT. This folder, called the *root user folder*, is created regardless of whether the user logs on locally or through a domain. Thus, the directory naming convention itself bears forensic value in identifying the user by their logon name. Figure 9.36 shows various root user folders created under Users for Windows Vista/7.

FIGURE 9.36   Root user folders created in Windows Vista

Reparse Points

As you look at Windows Vista and beyond, one of the most dramatic changes you see immediately is that folders were moved around and renamed. When you move things around and rename them, you risk wreaking havoc with programs that address the old locations. To avoid breaking legacy programs and thereby maintaining backward compatibility, *reparse points* are used where the old folders used to be.

There are different types of reparse points in Windows Vista. A reparse point to a folder is called a *junction*. The first and most obvious reparse point (junction) that you see in Windows Vista is Documents and Settings. If you click it with Windows Vista/2008/7 Explorer, you are greeted with an "Access Denied" message.

If you look at the same folder in EnCase, I'm pleased to report you won't be greeted by such a message. Rather, you'll see a symbolic link icon next to the folder name. If you look at the description column, you'll see it described as a symbolic link. If you look in the View pane on the Report tab, you see a line that again says "Symbolic Link" followed by the full path to folder to which the reparse point directs. In the case of Documents and Settings, the reparse point links to the path C:\Users.

Thus, any program that asks the operating system to address Documents and Settings will be redirected to C:\Users. You will see many reparse points representing the legacy Windows folders throughout Windows Vista/7. Now that you understand what they are and how they are used, you can move on with one more of Windows Vista/7's mysteries behind you.

Windows, for the most part, segregates or compartmentalizes that user's configuration, environment, and document files into subfolders under the root user folder. Further, by applying security credentials and permissions to each user's folders, users (except those with administrator or system privileges) are generally precluded from accessing other users' data. Forensically, this is most convenient: potential evidence for each user is neatly labeled and compartmentalized. Figure 9.37 shows the various subfolders created under the root user folder that are designed to contain the user's documents along with their configuration and user environment data.

At the same time that the root user folder and its subfolders are created at first logon, another significant file is created: the NTUSER.DAT file. This file is selected in the Table view pane in Figure 9.37. As you'll come to better appreciate in Chapter 10, this file comprises the user's registry hive.

FIGURE 9.37   Folders containing the user's documents, configuration, and environment data are created as subfolders under the root user folder.

Roaming Profiles in Windows

For Windows 2000, XP, and 2003, another file is created in the root user folder at first logon that is of interest to those working in domain environments where roaming profiles are in use.

Roaming profiles allow users to log onto various domain computers and have their user profiles follow them around. For the most part, this roaming profile consists of all the files and subfolders under the root user folder. There are exceptions, however, and they are defined in the ntuser.ini file, created at first logon.

Any folders listed after ExclusionList= in this file will not be included in the user's roaming profile. By default, the History, Temp, and Temporary Internet Files folders (found in the Local Settings folder) are excluded from the roaming profile.

In a domain setting where roaming profiles are used, files found in these three folders were created locally on that machine. They don't "follow" the user around in the domain. The ntuser.ini file can be modified on an individual basis or by group policy.

Windows Vista (and beyond) handles things differently. In AppData there are Local or Roaming folders. The data in the Local folders stays with the local host, and data in the Roaming folder follows the user in a domain.

The registry is a large database of system settings and configurations. The contents of the NTUSER.DAT file are specific to that user and their settings only. Chapter 10 covers some of the contents of this file. For now, you should understand that the file creation date for this file would normally indicate when the user first logged onto the computer under examination. This file is modified just as the user is logging off, so the last written date of this file would normally indicate when the user last used the computer under that username.

The operating system artifacts covered in the rest of this chapter are in the subfolders in the root user folder. Our approach will be that of examining the artifacts found in the folders that are generally the most significant ones for the examiner to analyze.

Recent Folder

When I discussed link files, I described how whenever a user opens a document, a link file is created in the Recent folder located in the root user folder, except for Windows Vista and beyond where it is located in the path C:\Users\%UserName%\AppData\Roaming\Microsoft\Windows\Recent. The user is unaware that this file is being created or modified. If the same document in the same location is later reopened, the link file is updated with the target file's updated information.

The purpose of the Recent folder is to provide a user interface that lists documents the user has recently created or modified. You can access this interface by clicking the Start button and then selecting My Recent Documents (older versions of Windows) or Recent Items (Windows Vista and beyond), as shown in Figure 9.38. By default, Windows displays the last 15 documents opened by the user.

FIGURE 9.38   The Recent folder contains link files that populate the Recent Items menu in Windows Vista with the last 15 files the user opened.

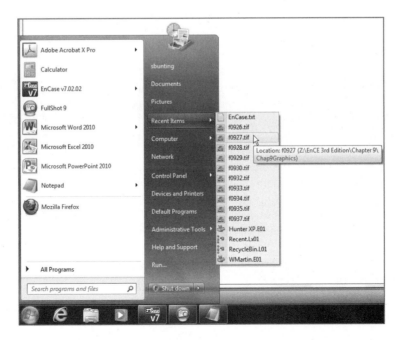

The Recent folder contains only link files. Windows looks to the MAC times of the link files to determine the most recent "link" file and looks to the content of the link file to display the information. If you select the properties of any file listed in My Recent Documents or Recent Items, you'll see the properties of the file that the link file points to and not necessarily those of the link file itself.

Although Windows displays only the last 15 documents, the Recent folder can contain hundreds of link files collected over months or years. For any one file in a specific path, there will be only one link file in the Recent folder for it. Each time it is accessed, the link file content is updated. Link files in the Recent folder are named after the file (including its extension) plus the extension .lnk. For example, a file named MyFile.doc would be given a filename of Myfile.doc.lnk in the Recent folder.

Link files in the Recent folder, probably as much as any other link file, are likely to be in RAM and from there are swapped out to the pagefile.sys file. Once in the swap file, an adjustment to the size of the swap file places them into the unallocated space. If a drive is formatted, these link files will lose their directory pointers, but the data is still there unless overwritten. The Link File Parser EnScript can recover much of this data from the unallocated clusters regardless of how the data was placed there.

Link files can reveal a wealth of information. Take the time to understand them, perform your own testing and research regarding their behavior, and then use that knowledge when conducting examinations.

One of the first places I examine in a case is the Recent folder. I quickly sort the files chronologically by last written time. It serves as a quick litmus test and timeline to see what kind of files the user has been accessing and, better yet, where those files are located on their system. This approach can quickly point the way to the user's favored or hidden storage locations, saving you lots of time and quickly focusing your resources in the right direction.

Desktop Folder

The files of any type located on your desktop are stored, in part, in the Desktop folder located in the root user folder. These files can be any type but are typically shortcuts (link files), applications, or documents. When a user first logs on and their root user folder is created, their Desktop folder has very little in it. (Currently Windows 7 Service Pack 1 deposits a shortcut file to the Windows Recycle Bin in the Desktop folder of all new users.)

Just because there is only one shortcut file in the user's Desktop folder does not mean the user has only one file or icon on their desktop. Interestingly, the files on your desktop have more than one source of origin. In older versions of Windows, any file that appears in the Desktop folder of the root user folder named All Users appears on the desktop of every user on that local host computer. Starting with Windows Vista, All Users has been replaced by Public, as shown in Figure 9.39. Thus, any file that appears in the Desktop folder in Public appears on the desktop of every user on that local host computer.

FIGURE 9.39 Starting with Windows Vista, the All Users folder has been replaced by a folder named Public

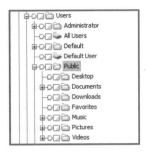

Other desktop objects are defined in the registry, such as the Recycle Bin. In addition to the Recycle Bin, the user may opt to have other desktop objects such as My Computer, My Network Places, Internet Explorer, or My Documents. You access the option to place these objects on the desktop by right-clicking the Windows Vista desktop and selecting Personalize. In the resulting dialog box, choose Change Desktop Icons under Tasks in the left pane. From there, as shown in Figure 9.40, it's a simple matter of checking the items you want to appear on your desktop. These settings are also stored in the registry.

FIGURE 9.40 The Desktop Icon Settings dialog box gives users the opportunity to select several items to be displayed on their desktop.

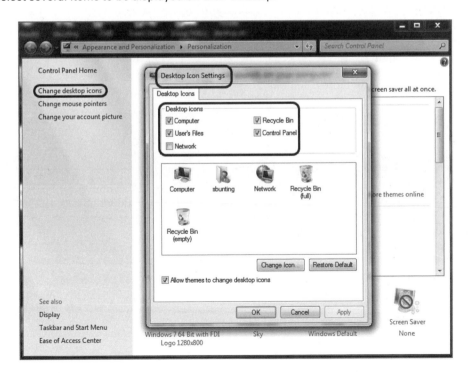

Thus, the contents that are displayed on the typical Windows desktop are derived from three sources: the registry, the All Users/Desktop or Public/Desktop folder, and the user's Desktop folder. If the host computer is in a domain environment and the user authenticates to a domain, the desktop can have yet another source. Group policy settings can direct that individual users or groups of users have a specified desktop, thereby providing a uniform fixed desktop to domain users.

Shortly after looking at the Recent folder, I typically examine the user's Desktop folder, which contains the files or shortcuts that a user placed there or caused to be placed there. Often, people place items they frequently access on their desktops, another good indicator of the user's activities and preferences.

My Documents/Documents

In older versions of Windows, under each root user folder there is, by default, a folder named My Documents. By default it contains a subfolder named My Pictures and most likely My Music and My eBooks, depending on the Windows version and service pack installed.

Of course, Windows Vista had to rearrange and rename things slightly just to keep everyone on their toes. In Windows Vista (and beyond), My Documents is called Documents and is still directly under the root user folder. My Pictures is called Pictures, and My Music is called Music. Both are directly under the root user folder instead of being subfolders of My Documents.

The purpose of these folders is to have secure and segregated locations for each user's files and folders. Most programs will default to saving files into the My Documents or Documents folder. The My Pictures or Pictures folder will typically contain several sample pictures of natural scenes, all of which are JPEG files. Beyond the default sample content, other files and folders in this folder are there as the result of user activity.

Send To Folder

The Send To folder contains the objects or links that will appear in the Explorer interface under the right-click option Send To. Several items appear here by default upon installation, and other items are created when various programs are installed. Although the user can add items here manually, this doesn't often happen. It is a good place to examine to locate attached media such as zip drives and the like.

Temp Folder

The Temp folder is a subfolder of the Local Settings folder. With Windows Vista (and beyond), this folder appears in the path Users\\%UserName%\\AppData\\Local\\Temp. As the name implies, the purpose of the Temp folder is to temporarily store files. There seems to be no end to the types of files you can find here. This is a good place to look after running a file-signature analysis because often programs create working copies of open documents in this area, changing their extensions. Some programs delete them when done, and others simply leave behind their garbage. I once found three files that were more than 2 GB each in this area. They apparently were created during a major system malfunction and were rich with evidence.

This area is normally hidden from the user and is certainly an area you want to examine carefully. In addition to having hidden or backup copies of files here, programs often write their temporary install files and folders in this area, as you can see in Figure 9.41.

FIGURE 9.41   The Temp folder can contain temporary files from program installation that are often overlooked when removing programs.

Often, a user will remove a program from an area they can access, such as Program Files, but will fail to remove files and folders in this area because it is out of the way and normally hidden. You may, therefore, find evidence here that refutes a claim that the user never had a given application installed on their system. You may find other Temp folders in other areas of the file system, but the important thing to remember is that this Temp folder (located in the Local Settings folder of the root user folder) is specific to the user.

Favorites Folder

The Favorites folder contains Internet shortcut files for Microsoft Internet Explorer. Internet shortcut files function in a similar way to link files in that they contain information about their target and the user accesses the target by clicking the shortcut file. In this case, the files have an extension of .url, which stands for Uniform Resource Locator. The target of an Internet shortcut is a URL, which is typically a web address but could just as easily be to a file on the local host or on a network resource.

A URL file has a unique header—[InternetShortcut], or at least it has remained so until recently. With Windows 7, that header has changed, as shown in Figure 9.42. Immediately following the string [InternetShortcut] will be the path to the URL target. The header (both formats) can be used to search for deleted shortcuts, depending on the version of Windows.

FIGURE 9.42   The data area of a URL file. This one is a default favorite that takes you to MSN.COM. Note the file header.

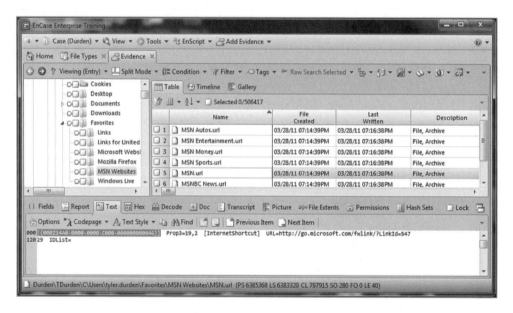

It is important to understand that some Internet shortcut files are loaded during installation. These default favorites can vary slightly depending on the Windows version and service pack. Additionally, some computer manufacturers use a customized original equipment manufacturer (OEM) version of Windows that may contain favorites to their company website or to those of their close affiliates. Figure 9.42 shows a default set of favorites for a standard installation of Windows 7.

You now understand the purpose of the Favorites folder and the structure and purpose of URL files. You also understand that you can expect, by default, that there will be some favorites preinstalled in this area. Some programs, when they are installed, may place a

URL to their company site in this area. Some may ask first, and others may not. Beyond those favorites, for the most part, what is placed in this area is done or at least caused by the user. Some websites may provide a mechanism by which they can be added to the user's favorites, with the user's permission.

Some malicious code may add favorites without the user's knowledge if their machine is vulnerable to such an action. Often, a telltale signature of such an act is that the creation time stamp for multiple favorites is within the same one- or two-second time period, making it clear that it was automated and not a manual act by the user.

When you examine this area, you will often find an elaborate tree of well-organized folders. When you compare this to the default, it is clear that such acts are carried out by the user. You will find that the Favorites folder is a valuable area to examine and that the evidence found here corroborates other findings. If a user claims that their visits to inappropriate websites were accidental, such can be easily refuted if the user has established an elaborate folder structure of favorites containing those same inappropriate websites.

Windows Vista Low Folders

As you go through the folders associated with the Windows 7 version of Internet Explorer 9, in addition to having new locations for these folders, you will see the presence of Low folders. The Cookies, History, and Temporary Internet Files folders will each have a subfolder named Low in which much of the structure of the Cookies, History, and Temporary Internet Files folders, subfolders, and files is repeated. Figure 9.43 shows how this structure appears for the Temporary Internet Files folder. You will note that the Content.IE5 folder appears normally as a subfolder in Temporary Internet Files. If you will look carefully, Temporary Internet Files has a new subfolder named Low in which the Content.IE5 folder appears again.

FIGURE 9.43   Temporary Internet Files structure including Low folder

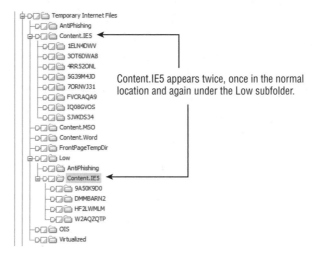

Content.IE5 appears twice, once in the normal location and again under the Low subfolder.

Before I explain what all of this means, I must first digress and explain some new security features that started with Windows Vista and persist through Server 2008 and Windows 7. With that understanding, the new folder structure will make a little more sense.

No doubt you have seen the commercials in which the Windows Vista operating system has been the target of humor over its warning messages asking you whether it is OK to proceed and so forth. These messages are part of Windows Vista's new security system, which, dare I say it, is something akin to the one used in OS X. Under either of these systems, the user's privileges upon login, even if they are administrators, are those of a mere user. When higher privileges are required by the task at hand, the process is interrupted until the user agrees to move forward.

The intent of this security model is to protect the system from malware. In the past, most Windows home users were administrators, and any process that was run by the user ran with administrator rights, which included malware. Under the new model, any process wanting to run with elevated privileges must do so with the express permission of the user.

Under Windows Vista (and beyond), the security system is a three-tiered, defense-in-depth system and is dubbed the UAC protected mode. The protected mode system uses the following three tiers of defense:

User Account Control (UAC)   The UAC implements the Principle of Least Privilege in which the user, despite being an administrator, functions at a lowest level needed to carry out normal user tasks.

Mandatory Integrity Control (MIC)   MIC implements a model in which data is configured or secured to prevent lower-integrity applications from accessing it. In Windows Vista and beyond, these data integrity levels are System, High, Medium, and Low. You should immediately pick up on the word *Low* and associate it with the Low folders. Let's call that a hint! Tasks that run from the Start menu run with a Medium integrity level. Files run by the user from the Explorer shell interface run with a Medium integrity level. Internet Explorer 7 runs files from the Internet at the Low integrity level. That's another hint!

User Interface Privilege Isolation (UIPI)   UIPI blocks lower-integrity processes from accessing higher-integrity processes. This mechanism prevents privilege escalation by means of blocking hooks into higher-level processes.

Without further digressing into the Windows Vista (and beyond) security model, you now have sufficient information to understand the Low folders. Internet Explorer 9 has a protected mode that leverages the Windows Vista security model by placing files from the Internet into the Low folders. Data placed in the Low folders runs at the lowest possible level of integrity and is therefore contained in a protective shell. By being isolated in a Low folder, its integrity is on the bottom on the Windows Vista (and beyond) security totem pole. Since this data can run only with the lowest possible privileges and can't climb or gain escalated privileges by virtue of UIPI, Internet browsing is made much safer.

Thus, normal Windows Vista (and beyond) Internet browsing activity will result in the data being placed in the Low folders. This goes for Cookies, History, and Temporary Internet Files. Because there is a normal or regular folder structure for Cookies, History, and Temporary

`Internet Files`, they must be there for a reason. They exist for holding data that is run at the higher integrity levels. Given the new security model, you might ask yourself how that could be. The answer lies in a series of exceptions.

As you may recall, files run from the Windows Explorer shell are tracked in the Internet history. For example, when you open a Word document, not only is a link file created but also an entry is made in the Internet history file. As I mentioned earlier in this section, Windows Explorer runs at the medium integrity level, and therefore history entries for files opened on the local host through Windows Explorer will be tracked in the regular `History` folder and not in the `Low` folder.

At first, you may think that you may now have a place for Internet activity (`Low` folders) and a place for local host activity (normal folders), but that logic must give may to more exceptions. Those exceptions are as follows:

- Disabling Internet Explorer 9 protected mode in the Internet Explorer 9 Internet Options Security tab is one exception. The user would have to disable the protected mode for each zone.

- Running Internet Explorer 9 in the administrator mode is another exception.

- Turning off the User Account Control (UAC) automatically disables Internet Explorer 9 protected mode because it has dependencies upon UAC, one of which is UIPI.

- Because the trusted sites security zone is considered safe, the protected mode does not apply to those sites, which includes sites added to this zone by the user. Thus, any site in the trusted zone runs with normal privileges.

- Viewing a local HTML page is considered trusted and runs in the unprotected mode, unless that local HTML page was saved locally from a website that was in the untrusted zone. If such is the case, even though viewed locally, the protected mode will be used to view this page.

Thus, the nice clean separation between data from the Internet (`Low` folders) and data from the local host (normal folders) is broken by a series of exceptions. In addition to these exceptions, for reasons Microsoft can't explain, there is some sporadic bleed over into the normal folders from data that should clearly be in the `Low` folders.

From a forensic standpoint, the examiner simply needs to make certain to process both the normal and `Low` folders to get all of the data. In Windows Vista/7, it is no longer in one convenient place. Generally speaking, except for the exceptions noted earlier, the data in the `Low` folder will be from normal Internet browsing, while the data in the normal folders will be from the local host or from Internet activity for which the protected mode did not apply.

Cookies Folder

In older versions of Windows, the `Cookies` folder is located in the root user folder. With Windows Vista (and beyond), because cookies follow the user in a domain, the `Cookies` folder is found at `\Users\%UserName%\AppData\Roaming\Microsoft\Windows\Cookies`.

Also with Windows Vista, in the `Cookies` folder you'll find a folder named `Low`, which was covered earlier. Thus, for Windows Vista (and beyond) Internet Explorer 9, you need to remember to examine and process both the normal `Cookies` folder and the `Low` folder, which is a subfolder of the `Cookies` folder.

Cookies are pieces of code created by websites and placed on the user's local computer. The code is supposed to be for the purpose of enhancing the user's browsing experience, in theory, but can be used for nefarious purposes. The data in a cookie is created by the website, and its true content or purpose is often unknown. Because of this, cookies are a serious security concern.

Cookie names have traditionally take the form of *username@domain name*.txt; however, recently (Microsoft patch in August 2011), they have evolved to take the format of an eight-character GUID with the .txt extension. The name changing convention is a security mechanism to prevent malicious data from being inserted into predictable cookie filenames. Each cookie is contained in one file, as shown in Figure 9.44. The total collection of cookie files is under the management of an `index.dat` file, which contains data about each cookie and pointers to the cookie file and to the originating web domain name. The `index.dat` file contains dates, and the cookie itself contains internal dates. The internal dates of a cookie describe when it was last modified by the website and its date of expiration.

FIGURE 9.44   Cookie files in the Cookies/Low subfolder. Microsoft apparently regards the site as untrusted by virtue of its appearance in the Low folder (an untrusted zone). The cookie data is visible in the View pane.

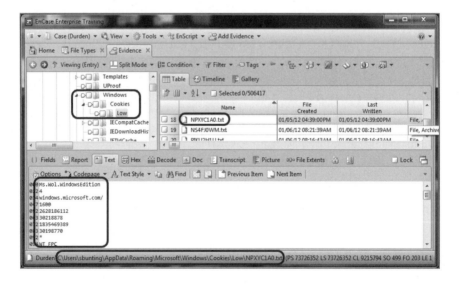

Some analytical examiners have been successful at using a cookie with a known expiration period to prove or disprove the accuracy of the system time when the cookie was last modified. Thus, there is certainly value in understanding cookie internals.

Several cookie decoders are available, but probably the best and easiest to use is CookieView, written by Craig Wilson. It is made to work in conjunction with EnCase as a viewer. When it is installed as a viewer, you can right-click a cookie in EnCase and use the Open with feature to pass the cookie file to CookieView, which will open externally and decode the values in the cookie, as shown in Figure 9.45. You can download CookieView from www.digital-detective.co.uk.

FIGURE 9.45   Cookie data decoded by CookieView, which can be installed as a viewer in EnCase

🌐 Real World Scenario

A Cookie Can Make Your Case

A woman was being stalked. She had, several years prior, preferred stalking charges against an individual, and it was her belief he was again stalking her, but he had learned many lessons, and he was very adept at concealing his identity.

Despite her extreme efforts to protect her identity, address, and so on, she received gifts in the mail, even ones for her newborn child, birthday electronic greetings, and other electronic communications. The stalker preferred public sites, especially ones in which Deep Freeze, or like programs, was installed. These programs refresh the OS and user data with each reboot, effectively sending evidence to the unallocated space and with considerable overwriting of data.

When a stalker gets comfortable with a routine, they make mistakes. This particular stalker favored a certain library with Deep Freeze. Arrangements were made with that library's staff to seize the machine as soon as possible the next time he used it. Naturally, he continued, and we seized the machine within just a few hours of the next offense and before Deep Freeze was permitted to run.

We easily recovered his electronic greeting, but that offered no evidence. Sometimes, though, people's habits and vices become their undoing. This was no exception. The stalker was addicted to a certain unnamed sports fantasy game by which one could win money. Thus, he couldn't help himself but to check in on his "game." When he did so, a cookie was left behind that contained the domain name of the game and a user ID.

After some testing using the same game, we found that the cookie expiration date and time was exactly one year from the time the site was visited, thus time stamping the cookie to coincide with the stalking event. Bingo!

Our next step was to send a subpoena to the sporting game's host to get a history and account information for the user ID. When that information came back, the name matched our suspect and the IP address history showed hundreds of logins from his home.

Naturally, we promptly visited him with a search warrant and arrest warrants in hand. The forensics examination of his machine revealed extensive searches for the victim, her family, and her friends, which was unsettling to all involved, given his obsession and persistence over the years.

A big question was also answered by the forensics, which was how he was getting information about the victim. Surprisingly, the answer was Amazon wish lists. The default list is public, and through this mechanism the stalker watched the victim's shopping habits and desires, including the birthday registry for her newborn.

One day a call came in from internal counsel for the sporting game company. He commented that this was the first time he was aware of that their service's artifacts were used to place a defendant at the scene of the crime. He was concerned, naturally, about publicity, and so on. As the stalker was entering a guilty plea, in the face of overwhelming evidence, the public knowledge issue was of no further concern.

The cyberstalker was incarcerated and subjected to a long probation period and mandatory post-incarceration psychological treatment.

History Folder

In older versions of Windows, the History folder is located in the Local Settings folder, which is in turn under the root user folder. For Windows Vista (and beyond) Internet Explorer 9, since history does not follow the user in a domain, history appears under the local folder in the path: C:\Users\%UserName%\AppData\Local\Microsoft\Windows\History. Under History, you'll find both History.IE5 and Low\History.IE5. As mentioned in the previous section, the latter is for Internet data resulting from browsing in the protected mode, while the former is from unprotected-mode activity, both local and internet.

The History folder, as the name implies, contains the history of the user's Internet browsing history. It enables you to go back and find websites they have recently visited. When you click the History button on the Internet Explorer toolbar (alternatively, View ➤ Explorer Bar ➤ History), the History window opens, usually on the left side of the browser window, as shown in Figure 9.46.

FIGURE 9.46   The Internet history feature shows the Internet history listing.

There is a top level or main index.dat database file that sits at the root level in the History.IE5 folder. All the history for the period covered is contained in this file. The default period is 20 days. In the History.IE5 folder are folders that have unique folder names. These folder names correspond with periods of time conforming to the convention MSHist01*DateRange*. The date range is in the format YEARMODAYEARMODA. These periods of time are in sync with the time periods you will see in the history window of your browser. Figure 9.47 depicts a typical History folder with the folders named after date ranges.

FIGURE 9.47   Folders named after Internet history date ranges have been located in the History.IE5 folder.

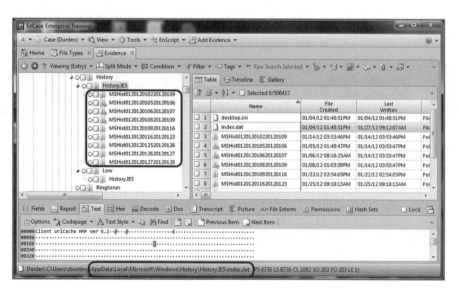

Table 9.4 maps a series of History folder names to the date ranges they represent as well as to their Internet history interface counterparts, specifically to those shown in Figures 9.46 and 9.47. It further describes which type of index.dat file (daily or weekly) is stored within that folder.

TABLE 9.4   History folder names are translated and linked to their browser History folder

History folder name	Date range	Browser History folder
MSHist012012010220120109 (index.dat File Type: Weekly)	2012 01 02 to 2012 01 09	Three weeks ago
MSHist012012010520120106 (index.dat File Type: Daily)	2012 01 05 to 2012 01 06	Deleted and recovered
MSHist012012010620120107 (index.dat File Type: Daily)	2012 01 06 to 2012 01 07	Deleted and recovered
MSHist012012010820120109 (index.dat File Type: Daily)	2012 01 08 to 2012 01 09	Deleted and recovered
MSHist012012010920120116 (index.dat File Type: Weekly)	2012 01 09 to 2012 01 16	Two weeks ago
MSHist012012011620120123 (index.dat File Type: Weekly)	2012 01 16 to 2012 01 23	Last week
MSHist012012012520120126 (index.dat File Type: Daily)	2012 01 25 to 2012 01 26	Wednesday
MSHist012012012620120127 (index.dat File Type: Daily)	2012 01 26 to 2012 01 27	Thursday
MSHist012012012720120128 (index.dat File Type: Daily)	2012 01 27 to 2012 01 28	Today

There is an index.dat Internet history database file located in each of the folders named after date ranges. The various history index.dat files (storing main history, daily history, and weekly history) are all slightly different in their internal structures. Fortunately, EnCase will decode the history for you and present it in a separate view that lets you analyze that information and bookmark it for inclusion in your report.

For EnCase to parse the history files and decode them for viewing, you must first direct EnCase to parse the Internet history, which beginning with EnCase 7 is carried out from within the EnCase Evidence Processor (EEP), as shown in Figure 9.48. With Find Internet Artifacts selected, run the EEP to begin the process. You should again note that you can optionally search the unallocated space, which provides for the most thorough search but will take additional processing time to complete.

FIGURE 9.48   Find Internet Artifacts is launched from within the EnCase Evidence Processor

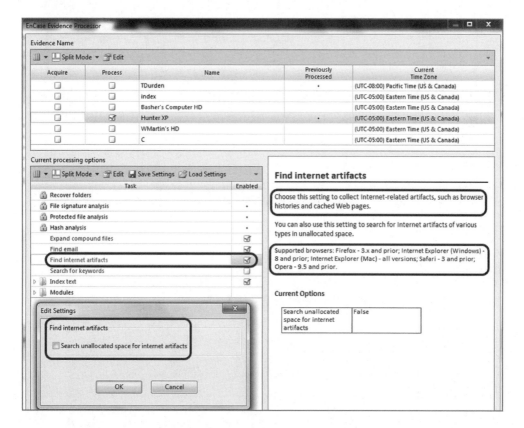

When the processing is finished, EnCase will have parsed and decoded both the Internet Explorer history and web cache, placing their results on the Records tab. Figure 9.49 shows the Records tab after the Internet history results have been processed and posted to this tab.

From the Records tab's Table view pane, you can sort by any of the columns. You can sort by date so as to view the history in a timeline. Using the conditions and filters, you can filter and view by host, user, name, or URL. You may prefer to select and bookmark individual entries or select them all and bookmark them all at once. When bookmarked, the entries are sent to the Bookmarks view for later inclusion in your report. Figure 9.50 shows a bookmarked Internet history report.

FIGURE 9.49   Records tab showing results of Internet history search with both History and Cache reported in separate folders

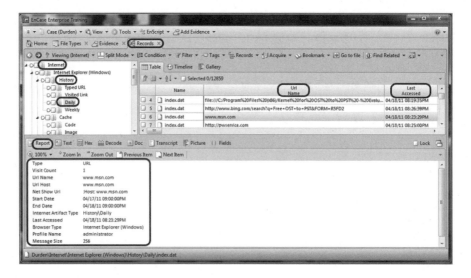

FIGURE 9.50   An Internet history entry is bookmarked and appears in Bookmarks view as they would appear in your final report.

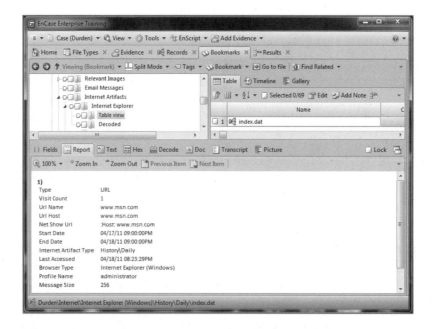

While the Records view contains the data from the EEP and you can work with it there, you can also use the Case Analyzer to summarize information from the Records view. Run the Case Analyzer and navigate to the Internet artifacts, as shown in Figure 9.51. As you can see, this view summarizes hosts by the number of visits, machines, and users. This information can be selected and sent to reports from this interface.

FIGURE 9.51   Case Analyzer used to summarize Internet history

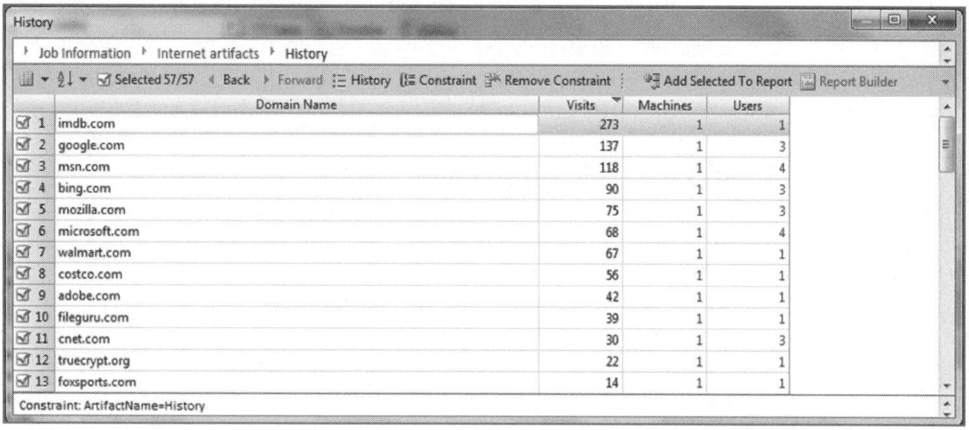

History

› Job Information › Internet artifacts › History

☐ ▾ ⫯↓ ▾ ☑ Selected 57/57 ◁ Back ▷ Forward ⫶≡ History ⫶≡ Constraint ⧉ Remove Constraint   ⧉ Add Selected To Report ⧉ Report Builder

	Domain Name	Visits	Machines	Users
☑ 1	imdb.com	273	1	1
☑ 2	google.com	137	1	3
☑ 3	msn.com	118	1	4
☑ 4	bing.com	90	1	3
☑ 5	mozilla.com	75	1	3
☑ 6	microsoft.com	68	1	4
☑ 7	walmart.com	67	1	1
☑ 8	costco.com	56	1	1
☑ 9	adobe.com	42	1	1
☑ 10	fileguru.com	39	1	1
☑ 11	cnet.com	30	1	3
☑ 12	truecrypt.org	22	1	1
☑ 13	foxsports.com	14	1	1

Constraint: ArtifactName=History

Internet History and Registered Local-Host Files

Figure 9.49 (entry #4 in Table view) illustrates a little-known or understood fact. Whenever a file on the host computer is opened or saved and that file is a registered file type, an entry is made in the history database (main, daily, and eventually weekly). The file is local and it is not cached, so don't expect to find it in the cache. Instead of the record beginning with URL, as would be the case with a web address, the record begins with file:///, followed by the full path and filename. Many believe the file must be opened in Internet Explorer for an entry to be here, but such is not the case. If you click a file and open it with its application, it will appear here. Expect to see Microsoft Office documents of all sorts as well as other file types.

In the earlier section "Windows Vista Low Folders," I discussed this topic in the context of where these files will be stored with Windows Vista. Because these local host files are being run via the Windows Explorer shell, they are running with Medium integrity and will not appear in the Low folders but rather in the normal folders in Windows Vista (and beyond).

Temporary Internet Files

In older versions of Microsoft Windows, the Temporary Internet Files folder, often called the "TIF folder" by many examiners, is located under the Local Settings folder. With Windows Vista (and beyond), since Internet cache does not follow a user in a domain, the TIF folder is a local setting and stored at C:\Users\%*UserName*%\AppData\Local\ Microsoft\Windows\Temporary Internet Files\. Also recall that with Windows Vista (and beyond), Low folders will be present. Data from protected-mode Internet activity is in the Low folders, while activity from unprotected-mode Internet will be in the normal folders.

The folders contained in the TIF folder store the files downloaded and cached from the Internet. By storing or caching these files, when a user returns to a site they visit often, the browser checks to see whether the files in cache are current. If so, there is no need to clog the Internet downloading files that are locally cached and current. In that case, the file in cache is used and not downloaded. In this manner, traffic on the Web is lessened, and the user sees their web page more quickly.

Naturally there must be a method to store and manage these files. By now you shouldn't be surprised to find that yet another index.dat file is used for this purpose. Although the name is the same as the other index.dat files I have thus far discussed, this one also differs somewhat in its structure and purpose from the others. The web cache index.dat file sits in the root of the Content.IE5 folder. In the Content.IE5 folder are at least four folders whose names consist of eight random alphanumeric characters each. As more cached files are created, a commensurate number of these folders are created to hold them. On systems where considerable browsing activity occurs, the presence of 16 or 20 of these folders is very typical.

The subfolders with random alphanumeric names under Content.IE5 are created by Windows in sets of four as they are needed. Thus, discounting recovered deleted folders, you will normal find these folders present in even multiples of four.

A typical web page consists of many files, typically a dozen or more. As those files are downloaded from the source website, they are written to the cache files. When they are written, the name of the cached file is usually modified slightly from its original name. A file that is downloaded and that has an original filename of menuicon.jpg will be stored in cache as menuicon[1].jpg unless a file by that name (menuicon[1].jpg) already exists, in which case it would be incremented by 1 and named menuicon[2].jpg.

The index.dat file keeps track of these filename changes, among other things. Each file in the cache has an entry in index.dat. That entry records its original filename and its complete URL and stores its cached filename so they can be linked back together. Each record tracks the folder number in which the cached filename is stored, along with several time stamps and other metadata. The cache folders are numbered starting at 0, and they are listed at the beginning of the index.dat file in numerical order. The first one listed is 01h, the second one listed is 02h, and so forth, until they are all listed and numbered. They are easy to spot at a glance.

As mentioned in the previous section when I discussed Internet history files as part of carrying out the Internet history search, EnCase will read the TIF index.dat files and parse the web cache for you in the Records tab. The various columns in the Table view describe the various attributes of each cached file, based on a combination of the cached file's attributes and the data from the index.dat.

If you go to the Records tab, after running the Internet history search, in the Tree view pane you will see both the Cache and History folders. If you select the cache folder, the Table view will list all of the files in the cache folders. If you select any file, you can see it in the View pane in any one of the normal views. The Document view will show the file in web format. Figure 9.52 shows a Bing search for *fight clubs* that was stored in the cache.

FIGURE 9.52   Bing search for fight clubs found in web cache

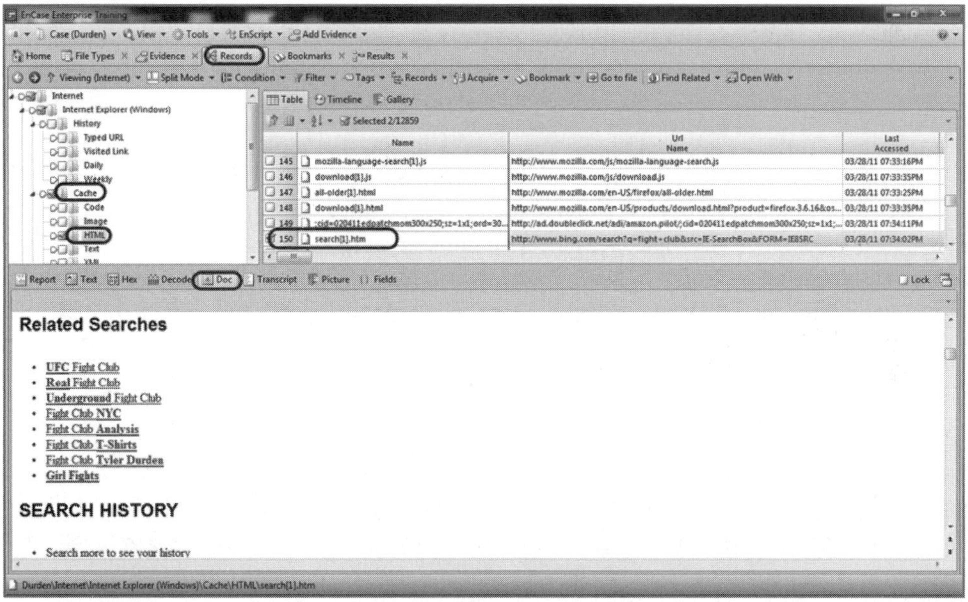

Cached items or files can be bookmarked just as any search hit or history entry. Select the cached files you want to bookmark, right-click, and bookmark the data. After you choose your destination folder in your bookmarks, click OK, and your cached file will appear in your Bookmarks view, ready for inclusion in your final report.

Cached files will show the Internet web page very close to how the user saw it. Obviously some minor formatting changes are done to make things fit in the EnCase viewing environment. While the format may change slightly, the content is otherwise present.

Real World Scenario

Artifact Recoveries After Formatting

A well-established publisher recently received a return-mail bundle from his local post office. As it turned out, the bundle of returned magazines did not belong to the publisher but belonged instead to a new competitor who had copied his publication so closely that the post office thought it belonged to their long-established postal patron and understandably mistakenly delivered the magazines being returned because of undeliverable addresses.

Upon closer inspection, the new magazine's editorial page revealed the new publisher as a recently departed employee of the original publisher. Upon an even closer inspection of the mailing address labels, the incorrect addresses being returned matched those in his customer database in both form and content, including a couple of misspellings.

Because theft of intellectual property was patently obvious, the publisher contacted counsel. Counsel in turn asked that I examine the former employee's hard drive to locate, to the extent possible, any evidence that would support their case.

Unfortunately, the hard drive had been used by the former employee's replacement for several weeks and problems occurred. To remedy the problem, the outsourced system administrator formatted the drive and reinstalled the OS after which it was again used by the former employee's replacement. Did I mention that they had also removed the former employee's files from the server? All this had transpired despite that they had prior knowledge that the former employee was leaving to start a business of his own!

There wasn't an intact file left belonging to the former employee. Nevertheless, all link files, FAT32 directory entries, and URLs were extracted from the unallocated clusters and slack spaces. That information was pulled together, and the events were reconstructed.

The link file content (file path and name, MAC times, and logical size) revealed that the former employee had accessed the customer database on the server at all times until he began his plans to start a competing business. His intent to start his own business was marked and time stamped by a sudden and extensive set of URL strings and web content for everything pertaining to starting one's business, from legal issues to supplies. It was at that critical juncture that the customer database was copied onto the employee's workstation. The database on the server was reduced to one-third its original size when he trashed thousands of entries. The target file sizes in the link files clearly showed this activity occurring within a 20-minute time period! From that point forward, the former employee never accessed the database on the server, or at least no evidence of such was found.

When the database was moved to the employee's workstation, the content from scores of recovered link files showed the file size of this database steadily increasing as he spent his last three months conducting searches, developing the customer database, and setting up his competing business on his former employer's time.

He created a competing website using some of his employer's images so much so that they appeared almost as a mirror site. The web mail traffic with his web developer was also recovered.

To top it off, there was even a link file that showed the customer database on a CD on his last day of his employment. The customer database, as he transferred it to CD, was 25 percent larger than it was when he started, while his employer's customer database was slashed by nearly two-thirds its original size. All this information was derived from recovered link file content, corroborated by URL entries.

When confronted with a substantial quantity of incriminating evidence, the former employee, through counsel, entered into an agreement with his former employer to avoid civil damages that would have bankrupted him. In the agreement, he admitted to the wrongdoing, agreed to shut down the website and cease his publication in its current format, permitted imaging of his company's computers to establish a baseline, and agreed to future imaging and examination of his data under certain agreed-upon conditions.

The agreement was far more restrictive upon his business than any judge would likely have ordered, but to avoid the expense and possible treble damages from an adverse ruling, he agreed to those conditions.

Most of the evidence that forced his hand resulted from recovered link file content along with other supporting data. All of it, without exception, was found in the unallocated clusters or in slack space. When the link file information was placed in a spreadsheet and accompanied by graphs and a timeline, the customer database story unfolded. When accompanied by other evidence relating to him starting up his business while on his former employer's time clock, the icing was on the cake.

Swap File

Windows and other operating systems have a limited supply of RAM with which to function. When they run out of RAM, they write some of the data that is in RAM to a file whose dedicated purpose is to cache RAM memory. This file is generically called a *swap file*, but more correctly called a *page file*. It is located in the root of the system drive, and its name is pagefile.sys on current versions of Windows.

The swap file can be configured for a drive other than the boot drive to optimize performance. If you don't see it on the root of the boot drive, you should examine other volumes to see whether it has been placed there. There is also the possibility that the user is security conscious and has configured their machine to delete this file during shutdown. If you can't find the file anywhere, look in the following registry key: HKEY_LOCAL_MACHINE\SYSTEM\CurrentControlSet\Control\Session Manager\Memory Management. If a value exists named ClearPageFileAtShutdown and its value is set at 1, the page file has been set to be deleted during shutdown.

When examining systems, you should always check this file. You may often find evidence that was written in RAM that was never in file format on the hard drive. You may find unencrypted text fragments in this file that are encrypted in their file format. If it was ever in RAM, it could be in the swap file. It is best to always search this file with the Unicode option enabled because files that appear normally in regular text can appear in Unicode when they are in RAM.

Hibernation File

With Windows 2000, XP, Vista, and Windows 7 allowing the computer to "hibernate" is an option. For a machine to power off and go to sleep and yet come back to life at the precise point where it went to sleep, the contents of RAM must be written to a file. Hence, you have the hibernation file, named hiberfil.sys, which is located in the root of the system drive.

Because the total contents of RAM are written to this file, this file will be the size of your system's RAM memory. If the computer has never been in a hibernation mode, the file will still be the same size as your system RAM but will be filled with 00h characters. Once it has been in the hibernation mode, the contents will reflect the last time the machine was in hibernation mode. The same processing guidelines apply to this file as with the swap file because they both store the contents of RAM at various points and for different reasons.

Figure 9.53 shows the location of the pagefile.sys swap file and the hiberfil.sys hibernation file on a Windows 7 system. The highlighted file is the swap file. Note that because the system from which it came had 8 GB of RAM, the swap file in this case is more than 12 GB. Normally the swap file will be 1.5 times the amount of RAM.

You may notice that Windows Server versions (2000, 2003, and 2008) weren't mentioned in the first paragraph as operating systems that allow machines to hibernate. That isn't to say that they can't hibernate, but server operating systems are typically not found on laptops, and servers usually run 24/7, making them unlikely candidates on which to find a hibernation file. So, while possible, don't expect it.

FIGURE 9.53 The swap file (pagefile.sys) and the hibernation file (hiberfil.sys) can hold valuable evidence.

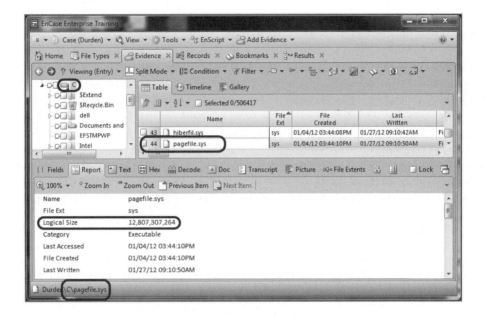

Print Spooling

When computers print files in a Windows environment, a print spooling process occurs. Spooling involves writing the print job to a couple of files so that the print job can run in the background while the user continues working with their applications. The print job is placed in a queue and prints as the printer is available to do the job. When the print job is done, the spooling files are deleted by the operating system.

When you set up your printer definition, you have the option of choosing either RAW or EMF mode. The RAW mode is a straight graphic dump of the print job. With the EMF mode, the graphics are converted to the EMF (Microsoft Enhanced Metafile) image format, and each printed page is represented by individual EMF files. These EMF files are not stand-alone files, but rather they are embedded within another file.

For each print job, two files are created. On Windows NT and 2000, these files will be located in `Winnt\system32\spool\printers`. On Windows XP/2003/Vista/2008/7 these files will be located in `Windows\system32\spool\printers`. The location is configurable by the user in the registry key `HKEY_LOCAL_MACHINE\SOFTWARE\Microsoft\Windows NT\CurrentVersion\Print\Printers\DefaultSpoolDirectory`. To that extent, it could exist almost anywhere.

If the workstation is connected to a network, spool files may also be sent to the server. Normally these temporary files are deleted at all locations after the print job is completed, and finding these files as allocated files is rare, unless the printer was offline and the spool files were in queue awaiting the printer to come back online—at which point the job would complete and the files would be deleted. However, I have seen hundreds of these spooled files on a Windows 2000 domain controller. For whatever reason, the server refused to delete these files when the print job was done. Bugs and poor configurations often leave added artifacts beyond your normal expectations.

Of the two temporary files created for each print job, one is called a *shadow file*, with the extension .shd, and the second is called the *spool file*, with the extension .spl. The filename will consist of five digits, and there will be a matching pair of files for each print job, differing only by their extension. For example, a print job may create the following two files: 00003.SHD and 00003.SPL. On some configurations you may find the five digits preceded by letters, such as FP00002.SHD and FP00002.SPL. The shadow file (SHD) is analogous to a job ticket. It contains information about the print job that includes the username, the printer, the name of the file being sent to print, and the print mode (RAW or EMF).

The spool file (SPL) contains the same kind of print job information, although formatted differently, and it contains the actual print job graphical data. When the mode is RAW, the graphic content is just that—a raw output of the graphical stream needed by the printer to output the job. Figure 9.54 shows two spool files created by a print job. The printer was offline, and the files are allocated files waiting for the printer to come back online. The spool file contains considerable information about the print job, including the filename, username, as so forth. This particular print job was done in the RAW mode, which is not commonly encountered because it is not the default mode.

FIGURE 9.54 Print job shadow and spool files on Windows XP. This print job was done in the RAW mode, which is not the default mode and is thus less common.

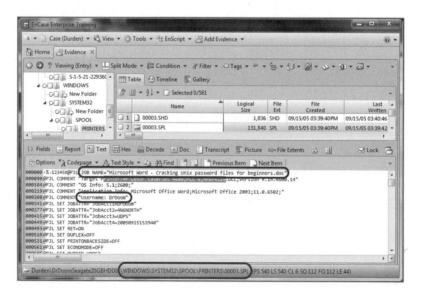

By default, printing is done using the EMF mode. Usually only special circumstances or issues warrant a change to the RAW mode, and it must be configured manually. Thus, most of the print jobs you will recover will be in the EMF mode, which are easily recovered.

In the EMF mode, each page of printed material will be represented by an EMF file embedded within the spool file in the order they will be printed. Figure 9.55 shows shadow and spool files for an EMF print job.

FIGURE 9.55   Print job shadow and spool files on Windows 7 (SP1). This print job was done in the EMF mode, which is the default mode.

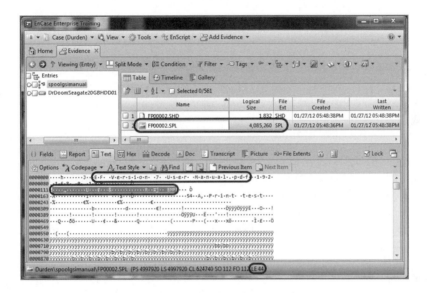

An EMF file has a unique header, which also varies with the operating system. Note that the EMF header is highlighted and circled in Figure 9.55. Table 9.5 lists the EMF header for each operating system that uses it. When attempting to recover print jobs, you should use the search string that applies to the operating system in use. Even then there are some variants with EMF headers even within the same version of Windows. If you fail to find any EMF headers, shorten your search string to the portion that is common to all, which is \x01\x00\x00\x00. Doing so will result in a significant number of false positives, and there are some better approaches to try first.

TABLE 9.5   EMF header search strings for different versions of Windows

Operating system	EMF header (GREP search strings)
Windows XP (very precise, few false positives)	\x01\x00\x00\x00\x5C\x01\x01 \x00\x00\x00\x84\x00
Windows 9x upgraded to XP	Use both: \x01\x00\x00\x00\x5C\x01 \x01\x00\x00\x00\x84\x00 and \x01\ x00\x00\x00\x58\x00\x00\x00

TABLE 9.5   EMF header search strings for different versions of Windows *(continued)*

Operating system	EMF header (GREP search strings)
Windows 2000 (very precise, few false positives)	\x01\x00\x00\x00\xD8\x17\x01\x00\x00\x00\x58\x6E
Windows NT and 2000	\x01\x00\x00\x00\x18\x17
Windows 9x*	\x01\x00\x00\x00\x58\x00
Windows 2000, XP, 2003, Vista, 2008, Windows 7 (very precise!)	\x01\x00\x00\x00..\x00.{34,34}EMF
Universal Search String (some false positives; can miss undocumented variants)	\x01\x00\x00\x00[\x5C\x84\xD8\x58\x18][\x01\x17\x6E\x00]

*Windows 9x handles print jobs differently, and the process is not described in this book.

You may search for EMF print jobs in spool files, but remember that you will rarely encounter them as allocated files, unless the printer was offline or some problem prevented the print job. Mostly, you can expect to find them in slack space, unallocated clusters, page files, and hibernation files. When you find a valid EMF embedded file or fragment, select the first few bytes of the search hit, bookmark the data, and view it as a picture. Figure 9.56 shows a search hit, in Hex view, for the EMF header. The cursor is on the first byte of the found string, which is all that is needed for EnCase to decode the data that follows.

With the cursor on the first byte, or first few if you'd like, simply switch to the Decode view and set the view type to picture, as shown in Figure 9.57. Assuming you have a valid EMF graphic, the picture will display in the right pane, as shown in Figure 9.57. I'm sure that most of you will recognize the print job as the first page of the EnCase Version 7 user manual. You should keep in mind that the SPL file will contain an embedded EMF graphic for each page of the print job, and you should step through the search hits in this file to view each page of the print job.

To automate the process of searching for EMF print jobs, you can use the EnCase Evidence Processor (EEP), specifically the File Carver module. As with any module in the EEP, you need to open the module to select options, which is in this case selecting the Enhanced Metafile Graphic in the Picture category, as shown in Figure 9.58. With that done, you run EEP and review the results.

There are reports from Microsoft that Windows Vista (any beyond) quickly and thoroughly deletes spool files. From my tests, it seems true that Windows Vista (any beyond) quickly deletes and overwrites the entries in the MFT; however, the data still persists in the unallocated clusters and should still remain a good artifact that can be recovered by searching for the EMF header. Also, as another bonus, Windows Vista (and beyond) adds some information to the end of the shadow (SHD) or job ticket file. Figure 9.59 shows this information. You can see that it includes the filename (if web page, the complete URL of the printed web page), printer type, user's name and SID, IP address of the printer, and so forth. It will be in Unicode, and Figure 9.59 shows this data after decoding it using the Decode view.

FIGURE 9.56   Search hit for EMF header string (circled). Note that the cursor is on the first byte of this string.

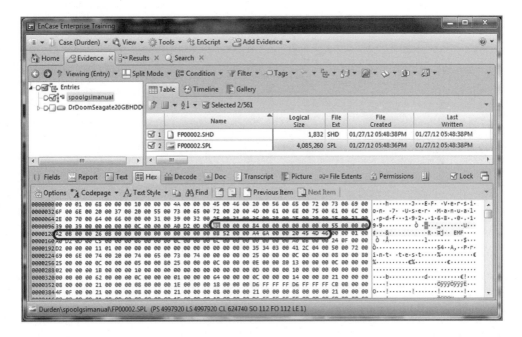

FIGURE 9.57   Using Decode feature to view an EMF print spool graphic

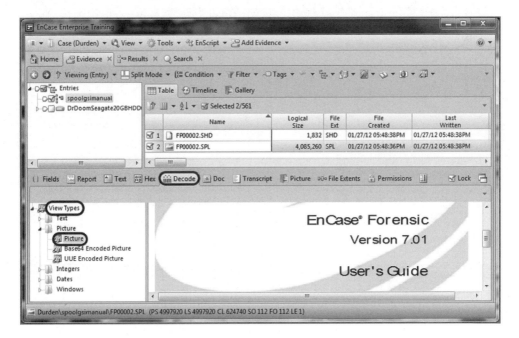

FIGURE 9.58   Using file carver in EEP to locate print spooler EMF graphics

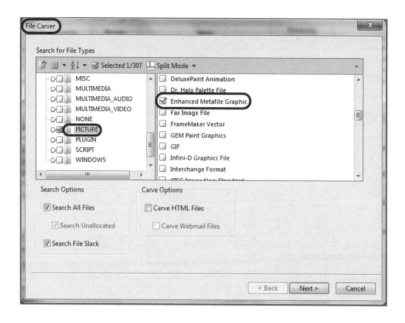

FIGURE 9.59   Windows 7 printer shadow file or job ticket showing considerable information about print job

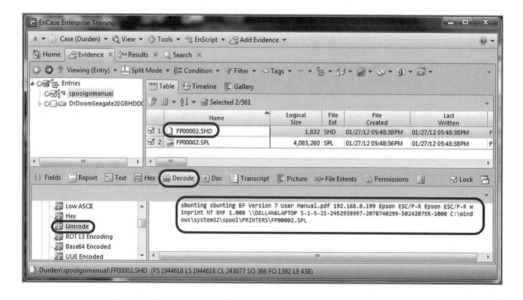

🌐 Real World Scenario

Print Jobs Artifacts Link Defendant to Crime Scene

A rather high-profile homicide case involved a lover's triangle consisting of three Russian students. The defendant stalked her former boyfriend for months. She drove to his apartment and remained outside overnight until he left the next morning, at which point she entered the apartment and killed her former boyfriend's new girlfriend.

Like many, she lived her life through her computer, and thus her computer provided substantial evidence throughout her trials (three mistrials due to hung juries). One significant piece of evidence surfaced, which was a recovered print job for directions from the defendant's apartment to the former boyfriend's apartment, printed minutes before she left on the eve of the homicide.

Recall that each page is a separate embedded graphic. This was a three-page set of directions, and there should have been three embedded graphics file; however, the first two were overwritten, and all the remained was page 3. Page 3 was almost overlooked because the page itself was blank, but at the bottom was the footer for the page, which included the defendant's address and the former boyfriend's address, including a date and time it was printed. Thus, take the time to look at what appear to be blank images when looking at thumbnails of recovered EMFs. Some of the best evidence is in the metadata!

Legacy Operating System Artifacts

Thus far, the artifacts mentioned have been for the most recent Windows operating systems, namely, Windows 2000/XP/2003 and Windows Vista and beyond. Windows 9x systems, while rapidly disappearing from the scene, are still encountered. Table 9.6 lists the locations of several artifacts on Windows 9x systems. Other than being located in a different place or named differently, they are functionally the same.

TABLE 9.6 Windows 9x artifacts and their paths

Description	Filename and path
Swap file.	C:\WIN386.SWP
Recent folder whose contents appear in the Windows 9x Start ➢ Documents menu.	C:\Recent
Desktop items.	C:\Desktop

TABLE 9.6   Windows 9*x* artifacts and their paths *(continued)*

Description	Filename and path
My Documents folder.	`C:\My Documents`
Internet cache and `index.dat`.	`C:\Windows\Temporary Internet Files\Content.IE5`
Cookies files.	`C:\Windows\Cookies`
Internet history files.	`C:\Windows\History`
User profiles (if configured). (Each user will have their own set of the files contained in this directory.)	`C:\Windows\Profiles\<user name>\`

Windows Volume Shadow Copy

In Chapter 10, I'll discuss restore points that are created by the system restore feature that appears in Windows XP and Windows Me. Windows Vista (and beyond) also uses restore points, but it stores its data in a much different and far more complex manner. As part of the system restore process, Windows Vista (and beyond) creates what are called *volume shadow copies* (VSCs). Whatever the Microsoft engineers may have taken away from forensic examiners with the introduction of Windows Vista, they gave back triple with this one!

What, therefore, is a volume shadow copy? Whereas Windows XP restore points took snapshots of critical system files, Windows Vista (and beyond) does much more. In essence, the Volume Shadow Service (VSS) takes snapshots of all data on the volume that has changed and does so from the block-level perspective, in 16 K blocks. Since it does all data, in addition to taking snapshots of important system file changes, it makes copies of user documents as well. Figure 9.60 shows the System Protection tab of the System Properties menu. On this tab, you can see which volumes have system restore configured.

In addition to protecting system files, starting with Vista, user files are protected with a feature dubbed "previous versions." Herein lies the forensic gold in Windows Vista (and beyond)! If a user deletes a file and dumps it from the Recycle Bin, there are often still copies of the deleted file existing as volume shadow copies within the restore point files. There are often as many copies as have been saved, and they are not typically fragmented when stored. The complexity of the storage system for Windows Vista (and beyond) restore points far exceeds that used in XP. Rather than store files in separate renamed files, Windows Vista (and beyond) stores everything in series of massive files; thus, these very large files are containers for hundreds of smaller files or file segments.

FIGURE 9.60   System Protection tab of Windows 7 System Properties menu

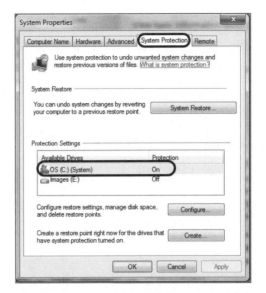

To appreciate the wealth of forensic gold maintained by Windows Vista (and beyond), one need only use one of the volume shadow copy administrator tools from the command line. To list all shadows, enter **vssadmin list shadows** at the command line. Figure 9.61 shows the amount of drive space used by the boot volume for shadow copies (enter **vssadmin list shadow storage**). For a drive that is 156 GB, 12.52 GB is currently being used to store shadow copies. There are a few tools under development to forensically process VSCs; however, none has yet arrived on the market, although one came very close. Reverse engineering the manner in which files, or portions thereof, are stored is underway and is clearly no simple process.

FIGURE 9.61   Command-line tool used to show storage space used by volume shadow copy

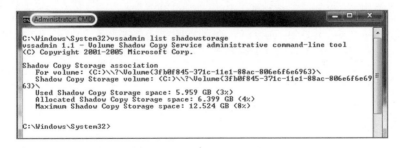

In the meantime, you can still work with these files. There are a couple of approaches that you can use. First, you can treat them very much as you would unallocated clusters, swap files, and so forth. You need only to locate them and search them. They are located in C:\System Volume Information. The easiest thing to do is to select all files in this folder and conduct specific searches depending on the type of files you seek or specific search keywords of interest in the case. You could also let EnCase's File Carver module do the heavy lifting.

Another method of working with the volume shadow copies created by VSS is to image them in the Windows environment, using a dd tool from George Garner's Forensic Acquisition Utility tools, which can be found at www.gmgsystemsinc.com/fau/03ddecb5-8262-4022-aaff-6559424ff8fc/fau-1.3.0.2390a.zip. In short, you list the Volume Shadow Copies using the command vssadmin list shadows, making sure you are running the command shell as an administrator. Figure 9.62 shows the output of this command for shadow copy number 5.

FIGURE 9.62   Command vssadmin list shadows output

```
Contents of shadow copy set ID: {b94d964b-ffd4-4da7-9270-3db026ecc379}
   Contained 1 shadow copies at creation time: 1/22/2012 1:03:06 PM
      Shadow Copy ID: {1e5597a9-d83b-4f62-9575-42dcc6f322d3}
         Original Volume: (C:)\\?\Volume{3fb0f845-371c-11e1-88ac-806e6f6e6963}\
         Shadow Copy Volume: \\?\GLOBALROOT\Device\HarddiskVolumeShadowCopy5
         Originating Machine: Dell4N6Laptop
         Service Machine: Dell4N6Laptop
         Provider: 'Microsoft Software Shadow Copy provider 1.0'
         Type: ClientAccessibleWriters
         Attributes: Persistent, Client-accessible, No auto release, Differentia
l, Auto recovered
```

Once you have the shadows listed, it is time to use Garner's dd tool. The syntax for running his tool to image the volume shadow copy is dd if=\\.\HarddiskVolumeShadowCopy5 of=E:\shadow5.img -localwrt, which will address and image VSC number 5, as shown in Figure 9.62. Figure 9.63 shows the output of this command after it has completed imaging. Since the target volume size here is approximately 160 GB, it does take some time. And by the way, there are five volume shadow copies. That means five times 160 GB (approximately) to get them and a commensurate amount of time. Ouch! No one said that good forensics was quick and easy.

FIGURE 9.63   Garner's dd tool used to successfully image a volume shadow copy

```
C:\fau\FAU.x64>dd if=\\.\HarddiskVolumeShadowCopy5 of=E:\shadow5.img --localwrt
Copying \\.\HarddiskVolumeShadowCopy5 to E:\shadow5.img
Output: E:\shadow5.img
168091475968 bytes
160304+1 records in
160304+1 records out
168091475968 bytes written

Succeeded!
```

If you didn't have the opportunity to image the volume shadow copies while it was running and before the machine was seized, you can still image the VSCs, but it becomes more complicated. You need to virtually mount the drive from within the forensic environment and then use Windows' vssadmin to address the volume shadow copies in that manner.

I often use the Voom Shadow to work with volume shadow copies. By inserting the Voom Shadow between the host system and its hard drive, Voom Shadow write protects the host hard drive but caches all writes to it on the Voom Shadow's hard drive, allowing a system to be booted and examined live in a forensically sound manner. Using this configuration, I can image the volume shadow copies. Further, I can install a third-party tool called Shadow Explorer and examine the contents of the various VSCs, as shown in Figure 9.64.

FIGURE 9.64   Shadow Explorer enables you to examine the contents of any of the available volume shadow copies, listed by the date and time created

To further understand how volume shadow copy works for the Windows user, let's say you created a file named Secrets.doc and listed all your nefarious activities in this file. Let's also say that you kept it updated over time. On a daily basis, or thereabouts, Windows makes a restore point, and with it the volume shadow copy feature creates copies of your file if it has changed since the last restore point. Let's say you become aware you are the focus of an investigation and decide it's in your best interest to delete this file. To do this, you sent the file to the Recycle Bin and dumped the Recycle Bin. The file is gone, or so you believe.

The forensic examiner might be able to recover the file by traditional forensic means, but in addition, there are copies of the file in the restore point files. If the machine were running, anyone could right-click the folder that contained the deleted file, select Properties, and then go to the Previous Versions tab. This tab would list the various versions of the file stored in restore points from which you could open, copy, or restore those files. Figure 9.65 shows the Previous Versions tab for the hypothetical file after it has been deleted and subsequently deleted again from the Recycle Bin.

FIGURE 9.65   The deleted file can be recovered from the Previous Versions tab of the Properties dialog box.

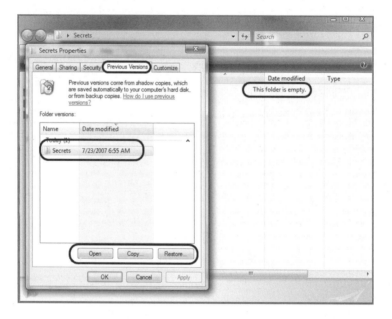

Once you've seen how this feature works in Windows Vista (and beyond), you'll see the forensic gold mine that Microsoft has created for computer forensics examiners. This should also open the door for some other methods of file recovery. You could use VMware to mount an image of a Windows drive. Once mounted, you could recover files from the Previous Versions tab, exporting to removable media.

Similarly, you could restore a copy of the image to a drive and boot the drive in the suspect's original machine. Again, once booted, you could recover files easily from the Previous Versions tab. In either method, you should take screen shots and notes of your activity as you proceed. The screen shots can be later presented to jury. It's much easier to understand how the recovery was done because most people do understand Windows basic functions.

The volume shadow copy technology is an evolving feature of Windows system restore feature. System restore and restore points began with Windows XP, and volume shadow copy was actually introduced into Windows Server 2003. Not much was said or known about volume shadow copy at the time; it was a quiet feature and not often encountered in computer forensics. With Windows Vista, however, the volume shadow copy feature hit the masses of the Windows user base.

Since Vista was a less-than-stellar version of Windows, Vista was never widely adopted by corporate users. Windows 7, compared to Vista, was far superior, and its acceptance by corporate users was much better. However, there is still a large XP user base among corporate users because there is no direct upgrade path from XP to Windows 7. That issue, coupled with slow economic times, slowed the conversion from XP to Windows 7. With time, Windows 7, and with it volume shadow copies, will be ubiquitous in the Windows user base. As its forensic worth becomes apparent, considerable effort will be expended in harvesting this evidence. Just as the volume shadow copy technology evolves, you can expect the forensic tools and methods to process it to follow suit.

Windows Event Logs

Since Windows was first released, it has always produced event logs of system and application activities. The logging has continually evolved over time, improving considerably in the process. Windows logs have always been rather cryptic and little understood. To make matters worse, by default Windows hasn't been very good at turning on the auditing features that are built in to the system. Thus, many people believe that Windows logging is not occurring or that what is being logged doesn't make much sense. Accordingly, the wealth of information available in logs hasn't been fully leveraged by the computer forensics community.

Kinds of Information Available in Event Logs

Even though Windows auditing is not enabled by default, it still captures valuable information in its event logs. Figure 9.66 shows the typical XP audit configuration, which is found in Administrative Tools ➢ Local Security Policy. Even though, quite obviously, no auditing is turned on, Windows still produces a considerable volume of data in the system and application event logs. Figure 9.67 clearly shows significant logging activity in the system event logs, despite the No Audit setting.

FIGURE 9.66 Default audit policy settings in Windows XP

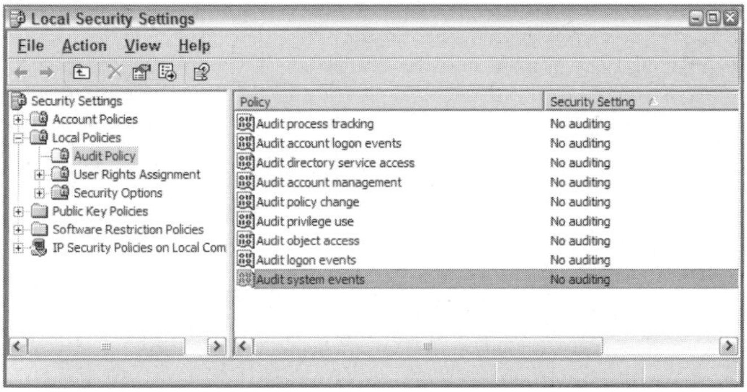

FIGURE 9.67 Event Viewer in Windows XP showing logging activity in system event logs despite a No Audit setting

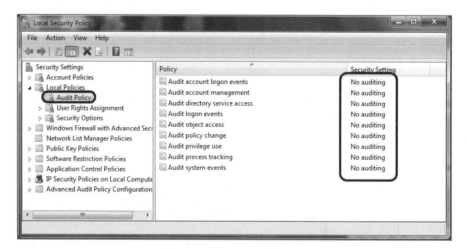

Windows Vista, as will be discussed further later in the chapter, changed the event log format. It also changed the amount of logging that occurred with the default no audit configuration. Figure 9.68 shows the default auditing policy for Windows 7 Enterprise (SP1), which on the surface appears the same as Windows XP in Figure 9.66. Despite the settings, however, Windows 7 security event logs will now contain event logs, as shown in Figure 9.69. With Windows XP, security event logs would contain one default entry; thus, there has been an improvement in the out-of-the-box logging with the introduction of Vista.

FIGURE 9.68 Default auditing policies for Windows 7 Enterprise (SP1)

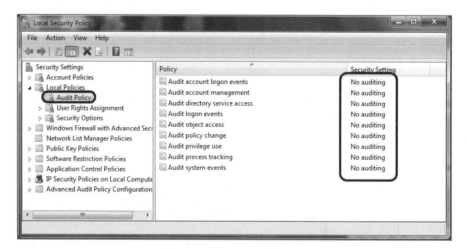

FIGURE 9.69   Despite "No Auditing" settings, some event logging still occurs

Windows, except for Windows Vista, stores data in three files in the folder C:\Windows\ System32\config:

- secevent.evt: The Security event log
- sysevent.evt: The System event log
- appevent.evt: The Application event log

The Windows interface for viewing event logs natively is the Event Viewer, which is found in the Administrative Tools menu.

In addition to Application, Security, and System logs, the careful observer will note the addition of Internet Explorer, Microsoft Office Diagnostics, and Microsoft Office Sessions. Internet Explorer will be present if there was an upgrade to Internet Explorer 7. The log is present, unpopulated with data, and there supposedly for future debugging purposes. The two logs related to Microsoft Office are present if there was an upgrade to Office 2007. The diagnostics log records data relative to the diagnostics routine for Office 2007. The sessions log records each time an Office 2007 application is opened and closed. It also records how it was closed, in other words, whether it closed normally or crashed.

Determining Levels of Auditing

One of the questions you often need to know is what level of auditing was enabled. Knowing what level of auditing was enabled provides the examiner with some expectations as to what kind of information might be found. Since the box in question is most often offline and being viewed in EnCase, you can't open the Local Security Policy menu and check the settings. The answer lies in the registry. If you're not comfortable yet with the registry, you may want to jump ahead to Chapter 10 first.

The audit event policy settings are stored at the following registry key: SECURITY\ Policy\PolAdtEv. The default value contains the information necessary to determine the audit policy settings. The first byte determines whether any auditing is configured. If it is 0, no auditing is enabled. If it is 1, auditing is enabled, and the various levels and types of auditing are defined in the bytes that follow.

Figure 9.70 shows the data in this value. Some of the data is relevant, and most is not. I have placed an overlay over this data such that only the relevant bytes are highlighted. In this manner, the information contained therein is much more visible and understandable.

FIGURE .9.70   Audit policy settings are highlighted.

To interpret the data in this registry value, refer to Tables 9.7 and 9.8. Table 9.7 describes the meaning of each byte offset as to which audit setting is affected. Table 9.8 describes the meaning of the value at the byte offset.

The following tables and audit policy definition scheme remain the same for Vista and beyond.

TABLE 9.7   Byte offsets and their corresponding audit types

Byte offset	Description
00	00 No Auditing/01 Auditing
04	System Events Audit Setting
08	Logon Events Audit Setting
12	Object Access Audit Setting
16	Privilege Use Audit Setting
20	Process Tracking Audit Setting

TABLE 9.7   Byte offsets and their corresponding audit types *(continued)*

Byte offset	Description
24	Policy Change Audit Setting
28	Account Management Audit Setting
32	Directory Service Access Audit Setting
36	Account Logon Audit Setting

TABLE 9.8   Bytes values and their corresponding audit settings

Byte value	Audit setting
00	No Auditing
01	Audit Successes
02	Audit Failures
03	Audit Success and Failures

With the information provided in these tables, you can interpret the data in Figure 9.62. Table 9.9 shows the audit settings configured and displayed in Figure 9.62.

TABLE 9.9   Audit settings in Figure 9.62 interpreted

Byte offset	Audit type	Value	Audit setting
00	00 No Auditing / 01 Auditing	01	Auditing Enabled
04	System Events Audit Setting	00	No Auditing
08	Logon Events Audit Setting	03	Audit Success & Failures
12	Object Access Audit Setting	00	No Auditing
16	Privilege Use Audit Setting	02	Audit Failures
20	Process Tracking Audit Setting	00	No Auditing
24	Policy Change Audit Setting	03	Audit Success & Failures
28	Account Management Audit Setting	03	Audit Success & Failures

TABLE 9.9   Audit settings in Figure 9.62 interpreted *(continued)*

Byte offset	Audit type	Value	Audit setting
32	Directory Service Access Audit Setting	02	Audit Failures
36	Account Logon Audit Setting	03	Audit Success & Failures

Windows Vista/7 Event Logs

Windows Vista (and beyond) event logging changed everything, or nearly everything. The event logs are now stored in the folder C:\Windows\system32\winevt\logs, and their file extension changed from .evt to .evtx. The filenames are now as follows:

- security.evtx: The Security event log
- system.evtx: The System event log
- application.evtx: The Application event log

In addition to these logs, there are nearly 100 files in this folder with event log extensions, as shown in Figure 9.71. That being said, there are considerably more logs in Windows Vista (and beyond) than in a pre–Windows Vista system. While they were changing things, the data format itself was changed to a binary XML format. Even the user interface changed. Figure 9.72 shows the new Windows Vista (and beyond) Event Viewer interface, in which you can see many of the logs.

FIGURE 9.71   Nearly 100 event logs in new location (\Windows\System32\winevt\Logs)

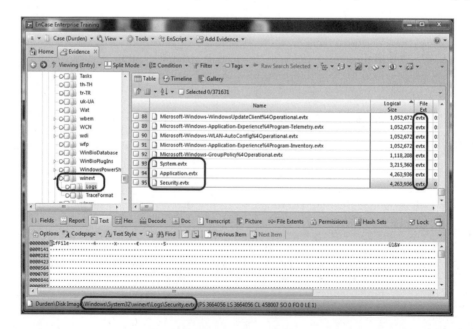

FIGURE 9.72   Windows Vista (and beyond) Event Viewer interface

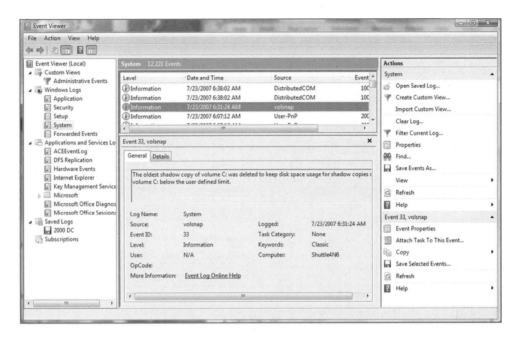

Those who used the features of the legacy Event Viewer to their fullest will recognize that much of what was under the hood with the old Event Viewer is now visible directly in the interface. For instance, the detailed information contained in the bottom pane used to require the user to open a record in a separate window. Most of the information in the right pane used to be in the Properties window or accessible via the contextual (right-click) menu.

Using the Windows Event Log Parser

Regardless of which event logs you are examining, Windows post-Vista or pre–Windows Vista, EnCase can process them all. Beginning with EnCase 6.6, Windows Vista (and beyond) event log parsing is available. EnCase does not rely upon the Windows API to parse the logs. Rather, it reads the raw data and parses it directly.

Figure 9.73 shows the EnCase 7 Windows Event Log Parser, which is a module in the EnCase Evidence Processor. Double-clicking the Windows Event Log Parser displays an options dialog box from which the user may configure conditions to apply to the parsing job. Figure 9.74 shows this dialog box.

FIGURE 9.73 Windows Event Log Parser is a module contained in the EnCase Evidence Processor.

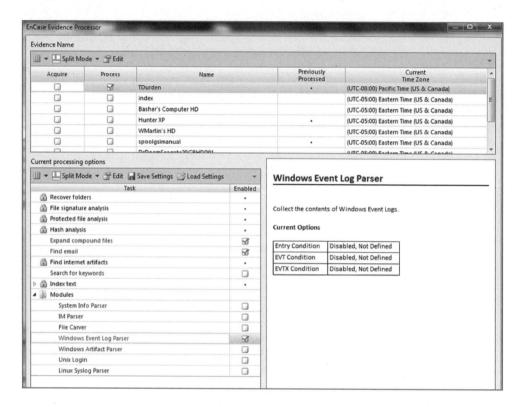

FIGURE 9.74 Windows Event Log Parser conditions options

Once the EnCase Evidence Processor has completed, some of the information from the parsed data is available from the records view; however, the Case Analyzer EnScript will produce a more usable format, as shown in Figure 9.76. From here you can add all or selected records to a report. Once the report is generated, you can save by right-clicking the report, and you can save the data in several formats, depending on your final needs.

FIGURE 9.75   Windows Event Log Parser output as generated by the Case Analyzer EnScript

		Event ID	Event Type	Generated	Description	Source	Cate.
☑	1	2	(0x4) Information	02/28/02 10:21:56AM		Serial	0
☑	2	6,009	(0x4) Information	02/28/02 10:22:27AM		EventLog	0
☑	3	6,005	(0x4) Information	02/28/02 10:22:27AM		EventLog	0
☑	4	6,011	(0x4) Information	02/28/02 04:41:23PM	The NetBIOS name and DNS host name of this machine have been changed from ...	EventLog	0
☑	5	60,054	(0x4) Information	02/28/02 05:03:20PM	Setup successfully installed Windows build 2600.%0	Setup	0
☑	6	6,009	(0x4) Information	02/28/02 05:05:40PM		EventLog	0
☑	7	6,005	(0x4) Information	02/28/02 05:05:40PM		EventLog	0
☑	8	115	(0x4) Information	02/28/02 05:06:55PM		SRService	0
☑	9	7,035	(0x4) Information	02/28/02 05:08:09PM	The Telephony service was successfully sent a start control.	Service Control Manager	0
☑	10	7,036	(0x4) Information	02/28/02 05:09:22PM		Service Control Manager	0
☑	11	7,035	(0x4) Information	02/28/02 05:11:28PM	The Network Connections service was successfully sent a start control.	Service Control Manager	0
☑	12	7,036	(0x4) Information	02/28/02 05:11:28PM		Service Control Manager	0
☑	13	7,035	(0x4) Information	02/28/02 05:11:28PM	The SSDP Discovery Service service was successfully sent a start control.	Service Control Manager	0
☑	14	7,036	(0x4) Information	02/28/02 05:11:29PM		Service Control Manager	0
☑	15	7,035	(0x4) Information	02/28/02 05:11:29PM	The Network Location Awareness (NLA) service was successfully sent a start control.	Service Control Manager	0
☑	16	7,036	(0x4) Information	02/28/02 05:11:29PM		Service Control Manager	0
☑	17	7,036	(0x4) Information	02/28/02 05:11:30PM		Service Control Manager	0
☑	18	7,035	(0x4) Information	02/28/02 05:11:30PM	The Remote Access Connection Manager service was successfully sent a start cont...	Service Control Manager	0

Constraint: None

In addition to all the other changes Windows Vista made to the event logging system, Microsoft also radically changed the event ID numbers. If you were used to the pre–Windows Vista event ID numbers, you will have to learn a completely new set of numbers.

The amount of information an examiner can extract from event logs is endless. IP connection information is often available and in places you'd least expect it. No examination can be considered complete without looking at the event logs for the time period in question. What can be revealed in these logs can often change the complexion of your case.

For More Information

Understanding Windows event logs is a complex topic and beyond the scope of this book. It could, in fact, be the topic of a book unto itself. For those wanting to understand Windows event logs, I suggest reading Chapters 12–15 of the book *Mastering Windows Network Forensics and Investigation*. Steve Anson and yours truly devoted nearly a third of the book to understanding and processing pre–Vista Windows event logs. The intent was to cover all facets of event logs from understanding the event ID numbers to understanding them on a binary level, including recovering event log fragments and processing them with EnCase. Recently, Ryan Johnson and Scott Pearson teamed with us on the second edition of this text. In newest release, the new post-Vista event log format has been covered extensively. More information on the book is available on the Wiley website at www.wiley.com/WileyCDA/WileyTitle/productCd1118163826.html.

It's one thing to read about Windows artifacts, but you'll get more out of this book if you engage in hands-on examination and recovery of those artifacts. Exercise 9.1 takes you through various Windows artifacts discussed in this chapter.

EXERCISE 9.1

Windows Artifacts Recovery

1. In the exercise, you will recover many of the artifacts discussed in this chapter. Before you start, go to the publisher's website for this book and download the set of evidence files named DellLaptopJohnyUser. The set of files weighs in at approximately 12 GBs, so allow ample time for the download before starting this exercise.

2. Open a new case in EnCase and name it something along the lines of Windows Artifacts Recovery.

3. From the home screen, choose Add Evidence and then choose Add Evidence File. Browse to the evidence file you downloaded and add it to your case.

4. From the Evidence view or tab, now visible after adding evidence, choose Process Evidence from the Evidence tab toolbar and allow the EnCase Evidence Processor (EEP) to initialize and load.

5. Before you can choose any modules to run or not, you must first select the evidence item for processing.

6. Select the modules you want to run at this time. For this exercise, I suggest selecting only Find Internet Artifacts and Windows Artifact Parser and turning off searching in unallocated clusters. File Signature Analysis is mandatory, and you can't deselect it. Click OK to run the EEP. This would be a good time to take a break to allow EEP to process.

7. Once EEP has successfully run (the progress bar in the lower right disappears), click View ➤ Records to go to the Records view.

8. From the Records view, in the Tree pane, open up Internet and drill down to Internet ➤ Internet Explorer ➤ History➤ Daily. In the Table pane, look over each entry's data in the View pane Report tab. Look for specifically, local files opened that may be of interest (file://), external drives or mapped drives, downloads of interest, and searches of interest. You should find some of each that should catch your interest when you see them.

9. From the Tree pane, drill down to Internet ➤ Mozilla 3 ➤ Downloads. Do you see any programs downloaded that should cause you some concern as an examiner, especially if you are investigating a matter in which data was exfiltrated from an employer? (Hint: Dropbox!)

10. From the Records view in the Tree pane, open Evidence Processor Module Results, and in the Table pane, among other items, you should see the Windows Artifact Parser – Records entry, which is blue and therefore hyperlinked. Click the blue hyperlinked entry and should open its own view within the Records view or tab.

11. Examine the Recycle Bin. From which folder were the three items dubbed "Geo Images" deleted? How does this discovery "complicate" your examination?

12. In the Tree pane, select the Link Parser. In the Table pane, double-click the Name column to sort the filenames in ascending order (arrow points up). You should see a link file near the top that begins with "08_iceland." You should note that this file is also blue, or hyperlinked. By clicking this hyperlinked file, you should be taken to the details for this file. You should immediately note that this link file points to a drive letter F, and that such is NOT included in the device you are examining, meaning your investigator has to locate this missing drive!

13. Bookmark your findings, save your case, and exit. Were this a real case, you should be contacting the investigator at this time and advising them that Dropbox is a factor in this case as well as another drive (F).

Summary

This chapter covered a wide array of artifacts produced by the Windows operating system. Before you could examine specific artifacts, you had to consider one artifact that was common to most artifacts: time. The NTFS file system stores its MAC times in GMT, whereas FAT file systems store their MAC times in local time. FAT uses an MS-DOS time stamp for MAC times; NTFS uses the Windows 64-bit time stamp for MAC times. The Windows 64-bit time stamp measures the number of 10 millionth-of-a-second intervals since January 1, 1601, at 00:00:00 GMT.

When displaying time to the user, NTFS file systems convert the GMT time to local time using the local time offset stored in the registry. EnCase uses the default offset based on the offset for the examiner's machine. If the offset on your evidence under examination differs from this offset, it can be modified. The registry can be manually examined for this information, or the Evidence Processor/System Info Parser module will return the same information with much less effort. You must set the correct time zone *before* running the core Evidence Processor functions that work with date and time, including Index Text, Find Internet Artifacts, and Find Email.

The Recycle Bin is the default location where Windows sends files that have been deleted. The directory entry from the file's original location is marked as deleted, and a new entry is created in the `Recycle Bin` folder. For Windows 2000/XP, the new name will begin with *D* for deleted. It will be followed by the letter of the volume from which the file was deleted. It will be followed next by the index number of the file in the `INFO2` record. The file will retain its original extension.

All files in the Recycle Bin are tracked and displayed to the user using the `INFO2` database. It consists of 800-byte records (280 bytes if Windows *9x*) for each file in the Recycle Bin. The record contains the index number, the original filename and path, and the date/time the file was deleted. If the Recycle Bin is on an NT system, the Recycle Bin will have folders for each user's deleted files, and the folders will be named after the user's SID number.

With Windows Vista (and beyond), the `INFO2` file was discarded and in its place are individual `$I`, or index, files that contain the metadata regarding the deleted file. The file renaming convention changed as well, with deleted files being renamed `$R` with a short GUID that corresponds with the index file GUID. The file extension remains the same for both the deleted file and the index file. As long as the `$I` file is intact, EnCase will report the `$R` file by its proper filename before it was deleted.

Link files are shortcut files. They are created by Windows, by programs, by user activity without their specific knowledge, or by deliberate intent of the user. The link file contains data about its target file. Among other information, this internal data contains the name and path of the target file; the volume serial number; the logical size of the target file; and the created, accessed, and written times (CAW) at byte offsets 28, 36, and 44, respectively.

Windows NT, 2000, XP, and 2003 create a series of files that are unique to each user. Windows NT stores them in `Profiles`, while Windows 2000, XP, and 2003 store them in `Documents and Settings`. Windows Vista (and beyond) is different still, storing them in `Users`. The first time a user logs onto one of these systems, a root user folder is created bearing the user's logon name. Nearly all data unique to that user is segregated and secured in these folders. Under the root user folder are several folders created by default, many of which are of forensic interest.

The `Recent` folder is one of the folders created under the root user folder. The `Recent` folder contains link files of files and documents opened by the user. Windows displays the most recent 15 of these link files in the My Recent Documents view. Windows Vista (and beyond) stores its `Recent` folder at `C:\Users\%UserName%\AppData\Roaming\Microsoft\Windows\Recent`.

The `Desktop` folder is another folder created under the root user folder. Although the user's actual desktop that they see has content from several possible sources, the contents of this folder, aside from the default content, are placed there by the user and are unique to that user's desktop.

The `My Documents` folder is another folder created under the root user folder. It contains, by default, at least a `My Pictures` subfolder and sometimes `My eBooks` and `My Music` subfolders, depending on the Windows version and service pack that created them. The purpose of `My Documents` is to create a unique and secure location for each user's documents. Generally, that which is under `My Documents`, aside from default folders and files, is attributable to the user to whom the folder belongs.

Windows Vista (and beyond), quite by contrast, uses `Documents` instead of `My Documents` and now places `Pictures`, `Music`, and so forth, in the root of the user's folder instead of being a subfolder of `My Documents`.

The `Send To` folder is another folder created under the root user folder. Its contents appear in the Windows Explorer right-click menu as Send To options. The user can (but doesn't typically) manually add items to this folder. It is most often populated by application installations and by Windows itself. It is a good place to look for external storage devices, such as zip drives and the like.

The `Temp` folder is another folder created under the root user folder. It is a vast dumping ground for temporary files. Looking at this area after a file signature analysis can prove quite beneficial. Files located here are specific to and attributable to the user.

The `Favorites` folder contains special link files for use with the Internet Explorer web browser. These special link files are called Internet Shortcut files and have the extension `.url`. The target file for these special shortcut files is a URL address. Some favorites are created by default, some are created by applications or websites, and some are created by the user. Very elaborate folder configurations are a telltale sign that the structure and contents were created by the user.

For each of the `Cookies`, `History`, and `Temporary Internet Files` folders, Windows Vista (and beyond) creates a `Low` subfolder. The purpose of the `Low` folder is to contain data that is being run in the protected-mode of Internet Explorer 9. Data for which the protected mode is not running is stored in the normal folders.

The `Cookies` folder contains individual files with pieces of code stored by websites to enhance the user's browsing experience, in theory. This code can likewise be misused or exploited. Each cookie is a file using the format username, followed by the @ symbol, followed by the website name. After August 2011, the format changed such that the filename is now an eight-character random alphanumeric. Each has a `.txt` extension. The cookies are managed by a database file named `index.dat`, which is located in the `Cookies` folder.

The `History` folder contains a series of `index.dat` files located in folders named after date ranges. The `History.IE5` folder contains the main history `index.dat` file. Each of the subfolders in the `History.IE5` folder contains an `index.dat` file for the time period referenced in the containing folder's date-range name. These files are parsed and displayed in the Records tab of EnCase after running the Internet History parsing tool from within the EnCase Evidence Processor.

The `Temporary Internet Files` (TIF) folder is used to store files that are downloaded from the Web and viewed in Internet Explorer. Other applications are known to use this area for file storage. Outlook Express and Hotmail both open attachments in the cache folders. Outlook creates a separate folder for opening its attachments and is located in TIF; the folder is named beginning with OLK. The `Content.IE5` folder contains an `index.dat` file that tracks the files cached by Internet Explorer (not other applications). This file tracks, among other information, the original URL and filename, the filename as stored in cache, and the cache folder in which the file is stored. This database is parsed, and the contents of the cache are displayed in the Records tab of EnCase after running the Internet History parsing tool from within the EnCase Evidence Processor.

The swap or paging file is used to temporarily store RAM memory when RAM space runs short for its current needs. This file is currently named `pagefile.sys` on current versions of Windows and is located in the root of the system drive. The hibernation file, named `hiberfil.sys`, is used by Windows 2000, XP, Vista, and Windows 7 to go into a hibernation mode to conserve power. The contents of RAM are written to this file so that when the system wakes up, RAM can be restored from this file. It is also located in the root of the system drive. Both these files should be routinely examined as they contain valuable data that can be found in no other location.

When Windows prints data, it caches the print job into two spool files per print job (Windows 2000, XP, 2003, Vista, 2008, and Windows 7). This process allows the print job to function behind the scenes, enabling the user to continue working. Print jobs are placed in queue, and it is essentially a first in, first out (FIFO) operation unless you are working in a networked environment in which certain users or machines have priority status with regard to printing. On a stand-alone workstation, the files are stored in `System32\spool\printers`. This path is a subfolder of the system root, which is either `WINNT` or `WINDOWS`. If the workstation under examination is in a domain environment, you will likely find the spool files on the server as well. When the print job completes, the two spool files are deleted.

The spool files have extensions of `.shd` and `.spl`. The former is called the *shadow file*, and the latter is called the *spool file*. The shadow file contains printer job information only. The spool file contains printer job information and the actual print job data itself. If the printer is configured for the RAW mode, the print job data will be one continuous stream of graphical output data. If the printer is configured for the EMF mode (the default and therefore most common), each printed page of output is represented by an EMF file embedded within the spool file. They appear sequentially arranged in the order that the pages will print.

EMF files have unique headers, but many variants of the header exist even within the same version of Windows. Headers can be located, and print jobs can be recovered. As spool files are deleted after the print job, rarely will you find them as allocated files. Most times, you will find them in unallocated clusters, in the swap file, in the hibernation file, or in file slack, but you should search everywhere to be thorough.

Windows Vista (and beyond) adds the Volume Shadow Service feature to the system restore system that was found in Windows XP. In addition to taking system snapshots, volume shadow copy makes copies of user files on a daily basis, placing this data in the system restore files. Even after a file has been deleted, it can be restored from the previous version tab of the containing folder's Property tab. The volume shadow copy feature is a forensic gold mine.

Windows event logs contain a wealth of information even when Windows auditing is disabled. Windows Vista increased the type and complexity of logging by using a new interface and by storing the data in a binary XML format. Starting with EnCase 6.6, Windows Vista (and beyond) event logs can be parsed with the same tool that processes pre–Windows Vista event logs.

Exam Essentials

Know and understand time stamps.   Understand and explain how NTFS differs from FAT in the method by which it stores MAC times. Be able to explain GMT and local time. Know how to determine the time zone offset for an evidence file. Explain how to modify the time zone offset for a device. Explain the 64-bit Windows date and time stamp as compared to the DOS and the Unix time stamp.

Understand the purpose and function of the Recycle Bin.   Explain how Windows 7 usually deletes files. Describe what happens to filenames (directory or MFT record entries) when a file is deleted from its original location and moved to the Recycle Bin. Explain the naming convention of a filename when it is located in the Recycle Bin. Describe how Windows 7 keeps this information in individual index files in the Recycle Bin that begin with $I. Know the remainder of the filename is an abbreviated GUID, and the file extension remains unchanged. Know the deleted filename, when placed in the Recycle Bin, is changed to a name that begins with $R. The remainder of the renamed deleted file (or folder) is also a GUID that matches that of its corresponding index file, and its file extension also remains unchanged.

Explain how Windows 7 usually deletes files.   Describe what happens to filenames (directory or MFT record entries) when a file is deleted from its original location and moved to the Recycle Bin. Explain the naming convention of a filename when it is located in the Recycle Bin. Describe how Windows 7 keeps this information in individual index files in the Recycle Bin that begin with $I. Know the remainder of the filename is an abbreviated GUID, and the file extension remains unchanged. Know the deleted filename, when placed in the Recycle Bin, is changed to a name that begins with $R. The remainder of the renamed deleted file (or folder) is also a GUID that matches that of its corresponding index file, and its file extension also remains unchanged.

Understand the purpose and function of link files.   Understand how, where, and why links files are created. Know what link files are created by the operating system, by applications, and by the user, both knowingly and unknowing. Describe how to create a desktop shortcut. Be able to explain, in detail, the contents or data portion of a link file. Know which time stamps are stored inside the link file, particularly the specific time stamps names (MAC), the correct order of their appearance, the byte offsets at which they are located, and the time stamp format. Explain the concept of a target file in the context of a link file.

Know and understand the root user folder and its default subfolders.   Understand and explain what a root user folder is and when it is created. Describe the folders created under the root user folder. Understand and explain the purpose and function of the Recent folder, specifically what kind of files it contains, how they are created, what purpose these files serve for the user, and the forensic significance of the files found in this folder.

Explain the purpose and function of the My Documents, Send To, Temp, and Favorites folders.   Explain how folders have changed or moved with the introduction of the Windows Vista operating system. Explain why the contents contained in the root user folder and its subfolders are usually attributable to the logged-in root user or owner of these folders and files.

Know and understand the contents, purpose, and function of the Cookies, History, and Temporary Internet Files folders and their contents.   Know and understand what a cookie is and the filenaming convention in which they are stored. Explain the purpose of the index.dat file found in the Cookies folder.

Explain the purpose of the History folder.   Know the purpose of the main history index.dat file located in History.IE5 folder. Explain the naming convention of the subfolders located in History.IE5. Describe the purpose of each index.dat file located in each of these subfolders as it relates to the user interface in Internet Explorer. Aside from containing Internet history, explain what other local file information may be found here and how it is created.

Explain the purpose of the Temporary Internet Files (TIF) folder.   Explain the purpose of the index.dat file located in the Content.IE5 folder. Know the contents of the subfolders in the Content.IE5 folder. Explain how and why files are cached in these folders. Describe how and why a filename is changed or modified when stored in cache. Know which file stores both the cached filename and the original filename (in the URL).

Explain where post–Windows Vista stores the cookies, history, and TIF folders.   Describe where Low folders are located and explain their purpose and function.

Explain how EnCase 7 parses and displays the contents of the Cookies, History, and Temporary InternettFiles.   Describe what other files, aside from cached web page content, are found in the TIF subfolders.

Understand the Windows printing process.   Understand and be able to explain how Windows prints data and which files are created in the process. Explain the concept of spooling. Explain the contents of a shadow file, and know what extension this file will have. Explain the contents of a spool file and know what extension this file will have. Describe the default location for printer spool files, and understand that it can be modified by the user. Be able to explain the differences between RAW and EMF modes. Explain which mode is the default and most commonly encountered mode. Explain what files are produced in the EMF mode and in which file they are stored. Explain how multiple-page printed documents are handled in the EMF mode. Explain the manual process by which EMF print jobs can be recovered.

Understand the Windows Vista/7 volume shadow copy feature.   Understand and be able to explain the purpose of the Windows Vista (and beyond) volume shadow copy feature. What does it do that the XP system restore feature did not do? Explain the forensic importance of the volume shadow copy feature.

Understand the Windows event logs.   Understand and be able to explain where pre–Windows Vista and post–Windows Vista store their event logs. Describe the kind of information stored in these files and their forensic importance. Explain how to determine the audit settings. Describe the process for processing Windows event logs using EnCase.

Review Questions

1. An operating system artifact can be defined as which of the following?

    A. Information specific to a user's preference

    B. Information about the computer's general settings

    C. Information stored about a user's activities on the computer

    D. Information used to simplify a user's experience

    E. All of the above

2. A FAT file system stores date and time stamps in _____, whereas the NTFS file system stores date and time stamps in _____.

    A. DOS directory, local time

    B. Zulu time, GMT

    C. Local time, GMT

    D. SYSTEM.DAT, NTUSER.DAT

3. Where does Windows store the time zone offset?

    A. BIOS

    B. Registry

    C. INFO2 file

    D. DOS directory or MFT

4. In Windows 7, the date and time of when a file was sent to the Recycle Bin can be found where?

    A. INFO2 file

    B. Original filename's last access date

    C. DOS directory or MFT

    D. $I index file

5. When a text file is sent a pre–Windows Vista Recycle Bin, Windows changes the short filename of the deleted file to DC0.txt in the Recycle Bin. Select the best choice that explains the deleted filename.

    A. D=DOS, C=character, 0=index number, file extension remains the same

    B. D=DOS, C=drive letter, 0=index number, file extension remains the same

    C. D=deleted, C=character, 0=index number, file extension remains the same

    D. D=deleted, C=drive letter, 0=index number, file extension remains the same

6. When a document is opened, a link file bearing the document's filename is created in the _____ folder.

    A. Shortcut

    B. Recent

    C. Temp

    D. History

7. Link files are shortcuts or pointers to actual items. These actual items can be what?

    A. Programs

    B. Documents

    C. Folders

    D. Devices

    E. All of the above

8. In NTFS, information unique to a specific user is stored in the _____ file.

    A. USER.DAT

    B. NTUSER.DAT

    C. SYSTEM.DAT

    D. None of the above

9. In Windows XP, Windows Vista, or Window 7, by default, how many recently opened documents are displayed in the My Recent Documents or Recent Items folder?

    A. 4

    B. 12

    C. 15

    D. Unlimited

10. Most of a user's desktop items on a Windows 7 operating system would be located in the _____ directory.

    A. C:\WINDOWS\Desktop

    B. C:\WinNT\Desktop

    C. C:\WINDOWS\System32\config\Desktop

    D. C:\Users\%User%\Desktop

11. Because this file will hold the contents of RAM when the machine is powered off, the _____ file will be the approximate size of the system RAM and will be in the root directory.

    A. hiberfil.sys

    B. WIN386.SWP

    C. PAGEFILE.SYS

    D. NTUSER.DAT

12. Where can you find evidence of web-based email such as from MSN Hotmail or Google Gmail on a Windows system?

    A. In `Temporary Internet Files` under `Local Settings` in the user's profile

    B. In `Unallocated Clusters`

    C. In the `pagefile.sys` file

    D. In the `hiberfil.sys` file

    E. All of the above

13. Filenames with the `.url` extension that direct web browsers to a specific website are normally located in which folder?

    A. `Favorites` folder

    B. `Cookies` folder

    C. `Send To` folder

    D. `History` folder

14. Data about Internet cookies such as URL names, date and time stamps, and pointers to the actual location of the cookie is stored where?

    A. INFO2 file

    B. `index.dat` file

    C. EMF file

    D. `pagefile.sys` file

15. On a Windows 98 machine, which folder is the swap or page file contained in?

    A. `WIN386.SWP`

    B. `pagefile.sys`

    C. `swapfile.sys`

    D. `page.swp`

16. When you are examining evidence that has been sent to a printer, which file contains an image of the actual print job?

    A. The Enhanced Metafile (EMF)

    B. The shadow file

    C. The spool file

    D. The RAW file

17. The two modes for printing in Windows are _____ and _____.

    A. spooled, shadowed

    B. spooled, direct

    C. spooled, EM

    D. EMF, RAW

18. Although the Windows operating system removed the EMF file upon a successful print job, the examiner may still recover the file as a result of a search on its unique header information in areas such as `Unallocated Clusters` or the swap file.

    A. True

    B. False

19. The `index.dat` files are system files that store information about other files. They track date and time stamps, file locations, and name changes. Select the folder that does *not* contain an `index.dat` file.

    A. `Cookies`

    B. `History`

    C. `Recycle Bin`

    D. `Temporary Internet Files`

20. The `Temporary Internet Files` directory contains which of the following?

    A. Web page files that are cached or saved for possible later reuse

    B. An `index.dat` file that serves as a database for the management of the cached files

    C. Web mail artifacts

    D. All of the above

Chapter

10

Advanced EnCase

ENCE EXAM TOPICS COVERED IN THIS CHAPTER:

✓ Locating and mounting partitions (partition recovery)

✓ Mounting files

✓ Windows registry

✓ EnScripts and filters

✓ Email

✓ Base64 encoding

✓ EnCase Decryption Suite (EDS)

✓ Virtual File System (VFS)

✓ Restoration

✓ Physical Disk Emulator (PDE)

This book's final chapter is a collection of advanced analysis concepts and tools. It begins with working with deleted partitions. I'll rely heavily on concepts covered in Chapter 2 as I explain the MBR, the VBR, and recovered deleted partitions.

There are a large number of complex files that can be "mounted" within EnCase for further examination and analysis. In this chapter, I'll describe the various ones supported, how they are mounted, and what to expect when they are mounted.

Among the files that EnCase can mount are the system registry files. A number of files comprise the system registry of the most current versions of Windows. I'll discuss how the files are mounted and the various registry keys that are derived from those files. Because understanding the registry is an important forensic skill, I'll explore some registry research techniques with the live Windows registry on a little-understood registry key. From that research, you'll better understand that particular key and develop valuable registry research skills in the process.

Throughout the text I've made reference to and used some basic EnScripts. In this chapter, I'll cover how to use the current EnScript feature set and its options.

Email seems to be a consistent factor in nearly every forensic examination. Email clients abound, and EnCase 7 provides support for most of the mainstream clients, with more under development. I'll describe which clients are currently covered and how EnCase 7 mounts and displays various email databases.

While I'm on the topic of email, I'll cover Base64 encoding, which is the most commonly encountered method for encoding email attachments. I'll cover how EnCase handles it automatically as well as how to manually extract it from the unallocated clusters.

EnCase 4, 5, and 6 have optional modules that you can purchase. However, many modules that were heretofore options for an added cost are included as part of EnCase 7. The EnCase Decryption Suite (EDS) decrypts data and files encrypted with the Windows Encrypted File System (EFS). I'll cover the basic features of this module.

There are two other modules now included: the Virtual File System (VFS) and the Physical Disk Emulator (PDE). VFS mounts the evidence file device as a file system so that it is available as a mounted volume in Windows. With this mounting, all data, including deleted folders and files, can be analyzed in Windows with third-party tools or Windows system tools. PDE is similar, but it mounts the evidence file device as a physical device in Windows. I'll discuss the similarities and differences in the two modules and how you can use them to further your examinations.

The EnCase FastBloc Software Edition (SE) is now included with EnCase 7. I covered this module extensively in Chapter 4, so I'll only briefly cover it in this chapter. EnCase 7 ships with another useful optional module called the CD-DVD module. By using this module, several features within EnCase can have their output written directly to a CD or DVD.

Occasionally you may need to restore an entire drive to boot and run the system as the suspect used it. That technique is called *restoration*, and I'll cover that as well.

Locating and Mounting Partitions

In this section, I'll make frequent references to concepts covered in detail in Chapter 2. If you aren't comfortable with MBRs, partition tables, VBRs, partition types, physical and logical sector addresses, CHS, and tracks, you may want to reread that chapter or at least refer to it frequently to refresh your understanding.

You should recall that the master boot record (MBR) is located at the first physical sector of a hard drive. Although it contains important boot code, it also contains the partition table, which can describe up to four partitions on that hard drive. The partition table consists of 64 bytes and starts in physical sector 0 at byte offsets 446 through 509. Each of four possible partitions is described by a 16-byte string.

Figure 10.1 shows the partition table in which sector 0, byte offsets 446 through 509, are selected. You should note that I'm working in the Disk view in the Table pane and in the Hex view in the View pane.

FIGURE 10.1 The partition table in sector 0 of the MBR type partition scheme is selected.

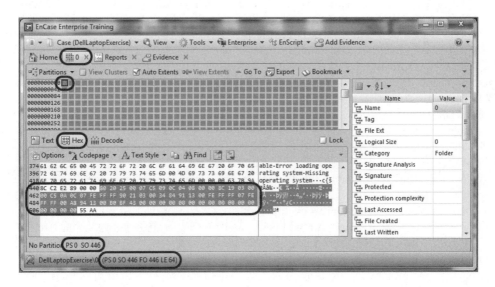

To have EnCase interpret or parse the information in the 64-byte partition table, we need only switch to the Decode view and choose the Partition Entry view type, as shown in Figure 10.2.

FIGURE 10.2   This is a 64-byte partition table selected and viewed as a Windows Partition Entry in the Decode view.

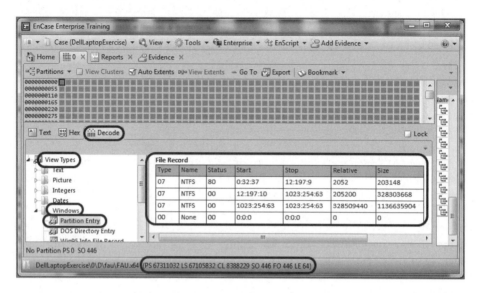

In this case, there are three partitions on this drive, and all three partitions are of type 07h, which is NTFS. This is shown in the first column. The first partition on this Windows 7 system is a 100 MB, hidden-system partition that handles the boot, and its status is 80h, which means the partition is the active, bootable partition. Using the legacy Cylinder Head Sector (CHS) system, the start point for the first partition is 0:32:37, and the stop point is 12:197:9. The more meaningful information follows the legacy CHS addressing, which is the starting sector (in the Relative column) and the size in sectors. The size of the first partition is 203,148 sectors (approximately 100 MB), relative to sector 2,052, which is the starting sector for the partition. If you add 2,052 to 203,148 and subtract 1, you arrive at 205,199, which is the sector number of the last sector in the partition. Since this is an NTFS partition, if you go to that last sector of the partition (sector 205,199), you will expect to find a backup copy of the VBR, and you do, as shown in Figure 10.3.

Since you know the starting sector of the partition from the partition table, you can easily go to that sector to view the first sector of the partition, which you have learned is the volume boot record (VBR). In this example, the first sector of the first partition is at sector 2,052. If you go to that sector, you will be at the VBR. Figure 10.4 shows the data found at sector 2,052, which is the VBR. The position indicator (GPS) confirms you are at physical sector (PS) 2,052. VBRs have headers or signatures that will eventually allow you to find them if the partition table entries are deleted. One of these signatures or headers is selected (first 7 bytes) in Figure 10.4. As you'll probably recall from Chapter 2, the first 3 bytes are the jump instructions, and the string that follows describes the operating system that did the formatting.

FIGURE 10.3   The last sector of the NTFS partition contains a backup copy of the VBR.

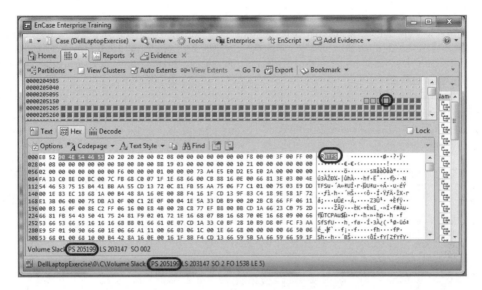

FIGURE 10.4   This partition starts at sector 2,052, which contains the VBR for an NTFS partition.

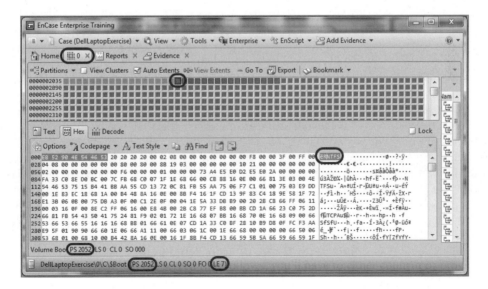

If a partition utility such as FDISK is used to remove a partition, the 16 bytes for that partition in the partition table are changed to zeros. Figure 10.5 shows a partition table after FDISK was used to remove all partitions. The partition itself, however, and all of its data are untouched by the process. It is similar to the process of deleting a file—only the pointers to the data are removed or altered; the data remains unchanged. With that in mind, it should be apparent that a partition can be easily recovered under these circumstances.

FIGURE 10.5   The partition table contains all zeros after FDISK was used to remove all partitions. There is no directory structure, and all squares in the Disk view indicate "no partition."

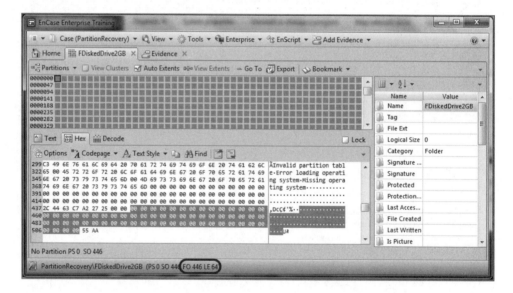

To recover deleted partitions, you must locate the beginning of the partition by locating the VBR. Because VBRs have telltale signatures, they are relatively easy to locate. While looking for VBRs, you will encounter a few search hits that are not partitions. Each NTFS partition keeps a backup copy of the VBR in the last sector of that partition. Of course, knowing where a partition ends is also useful information. The recommended method of recovering partitions is to start with the partition found nearest to the beginning of the drive and work from that direction, restoring partitions as you go. When you do, you'll find that many of your "hits" will be within allocated files or within the restored partition, as in the case of the backup VBR.

You know that the MBR is in the first sector of an MBR partitioned drive, which is sector 0. Because most drives currently have 63 sectors per track and the remainder of the first track is unused, you can expect sector 1 through sector 62 to be all zeros. Some tracking utilities write data in this space, but most of the time it will contain zeros. Sector 63 is the first sector of the second track and where you will usually find the beginning of the first partition for operating system drives before Vista. Starting with Vista, the VBR (the beginning of the NTFS partition) is normally installed at sector 2048 on a new installation of an operating system, as shown in Figure 10.6. While it's not often encountered anymore, on older drives, where there were 39 sectors per track, look at sector 39 for the beginning of the first partition.

FIGURE 10.6 VBR or beginning of NTFS partition on a Windows 7 operating system drive (new installation)

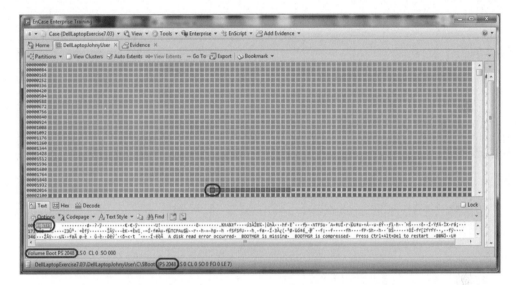

Most certainly you could have crafted a search term to locate this VBR, but because you know the common places to look, it is often quicker to go to those sectors (39, 63, 2048) first. The drive in this example is an XP operating system on a drive with 63 sectors per track and has had its partition removed, as you can recall from Figure 10.5. If you take a shortcut and go immediately to sector 63, you'll see a VBR at that location. While in the Disk view, place your cursor on the sector containing the VBR (the beginning of the partition), which is sector 63 in our example. On the Disk view menu bar, under Partitions, choose Add Partition, as shown in Figure 10.7. You will see the Add Partition dialog box, as shown in Figure 10.8. EnCase will parse the data in the VBR and use that information to populate the fields in the dialog box, which will be used to correctly rebuild the partition. Click OK; EnCase will restore the partition. To view the restored partition, you must go back to the Table tab on the Evidence tab and reopen the evidence item, and the directory structure will then be visible in the Tree pane view.

FIGURE 10.7   Sector 63 is selected, and under the Partitions menu, Add Partition is chosen.

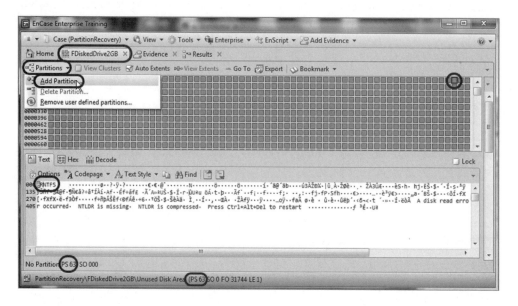

FIGURE 10.8   Add Partition dialog box—values therein are obtained when EnCase reads the data from the volume boot record

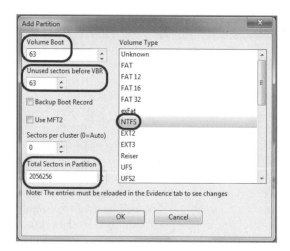

It is important to note that the evidence file is not changed by this process. Even after you have restored the partition, if you go back and check, you will find that the partition table still contains all zeros. EnCase restores the partition virtually with pointers contained within the case file. Figure 10.9 shows the correct directory structure after the partition was restored.

FIGURE 10.9   After the partition is recovered, the directory structure is restored to normal.

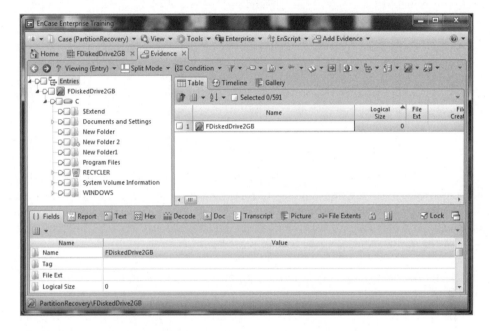

If you need to remove a partition, from the Disk view, go to the sector where you created the partition, and from the Partitions menu, choose Delete Partition. Alternatively, you could choose Remove User Defined Partitions, and any user-defined partition will be deleted.

If you have more than one partition to restore or you have the potential for other than the run-of-the-mill Windows partition types to exist, it then becomes advantageous to search for partitions. You could create a series of search strings and search for them manually; however, EnCase has a well-designed EnScript to do that work for you. It is an option or module within the Case Processor EnScript. When you run the Case Processor EnScript, located on the application toolbar under EnScript, you will see a dialog box asking you for a Bookmark Folder Name, as shown in Figure 10.10.

FIGURE 10.10 In the first stage, you are prompted for a Bookmark Folder Name.

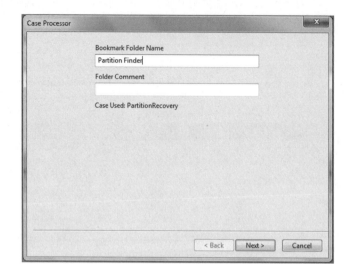

Once you enter a Bookmark Folder Name, choose Next and then select Partition Finder with a blue check mark, as shown in Figure 10.11. If you double-click Partition Finder, you'll see a Help screen, explaining how the parser works and what to expect, which is also shown in Figure 10.11. Click Finish to run the EnScript, and when done, go to the Bookmarks tab and view the results under the folder, in this case Partition Finder.

FIGURE 10.11 The Partition Finder EnScript will locate partitions and note them in a bookmark.

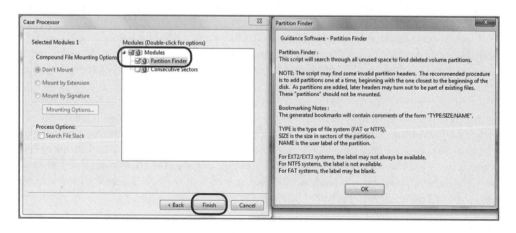

If you go to the Bookmarks tab after running the EnScript, you'll typically find the partitions located by the EnScript along with, very often, some false positives. The bookmark will contain a comment for each hit that describes the partition parameters in the format *Partition Type : Size in Sectors : Name (if available), along with Bookmark Start and Bookmark Sector.* Figure 10.12 shows the results of running the Partition Finder. You will note that five hits were reported, and the Comment column shows the information about the partition. Note that the columns have been arranged in an optimal manner for this task.

- Name column: Contains name of area where search hit found

- Comment column: Contains partition information

FIGURE 10.12   The Bookmark view shows the results of the Partition Finder. Note the columns and their arrangement.

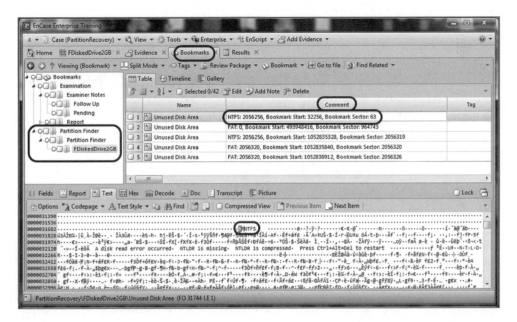

By arranging the columns as shown in Figure 10.12, you can see at a glance which bookmarks are most likely partitions and which are most likely not. Now it is time to logically examine the results. While in another view, I examined the device before I started this process and determined it contained 4,124,736 total sectors. The first bookmarked item starts at sector 63. Because the device has 63 sectors per track, sectors 0–62 (63 sectors) appear on the first track. Sector 63 marks the beginning of the second track and the normal location for the first partition. It makes sense, therefore, that this search hit is describing a valid partition. If you look at its size, which is 2,056,256 sectors, you find that it covers about half the drive.

If you examine the other search hit, located at sector 118,911, you see that it is contained within the recovered partition. You might therefore conclude that it is a false hit, such as a backup VBR, or data within a file. With that conclusion, you could dismiss it and move on—or you could consider one more possibility. Suppose there were, at one time, two partitions on this drive and the user removed them and partitioned the device in a different partition sizing layout. The first partition starting at sector 63 would have been overwritten immediately, but the partition starting somewhere out there in the middle of the drive might still exist and be recoverable. That said, in most cases, you'd want to investigate this possibility by restoring a partition in that location and reviewing the results.

In our example, we want to proceed by restoring the first partition found, which is located at physical sector 63. On the first search hit showing on the Bookmarks tab, right-click it and choose Go To File, as shown in Figure 10.13.

FIGURE 10.13   Right-click the search hit on the Bookmarks tab, and choose Go To File.

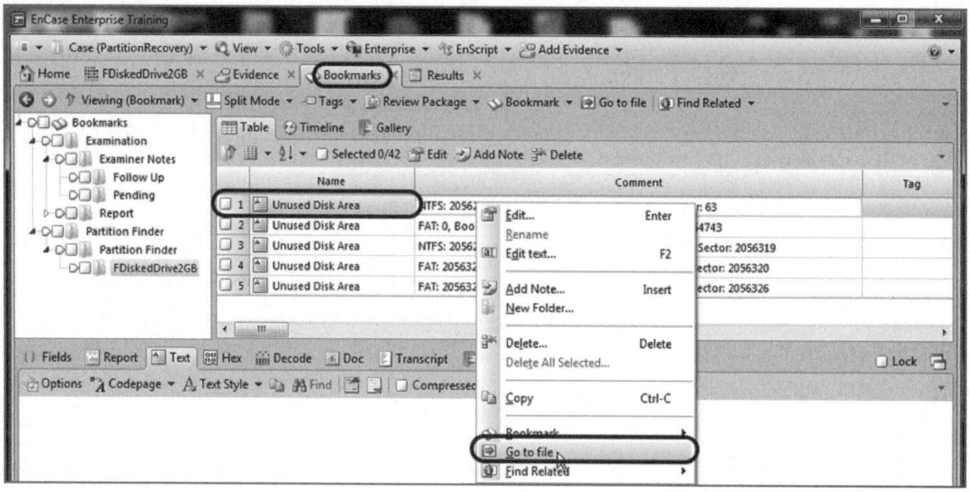

This will launch a separate tab within Bookmarks tab showing the containing file (in this case Unused Disk Area) with the cursor on the offset containing the search hit in the Text view, as shown in Figure 10.14.

While in this view, from either the Table view or the Text view, right-click and choose Device ➢ Disk View, as shown in Figure 10.15; you'll be taken to the Disk view and directly to the sector containing the start of the partition, based on the selected search hit.

FIGURE 10.14   New tab under Bookmarks tab showing the Text view

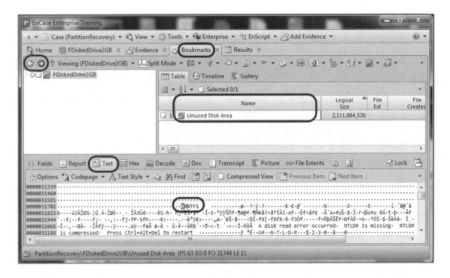

FIGURE 10.15   Right-click in Table view or Text view and choose Device ➤ Disk View.

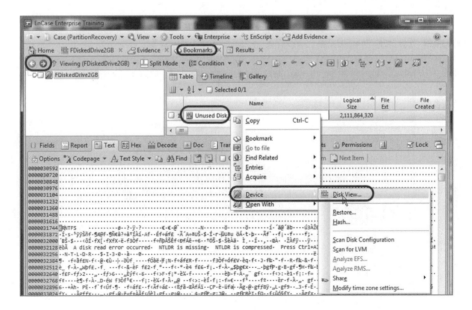

With sector 63 selected, as shown in Figure 10.16, go to the Partitions menu, as shown in Figure 10.17, and choose Add Partition. Accept the defaults, shown in the Add Partition menu, which are shown in Figure 10.18, and choose OK, which inserts the defined partition. As before, you need to reload the evidence entries on the Evidence tab to see the restored partition.

FIGURE 10.16   Disk view that lands on sector containing selected search hit, which is also the volume boot record where the partition is to be inserted

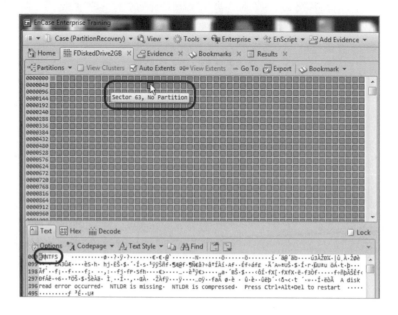

FIGURE 10.17   Partitions menu is accessed from Disk view

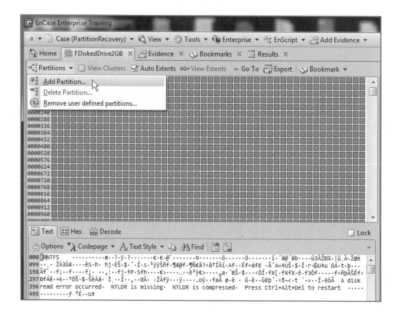

FIGURE 10.18   Add Partition dialog box

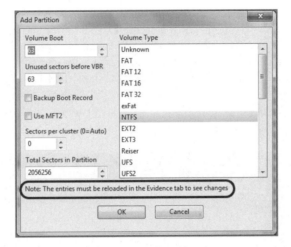

As previously mentioned, this partition occupies about half of the device, which means either that the rest of the device is unpartitioned or that another partition exists and needs to also be restored. If you go back to the Bookmarks tab and carefully review the other partition signature search hits, shown in Figure 10.19, you'll note that the third search hit is the backup VBR existing in the last sector (2,056,319) of the partition we just restored. You'll also note that the fourth search hit appears to be a valid FAT partition (VBR) starting in the first sector immediately after the partition we just inserted, which is sector 2,056,320. Further, there is a backup VBR in the seventh sector after this VBR, which is the earmark of a valid FAT32 partition. Thus, it seems clear that we have another partition to insert at sector 2,056,320 (the fourth search hit).

FIGURE 10.19   The fourth search hit is a VBR for a FAT32 partition that needs to be restored.

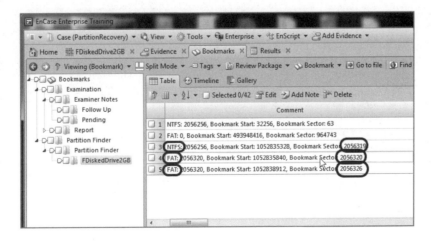

If we follow the same steps for restoring the first partition—right-clicking the fourth search hit, choosing Go To File, and then right-clicking in the Table view of the resulting screen and choosing Device ➢ Disk View—we end up in the Disk view with our focus on the sector where we need to insert the FAT partition, which is sector 2,056,320 and shown in Figure 10.20. With our focus on that partition, simply choose Add Partition from the Partition menu, accept the defaults, and choose OK. Remember to reload the evidence item in the Evidence tab. Now both partitions should be available in the Tree pane, as shown in Figure 10.21.

FIGURE 10.20   Disk view with focus on sector 2,056,320, which is the VBR for a FAT32

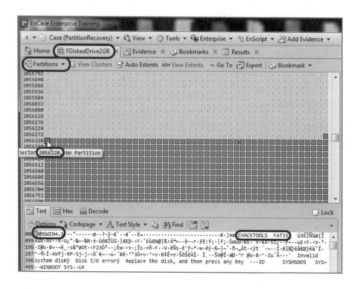

FIGURE 10.21   Tree view showing both restored partitions

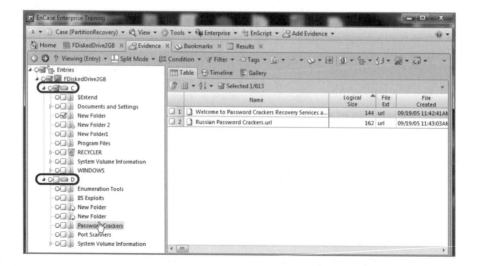

As with most knowledge, it is enhanced by practical skills that make use of that knowledge. In Exercise 10.1, you recover a partition. You should do this exercise now while the concepts are fresh in your mind. You'll understand it better and will retain the knowledge longer.

EXERCISE 10.1

Partition Recovery

In this exercise, you will examine a drive on which the partitions have been deleted using FDISK. You'll locate and recover those partitions.

1. Create a new case, naming your case Partition Recovery. Locate an evidence file on the publisher's website for this book, named Advanced\FDiskedDrive2GB.E01. Place it in an evidence folder along with those created by EnCase 7 for your newly created case.

2. With a new case created, from the Home tab, click Add Evidence and next choose Add Evidence File. Browse to the location where you placed the file FDiskedDrive2GB .E01. Once you have located it, select it, and click Open.

3. You will now be in the Evidence view with the one evidence item showing. Double-click this evidence item to have it parse and appear in the Entries view. When you do, you will immediately note that no partitions are present and that all data appears as Unused Disk Area. If you closely examine the first physical sector, you will see that it contains data but that the partition table area (byte offsets 446-509) contains all zeros, indicating that the partition table has been zeroed out and any defined partitions deleted.

4. From the Table view, right-click the device and choose Device ➢ Disk View. Knowing that often the first partition can be found at sector 63, examine the contents of that sector, and you will note that it appears to contain the VBR for an NTFS partition. Let's insert a partition at this point and examine the results.

5. From within the Disk view, with your cursor on sector 63, choose the Partitions menu and choose Add Partition. Accept the defaults and click OK.

6. Return to the Evidence tab and the Entries view. You will note that view at this point remains unchanged by the addition of the partition. This is expected as we must return to the Evidence tab Table view and force our evidence item to be reparsed. To do so, click the green left arrow to the left of the words *Viewing (Entry)*. Next, simply double-click the evidence item; you will be returned to the Entries view, and your added partition will be fully viewable.

7. One might consider the work done at this point, but one should always account for all drive geometry because there could be yet another deleted partition. In fact, if you force the device to appear in the Table view and look at the Report view for that device in the View pane, you will note that the device contains 4,124,736 sectors and that the recovered partition accounts for only 2,056,319 sectors or about half of the total drive space.

8. There are essentially two approaches to handling this situation. You could use the Partition Finder contained within the EnCase Evidence Processor to locate partition signatures and work through the results, adding the partition when found. Alternatively, and often much more quickly, you could go to the end of the recovered partition and examine the sectors in the area for the presence of another partition. Let's do the latter.

9. From the Disk view, right-click any sector and choose Go To. In the Go To window, type in **2,056,318** and click OK, which should take you to the last sector in the recovered partition. If you step over to the next sector (2,056,319), you will see the backup VBR for the recovered partition. Continuing to the next sector (2,056, 320), you will see what appears to be the VBR for a FAT32 partition. If this is a valid FAT32 partition, you would expect to see a backup VBR located six sectors from here at sector 2,056,326. When we examine this, we confirm the presence of the backup VBR and realize that we need to add a partition at the primary VBR located at sector 2,056,320. Place your cursor on that sector and, from the Partition menu, choose Add Partition. In the input block Unused Sectors Before VBR, change the value of 63 to 0, and click OK.

10. As before, return to the Evidence tab Table view and double-click the evidence item to force it to reparse. The result will be displayed on the Evidence tab Entries view, and both user-added partitions will now be visible. Be sure to save your work at this point!

Mounting Files

Many files are compound in nature. A compound file contains data that may be hierarchical, compressed, encrypted, or a combination of these methods. Its raw data is often illogical, difficult, or even impossible to view in its native state. EnCase can decode and mount these files so they are displayed in a logical or hierarchical format. In this manner, the examiner can see the data in the file in a more meaningful and logical format.

It is important to understand which files can be searched without mounting and which files can't be searched until they are mounted. Also, it is important to understand that certain files are mounted as part of other processing.

The process is the same for mounting any compound file. You simply right-click the file, under the Entries option select the View File Structure option, and then click OK in the resulting dialog box. Figure 10.22 shows the right-click menu with the option View File Structure selected.

FIGURE 10.22   To mount a compound file, right-click it and choose View File Structure under the Entries option.

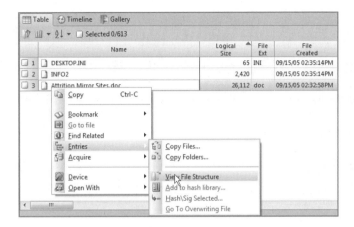

EnCase mounts the compound file, and the mounted file will be visible in blue to indicate that it is a hyperlinked object. If you hold your cursor over the hyperlink, the cursor will change to a hand, which is depicted in Figure 10.23. In past versions of EnCase, a mounted file was stored in RAM and consumed significant resources, especially when many large compound files were mounted. EnCase 7, by contrast, mounts compound files by creating logical evidence files for each mounted file and stores them in the EvidenceCache folder. This is a far more efficient method of mounting compound files and negates the need to dismount them. Currently, as of EnCase 7.04 there is no method by which to unmount or close a mounted file, but a future release may provide that option, even though it is not really necessary.

FIGURE 10.23   A mounted compound file is shown in blue indicating its hyperlinked status. The cursor changes to a hand when placed over a mounted compound file.

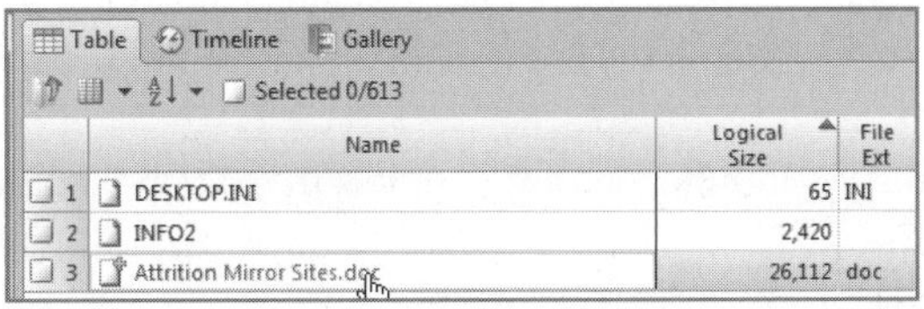

To view a mounted compound file, simply click the blue hyperlink, and the mounted file will launch in its own window within the Evidence tab, as shown in Figure 10.24. From this view, you can navigate its structure from within the Tree pane beginning at the special icon denoting the root of the mounted compound file, which is also shown in Figure 10.24. Any object within the mounted structure can be bookmarked and subsequently included in your final report.

FIGURE 10.24   Mounted files are viewable in their own separate window on the Evidence tab.

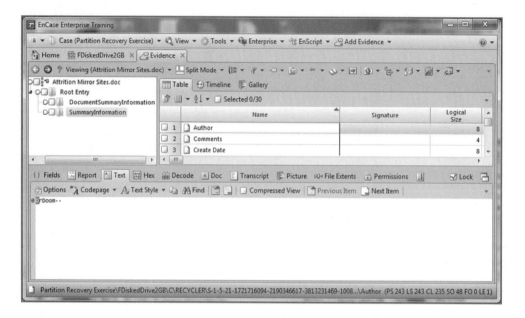

    Often there are temp files that are compound files. Running a file signature analysis reveals these file as having an alias of * Compound Document File in the file signature column. These files are good candidates to mount and examine.

The list of files that can be mounted seems to grow with each release of EnCase. Table 10.1 describes the most common files that can be mounted within the EnCase environment. There is a brief description of the file and what data can be seen upon mounting.

TABLE 10.1   Listing of common compound files that can be mounted in EnCase

File	Type	Description
.dbx extension	Outlook Express email	Mounting places emails in a hierarchical structure instead of viewing in a flat file.
.mbx extension	Outlook Express email (earlier versions)	Mounting places emails in a hierarchical structure instead of viewing in a flat file.

TABLE 10.1   Listing of common compound files that can be mounted in EnCase *(continued)*

File	Type	Description
`.doc/.docx` extension	Microsoft Word document	Mounting places various objects in a folder structure so that you can view the document properties, including the data, document summary information, and so on.
`.xls/.xlsx` extension	Microsoft Excel spreadsheet	Mounting places various objects in a folder structure so that you can view the various document properties such as the data, document summary information, and so on.
`.ppt/.pptx` extension	Microsoft PowerPoint document	Mounting places various objects in a folder structure so you can view the various document properties such as the data, document summary information, and so on.
`.zip` extension	WinZip-compressed file	Mounting decompresses the archives, presenting the individual files for examination.
`.pst` extension	Outlook email	Mounting places emails in a hierarchical structure instead of viewing in a flat file. Outlook's structure is very detailed.
`.MailDB` extension	MSN mail (has `.dbx` header and structure)	Mounting places emails in a hierarchical structure instead of viewing in a flat file.
`.msi` extension	Microsoft Installer	Mounting shows some of the properties of this installer package.
`Thumbs.db`	Hidden system file created when using Windows Explorer in the thumbnail view	Mounted file shows thumbnails of images in folder on the last occasion the user viewed thumbnails. Can show thumbnail images of files that were deleted. It also shows that user saw images and was aware of contents, which is useful in cases where inappropriate or unlawful images are at issue.
`SYSTEM.DAT` `USER.DAT` System Security Software SAM Default `NTUSER.DAT`	Registry files for Windows 9*x* and NT systems	Mounting these files parses the specific registry hive and allows the examiner to navigate that branch of the registry in a hierarchical view. See the next section, "Registry."

TABLE 10.1 Listing of common compound files that can be mounted in EnCase *(continued)*

File	Type	Description
.tar extension	tar-compressed file	Mounting decompresses the archives, presenting the individual files for examination.
.rar extension	rar-compressed file	Mounting decompresses the archives, presenting the individual files for examination.
.bzip2	bzip2-compressed file	Mounting decompresses the archives, presenting the individual files for examination.
.CLOOP	CLOOP-compressed archive	Mounting decompresses the archives, presenting the individual files for examination.
.rzip extension	rzip-compressed file	Mounting decompresses the archives, presenting the individual files for examination.
.gzip extension	gzip-compressed file	Mounting decompresses the archives, presenting the individual files for examination.
.arc extension	arc-compressed file	Mounting decompresses the archives, presenting the individual files for examination.
.cab extension	Microsoft Installation Archive	Mounting decompresses the archives, presenting the individual files for examination.
.pfc extension	AOL Personal File Cabinet	Mounting makes available the content of the PFC.
.nsf extension	Lotus Notes data stores	Mounting places emails in a hierarchical structure instead of viewing in a flat file.
.edb extension	Microsoft Exchange email database file	Mounting places emails in a hierarchical structure instead of viewing in a flat file.
.mbox extension	Unix email	Mounting places emails in a hierarchical structure instead of viewing in a flat file
Cpio	Macintosh PAX archive	Mounting decompresses the archives, presenting the individual files for examination.
.stf extension	Archive file associated with ShrinkToFit	Mounting decompresses the archives, presenting the individual files for examination.

Some compound files can be searched without mounting them; others require mounting before they can be searched. For the most part, the determining factor is whether the data is compressed, encrypted, or both. For example, ZIP or TAR files are compressed, and a normal search using the active code page won't find data within them. If you mount them, however, the compressed text is uncompressed during mounting, and they can then be searched.

An Outlook PST file, for example, stores its data using Outlook compressible encryption. Thus, it is compressed and encrypted. If you search this file using the active code page, don't expect to find any meaningful data. If you mount this file, the data is uncompressed, decrypted, and displayed in a hierarchical structure. In this format, it can be easily searched.

When you search for email or Internet history, EnCase mounts the various files you have selected (choosing Outlook causes the PST file to be mounted, Outlook Express causes the DBX and MBX files to be mounted, and so on). Once you have them mounted, you can effectively search them.

Microsoft Office documents can be searched without mounting. Mounting Office doesn't decrypt or uncompress data; it simply places data in a hierarchical format for organized or logical viewing.

The EnCase Evidence Processor contains an option to mount certain compound files, as shown in Figure 10.25. Currently the feature supports the following archives: ZIP, GZIP, TAR, RAR, THUMBS.DB, CLOOP, and BZIP2.

FIGURE 10.25   EnCase Evidence Processor's compound file mounting feature

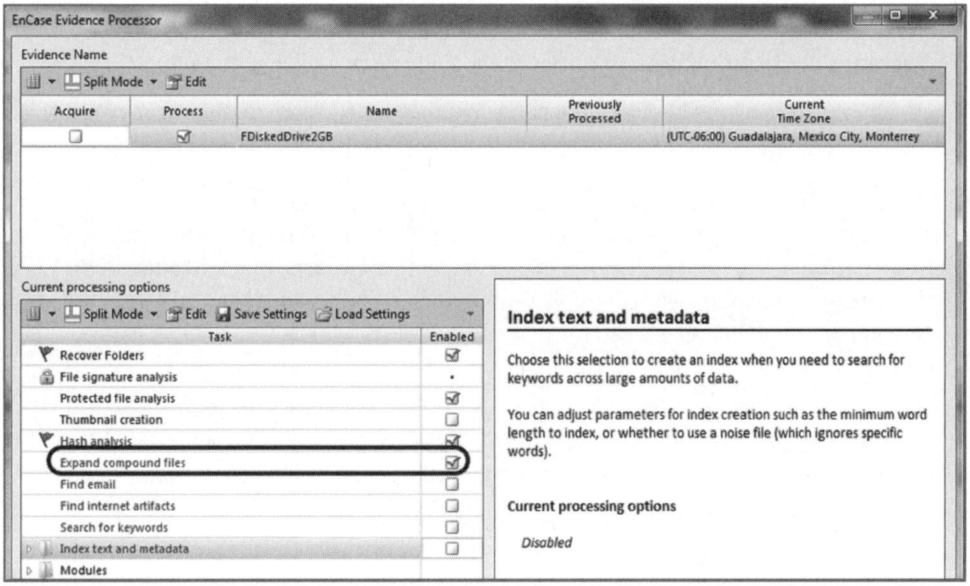

File Signatures and Non-Windows Systems

If you'll recall, Macintosh, Unix, Linux, and so forth, do not use file extensions for application binding. Although Macintosh is moving into that area, you can't count on having file extensions in these environments. Thus, when using the File Mounter, you will want to search for compound files by both extension and signature if you are working on a non-Windows system. In fact, you may want to use it almost always because compound files created on other than Windows machines often find their way onto Windows systems from downloads, email attachments, and the like. Also, some browsers store Internet cache files in renamed files with no file extensions.

Thus, if you want to be thorough and find and mount all compound files, search by both file extension and file signature on both Windows and non-Windows systems.

Searching for Outlook PST Data in the Unallocated Clusters

Outlook leaves fragments of its data throughout the hard drive in slack space, in unallocated space, in the swap file, and in the hibernation file. This space can't be mounted as a PST file, but it can be effectively searched for Outlook data.

1. The first step is to create a keyword to search. When you create the keyword, you need to select a Unicode search and uncheck the current active code page.

2. Next, go to the Code page tab. Go down the list of available code pages until you reach the Outlook Compressible Encryption code page, which is code 65003.

3. Place a check mark next to this code page, and then click OK to create your keyword.

4. Search your case using this keyword.

5. Go to the Results view and review your search hits in the View pane, using the Text tab. Any search hits that appear immediately in clear text are not ones that are in Outlook Compressible Encryption. To see those search hits, go to the Code Page menu and change into Outlook Compressible Encryption. Now your results will appear in gibberish, except for those in clear text, which are decoded from Outlook Compressible Encryption.

6. Bookmark any hits of import and then view the results in the Bookmark view. You will find that the code page used when the bookmark was created follows the bookmark, and you don't need to make any further adjustments as in past versions of EnCase.

Registry

The Windows registry is a central repository or database of the configuration data for the operating system and most of its programs. Although the registry creates a convenient central location for this data, it also creates the potential for a single point of failure that can bring the system to a halt. Because of that vulnerability, the operating system uses safeguards to enable recovery to safe configurations through the use of "last known good configuration" and restore points in Windows XP/2003/Vista/2008/7.

WARNING   To understand the registry as seen in EnCase, you need to understand the live registry as seen in Windows. As you go through this chapter, you will explore and in some cases make changes to your system registry. No discussion of registry changes would be complete without the customary warning: changing your system registry could harm your operating system. Consequently, if you aren't comfortable with doing so, don't. If you want to make changes, back up your registry first, or create a restore point before proceeding.

With the warnings behind us, let's proceed. To be certain, the registry is a gold mine of forensic evidence. Since Microsoft discourages users, administrators included, from accessing or modifying the registry, it is doing its part in helping us preserve evidence, for which we are most grateful. As an examiner, you need to be very comfortable navigating within and working with the data in the registry. Comfort comes with knowledge, understanding, and experience, which are the precise goals of this section.

In the following sections, I'll provide a background of the registry, including its history and its current structure. I'll introduce you to the terminology associated with the registry, such as hives, keys, subkeys, and values.

Once I describe the terminology and structure, I'll cover research techniques that will enable you to truly understand the internal workings of the registry. I'll target an obscure and little-understood registry key for this research. When you are done with this chapter, you will join a relatively elite group of examiners who understand and properly interpret the function and values contained in this key. Its forensic usefulness will unfold before your eyes!

If you are going to testify about what a particular value in the registry means, you need to be able to demonstrate and explain those values. After completing this section, you should have the tools and techniques to do so.

Registry History

If you trace Windows back to its roots, its predecessor was MS-DOS. MS-DOS was a command-line interface whose configuration settings, by today's standards, were anemic. MS-DOS received its configuration settings from two modest little files: config.sys and autoexec.bat. The config.sys file primarily loaded device drivers, and autoexec.bat was for setting environment variables, running programs, and the like.

The first Windows GUI was Microsoft Windows 3.0. This first version of Windows introduced INI files as containers for configuration information. These were flat text files with no hierarchical structure, and related configuration data was stored in sections. Text files made it difficult to store binary data, and the INI files were numerous and lacking in organization.

Windows 3.1 followed shortly after Windows 3.0, and with it came the rudiments of the system registry as a repository for system configuration settings. Windows 95 and NT 3.5 expanded the registry to the structure and interface that we recognize today in Windows 7, although it was a fraction of the size and complexity of today's registry. The files in which the registry values are stored have gone from two with Windows 9x to six or more with Windows 2000/XP/2003/Vista/2008/7.

Registry Organization and Terminology

The Windows registry is stored in files called *hives* at a physical level. The interface for the user and applications takes on a logical scheme or format that resembles the directory structure used by Windows Explorer to store data in files and folders. Instead of using folders, the registry uses keys. Instead of using files, the registry uses values. If you think of it using that analogy, you are well along your way to understanding the hierarchy and terminology.

The user primarily views or modifies the registry with the registry editor tool. With Windows 2000, you had to choose between two registry editors (regedit.exe or regedt32.exe) depending on the task at hand. Either would allow you to view and navigate the registry, but each had capabilities and limitations that the other did not have, forcing a choice at times. Fortunately, Microsoft resolved that problem with the release of Windows XP/2003 and combined all features into one registry editor known simply as *regedit*.

Microsoft does not provide a shortcut to the registry editor in any known dialog box. In fact, Microsoft keeps the registry well below the radar screen, making only brief mention of the registry in the Windows help feature. At every stage Microsoft recommends against editing the registry, even to the point of recommending that administrators edit the registry as a last resort. That being said, you'll find regedit.exe in the root of Windows, and you can usually access it from the Run command. To open the Run command, hold down the Windows key, and press R (for run). In the resulting window, type **regedit**, and press Enter. Figure 10.26 shows the Windows 7 registry editor when you open it. The left pane is known as the *key pane*, and the right pane is known as the *value pane*.

The Windows registry consists of five root-level keys, shown in Figure 10.26. Table 10.2 describes these root keys. Of those five root keys, only two are master keys, while the remaining three are derived keys that are linked to keys within the two master keys.

FIGURE 10.26   The Windows 7 registry editor

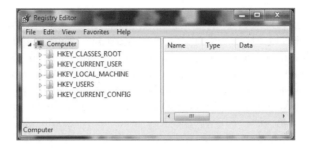

TABLE 10.2   Five root keys of the registry

Root key name	Description
HKEY_CLASSES_ROOT	Used to associate file types with programs that open them and also used to register classes for Component Object Model (COM) objects. It is the largest of the root keys in terms of the registry space it occupies. This key is derived from a linked merger of two keys, which are HKLM\Software\Classes and HKCU\Software\Classes. This merger effectively blends default settings with per-user settings.
HKEY_CURRENT_USER	Used to configure the environment for the console user. It is a per-user setting (specific only to this user) and is derived from a link to HKU\SID, where the SID is the user's security identifier.
HKEY_CURRENT_CONFIG	Used to establish the current hardware configuration profile. This key is derived from a link to HKLM\SYSTEM\CurrentControlSet\Hardware Profiles\Current. Current is derived from a link to HKLM\SYSTEM\CurrentControlSet\Hardware Profiles\####, where #### is a number that increments starting at 0000. HKLM\SYSTEM\CurrentControlSet, in turn, is a link to HKLM\SYSTEM\ControlSet###, where ### is a number that increments starting at 000. Which control set is current and used to create this key and subsequent link is determined by the value located in HKLM\SYSTEM\Select\Current.
HKEY_LOCAL_MACHINE	Used to establish the per-computer settings. Settings found in this key apply to the machine and all of its users, covering all facets of the computer's function. This key is a master key and is not, therefore, derived from any link as are the previous three keys.
HKEY_USERS	Used for environment settings for the console user as well as other users who have logged onto the system. There will be at least three subkeys—.DEFAULT, SID, and SID_Classes, where the SID is that of the console user. You may also find SIDs S-1-5-18, S-1-5-19, and S-1-5-20, which are for the LocalSystem, LocalService, and NetworkService accounts, respectively. Any other SIDs found here will belong to other users who have logged on to the machine. This key is a master key and is not, therefore, derived from any link.

At a physical level, each of the logical master keys has its source data stored in a file that is called a *hive*. In each of the two master keys (HKLM and HKU), there are subkeys named for each of the hive files. Table 10.3 shows the hive keys and the associated hive files from which they originate. These hive files are located in the folder *%SYSTEMROOT%*\System32\config, except for the new hive key that was introduced in Vista, which is the BCD, or Boot Configuration Data, hive. This hive file is located in the first partition, which is a hidden system partition. This file replaces the legacy boot.ini file. This file previously existed as a text file and was an easy target for malware. Part of the rationale for placing the boot data in the registry hive file was to make it more difficult for malware to utilize for start-up purposes. While it remains to be seen whether that rationale was valid, clearly the registry hive file format allows binary data storage and considerable extensibility for boot configuration data storage.

TABLE 10.3   HKLM hive keys and their corresponding hive files

Hive key	Hive file
HKLM\BDC00000000	**\Boot\BCD (located on first partition!)**
HKLM\SAM	*%SYSTEMROOT%*\System32\config\SAM
HKLM\SECURITY	*%SYSTEMROOT%*\System32\config\SECURITY
HKLM\SOFTWARE	*%SYSTEMROOT%*\System32\config\software
HKLM\SYSTEM	*%SYSTEMROOT%*\System32\config\system

If you look at the live registry under the master key HKLM, you see the five hive keys listed in Table 10.3, plus you will see one more that is named HARDWARE. Interestingly, HARDWARE is a dynamic key with no source hive file at the physical level. It is created as a dynamic key in RAM when Windows boots. When the system shuts down, the data in this key is gone.

Thus far, we've covered the hive keys and files located in HKLM. The master key HKU has its share of hive files as well. In fact, each subkey under HKU is a hive key with a corresponding hive file. The hive files for HKU are found in several locations. Table 10.4 shows the various hive keys in HKU and their source hive files. When SID is referenced, it is the SID of the console user or other past logged-on user. When UserName is referenced, it is the username that corresponds to the SID.

TABLE 10.4   HKU hive keys and their corresponding hive files

Hive key	Hive file
HKU\.DEFAULT	*%SYSTEMROOT%*\System32\config\default
HKU\S-1-5-19	Documents and Settings\LocalService\NTUSER.DAT
HKU\S-1-5-19_Classes	Documents and Settings\LocalService\Local Settings\Application Data\Microsoft\Windows\UsrClass.dat
HKU\S-1-5-20	Documents and Settings\NetworkService\NTUSER.DAT
HKU\S-1-5-20_Classes	Documents and Settings\NetworkService\Local Settings\Application Data\Microsoft\Windows\UsrClass.dat
HKU\SID	Documents and Settings\UserName\NTUSER.DAT
HKU\SID_Classes	Documents and Settings\UserName\Local Settings\Application Data\Microsoft\Windows\UsrClass.dat

When the system loads these hives into the registry, there is one key that lists or maps the loaded hive files with their corresponding registry hive keys. This key is an excellent one to visit because it shows the relationships between hive files and hive keys that are loaded on the system (see Figure 10.27). You can find this key at HKEY_LOCAL_MACHINE\SYSTEM\CurrentControlSet\Control\hivelist but only in the live registry. When the system is shut down, none of the hives is loaded.

FIGURE 10.27   The key "hive list" shows currently loaded hive files and their mapping to registry hive keys.

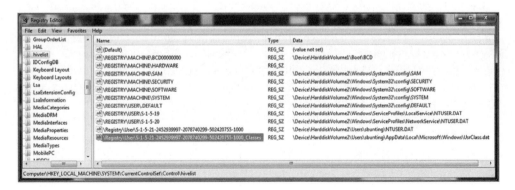

As I mentioned earlier, the registry keys are displayed in the left, or key, pane of the registry editor. It is from this pane that you can navigate among the various registry keys. The right, or value, pane is the pane in which you view or access the registry values. A value has three components: its name, its data type, and its data. Figure 10.28 shows the registry editor in which a series of values is shown in the right, or value, pane. In the value pane there is a column for each of the three value attributes (Name, Type, and Data).

FIGURE 10.28   Registry editor showing registry values in the right, or value, pane

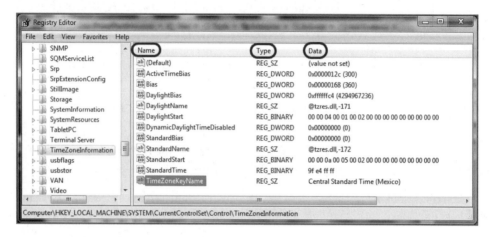

All values have names; there can't be a null name. A value's name is analogous to a file's name. A value name can be up to 512 ANSI characters in length (256 Unicode characters), except for the special characters: question mark (?), backslash (\), and asterisk (*). Furthermore, Windows reserves all value names that begin with a period (.). Just as no folder can contain two files with the same name, no key can contain two values with the same name.

Each value contains data of a specified data type. That type is specified by a number, which is interpreted by the registry API so that the user sees the data type in plain text. Table 10.5 shows each of the data types, their corresponding number, and a brief description of what the data type means. When you see a registry value in EnCase versions older than version 5, only the data type number will be shown, not the plain-text version rendered by the registry API. EnCase 5 and 6 interpret the numeric value and return the plain-text data type, as shown in Table 10.5. In all versions, the data type appears in the file type column. With EnCase 7, the file type column does not appear, and there is no information provided regarding the value data type.

TABLE 10.5 Listing of registry value data types

Data type	Number	Description
REG_NONE	0	Data type is not defined.
REG_SZ	1	Fixed-length text string expressed in user-friendly format, often used to describe components.
REG_EXPAND_SZ	2	Variable or expandable length data string.
REG_BINARY	3	Binary data, displayed in editor as hex.
REG_DWORD	4	32-bit double word value—the most common data type found in the registry.
REG_DWORD_LITTLE_ENDIAN	4	32-bit double word value with bytes in reverse order. Because Intel already stores data in this format, this term is synonymous with REG_DWORD, and they have the same numeric value.
REG_DWORD_BIG_ENDIAN	5	32-bit double word value with bytes in normal order, with the highest bit appearing first.
REG_LINK	6	An internal-use-only data type for Unicode symbolic link.
REG_MULTI_SZ	7	Multiple-string field in which each string is separated by a null (00h) and with two nulls (00 00) marking the end of the list of strings.
REG_RESOURCE_LIST	8	Listing of resource lists for devices or device drivers (REG_FULL_RESOURCE_DESCRIPTOR). You can view but not edit these lists.

Using EnCase to Mount and View the Registry

I've now covered the basics of the live registry as seen by the user in a registry editor. It is the logical interface by which the registry hive files are addressed, viewed, and edited. The live registry, as thus far depicted, and the registry as seen in EnCase will have noticeable differences.

When you view the registry in EnCase, you are looking at only the hive files, and the view will differ from a live registry view in many ways. For example, you will not see the HARDWARE key that exists in the live registry under HKLM. This key is a dynamic key, created at boot, and exists only in RAM while the system is loaded and running. There is no hive file for this dynamic key.

You have seen that certain keys exist only virtually as links to keys on the master keys. You should not expect to see the virtual keys, but you can certainly view their data by going to the key to which they are linked. For example, don't expect to see HKEY_CURRENT_ USER in the EnCase registry. However, you know that this key is derived from the SID key under HKEY_USERS and that the SID key is actually a hive key whose source file is NTUSER.DAT, which is located in the root of the SID user's folder (root user folder). By mounting and viewing a particular user's NTUSER.DAT, you are looking at what was their HKEY_CURRENT_USER key and its content (user environment/profile) when they were last logged on.

In the previous section, "Mounting Files," I described the registry files as being *mountable* files within EnCase. As with any other mountable file, to mount a registry hive file, you need only to right-click one of the hive files and choose to view its file structure from the Entries option.

If you look at the five hive files (SAM, SECURITY, SOFTWARE, SYSTEM, and DEFAULT) located in the *%SystemRoot%*\system32\config folder, you will note that they have counterparts by the same names located in the *%SystemRoot%*\repair folder. The ones in the repair folder are basic configurations for repair purposes if things go wrong. Here you want the active registry hive files in the config folder. Don't confuse the two!

To mount any of the hive files, simply right-click the desired file and choose to view its file structure from the Entries option. Because some of these files are very large and complex, mounting them may take some time, but it's usually less than a minute.

When the file mounts, you can navigate through the various keys as you would any hierarchical file structure. When a value is displayed in the Table view pane, you will see its name in the Name column and its data in the View pane in either the Text or Hex view.

Figure 10.29 shows the system hive file mounted. The Select key contains four values. Although the others are important, you want to know which control set is current, and the value named Current contains the data that makes that determination. In this case, the data for the value named Current is a Dword data type and the data reads 01 00 00 00. This value translates to 1, and the current control set is 1. Forensically, we look to the values contained in ControlSet001 to be those of the CurrentControlSet.

With Vista, registry virtualization was born, by which applications that do not follow the rules (principle of least privilege) and attempt to write to read-only areas of the registry (HKLM, for example) have their writes redirected to a special area dedicated for this purpose. The application is unaware that its data is stored in a new location as the calls are redirected to the virtualized area, and everyone is happy. For the examiner, however, the virtualized registry key is yet another area to examine so as to conduct a complete examination. This key is located at HKU\(User's SID)_Classes\VirtualStore and is shown in Figure 10.30.

FIGURE 10.29   The system hive file is mounted. The Select key contains a value named Current whose data determines the CurrentControlSet.

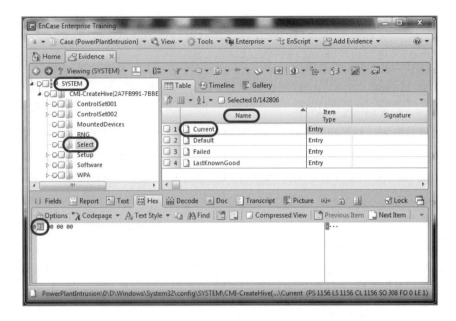

FIGURE 10.30   Location of VirtualStore and data located therein

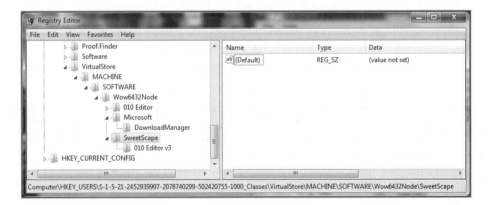

Registry Hive Files in the Restore Points

Starting with Windows ME/XP, Windows creates restore points every 24 hours and retains them for up to 90 days, hard drive space permitting. Additionally, restore points are created before Windows updates, when software is installed, when an unsigned drive is installed, and when a user decides to restore to another restore point. They are also turned on by default, so you should usually expect to see them unless they have been disabled by the user or the hard drive is nearing its capacity.

Restore points are stored in the root-level folder \System Volume Information\-restore{GUID}\RP##, where ## are sequential numbers as restore points are created. Although the date the restore point was created is stored in the last eight bytes of the rp.log file, the file creation time for the RP## folder itself is also evidence of the restore point's creation time.

As part of the restore point data gathering, Windows makes copies of the registry files and places them in the Snapshot folder, renaming them in the process. The Snapshot folder appears under each of the RP## folders. Thus, if you look in the Snapshot folders, you'll see, among other data, renamed registry files. Table 10.6 shows the names of the more forensically significant registry hive files and their new filenames as stored in the restore points. Even though they've been renamed, you need only right-click them and choose View File Structure, and then they will be mounted.

With the advent of Windows Vista, restore points became much more sophisticated with the implementation of the Volume Shadow Service (VSS). Instead of just capturing snapshots of critical operating system and program files and settings, VSS contains snapshots of *all* data from a volume that has changed and does so from a block perspective, with each block being a 16 KB unit. Extracting data from the VSS copies is a somewhat onerous process but can be done. The result is a gold mine of forensic data, often containing copies of files long ago deleted and forgotten.

The ability to go back and view registry data at various points in time is a tremendous investigative tool with endless forensic possibilities. You can examine for changed settings before and after intrusions, old search histories, old most recently used (MRU) lists, and so on. Steve Anson and I teamed up to write the book *Mastering Windows Network Forensics and Investigation*, in which restore points are covered extensively. Recently Ryan Johnson and Scott Pearson joined the authors' team and completed the second edition, updating the material significantly. The books are available here:

www.wiley.com/WileyCDA/WileyTitle/productCd-0470097620.html

www.wiley.com/WileyCDA/WileyTitle/productCd-1118163826.html

TABLE 10.6   Mapping of hive filenames to their restore point filenames

Original hive filenames	Restore point filenames
SAM	_REGISTRY_MACHINE_SAM
SECURITY	_REGISTRY_MACHINE_SECURITY
SOFTWARE	_REGISTRY_MACHINE_SOFTWARE
SYSTEM	_REGISTRY_MACHINE_SYSTEM
NTUSER.DAT	_REGISTRY_USER_NTUSER_SID*

* SID is the security identifier for the individual user. To locate a particular user's NTUSER.DAT file, you need to know a SID number for the user in question.

Registry Research Techniques

You should, by now, have a good understanding of the registry and how it is logically organized. You should be familiar with the registry editor and navigating the registry keys. You should be able to determine a value's name, data type, and data. You should also grasp the differences between the live registry in Windows and the offline registry as viewed in EnCase.

There will be times when you will want to know where a particular setting is located in the registry. Rather than ask and be forced to accept the word of a third party, wouldn't it be better to research the issue and be able to testify in court, first hand, that you've tested and validated the result? Most certainly it would. In this manner, you can speak more authoritatively and confidently about your findings.

To conduct research into the live registry, there is no better tool than the free tools from Microsoft designed specifically for this purpose. Originally they were all separate tools (regmon, filemon, and so on), but they have now been rolled into one tool set named Process Monitor, available at http://technet.microsoft.com/en-us/sysinternals/bb896645.

Once you've downloaded the tool, you need only run it because it requires no installation, making it also convenient to run from a thumb drive at times. By default, at launch, you are monitoring almost everything, and the result is simply too much data. To begin with, turn off File System, Network, and Process activity by clicking their icon buttons on the toolbar, as shown in Figure 10.31. This will leave only Registry Monitoring active.

FIGURE 10.31   Only registry-monitoring activity is enabled

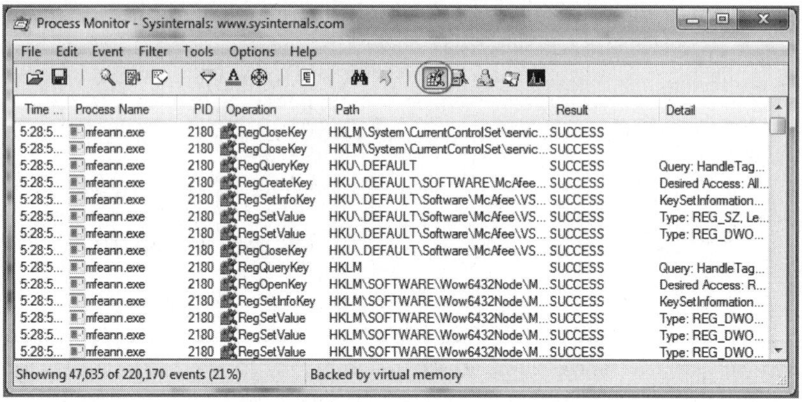

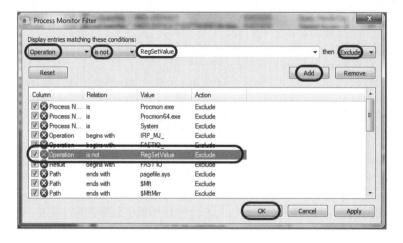

Next, you'll want to filter for successful writes to the registry; otherwise, you are seeing reads and much else, which again results in too much data. To apply this filter, click Filter on the toolbar and choose Filter again. In the resulting menu, set the filter for Operation Is Not RegSetValue and then set Exclude. With those settings in place, click Add to place the filter in the list, as shown in Figure 10.32. When you click OK, the filter is applied.

FIGURE 10.32   Filter is set to exclude anything except operations that set registry values.

You are almost ready to go to work. The next thing you'll want to do is to familiarize yourself with the button that toggles capture on and off, as well as the button to clear out data. Figure 10.33 shows the Capture button under the cursor. Two buttons to the right you will find the Clear button. Toggle off Data Capture and clear out any existing data. You are now set to investigate the registry.

FIGURE 10.33   The button to toggle data capture on and off is under the cursor. The Clear button is circled.

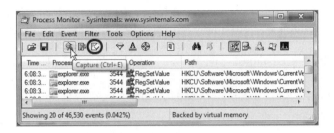

Let's suppose we want to know which registry setting indicates whether Remote Desktop is enabled. If Remote Desktop is enabled, naturally this adds a new dimension to any case because the computer can be accessed remotely. Therefore, this should be a setting that we usually inspect on a routine basis. We must, however, first know where it is. Let's allow Process Monitor to give us the answer.

Leave Process Monitor off for now. You want to capture data only for the brief instant that you apply a setting to minimize data and to zoom in on your finding.

To enable or disable Remote Desktop, right-click Computer and click Properties. On the screen that follows, you will see Remote Settings on the left side of the screen. Click Remote Settings, which will open a System Properties menu that is opened to the Remote tab. In the bottom half of this menu are three settings pertaining to Remote Desktop. We'll go forward with the presumption that the first option is enabled, which is to not allow remote connections to this computer. Click the middle button, which enables Remote Desktop from any version, as shown in Figure 10.34. Do *not* click OK or Apply just yet!

FIGURE 10.34   System Properties dialog box open to Remote tab from which Remote Desktop is enabled or disabled

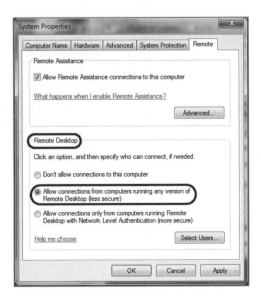

The next step is to get your Process Monitor window and your System Properties menu side by side and visible at the same time. When ready, you toggle on Data Capture, click Apply to apply the Remote Desktop settings, and immediately thereafter turn off the data capture. You should then see, among other data, the entry in the registry that enables Remote Desktop. As you can see in Figure 10.35, the registry key HKLM\System\ CurrentControlSet\Control\Terminal Server\fDenyTSConnections will be set to zero when Remote Desktop is enabled. The default setting, 1, denies connections.

FIGURE 10.35   Process Monitor used to capture registry setting for enabling Remote Desktop

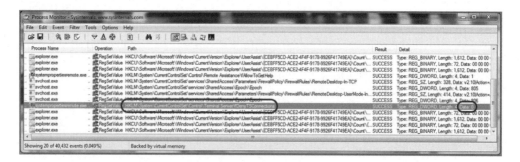

You can easily see how useful this tool can be in your examinations. Whenever you have a question about a setting, you can verify it on the spot in most cases. In the previous example, you could repeatedly toggle the feature on and off, capturing data each time. You could even tweak the registry directly to establish that it works. For those times when you encounter malware and have to test its impact and behavior on a test system or, better yet, a virtual machine, running this tool from a thumb drive can allow you to see all system activity that occurs. It is an incredibly useful tool in the advanced examiner's toolbox.

EnScript and Filters

EnScript is a proprietary programming language and application programming interface (API) that exists within the EnCase program environment, which means EnCase must be running to run EnScripts. EnScript adheres to the ANSI C++ and Java standards for expression evaluation and operator meanings, making for an easy transition for those accustomed to programming in those languages. Even though EnScript adheres to those standards, only a small subset of C++ features is incorporated. In short, EnScript uses C++ operators and general syntax but uses different classes and functions.

EnScripts are scripts or small pieces of code that automate various forensic processing tasks. Examiners can use the EnScripts provided by Guidance Software, Inc., or they can create their own or share them with other examiners. For those interested in creating their own EnScripts, some programming background, particularly in object-oriented programming (OOP), is most helpful. Guidance Software offers a four-day class in EnScript programming for those seeking training in this area.

With EnCase 7, EnScripts are now conveniently accessed from their own drop-down menu on the application toolbar. Upon opening the drop-down menu, as shown in Figure 10.36, you have the option of accessing and running any of the five most recent EnScripts. Additionally, by selecting Run, you can browse to and run any EnScript. Finally, you can create a new EnScript or edit an existing one.

FIGURE 10.36   EnScript menu accessible from application toolbar

Running EnScripts

Running an EnScript, as you have seen, is as simple as double-clicking the EnScript name in the recent list or navigating to it under Run and launching it. As you have also seen, many EnScripts have several modules, and modules may have additional options. Many of you are probably familiar with the Case Processor from past versions of EnCase. In Figure 10.36, you may have noted the Case Processor. You will find that with EnCase 7, nearly all of the functions that used to be in the Case Processor are now included in the various modules found in the EnCase Evidence Processor. Currently, the Case Processor has two EnScript modules available, which are Partition Finder and Consecutive Sectors, as shown in Figure 10.37.

FIGURE 10.37 Case Processor features have moved to the EnCase Evidence Processor, leaving behind Partition Finder and Consecutive Sectors

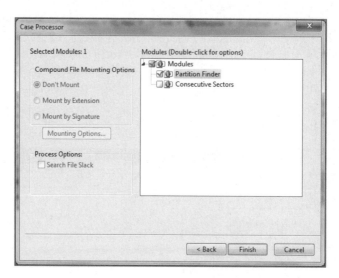

New to EnCase 7 is the Case Analyzer EnScript, which is a very powerful and easy-to-overlook set of analysis and summarization tools. This tool takes in and processes considerable case data from various sources and brings it together in a summary screen that you can drill down into and report upon at various levels of granularity. Figure 10.38 shows the Job Summary menu from which to start the drill-down process. Figure 10.39 shows having drilled down into the Windows Artifact Parser for the Hitachi Travelstar device and having chosen Link Files from among other options. The link file list can be sorted by any column, reports can be generated from selected items, or more information can be derived by clicking any particular link file. The information and reports available from this tool are vast and should offer something for nearly any case under examination. The best way to see what this tool can do is to simply explore and experiment.

FIGURE 10.38 Case Analyzer EnScript Job Summary report

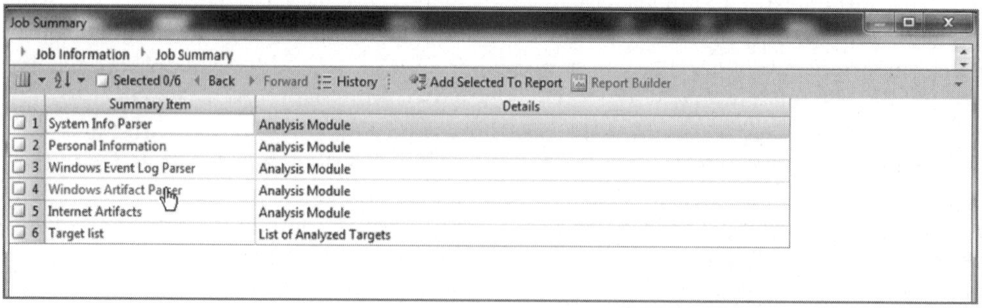

FIGURE 10.39   Results of link file analysis report—note the hyperlinked path bar that is circled

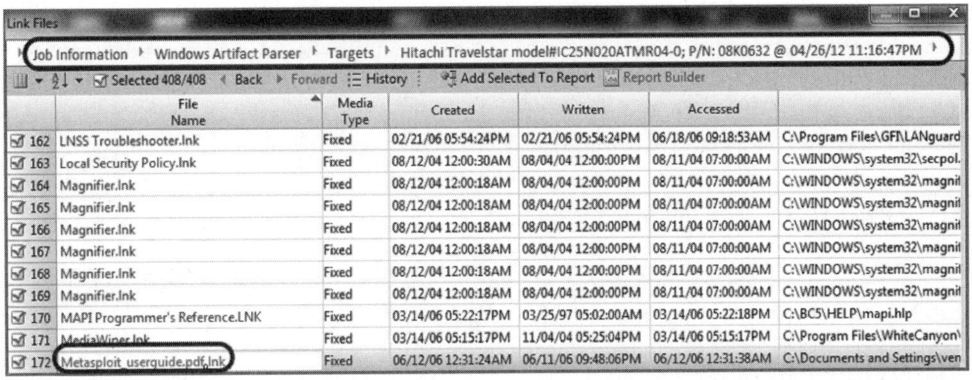

EnScripts are constantly undergoing improvements and additions. You should take the time to try them all on small test sets of data, so you understand how they work and how they can help you process more evidence in less time.

Filters and Conditions

Filters are specialized EnScripts that allow you to filter your case based on a set of parameters. For example, you could filter for all files with the .xls extensions to view only spreadsheets. Several filters are included in EnCase when you install it. Filters are available, quite appropriately, from the Evidence tab toolbar between the Condition and Tags menus, as shown in Figure 10.40. Filters, like EnScripts, need only to be double-clicked to launch. There are often options after launch from which the user can apply added filter criteria.

FIGURE 10.40   Filter menu on Evidence tab toolbar

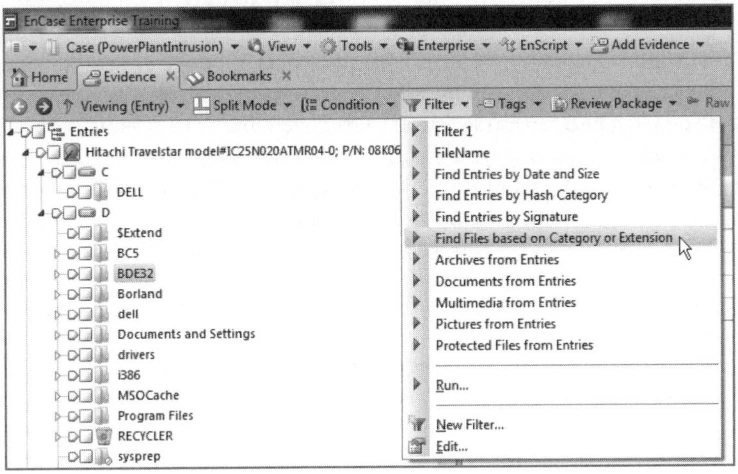

If you want to create a filter, you'll have to do so using code. Conditions are much easier to create because they allow you to create filters using preset parameters available through dialog box choices. Conditions are available also from the Evidence tab toolbar. You can build powerful and useful conditions in addition to the ones that have been provided. Probably the easiest way to get started creating new conditions is to edit a condition (right-click and choose Edit) that approximates what you are trying to create. Figure 10.41 shows a condition in the Edit mode. Once you visit the various filter conditions in the Edit mode, the road map becomes very clear for creating your own conditions.

FIGURE 10.41   Condition in the Edit mode

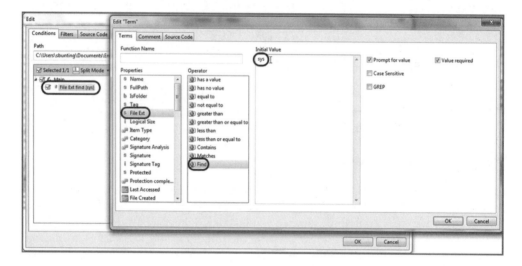

When you run a filter or condition, the results, or found set, are returned in a Results tab and window. For EnCase veterans, this is a significant change in behavior but is clearly one for the better once you get beyond the change. You can do anything that you need to do to the found set on the Results tab. You can send multiple filters or queries to the Results tab, and from there, you can combine them and apply AND or OR logic to the combinations.

You combine them by selecting them and then choosing the logic to apply, as shown in Figure 10.42. Each combination is required to have a name, for which you will be prompted. By having this feature, you can save varying sets of combined filters and conditions. Figure 10.43 shows the end result. In this case, I created a condition to find all files in the case with .evt extensions and another condition to find all files with System32\config in their path. By combining them, I find only the .evt extensions in the previous path.

FIGURE 10.42   Combining two conditions with AND logic

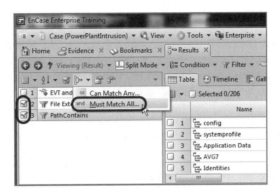

FIGURE 10.43   The combination is "named," and the result of combining two conditions is shown.

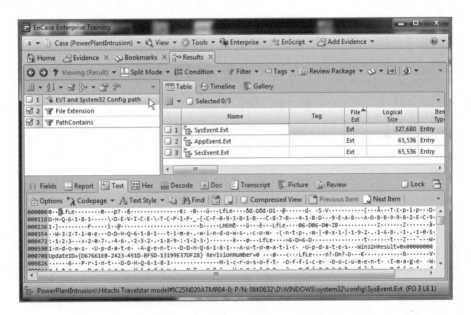

For those seeking more information on the syntax for EnScripts or filters, visit the Guidance Software website at www.guidancesoftware.com, and go to the EnScript Language Reference section. Also, the various EnScript classes and functions are available from the EnScript editor interface that launches when you choose to create or edit an EnScript. There is also a separate and extensive EnScript help file that is included during the installation of EnCase.

Email

You probably recall from our discussions regarding the EnCase Evidence Processor (EEP) that it processes email as one of it feature sets. In this section, I'll first review the EEP email-processing options. Next, I'll cover how to examine the results of the email processor and bookmark those results into your report. The EnCase Evidence Processor has a Find Email module that will currently process the following email types:

- Outlook (PST)
- Outlook Express (DBX/MBX)
- AOL
- MBOX (a common flat file format)
- Lotus Notes (NSF data stores)
- Microsoft Exchange Email Server (EDB files)

To run the Find Email module, simply launch EEP, check the Find Email feature, and choose which email types you want to find, as shown in Figure 10.44.

FIGURE 10.44   Find Email feature in EnCase Evidence Processor

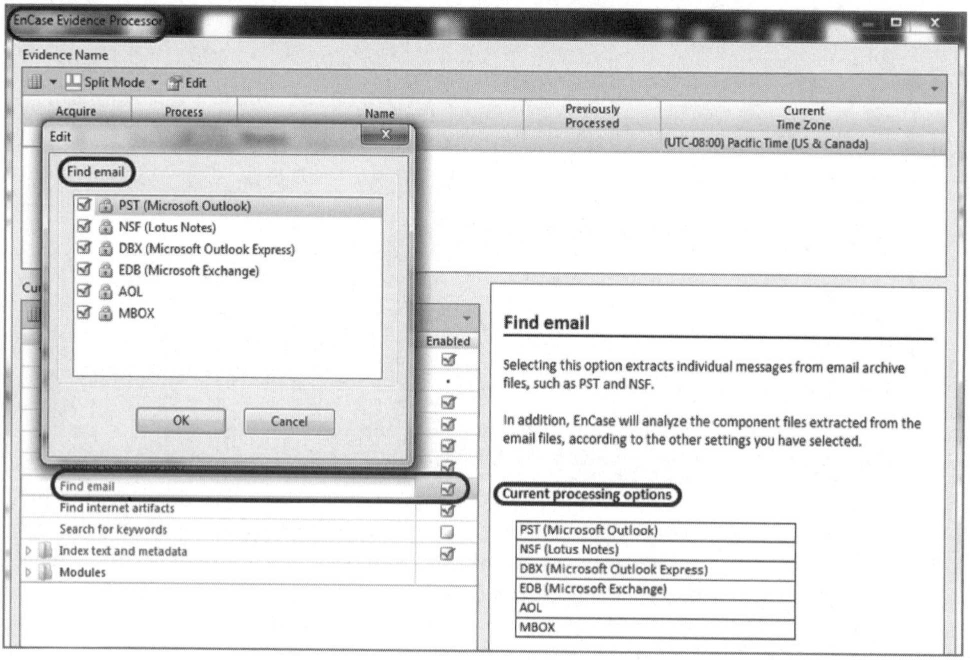

The results of the email finder are sent to the Records tab, which will be our work area for viewing them in a logical format. The email messages will displayed in a typical email

format with headers such as From, To, Subject, Created Date, Sent Date, Received Date, Header, and Attachments; this information exists within any given email database.

You will notice the absence of any web mail options in the Find Email feature. Web mail has become increasingly more secure with time, and finding entire HTML web pages containing email is largely a thing of the past. Nevertheless, some web mail or fragments thereof can still be recovered, as can some important web mail that is residual from long ago in some cases. As part of a thorough examination, we always must look. To search for webmail, use the File Carver in the EEP, and in the bottom section, choose Carve HTML Files; under that option, also choose Carve Webmail Files.

There are some really good third-party tools available that have sought to fill a void by specializing in recovering Internet artifacts from the vast array of web-related communications services. Internet Evidence Finder from JAD Software is a very powerful tool that I highly recommend to expand your ability to recover these types of Internet communications. To the extent that Gmail fragments exist, it recovers more than any other tool with which I've worked.

With past versions of EnCase, you could use the View File Structure feature to both mount a compound email file, such as a PST, OST, and so forth, and populate the Records tab. With EnCase 7, using the View File Structure feature will mount a PST/OST and launch it in a separate tab within the Evidence tab, but it will not populate the Records tab. Unless you have a reason to do otherwise, I recommend processing email stores with the EEP. If you have to quickly review an email store, quickly mounting it with the View File Structure feature will certainly work for you in a pinch.

Once the EEP completes with the Find Email feature enabled, you can see the results on the Records tab. In the Tree pane, you will see, among other record folders, an email record folder. When you select it, the Table view will populate with the email stores found and parsed, as shown in Figure 10.45. The various email stores will appear in blue as hyperlinked. To view any one of them, merely click it for it to open in its own view within the Records tab.

FIGURE 10.45   Records tab containing, among other things, the results of the email finder

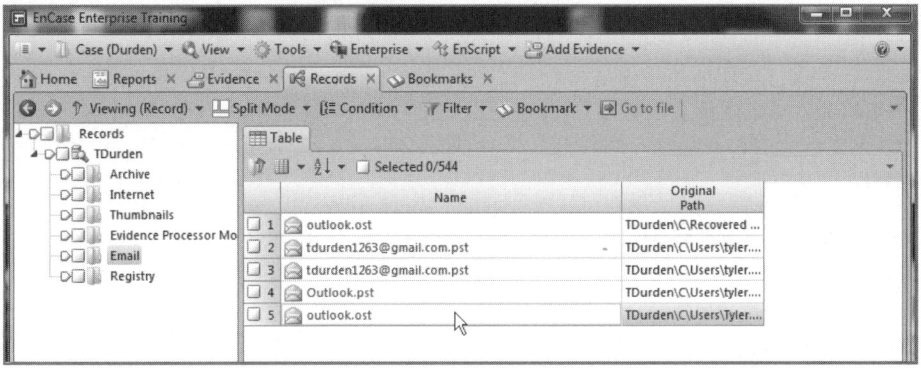

When you click an email store, a separate view or window will launch within the Records tab containing the parsed results for that particular email store. The Tree view will display a hierarchical view of the mail store, showing the various folders or mailboxes. Within them will be the emails themselves. The email will display in the Table view on the Report tab much as the user saw it, complete with attachments in view if viewable, as shown in Figure 10.46.

FIGURE 10.46   Email tree structure in Tree pane with individual email and attachments viewed in Table pane

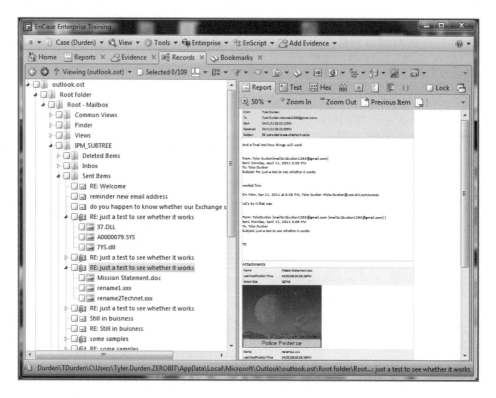

You may easily right-click and bookmark any email from the Table view. As with other EnCase views, you may select multiple emails and bookmark them. Once bookmarked and placed in a destination folder, the bookmarked emails are viewable from the Bookmark view and subsequently viewable in your report.

In the Table pane, you can select the field table, which will in turn display more than 100 fields (103 fields with version 7.03), as shown in Figure 10.47. Each field provides data for a specific property of each email, with some fields having null values when no data exists for that field.

FIGURE 10.47 Field tab displaying more than 100 fields with each containing data pertaining to a specific property for that email

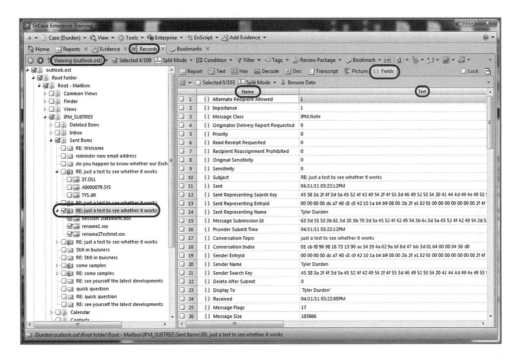

In Exercise 10.2, you'll get to work with the email finder in the EnCase Evidence Processor. You should take the time now to enhance your learning experience by doing this exercise.

EXERCISE 10.2

Conducting Email Examinations

In this exercise, you will examine email artifacts located using the Find Email feature of EnCase Evidence Processor.

1. Create a new case and name it Email Examination. Locate an evidence file on the publisher's website for this book that is named Advanced\DrDoomRootUserFolder_ CD001.E01. Place it in the evidence folder for your newly created case.

2. From the Home page, select Add Evidence ➤ Add Evidence File. Browse to the location of the above evidence file and open it. From the Evidence tab Table view, check that the evidence file passed the file integrity test.

3. Launch the EnCase Evidence Processor, select the evidence item, and at the very least select the Find Email option, choosing DBX minimally as an email type for the search. If you'd care to explore other features, feel free to check them. It is a small evidence file and everything will process quickly.

4. When the EEP completes, double-click the evidence item to cause it to parse and display in the Entries view of the Evidence tab. From the View menu, open the Records view. From the Records view, click Email.

5. With email selected in the Tree pane, click the first inbox you see in the Table pane, which will open the inbox in a separate view. From the Tree pane, locate an email with a subject of "1st target." Force it to display in the Table pane, using the Report tab.

6. From the Table pane Report tab, right-click the email and create a bookmark, placing it in the Email Messages folder. Go to the Bookmarks view and locate the bookmarked email. Highlight it in the Table pane and view it in the View pane in the Report view. You should see the email and the attachment.

7. Save your case and exit.

 Real World Scenario

Email Is Great, But...

Email is a rich source of evidence. Usually its content is less formal than traditional business communications and often captures facts, opinions, comments, actions, and so forth, that would never be found in any other evidence.

Sometimes, however, nefarious individuals are email wary, and their email appears quite sterile and uninteresting. In a recent examination, such was the case. Two public officials exchanged email that was quite boring. The investigators knew something was going on, but they lacked the evidence to prove their case after five months of investigating.

I was asked to do a computer forensics examination of the involved computer systems. While looking at their corporate web mail in the temporary Internet files, yawning from the boredom, something jumped out at me. There were hundreds of files that were either wwwpage[#].htm or wwwtwoway[#].htm. Upon opening them, the evidence displayed was incredible. The two officials were communicating below the radar screen using text messaging from computer to computer and from computer to pagers. The text messages and the pager numbers were completely cached in the temporary Internet files. There were several hundred of them going back nearly three years.

As boring as the email was, the text messages were just the opposite. The content was raw, uninhibited, and quite incriminating. Needless to say, the investigators were ecstatic, and the investigation accelerated rapidly with a government official resigning within hours of these findings.

There are thousands of ways to communicate, and most have web interfaces, which means there's probably something cached. Sometimes if you don't know what you are looking for, there is no substitution for sifting through the web cache and looking for patterns, significant visits to a particular site, and so forth. It's slow and tedious, but sometimes the reward is worth the effort. You can also use the Case Analysis Tool in EnCase 7 to assist in this area. After the EnScript runs, go to the Internet Artifacts, and you will find a frequency summary for websites visited. This can often reveal patterns that are not readily apparent, which can in turn lead to communications patterns. Once you figure out how communications are taking place, you then know what to look for, and the rest is easy.

Base64 Encoding

While I'm on the topic of email, it is a good time to discuss email attachments. If you'll recall from the discussion of the ASCII table, all of the printable characters are contained within the first 128 bytes of the 256-byte table. These first 128 bytes are also called *low-bit ASCII* because all 128 characters can be represented using 7 bits.

When the first protocols were developed for communicating between computers, the characters transmitted were low-bit ASCII (7 bits), and the 8th bit of each byte was used for parity or error checking to make sure the 7 bits arrived accurately. All was well for a while until programs or other files containing binary data needed to be sent. Such a data transfer involved sending characters greater than 128; this meant using the 8th bit, which was needed for parity.

Thus, the need to transmit binary data led to the development of various encoding schemes to facilitate this transfer. Encoding allows 8-bit data (binary) to travel through data paths that support only 7-bit data (text). The first encoding method, historically, was *uuencoding*. This simple method used spaces in the encoding scheme. Because a space could occur at the end of a line and some gateways strip spaces at the end of lines, the method resulted in corrupted data at unacceptable levels.

A second encoding method, called *xxencoding*, was developed. Although it fixed some of the problems with uuencoding, it never became popular and is rarely used.

The third encoding method is the most popular and widely used: *Base64 encoding*. Base64 was introduced with the Multipurpose Internet Mail Extensions standard, better known as the MIME standard. Because the MIME standard provides many other benefits and Base64 avoids the pitfalls of the previous methods, Base64 has become the most widely used encoding method and is also the most secure method.

There is a fourth method of encoding that you may encounter known as *BinHex*. It is used primarily for transferring files among Macintosh systems. The Macintosh file system uses a data fork and a resource fork, and BinHex creates a third part called a *header*. The three parts (data fork, resource fork, and header) are combined into a single data stream that is slightly compressed and encoded. Using this encoding scheme, Macintosh files, complete with metadata, can be transmitted to other Macintosh machines.

Since Base64 is the most commonly encountered approach, I'll focus on that particular encoding scheme in this chapter. In the previous section covering email, you saw how EnCase automatically decoded email attachments, placing them on a separate tab. Figure 10.48 shows an email attachment in the Table view pane that is already decoded and displays as an image in the View pane. This automated processing saves considerable time, and the results are easily bookmarked for your report.

FIGURE 10.48   Base64 email image attachment automatically processed and displayed in EnCase 7

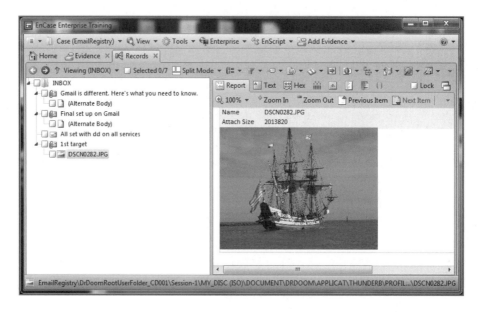

Often, examiners encounter non-image Base64 attachments, such as documents, spreadsheets, ZIP files, and the like. EnCase automatically processes them as well. They are also decoded and displayed as they were attached by the sender. If you wanted to see its contents, you could right-click and tag the file. Once in the Entries view, you could double-click the ZIP file. EnCase would pass the file to the application registered by Windows to open ZIP files, and you could view the contents of the ZIP file in the Windows environment. Alternatively, you could go to the Entries view, locate the ZIP file, mount it (right-click and choose View File Structure), and view its contents within EnCase.

When Base64 attachments appear in the unallocated clusters, they usually require manual processing to extract them. Before you can extract them, you must find them. Base64 encoding has header information, some of which is unique and consistent, and it has a footer or marker to establish its endpoint. Figure 10.49 shows the header information that precedes Base64 data. By searching for strings associated with these headers and footers, you can locate Base64-encoded data in the unallocated clusters or wherever it may occur. These strings are `base64` and `_NextPart_` (these strings are case-sensitive).

If the Base64 attachment is an image, finding the header information is usually sufficient because EnCase's internal viewer can view the encoded data by simply bookmarking the first byte of the encoded data. In Figure 10.49, I have placed the cursor on the first couple of bytes of the Base64-encoded data of a JPEG image. To display the image, simply switch to the Decode tab, and under View Types, choose Picture, and under Picture, chose the Base64 Encoded Picture option, as shown in Figure 10.50.

FIGURE 10.49 Base64 header information that precedes Base64 data, noting the search hits on the previous strings

FIGURE 10.50 Place the cursor on the first byte (or more) of Base64 image data and view it in the Decode tab as a Base64 Encoded Picture.

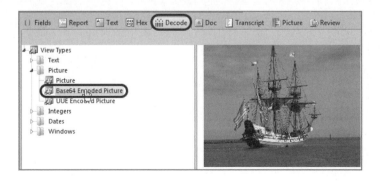

Just as you can search for JPEG headers by searching for the string \xFF\xD8\xFF[\xFE\xE0\xE1], you can search for a JPEG image encoded in Base64 by using its unique header. The string for this search is /9j/4Yh. This is *not* a GREP search and should be run with case sensitivity enabled to make your search both fast and precise.

EnCase Decryption Suite

EnCase Decryption Suite (EDS) in previous versions of Encase was an extra-cost module; however, with EnCase 7, EDS is integrated into the program at no extra charge. EDS has grown and evolved with the growth of encryption schemes and products. The help screen in EnCase, shown in Figure 10.51, shows quite vividly the depth of complexity and support offered with this feature. Currently (version 7.04), EDS supports the following forms of encryption:

- Disk and volume encryption
  - Microsoft BitLocker
  - GuardianEdge Encryption Plus/Encryption Anywhere/Hard Disk Encryption
  - Utimaco Safeguard Easy
  - McAfee SafeBoot
  - WinMagic SecureDoc Full Disk Encryption
  - PGP Whole Disk Encryption
  - Checkpoint FDE (Full Disk Encryption)
- File-based encryption
  - Microsoft Encrypting File System (EFS)
  - CREDANT Mobile Guardian
  - RMS
- Mounted files
  - PST (Microsoft Outlook)
  - S/MIME-encrypted email in PST files
  - NSF (Lotus Notes)
  - Protected Storage (NTUSER.DAT)
  - Security hive
  - Active Directory 2003 (NTDS.DIT)
  - EnCase Logical Evidence file Version 2 Encryption

FIGURE 10.51   The EnCase help feature for EDS depicts supported encryption products.

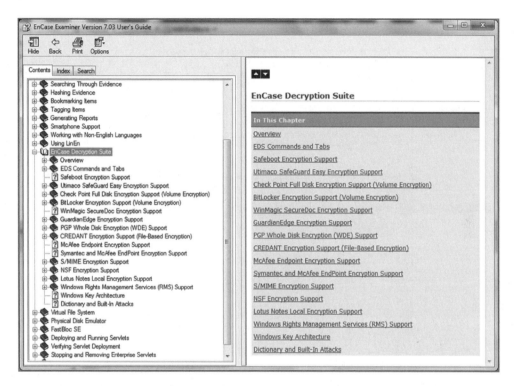

Much of what EDS does is in the background, while some of its functionality requires examiner action. For example, when an image is added to a case, the master boot record area of the drive is scanned for signatures of known encryption schemes. If encryption is found, EDS will intervene and prompt the user for the credentials for that product so it will be able to decrypt it.

Soon after adding an evidence item to a case, an examiner should run the analyze EFS routine against each volume in the case. This will allow the EDS module to extract valuable information from the operating system drive for the purposes of decrypting various encrypted files or data streams. The information will be used to populate the Secure Storage view.

To run the Analyze EFS module, right-click the device in the Tree pane. Under Device options, choose Analyze EFS, as shown in Figure 10.52. You will immediately receive a confirmation menu advising you what you are about to do and to which volume; simply click Next to proceed. On the screen that follows, you'll have to either confirm or provide the path information for the Documents and Settings folder and the registry, as shown in Figure 10.53. Once you confirm these settings and click Next, the Scan EFS module will run. Upon completion, a screen will appear indicating the result of the scan, as shown in Figure 10.54.

FIGURE 10.52 Analyze EFS on right-click menu under device options

FIGURE 10.53 Menu by which to confirm or edit paths to Documents and Settings and registry

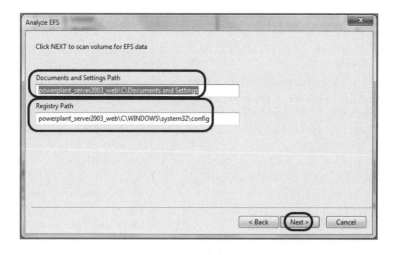

FIGURE 10.54 Results of EFS scan

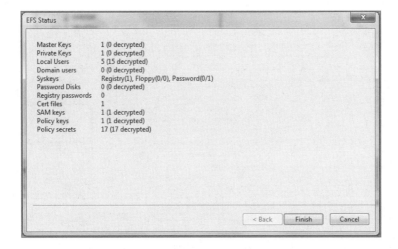

The Secure Storage view, found on the View menu, is the repository and interface for the EDS module, which includes the results of the EFS scan, as shown in Figure 10.55. From this view, many types of security data can be manually entered, including passwords, user/ SID combinations, keys, and so forth. The super-secret menu button at the far right of the Table toolbar provides access to several data-entry tools, as shown in Figure 10.56. The Enter menu, shown in Figure 10.57, allows you many types of password/security entries, all of which are fully explained in the EnCase User Manual. The User List menu, shown in Figure 10.58, allows you export usernames, SIDs, and hashes. Additionally, there are tabs adding users in both Windows Domains and Unix environments.

FIGURE 10.55 Secure Storage view populated with data from EFS scan

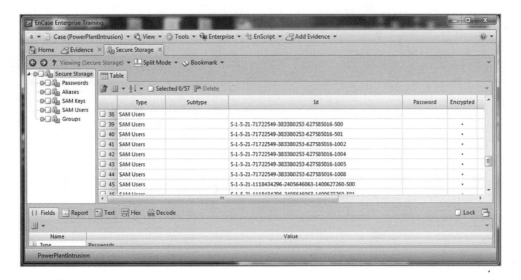

FIGURE 10.56 This super-secret menu (circled triangle) provides access to various entry menus (circled).

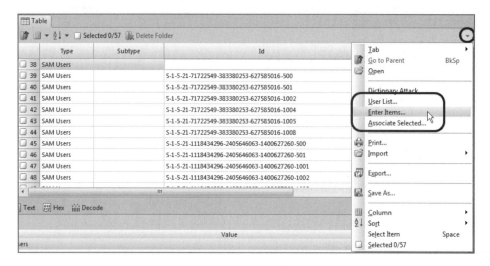

FIGURE 10.57 Enter items dialog box allows entry of various passwords and keys

FIGURE 10.58 User List dialog box allows exporting of hashes for password cracking and entry of Windows or Unix users

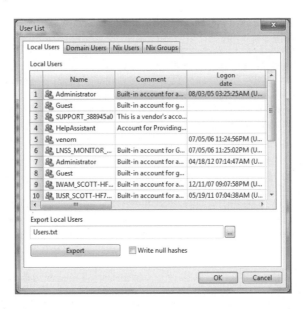

Guidance Software publishes a manual for EnCase, which includes extensive documentation for the EDS module. Working with encryption can become rather involved, and this manual covers the topic in depth. It is updated periodically as new releases of EnCase become available and new encryption products are supported. You can locate it easily on Guidance Software's website under Download Center in the Support section. It also is provided in an email link when you register your dongle.

Cool Tool in EDS!

When you right-click a volume in the Tree pane view and choose Analyze EFS, many things happen, most of which are complex and far exceed the scope of this book. One thing that happens is that the syskey is extracted from the system file and used to decrypt the password hashes stored in the Security Accounts Manager (SAM). That this occurs is not readily apparent, and likewise getting at this information is even more obscure. If, however, you go to the Secure Storage view, after running Analyze EFS, you can easily access this information. In the Secure Storage view, right-click in either the Tree view or Table view pane, choose User List, and look at the Local Users view. Because this window is fixed size, the good information is not in view. If you use your horizontal scroll bar, you can look at the password hashes hidden to the right.

In the browse feature in the lower half of the window, choose a convenient location, call the file something like hashes.txt, and choose Export. What you now have is a password hash file created in the pwdump format and ready for additional processing. It should look something like this:

```
Administrator:500:99050cc8594bac75889941946374a88f:
e2161704a3fe4fa087babc097f25249b:Built-in account for administering the
computer/domain::

Jay L. Bird:1003:f03fd06248a220c9648d2484dbc4b29d:
f9adf23e9ec3a3c60aa1aee6de72d433:::
```

This functionality saves the user from exporting out of EnCase the system and SAM files and having to use third-party tools to extract the syskey and subsequently use it to decrypt the hashes from the SAM. EFS does this for you all within EnCase. You need export only the resultant text file as described earlier.

If you're not familiar with the next step, you can use several tools to crack the password from the hash. Some use dictionary attacks, while others use brute force, but you can't beat rainbow tables for the task at hand.

To use rainbow tables, you first must have them. Shmoo's website (http://rainbowtables.shmoo.com/) has a torrent you can use with BitTorrent to download the tables. The best to get is the alphanumeric-symbol32-space LanMan tables. It will take you three or four days to download them on a fast connection. When they're unpacked, they occupy about 64 GB of drive space. That being said, you'll need to plan for significant drive space on which to store the download and subsequent decompressed files.

Once you have the tables and Rainbow Crack, both of which are free, you need run only the Rainbow Crack command-line tool, pointing it at the tables and the file you extracted from EnCase. You will also be using the -f switch, which signifies the file is in the pwdump format. Assuming the hash text file exported from EnCase is in the same location as the rcrack tool and that the tables are in subfolder of the same location, the command will take on the following syntax:

```
rcrack \tables\*.rt -f hashes.txt
```

After you run this command, go on about your business. If you have two accounts, such as those shown earlier, to process on an average-speed machine, you have your passwords cracked in less than two hours. In a recent test of more than 200 users from an Active Directory pwdump, Rainbow Crack resolved 100 percent of the passwords in just less than 24 hours.

Naturally, this technique won't work if the LanMan hashes are disabled or the user has a password that is 15 characters or longer in length. In practice, however, rarely will you encounter either circumstance with the typical user.

Bad and Good News from Microsoft

Windows Vista (and Windows 7 as well) ships with the LanMan hash disabled, meaning that there is no more easy cracking with rainbow tables. Instead, you'll have to attack the stronger NTLM hash, which you can export from the User List as described earlier and use the NTLM hashes and against NTLM rainbow tables instead. That's the bad news.

There is, however, some good news. Microsoft has provided some rather surprising assistance because Windows Vista has a new registry value in the SAM at Domains\Account\Users\<RID>\. The value name is UserPasswordHint. If you can believe this, the value is stored in plain text. This appears, naturally, only if the user has provided a password hint, but many do, and it appears in the clear. Thus, if you have to attack the NTLM hash, look here first!

Virtual File System (VFS)

VFS enables you to mount evidence as a read-only, offline network drive. As such, the mounted volume is available in Windows and can be browsed with Windows Explorer or examined by third-party tools. VFS is no longer a separately purchased module but rather included in EnCase 7, thus providing added functionality with the basic software package.

EnCase treats the unallocated clusters as though they were logical files, and when the evidence volume is mounted, the unallocated clusters are addressable within Windows. As an added bonus, all deleted files and folders are available as well. Figure 10.59 shows an EnCase evidence image that has been mounted using VFS and is then available as a network drive in Windows. The unallocated clusters are showing as one 23 GB file; you also have access to the Lost Files folder and all files and folders in it.

FIGURE 10.59 An EnCase evidence file mounted with VFS and appearing as a network drive in Windows

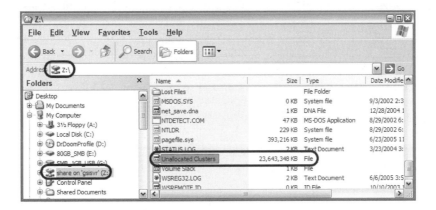

If EnCase supports the image file type, VFS will mount it. EnCase supports EnCase Evidence Files, dd images, SafeBack (V2) images, and VMware images. In addition, live computer forensic devices can be mounted with VFS and include a local machine preview of removable media, a local machine preview using any of the FastBloc or Tableau write-blocking devices, and EnCase Enterprise or FIM (version 6) live network previews.

Interestingly, all file systems that EnCase supports can be mounted with VFS in Windows Explorer. Currently, the list of supported file systems includes the following:

- Windows file systems (FAT 12, 16, and 32 and NTFS)
- Linux file systems (Reiser, EXT2, EXT3)
- Unix file systems (Solaris UFS)
- AIX Journaling File System (JFS and `.jfs`)
- LVM8
- Macintosh (HFS, HFS+)
- BSD (FFS, UFS_2, which is also called FFS_2)
- TiVo 1 and 2
- Novell NWFS and NSS
- CD/DVD (Joliet, ISO 9660, UDF, DVD, HFS)
- Palm (Palm OS)

VFS can mount only one mount point at a time, but it can mount at four different levels: the case level, the disk/device level, the volume level, or the folder level. Whichever level you choose, before you can change to another level, you must first dismount the current mount, because you can have only one mount point at any time.

To perform a VFS mount, choose the level for your mount by placing it in the Table pane and highlighting it. Right-click the level/object to mount, and choose Mount As Network Share from the Device ➤ Share menu, as shown in Figure 10.60.

You will be prompted next with a Mount As Network Share dialog box, where you will click OK, accepting all defaults. Figure 10.61 shows this dialog box.

After you click OK, the mount will occur, and you will see a pop-up box informing you of a successful mount and the location of the mount, as shown in Figure 10.62.

When you are done, the various devices in your case will be available under one network share drive letter in Windows. In the previous example, we simply mounted a Windows volume. As an example of the versatility and power of this future, in another case we had evidence devices that consisted of two Windows file systems (FAT 32 and NTFS), a Macintosh OS X file system (HFS+), and two Linux file systems (EXT2). Amazingly enough, all these disparate file systems were made available in Windows Explorer by applying VFS at the case level, as shown in Figure 10.63. VFS can also mount EnCase Logical Evidence Files, and it is an integration point for processing collected and preserved data for electronic evidence discovery (eDiscovery) in civil litigation.

FIGURE 10.60 VFS is activated from the right-click Device ➤ Share ➤ Mount As Network Share menu.

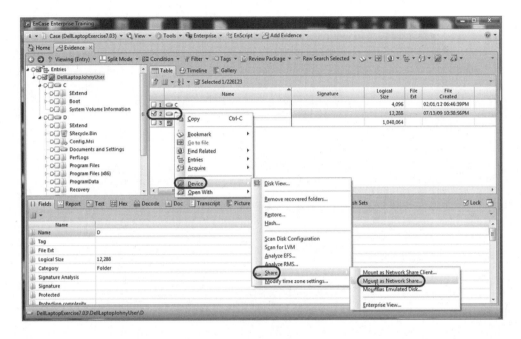

FIGURE 10.61 The Mount As Network Share dialog box; accept the defaults and click OK

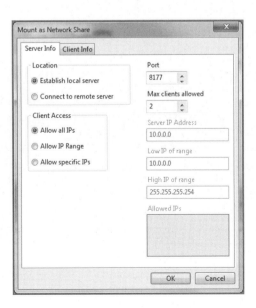

Virtual File System is running and gives the drive letter for

FIGURE 10.63 Windows, Macintosh, and Linux file systems are all available simultaneously in a Windows interface through one VFS mount point applied at the case level.

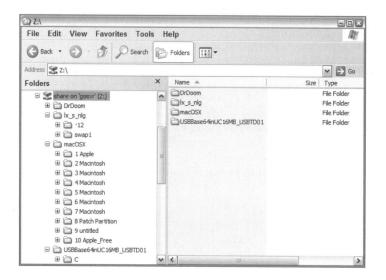

Once mounted, the possibilities for third-party examinations are seemingly endless. At the least, a thorough examination should include a virus scan and a spyware/Trojan scan with at least two different products to be thorough. VFS simplifies this task greatly, saving much time and money compared to other methods of achieving the same task.

To dismount or end VFS, the user must double-click in the lower right of the EnCase screen where the label Virtual File System is constantly blinking while VFS is running. When you double-click this blinking label, you will receive a prompt asking whether you want to cancel the VFS process, which you confirm by clicking Yes.

As with the EDS, Guidance Software documents the VFS function in the EnCase User Manual, which is available on its website. Advanced features and techniques are described in this publication.

Restoration

Restoring the evidence file to another drive produces a cloned drive that can be used for many purposes. Often, this technique is used to boot the suspect's machine with the cloned drive to conduct a myriad of special examinations, ranging from restore point analysis to using applications on the system. Also, using this method, you can see the system very much as the suspect did, which can provide valuable information that is difficult to obtain any other way.

EnCase provides the option to restore either the logical or physical drive. If your original evidence is a physical device, restoring the logical device only does not allow for verification as an exact copy. Usually, the physical drive is the best method for restoration, especially if your intent is to boot the suspect drive after restoration.

When restoring, EnCase copies everything at the level selected (logical or physical), sector by sector, to the target media. The drive you're restoring to must be of equal or larger size. When the restoration is complete, EnCase will verify the restoration and provide hash values of the restored drive. If the target drive is larger, as it often will be, the excess sectors are not included in the verification hash because the hash value represents only the number of sectors restored. The examiner should understand this, and a separate MD5 hash of the restored drive must be conducted only on the restored sectors for the values to match.

One 500 GB hard drive model will most likely have the same number of sectors as another model rated at 500 GB, but then again it may not. When you select a drive to restore to, compare the number of sectors to determine whether the target drive is of equal or larger capacity.

You may optionally wipe the target drive before restoring to it, but this is not necessary because EnCase provides the option to wipe any remaining or unused portion of the drive after all the sectors have been restored. Once you have selected an appropriate target device, mount it in Windows.

To restore an image, at either the logical or physical level, begin in the Tree pane of the Case view. Alternatively, you could force the physical or logical device, from which you want to restore, into the Table pane and work from there as well. From either location, select either the logical or physical device icon, right-click it, and choose Restore, under the Device options. EnCase displays the Restore dialog box, which is a large, boring gray box with the choice of only Cancel or Next. Choose Next, which will collect local devices to which you can restore. In the screen that follows, shown in Figure 10.64, you specify the local device for restoration. Since the source of my restoration is the physical drive, I plan to restore to the physical drive. Thus, I have chosen physical device #1, which is a 4 GB USB drive. Click Next for the next step, which is to select some final options.

As a safety measure, EnCase will not display the volume (drive letter) on which Windows is running.

FIGURE 10.64 This dialog box lets you select the target drive for restoration.

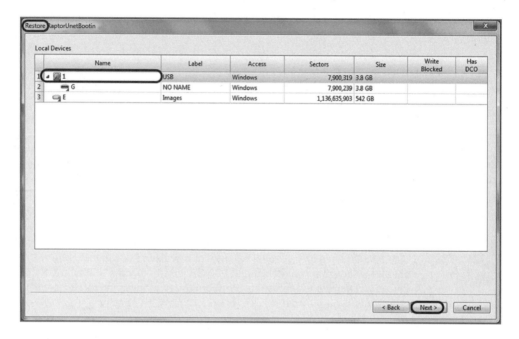

After you choose the target drive for the restoration, EnCase provides some final options before the restoration begins. Those final options are displayed in the Drives dialog box, as shown in Figure 10.65. The first option is Wipe Remaining Sectors On Target, which, when selected, causes any remaining sectors on the drive to be wiped. The second option is Verify Wiped Sectors. This option name does not accurately describe its function. Its actual purpose is to cause EnCase to verify the *restored* sectors, comparing the acquisition hash value with the hash value of the restored sectors. The final option is to choose the characters used for wiping the remaining sectors. The default value is 00h but can be any hex value you specify. When you are ready, click Finish. EnCase will prompt you by asking you whether you want to proceed, as shown in Figure 10.66. Type **Yes**, and click OK to confirm and start the restoration.

FIGURE 10.65   Drives menu in which final options are selected. Accept all defaults!

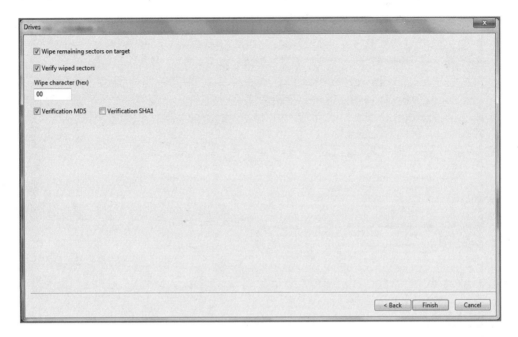

FIGURE 10.66   Final confirmation and warning

When the restoration is complete, the progress bar will disappear, and there will be no pop-up completion reports as with past versions of EnCase. Immediately remove the drive from Windows to prevent Windows from eventually discovering it and writing to it. The information pertaining to the restoration task will be recorded in a log record. From the View menu, choose and open Log Records. In the Log Record view, locate the Restore task, open it, and review the details. The acquisition and verification hashes should match. Other information will be available, as shown in Figure 10.67.

FIGURE 10.67   Restore and verification data is contained in a log record.

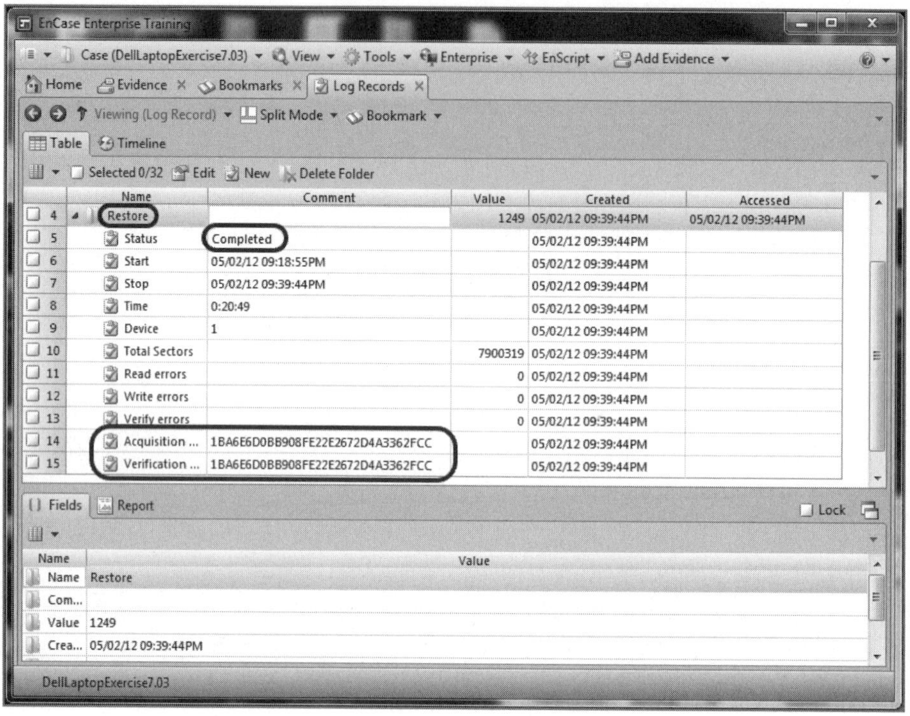

As a final note, if the restoration is to be made of a logical device, your preparation will be somewhat different. A logical volume must be restored to a volume of the same type and of equal or greater size. If the evidence file volume to be restored is NTFS and 500 MB in size, the target volume must be formatted to NTFS and must be 500 MB or larger in size. To determine the size and properties (partition type) of the evidence file volume, refer to the Report view for the volume. When you restore the logical volume, make sure you select the logical drive letter of the target drive.

Physical Disk Emulator (PDE)

The Physical Disk Emulator (PDE) module is similar to the VFS in many ways, but there are some clear and distinct differences:

- PDE can mount only a physical disk or volume. VFS can also mount an image file.

- When PDE mounts a disk or volume, Windows treats it as a disk or volume. Windows treats a VFS-mounted item as a network share.

- PDE mounts file systems supported by Windows. VFS mounts any file system supported by EnCase.

- With VFS you can see unallocated clusters, deleted files, and recovered partitions.

- With PDE, you can use VMware to mount a disk as a virtual machine.

When PDE mounts a disk or volume, it will appear in the Windows Logical Disk Manager, which is a service that starts when there is a need to configure hard disk drives and volumes and stops when that process is done. Figure 10.68 shows the Windows Logical Disk Manager after a 1.8 GB physical drive has been mounted within EnCase using PDE. This mounted drive shows as physical disk 3 and is further mounted as drive letter F.

FIGURE 10.68   Windows Logical Disk Manager displays a PDE-mounted disk.

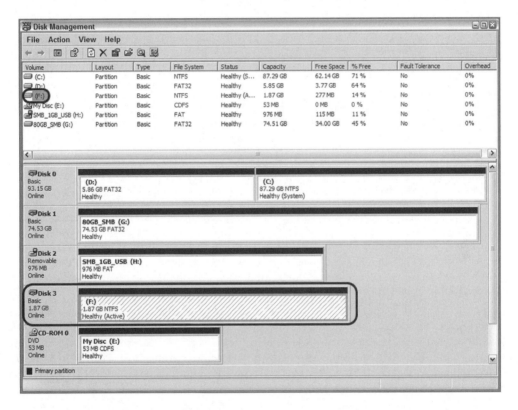

The process of mounting a physical device or volume with PDE is similar to that of mounting with VFS. First, select the physical or logical device to mount by placing your cursor on it, right-click, and choose Mount As Emulated Disk, which will be under the Devices ➢ Sharing options, as shown in Figure 10.69.

FIGURE 10.69   Location of Mount As Emulated Disk feature

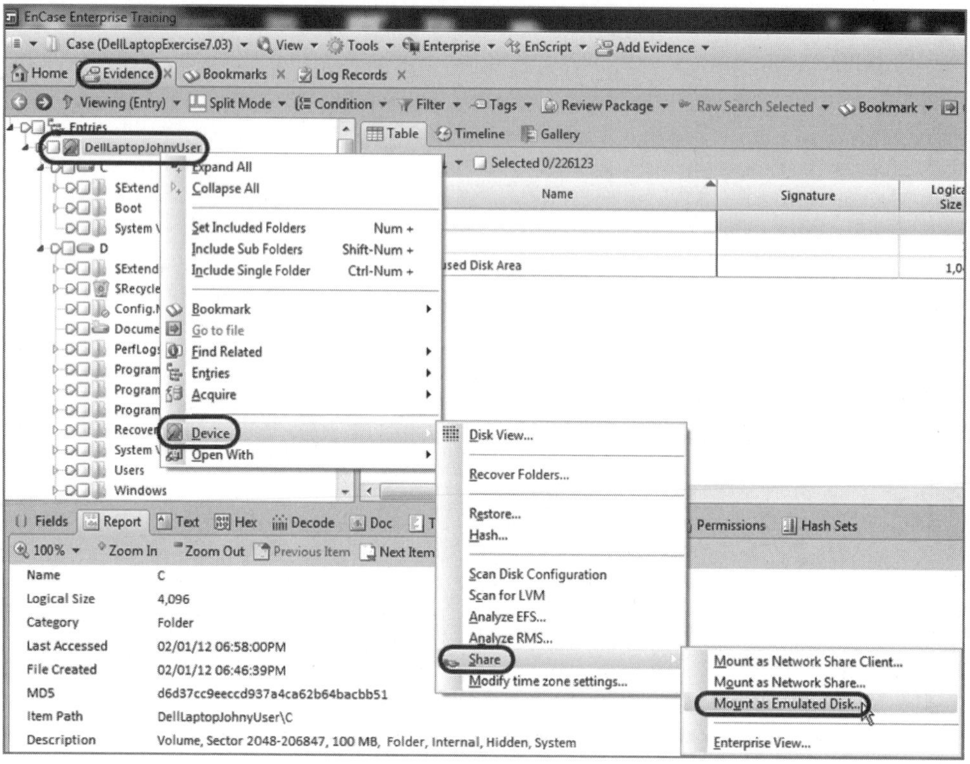

You will see the Mount As Emulated Disk dialog box, which should default to the Server Info tab, as shown in Figure 10.70. A local port is assigned to the mount, and the number will appear in the window, which can be changed if you like. Once the port is in use, it remains assigned for all future mounts. To release this port and assign another port, you need to restart Windows. (This issue or process is really rather academic because I've never seen a reason to change the default port or change it after it was assigned. But if you encounter that need, you now know the rules!)

A second tab is available in the Mount As Emulated Disk dialog box. The Client Info tab, as shown in Figure 10.71, provides certain advanced options. If a multisession CD is mounted, you can choose which sessions you want to mount. If you are using VMware (discussed later in this section), you need to enable caching per the set of instructions for setting up VMware. Caching allows files to be added, modified, or deleted as needed and to have these changes cached to a file for use by VMware. In addition, these cached files can be saved and reused in future sessions. When you start the mount, you will likely get a warning from Windows that the publisher of the driver can't be verified. If so, choose the option to install the driver anyway. You stop or end PDE in the same way you would VFS, which is by double-clicking the blinking Physical Disk Emulator in the lower-right corner.

FIGURE 10.70   The Mount As Emulated Disk dialog box showing the Server Info tab

FIGURE 10.71   The Client Info tab of the Mount As Emulated Disk dialog box

PDE supports the same evidence file formats and live computer forensics evidence as does VFS. When PDE mounts in Windows; however, only file systems recognized by Windows will be supported and mounted, which means only NTFS and FAT. If neither the NTFS nor FAT file system is present, no file system will mount, but the physical device will be available. As you'll recall, by contrast, VFS will mount in Windows any file system supported by EnCase.

Don't use PDE to mount EnCase images or previews of a local hard drive. If Windows detects multiple instances of the same drive on the local box, you will likely experience the proverbial Blue Screen of Death (BSOD).

Another subtle difference between PDE and VFS is that PDE presents the physical disk or volume as is to Windows, whereas VFS presents the file system as EnCase sees it. What does this really mean? Windows can't see unallocated clusters, and when PDE presents a physical disk to Windows to mount, you won't see unallocated clusters in Windows Explorer. Quite by contrast, when you mount using VFS, EnCase treats the unallocated clusters as one contiguous logical file, and that logical construct is passed to Windows when VFS mounts. With VFS, unallocated clusters are viewable in the Explorer interface.

The same rule or logic applies to deleted files. As EnCase undeletes deleted files and displays them, VFS presents this logical reconstruction of deleted files to Windows when VFS mounts; thus, deleted files will be viewable in Windows Explorer with VFS. With PDE, don't expect to see deleted files.

These differences are subtle, but the difference is truly magnified in the case of a recovered partition. If you recover a partition with EnCase and mount the physical drive with PDE, Windows sees only the physical disk and can't mount the recovered partition since it is not there. By extreme contrast, if you mount the same physical drive with the recovered partition using VFS, the recovered partition as EnCase sees it is passed along to Windows, and you can see the entire partition in Windows Explorer.

It is important to understand the similarities and the differences between the two modules; clearly some tasks are module specific, while some tasks can be carried out in either. For example, if your intent is to process the unallocated clusters, you need to use VFS. If your intent is to scan for viruses or malware, either module will suffice.

One of the most popular capabilities of PDE is that of using it in conjunction with VMware. When you have the physical disk or volume mounted in Windows as a physical disk, VMware can take that physical disk and mount it as a virtual machine. This means you can often virtually boot and run your suspect's drive totally within the EnCase and VMware combined environments. This can save considerable time and expense compared with the traditional method of restoring the image to a drive and booting it in the suspect's box.

The entire process of using VMware with PDE as well as the advanced features of the PDE module are well documented in the EnCase User Manual provided by Guidance

Software. PDE, like VFS, is now included with EnCase and no longer requires a separate license and fees.

Often the question arises as to which module, PDE or VFS, should be used for which task. Table 10.7 lists various tasks and the proper module (VFS or PDE) for the job, along with a brief description of the reason.

TABLE 10.7 Forensic tasks and the proper module (VFS or PDE) for the job

Task	Module	Rationale
Running a virtual machine using VMware	PDE	VMware needs access to a physical disk.
Virus or malware scan	PDE or VFS	If not interested in deleted files, use PDE. If interested in deleted files, use VFS.
Extracting Internet history from unallocated clusters	VFS	PDE does not provide access to unallocated clusters. Only VFS provides this access.
Using Windows Explorer to peruse Linux or Macintosh file systems	VFS	PDE allows the mounting of only those file systems supported by Windows. VFS mounts any file system supported within EnCase.
Using any third-party tool in Windows to examine a partition recovered in EnCase	VFS	With PDE, Windows won't see the recovered partition. VFS presents the file system as EnCase has restored it.

Putting It All Together

Together we have covered the gamut of the major features of EnCase 7. The order in which we have proceeded was largely determined by the most logical learning progression, which has no connection to the order in which you might conduct a forensic examination. So, what is the best order in which to conduct a forensic examination? Clearly, there are a few basic steps that progress in a certain sequence, but beyond that, the order is most often determined by the examiner based on the nature and urgency of the case.

Over the years, many examiners have asked for a list of suggested steps for an examination. Over time, with input and suggestions from many colleagues, I have assembled such a list. It should never be regarded as mandatory or as a standard. Rather, consider it a suggested approach that is dynamic, flexible, and rarely if ever all-inclusive. Every case is different, and both the tools and the computing environment are in a constant state of change. Also, please keep in mind that any search (hash analysis included) must be conducted within the scope of your search authority. With those caveats and conditions stated, the list of suggested steps follows:

1. Log your case information into your lab case management database or casebook.

2. Examine and document the computer systems under examination, taking care to conduct both an internal and external inspection and carefully recording your findings in photos, notes, or forms created for that purpose.

3. Determine the method of acquisition, preview (if applicable), and acquire the image of the media.

4. Make certain that all sectors on the drive have been identified and actually acquired (determine whether HPA or DCO is present).

5. Make a backup copy of all images, store the original in a secure location, and conduct your examination on copies.

6. Obtain the system times from all machines under examination, and simultaneously record the known time from an accepted time standard.

7. Once images are acquired and brought into the case, make certain that the file integrity is verified.

8. Preview the images acquired. Determine the total sectors on the various devices; reconcile those sectors with sectors in partitions to make certain all partitions are mounted and accounted for. Recover and mount any deleted partitions.

9. Determine time zone offsets for all devices and modify time zone offsets according to case requirements. Usually you want all offsets to be uniform across the case.

10. Run Analyze EFS on all volumes.

11. Run the EnCase Evidence Processor. Run: Recover Folders, File Signature Analysis, Expand Compound Files, Hash Analysis, and Protected File Analysis at a minimum. Depending on your case (nature of investigation, time constraints, and so on), also run Find Email, Find Internet Artifacts, Index Text, Windows Event Log Parser, File Carver with web mail option, and Windows Artifact Parser.

12. While EEP is running, review obvious artifacts in the folder structure. Look at the user's desktop, documents, pictures, favorites, and recent folders. Review the Internet cache in Gallery view to get an overview, pictorially, of the browsing activity. Look in the Recycle Bins for deleted files or signs of recent purging of files. Process the UserAssist key with a third-party tool to see what programs have been recently run and how frequently. Follow this up with a review of the prefetch files. Look in the program folders and see what programs are installed. In short, get a good handle on the user's activities. If any programs of import are being used, take note and follow up (hacking tools, forgery tools, and so forth, for example)

13. While EEP is running, review information collected during incident response. Review the volatile data capture report, noting any anomalies regarding running processes, open ports, and so forth, that may have a bearing on the case. If the case warrants, examine RAM memory that was acquired.

14. Determine whether the computer is being used remotely via Remote Desktop, or other like tool.

15. Run a condition to determine whether EFS encryption is applied anywhere (the description contains *encrypted*).

16. Using VFS or like tool, conduct a malware scan. If machine is compromised, you need to know early on in the case, not near the end.

17. Review link file analysis (completed by EEP) and determine whether there are other drives (external or network) that are missing. Review also the USBStor registry key for recently attached USB drives. In short, make sure all media being accessed and of apparent import has been secured for examination. If not, make certain to take proper action to obtain it.

18. Complete link file analysis, following up as needed.

19. Run Case Analyzer EnScript. Under Windows Artifacts, review Link Files, Recycle Bin, MFT Transactions, and other reported data. Under Internet Artifacts, review history, cache, cookies, bookmarks, and downloads. When reviewing history, look for frequency patterns in browsing activity. Under System Info, review users and accounts, network settings, shares, and mapped drives. If Personal Information is parsed, review.

20. Review results of file signature analysis (use condition to focus on files having an alias in the Signature column).

21. Review results of hash analysis. Look for presence of notable files first and those in hash sets next. Conditions are great for this task.

22. On Records tab, review thumbnails for images of import.

23. On Records tab, review email for messages and attachments of import.

24. As review of documents, files, and so forth, occurs, if password protection is encountered, develop strategy to decrypt (low-hanging fruit passwords, create lists of strings for dictionaries, compile biography of suspect for added dictionary words, determine best decryption tools, and commence cracking task).

25. Search index for relevant keywords. If necessary, conduct raw keyword searches for relevant keywords.

26. Process restore points/volume shadow copies as indicated by case specifics. Such may require restoration of drive and booting of suspect's machine. Voom Shadow drives are quite useful for this purpose.

27. Search for and process artifacts of past print jobs from deleted spool files.

28. Locate instant messaging clients and process any artifacts or messages that may be logged.

29. Locate any peer-to-peer file sharing software. Process the associated artifacts.

30. Locate financial software and process any associated databases in their native environment.

31. Examine Photoshop files in their native environment to check for images or text data that may be hidden in layers. EnCase doesn't see underlying hidden layers!

32. Run third-party tools on mounted devices using VFS or PDE as may be indicated.

33. Examine log files (Windows event logs, `setupapi.log`, web server logs, FTP logs, error logs, AOL logs, and so on).

34. Examine the Windows event logs for the time period in question. Make certain the sequential numbering of the records is in sync with the chronological sequencing. (In short, examine for alterations of the system time.)

35. Carve files from free spaces of file types indicated by case.

35. Conduct any other specialized inquiries as may be dictated by the specifics of the case.

36. Use PDE to mount physical device and run VMware to boot the suspect's drive to see it as the suspect saw it. Alternatively, restore the image out to a drive and use the restored drive to boot the suspect's computer, again viewing their system as the suspect saw it.

37. Run an end-of-case Verify File Integrity check, and bookmark your findings.

38. Bookmark all significant findings, organize bookmarks, and create your final report.

39. Use the Create Package feature to archive all case data onto archival media, verifying copies of evidence files.

This is, again, a suggested list and one that you can customize and modify as circumstances warrant. You will probably find that the first half of the list contains steps you'll need to do in most every case and quite often in the order presented. After that, the nature of the case starts to guide your approach. The last three steps trend back to obligatory tasks or best practices. Lists are helpful, but you should avoid getting into a checklist trap, where you methodically process according to a standardized checklist. Such an approach becomes habitual and can inhibit creativity and examinations that are beyond the list or out of the box.

Computer forensics is an extremely dynamic field, one in which the playing field is constantly changing. New technologies are evolving daily. As examiners, we should be reactive to trends and be able to adapt rapidly to changes.

Up until around 2005, give or take a couple of years, computer forensics examiners were generalists. Today, things have changed. Computing in general has become far more complex than it was seven years ago. One can no longer be an expert in all areas; the field has become too vast. Specialty areas are emerging. Not only must you be a generalist, but you must also develop specialties based on the type of work in which you are immersed. The age of computer forensic specialty areas is here, and there's only one direction it can go: up.

If you think about the development over the past 5 to 10 years and try to imagine what computing will be like in 5, 10, or 15 years, it is simply too much to even comprehend. Computers are trending toward smart devices that we carry with us. Just how those trends will play out, only time will tell. We will be facing technologies that we cannot even begin to imagine today. As always, training and education will be the keys to meeting these new challenges.

Although training and education are important, they aren't the complete solution. One person can't possibly begin to be an expert in all areas, so we must develop strong informational networks among computer forensics examiners. Information-sharing networks allow us to share knowledge and techniques and foster problem solving in real time, regardless of your geographical location.

With those parting thoughts in mind, if we are to meet the challenges of the future of computer forensics, we all need to embrace a couple of simple goals. First, we must put aside our differences and all work together to form and nurture informational networks. Finally, each of us must make a commitment to excellence and seek out all possible education and training opportunities. We now live in an information age, and the more information we have, the better off we'll be in facing the challenges of the future.

In the field of computer forensics, excellence is not an option; it is an operational necessity. Excellence, on the individual level, is a combination of integrity, perseverance, a commitment to the highest standards of the profession, and a never-ending thirst for knowledge through research and education.

My best wishes and regards to you on your EnCE certification testing and in your career.

Summary

In this chapter, I covered a wide array of advanced techniques and concepts. I began with a review of the previous discussions of partitions as a predecessor to recovering them when deleted. The partition table is located in the MBR at byte offsets 446–509. In those 64 bytes, up to four partitions can be described in 16-byte strings. When one or more partitions are deleted, their corresponding entries in this table are removed and replaced with zeros. This is often described as *fdisking*.

Even though the entry in the table may be zeroed out, the VBR marking the beginning and containing the parameters of the partition often remains untouched, depending on where it is and what subsequent actions have taken place.

When the first partition is missing, you can usually look to the first sector of the second track to find the VBR. With that located, you can restore the partition by right-clicking that sector in the Disk view and choosing Add Partition. Usually you accept the default values, and the partition is restored by clicking OK.

When the partition is missing elsewhere on the drive, using the Partition Finder EnScript to locate VBRs works well. It is best to work in one direction, starting from the beginning of the drive, and restore partitions as they are found.

Many files are compound in nature. They can be flat files that contain objects (Office documents), they may be flat files that have a hierarchical structure (registry hive files), they can be files that are compressed (ZIP files), or they may be files that are compressed and encrypted (Outlook PST files). EnCase supports and mounts many different types of compound files. To mount a compound file, right-click it, and choose View File Structure. The resultant mounted structure may be browsed from the Tree pane/Evidence Entries tab.

The Windows registry is an enormous database containing configuration information for your hardware and software environment. The data is contained, at a physical level, in a series of hive files. The hive files are addressed by the user and programs by a logical addressing scheme that is hierarchical and similar to the files and folders used in the Explorer interface.

Instead of Explorer, the interface by which to view or edit the registry is called *regedit*. Instead of folders, the registry uses the term *keys*. The term *subkey* is used when it is showing a subordinate relationship between keys. Instead of files, the registry uses *values*. Values have three components: the value name, the data type, and the data. In regedit, the left pane is called the *key pane*, and only keys are viewed in this pane. The right pane is called the *value pane*, and only values are viewed in this pane.

The live registry consists of five root keys: HKEY_CLASSES_ROOT, HKEY_CURRENT_USER, HKEY_CURRENT_CONFIG, HKEY_LOCAL_MACHINE, and HKEY_USERS. Of these five, only the last two are master keys. The first three are derived keys that exist as links to keys within the master keys. The two master keys are the logical representation of the various physical hive files.

The hive files (BCD, SAM, SECURITY, SOFTWARE, and SYSTEM) form the hive keys under HKEY_LOCAL_MACHINE by the same names. These hive files are located in the folder *%SYSTEMROOT%*\System32\config, except that BCD is located on the first partition that is hidden boot partition. There is no hardware hive file because the HKLM\HARDWARE key is dynamic, created at boot, supports the booted hardware configuration, and is gone when the system shuts down.

The HKEY_USERS key consists of many hive files representing the SID numbers of the various users who have logged onto the system. Usually, there are at least three: .DEFAULT, SID, and SID_Classes, where the SID is that of the console user. The hive file for the .DEFAULT key is at *%SYSTEMROOT%*\System32\config\default. The hive file for the SID key is the file NTUSER.DAT, located in the root of the root user folder for the username corresponding to the SID. The hive file for the SID_Classes key is the file UsrClass.dat, located in Documents and Settings\UserName\Local Settings\Application Data\Microsoft\ Windows\, where the UserName corresponds to the SID.

Registry virtualization started with Windows Vista and applications that attempt to write to protected areas of the registry have their writes seamlessly redirected to HKU\ (User's SID)_Classes\VirtualStore. Thus, this is an added area for the examiner to review.

The live registry as seen in Windows differs from the offline registry as viewed in EnCase. Volatile keys such as the HARDWARE key under HKLM will be nonexistent. Three of the five root keys are derived keys and won't be seen as such; however, the subkeys within the master keys from which they are derived from links can be viewed. To view the registry in EnCase, simply mount any of the hive keys by right-clicking and choosing View File Structure.

EnScripts are short pieces of code that automate forensic processing or tasks. EnScripts can be used as shipped with EnCase by simply double-clicking the desired EnScript and following any prompts to configure options. For those with the proper skills, EnScripts can be created or edited within the EnCase environment. EnScripts are accessible directly from the application toolbar under EnScripts. EnCase 7 provides conditions and filters for narrowing data sets. Filters are simply specialized EnScripts that allow you to filter the case for various attributes, such as extension or file type. To create a filter, you must enter code. Conditions are filters, but the interface by which they are created is a set of dialog box options that build the code in the background for you. Filters and conditions are powerful tools. Many ship with EnCase, and conditions are easy to create. The results of filters and conditions are sent to the Results view where they can be combined into named sets using Boolean logic operators (AND and OR).

EnCase 7 (as of 7.35) supports the following email types: Outlook (PST), Outlook Express (DBX/MBX), AOL, mbox, Lotus Notes, and Microsoft Exchange Server. Email is processed within the EnCase Evidence Processor, and the results are sent to the Records view. To search for web mail, the web mail parser is selected from the File Carver, again in the EnCase Evidence Processor. Internet history and cache is parsed by the Internet Artifacts finder in the EnCase Evidence Processor. Email, web mail, Internet history, and Internet cache are all found on the Records tab. Any of these can be bookmarked individually or in selected groups. You can view the results in the Bookmark view and include them in your final report.

The EDS feature is used to decrypt data encrypted with Microsoft Encrypting File System. In some cases, the decryption is automatic, and in other cases, the password must be obtained through various cracking methods. In addition to decrypting EFS, the EDS module automatically decrypts data stored in the protected storage area of the registry. This data consists of passwords that Windows remembered for the user, and it consists of data stored for use with the autofill feature. The EDS feature has expanded to support several leading disk encryption packages, with more being added.

The VFS module mounts any file system supported by EnCase as an offline, read-only network drive. In this manner, the user can access all logical files, all deleted files that EnCase can recover, and the unallocated clusters within the Windows environment. In this way, third-party tools can be used against those logical file system objects as seen by EnCase.

The PDE module mounts the physical device or volume as a physical disk in Windows. Only file systems supported by Windows can be mounted. All other file systems will be available at a physical level only. PDE can work in conjunction with VMware to mount the suspect's drive as a virtual machine, boot it, and see it as the suspects saw it, saving considerable time and money, plus providing another valuable examination tool.

Exam Essentials

Understand partitions, partition tables, MBRs, and VBRs. Know the location of the main partition table on a hard drive. Describe what the partition table does and what information it contains. Explain what happens when a partition is removed, particularly what is affected and what is not. Understand how to locate deleted partitions and restore them using EnCase.

Understand compound files and how they are mounted. Describe different types of compound files, and be able to provide examples. Know which compound files can be mounted in EnCase 7. Be able to describe the process of mounting files within EnCase. Explain the importance of mounting files.

Understand the purpose and function of the Windows registry. Explain the purpose of the Windows registry. List the five root keys of the Windows registry. Know which of the five keys are master keys and which are derived keys. Explain a hive file. Know the names and locations of the hive files. Understand and explain the logical structure of the registry. Explain the difference between keys and values. Know the three attributes of a value. Describe the registry interface tool and how it is launched. Explain the difference between the live registry in Windows and the offline registry in EnCase. Explain how to mount the registry in EnCase. Explain which hive files correspond with which logical keys in the live registry.

Understand EnScripts, filters, and conditions. Explain the function of EnScripts. Know how to navigate to and run a typical EnScript. Explain the purpose of filters and conditions. Describe the differences between filters and conditions. Describe the process of creating a condition. Explain how to navigate to and run a filter or condition. Understand how to combine filter and query results and how to change the Boolean logic.

Understand and know how to conduct email examinations. Explain the various types of email clients, applications, and services. Explain the difference between an email client and web mail. Describe which email types are supported currently within EnCase. Explain the method by which email is parsed. Explain how web mail works and where to look for artifacts. Explain where parsed email can be found and how to navigate the interface and bookmark emails and/or attachments.

Understand the purpose and function of the EDS module. Explain what EFS means. Describe the system used by Windows to encrypt data. Explain what happens when a drive is mounted in EnCase and what occurs when disk encryption is encountered. Explain how to carry out Analyze EFS and where the results will be located. Describe how users' hashes can be exported for cracking by third-party tools.

Understand the purpose and function of the VFS and PDE modules. Understand the function of the VFS module. Know which file systems will be displayed in Windows when using the VFS module. Explain the type of mount that VFS will present to Windows. Describe the various levels at which VFS can mount. Understand the function of the PDE module. Explain which file systems will be displayed in Windows when using the PDE module. Describe the primary differences between the VFS and PDE modules. Explain which module mounts deleted files and unallocated clusters in Windows.

Review Questions

1. How many sector(s) on a hard drive are reserved for the master boot record (MBR)?

    A. 1

    B. 4

    C. 16

    D. 62

    E. 63

2. The very first sector of a formatted hard drive that contains an operating system is referred to as which of the following?

    A. Absolute sector 0

    B. Boot sector

    C. Containing the master boot record (MBR)

    D. All of the above

3. How many logical partitions does the partition table in the master boot record allow for a physical drive?

    A. 1

    B. 2

    C. 4

    D. 24

4. The very first sector of a partition is referred to as which of the following?

    A. Master boot record

    B. Physical sector 0

    C. Active primary partition

    D. Volume boot record

5. If a hard drive has been fdisked, EnCase can still recover the deleted partition(s), if you point to the _____ and select Add Partition from the Partition menu.

    A. master boot record

    B. volume boot record

    C. partition table

    D. unallocated space

6. In an NTFS partition, where is the backup copy of the volume boot record (VBR) stored?

    A. In the partition table.

    B. Immediately after the VBR.

    C. The last sector of the partition.

    D. An NTFS partition does not store a backup of the VBR.

7. EnCase can mount a compound file, which can then be viewed in a hierarchical format. Select an example of a compound file.

    A. Registry file (that is, .dat)

    B. Email file (that is, .edb, .nsf, .pst, .dbx)

    C. Compressed file (that is, .zip)

    D. Thumbs.db

    E. All of the above

8. Windows 7 contains two master keys in its registry. They are HKEY_LOCAL_MACHINE and which of the following?

    A. HKEY_USERS

    B. HKEY_CLASSES_ROOT

    C. HKEY_CURRENT_USER

    D. HKEY_CURRENT_CONFIG

9. In Windows 7, information about a specific user's preference is stored in the NTUSER.DAT file. This compound file can be found where?

    A. C:\

    B. C:\WINDOWS\

    C. C:\Users\username

    D. C:\Documents and Settings\All Users\Application Data

10. In an NTFS file system, the date and time stamps recorded in the registry are stored where?

    A. Local time based on the BIOS settings

    B. GMT and converted based on the system's time zone settings

11. EnScript is a proprietary programming language and application programming interface (API) developed by Guidance Software, designed to function properly only within the EnCase environment.

    A. True

    B. False

12. Since EnScript is a proprietary programming language developed by Guidance Software, EnScripts can be created by and obtained only from Guidance Software.

    A. True

    B. False

13. Filters are a type of EnScript that "filters" a case for certain file properties such as file types, dates, and hash categories. Like EnScripts, filters can also be changed or created by a user.

    A. True

    B. False

14. Select the type of email that EnCase 6 is *not* capable of recovering.

    A. Microsoft Outlook

    B. AOL

    C. Microsoft Outlook Express

    D. Lotus Notes and Microsoft Exchange Server

    E. None of the above

15. Which method is used to view the contents of a compound file that contains emails such as a PST file in EnCase 7?

    A. Select View File Structure from the Entries options.

    B. Run Find Email from within the EnCase Evidence Processor.

    C. Both A and B.

    D. None of the above.

16. EnCase 7 cannot process web-based email such as MSN Hotmail or Yahoo! Mail because the information can be found only on the mail servers.

    A. True

    B. False

17. The EnCase Decryption Suite (EDS) will *not* decrypt Microsoft's Encrypting File System (EFS) on the _____ operating system.

    A. Windows 2000 Professional and Server

    B. Windows XP Professional

    C. Windows 2003 Server

    D. Windows 7 Home Edition

18. At which levels can the VFS module mount objects in the Windows environment?

    A. The case level

    B. The disk or device level

    C. The volume level

    D. The folder level

    E. All of the above

19. The Physical Disk Emulator (PDE) module is similar to the Virtual File System (VFS); the module can mount a piece of media that is accessible in the Windows environment. Select the type(s) of media that the Physical Disk Emulator *cannot* mount.

    A. Cases

    B. Folders

    C. Volumes

    D. Physical disks

    E. Both A and B

20. The Virtual File System (VFS) module mounts data as _____, while the Physical Disk Emulator (PDE) module mounts data as _____.

   A. network share, emulated disk

   B. emulated disk, network share

   C. virtual drive, physical drive

   D. virtual file, physical disk

Appendix A

Answers to Review Questions

Chapter 1: Computer Hardware

1. C. A CPU is the central processing unit, which means it's a microprocessor that performs data processing, in other words, interprets and executes instructions.

2. A. BIOS stands for Basic Input Output System and consists of all the low-level software that is the interface between the system hardware and its operating system. It loads, typically, from three sources: the ROM/BIOS on the motherboard; the various BIOS ROMs on video cards, SCSI cards, and so forth; and finally, the device drivers.

3. D. Power On Self-Test is a diagnostic test of the computer's hardware, such as the motherboard, memory, CD-ROM drive, and so forth. POST does not test the computer's software.

4. B. Information contained on a ROM chip, read-only memory, is not lost after the computer has been shut down.

5. B. Unlike a ROM chip, information contained on a computer's RAM chip is not readily accessible after a proper shutdown.

6. A. Although not very common, information stored in the BIOS can change, such as when the BIOS needs to be upgraded to support new hardware.

7. A. Read-only memory (ROM) contains information about the computer, such as hardware configuration. Unlike RAM, the information is not lost once power is disconnected.

8. A. Information contained in RAM memory is considered volatile, which means the data is lost after the computer has been disconnected.

9. C. The answer is 24 drive letters (C–Z), with drive letters *A* and *B* reserved for floppy drives.

10. B. Data is written to sectors, and files are written to clusters.

11. E. Multiplying C, H, and S gives the total amount of sectors in older systems if the number of sectors per track is constant. When it's not, total LBA sectors give total sectors. Multiplying the total number of sectors from the appropriate method by 512 bytes per sector gives the total number of bytes for the physical drive. Adding up the total size of partitions does not include areas outside the partitions, such as unused disk area.

12. C. A CD-RW (rewritable) drive is both an input and output device, as opposed to a CD drive, which only reads and inputs data to the computer system.

13. A. A bus performs two functions: it transports data from one place to another and directs the information where to go.

14. B. The motherboard is the main circuit board used to attach internal hardware devices to its connectors.

15. D. Integrated Drive Electronics (IDE), Small Computer System Interface (SCSI), and Serial Advanced Technology Attachment (SATA) describe different hard drive interfaces.

16. C. Master, Slave, and Cable Select are settings for internal devices such as IDE hard drives and CD drives to identify and differentiate the devices on the same channel.

17. A. SATA and SCSI hard drives do not require jumper setting configurations.

18. A. The master boot record is always located at the first physical sector on a hard drive. This record stores key information about the drive itself, such as the master partition table and master boot code.

19. B. The first sector on a volume is called the volume boot record or volume boot sector. This sector contains the disk parameter block and volume boot code.

20. D. All are true statements, except for a portion of D. The partition table is contained within the MBR and consists of a total of 64 bytes, not 16 bytes, which describes up to four partitions using 16 bytes each to do so, not 4 bytes each.

Chapter 2: File Systems

 The word "FAT" applies to FAT12, FAT16, and FAT32 file systems, unless exFAT is specifically mentioned.

1. B. The file allocation table is created by the file system during format and contains pointers to clusters located on a drive.

2. D. When the FAT marks a cluster as being bad, the entire cluster is prevented from being written to.

3. D. A partition table is located in the master boot record and is always located in the very first sector of a physical drive. The partition table keeps track of the partitions located on the physical drive.

4. A. The FAT assigns numbers to each cluster entry pointing to the next cluster in the cluster run until the last cluster is reached, which is marked as EOF.

5. D. When the FAT marks a cluster as 0, it is in unallocated blusters, which means it is freely available to store data.

6. D. The volume boot record is always located at the first sector of its logical partition and contains the BIOS parameter block and volume boot code.

7. D. The NTFS file system supports long filenames, compresses files and directories, and supports file sizes in excess of 4 GB.

8. D. A FAT32 file system theoretically allows up to 228 = 268,435,456 clusters. The extra 4 bits are reserved by the file system, however, and there is an MBR-imposed limit of 67,092,481 clusters, which means FAT32 is capable of supporting a partition size of 2 terabytes.

9. C. The FAT tracks the location of the last cluster for a file (EOF), while the directory entry maintains the file's starting cluster number.

10. B. Each volume maintains two copies (one for backup): FAT1 and FAT2.

11. D. A, B, and C are all true statements regarding NTFS; however, there is no FAT in an NTFS file system. FAT is an element of the FAT file system.

12. B. A file's physical size is the number of bytes to the end of the last cluster, and a file's logical size is the number of bytes that the actual file contains. A file's physical size can be the same as its logical size.

13. A. A directory entry in a FAT file system has no logical size.

14. D. In a FAT file system, each directory entry is 32 bytes in length.

15. B. Because directory entries are just names with no logical size and because they do not contain any actual data, EnCase displays the information in red.

16. D. The area between a file's logical size and its physical size is commonly referred to as *slack space*.

17. A. The directory structure records the file's information, the FAT tracks the number of clusters allocated to the file, and the file's data is filled in to the assigned clusters.

18. C. EnCase recovers deleted files by first obtaining the file's starting cluster number and its size from the directory entry. Then, EnCase determines the number of clusters needed based on the file's size and then attempts to recover the data from the starting extent through the amount of clusters needed.

19. C. When EnCase determines that the starting cluster listed in the FAT has been reassigned to an existing file, it reports the previously deleted file as being overwritten.

20. A. All are true regarding exFAT except A, since cluster allocation is not tracked by the FAT but rather by an allocation bitmap.

Chapter 3: First Response

1. A. Without consideration for your own personal safety, none of the other considerations can be accomplished.

2. E. When responding to a facility, your most helpful ally is prior knowledge of the location, its hours of activity, and the people who occupy it.

3. E. When responding to a facility, having prior knowledge of the types and functions of the computers and their locations will help reduce any unforeseen complications, thus easing the task.

4. C. Pulling the plug on a workstation, unlike doing so on a server, will not lose any critical information.

5. A. Unlike with a Windows desktop computer, certain information may not be recovered if a server is not properly shut down. It is best to properly shut down a Windows server and document your actions.

6. A. Unix/Linux machines can store critical information that may be lost if the machine is improperly shut down.

7. A. When unplugging a desktop computer, it is best to unplug a power cord from the back of the computer at the power supply. Unplugging a cord from the outlet connected to an uninterrupted power supply (UPS) will not shut down the computer.

8. D. Removing both the power cord (AC) and the battery (DC) will ensure that no electricity is being fed to the computer.

9. C. A Mac should generally be shut down by pulling the power plug from the back of the computer.

10. D. The best way to shut down a Linux/Unix system is to perform a proper shutdown using the operating system.

11. E. When the system is shut down normally or the plug is pulled, all the other live system-state data mentioned is lost.

12. C. A plastic garbage bag has properties that are conducive to static electricity discharge, which could damage sensitive computer components, including media.

13. E. In all circumstances described, the best course of action would be a normal shutdown, and thus pulling the plug is considered best practice for any of these.

14. E. The evidence steps described here are an important component in maintaining the chain of custody and hence the integrity of the evidence.

15. B. In a business setting, anything is possible. A large business database could be hosted on a Windows 7 Enterprise operating system, as could a number of other critical applications, which include access control systems, critical process control software, life-support systems, life-safety alarm monitoring, and so forth.

16. C. Generally, unless configured otherwise, you must be root to shut down a Linux/ Unix system in a production environment. This prevents a typical user from stopping the system and halting mission-critical computing processes.

17. E. Certain information may not be retrievable after the system has been shut down. Given that, it is acceptable to access a system to retrieve information of evidentiary value as long as the actions are justified, documented, and explained.

18. D. Microsoft PC operating systems use backslashes (\) for the directory path structure, whereas Linux/Unix uses forward slashes (/) for the same purpose.

19. B. Although most of the time the network administrator knows much more about the computers than the responding examiner and may be of great help, requesting that person's assistance may be detrimental to the investigation if the network administrator is the target of the investigation. As part of your preplanning, you must determine whether the administrator is part of the problem or part of the solution before you make such an approach.

20. E. Upon leaving the scene of a search, you should leave behind a copy of the signed search warrant and a list of items seized.

Chapter 4: Acquiring Digital Evidence

1. C. When partitions have been removed or the partitions are not recognized by Linux, EnCase still recognizes the physical drive and acquires it as such.

2. B. LinEn does not have a built-in write blocker. Rather, it relies upon Linux's automount feature having been disabled.

3. B. Although EnCase only examines the contents within the evidence files, it is still good forensic practice to wipe/sterilize each hard drive prior to reusing it to eliminate the argument of possible cross-contamination.

4. E. You should suspect an HPA or a DCO. Booting with LinEn or using Tableau or FastBloc SE should enable you to see all sectors.

5. C. Digital evidence must be treated like any other evidence, whereas a chain of custody must be established to account for everyone who has access to the property.

6. A and B. HPA stands for Host Protected Area and is not normally seen by the BIOS. It was introduced in the ATA-4 specification, not ATA-6, and is seen when directly accessed via the Direct ATA mode.

7. E. All are correct statements with regard to DCO.

8. C. LinEn runs on the Linux OS, and the user must be the root user to successfully work with LinEn.

9. B. When reacquiring an image, the MD5 of the original data stream remains the same despite the compression applied.

10. B. When reacquiring, you can change the compression, you can add or remove a password, you can change the file segment size, you can change the block and error granularity sizes, or you can change the start and stop sectors. Other properties can't be changed.

11. F. All of the above are correct answers. Linux can read or write to both FAT and NTFS file systems.

12. B and D. Here, hdb2 refers to the second partition on the primary slave.

13. B, C, and D. Linux will name an IDE device, normally, with hda, hdb, hdc, or hdd, to denote their position on the ATA controller (primary master, primary slave, secondary master, secondary slave, respectively). sdb is the second SCSI device, and since Linux calls USB or FireWire devices SCSI devices, any of the three (B, C, or D) could be represented by sdb.

14. F. All are methods of write-protecting USB devices, some arguably better than others, but methods nevertheless.

15. A, B, C, and D. All of these statements are true regarding EnCase Portable.

16. B. LinEn can't be run under DOS and can't be run under Windows. Rather, LinEn must be run under the Linux OS.

17. C. The level of support for USB, FireWire, SCSI, and other devices is totally dependent on the Linux distribution being used to run LinEn. For the most support, try to use the latest Linux distribution available.

18. B. CDs can be safely acquired in the Windows environment.

19. A, B, C, and D. A FIM can be licensed only to law enforcement or military customers. All other statements are correct.

20. A. Only A is correct. LinEn has no onboard drivers for write blocking, relying on the host OS to have its automount feature disabled. LinEn can't format to any format because formatting is not included within the tool. EnCase for DOS contained an unlock feature by which the target drive was unlocked for writing. LinEn contains no such feature.

Chapter 5: EnCase Concepts

1. D. An EnCase evidence file is a bitstream image of a source device such as a hard drive, CD-ROM, or floppy disk written to a file (.Ex01) or several file segments (.Ex02, .Ex03, and so on).

2. D. EnCase writes a CRC value for every 64 sectors copied, by default. If the block size has been increased, the CRC frequency will be adjusted accordingly.

3. D. The smallest file size that an EnCase evidence file can be saved as is 30 MB.

4. D. The largest file size that an EnCase evidence file can be saved as is now 8,589,934,588 GB with EnCase 7. Naturally the file system storing the file must support this file size.

5. A. EnCase compares the MD5 hash value (alternatively SHA-1 or both) of the source device to the MD5 hash value (alternatively SHA-1 or both) of just the data stored in the evidence file, not the entire contents of the evidence file, such as case information and CRC values of each data block.

6. C. EnCase calculates a CRC value for the case information, which is verified when the evidence file is added to a case.

7. B. When an evidence file is added to a case, EnCase verifies both the CRC and MD5 hash values (alternatively SHA-1 or both). All acquisition values (CRCs and hashes) must match the recalculated verification values.

8. C. The MD5 hash algorithm produces a 128-bit value.

9. E. Starting with EnCase 7.04, the backup process has been greatly enhanced and .cbak files are no longer used, making A no longer correct. Options B and C are true statements regarding the backup process.

10. B. EnCase will no longer (as of version 5) detect corrupted data on the fly. Therefore, EnCase will show and allow corrupted data to be searched, bookmarked, and so on. Post-verification corruption, although rare, can occur, and therefore every case should be subjected to verification at the end of the case to assure no corruption has occurred.

11. D. The evidence file size can be changed during a reacquire.

12. B. EnCase can verify independent evidence file segments by comparing the CRC values of the data blocks. This function is accessed from the Tools menu and is called Verify Evidence Files.

13. D. EnCase does not write to the evidence file after the acquisition is complete.

14. D. As with any forensic tool, the investigator should test the tools to better understand how the tool performs and to verify that it is functioning properly.

15. A. Compressing an evidence file does not change its MD5 and/or SHA-1 hash value(s).

16. B. The three parts are the Ev2 Header, Data, and Link Record. There is no such part called CRC record.

17. A. An EnCase evidence file's logical filename can be renamed without affecting the verification of the acquired evidence.

18. A. EnCase evidence files can be moved without affecting the file verification.

19. C. When an evidence file has moved from the previous path, EnCase will prompt for the new location of the evidence file.

20. A, B, D, and E. All may be changed during reacquisition with the exception of the investigator's name.

Chapter 6: EnCase Environment

1. A. You must first create a new case before the Add Device option is available.

2. C. EnCase 7 creates Email, Export, Tags, and Temp. The Evidence folder would have to be created manually by the user if the user opted to place it in this location.

3. E. A, B, C, and D can all be carried out from the Home screen.

4. E. The Case Options dialog box asks for all the options listed when a new case is created.

5. B. The data in the File Types database (stored in the FILETYPES.INI file) determines which file types will be opened by which viewers upon double-clicking or opening the file.

6. C. External viewers are programs that EnCase uses to open specific file types and are configured by the user

7. D. The VIEWERS.INI file stores information on external programs that EnCase uses to open specific file types.

8. C. When EnCase sends a file to an external viewer, the file is placed in the temp folder.

9. B. It is launched as an option from the Device menu.

10. D. All are true regarding the Gallery view.

11. A. The right-side menu is a collection of the menus and tools found on the toolbar to its left. It is akin to the content formerly found on the right-click mouse button.

12. B. When a filter or condition is run, the results are shown in the Results view or tab.

13. C. To adjust the amount of minutes the backup file is saved, select Tools in the menu bar, select Options, and then change the time in the Auto Save Minutes box on the Global tab of the resulting dialog box.

14. C. EnCase allows the user to sort up to six columns in the Table view tab.

15. C. The user can use either method to reverse-sort on a column.

16. E. All four methods will hide selected columns from the Table view.

17. B. The Gallery view displays images based on the File Category – Picture setting, which is determined by file extensions until such time that a file signature analysis is run.

18. C. When a signature analysis is performed, EnCase will update or correct the file category to Picture, in this particular case, based on the information contained in the file header.

19. D. A user can change the way colors and fonts appear by selecting the Tools tab and then clicking Options to change colors and fonts.

20. A. Navigation Data (also called the GPS bar in the field) displays the selected data's exact location, including the full path, physical sector, logical sector number, cluster number, sector offset, and file offset.

Chapter 7: Understanding, Searching For, and Bookmarking Data

1. C. Binary is a numbering system consisting of 0 and 1 used by computers to process information.

2. A. *Bi* refers to two; therefore, a bit can have only two values, 0 or 1.

3. C. A byte consists of 8 bits or two 4-bit nibbles, commonly referred to as the *left nibble* and *right nibble*.

4. D. 2^8 is 2×2 eight times, or $2 \times 2 \times 2 \times 2 \times 2 \times 2 \times 2 \times 2 = 256$.

5. A. Values expressed with the letter *h* as a suffix are hexadecimal characters. EnCase can display the letter *A* in text or hexadecimal formats

6. B. Starting from the right, the bits are "on" for bit positions 1 and 8, which totals 9.

7. C and D. A Dword is a 32-bit value. A is incorrect because it depicts 8 binary bits or one byte. B is incorrect because it depicts 4 binary bits or one nibble. C is correct because it represents four hexadecimal values with each being 8 bits ($4 \times 8 = 32$ bits). D is correct because it represents 32 binary bits.

8. D. 2^7 is 2×2 seven times or $2 \times 2 \times 2 \times 2 \times 2 \times 2 \times 2 = 128$, while 2^{16} is 2×2 sixteen times $= 65,536$.

9. C. A device must be an image or be acquired first by the EnCase Evidence Processor. Live devices can be subjected to direct processing by the EnCase Evidence Processor. Red flags denote items that must be run during the first run of the processor. If you don't run them then, you can't run them later. It's now or never, so to speak.

10. C. EnCase performs a search not only of logical files but of the entire disk to include unallocated clusters and unused disk areas outside the logical partition.

11. B. By default, the Case Sensitive option is not selected; therefore, search terms are not case sensitive unless you select that option.

12. A. By selecting the Unicode box, EnCase will search for both ASCII and Unicode formats.

13. D. EnCase can perform both physical searches as well as logical searches for keyword(s) that span noncontiguous clusters.

14. E. Since the entry allows for characters to precede and follow the keyword and the default setting does not have the Case Sensitive option enabled, all the selections apply.

15. C. The GREP symbol ^ means to exclude the following characters. So, the GREP expression in the question excludes the alpha characters (*a* through *z*) before and after the keyword but will find nonalpha characters such as numbers.

16. B. The GREP expression in the question permits a hexadecimal range from 00 through 07 followed by hexadecimal values 00 00 00 and any other characters.

17. A. This index search expression calls first for a case-sensitive search, because of the <c>. The npre/3 means at least three words apart *and* Saddam must precede Hussein. Only A meets this query.

18. A. The GREP expression [^#] means that it cannot be a number, meaning the first character and last character following the 9 can't be numbers. Therefore, A will not return as a search hit because the number 0 follows the number 9.

19. C. The highlighted data bookmark is a sweep or highlight of a specific text fragment.

20. A and C. An index is required first before searching but is created by the EnCase Evidence Processor and *not* by an EnScript named Create Index. Queries are case insensitive, by default, but do have the ability to be case sensitive if preceded by <c>.

Chapter 8: File Signature Analysis and Hash Analysis

1. D. A signature analysis will compare a file's header or signature to its file extension.

2. A. A file header identifies the type of file and is located at the beginning of the file's data area.

3. C. The Windows operating system uses a file's extension to associate the file with the proper application.

4. B. Unix (including Linux) operating systems use a file's header information to associate file types to specific applications.

5. D. When determining which application to use to open a file, Mac OS X gives first precedence to "user defined" settings, second precedence to creator code metadata, and third precedence to filename extensions. If none of these are present, other rules come into play.

6. A. Information about a file's header and extension is saved in the FileTypes.ini file.

7. B. When a file's signature is unknown and a valid extension is present, EnCase will display the status as being Bad Signature.

8. A. When a file's signature is known and an inaccurate file extension is present, EnCase reports Alias in the Signature Analysis column, displays the true signature in the Signature column, and may update the Category column.

9. D. When a file's signature is known and an accurate file extension is present, EnCase will display the result as a Match.

10. C. When a file's signature and extension are not recognized, EnCase will display the result as Unknown.

11. A. A unique file header can share multiple file extensions. An example of such as case is a .jpeg or .jpg file, which shares the same file header \xFF\xD8\xFF[\xFE\xE0\xE1].

12. C. A user can manually add new file headers and extensions by accessing the File Types view and creating a new entry, with new header and extension.

13. D. An MD5 hash is a 128-bit hash value, and the odds of two different files having the same value is one in $2^{128.}$ A file's MD5 hash value is based on the file's data area, not its filename, which resides outside the data area.

14. D. EnCase can calculate hash values for any of the options listed.

15. B. EnCase 7 allows two hash libraries to be applied to a case at any given time.

16. B. Merely changing a file's name will not affect its MD5 or SHA1 hash value because the hash value is based on the file's data, not its filename.

17. A. These hash sets have been produced from known safe sources and are categorized as Known. In most cases, they are nonevidentiary and can be ignored when conducting searches and other analyses.

18. B. Evidentiary files or files of interest are usually categorized as Notable.

19. A. Regardless of the MD5 or SHA1 hashing utility, the hash value generated will have the same result, because the MD5 or SHA1 hash is an industry-standard algorithm.

20. C. A hash library is comprised of hash sets, which are comprised of hash values.

Chapter 9: Windows Operating System Artifacts

1. E. Operating system artifacts serve as information used by the computer to fulfill certain user- and system-specific requirements and needs.

2. C. A FAT file system stores date and time stamps in local time while the NTFS file system stores date and time stamps in GMT.

3. B. Windows stores the time zone offset in the registry.

4. D. If it is a Windows Vista (or beyond) Recycle Bin, the date and time when the file was deleted is saved in the $I index file that corresponds with the deleted file. If it is a pre-Vista operating system, when a file is sent to the Recycle Bin, the date and time of when the file was deleted is saved in the INFO2 file.

5. D. When a file is sent to the Recycle Bin, Windows changes the short filename to D for Deleted, followed by the drive letter and the index number. The file extension for the deleted file remains the same.

6. B. When a user opens a document, a link file bearing the document's filename is created in the Recent folder.

7. E. Link files are shortcuts to a variety of items such as programs, documents, folders, and devices such as removable media.

8. B. In NTFS, information unique to a specific user is stored in the NTUSER.DAT file.

9. C. By default, the My Recent Documents folder displays 15 recently opened documents; however, the actual folder may contain hundreds more.

10. D. A specific user's desktop items are located in the path C:\Users\%User%\Desktop in a Windows 7 operating system.

11. A. When the system goes into hibernation, the contents of RAM are written to the file hiberfil.sys, which is the exact size of RAM and located in the root of the system drive.

12. E. Evidence of web-based email is commonly viewed but not saved. Therefore, its contents may be found in the Temporary Internet Files folder, Unallocated Clusters, or the pagefile.sys and hiberfil.sys folders.

13. A. The Favorites folder contains link files that direct the browser to certain websites. These link files usually have a name that describes the website followed with the .url extension.

14. B. Information about an Internet cookie such as the URL name, date and time stamps, and pointers to the actual cookie are stored in the index.dat file.

15. A. The swap file is saved as WIN386.SWP in a Windows 98 machine and as pagefile.sys in Windows XP and newer.

16. C. The .spl, or spool, file contains an image of what is sent to the printer to be printed.

17. D. The two printing modes in Windows are RAW and EMF.

18. A. Even though Windows deletes the EMF file after a print job has been completed, EnCase may still be able to recover the file by doing a search of its unique header information.

19. C. The Recycle Bin does not contain an index.dat file; in Windows 2000/XP, it contains the INFO2 file.

20. D. The Temporary Internet Files directory contains all the previously mentioned items.

Chapter 10: Advanced EnCase

1. E. The first 63 sectors of a hard drive are reserved for the MBR even though its contents are contained in the very first sector.

2. D. The first sector of a formatted hard drive with an operating system is referred to as a *boot sector*, which contains the MBR and is located at absolute sector 0.

3. C. The partition table allows for four logical partitions. It consists of 64 bytes, and each of the four partitions is described by 16-byte string.

4. D. The first sector of a partition contains the volume boot record.

5. B. EnCase can still recover deleted partitions if you point to the first sector of the partition, which is the volume boot record, and select the Add Partition command from the Partition menu.

6. C. When a hard drive is formatted with an NTFS partition, a backup of the VBR is stored in the last sector of the partition.

7. E. These file types are all examples of compound files that EnCase is able to display their contents in a hierarchical format.

8. A. The other master key is HKEY_USERS. The other choices are derived keys that are linked to keys within the two master keys.

9. C. Each time a profile or username is created, the NTUSER.DAT file is also created for the specific profile. This compound file is stored locally in the root of C:\Users\ %USERNAME%.

10. B. In an NTFS file system, the date and time stamps recorded in the registry are recorded in GMT, which is then displayed in local time based on the system's time zone settings.

11. A. Since EnScript is a proprietary programming language, it is designed to function properly only in the EnCase environment.

12. B. Although EnScript was developed by Guidance Software, anyone with computer programming skills and knowledge of the programming language can develop their own EnScripts.

13. A. Since filters are in essence EnScripts, any user can modify an existing filter or create their own.

14. E. EnCase 7 can recognize and parse all these types of emails.

15. C. EnCase 7 allows the user to view the contents of compound files containing emails either by selecting View File Structure or by running Find Email from within the EnCase Evidence Processor. While both will allow viewing the compound file, per se, only the latter method will send the output to the Records view.

16. B. Contents of web-based emails may reside in areas such as Temporary Internet History, cache (pagefile.sys), hiberfil.sys, and unallocated clusters. Using the web mail finder option from the File Carver, EnCase can locate web mail fragments.

17. D. Microsoft Windows 7 Home Edition does not include the EFS feature nor does it support BitLocker.

18. E. The VFS module can also mount data at the case, disk or device, volume, and folder levels.

19. E. The Physical Disk Emulator can mount volumes and physical disks in the Windows environment; however, it does not mount cases or folders.

20. A. When a user selects the VFS module, EnCase will prompt the user with a Mount As Network Share dialog box. When a user selects the PDE module, EnCase will prompt the user with a Mount As Emulated Disk dialog box.

Appendix B

Creating Paperless Reports

In the not too distant past, computer forensics reports were typically printed documents. As the volume and complexity of computing in general has grown, computer forensics reports have likewise grown and evolved. The current trend is toward paperless web page–style reports that are contained on CDs or DVDs. As media continues to grow in size and with it the size of cases and their reports, you may find that you are exceeding the capacity of high-capacity DVDs. In those cases, you may need to package your report on external hard disks.

Often is the case that you must deliver your electronic report securely, which usually translates into encrypted reports. When your reader is nontechnical, submitting encrypted data often does not work because the reader simply lacks the skill set to work with encrypted data. Aegis Padlock Pro is a great solution for delivering secure reports. The data on the drive is encrypted using the firmware in the drive housing. Simply plug it in, press a couple of buttons, enter a PIN on a keypad, and press the unlock button. If your reader can use an ATM, they can work with this device. The device comes in several different capacities to suit your needs.

EnCase's web page reports provide a powerful tool to convey your findings. They are extremely flexible; you create the hierarchy and structure when you create your bookmarks. The more organized and articulate you are as you create folder structures and names, the better your reports will appear in either format, but especially in the web page version.

Although content is always important, presentation is probably even more important. It is the first thing seen by everyone, and it is the medium by which your content is delivered. You may be the sharpest examiner around, and every examination you do may be the epitome of computer forensics, but if your report is ugly and technically intimidating, case agents and prosecutors will shy away. Your challenge is to package your technical findings into a report that looks good, that is easy to read, and that tells a story with links to technical findings.

If you are to be a successful examiner, at some point you will have to convey your findings to a third party who has very little understanding of computers. These third parties are typically case investigators, attorneys, judges, hearing boards, juries, and the like. You will have to explain, verbally and in written reports, very technical concepts in terms that the layperson can understand. It takes time, practice, skill, experience, and creativity. Most of all, it requires that you be willing to take the extra effort to make it happen. When you create reports that your readers can easily read and understand, the results you see will speak for themselves.

It is beyond the scope of this book to transform you into a brilliant technical writer, but I can provide you with a presentation-grade template that you can adapt that will greatly improve the appearance and readability of your reports. I'll also give you some ideas and suggestions that can help you with your reports. The template you will adapt is one that has its roots in a template developed by Roy Rector a few years ago. Rector is a police officer in Austin, Texas, and a part-time instructor with Guidance Software, Inc. In the latter capacity, he shared this template with the many classes he taught.

I have made many changes to the original template, but the most significant change was that of making it easily adaptable for other users to employ. To make it work for you, you need only rename your agency seal filename to `agency.jpg`, insert your signature in place of mine, change the agency name and address information on the headers, and insert your biographical information in place of mine. Assuming your bio is relatively current, all the changes can be done in minutes.

When done, this template gives you an organized and attractive shell in which to write your narrative and create links to the EnCase report. In this manner, the reader can read a narrative in which you explain what you did and what you found. As you describe significant findings, you will create hyperlinks to the EnCase report where the actual evidence exists. The reader can follow the link, view the evidence, and return to reading your narrative. It makes reading and navigating your report a pleasure.

In addition, the shell or template has separate pages on which to describe your hardware analysis, which can be accessed by hyperlinks. If terminology is an issue, there is a glossary page that can be accessed via hyperlinks. There is also a page on which you can place your bio so it is readily viewable.

At the center of these pages is your EnCase report, which will have links to it from many different sources. You can add third-party reports and provide links to them as you want. It is almost limitless what you can do when you create your reports in this manner. When this appendix concludes, I'll show you how to arrange your files for placement on a CD or DVD (or external hard drive), including a couple of files needed to automatically run your media when placed in the drive. Once you've created and submitted one paperless report, both you and your readers will insist on them in the future.

Exporting the Web Page Report

After you have bookmarked all of your findings and your report is finished, fully reflecting your findings and formatted to appear to your liking, it is time to export your report. From the Report view, right-click the report body and choose Save As. When you do, you'll see the Report – Save As dialog box, as shown in Figure B.1. Use the HTML format and direct the output to a folder named Reports, which you will create in the root of your case folder.

FIGURE B.1 Report – Save As menu with HTML format selected and being directed to a folder named Reports

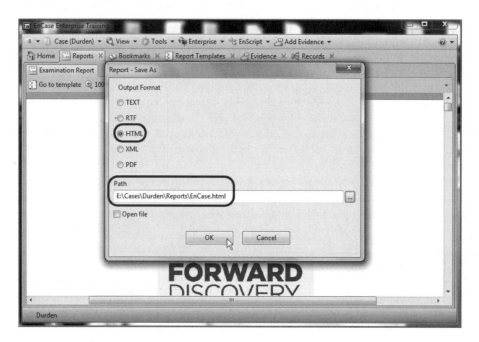

When done, you can open your report in your browser. In this case, the filename I used to contain my report was named EnCase.html. EnCase will create a folder named EnCase_files in which it will place any files needed in support of the report. Figure B.2 shows the file and folder created for the exported case report.

FIGURE B.2 File and folder created for EnCase case report

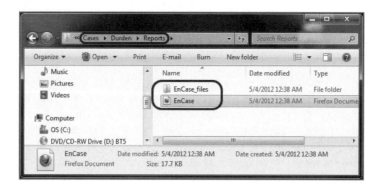

Now that you understand the files created by an EnCase web page report, you are ready to create a report around them. Before going further, it is always a good idea to launch the EnCase report by double-clicking the EnCase.html file, as shown in Figure B.2, and reviewing the contents in your browser. Make sure everything is the way you want it to appear before going further. If there are problems, fix them in EnCase now, and export the file again.

If your full report file is excessively large, it may take a long time to load in your browser. If the load time is long on your forensics machine with robust resources, you need to consider what the load time is going to be on your reader's machine, which usually has minimal resources. If that is a concern, now is the time to go back into EnCase and export your report in as many sections as it takes to make it manageable in a browser. Place the first section in the folder Reports, the second in folder Reports2, and so forth. You can tie them together later with hyperlinks in an index.

Creating Your Container Report

Now that you have created and exported your EnCase report, it is time to place it within your container report. This container report is the polished gateway or front end to your EnCase report. It contains the splash screen/full narrative report, hardware analysis report, general procedures, a glossary, and the examiner's bio. Each of these reports, pages, or tabs, or whatever you prefer to call them, has a standard format and a standard set of navigation menus. Table B.1 lists each report, page, or tab by filename, along with its description and a listing of standard and suggested or optional hyperlinks found within it.

TABLE B.1   Individual reports found in the container report

Name	Filename	Description	Hyperlinks
Initial Splash Screen	index.htm	Home screen—initial screen that is first seen upon autorun. Edit, for each case, the case name, number, and case officer information. This is the main body of the report, containing your full narrative with links throughout.	Standard links: Home About the Examiner Hardware Analysis General Procedures Glossary

TABLE B.1   Individual reports found in the container report *(continued)*

Name	Filename	Description	Hyperlinks
About the Examiner	about.htm	Examiner's bio that is updated periodically as needed. Including it in the report makes it available to all readers at the outset.	Standard links: Home About the Examiner Hardware Analysis General Procedures Glossary
Hardware Analysis	hardware_analysis.htm	Describes all hardware in the case, including a report of system time compared to known time standard.	Standard links: Home About the Examiner Hardware Analysis General Procedures Glossary Links to photographs of computer equipment associated with the case
General Procedures	general_procedures.htm	Lists the general procedures typically employed in a case. This doesn't usually require editing unless you introduce significant changes to your processing routine.	Standard links: Home About the Examiner Hardware Analysis General Procedures Glossary
Glossary	glossary.htm	Definitions of terms typically encountered in a computer forensics report.	Standard links: Home About the Examiner Hardware Analysis General Procedures Glossary

Before going further, it is important to understand that you will be editing web pages that contain Hypertext Markup Language (HTML) as its source code. This is the language of the Web. It is not necessary to edit raw code, nor is it particularly desirable to do so even if you have the requisite skills, because coding is slow and tedious. Rather, you should use a full-featured HTML editor so that you can quickly get the job done. Many such editors are available, and some are free. You can use Microsoft Word as an HTML editor, but it is not the best tool for this task. I used Microsoft FrontPage to create the narrative and links shown in this section, but a newer product from Microsoft is Microsoft Expression Studio. Either will do a great job.

 Examiners should be aware that FrontPage uses a Temp folder under the Local Settings folder of the user account on the examination machine. This can be an issue if working with contraband or sensitive files and may require cleanup. Some examiners use a clean restoration of their examination machine for each case to mitigate such concerns.

Before you start editing, you need to get all your folders and files in place so that the paths you create with your hyperlinks will remain intact. On the publisher's website for this book, locate the CD Container Report. Figure B.3 shows the files and folders contained in that folder. You should create a folder, name it with your case name, and copy these files and folders into that folder.

FIGURE B.3   Files and folders needed for paperless report

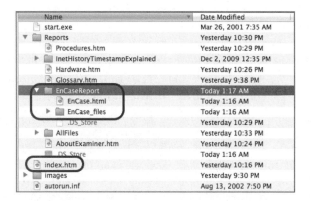

Once you have created a folder dedicated to your report and have copied the container report files and folders into it, you should locate the folder named Reports in your EnCase case folder. The EnCaseReport folder contains the EnCase web report you exported. There is a folder by the same name (Reports) in the container report files and folders. Your final step in organizing and setting up your files and folders is to copy all files and folders (see Figure B.2) in the EnCase web report folder named Reports into the folder by the same name (Reports) located in the folder you named to contain your paperless report.

 On the publisher's website for this book is a Reports folder already containing the files and folders from the EnCaseReport folder (see circled area in Figure B.3) to show you the finished product. Ordinarily you should keep this folder empty after you create your working template to avoid the possibility of mixing report files from old cases.

Once you have the folder created and it contains the files and folders shown in Figure B.3, and once the Reports folder contains the files and folders from the EnCase web report folder (named EnCaseReport), you are ready to edit and prepare your paperless report.

If this is the first time you've set up your paperless report, take a couple of minutes to customize this report for you and your agency. You will need to do the following:

1. Obtain your agency seal in a JPEG format. Name it agency.jpg, and place it in the images folder of the paperless report, overwriting the one there by the same name. The sample agency seal is 188 pixels wide and 133 pixels high. If you keep your agency seal size within these parameters, it should fit nicely with little or no adjustment.

2. Scan your signature, and save it as a GIF file with the name signature.gif, placing it in the images folder, again overwriting the one there by the same name. The present signature is 559 pixels wide and 259 pixels high. If you keep your signature size within these parameters, it should fit nicely with little or no adjustment.

3. Using FrontPage or your editor, open the file index.htm. Edit the top-right section, entering your agency, name, address, and contact information in place of the generic information. Copy this block to your Clipboard. Save your changes to index.htm. Make the same changes (pasting from the Clipboard) to the following files: about.htm, general_procedures.htm, hardware_analysis.htm, and glossary.htm. As you make the changes, save each file, and close it.

4. Using FrontPage, open the file about.htm. Place your bio information on this page, overwriting the current bio information. Save this file when complete.

5. Using FrontPage, open the file index.htm. Place your name and information under the signature on this page, overwriting the current information. Save this file when complete.

6. You have now completed customizing the container report for your paperless report. Create a folder on your desktop, and name it **Paperless Report Template**. Copy the files and folders in Figure B.3 into this template folder. Open index.htm and hardware_analysis .htm. Remove information that is specific to the example case (very little actually), leaving behind all the generic information that you want to remain in your template. Save your changes as you go. Delete the folders and files in the Reports folder in order to leave it empty and clean for your subsequent case reports.

With little effort, you have customized the current paperless report for you and your agency. Further, by copying your work into a separate folder, you have created a template to use for future reports that is ready to be copied and used as is.

For each report you create, as a matter of routine, you will place case-specific information in each of the following files: index.htm and hardware_analysis.htm. You will, from time to time, update your bio (about.htm). You probably won't change the general procedures or glossary files often.

Now turn your attention back to the paperless report you are creating. For the most part, you are ready to use FrontPage or your editor to create your narrative in the narrative report (index.htm) that describes your examination process and findings. It is beyond the scope of this book to delve into technical writing or style issues. To help you complete your report, I need to address two issues: creating bookmarks and hyperlinks, and burning your final report to a CD that will run automatically.

Bookmarks and Hyperlinks

Turn your attention now to creating bookmarks and hyperlinks, which are the features that truly make paperless reports appealing. A bookmark in an HTML document is different from a bookmark created in EnCase. A *bookmark* is a Microsoft term for the HTML code or tag that is called an *anchor*. An anchor, or bookmark, simply creates a specific point in a document to which you can direct a hyperlink. Instead of saying "See EnCase report for details," you'll create a significant number of bookmarks within the EnCase report pointing the various pieces of evidence contained within it. As you write your report narrative, you'll create hyperlinks pointing to these bookmarks (document anchors) that will allow the reader to click the hyperlink and be immediately taken to the section of the EnCase report that provides the evidence described in the narrative.

I have placed an extra folder in the reports folder named Reports, which holds the EnCase 6 report from the following referenced case. It is included only for the purposes of allowing you to practice creating bookmarks (anchors) with the following referenced files. When you are done, remove it completely because it serves no other purpose. The folder EnCaseReport holds a shell EnCase 7 report so you can launch it, look over the format, and leave it there as a placeholder.

Let's create a bookmark. Using FrontPage, open the file Terrorist_Hacker.html, which is located in the Reports folder and contains the main body of the EnCase report. You want to take your reader directly to the files that were found to match the hash values from another system under examination in a possible terrorism case. With experience, you'll quickly determine where to place bookmarks. It is both an art and a technical skill.

In this case, say you have decided to create a bookmark on the title leading to these images. Select the text where you want to create your bookmark and choose Insert ➢ Bookmark (press Ctrl+G when you're using FrontPage 2003). Figure B.4 shows the selected text and the dialog box that opens when you insert a bookmark. You should note that the bookmark name is, by default, the selected text with underscores inserted where spaces existed. If your HTML editor doesn't insert underscores for spaces, it is a good practice to insert them. Click OK to create your bookmark. For you to be able to create a hyperlink to this newly created bookmark, you must save the file in FrontPage first by choosing File ➢ Save or pressing Ctrl+S.

Now that you have created a bookmark or anchor, let's create a hyperlink to it. In this sample case, finding image files that match image files on another possible terrorist's computer is a significant finding and one you decide is worthy of placement on your summary page. Using FrontPage, open the file index.htm, which is your full narrative report page. You'll use this report page to provide a full report and statement of findings. It is a place for the reader to go to read the findings in a case. After creating the text for the report page, you have decided you want to create a hyperlink in the sentence where you described having found images matching the hash values in another case. In this manner, the reader can read about your findings and follow a link to see the images right away.

FIGURE B.4   Inserting a bookmark

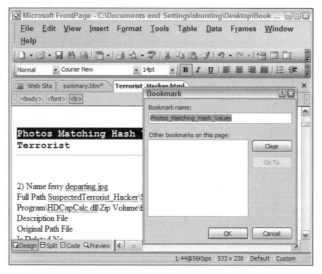

 I have inserted the paragraph shown in Figures B.5 and B.7 that starts off reading "Abbreviated Findings: Upon hash analysis, four images were found" into the file `index.htm`. You won't miss it! You should later delete this paper from your template. It is included only to assist you in practicing creating hyperlinks, as described next.

Generally, it is not considered good style to hyperlink entire sentences within a body of text. Rather, you should select brief phrases or strings of words within a sentence for your hyperlink. These words should readily describe what could be found at the hyperlink. You can start to see that you need to carefully compose your sentences to accommodate your hyperlinks. You will develop this style and technique with practice.

Let's create a hyperlink using the two words *four images*. As shown in Figure B.5, select those two words, and then choose Insert ➤ Hyperlink or press Ctrl+K to open the Insert Hyperlink dialog box. This bookmark is contained in the file `Reports\Terrorist_Hacker .html`, so navigate to and highlight that file, as shown in Figure B.5.

At this stage, if you clicked OK, you would create a hyperlink to the file. A hyperlink to a file will take you to the beginning of a file. Since you want to take your reader to a specific point in a very large file, you must point the hyperlink to a bookmark or anchor contained within the file. To do so, highlight the file containing the bookmark, and click the Bookmark button on the right side of the Insert Hyperlink dialog box. Figure B.6 shows the Select Place In Document dialog box that results from clicking the Bookmark button. Select the name of the bookmark, click OK to close this dialog box, and then click OK again to close the Insert Hyperlink dialog box.

FIGURE B.5   The Insert Hyperlink dialog box in Microsoft FrontPage 2003

FIGURE B.6   The Select Place In Document dialog box enables you to create a hyperlink to a bookmark within a file.

You have created your hyperlink, and as you can see, the two words *four images* appear in blue and are underscored, indicating a hyperlink. If you place your cursor over the hyperlink, you can see the path for the hyperlink in the lower left of the FrontPage window, as shown in Figure B.7. In this example, the path is *Reports*/Terrorist_Hacker .html#Photos_Matching_Hash_Values, where *Reports* is the folder name containing the file named Terrorist_Hacker.html. The # sign denotes an anchor or bookmark, which in this example is named Photos_Matching_Hash_Values.

FIGURE B.7   A hyperlink and its path in Microsoft FrontPage

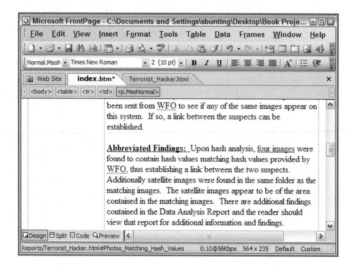

If you want to test your hyperlink, you can save your file in FrontPage and then open the file summary.htm with your browser. If you click your new hyperlink, it will take you directly the bookmark you created in your EnCase web report.

The next step is to complete your various reports using a combination of bookmarks and hyperlinks to allow readers to quickly view exhibits and evidence and then use their browser's Back button to continue reading. Once your report is done, you are ready to burn your paperless report to a CD or DVD.

Burning the Report to CD or DVD

The final step is the easiest part. The more difficult task is making sure your report is complete and accurate and that all the hyperlinks work before committing it to a CD or DVD. It is good practice to have another examiner in your office walk through the report when you are finished. When you are ready, you simply need to start your favorite CD- or DVD-burning software and create a data CD or DVD. The files and folders that you need to place on your CD or DVD are all of those files and folders in the folder you created to contain your paperless report. Figure B.8 shows the files and folders in Nero Express as they are about to be burned to a CD.

FIGURE B.8   Files and folders needed on the CD for a paperless report

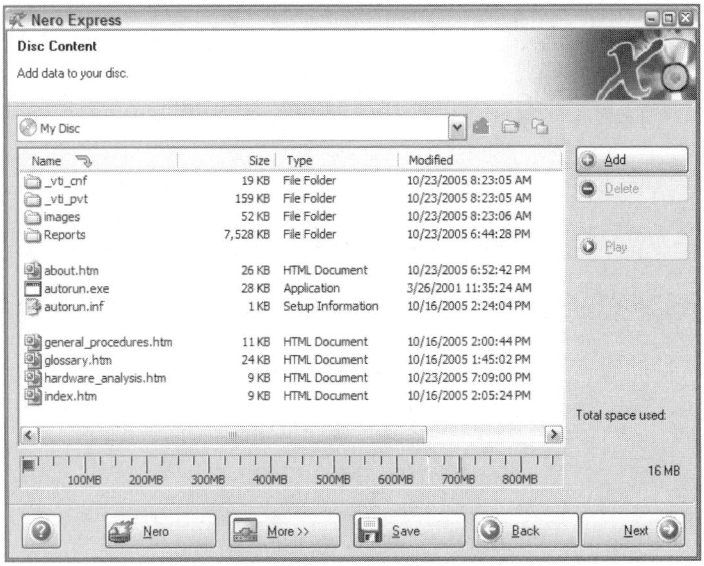

Most of the files and folders have been thoroughly discussed thus far. The HTML documents are simply the various reports you have been editing and are described in Table B.1. The EnCaseReport folder contains the EnCase web-based report. The images folder contains the various images needed to display the container report. The _vti_cnf and _vti_pvt folders contain metadata used by FrontPage. You need them, but they are best left alone. There are two files in the root of the CD needed for the CD to autorun when inserted: autorun.exe and autorun.inf. You need not do anything with them other than make sure they are present. They work in unison to open your CD, launching the file index.htm when the CD autoruns.

At this point, once you finish burning your CD or DVD, your paperless report is complete. It is advisable to burn one CD or DVD and test it thoroughly before continuing. When you are satisfied, burn as many copies as are needed. If your reader's machine is configured to allow CDs or DVDs to autorun, they need only to insert the media and start following links. For those whose autorun capability has been disabled, they will need to know on which file to click to run your report. For those readers, I simply affix a label to the CD case advising to click the file index.htm to begin the report if it doesn't autorun.

The entire set of files and folders shown in Figure B.8, which are about to be burned to a CD by Nero Express, are included on the publisher's website for this book in the folder CD Container Report. If you burn those folders to a CD, you will have the paperless report that I just showed how to create in this appendix. You can read it, see how it works, and get ideas for your own paperless reports. Best of all, you can use it as a template with just a few minor adjustments. Once you start submitting paperless reports of this caliber, your readers will prefer them, as will you.

Appendix C

About the Additional Study Tools

IN THIS APPENDIX:

✓ Additional study tools

✓ System requirements

✓ Using the study tools

✓ Troubleshooting

Additional Study Tools

The following sections summarize the software and other goodies you'll find on the companion website. If you need help with installing the items, refer to the installation instructions in the "Using the Study Tools" section of this appendix.

NOTE

The additional study tools can be found at www.sybex.com/go/ence3e. There you will get instructions on how to download the files to your hard drive.

Sybex Test Engine

The files contain the Sybex test engine, which includes two bonus practice exams, as well as the Assessment Test and the Chapter Review Questions, which are also included in this book.

Electronic Flashcards

These handy electronic flashcards are just what they sound like. One side contains a question, and the other side shows the answer.

PDF of Glossary of Terms

We have included an electronic version of the Glossary in PDF. You can view the electronic version of the Glossary with Adobe Reader.

Adobe Reader

We've also included a copy of Adobe Reader so you can view PDF files that accompany the book's content. For more information on Adobe Reader or to check for a newer version, visit Adobe's website at www.adobe.com/products/reader/.

Additional Author Files

Also included are the *EnCase Legal Journal*, sample evidence files to complete the exercises in the book, and more.

System Requirements

Make sure your computer meets the minimum system requirements shown in the following list. If your computer doesn't match up to most of these requirements, you may have problems using the software and files. For the latest and greatest information, please refer to the ReadMe file located in the downloads.

- A PC running Microsoft Windows 98, Windows 2000, Windows NT4 (with SP4 or newer), Windows Me, Windows XP, Windows Vista, or Windows 7
- An Internet connection

Using the Study Tools

To install the items, follow these steps:

1. Download the .ZIP file to your hard drive, and unzip it to an appropriate location. Instructions on where to download this file can be found at www.sybex.com/go/ence3e.
2. Click the Start.EXE file to open the study tools file.
3. Read the license agreement, and then click the Accept button if you want to use the study tools.

   The main interface appears. The interface allows you to access the content with just one or two clicks.

Troubleshooting

Wiley has attempted to provide programs that work on most computers with the minimum system requirements. Alas, your computer may differ, and some programs may not work properly for some reason.

The two likeliest problems are that you don't have enough memory (RAM) for the programs you want to use or you have other programs running that are affecting installation or running of a program. If you get an error message such as "Not enough memory" or "Setup cannot continue," try one or more of the following suggestions and then try using the software again:

Turn off any antivirus software running on your computer.   Installation programs sometimes mimic virus activity and may make your computer incorrectly believe that it's being infected by a virus.

Close all running programs.   The more programs you have running, the less memory is available to other programs. Installation programs typically update files and programs, so if you keep other programs running, installation may not work properly.

Have your local computer store add more RAM to your computer.   This is, admittedly, a drastic and somewhat expensive step. However, adding more memory can really help the speed of your computer and allow more programs to run at the same time.

Customer Care

If you have trouble with the book's companion study tools, please call the Wiley Product Technical Support phone number at (800) 762-2974, or email them at `http://sybex.custhelp.com/`.

Index

Note to the Reader: Throughout this index **boldfaced** page numbers indicate primary discussions of a topic. *Italicized* page numbers indicate illustrations.

D

G

H

I

M

N

S

X

Y

Z

Free Online Study Tools

Register on Sybex.com to gain access to a complete set of study tools to help you prepare for your EnCE Certification

Comprehensive Study Tool Package includes:

- **Assessment Test** to help you focus your study to specific objectives

- **Chapter Review Questions** for each chapter of the book

- **Two Full-Length Practice Exams** to test your knowledge of the material

- **Electronic Flashcards** to reinforce your learning and give you that last-minute test prep before the exam

- **Searchable Glossary** gives you instant access to the key terms you'll need to know for the exam

- **And More** including sample evidence files and the *EnCase® Legal Journal*

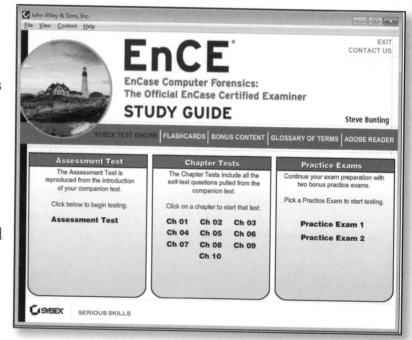

Go to **www.sybex.com/go/ence3e** to register and gain access to this comprehensive study tool package.